# WEST ACADEMIC PUBLISHING'S LAW SCHOOL ADVISORY BOARD

# PUBLIC LAW

## A CASEBOOK FOR MASTER'S DEGREE STUDENTS

■ ■ ■

**Peter L. Reich**
*Continuing Lecturer in Law*
*Director, Law & Communication Intensive*
*UCLA School of Law*

AMERICAN CASEBOOK SERIES®

WEST ACADEMIC

860 Blue Gentian Road, Suite 350
Eagan, MN 55121
1-877-888-1330



Published in the United States of America

**ISBN:** 978-1-68561-110-1

*To my students, who inspired this book.*

# INTRODUCTION

This casebook is designed for students in master's programs, including those for non-lawyers and for lawyers from foreign countries, as well as for advanced undergraduates. It provides materials for class discussions on U.S. federal constitutional law, state constitutional law, and statutes. As such it concentrates on "public law," the rules regulating the relationship between individuals and government. The subject matter is distinguished from, and complements, "private law," or rules regulating relations between individuals. There is necessarily some blurring of these categories, both in European civil law (code-based) jurisdictions and in common law (judicial decision-based) countries such as England and the United States.[1]

The origins of the public-private law division can be traced to the classical period of ancient Rome (27 B.C.E.–284 C.E.) when the state protected the scope of magistrates' and priests' judicial power while all other conflicts were considered private.[2] Despite the narrowness of the public sphere, all disputes had to be resolved in accordance with *utilitas publica*, or the common good.[3] In addition, limits were placed on the ability of officials and judges to impose fines on individuals and dispose of private property.[4] The distinction was further muddied in medieval law's reference to both private ownership and governmental power over property as *dominium*, or the capacity to control and dispose.[5] In the United States, the precise limits of the public versus the private spheres continue to be debated—a question exacerbated by the post-Civil War expansion of the administrative state, with its jurisdiction over a broad range of disputes between the government and private parties.[6]

In teaching Public Law to master's degree students at UCLA, I have developed a set of course materials that introduce students to constitutional and statutory analysis at both the federal and state levels, which I provide here. Rather than cover every aspect of these categories, I have chosen topics that give a sense of the overall structure of public law

---

[1] ELIZABETH ZOLLER, INTRODUCTION TO PUBLIC LAW: A COMPARATIVE STUDY 1–2 (2008). To simplify the private-public law separation, some civil law nations, such as France, have two court systems; common law systems adjudicate both in the same system but provide distinct private and public law remedies.

[2] David Johnston, *The General Influence of Roman Institutions of State and Public Law*, *in* THE CIVILIAN TRADITION AND SCOTS LAW 87, 88–89 (David L. Carey Miller & Reinhard Zimmerman eds. 1997).

[3] *Id.* at 89 (*citing* Ulpian's Digest).

[4] TONY HONORÉ, ULPIAN 236–46 (1982) (*citing* Ulpian's Digest).

[5] FREDERIC WILLIAM MAITLAND, DOMESDAY BOOK AND BEYOND 224 (Bruce Lyon ed., 1966) (1897).

[6] *See generally* BLAKE EMERSON, THE PUBLIC'S LAW: ORIGINS AND ARCHITECTURE OF PROGRESSIVE DEMOCRACY (2019).

in the United States. After an introduction to constitutional interpretation, judicial power, and federalism, this book presents chapters on standing, the Commerce Clause, the Dormant Commerce Clause, taxing and spending, the President's foreign affairs and military roles, executive authority and individual rights, judicial limitations on the executive, economic regulation, takings, equal protection and race, equal protection and gender/education, the First Amendment, and the Fourth Amendment. Departing from federal constitutional law, the text continues with chapters on state constitutional parallels to the U.S. Constitution, state constitutional positive rights, statutory interpretation, and administrative law. Then, decisions interpreting specific statutes have been chosen to illustrate how courts have resolved questions in various aspects of public law: the National Environmental Policy Act, the Endangered Species Act, plenary power and immigrant status, persecution and asylum, corporate criminal liability and privilege, Title VII discrimination, occupational safety and workers' compensation. The book's concluding chapter shows how government regulation of private action also takes place through the common law, under the Public Trust doctrine. For each chapter I provide a brief introduction to the topic, followed by references to contextual background readings—something my students regularly request—and questions to spark discussion.

A word is in order about the case method, widely used in U.S. law schools, and which this book encourages for master's students. This approach began in the late nineteenth century and employed the analysis of judicial decisions to explain how common law developed and changed. Designed at Harvard Law School, the method follows the analogy of natural science investigation: Students read cases (as well as essays and statutes), and with an instructor's guidance discover the workings of the legal system, just as a laboratory researcher examines specimens to ascertain the principles of botany or zoology. In the law school context this inductive approach has been found to engage students far more effectively than top-down lectures.[7] The selection of cases and other materials presented here, along with the discussion questions, are informed by this pedagogy.

For encouraging me to embark on this project, as well as for helpful comments, I am particularly grateful to Russell Korobkin, Vice Dean and Professor at UCLA School of Law; Jason Fiske, Assistant Dean for Graduate Studies and Professional Programs; and my editors at West Academic Publishing, Louis Higgins and Jon Harkness. My students have been indispensable in telling me which cases work well, which don't, and

---

[7] BRUCE A. KIMBALL & DANIEL R. COQUILETTE, THE INTELLECTUAL SWORD: HARVARD LAW SCHOOL, THE SECOND CENTURY 51 (2020).

how the material might be better explained. If those who assign this casebook have suggestions for improvement, I welcome any feedback.

Los Angeles, November 2024

# SUMMARY OF CONTENTS

# TABLE OF CONTENTS

# TABLE OF CASES

**The principal cases are in bold type.**

# PUBLIC LAW

## A CASEBOOK FOR MASTER'S DEGREE STUDENTS

# CHAPTER 1

# JUDICIAL REVIEW AND FEDERALISM

■ ■ ■

## CONTEXT & SOURCES

The U.S. Constitution emerged as the governing structure of public law in response to the more decentralized system established by the Articles of Confederation (1781–1789). This chapter introduces themes that run through the book: the judicial role in reviewing legislation, courts' different interpretive approaches, and the federalist allocation of power between the national and state governments. The national government, including federal law and international treaties are made binding on the states in Article 6, referred to as the Supremacy Clause. Another important component of federalism stems from the Constitution's Article I, § 8, para. 18, Congress's authority "[t]o make all Laws which shall be necessary and proper for carrying into execution" the specifically enumerated powers in the section. In this chapter, selections present the doctrine of judicial review; the two basic doctrines of constitutional interpretation—"originalism" and "living constitutionalism;" and the federal structure as expressed through national government supremacy and the Necessary and Proper Clause.

For a deep dive into the history of the Constitution's drafting and ratification, see Jack N. Rakove, *Original Meanings: Politics and Ideas in the Making of the Constitution* (1996). *Judicial Review and American Democracy* (Albert P. Melone & George Mace eds., Iowa State University Press, 1988) is a selection of classic and more recent writings on the tension between the judiciary's evolving constitutional function and majoritarian rule. A useful summary of the major interpretative approaches is provided by Sotirios A. Barber and James E. Fleming, *Constitutional Interpretation: The Basic Questions* (Oxford University Press, 2007). An older but still highly useful discussion of how federalism informs the Supreme Court's jurisprudence can be found in Charles L. Black, Jr., *Structure and Relationship in Constitutional Law* (Louisiana State University Press, 1969). For an incisive study of how *Missouri v. Holland* applied the Supremacy Clause to international treaties, see Charles A. Lofgren, *"Government from Reflection and Choice." Constitutional Essays on War, Foreign Relations, and Federalism* (Oxford University Press, 1986), 116–166. Mark R. Killenbeck, *M'Culloch v. Maryland: Securing a Nation*

(University Press of Kansas, 2006) presents the context, process, and legacy of the first Necessary and Proper Clause decision.

## THE JUDICIAL ROLE

### FEDERALIST NO. 78

Alexander Hamilton, 1788

To the People of the State of New York:

WE PROCEED now to an examination of the judiciary department of the proposed government.

* * *

The complete independence of the courts of justice is peculiarly essential in a limited Constitution. By a limited Constitution, I understand one which contains certain specified exceptions to the legislative authority; such, for instance, as that it shall pass no bills of attainder, no ex-post-facto laws, and the like. Limitations of this kind can be preserved in practice no other way than through the medium of courts of justice, whose duty it must be to declare all acts contrary to the manifest tenor of the Constitution void. Without this, all the reservations of particular rights or privileges would amount to nothing.

Some perplexity respecting the rights of the courts to pronounce legislative acts void, because contrary to the Constitution, has arisen from an imagination that the doctrine would imply a superiority of the judiciary to the legislative power. It is urged that the authority which can declare the acts of another void, must necessarily be superior to the one whose acts may be declared void. As this doctrine is of great importance in all the American constitutions, a brief discussion of the ground on which it rests cannot be unacceptable.

There is no position which depends on clearer principles, than that every act of a delegated authority, contrary to the tenor of the commission under which it is exercised, is void. No legislative act, therefore, contrary to the Constitution, can be valid. To deny this, would be to affirm, that the deputy is greater than his principal; that the servant is above his master; that the representatives of the people are superior to the people themselves; that men acting by virtue of powers, may do not only what their powers do not authorize, but what they forbid.

If it be said that the legislative body are themselves the constitutional judges of their own powers, and that the construction they put upon them is conclusive upon the other departments, it may be answered, that this cannot be the natural presumption, where it is not to be collected from any particular provisions in the Constitution. It is not otherwise to be supposed, that the Constitution could intend to enable the representatives of the people to substitute their WILL to that of their constituents. It is far more rational to suppose, that the courts were designed to be an intermediate body between the people and the legislature, in order, among other things, to keep the latter within the limits assigned to their authority. The interpretation of the laws is the proper and peculiar province of the courts. A constitution is, in fact, and must be regarded by the judges, as a fundamental law. It therefore belongs to them to ascertain its meaning, as well as the meaning of any particular act proceeding from the legislative body. If there should happen to be an irreconcilable variance between the two, that which has the superior obligation and validity ought, of course, to be preferred; or, in other words, the Constitution ought to be preferred to the statute, the intention of the people to the intention of their agents.

Nor does this conclusion by any means suppose a superiority of the judicial to the legislative power. It only supposes that the power of the people is superior to both; and that where the will of the legislature, declared in its statutes, stands in opposition to that of the people, declared in the Constitution, the judges ought to be governed by the latter rather than the former. They ought to regulate their decisions by the fundamental laws, rather than by those which are not fundamental.

* * *

*PUBLIUS.*

---

**Questions:** Is Hamilton's concept of the judiciary's role consistent with that set out in the Constitution? In *Marbury v. Madison,* 5 U.S. 137 (1803), the U.S. Supreme Court first applied judicial review, but ironically did so to strike down a federal statute expanding its own jurisdiction. Does this approach satisfy the criticism that judicial review is incompatible with democracy?

## CONSTITUTIONAL INTERPRETATION

> "Words do have a limited range of meaning, and no interpretation that goes beyond that range is permissible."
>
> "There is plenty of room for disagreement as to what original meaning was, and even more as to how that original meaning applies to the situation before the court. But the originalist at least knows what he is looking for: the original meaning of the text. . . ."[T]he difficulties and uncertainties of determining original meaning and applying it to modern circumstances are negligible compared with the difficulties and uncertainties of the philosophy which says that the Constitution *changes* . . . ."

Antonin Scalia, *A Matter of Interpretation: Federal Courts and the Law* (Princeton University Press, 1997), 24, 45.

> "[T]he founders stated a commitment in the Declaration of Independence to equality and in the Bill of Rights to individual liberty. These commitments had growth potential. . . .[A] prime portion of the history of the U.S. Constitution is the story of the extension (through amendment, judicial interpretation, and practice) of constitutional rights and protections to once-excluded groups: to people who were once held in bondage, to men without property, to Native Americans, and to women."

Ruth Bader Ginsburg, *My Own Words* (Simon & Schuster, 2016), 231.

---

**Question:** The Constitution neither prescribes Justice Scalia's originalist (or "textualist") approach nor Justice Ginsburg's living constitutionalism as a preferred interpretative method. Which provides greater latitude for judges? For a former Supreme Court justice's view that pure originalism does not reflect the Founders' intentions, which are often difficult to ascertain, *see* Stephen Breyer, *Reading the Constitution: Why I Chose Pragmatism,* Not *Textualism* (Simon & Schuster, 2024).

## FEDERAL STRUCTURE

### FEDERALIST 10

James Madison, 1787

To the People of the State of New York:

AMONG the numerous advantages promised by a well constructed Union, none deserves to be more accurately developed than its tendency to break and control the violence of faction. The friend of popular governments never finds himself so much alarmed for their character and fate, as when he contemplates their propensity to this dangerous vice. He will not fail, therefore, to set a due value on any plan which, without violating the principles to which he is attached, provides a proper cure for it. The instability, injustice, and confusion introduced into the public councils, have, in truth, been the mortal diseases under which popular governments have everywhere perished; as they continue to be the favorite and fruitful topics from which the adversaries to liberty derive their most specious declamations. The valuable improvements made by the American constitutions on the popular models, both ancient and modern, cannot certainly be too much admired; but it would be an unwarrantable partiality, to contend that they have as effectually obviated the danger on this side, as was wished and expected. Complaints are everywhere heard from our most considerate and virtuous citizens, equally the friends of public and private faith, and of public and personal liberty, that our governments are too unstable, that the public good is disregarded in the conflicts of rival parties, and that measures are too often decided, not according to the rules of justice and the rights of the minor party, but by the superior force of an interested and overbearing majority. However anxiously we may wish that these complaints had no foundation, the evidence, of known facts will not permit us to deny that they are in some degree true. It will be found, indeed, on a candid review of our situation, that some of the distresses under which we labor have been erroneously charged on the operation of our governments; but it will be found, at the same time, that other causes will not alone account for many of our heaviest misfortunes; and, particularly, for that prevailing and increasing distrust of public engagements, and alarm for private rights, which are echoed from one end of the continent to the other. These must be chiefly, if not wholly, effects of the unsteadiness and injustice with which a factious spirit has tainted our public administrations.

By a faction, I understand a number of citizens, whether amounting to a majority or a minority of the whole, who are united and actuated by some common impulse of passion, or of interest, adversed to the rights of other citizens, or to the permanent and aggregate interests of the community.

There are two methods of curing the mischiefs of faction: the one, by removing its causes; the other, by controlling its effects.

There are again two methods of removing the causes of faction: the one, by destroying the liberty which is essential to its existence; the other, by giving to every citizen the same opinions, the same passions, and the same interests.

It could never be more truly said than of the first remedy, that it was worse than the disease. Liberty is to faction what air is to fire, an aliment without which it instantly expires. But it could not be less folly to abolish liberty, which is essential to political life, because it nourishes faction, than it would be to wish the annihilation of air, which is essential to animal life, because it imparts to fire its destructive agency.

The second expedient is as impracticable as the first would be unwise. As long as the reason of man continues fallible, and he is at liberty to exercise it, different opinions will be formed. As long as the connection subsists between his reason and his self-love, his opinions and his passions will have a reciprocal influence on each other; and the former will be objects to which the latter will attach themselves. The diversity in the faculties of men, from which the rights of property originate, is not less an insuperable obstacle to a uniformity of interests. The protection of these faculties is the first object of government. From the protection of different and unequal faculties of acquiring property, the possession of different degrees and kinds of property immediately results; and from the influence of these on the sentiments and views of the respective proprietors, ensues a division of the society into different interests and parties.

The latent causes of faction are thus sown in the nature of man; and we see them everywhere brought into different degrees of activity, according to the different circumstances of civil society. A zeal for different opinions concerning religion, concerning government, and many other points, as well of speculation as of practice; an attachment to different leaders ambitiously contending for pre-eminence and power; or to persons of other descriptions whose fortunes have been interesting to the human passions, have, in turn, divided mankind into parties, inflamed them with mutual animosity, and rendered them much more disposed to vex and oppress each other than to co-operate for their common good. So strong is this propensity of mankind to fall into mutual animosities, that where no substantial occasion presents itself, the most frivolous and fanciful distinctions have been sufficient to kindle their unfriendly passions and excite their most violent conflicts. But the most common and durable source of factions has been the various and unequal distribution of property. Those who hold and those who are without property have ever formed distinct interests in society. Those who are creditors, and those who are debtors, fall under a like discrimination. A landed interest, a manufacturing interest, a mercantile interest, a moneyed interest, with many lesser interests, grow up of necessity in civilized nations, and divide them into different classes, actuated by different sentiments and views. The regulation of these various and interfering interests forms the principal task of modern legislation, and involves the spirit of party and faction in the necessary and ordinary operations of the government.

No man is allowed to be a judge in his own cause, because his interest would certainly bias his judgment, and, not improbably, corrupt his integrity. With equal, nay with greater reason, a body of men are unfit to be both judges and parties at the same time; yet what are many of the most important acts of legislation, but so many judicial determinations, not indeed concerning the rights of single persons, but concerning the rights of large bodies of citizens? And what are the different classes of legislators but advocates and parties to the causes which they determine? Is a law proposed concerning private debts? It is a question to which the creditors are parties on one side and the debtors on the other. Justice ought to hold the balance between them. Yet the parties are, and must be, themselves the judges; and the most numerous party, or, in other words, the most powerful faction must be expected to prevail. Shall domestic manufactures be encouraged, and in what degree, by restrictions on foreign manufactures? are questions which would be differently decided by the landed and the manufacturing classes, and probably by neither with a sole regard to justice and the public good. The apportionment of taxes on the various descriptions of property is an act which seems to require the most exact impartiality; yet there is, perhaps, no legislative act in which greater opportunity and temptation are given to a predominant party to trample on the rules of justice. Every shilling with which they overburden the inferior number, is a shilling saved to their own pockets.

It is in vain to say that enlightened statesmen will be able to adjust these clashing interests, and render them all subservient to the public good. Enlightened statesmen will not always be at the helm. Nor, in many cases, can such an adjustment be made at all without taking into view indirect and remote considerations, which will rarely prevail over the immediate interest which one party may find in disregarding the rights of another or the good of the whole.

The inference to which we are brought is, that the CAUSES of faction cannot be removed, and that relief is only to be sought in the means of controlling its EFFECTS.

If a faction consists of less than a majority, relief is supplied by the republican principle, which enables the majority to defeat its sinister views by regular vote. It may clog the administration, it may convulse the society; but it will be unable to execute and mask its violence under the forms of the Constitution. When a majority is included in a faction, the form of popular government, on the other hand, enables it to sacrifice to its ruling passion or interest both the public good and the rights of other citizens. To secure the public good and private rights against the danger of such a faction, and at the same time to preserve the spirit and the form of popular government, is then the great object to which our inquiries are directed. Let me add that it is the great desideratum by which this form of government can be rescued from the opprobrium under which it has so long labored, and be recommended to the esteem and adoption of mankind.

By what means is this object attainable? Evidently by one of two only. Either the existence of the same passion or interest in a majority at the same time must be prevented, or the majority, having such coexistent passion or interest, must be rendered, by their number and local situation, unable to concert and carry into effect schemes of oppression. If the impulse and the opportunity be suffered to coincide, we well know that neither moral nor religious motives can be relied on as an adequate control. They are not found to be such on the injustice and violence of individuals, and lose their efficacy in proportion to the number combined together, that is, in proportion as their efficacy becomes needful.

From this view of the subject it may be concluded that a pure democracy, by which I mean a society consisting of a small number of citizens, who assemble and administer the government in person, can admit of no cure for the mischiefs of faction. A common passion or interest will, in almost every case, be felt by a majority of the whole; a communication and concert result from the form of government itself; and there is nothing to check the inducements to sacrifice the weaker party or an obnoxious individual. Hence it is that such democracies have ever been spectacles of turbulence and contention; have ever been found incompatible with personal security or the rights of property; and have in general been as short in their lives as they have been violent in their deaths. Theoretic politicians, who have patronized this species of government, have erroneously supposed that by reducing mankind to a perfect equality in their political rights, they would, at the same time, be perfectly equalized and assimilated in their possessions, their opinions, and their passions.

A republic, by which I mean a government in which the scheme of representation takes place, opens a different prospect, and promises the cure for which we are seeking. Let us examine the points in which it varies from pure democracy, and we shall comprehend both the nature of the cure and the efficacy which it must derive from the Union.

The two great points of difference between a democracy and a republic are: first, the delegation of the government, in the latter, to a small number of citizens elected by the rest; secondly, the greater number of citizens, and greater sphere of country, over which the latter may be extended.

The effect of the first difference is, on the one hand, to refine and enlarge the public views, by passing them through the medium of a chosen body of citizens, whose wisdom may best discern the true interest of their country, and whose patriotism and love of justice will be least likely to sacrifice it to temporary or partial considerations. Under such a regulation, it may well happen that the public voice, pronounced by the representatives of the people, will be more consonant to the public good than if pronounced by the people themselves, convened for the purpose. On the other hand, the effect may be inverted. Men of factious tempers, of local prejudices, or of sinister designs, may, by intrigue, by corruption, or by other means, first obtain the suffrages, and then betray the interests, of the people. The question resulting is, whether small or extensive republics are more favorable to the election of proper guardians of the public weal; and it is clearly decided in favor of the latter by two obvious considerations:

In the first place, it is to be remarked that, however small the republic may be, the representatives must be raised to a certain number, in order to guard against the cabals of a few; and that, however large it may be, they must be limited to a certain number, in order to guard against the confusion of a multitude. Hence, the number of representatives in the two cases not being in proportion to that of the two constituents, and being proportionally greater in the small republic, it follows that, if the proportion of fit characters be not less in the large than in the small republic, the former will present a greater option, and consequently a greater probability of a fit choice.

In the next place, as each representative will be chosen by a greater number of citizens in the large than in the small republic, it will be more difficult for unworthy candidates to practice with success the vicious arts by which elections are too often carried; and the suffrages of the people being more free, will be more likely to centre in men who possess the most attractive merit and the most diffusive and established characters.

It must be confessed that in this, as in most other cases, there is a mean, on both sides of which inconveniences will be found to lie. By enlarging too much the number of electors, you render the representatives too little acquainted with all their local circumstances and lesser interests; as by reducing it too much, you render him unduly attached to these, and too little fit to comprehend and pursue great and national objects. The federal Constitution forms a happy combination in this respect; the great and aggregate interests being referred to the national, the local and particular to the State legislatures.

The other point of difference is, the greater number of citizens and extent of territory which may be brought within the compass of republican than of democratic government; and it is this circumstance principally which renders factious combinations less to be dreaded in the former than in the latter. The smaller the society, the fewer probably will be the distinct parties and interests composing it; the fewer the distinct parties and interests, the more frequently will a majority be found of the same party; and the smaller the number of individuals composing a majority, and the smaller the compass within which they are placed, the more easily will they concert and execute their plans of oppression. Extend the sphere, and you take in a greater variety of parties and interests; you make it less probable that a majority of the whole will have a common motive to invade the rights of other citizens; or if such a common motive exists, it will be more difficult for all who feel it to discover their own strength, and to act in unison with each other. Besides other impediments, it may be remarked that, where there is a consciousness of unjust or dishonorable purposes, communication is always checked by distrust in proportion to the number whose concurrence is necessary.

Hence, it clearly appears, that the same advantage which a republic has over a democracy, in controlling the effects of faction, is enjoyed by a large over a small republic,—is enjoyed by the Union over the States composing it. Does the advantage consist in the substitution of representatives whose enlightened views and virtuous sentiments render them superior to local prejudices and schemes of injustice? It will not be denied that the representation of the Union will be most likely to possess these requisite endowments. Does it consist in the greater security afforded by a greater variety of parties, against the event of any one party being able to outnumber and oppress the rest? In an equal degree does the increased variety of parties comprised within the Union, increase this security. Does it, in fine, consist in the greater obstacles opposed to the concert and accomplishment of the secret wishes of an unjust and interested majority? Here, again, the extent of the Union gives it the most palpable advantage.

The influence of factious leaders may kindle a flame within their particular States, but will be unable to spread a general conflagration through the other States. A religious sect may degenerate into a political faction in a part of the Confederacy; but the variety of sects dispersed over the entire face of it must secure the national councils against any danger from that source. A rage for paper money, for an abolition of debts, for an equal division of property, or for any other improper or wicked project, will be less apt to pervade the whole body of the Union than a particular member of it; in the same proportion as such a malady is more likely to taint a particular county or district, than an entire State.

In the extent and proper structure of the Union, therefore, we behold a republican remedy for the diseases most incident to republican government. And according to the degree of pleasure and pride we feel in being republicans, ought to be our zeal in cherishing the spirit and supporting the character of Federalists.

PUBLIUS.

---

**Question:** What did Madison and the other drafters not foresee about the historical development of factions, and how they might evolve beyond federalism's ability to control them?

## STATE OF MISSOURI V. HOLLAND

252 U.S. 416 (1920)

MR. JUSTICE HOLMES delivered the opinion of the Court.

This is a bill in equity brought by the State of Missouri to prevent a game warden of the United States from attempting to enforce the Migratory Bird Treaty Act of July 3, 1918, c. 128, 40 Stat. 755, and the regulations made by the Secretary of Agriculture in pursuance of the same. The ground of the bill is that the statute is an unconstitutional interference with the rights reserved to the States by the Tenth Amendment, and that the acts of the defendant done and threatened under that authority invade the sovereign right of the State and contravene its will manifested in statutes. The State also alleges a pecuniary interest, as owner of the wild birds within its borders and otherwise, admitted by the Government to be sufficient, but it is enough that the bill is a reasonable and proper means to assert the alleged quasi sovereign rights of a State. [citations]. A motion to dismiss was sustained by the District Court on the ground that the Act of Congress is constitutional. [citations]. The State appeals.

On December 8, 1916, a treaty between the United States and Great Britain was proclaimed by the President. It recited that many species of birds in their annual migrations traversed many parts of the United States and of Canada, that they were of great value as a source of food and in destroying insects injurious to vegetation, but were in danger of extermination through lack of adequate protection. It therefore provided for specified closed seasons and protection in other forms, and agreed that the two powers would take or propose to their lawmaking bodies the necessary measures for carrying the treaty out. 39 Stat. 1702. The above mentioned act of July 3, 1918, entitled an act to give effect to the convention, prohibited the killing, capturing or selling any of the migratory birds included in the terms of the treaty except as permitted by regulations compatible with those terms, to be made by the Secretary of Agriculture. Regulations were proclaimed on July 31, and October 25, 1918. 40 Stat. 1812, 1863. It is unnecessary to go into any details, because, as we have said, the question raised is the general one whether the treaty and statute are void as an interference with the rights reserved to the States.

To answer this question it is not enough to refer to the Tenth Amendment, reserving the powers not delegated to the United States, because by Article 2, Section 2, the power to make treaties is delegated expressly, and by Article 6 treaties made under the authority of the United States, along with the Constitution and laws of the United States made in pursuance thereof, are declared the supreme law of the land. If the treaty is valid there can be no dispute about the validity of the statute under Article 1, Section 8, as a necessary and proper means to execute the powers of the Government. The language of the Constitution as to the supremacy of treaties being general, the question before us is narrowed to an inquiry into the ground upon which the present supposed exception is placed.

It is said that a treaty cannot be valid if it infringes the Constitution, that there are limits, therefore, to the treaty-making power, and that one such limit is that what an act of Congress could not do unaided, in derogation of the powers reserved to the States, a treaty cannot do. An earlier act of Congress that attempted by itself and not in pursuance of a treaty to regulate the killing of migratory birds within the States had been held bad in the District Court. [citations]. Those decisions were supported by arguments that migratory birds were owned by the States in their sovereign capacity for the benefit of their people, and that under cases like [citation], this control was one that Congress had no power to displace. The same argument is supposed to apply now with equal force.

Whether the two cases cited were decided rightly or not they cannot be accepted as a test of the treaty power. Acts of Congress are the supreme law of the land only when made in pursuance of the Constitution, while treaties are declared to be so when made under the authority of the United States. It is open to question whether the authority of the United States means more than the formal acts prescribed to make the convention. We do not mean to imply that there are no qualifications to the treaty-making power; but they must be ascertained in a different way. It is obvious that there may be matters of the sharpest exigency for the national well being that an act of Congress could not deal with but that a treaty followed by such an act could, and it is not lightly to be assumed that, in matters requiring national action, 'a power which must belong to and somewhere reside in every civilized government' is not to be found. [citation]. What was said in that case with regard to the powers of the States applies with equal force to the powers of the nation in cases where the States individually are incompetent to act. We are not yet discussing the particular case before us but only are considering the validity of the test proposed. With regard to that we may add that when we are dealing with words that also are a constituent act, like the Constitution of the United States, we must realize that they have called into life a being the development of which could not have been foreseen completely by the most gifted of its begetters. It was enough for them to realize or to hope that they had created an organism; it has taken a century and has cost their successors much sweat and blood to prove that they created a nation. The case before us must be considered in the light of our whole experience and not merely in that of what was said a hundred years ago. The treaty in question does not contravene any prohibitory words to be found in the Constitution. The only question is whether it is forbidden by some invisible radiation from the general terms of the Tenth Amendment. We must consider what this country has become in deciding what that amendment has reserved.

The State as we have intimated founds its claim of exclusive authority upon an assertion of title to migratory birds, an assertion that is embodied in statute. No doubt it is true that as between a State and its inhabitants the State may regulate the killing and sale of such birds, but it does not follow that its authority is exclusive of paramount powers. To put the claim of the State upon title is to lean upon a slender reed. Wild birds are not in the possession of anyone; and possession is the beginning of ownership. The whole foundation of the State's rights is the presence within their jurisdiction of birds that yesterday had not arrived, tomorrow may be in another State and in a week a thousand miles away. If we are to be accurate we cannot put the case of the State upon higher ground than that the treaty deals with creatures that for the moment are within the state borders, that it must be carried out by officers of the United States within the same territory, and that but for the treaty the State would be free to regulate this subject itself.

As most of the laws of the United States are carried out within the States and as many of them deal with matters which in the silence of such laws the State might regulate, such general grounds are not enough to support Missouri's claim. Valid treaties of course 'are as binding within the territorial limits of the States as they are elsewhere throughout the dominion of the United States.' [citation]. No doubt the great body of private relations usually fall within the control of the State, but a treaty may override its power. We do not have to invoke the later developments of constitutional law for this proposition; it was recognized as early as [citation], with regard to statutes of limitation, and even earlier, as to confiscation, in [citation]. It was assumed by Chief Justice Marshall with regard to the escheat of land to the State in [citations]. So as to a limited jurisdiction of foreign consuls within a State. [citations]. Further illustration seems unnecessary, and it only remains to consider the application of established rules to the present case.

Here a national interest of very nearly the first magnitude is involved. It can be protected only by national action in concert with that of another power. The subject matter is only transitorily within the State and has no permanent habitat therein. But for the treaty and the statute there soon might be no birds for any powers to deal with. We see nothing in the Constitution that compels the Government to sit by while a food supply is cut off and the protectors of our forests and our crops are destroyed. It is not sufficient to rely upon the States. The reliance is vain, and were it otherwise, the question is whether the United States is forbidden to act. We are of opinion that the treaty and statute must be upheld. [citation].

Decree affirmed.

MR. JUSTICE VAN DEVANTER and MR. JUSTICE PITNEY dissent.

---

**Questions:** To what extent is Justice Holmes's view of federalism in *Missouri v. Holland* rooted in the Constitution's text? Can an individual who allegedly poisoned her husband's mistress with toxic chemicals be federally charged with violating a U.S.-signed international treaty barring the possession of chemical weapons? See *Bond v. United States,* 573 U.S. 844 (2014).

## MCCULLOCH V. MARYLAND

4 Wheaton (17 U.S.) 316 (1819)

[Maryland required banks operating in the state to pay an annual tax of either two percent of the value of banknotes issued or $15,000. The Baltimore branch of the Bank of the United States refused to pay the tax and challenged its constitutionality].

MARSHALL, CH. J., delivered the opinion of the court.

* * *

The first question made in the cause is—has congress power to incorporate a bank?

* * *

This government is acknowledged by all, to be one of enumerated powers.

* * *

Among the enumerated powers, we do not find that of establishing a bank or creating a corporation. But there is no phrase in the instrument which, like the articles of confederation, excludes incidental or implied powers; and which requires that everything granted shall be expressly and minutely described. Even the 10th amendment, which was framed for the purpose of quieting the excessive jealousies which had been excited, omits the word 'expressly,' and declares only, that the powers 'not delegated to the United States, nor prohibited to the states, are reserved to the states or to the people;' thus leaving the question, whether the particular power which may become the subject of contest, has been delegated to the one government, or prohibited to the other, to depend on a fair construction of the whole instrument. The men who drew and adopted this amendment had experienced the embarrassments resulting from the insertion of this word in the articles of confederation, and probably omitted it, to avoid those embarrassments. A constitution, to contain an accurate detail of all the subdivisions of which its great powers will admit, and of all the means by which they may be carried into execution, would partake of the prolixity of a legal code, and could scarcely be embraced by the human mind. It would, probably, never be understood by the public. Its nature, therefore, requires, that only its great outlines should be marked, its important objects designated, and the minor ingredients which compose those objects, be deduced from the nature of the objects themselves. That this idea was entertained by the framers of the American constitution, is not only to be inferred from the nature of the instrument, but from the language. Why else were some of the limitations, found in the 9th section of the 1st article, introduced? It is also, in some degree, warranted, by their having omitted to use any restrictive term which might prevent its receiving a fair and just interpretation. In considering this question, then, we must never forget that it is a *constitution* we are expounding.

Although, among the enumerated powers of government, we do not find the word 'bank' or 'incorporation,' we find the great powers, to lay and collect taxes; to borrow money; to regulate commerce; to declare and conduct a war; and to raise and support armies and navies. The sword and the purse, all the external relations, and no inconsiderable portion of the industry of the nation, are intrusted to its government. It can never be pretended, that these vast powers draw after them others of inferior importance, merely because they are inferior. Such an idea can never be advanced. But it may with great reason be contended, that a government, intrusted with such ample powers, on the due execution of which the happiness and prosperity of the nation so vitally depends, must also be intrusted with ample means for their execution. The power being given, it is the interest of the nation to facilitate its execution. It can never be their interest, and cannot be presumed to have been their intention, to clog and embarrass its execution, by withholding the most appropriate means . . . .The exigencies of the nation may require, that the treasure raised in the north should be transported to the south, that raised in the east, conveyed to the west, or that this order should be reversed. Is that construction of the constitution to be preferred, which would render these operations difficult, hazardous and expensive? Can we adopt that construction (unless the words imperiously require it), which would impute to the framers of that instrument, when granting these powers for the public good, the intention of impeding their exercise, by withholding a choice of means?

* * *

The creation of a corporation, it is said, appertains to sovereignty. This is admitted. But to what portion of sovereignty does it appertain? Does it belong to one more than to another? In America, the powers of sovereignty are divided between the government of the Union, and those of the states. They are each sovereign, with respect to the objects committed to it, and neither sovereign, with respect to the objects committed to the other. We cannot comprehend that train of reasoning, which would maintain, that the extent of power granted by the people is to be ascertained, not by the nature and terms of the grant, but by its date. Some state constitutions were formed before, some since that of the United States. We cannot believe, that their relation to each other is in any degree dependent upon this circumstance. Their respective powers must, we think, be precisely the same, as if they had been formed at the same time. Had they been formed at the same time, and had the people conferred on the general government the power contained in the constitution, and on the states the whole residuum of power, would it have been asserted, that the government of the Union was not sovereign, with respect to those objects which were intrusted to it, in relation to which its laws were declared to be supreme? If this could not have been asserted, we cannot well comprehend the process of reasoning which maintains, that a power appertaining to sovereignty cannot be connected with that vast portion of it which is granted to the general government, so far as it is calculated to subserve the legitimate objects of that government. The power of creating a corporation, though appertaining to sovereignty, is not, like the power of making war, or levying taxes, or of regulating commerce, a great substantive and independent power, which cannot be implied as incidental to other powers, or used as a means of executing them. It is never the end for which other powers are exercised, but a means by which other objects are accomplished.

* * *

But the constitution of the United States has not left the right of congress to employ the necessary means, for the execution of the powers conferred on the government, to general reasoning. To its enumeration of powers is added, that of making 'all laws which shall be necessary and proper, for carrying into execution the foregoing powers, and all other powers vested by this constitution, in the government of the United States, or in any department thereof.'

* * *

To employ the means necessary to an end, is generally understood as employing any means calculated to produce the end, and not as being confined to those single means, without which the end would be entirely unattainable. Such is the character of human language, that no word conveys to the mind, in all situations, one single definite idea; and nothing is more common than to use words in a figurative sense. Almost all compositions contain words, which, taken in a their rigorous sense, would convey a meaning different from that which is obviously intended. It is essential to just construction, that many words which import something excessive, should be understood in a more mitigated sense—in that sense which common usage justifies. The word 'necessary' is of this description. It has not a fixed character, peculiar to itself. It admits of all degrees of comparison; and is often connected with other words, which increase or diminish the impression the mind receives of the urgency it imports. A thing may be necessary, very necessary, absolutely or indispensably necessary. To no mind would the same idea be conveyed by these several phrases. The comment on the word is well illustrated by the passage cited at the bar, from the 10th section of the 1st article of the constitution. It is, we think, impossible to compare the sentence which prohibits a state from laying 'imposts, or duties on imports or exports, except what may be *absolutely* necessary for executing its inspection laws,' with that which authorizes congress 'to make all laws which shall be necessary and proper for carrying into execution' the powers of the general government, without feeling a conviction, that the convention understood itself to change materially the meaning of the word 'necessary,' by prefixing the word 'absolutely.' This word, then, like others, is used in various senses; and, in its construction, the subject, the context, the intention of the person using them, are all to be taken into view.

Let this be done in the case under consideration. The subject is the execution of those great powers on which the welfare of a nation essentially depends. It must have been the intention of those who gave these powers, to insure, so far as human prudence could insure, their beneficial execution. This could not be done, by confiding the choice of means to such narrow limits as not to leave it in the power of congress to adopt any which might be appropriate, and which were conducive to the end. This provision is made in a constitution, intended to endure for ages to come, and consequently, to be adapted to the various *crises* of human affairs. To have prescribed the means by which government should, in all future time, execute its powers, would have been to change, entirely, the character of the instrument, and give it the properties of a legal code. It would have been an unwise attempt to provide, by immutable rules, for exigencies which, if foreseen at all, must have been seen dimly, and which can be best provided for as they occur. To have declared, that the best means shall not be used, but those alone, without which the power given would be nugatory, would have been to deprive the legislature of the capacity to avail itself of experience, to exercise its reason, and to accommodate its legislation to circumstances. If we apply this principle of construction to any of the powers of the government, we shall find it so pernicious in its operation that we shall be compelled to discard it.

* * *

But the argument which most conclusively demonstrates the error of the construction contended for by the counsel for the state of Maryland, is founded on the intention of the convention, as manifested in the whole clause.

* * *

We think so for the following reasons: 1st. The clause is placed among the powers of congress, not among the limitations on those powers. 2d. Its terms purport to enlarge, not to diminish the powers vested in the government. It purports to be an additional power, not a restriction on those already granted. No reason has been, or can be assigned, for thus concealing an intention to narrow the discretion of the national legislature, under words which purport to enlarge it. The framers of the Constitution wished its adoption, and well knew that it would be endangered by its strength, not by its weakness. Had they been capable of using language which would convey to the eye one idea, and, after deep reflection, impress on the mind, another, they would rather have disguised the grant of power, than its limitation. If, then, their intention had been, by this clause, to restrain the free use of means which might otherwise have been implied, that intention would have been inserted in another place, and would have been expressed in terms resembling these. 'In carrying into execution the foregoing powers, and all others,' &c., 'no laws shall be passed but such as are necessary and proper.' Had the intention been to make this clause restrictive, it would unquestionably have been so in form as well as in effect.

The result of the most careful and attentive consideration bestowed upon this clause is, that if it does not enlarge, it cannot be construed to restrain the powers of congress, or to impair the right of the legislature to exercise its best judgment in the selection of measures to carry into execution the constitutional powers of the government. If no other motive for its insertion can be suggested, a sufficient one is found in the desire to remove all doubts respecting the right to legislate on that vast mass of incidental powers which must be involved in the Constitution, if that instrument be not a splendid bauble.

We admit, as all must admit, that the powers of the government are limited, and that its limits are not to be transcended. But we think the sound construction of the constitution must allow to the national legislature that discretion, with respect to the means by which the powers it confers are to be carried into execution, which will enable that body to perform the high duties assigned to it, in the manner most beneficial to the people. Let the end be legitimate, let it be within the scope of the constitution, and all means which are appropriate, which are plainly adapted to that end, which are not prohibited, but consist with the letter and spirit of the Constitution, are constitutional.

That a corporation must be considered as a means not less usual, not of higher dignity, not more requiring a particular specification than other means, has been sufficiently proved. If we look to the origin of corporations, to the manner in which they have been framed in that government from which we have derived most of our legal principles and ideas, or to the uses to which they have been applied, we find no reason to suppose, that a constitution, omitting, and wisely omitting, to enumerate all the means for carrying into execution the great powers vested in government, ought to have specified this. Had it been intended to grant this power, as one which should be distinct and independent, to be exercised in any case whatever, it would have found a place among the enumerated powers of the government. But being considered merely as a means, to be employed only for the purpose of carrying into execution the given powers, there could be no motive for particularly mentioning it.

* * *

After the most deliberate consideration, it is the unanimous and decided opinion of this court, that the act to incorporate the Bank of the United States is a law made in pursuance of the constitution, and is a part of the supreme law of the land.

* * *

It being the opinion of the court, that the act incorporating the bank is constitutional; and that the power of establishing a branch in the state of Maryland might be properly exercised by the bank itself, we proceed to inquire—

Whether the state of Maryland may, without violating the constitution, tax that branch? That the power of taxation is one of vital importance; that it is retained by the states; that it is not abridged by the grant of a similar power to the government of the Union; that it is to be concurrently exercised by the two governments—are truths which have never been denied. But such is the paramount character of the Constitution, that its capacity to withdraw any subject from the action of even this power, is admitted. The states are expressly forbidden to lay any duties on imports or exports, except what may be absolutely necessary for executing their inspection laws. If the obligation of this prohibition must be conceded—if it may restrain a state from the exercise of its taxing power on imports and exports—the same paramount character would seem to restrain, as it certainly may restrain, a state from such other exercise of this power, as is in its nature incompatible with, and repugnant to, the constitutional laws of the Union. A law, absolutely repugnant to another, as entirely repeals that other as if express terms of repeal were used.

On this ground, the counsel for the bank place its claim to be exempted from the power of a state to tax its operations. There is no express provision for the case, but the claim has been sustained on a principle which so entirely pervades the Constitution, is so intermixed with the materials which compose it, so interwoven with its web, so blended with its texture, as to be incapable of being separated from it, without rending it into shreds. This great principle is, that the Constitution and the laws made in pursuance thereof are supreme; that they control the Constitution and laws of the respective states, and cannot be controlled by them. From this, which may be almost termed an axiom, other propositions are deduced as corollaries, on the truth or error of which, and on their application to this case, the cause has been supposed to depend. These are, 1st. That a power to create implies a power to preserve: 2d. That a power to destroy, if wielded by a different hand, is hostile to, and incompatible with these powers to create and to preserve: 3d. That where this repugnancy exists, that authority which is supreme must control, not yield to that over which it is supreme.

These propositions, as abstract truths, would, perhaps, never be controverted. Their application to this case, however, has been denied; and both in maintaining the affirmative and the negative, a splendor of eloquence, and strength of argument, seldom, if ever, surpassed, have been displayed.

The power of congress to create, and of course, to continue, the bank, was the subject of the preceding part of this opinion; and is no longer to be considered as questionable. That the power of taxing it by the states may be exercised so as to destroy it, is too obvious to be denied. But taxation is said to be an absolute power, which acknowledges no other limits than those expressly prescribed in the constitution, and like sovereign power of every other description, is intrusted to the discretion of those who use it. But the very terms of this argument admit, that the sovereignty of the state, in the article of taxation itself, is subordinate to, and may be controlled by the Constitution of the United States. How far it has been controlled by that instrument, must be a question of construction. In making this construction, no principle, not declared, can be admissible, which would defeat the legitimate operations of a supreme government. It is of the very essence of supremacy, to remove all obstacles to its action within its own sphere, and so to modify every power vested in subordinate governments, as to exempt its own operations from their own influence. This effect need not be stated in terms. It is so involved in the declaration of supremacy, so necessarily implied in it, that the expression of it could not make it more certain. We must, therefore, keep it in view, while construing the Constitution.

* * *

If we apply the principle for which the state of Maryland contends, to the Constitution, generally, we shall find it capable of changing totally the character of that instrument. We shall find it capable of arresting all the measures of the government, and of prostrating it at the foot of the states. The American people have declared their constitution and the laws made in pursuance thereof, to be supreme; but this principle would transfer the supremacy, in fact, to the states. If the states may tax one instrument, employed by the government in the execution of its powers, they may tax any and every other instrument. They may tax the mail; they may tax the mint; they may tax patent-rights; they may tax the papers of the custom-house; they may tax judicial process; they may tax all the means employed by the government, to an excess which would defeat all the ends of government. This was not intended by the American people. They did not design to make their government dependent on the states.

* * *

The court has bestowed on this subject its most deliberate consideration. The result is a conviction that the states have no power, by taxation or otherwise, to retard, impede, burden, or in any manner control, the operations of the constitutional laws enacted by congress to carry into execution the powers vested in the general government. This is, we think, the unavoidable consequence of that supremacy which the constitution has declared. We are unanimously of opinion, that the law passed by the legislature of Maryland, imposing a tax on the Bank of the United States, is unconstitutional and void.

This opinion does not deprive the states of any resources which they originally possessed. It does not extend to a tax paid by the real property of the bank, in common with the other real property within the state, nor to a tax imposed on the interest which the citizens of Maryland may hold in this institution, in common with other property of the same description throughout the state. But this is a tax on the operations of the bank, and is, consequently, a tax on the operation of an instrument employed by the government of the Union to carry its powers into execution. Such a tax must be unconstitutional.

JUDGMENT.—This cause came on to be heard, on the transcript of the record of the court of appeals of the state of Maryland, and was argued by counsel: on consideration whereof, it is the opinion of this court, that the act of the legislature of Maryland is contrary to the constitution of the United States, and void

* * *

In **UNITED STATES v. COMSTOCK**, 560 U.S. 126 (2010), a federal statute authorized the U.S. Department of Justice to detain mentally ill sexual predators beyond their release dates from state prisons. Justice Breyer held for a 7–2 majority that the Necessary and Proper Clause gave Congress the authority to enact criminal laws in furtherance of its statutory authority to provide prisoners with mental health care. Justice Scalia's dissent argued that the Clause did not extend to furthering legislation rather than constitutionally enumerated powers.

---

**Questions:** Is the *McCulloch* an example of originalism or of living constitutionalism? Comparing *Missouri* and *McCulloch,* which looks more like a case of judicial overreach?

# CHAPTER 2

# STANDING

■ ■ ■

## CONTEXT & SOURCES

Standing, the doctrine by which parties are allowed to have a court decide their dispute, arises out of the "cases and controversies" limitation on federal jurisdiction set forth in the Constitution's Article III, § 2, paragraph 1. The scope of standing has evolved over time: Pure "interest" litigation has been discouraged, but states have been given greater flexibility to protect their sovereign interests, such as the quality of their natural resources.

For further reading, students should consult Daniel P. Selmi, *Dawn at Mineral King Valley* (University of Chicago Press, 2022), which dissects the Sierra Club's lawsuit against Disney and the Supreme Court's development of standing doctrine. Christopher Stone, the scholar who inspired Justice Douglas's *Sierra Club* dissent, makes the case for broader litigation opportunities in *Should Trees Have Standing? Law, Morality and the Environment* (3d ed., Oxford University Press, 2010). On a key decision expanding standing, *see* Richard J. Lazarus, *The Rule of Five: Making Climate History at the Supreme Court* (Harvard University Press, 2020) which studies in depth how *Massachusetts v. E.P.A.* was argued and decided.

### SIERRA CLUB V. MORTON

405 U.S. 727 (1972)

* * *

MR. JUSTICE STEWART delivered the opinion of the Court.

The Mineral King Valley is an area of great natural beauty nestled in the Sierra Nevada Mountains in Tulare County, California, adjacent to Sequoia National Park. It has been part of the Sequoia National Forest since 1926, and is designated as a national game refuge by special Act of Congress. Though once the site of extensive mining activity, Mineral King is now used almost exclusively for recreational purposes. Its relative inaccessibility and lack of development have limited the number of visitors each year, and at the same time have preserved the valley's quality as a quasi-wilderness area largely uncluttered by the products of civilization.

The United States Forest Service, which is entrusted with the maintenance and administration of national forests, began in the late 1940's to give consideration to Mineral King as a potential site for recreational development. Prodded by a rapidly increasing demand for skiing facilities, the Forest Service published a prospectus in 1965, inviting bids from private developers for the construction and operation of a ski resort that would also serve as a summer recreation area. The proposal of Walt Disney Enterprises, Inc., was chosen from those of six bidders, and Disney received a three-year permit to conduct surveys and explorations in the valley in connection with its preparation of a complete master plan for the resort.

The final Disney plan, approved by the Forest Service in January 1969, outlines a $35 million complex of motels, restaurants, swimming pools, parking lots, and other structures designed to accommodate 14,000 visitors daily. This complex is to be constructed on 80 acres of the valley floor under a 30-year use permit from the Forest Service. Other facilities, including ski lifts, ski trails, a cog-assisted railway, and utility installations, are to be constructed on the mountain slopes and in other parts of the valley under a revocable special-use permit. To provide access to the resort, the State of California proposes to construct a highway 20 miles in length. A section of this road would traverse Sequoia National Park, as would a proposed high voltage power line needed to provide electricity for the resort. Both the highway and the power line require the approval of the Department of the Interior, which is entrusted with the preservation and maintenance of the national parks.

Representatives of the Sierra Club, who favor maintaining Mineral King largely in its present state, followed the progress of recreational planning for the valley with close attention and increasing dismay. They unsuccessfully sought a public hearing on the proposed development in 1965, and in subsequent correspondence with officials of the Forest Service and the Department of the Interior, they expressed the Club's objections to Disney's plan as a whole and to particular features included in it. In June 1969 the Club filed the present suit in the United States District Court for the Northern District of California, seeking a declaratory judgment that various aspects of the proposed development contravene federal laws and regulations governing the preservation of national parks, forests, and game refuges, and also seeking preliminary and permanent injunctions restraining the federal officials involved from granting their approval or issuing permits in connection with the Mineral King project. The petitioner Sierra Club sued as a membership corporation with 'a special interest in the conservation and the sound maintenance of the national parks, game refuges and forests of the country,' and invoked the judicial-review provisions of the Administrative Procedure Act, 5 U.S.C. § 701 et seq.

After two days of hearings, the District Court granted the requested preliminary injunction. It rejected the respondents' challenge to the Sierra Club's standing to sue, and determined that the hearing had raised questions 'concerning possible excess of statutory authority, sufficiently substantial and serious to justify a preliminary injunction. . . .' The respondents appealed, and the Court of Appeals for the Ninth Circuit reversed. 433 F.2d 24. With respect to the petitioner's standing, the court noted that there was 'no allegation in the complaint that members of the Sierra Club would be affected by the actions of (the respondents) other than the fact that the actions are personally displeasing or distasteful to them,' id., at 33, and concluded:

'We do not believe such club concern without a showing of more direct interest can constitute standing in the legal sense sufficient to challenge the exercise of responsibilities on behalf of all the citizens by two cabinet level officials of the government acting under Congressional and Constitutional authority.' Id., at 30.

Alternatively, the Court of Appeals held that the Sierra Club had no made an adequate showing of irreparable injury and likelihood of success on the merits to justify issuance of a preliminary injunction. The court thus vacated the injunction. The Sierra Club filed a petition for a writ of certiorari which we granted to review the questions of federal law presented.

The first question presented is whether the Sierra Club has alleged facts that entitle it to obtain judicial review of the challenged action. Whether a party has a sufficient stake in an otherwise justiciable controversy to obtain judicial resolution of that controversy is what has traditionally been referred to as the question of standing to sue. Where the party does not rely on any specific statute authorizing invocation of the judicial process, the question of standing depends upon whether the party has alleged such a 'personal stake in the outcome of the controversy,' Baker v. Carr, 369 U.S. 186, 204 as to ensure that 'the dispute sought to be adjudicated will be presented in an adversary context and in a form historically viewed as capable of judicial resolution.' Flast v. Cohen, 392 U.S. 83, 101. Where, however, Congress has authorized public officials to perform certain functions according to law, and has provided by statute for judicial review of those actions under certain circumstances, the inquiry as to standing must begin with a determination of whether the statute in question authorizes review at the behest of the plaintiff.

The Sierra Club relies upon § 10 of the Administrative Procedure Act (APA), 5 U.S.C. § 702, which provides:

'A person suffering legal wrong because of agency action, or adversely affected or aggrieved by agency action within the meaning of a relevant statute, is entitled to judicial review thereof.'

Early decisions under this statute interpreted the language as adopting the various formulations of 'legal interest' and 'legal wrong' then prevailing as constitutional requirements of standing. But, in Association of Data Processing Service Organizations, Inc. v. Camp, 397 U.S. 150, 90 S.Ct. 827, and Barlow v. Collins, 397 U.S. 159, decided the same day, we held more broadly that persons had standing to obtain judicial review of federal agency action under § 10 of the APA where they had alleged that the challenged action had caused them 'injury in fact,' and where the alleged injury was to an interest 'arguably within the zone of interests to be protected or regulated' by the statutes that the agencies were claimed to have violated.

In Data Processing, the injury claimed by the petitioners consisted of harm to their competitive position in the computer-servicing market through a ruling by the Comptroller of the Currency that national banks might perform data-processing services for their customers. In Barlow, the petitioners were tenant farmers who claimed that certain regulations of the Secretary of Agriculture adversely affected their economic position vis-a-vis their landlords. These palpable economic injuries have long been recognized as sufficient to lay the basis for standing, with or without a specific statutory provision for judicial review. Thus, neither Data Processing nor Barlow addressed itself to the question, which has arisen with increasing frequency in federal courts in recent years, as to what must be alleged by persons who claim injury of a noneconomic nature to interests that are widely shared. That question is presented in this case.

The injury alleged by the Sierra Club will be incurred entirely by reason of the change in the uses to which Mineral King will be put, and the attendant change in the aesthetics and ecology of the area. Thus, in referring to the road to be built through Sequoia National Park, the complaint alleged that the development 'would destroy or otherwise adversely affect the scenery, natural and historic objects and wildlife of the park and would impair the enjoyment of the park for future generations.' We do not question that this type of harm may amount to an 'injury in fact' sufficient to lay the basis for standing under § 10 of the APA. Aesthetic and environmental well-being, like economic well-being, are important ingredients of the quality of life in our society, and the fact that particular environmental interests are shared by the many rather than the few does not make them less deserving of legal protection through the judicial process. But the 'injury in fact' test requires more than an injury to a cognizable interest. It requires that the party seeking review be himself among the injured.

The impact of the proposed changes in the environment of Mineral King will not fall indiscriminately upon every citizen. The alleged injury will be felt directly only by those who use Mineral King and Sequoia National Park, and for whom the aesthetic and recreational values of the area will be lessened by the highway and ski resort. The Sierra Club failed to allege that it or its members would be affected in any of their activities or pastimes by the Disney development. Nowhere in the pleadings or affidavits did the Club state that its members use Mineral King for any purpose, much less that they use it in any way that would be significantly affected by the proposed actions of the respondents.

The Club apparently regarded an allegations of individualized injury as superfluous, on the theory that this was a 'public' action involving questions as to the use of natural resources, and that the Club's longstanding concern with and expertise in such matters were sufficient to give it standing as a 'representative of the public.' This theory reflects a misunderstanding of our cases involving so-called 'public actions' in the area of administrative law.

The origin of the theory advanced by the Sierra Club may be traced to a dictum in Scripps-Howard Radio v. FCC, 316 U.S. 4, in which the licensee of a radio station in Cincinnati, Ohio, sought a stay of an order of the FCC allowing another radio station in a nearby city to change its frequency and increase its range. In discussing its power to grant a stay, the Court noted that 'these private litigants have standing only as representatives of the public interest.' Id., at 14. But that observation did not describe the basis upon which the appellant was allowed to obtain judicial review as a 'person aggrieved' within the meaning of the statute involved in that case, since Scripps-Howard was clearly 'aggrieved' by reason of the economic injury that it would suffer as a result of the Commission's action. The Court's statement was, rather directed to the theory upon which Congress had authorized judicial review of the Commission's actions. That theory had been described earlier in FCC v. Sanders Bros. Radio Station, 309 U.S. 470, 477, as follows:

'Congress had some purpose in enacting section 402(b)(2). It may have been of opinion that one likely to be financially injured by the issue of a license would be the only person having a sufficient interest to bring to the attention of the appellate court errors of law in the action of the Commission in granting the license. It is within the power of Congress to confer such standing to prosecute an appeal.'

Taken together, Sanders and Scripps-Howard thus established a dual proposition: the fact of economic injury is what gives a person standing to seek judicial review under the statute, but once review is properly invoked, that person may argue the public interest in support of his claim that the agency has failed to comply with its statutory mandate. It was in the latter sense that the 'standing' of the appellant in Scripps-Howard, existed only as a 'representative of the public interest.' It is in a similar sense that we have used the phrase 'private attorney general' to describe the function performed by persons upon whom Congress has conferred the right to seek judicial review of agency action. See Data Processing, supra, 397 U.S., at 154.

The trend of cases arising under the APA and other statutes authorizing judicial review of federal agency action has been toward recognizing that injuries other than economic harm are sufficient to bring a person within the meaning of the statutory language, and toward discarding the notion that an injury that is widely shared is ipso facto not an injury sufficient to provide the basis for judicial review. We noted this development with approval in Data Processing, 397 U.S., at 154, in saying that the interest alleged to have been injured 'may reflect 'aesthetic, conservational, and recreational' as well as economic values.' But broadening the categories of injury that may be alleged in support of standing is a different matter from abandoning the requirement that the party seeking review must himself have suffered an injury.

Some courts have indicated a willingness to take this latter step by conferring standing upon organizations that have demonstrated 'an organizational interest in the problem' of environmental or consumer protection. Environmental Defense Fund, Inc. v. Hardin, 428 F.2d 1093, 1097. It is clear that an organization whose members are injured may represent those members in a proceeding for judicial review. See, e.g., NAACP v. Button, 371 U.S. 415, 428. But a mere 'interest in a problem,' no matter how longstanding the interest and no matter how qualified the organization is in evaluating the problem, is not sufficient by itself to render the organization 'adversely affected' or 'aggrieved' within the meaning of the APA. The Sierra Club is a large and long-established organization, with a historic commitment to the cause of protecting our Nation's natural heritage from man's depredations. But if a 'special interest' in this subject were enough to entitle the Sierra Club to commence this litigation, there would appear to be no objective basis upon which to disallow a suit by any other bona fide 'special interest' organization however small or short-lived. And if any group with a bona fide 'special interest' could initiate such litigation, it is difficult to perceive why any individual citizen with the same bona fide special interest would not also be entitled to do so.

The requirement that a party seeking review must allege facts showing that he is himself adversely affected does not insulate executive action from judicial review, nor does it prevent any public interests from being protected through the judicial process. It does serve as at least a rough attempt to put the decision as to whether review will be sought in the hands of those who have a direct stake in the outcome. That goal would be undermined were we to construe the APA to authorize judicial review at the behest of organizations or individuals who seek to do no more than vindicate their own value preferences through the judicial process. The principle that the Sierra Club would have us establish in this case would do just that.

As we conclude that the Court of Appeals was correct in its holding that the Sierra Club lacked standing to maintain this action, we do not reach any other questions presented in the petition, and we intimate no view on the merits of the complaint. The judgment is

Affirmed.

MR. JUSTICE POWELL and MR. JUSTICE REHNQUIST took no part in the consideration or decision of this case.

MR. JUSTICE DOUGLAS, dissenting.

I share the views of my Brother BLACKMUN and would reverse the judgment below.

The critical question of 'standing' would be simplified and also put neatly in focus if we fashioned a federal rule that allowed environmental issues to be litigated before federal agencies or federal courts in the name of the inanimate object about to be despoiled, defaced, or invaded by roads and bulldozers and where injury is the subject of public outrage. Contemporary public concern for protecting nature's ecological equilibrium should lead to the conferral of standing upon environmental objects to sue for their own preservation. See Stone, Should Trees Have Standing? Toward Legal Rights for Natural Objects, 45 S.Cal.L.Rev. 450 (1972). This suit would therefore be more properly labeled as Mineral King v. Morton.

Inanimate objects are sometimes parties in litigation. A ship has a legal personality, a fiction found useful for maritime purposes. The corporation sole—a creature of ecclesiastical law is an acceptable adversary and large fortunes ride on its cases. The ordinary corporation is a 'person' for purposes of the adjudicatory processes, whether it represents proprietary, spiritual, aesthetic, or charitable causes.

So it should be as respects valleys, alpine meadows, rivers, lakes, estuaries, beaches, ridges, proves of trees, swampland, or even air that feels the destructive pressures of modern technology and modern life. The river, for example, is the living symbol of all the life it sustains or nourishes—fish, aquatic insects, water ouzels, otter, fisher, deer, elk, bear, and all other animals, including man, who are dependent on it or who enjoy it for its sight, its sound, or its life. The river as plaintiff speaks for the ecological unit of life that is part of it. Those people who have a meaningful relation to that body of water—whether it be a fisherman, a canoeist, a zoologist, or a logger—must be able to speak for the values which the river represents and which are threatened with destruction.

I do not know Mineral King. I have never seen it nor traveled it, though I have seen articles describing its proposed 'development' notably Hano,

Protectionists vs. recreationists—The Battle of Mineral King, N.Y. Times Mag., Aug. 17, 1969, p. 25; and Browning, Mickey Mouse in the Mountains, Harper's, March 1972, p. 65. The Sierra Club in its complaint alleges that '(o)ne of the principal purposes of the Sierra Club is to protect and conserve the national resources of the Sierra Nevada Mountains.' The District Court held that this uncontested allegation made the Sierra Club 'sufficiently aggrieved' to have 'standing' to sue on behalf of Mineral King.

Mineral King is doubtless like other wonders of the Sierra Nevada such as Tuolumne Meadows and the John Muir Trail. Those who hike it, fish it, hunt it, camp in it, frequent it, or visit it merely to sit in solitude and wonderment are legitimate spokesmen for it, whether they may be few or many. Those who have that intimate relation with the inanimate object about to be injured, polluted, or otherwise despoiled are its legitimate spokesmen.

The Solicitor General, whose views on this subject are in the Appendix to this opinion, takes a wholly different approach. He considers the problem in terms of 'government by the Judiciary.' With all respect, the problem is to make certain that the inanimate objects, which are the very core of America's beauty, have spokesmen before they are destroyed. It is, of course, true that most of them are under the control of a federal or state agency. The standards given those agencies are usually expressed in terms of the 'public interest.' Yet 'public interest' has so many differing shades of meaning as to be quite meaningless on the environmental front. Congress accordingly has adopted ecological standards in the National Environmental Policy Act of 1969, Pub.L. 91–90, 83 Stat. 852, 42 U.S.C. § 4321 et seq., and guidelines for agency action have been provided by the Council on Environmental Quality of which Russell E. Train is Chairman. See 36 Fed.Reg. 7724.

Yet the pressures on agencies for favorable action one way or the other are enormous. The suggestion that Congress can stop action which is undesirable is true in theory; yet even Congress is too remote to give meaningful direction and its machinery is too ponderous to use very often. The federal agencies of which I speak are not venal or corrupt. But they are notoriously under the control of powerful interests who manipulate them through advisory committees, or friendly working relations, or who have that natural affinity with the agency which in time develops between the regulator and the regulated. As early as 1894, Attorney General Olney predicted that regulatory agencies might become 'industry-minded,' as illustrated by his forecast concerning the Interstate Commerce Commission:

'The Commission . . . is, or can be made, of great use to the railroads. It satisfies the popular clamor for a government supervision of railroads, at the same time that that supervision is almost entirely nominal. Further, the older such a commission gets to be, the more inclined it will be found to take the business and railroad view of things.' M. Josephson, The Politicos 526 (1938).

Years later a court of appeals observed, 'the recurring question which has plagued public regulation of industry (is) whether the regulatory agency is unduly oriented toward the interests of the industry it is designed to regulate, rather than the public interest it is designed to protect.' Moss v. CAB, 430 F.2d 891, 893.

* * *

The Forest Service—one of the federal agencies behind the scheme to despoil Mineral King—has been notorious for its alignment with lumber companies, although its mandate from Congress directs it to consider the various aspects of multiple use in its supervision of the national forests.

The voice of the inanimate object, therefore, should not be stilled. That does not mean that the judiciary takes over the managerial functions from the federal agency. It merely means that before these priceless bits of Americana (such as a valley, an alpine meadow, a river, or a lake) are forever lost or are so transformed as to be reduced to the eventual rubble of our urban environment, the voice of the existing beneficiaries of these environmental wonders should be heard.

Perhaps they will not win. Perhaps the bulldozers of 'progress' will plow under all the aesthetic wonders of this beautiful land. That is not the present question. The sole question is, who has standing to be heard?

Those who hike the Appalachian Trail into Sunfish Pond, New Jersey, and camp or sleep there, or run the Allagash in Maine, or climb the Guadalupes in West Texas, or who canoe and portage the Quetico Superior in Minnesota, certainly should have standing to defend those natural wonders before courts or agencies, though they live 3,000 miles away. Those who merely are caught up in environmental news or propaganda and flock to defend these waters or areas may be treated differently. That is why these environmental issues should be tendered by the inanimate object itself. Then there will be assurances that all of the forms of life which it represents will stand before the court—the pileated woodpecker as well as the coyote and bear, the lemmings as well as the trout in the streams. Those inarticulate members of the ecological group cannot speak. But those people who have so frequented the place as to know its values and wonders will be able to speak for the entire ecological community.

Ecology reflects the land ethic; and Aldo Leopold wrote in A Sand County Almanac 204 (1949), 'The land ethic simply enlarges the boundaries of the community to include soils, waters, plants, and animals, or collectively: the land.'

That, as I see it, is the issue of 'standing' in the present case and controversy.

* * *

---

**Question:** Why didn't the plaintiff in *Sierra Club* argue that their members actually used the area at issue?

## LUJAN V. DEFENDERS OF WILDLIFE

504 U.S. 555 (1992)

* * *

SCALIA, J., announced the judgment of the Court and delivered the opinion of the Court with respect to Parts I, II, III-A, and IV, in which REHNQUIST, C.J., and WHITE, KENNEDY, SOUTER, and THOMAS, JJ., joined, and an opinion with respect to Part III-B, in which REHNQUIST, C.J., and WHITE and THOMAS, JJ., joined. KENNEDY, J., filed an opinion concurring in part and concurring in the judgment, in which SOUTER, J., joined. STEVENS, J., filed an opinion concurring in the judgment. BLACKMUN, J., filed a dissenting opinion, in which O'CONNOR, J., joined.

* * *

This case involves a challenge to a rule promulgated by the Secretary of the Interior interpreting § 7 of the Endangered Species Act of 1973 (ESA), 87 Stat. 884, 892, as amended, 16 U.S.C. § 1536, in such fashion as to render it applicable only to actions within the United States or on the high seas. The preliminary issue, and the only one we reach, is whether the respondents here, plaintiffs below, have standing to seek judicial review of the rule.

The ESA, 87 Stat. 884, as amended, 16 U.S.C. § 1531 et seq., seeks to protect species of animals against threats to their continuing existence caused by man. See generally TVA v. Hill, 437 U.S. 153, 98 S.Ct. 2279, 57 L.Ed.2d 117 (1978). The ESA instructs the Secretary of the Interior to promulgate by regulation a list of those species which are either endangered or threatened under enumerated criteria, and to define the critical habitat of these species. 16 U.S.C. §§ 1533, 1536. Section 7(a)(2) of the Act then provides, in pertinent part:

"Each Federal agency shall, in consultation with and with the assistance of the Secretary [of the Interior], insure that any action authorized, funded, or carried out by such agency . . . is not likely to jeopardize the continued existence of any endangered species or threatened species or result in the destruction or adverse modification of habitat of such species which is determined by the Secretary, after consultation as appropriate with affected States, to be critical." 16 U.S.C. § 1536(a)(2).

In 1978, the Fish and Wildlife Service (FWS) and the National Marine Fisheries Service (NMFS), on behalf of the Secretary of the Interior and the Secretary of Commerce respectively, promulgated a joint regulation stating that the obligations imposed by § 7(a)(2) extend to actions taken in foreign nations. 43 Fed.Reg. 874 (1978). The next year, however, the Interior Department began to reexamine its position. Letter from Leo Kuliz, Solicitor, Department of the Interior, to Assistant Secretary, Fish and Wildlife and Parks, Aug. 8, 1979. A revised joint regulation, reinterpreting § 7(a)(2) to require consultation only for actions taken in the United States or on the high seas, was proposed in 1983, 48 Fed.Reg. 29990 (1983), and promulgated in 1986, 51 Fed.Reg. 19926 (1986); 50 C.F.R. 402.01 (1991).

Shortly thereafter, respondents, organizations dedicated to wildlife conservation and other environmental causes, filed this action against the Secretary of the Interior, seeking a declaratory judgment that the new regulation is in error as to the geographic scope of § 7(a)(2), and an injunction requiring the Secretary to promulgate a new regulation restoring the initial interpretation. The District Court granted the Secretary's motion to dismiss for lack of standing. Defenders of Wildlife v. Hodel, 658 F.Supp. 43, 47–48 (Minn.1987). The Court of Appeals for the Eighth Circuit reversed by a divided vote. Defenders of Wildlife v. Hodel, 851 F.2d 1035 (1988). On remand, the Secretary moved for summary judgment on the standing issue, and respondents moved for summary judgment on the merits. The District Court denied the Secretary's motion, on the ground that the Eighth Circuit had already determined the standing question in this case; it granted respondents' merits motion, and ordered the Secretary to publish a revised regulation. Defenders of Wildlife v. Hodel, 707 F.Supp. 1082 (Minn.1989). The Eighth Circuit affirmed. 911 F.2d 117 (1990). We granted certiorari, 500 U.S. ___, 111 (1991).

While the Constitution of the United States divides all power conferred upon the Federal Government into "legislative Powers," Art. I, § 1, "[t]he executive Power," Art. II, § 1, and "[t]he judicial Power," Art. III, § 1, it does not attempt to define those terms. To be sure, it limits the jurisdiction of federal courts to "Cases" and "Controversies," but an executive inquiry can bear the name "case" (the Hoffa case) and a legislative dispute can bear the name "controversy" (the Smoot-Hawley controversy). Obviously, then, the Constitution's central mechanism of separation of powers depends largely upon common understanding of what activities are appropriate to legislatures, to executives, and to courts. In The Federalist No. 48, Madison expressed the view that "[i]t is not infrequently a question of real nicety in legislative bodies whether the operation of a particular measure will, or will not, extend beyond the legislative sphere," whereas "the executive power [is] restrained within a narrower compass and . . . more simple in its nature," and "the judiciary [is] described by landmarks still less uncertain." The Federalist No. 48, p. 256 (Carey and McClellan eds. 1990). One of those landmarks, setting apart the "Cases" and "Controversies" that are of the justiciable sort referred to in Article III—"serv[ing] to identify those disputes which are appropriately resolved through the judicial process," Whitmore v. Arkansas, 495 U.S. 149, 155 (1990)—is the doctrine of standing. Though some of its elements express merely prudential considerations that are part of judicial self-government, the core component of standing is an essential and unchanging part of the case-or-controversy requirement of Article III. See, e.g., Allen v. Wright, 468 U.S. 737, 751 (1984).

Over the years, our cases have established that the irreducible constitutional minimum of standing contains three elements: First, the plaintiff must have suffered an "injury in fact"—an invasion of a legally-protected interest which is (a) concrete and particularized, see id., at 756, 104 S.Ct., at 3327; Sierra Club v. Morton, 405 U.S. 727, 740–741 (1972);1 and (b) "actual or imminent, not 'conjectural' or 'hypothetical,' " Whitmore, supra, 495 U.S., at 155 (1983)). Second, there must be a causal connection between the injury and the conduct complained of—the injury has to be "fairly . . . trace[able] to the challenged action of the defendant, and not . . . th[e] result [of] the independent action of some third party not before the court." Simon v. Eastern Kentucky Welfare Rights Org., 426 U.S. 26, 41–42 (1976). Third, it must be "likely," as opposed to merely "speculative," that the injury will be "redressed by a favorable decision." Id., at 38.

The party invoking federal jurisdiction bears the burden of establishing these elements. See FW/PBS, Inc. v. Dallas, 493 U.S. 215, 231 (1990). Since they are not mere pleading requirements but rather an indispensable part of the plaintiff's case, each element must be supported in the same way as any other matter on which the plaintiff bears the burden of proof, i.e., with the manner and degree of evidence required at the successive stages of the litigation. See Lujan v. National Wildlife Federation, 497 U.S. 871, 883–889; Gladstone, Realtors v. Village of Bellwood, 441 U.S. 91, 114–115; [additional citations]. * * * In response to a summary judgment motion, . . . the plaintiff can no longer rest on . . . "mere allegations," but must "set forth" by affidavit or other evidence "specific facts," Fed.Rule Civ.Proc. 56(e), which for purposes of the summary judgment motion will be taken to be true. And at the final stage, those facts (if controverted) must be "supported adequately by the evidence adduced at trial," Gladstone, supra, 441 U.S., at 115, n. 31.

* * *

We think the Court of Appeals failed to apply the foregoing principles in denying the Secretary's motion for summary judgment. Respondents had not made the requisite demonstration of (at least) injury and redressability.

Respondents' claim to injury is that the lack of consultation with respect to certain funded activities abroad "increas[es] the rate of extinction of endangered and threatened species." Complaint ¶ 5, App. 13. Of course, the desire to use or observe an animal species, even for purely aesthetic purposes, is undeniably a cognizable interest for purpose of standing. See, e.g., Sierra Club v. Morton, 405 U.S., at 734. "But the 'injury in fact' test requires more than an injury to a cognizable interest. It requires that the party seeking review be himself among the injured." Id., at 734–735. To survive the Secretary's summary judgment motion, respondents had to submit affidavits or other evidence showing, through specific facts, not only that listed species were in fact being threatened by funded activities abroad, but also that one or more of respondents' members would thereby be "directly" affected apart from their " 'special interest' in th[e] subject." Id., at 735, 739.

With respect to this aspect of the case, the Court of Appeals focused on the affidavits of two Defenders' members—Joyce Kelly and Amy Skilbred. Ms. Kelly stated that she traveled to Egypt in 1986 and "observed the traditional habitat of the endangered nile crocodile there and intend[s] to do so again, and hope[s] to observe the crocodile directly," and that she "will suffer harm in fact as a result of [the] American . . . role . . . in overseeing the rehabilitation of the Aswan High Dam on the Nile . . . and [in] develop[ing] . . . Egypt's . . . Master Water Plan." App. 101. Ms. Skilbred averred that she traveled to Sri Lanka in 1981 and "observed th[e] habitat" of "endangered species such as the Asian elephant and the leopard" at what is now the site of the Mahaweli Project funded by the Agency for International Development (AID), although she "was unable to see any of the endangered species;" "this development project," she continued, "will seriously reduce endangered, threatened, and endemic species habitat including areas that I visited . . . [, which] may severely shorten the future of these species;" that threat, she concluded, harmed her because she "intend[s] to return to Sri Lanka in the future and hope[s] to be more fortunate in spotting at least the endangered elephant and leopard." Id., at 145–146. When Ms. Skilbred was asked at a subsequent deposition if and when she had any plans to return to Sri Lanka, she reiterated that "I intend to go back to Sri Lanka," but confessed that she had no current plans: "I don't know [when]. There is a civil war going on right now. I don't know. Not next year, I will say. In the future." Id., at 318.

We shall assume for the sake of argument that these affidavits contain facts showing that certain agency-funded projects threaten listed species—though that is questionable. They plainly contain no facts, however, showing how damage to the species will produce "imminent" injury to Mss. Kelly and Skilbred. That the women "had visited" the areas of the projects before the projects commenced proves nothing. As we have said in a related context, " '[p]ast exposure to illegal conduct does not in itself show a present case or controversy regarding injunctive relief . . . if unaccompanied by any continuing, present adverse effects.' " Los Angeles v. Lyons, 461 U.S., at 102 (1983). And the affiants' profession of an "inten[t]" to return to the places they had visited before—where they will presumably, this time, be deprived of the opportunity to observe animals of the endangered species—is simply not enough. Such "some day" intentions—without any description of concrete plans, or indeed even any specification of when the some day will be—do not support a finding of the "actual or imminent" injury that our cases require. See supra, at 560.

Besides relying upon the Kelly and Skilbred affidavits, respondents propose a series of novel standing theories. The first, inelegantly styled "ecosystem nexus," proposes that any person who uses any part of a "contiguous ecosystem" adversely affected by a funded activity has standing even if the activity is located a great distance away. * * * [But] [t]o say that the Act protects ecosystems is not to say that the Act creates (if it were possible) rights of action in persons who have not been injured in fact, that is, persons who use portions of an ecosystem not perceptibly affected by the unlawful action in question.

Respondents' other theories are called, alas, the "animal nexus" approach, whereby anyone who has an interest in studying or seeing the endangered animals anywhere on the globe has standing; and the "vocational nexus" approach, under which anyone with a professional interest in such animals can sue. Under these theories, anyone who goes to see Asian elephants in the Bronx Zoo, and anyone who is a keeper of Asian elephants in the Bronx Zoo, has standing to sue because the Director of AID did not consult with the Secretary regarding the AID-funded project in Sri Lanka. This is beyond all reason. Standing is not "an ingenious academic exercise in the conceivable," United States v. Students Challenging Regulatory Agency Procedures (SCRAP), 412 U.S. 669 (1973), but as we have said requires, at the summary judgment stage, a factual showing of perceptible harm. It is clear that the person who observes or works with a particular animal threatened by a federal decision is facing perceptible harm, since the very subject of his interest will no longer exist. It is even plausible—though it goes to the outermost limit of plausibility—to think that a person who observes or works with animals of a particular species in the very area of the world where that species is threatened by a federal decision is facing such harm, since some animals that might have been the subject of his interest will no longer exist, see Japan Whaling Assn. v. American Cetacean Soc., 478 U.S. 221, 231, n. 4 (1986). It goes beyond the limit, however, and into pure speculation and fantasy, to say that anyone who observes or works with an endangered species, anywhere in the world, is appreciably harmed by a single project affecting some portion of that species with which he has no more specific connection.

Besides failing to show injury, respondents failed to demonstrate redressability. Instead of attacking the separate decisions to fund particular projects allegedly causing them harm, the respondents chose to challenge a more generalized level of government action (rules regarding consultation), the invalidation of which would affect all overseas projects.

* * *

Since the agencies funding the projects were not parties to the case, the District Court could accord relief only against the Secretary: He could be ordered to revise his regulation to require consultation for foreign projects. But this would not remedy respondents' alleged injury unless the funding agencies were bound by the Secretary's regulation, which is very much an open question.

* * *

During the period when the Secretary took the view that § 7(a)(2) did apply abroad, AID and FWS engaged in a running controversy over whether consultation was required with respect to the Mahaweli project, AID insisting that consultation applied only to domestic actions.

* * *

The Court of Appeals found that respondents had standing for an additional reason: because they had suffered a "procedural injury." The so-called "citizen-suit" provision of the ESA provides, in pertinent part, that "any person may commence a civil suit on his own behalf (A) to enjoin any person, including the United States and any other governmental instrumentality or agency . . . who is alleged to be in violation of any provision of this chapter." 16 U.S.C. § 1540(g). The court held that, because § 7(a)(2) requires interagency consultation, the citizen-suit provision creates a "procedural righ[t]" to consultation in all "persons"—so that anyone can file suit in federal court to challenge the Secretary's (or presumably any other official's) failure to follow the assertedly correct consultative procedure, notwithstanding their inability to allege any discrete injury flowing from that failure. 911 F.2d, at 121–122. To understand the remarkable nature of this holding one must be clear about what it does not rest upon: This is not a case where plaintiffs are seeking to enforce a procedural requirement the disregard of which could impair a separate concrete interest of theirs (e.g., the procedural requirement for a hearing prior to denial of their license application, or the procedural requirement for an environmental impact statement before a federal facility is constructed next door to them). Nor is it simply a case where concrete injury has been suffered by many persons, as in mass fraud or mass tort situations. Nor, finally, is it the unusual case in which Congress has created a concrete private interest in the outcome of a suit against a private party for the government's benefit, by providing a cash bounty for the victorious plaintiff. Rather, the court held that the injury-in-fact requirement had been satisfied by congressional conferral upon all persons of an abstract, self-contained, non-instrumental "right" to have the Executive observe the procedures required by law. We reject this view.

* * *

We have consistently held that a plaintiff raising only a generally available grievance about government—claiming only harm to his and every citizen's interest in proper application of the Constitution and laws, and seeking relief that no more directly and tangibly benefits him than it does the public at large—does not state an Article III case or controversy. For example, in Fairchild v. Hughes, 258 U.S. 126, 129–130 (1922), we dismissed a suit challenging the propriety of the process by which the Nineteenth Amendment was ratified. Justice Brandeis wrote for the Court:

"[This is] not a case within the meaning of . . . Article III. . . . Plaintiff has [asserted] only the right, possessed by every citizen, to require that the Government be administered according to law and that the public moneys be not wasted. Obviously this general right does not entitle a private citizen to institute in the federal courts a suit. . . ." Ibid.

* * *

More recent cases are to the same effect. In United States v. Richardson, 418 U.S. 166 (1974), we dismissed for lack of standing a taxpayer suit challenging the Government's failure to disclose the expenditures of the Central Intelligence Agency, in alleged violation of the constitutional requirement, Art. I, § 9, cl. 7, that "a regular Statement and Account of the Receipts and Expenditures of all public Money shall be published from time to time." We held that such a suit rested upon an impermissible "generalized grievance," and was inconsistent with "the framework of Article III" because "the impact on [plaintiff] is plainly undifferentiated and common to all members of the public." Richardson, supra, at 171, 176–177.

* * *

To be sure, our generalized-grievance cases have typically involved Government violation of procedures assertedly ordained by the Constitution rather than the Congress. But there is absolutely no basis for making the Article III inquiry turn on the source of the asserted right. Whether the courts were to act on their own, or at the invitation of Congress, in ignoring the concrete injury requirement described in our cases, they would be discarding a principle fundamental to the separate and distinct constitutional role of the Third Branch—one of the essential elements that identifies those "Cases" and "Controversies" that are the business of the courts rather than of the political branches. "The province of the court," as Chief Justice Marshall said in Marbury v. Madison, 5 U.S. (1 Cranch) 137, 170 (1803) "is, solely, to decide on the rights of individuals." Vindicating the public interest (including the public interest in government observance of the Constitution and laws) is the function of Congress and the Chief Executive. The question presented here is whether the public interest in proper administration of the laws (specifically, in agencies' observance of a particular, statutorily prescribed procedure) can be converted into an individual right by a statute that denominates it as such, and that permits all citizens (or, for that matter, a subclass of citizens who suffer no distinctive concrete harm) to sue. If the concrete injury requirement has the separation-of-powers significance we have always said, the answer must be obvious: To permit Congress to convert the undifferentiated public interest in executive officers' compliance with the law into an "individual right" vindicable in the courts is to permit Congress to transfer from the President to the courts the Chief Executive's most important constitutional duty, to "take Care that the Laws be faithfully executed," Art. II, § 3. It would enable the courts, with the permission of Congress, "to assume a position of authority over the governmental acts of another and co-equal department," Frothingham v. Mellon, 262 U.S., at 489 (1923) . . . We have always rejected that vision of our role.

* * *

We hold that respondents lack standing to bring this action and that the Court of Appeals erred in denying the summary judgment motion filed by the United States. The opinion of the Court of Appeals is hereby reversed, and the cause remanded for proceedings consistent with this opinion.

It is so ordered.

---

**Question:** In *Lujan,* why weren't plaintiffs' plans to visit the affected areas sufficient to give them standing?

## MASSACHUSETTS V. ENVIRONMENTAL PROTECTION AGENCY

549 U.S. 497 (2007)

JUSTICE STEVENS delivered the opinion of the Court.

A well-documented rise in global temperatures has coincided with a significant increase in the concentration of carbon dioxide in the atmosphere. Respected scientists believe the two trends are related. For when carbon dioxide is released into the atmosphere, it acts like the ceiling of a greenhouse, trapping solar energy and retarding the escape of reflected heat. It is therefore a species—the most important species—of a "greenhouse gas."

Calling global warming "the most pressing environmental challenge of our time," a group of States, local governments, and private organizations, alleged in a petition for certiorari that the Environmental Protection Agency (EPA) has abdicated its responsibility under the Clean Air Act to regulate the emissions of four greenhouse gases, including carbon dioxide. Specifically, petitioners asked us to answer two questions concerning the meaning of § 202(a)(1) of the Act: whether EPA has the statutory authority to regulate greenhouse gas emissions from new motor vehicles; and if so, whether its stated reasons for refusing to do so are consistent with the statute.

In response, EPA, supported by 10 intervening States and six trade associations, correctly argued that we may not address those two questions unless at least one petitioner has standing to invoke our jurisdiction under Article III of the Constitution. Notwithstanding the serious character of that jurisdictional argument and the absence of any conflicting decisions construing § 202(a)(1), the unusual importance of the underlying issue persuaded us to grant the writ. 548 U. S. ___ (2006).

Section 202(a)(1) of the Clean Air Act, as added by Pub. L. 89–272, § 101(8), 79 Stat. 992, and as amended by, *inter alia*, 84 Stat. 1690 and 91 Stat. 791, 42 U. S. C. § 7521(a)(1), provides:

"The [EPA] Administrator shall by regulation prescribe (and from time to time revise) in accordance with the provisions of this section, standards applicable to the emission of any air pollutant from any class or classes of new motor vehicles or new motor vehicle engines, which in his judgment cause, or contribute to, air pollution which may reasonably be anticipated to endanger public health or welfare . . . ."

The Act defines "air pollutant" to include "any air pollution agent or combination of such agents, including any physical, chemical, biological, radioactive . . . substance or matter which is emitted into or otherwise enters the ambient air." § 7602(g). "Welfare" is also defined broadly: among other things, it includes "effects on . . . weather . . . and climate." § 7602(h).

When Congress enacted these provisions, the study of climate change was in its infancy. In 1959, shortly after the U. S. Weather Bureau began monitoring atmospheric carbon dioxide levels, an observatory in Mauna Loa, Hawaii, recorded a mean level of 316 parts per million. This was well above the highest carbon dioxide concentration—no more than 300 parts per million—revealed in the 420,000-year-old ice-core record. By the time Congress drafted § 202(a)(1) in 1970, carbon dioxide levels had reached 325 parts per million.

In the late 1970's, the Federal Government began devoting serious attention to the possibility that carbon dioxide emissions associated with human activity could provoke climate change. In 1978, Congress enacted the National Climate Program Act, 92 Stat. 601, which required the President to establish a program to "assist the Nation and the world to understand and respond to natural and man-induced climate processes and their implications," *id.,* § 3. President Carter, in turn, asked the National Research Council, the working arm of the National Academy of Sciences, to investigate the subject. The Council's response was unequivocal: "If carbon dioxide continues to increase, the study group finds no reason to doubt that climate changes will result and no reason to believe that these changes will be negligible. . . . A wait-and-see policy may mean waiting until it is too late."

* * *

Meanwhile, the scientific understanding of climate change progressed. In 1990, the Intergovernmental Panel on Climate Change (IPCC), a multinational scientific body organized under the auspices of the United Nations, published its first comprehensive report on the topic. Drawing on expert opinions from across the globe, the IPCC concluded that "emissions resulting from human activities are substantially increasing the atmospheric concentrations of . . . greenhouse gases [which] will enhance the greenhouse effect, resulting on average in an additional warming of the Earth's surface."

* * *

On October 20, 1999, a group of 19 private organizations filed a rulemaking petition asking EPA to regulate "greenhouse gas emissions from new motor vehicles under § 202 of the Clean Air Act." App. 5. Petitioners maintained that 1998 was the "warmest year on record"; that carbon dioxide, methane, nitrous oxide, and hydrofluorocarbons are "heat trapping greenhouse gases"; that greenhouse gas emissions have significantly accelerated climate change; and that the IPCC's 1995 report warned that "carbon dioxide remains the most important contributor to [man-made] forcing of climate change." *Id.,* at 13 (internal quotation marks omitted). The petition further alleged that climate change will have serious adverse effects on human health and the environment. *Id.,* at 22–35. As to EPA's statutory authority, the petition observed that the agency itself had already confirmed that it had the power to regulate carbon dioxide. See *id.,* at 18, n. 21. In 1998, Jonathan Z. Cannon, then EPA's General Counsel, prepared a legal opinion concluding that "CO2 emissions are within the scope of EPA's authority to regulate," even as he recognized that EPA had so far declined to exercise that authority. *Id.,* at 54 (memorandum to Carol M. Browner, Administrator (Apr. 10, 1998) (hereinafter Cannon memorandum)). Cannon's successor, Gary S. Guzy, reiterated that opinion before a congressional committee just two weeks before the rulemaking petition was filed. See *id.*, at 61.

Fifteen months after the petition's submission, EPA requested public comment on "all the issues raised in [the] petition," adding a "particular" request for comments on "any scientific, technical, legal, economic or other aspect of these issues that may be relevant to EPA's consideration of this petition." 66 Fed. Reg. 7486, 7487 (2001). EPA received more than 50,000 comments over the next five months. See 68 Fed. Reg. 52924 (2003).

Before the close of the comment period, the White House sought "assistance in identifying the areas in the science of climate change where there are the greatest certainties and uncertainties" from the National Research Council, asking for a response "as soon as possible." App. 213. The result was a 2001 report titled Climate Change: An Analysis of Some Key Questions (NRC Report), which, drawing heavily on the 1995 IPCC report, concluded that "[g]reenhouse gases are accumulating in Earth's atmosphere as a result of human activities, causing surface air temperatures and subsurface ocean temperatures to rise. Temperatures are, in fact, rising." NRC Report 1.

On September 8, 2003, EPA entered an order denying the rulemaking petition. 68 Fed. Reg. 52922. The agency gave two reasons for its decision: (1) that contrary to the opinions of its former general counsels, the Clean Air Act does not authorize EPA to issue mandatory regulations to address global climate change, see *id.*, at 52925–52929; and (2) that even if the agency had the authority to set greenhouse gas emission standards, it would be unwise to do so at this time, *id.*, at 52929–52931.

In concluding that it lacked statutory authority over greenhouse gases, EPA observed that Congress "was well aware of the global climate change issue when it last comprehensively amended the [Clean Air Act] in 1990," yet it declined to adopt a proposed amendment establishing binding emissions limitations.

* * *

In essence, EPA concluded that climate change was so important that unless Congress spoke with exacting specificity, it could not have meant the agency to address it.

Having reached that conclusion, EPA believed it followed that greenhouse gases cannot be "air pollutants" within the meaning of the Act. See *ibid.* ("It follows from this conclusion, that [greenhouse gases], as such, are not air pollutants under the [Clean Air Act's] regulatory provisions . . ."). The agency bolstered this conclusion by explaining that if carbon dioxide were an air pollutant, the only feasible method of reducing tailpipe emissions would be to improve fuel economy. But because Congress has already created detailed mandatory fuel economy standards subject to

Department of Transportation (DOT) administration, the agency concluded that EPA regulation would either conflict with those standards or be superfluous. *Id.*, at 52929.

Even assuming that it had authority over greenhouse gases, EPA explained in detail why it would refuse to exercise that authority. The agency began by recognizing that the concentration of greenhouse gases has dramatically increased as a result of human activities, and acknowledged the attendant increase in global surface air temperatures. *Id.*, at 52930. EPA nevertheless gave controlling importance to the NRC Report's statement that a causal link between the two " 'cannot be unequivocally established.' " *Ibid.* (quoting NRC Report 17). Given that residual uncertainty, EPA concluded that regulating greenhouse gas emissions would be unwise. 68 Fed. Reg. 52930.

The agency furthermore characterized any EPA regulation of motor-vehicle emissions as a "piecemeal approach" to climate change, *id.*, at 52931, and stated that such regulation would conflict with the President's "comprehensive approach" to the problem, *id.*, at 52932. That approach involves additional support for technological innovation, the creation of nonregulatory programs to encourage voluntary private-sector reductions in greenhouse gas emissions, and further research on climate change—not actual regulation. *Id.*, at 52932–52933. According to EPA, unilateral EPA regulation of motor-vehicle greenhouse gas emissions might also hamper the President's ability to persuade key developing countries to reduce greenhouse gas emissions. *Id.*, at 52931.

Petitioners, now joined by intervenor States and local governments, sought review of EPA's order in the United States Court of Appeals for the District of Columbia Circuit. Although each of the three judges on the panel wrote a separate opinion, two judges agreed "that the EPA Administrator properly exercised his discretion under § 202(a)(1) in denying the petition for rule making." 415 F. 3d 50, 58 (2005). The court therefore denied the petition for review.

In his opinion announcing the court's judgment, Judge Randolph avoided a definitive ruling as to petitioners' standing, *id.*, at 56, reasoning that it was permissible to proceed to the merits because the standing and the merits inquiries "overlap[ped]," *ibid.* Assuming without deciding that the statute authorized the EPA Administrator to regulate greenhouse gas emissions that "in his judgment" may "reasonably be anticipated to endanger public health or welfare," 42 U. S. C. § 7521(a)(1), Judge Randolph concluded that the exercise of that judgment need not be based solely on scientific evidence, but may also be informed by the sort of policy judgments that motivate congressional action. 415 F. 3d, at 58. Given that framework, it was reasonable for EPA to base its decision on scientific uncertainty as well as on other factors, including the concern that unilateral regulation of U. S. motor-vehicle emissions could weaken efforts to reduce greenhouse gas emissions from other countries. *Ibid.*

Judge Sentelle wrote separately because he believed petitioners failed to "demonstrat[e] the element of injury necessary to establish standing under Article III." *Id.*, at 59 (opinion dissenting in part and concurring in judgment). In his view, they had alleged that global warming is "harmful to humanity at large," but could not allege "particularized injuries" to themselves. *Id.*, at 60 (citing *Lujan* v. *Defenders of Wildlife*, 504 U. S. 555, 562 (1992)). . . .

Judge Tatel dissented. Emphasizing that EPA nowhere challenged the factual basis of petitioners' affidavits, *id.*, at 66, he concluded that at least Massachusetts had "satisfied each element of Article III standing—injury, causation, and redressability," *id.*, at 64. In Judge Tatel's view, the " 'substantial probability,' " *id.*, at 66, that projected rises in sea level would lead to serious loss of coastal property was a "far cry" from the kind of generalized harm insufficient to ground Article III jurisdiction. *Id.*, at 65. * * * On the merits, Judge Tatel explained at length why he believed the text of the statute provided EPA with authority to regulate greenhouse gas emissions, and why its policy concerns did not justify its refusal to exercise that authority. 415 F. 3d, at 67–82.

Article III of the Constitution limits federal-court jurisdiction to "Cases" and "Controversies." Those two words confine "the business of federal courts to questions presented in an adversary context and in a form historically viewed as capable of resolution through the judicial process." *Flast* v. *Cohen*, 392 U. S. 83, 95 (1968). It is therefore familiar learning that no justiciable "controversy" exists when parties seek adjudication of a political question, *Luther* v. *Borden*, 7How. 1 (1849), when they ask for an advisory opinion, *Hayburn's Case*, 2 Dall. 409 (1792), see also *Clinton* v. *Jones*, 520 U. S. 681, 700, n. 33 (1997), or when the question sought to be adjudicated has been mooted by subsequent developments, *California* v. *San Pablo & Tulare R. Co.*, 149 U. S. 308 (1893). This case suffers from none of these defects.

The parties' dispute turns on the proper construction of a congressional statute, a question eminently suitable to resolution in federal court. Congress has moreover authorized this type of challenge to EPA action. See 42 U. S. C. § 7607(b)(1). That authorization is of critical importance to the standing inquiry: "Congress has the power to define injuries and articulate chains of causation that will give rise to a case or controversy where none existed before." *Lujan*, 504 U. S., at 580 (Kennedy, J., concurring in part and concurring in judgment). "In exercising this power, however, Congress must at the very least identify the injury it seeks to vindicate and relate the injury to the class of persons entitled to bring suit." *Ibid.* We will not, therefore, "entertain citizen suits to vindicate the public's nonconcrete interest in the proper administration of the laws." *Id.*, at 581.

EPA maintains that because greenhouse gas emissions inflict widespread harm, the doctrine of standing presents an insuperable jurisdictional obstacle. We do not agree. At bottom, "the gist of the question of standing" is whether petitioners have "such a personal stake in the outcome of the controversy as to assure that concrete adverseness which sharpens the presentation of issues upon which the court so largely depends for illumination." *Baker* v. *Carr*, 369 U. S. 186, 204 (1962).

* * *

To ensure the proper adversarial presentation, *Lujan* holds that a litigant must demonstrate that it has suffered a concrete and particularized injury that is either actual or imminent, that the injury is fairly traceable to the defendant, and that it is likely that a favorable decision will redress that injury. See *id.*, at 560–561. However, a litigant to whom Congress has "accorded a procedural right to protect his concrete interests," *id.*, at 572, n. 7—here, the right to challenge agency action unlawfully withheld, § 7607(b)(1)—"can assert that right without meeting all the normal standards for redressability and immediacy," *ibid.* When a litigant is vested with a procedural right, that litigant has standing if there is some possibility that the requested relief will prompt the injury-causing party to reconsider the decision that allegedly harmed the litigant. *Ibid.*; see also *Sugar Cane Growers Cooperative of Fla.* v. *Veneman*, 289 F. 3d 89, 94–95 (CADC 2002) ("A [litigant] who alleges a deprivation of a procedural protection to which he is entitled never has to prove that if he had received the procedure the substantive result would have been altered. All that is necessary is to show that the procedural step was connected to the substantive result").

Only one of the petitioners needs to have standing to permit us to consider the petition for review. See *Rumsfeld* v. *Forum for Academic and Institutional Rights, Inc.*, 547 U. S. 47, n. 2 (2006). We stress here, as did Judge Tatel below, the special position and interest of Massachusetts. It is of considerable relevance that the party seeking review here is a sovereign State and not, as it was in *Lujan*, a private individual.

Well before the creation of the modern administrative state, we recognized that States are not normal litigants for the purposes of invoking federal jurisdiction. As Justice Holmes explained in *Georgia* v. *Tennessee Copper Co.*, 206 U. S. 230, 237 (1907), a case in which Georgia sought to protect its citizens from air pollution originating outside its borders:

"The case has been argued largely as if it were one between two private parties; but it is not. The very elements that would be relied upon in a suit between fellow-citizens as a ground for equitable relief are wanting here.

The State owns very little of the territory alleged to be affected, and the damage to it capable of estimate in money, possibly, at least, is small. This is a suit by a State for an injury to it in its capacity of *quasi*-sovereign. In that capacity the State has an interest independent of and behind the titles of its citizens, in all the earth and air within its domain. It has the last word as to whether its mountains shall be stripped of their forests and its inhabitants shall breathe pure air."

Just as Georgia's "independent interest . . . in all the earth and air within its domain" supported federal jurisdiction a century ago, so too does Massachusetts' well-founded desire to preserve its sovereign territory today. Cf. *Alden* v. *Maine*, 527 U. S. 706, 715 (1999) (observing that in the federal system, the States "are not relegated to the role of mere provinces or political corporations, but retain the dignity, though not the full authority, of sovereignty"). That Massachusetts does in fact own a great deal of the "territory alleged to be affected" only reinforces the conclusion that its stake in the outcome of this case is sufficiently concrete to warrant the exercise of federal judicial power.

When a State enters the Union, it surrenders certain sovereign prerogatives. Massachusetts cannot invade Rhode Island to force reductions in greenhouse gas emissions, it cannot negotiate an emissions treaty with China or India, and in some circumstances the exercise of its police powers to reduce in-state motor-vehicle emissions might well be pre-empted.

* * *

These sovereign prerogatives are now lodged in the Federal Government, and Congress has ordered EPA to protect Massachusetts (among others) by prescribing standards applicable to the "emission of any air pollutant from any class or classes of new motor vehicle engines, which in [the Administrator's] judgment cause, or contribute to, air pollution which may reasonably be anticipated to endanger public health or welfare." 42 U. S. C. § 7521(a)(1). Congress has moreover recognized a concomitant procedural right to challenge the rejection of its rulemaking petition as arbitrary and capricious. § 7607(b)(1). Given that procedural right and Massachusetts' stake in protecting its quasi-sovereign interests, the Commonwealth is entitled to special solicitude in our standing analysis.

With that in mind, it is clear that petitioners' submissions as they pertain to Massachusetts have satisfied the most demanding standards of the adversarial process. EPA's steadfast refusal to regulate greenhouse gas emissions presents a risk of harm to Massachusetts that is both "actual" and "imminent." *Lujan*, 504 U. S., at 560. There is, moreover, a "substantial likelihood that the judicial relief requested" will prompt EPA to take steps to reduce that risk. *Duke Power Co.* v. *Carolina Environmental Study Group, Inc.*, 438 U. S. 59, 79 (1978).

The Injury

The harms associated with climate change are serious and well recognized. Indeed, the NRC Report itself—which EPA regards as an "objective and independent assessment of the relevant science," 68 Fed. Reg. 52930—identifies a number of environmental changes that have already inflicted significant harms, including "the global retreat of mountain glaciers, reduction in snow-cover extent, the earlier spring melting of rivers and lakes, [and] the accelerated rate of rise of sea levels during the 20th century relative to the past few thousand years . . . ." NRC Report 16.

Petitioners allege that this only hints at the environmental damage yet to come. According to the climate scientist Michael MacCracken, "qualified scientific experts involved in climate change research" have reached a "strong consensus" that global warming threatens (among other things) a precipitate rise in sea levels by the end of the century, MacCracken Decl. ¶ 15, Stdg. App. 207, "severe and irreversible changes to natural ecosystems," *id.*, ¶ 5(d), at 209, a "significant reduction in water storage in winter snowpack in mountainous regions with direct and important economic consequences," *ibid.*, and an increase in the spread of disease, *id.*, ¶ 28, at 218–219. He also observes that rising ocean temperatures may contribute to the ferocity of hurricanes. *Id.*, ¶¶ 23–25, at 216–217.

* * *

According to petitioners' unchallenged affidavits, global sea levels rose somewhere between 10 and 20 centimeters over the 20th century as a result of global warming. MacCracken Decl. ¶ 5(c), Stdg. App. 208. These rising seas have already begun to swallow Massachusetts' coastal land. *Id.*, at 196 (declaration of Paul H. Kirshen ¶ 5), 216 (MacCracken Decl. ¶ 23). Because the Commonwealth "owns a substantial portion of the state's coastal property," *id.*, at 171 (declaration of Karst R. Hoogeboom ¶ 4), it has alleged a particularized injury in its capacity as a landowner. The severity of that injury will only increase over the course of the next century: If sea levels continue to rise as predicted, one Massachusetts official believes that a significant fraction of coastal property will be "either permanently lost through inundation or temporarily lost through periodic storm surge and flooding events." *Id.*, ¶ 6, at 172. Remediation costs alone, petitioners allege, could run well into the hundreds of millions of dollars. *Id.*, ¶ 7, at 172; see also Kirshen Decl. ¶ 12, at 198.

Causation

EPA does not dispute the existence of a causal connection between man-made greenhouse gas emissions and global warming. At a minimum, therefore, EPA's refusal to regulate such emissions "contributes" to Massachusetts' injuries.

EPA nevertheless maintains that its decision not to regulate greenhouse gas emissions from new motor vehicles contributes so insignificantly to petitioners' injuries that the agency cannot be haled into federal court to answer for them. For the same reason, EPA does not believe that any realistic possibility exists that the relief petitioners seek would mitigate global climate change and remedy their injuries. That is especially so because predicted increases in greenhouse gas emissions from developing nations, particularly China and India, are likely to offset any marginal domestic decrease.

But EPA overstates its case. Its argument rests on the erroneous assumption that a small incremental step, because it is incremental, can never be attacked in a federal judicial forum. Yet accepting that premise would doom most challenges to regulatory action. Agencies, like legislatures, do not generally resolve massive problems in one fell regulatory swoop. See *Williamson* v. *Lee Optical of Okla., Inc.*, 348 U. S. 483, 489 (1955) ("[A] reform may take one step at a time, addressing itself to the phase of the problem which seems most acute to the legislative mind"). They instead whittle away at them over time, refining their preferred approach as circumstances change and as they develop a more-nuanced understanding of how best to proceed. . . . . That a first step might be tentative does not by itself support the notion that federal courts lack jurisdiction to determine whether that step conforms to law.

And reducing domestic automobile emissions is hardly a tentative step. Even leaving aside the other greenhouse gases, the United States transportation sector emits an enormous quantity of carbon dioxide into the atmosphere—according to the MacCracken affidavit, more than 1.7 billion metric tons in 1999 alone. ¶ 30, Stdg. App. 219. That accounts for more than 6% of worldwide carbon dioxide emissions. *Id.,* at 232 (Oppenheimer Decl. ¶ 3); see also MacCracken Decl. ¶ 31, at 220. To put this in perspective: Considering just emissions from the transportation sector, which represent less than one-third of this country's total carbon dioxide emissions, the United States would still rank as the third-largest emitter of carbon dioxide in the world, outpaced only by the European Union and China. Judged by any standard, U. S. motor-vehicle emissions make a meaningful contribution to greenhouse gas concentrations and hence, according to petitioners, to global warming.

The Remedy

While it may be true that regulating motor-vehicle emissions will not by itself *reverse* global warming, it by no means follows that we lack jurisdiction to decide whether EPA has a duty to take steps to *slow* or *reduce* it. See also *Larson* v. *Valente,* 456 U. S. 228, n. 15 (1982) ("[A] plaintiff satisfies the redressability requirement when he shows that a favorable decision will relieve a discrete injury to himself. He need not show that a favorable decision will relieve his *every* injury"). Because of the enormity of the potential consequences associated with man-made climate change, the fact that the effectiveness of a remedy might be delayed during the (relatively short) time it takes for a new motor-vehicle fleet to replace an older one is essentially irrelevant. Nor is it dispositive that developing countries such as China and India are poised to increase greenhouse gas emissions substantially over the next century: A reduction in domestic emissions would slow the pace of global emissions increases, no matter what happens elsewhere.

We moreover attach considerable significance to EPA's "agree[ment] with the President that 'we must address the issue of global climate change,'" 68 Fed. Reg. 52929 (quoting remarks announcing Clear Skies and Global Climate Initiatives, 2002 Public Papers of George W. Bush, Vol. 1, Feb. 14, p. 227 (2004)), and to EPA's ardent support for various voluntary emission-reduction programs, 68 Fed. Reg. 52932. As Judge Tatel observed in dissent below, "EPA would presumably not bother with such efforts if it thought emissions reductions would have no discernable impact on future global warming." 415 F. 3d, at 66.

In sum—at least according to petitioners' uncontested affidavits—the rise in sea levels associated with global warming has already harmed and will continue to harm Massachusetts. The risk of catastrophic harm, though remote, is nevertheless real. That risk would be reduced to some extent if petitioners received the relief they seek. We therefore hold that petitioners have standing to challenge the EPA's denial of their rulemaking petition.

* * *

EPA concluded in its denial of the petition for rulemaking that it lacked authority under 42 U. S. C. § 7521(a)(1) to regulate new vehicle emissions because carbon dioxide is not an "air pollutant" as that term is defined in § 7602. In the alternative, it concluded that even if it possessed authority, it would decline to do so because regulation would conflict with other administration priorities. As discussed earlier, the Clean Air Act expressly permits review of such an action. § 7607(b)(1). We therefore "may reverse any such action found to be . . . arbitrary, capricious, an abuse of discretion, or otherwise not in accordance with law." § 7607(d)(9).

On the merits, the first question is whether § 202(a)(1) of the Clean Air Act authorizes EPA to regulate greenhouse gas emissions from new motor vehicles in the event that it forms a "judgment" that such emissions contribute to climate change. We have little trouble concluding that it does. In relevant part, § 202(a)(1) provides that EPA "shall by regulation prescribe . . . standards applicable to the emission of any air pollutant from any class or classes of new motor vehicles or new motor vehicle engines, which in [the Administrator's] judgment cause, or contribute to, air pollution which may reasonably be anticipated to endanger public health or welfare." 42 U. S. C. § 7521(a)(1). Because EPA believes that Congress did not intend it to regulate substances that contribute to climate change, the agency maintains that carbon dioxide is not an "air pollutant" within the meaning of the provision.

The statutory text forecloses EPA's reading. The Clean Air Act's sweeping definition of "air pollutant" includes "*any* air pollution agent or combination of such agents, including *any* physical, chemical . . . substance or matter which is emitted into or otherwise enters the ambient air . . . ." § 7602(g) (emphasis added). On its face, the definition embraces all airborne compounds of whatever stripe, and underscores that intent through the repeated use of the word "any." Carbon dioxide, methane, nitrous oxide, and hydrofluorocarbons are without a doubt "physical [and] chemical . . . substance[s] which [are] emitted into . . . the ambient air." The statute is unambiguous.

* * *

While the Congresses that drafted § 202(a)(1) might not have appreciated the possibility that burning fossil fuels could lead to global warming, they did understand that without regulatory flexibility, changing circumstances and scientific developments would soon render the Clean Air Act obsolete. The broad language of § 202(a)(1) reflects an intentional effort to confer the flexibility necessary to forestall such obsolescence. See *Pennsylvania Dept. of Corrections* v. *Yeskey*, 524 U. S. 206, 212 (1998) ("[T]he fact that a statute can be applied in situations not expressly anticipated by Congress does not demonstrate ambiguity. It demonstrates breadth" (internal quotation marks omitted)). Because greenhouse gases fit well within the Clean Air Act's capacious definition of "air pollutant," we hold that EPA has the statutory authority to regulate the emission of such gases from new motor vehicles.

[EPA's argument] that even if it does have statutory authority to regulate greenhouse gases, it would be unwise to do so at this time—rests on reasoning divorced from the statutory text. While the statute does condition the exercise of EPA's authority on its formation of a "judgment," 42 U. S. C. § 7521(a)(1), that judgment must relate to whether an air pollutant "cause[s], or contribute[s] to, air pollution which may reasonably be anticipated to endanger public health or welfare," *ibid.* Put another way, the use of the word "judgment" is not a roving license to ignore the statutory text. It is but a direction to exercise discretion within defined statutory limits.

If EPA makes a finding of endangerment, the Clean Air Act requires the agency to regulate emissions of the deleterious pollutant from new motor vehicles. *Ibid.* (stating that "[EPA] shall by regulation prescribe . . . standards applicable to the emission of any air pollutant from any class of new motor vehicles"). EPA no doubt has significant latitude as to the manner, timing, content, and coordination of its regulations with those of other agencies. But once EPA has responded to a petition for rulemaking, its reasons for action or inaction must conform to the authorizing statute. Under the clear terms of the Clean Air Act, EPA can avoid taking further action only if it determines that greenhouse gases do not contribute to climate change or if it provides some reasonable explanation as to why it cannot or will not exercise its discretion to determine whether they do. *Ibid.* To the extent that this constrains agency discretion to pursue other priorities of the Administrator or the President, this is the congressional design.

EPA has refused to comply with this clear statutory command. Instead, it has offered a laundry list of reasons not to regulate. For example, EPA said that a number of voluntary executive branch programs already provide an effective response to the threat of global warming, 68 Fed. Reg. 52932, that regulating greenhouse gases might impair the President's ability to negotiate with "key developing nations" to reduce emissions, *id.*, at 52931, and that curtailing motor-vehicle emissions would reflect "an inefficient, piecemeal approach to address the climate change issue." Ibid.

Although we have neither the expertise nor the authority to evaluate these policy judgments, it is evident they have nothing to do with whether greenhouse gas emissions contribute to climate change. Still less do they amount to a reasoned justification for declining to form a scientific judgment.

* * *

Nor can EPA avoid its statutory obligation by noting the uncertainty surrounding various features of climate change and concluding that it would therefore be better not to regulate at this time. See 68 Fed. Reg. 52930–52931. If the scientific uncertainty is so profound that it precludes EPA from making a reasoned judgment as to whether greenhouse gases contribute to global warming, EPA must say so. . . . The statutory question is whether sufficient information exists to make an endangerment finding.

In short, EPA has offered no reasoned explanation for its refusal to decide whether greenhouse gases cause or contribute to climate change. Its action was therefore "arbitrary, capricious, . . . or otherwise not in accordance with law." 42 U. S. C. § 7607(d)(9)(A).

* * *

The judgment of the Court of Appeals is reversed, and the case is remanded for further proceedings consistent with this opinion.

It is so ordered.

---

**Question:** Why is the injury in *Massachusetts v. E.P.A.* more specific than in the prior standing decisions? How do the standing cases treat individuals and states differently?

Following the 2020 U.S. presidential election, the state of Texas, which awarded its Electoral College votes to incumbent Donald Trump, challenged Pennsylvania's announcement that its votes were going to candidate Joseph Biden, based on alleged discrepancies in Pennsylvania's tabulation process. Texas applied to the Supreme Court for leave to file a bill of complaint. The Court responded: "The State of Texas's motion for leave to file a bill of complaint is denied under Article III of the Constitution. Texas has not demonstrated a judicially cognizable interest in the manner in which another State conducts its elections." **TEXAS v. PENNSYLVANIA**, Order in Pending Case, 141 S.Ct. 1230 ( 2020).

**Questions:** A human rights organization sues the U.S. government based on the existence of a program allowing wiretaps of phone conversations between the organization and foreign contacts. Should the plaintiff have standing? See *Clapper v. Amnesty International,* 568 U.S. 398 (2013). A "traditional values" organization sponsored a ballot referendum banning same-sex marriage. The referendum passed and became state law. When opponents of the measure challenged its constitutionality, the state attorney general's office refused to defend it, and the sponsor organization claimed it had the right to substitute for the state and protect the law in court. Standing? See *Hollingsworth v. Perry,* 570 U.S. 693 (2013). Which decision in this chapter is similar, and why?

# CHAPTER 3

# COMMERCE CLAUSE

■ ■ ■

## CONTEXT & SOURCES

Article I, § 8, para. 3 of the Constitution gave Congress the power "[t]o regulate Commerce . . . among the several states . . . ." Responding to the desire during the early republic to create a national market, the Supreme Court first applied the Commerce Clause to bar discrimination by one state against another's business, at least when such action contradicted a federal statute, in *Gibbons v. Ogden,* 22 U.S. 1 (1824). This chapter surveys the Court's move from a narrow interpretation in the late nineteenth century to its broad upholding of New Deal legislation and then back again to a more skeptical view of regulation since the 1990s. Shifts between narrower and broader interpretations reflect the oscillation between doctrinal theories of "formalism" and "realism" that the Court expounded in response to changing political realities.

The origins and influence of Commerce Clause jurisprudence are explained in Herbert A. Johnson, *Gibbons v. Ogden: John Marshall, Steamboats and the Commerce Clause* (University Press of Kansas, 2010), which includes an excellent chapter on subsequent cases. A classic historical survey of the New Deal reinterpretation of the Commerce Clause, and its aftermath, is Paul R. Benson, Jr., *The Supreme Court and the Commerce Clause, 1937–1970* (Dunellen Publishing Co., 1970). For details on a key New Deal decision, see Jim Chen, "The Story of *Wickard v. Filburn*: Agriculture, Aggregation, and Commerce," in *Constitutional Law Stories* (Michael Dorf ed., Foundation Press 2009), 69–109.

### UNITED STATES V. E. C. KNIGHT CO. ET AL.

156 U.S. 1 (1895)

* * *

This was a bill filed by the United States against E. C. Knight Company and others, in the circuit court of the United States for the Eastern district of Pennsylvania, charging that the defendants had violated the provisions of an act of congress approved July 2, 1890, entitled, 'An act to protect trade and commerce against unlawful restraints and monopolies' (26 Stat. 209, c. 647), 'providing that every contract, combination in the form of trust, or otherwise, or conspiracy in restraint of trade and commerce among the several states is illegal, and that persons who shall monopolize or shall attempt to monopolize, or combine or conspire with other persons to monopolize trade and commerce among the several states, shall be guilty of a misdemeanor.'

* * *

MR. CHIEF JUSTICE FULLER, after stating the facts in the foregoing language, delivered the opinion of the court.

By the purchase of the stock of the four Philadelphia refineries with shares of its own stock the American Sugar Refining Company acquired nearly complete control of the manufacture of refined sugar within the United States. The bill charged that the contracts under which these purchases were made constituted combinations in restraint of trade, and that in entering into them the defendants combined and conspired to restrain the trade and commerce in refined sugar among the several states and with foreign nations, contrary to the act of congress of July 2, 1890.

The relief sought was the cancellation of the agreements under which the stock was transferred, the redelivery of the stock to the parties respectively, and an injunction against the further performance of the agreements and further violations of the act. As usual, there was a prayer for general relief, but only such relief could be afforded under that prayer as would be agreeable to the case made by the bill and consistent with that specifically prayed. And as to the injunction asked, that relief was ancillary to and in aid of the primary equity, or ground of suit, and, if that failed, would fall with it. That ground here was the existence of contracts to monopolize interstate or international trade or commerce, and to restrain such trade or commerce which, by the provisions of the act, could be rescinded, or operations thereunder arrested.

* * *

The fundamental question is whether, conceding that the existence of a monopoly in manufacture is established by the evidence, that monopoly can be directly suppressed under the act of congress in the mode attempted by this bill.

It cannot be denied that the power of a state to protect the lives, health, and property of its citizens, and to preserve good order and the public morals, 'the power to govern men and things within the limits of its dominion,' is a power originally and always belonging to the states, not surrendered by them to the general government, nor directly restrained by the constitution of the United States, and essentially exclusive. The relief of the citizens of each state from the burden of monopoly and the evils resulting from the restraint of trade among such citizens was left with the states to deal with, and this court has recognized their possession of that power even to the extent of holding that an employment or business carried on by private individuals, when it becomes a matter of such public interest and importance as to create a common charge or burden upon the citizen,—in other words, when it becomes a practical monopoly, to which the citizen is compelled to resort, and by means of which a tribute can be exacted from the community,—is subject to regulation by state legislative power. On the other hand, the power of congress to regulate commerce among the several states is also exclusive. The constitution does not provide that interstate commerce shall be free, but, by the grant of this exclusive power to regulate it, it was left free, except as congress might impose restraints. Therefore it has been determined that the failure of congress to exercise this exclusive power in any case is an expression of its will that the subject shall be free from restrictions or impositions upon it by the several states, and if a law passed by a state in the exercise of its acknowledged powers comes into conflict with that will, the congress and the state cannot occupy the position of equal opposing sovereignties, because the constitution declares its supremacy, and that of the laws passed in pursuance thereof; and that which is not supreme must yield to that which is supreme. 'Commerce undoubtedly is traffic,' said Chief Justice Marshall, 'but it is something more; it is intercourse. It describes the commercial intercourse between nations and parts of nations in all its branches, and is regulated by prescribing rules for carrying on that intercourse.' That which belongs to commerce is within the jurisdiction of the United States, but that which does not belong to commerce is within the jurisdiction of the police power of the state. Gibbons v. Ogden, 9 Wheat. 1, 210; [additional citations].

The argument is that the power to control the manufacture of refined sugar is a monopoly over a necessary of life, to the enjoyment of which by a large part of the population of the United States interstate commerce is indispensable, and that, therefore, the general government, in the exercise of the power to regulate commerce, may repress such monopoly directly, and set aside the instruments which have created it. But this argument cannot be confined to necessaries of life merely, and must include all articles of general consumption. Doubtless the power to control the manufacture of a given thing involves, in a certain sense, the control of its disposition, but this is a secondary, and not the primary, sense; and, although the exercise of that power may result in bringing the operation of commerce into play, it does not control it, and affects it only incidentally and indirectly. Commerce succeeds to manufacture, and is not a part of it. The power to regulate commerce is the power to prescribe the rule by which commerce shall be governed, and is a power independent of the power to suppress monopoly. But it may operate in repression of monopoly whenever that comes within the rules by which commerce is governed, or whenever the transaction is itself a monopoly of commerce.

It is vital that the independence of the commercial power and of the police power, and the delimitation between them, however sometimes perplexing, should always be recognized and observed, for, while the one furnishes the strongest bond of union, the other is essential to the preservation of the autonomy of the states as required by our dual form of government; and acknowledged evils, however grave and urgent they may appear to be, had better be borne, than the risk be run, in the effort to suppress them, of more serious consequences by resort to expedients of even doubtful constitutionality.

It will be perceived how far-reaching the proposition is that the power of dealing with a monopoly directly may be exercised by the general government whenever interstate or international commerce may be ultimately affected. The regulation of commerce applies to the subjects of commerce, and not to matters of internal police. Contracts to buy, sell, or exchange goods to be transported among the several states, the transportation and its instrumentalities, and articles bought, sold, or exchanged for the purposes of such transit among the states, or put in the way of transit, may be regulated; but this is because they form part of interstate trade or commerce. The fact that an article is manufactured for export to another state does not of itself make it an article of interstate commerce, and the intent of the manufacturer does not determine the time when the article or product passes from the control of the state and belongs to commerce. This was so ruled in Coe v. Errol, 116 U. S. 517, in which the question before the court was whether certain logs cut at a place in New Hampshire, and hauled to a river town for the purpose of transportation to the state of Maine, were liable to be taxed like other property in the state of New Hampshire. Mr. Justice Bradley, delivering the opinion of the court, said: 'Does the owner's state of mind in relation to the goods—that is, his intent to export them, and his partial preparation to do so—exempt them from taxation? This is the precise question for solution. * * * There must be a point of time when they cease to be governed exclusively by the domestic law, and begin to be governed and protected by the national law of commercial regulation; and that moment seems to us to be a legitimate one for this purpose in which they commence their final movement from the state of their origin to that of their destination.'

And again, in Kidd v. Pearson, 128 U. S. 1, 20, where the question was discussed whether the right of a state to enact a statute prohibiting within its limits the manufacture of intoxicating liquors, except for certain purposes, could be overthrown by the fact that the manufacturer intended to export the liquors when made, it was held that the intent of the manufacturer did not determine the time when the article or product passed from the control of the state and belonged to commerce, and that, therefore, the statute, in omitting to except from its operation the manufacture of intoxicating liquors within the limits of the state for export, did not constitute an unauthorized interference with the right of congress to regulate commerce. And Mr. Justice Lamar remarked: 'No distinction is more popular to the common mind, or more clearly expressed in economic and political literature, than that between manufacture and commerce. Manufacture is transformation,—the fashioning of raw materials into a change of form for use. The functions of commerce are different. The buying and selling, and the transportation incidental thereto, constitute commerce; and the regulation of commerce in the constitutional sense embraces the regulation at least of such transportation. * * * If it be held that the term includes the regulation of all such manufactures as are intended to be the subject of commercial transactions in the future, it is impossible to deny that it would also include all productive industries that contemplate the same thing. The result would be that congress would be invested, to the exclusion of the states, with the power to regulate, not only manufactures, but also agriculture, horticulture, stock-raising, domestic fisheries, mining; in short, every branch of human industry. For is there one of them that does not contemplate, more or less clearly, an interstate or foreign market? Does not the wheat grower of the Northwest, and the cotton planter of the South, plant, cultivate, and harvest his crop with an eye on the prices at Liverpool, New York, and Chicago? The power being vested in congress and denied to the states, it would follow as an inevitable result that the duty would devolve on congress to regulate all of these delicate, multiform, and vital interests, interests which in their nature are, and must be, local in all the details of their successful management. * * * The demands of such supervision would require, not uniform legislation generally applicable throughout the United States, but a swarm of statutes only locally applicable, and utterly inconsistent. Any movement towards the establishment of rules of production in this vast country, with its many different climates and opportunities, would only be at the sacrifice of the peculiar advantages of a large part of the localities in it, if not of every one of them. On the other hand, any movement towards the local, detailed, and incongruous legislation required by such interpretation would be about the widest possible departure from the declared object of the clause in question. Nor this alone. Even in the exercise of the power contended for, congress would be confined to the regulation, not of certain branches of industry, however numerous, but to those instances in each and every branch where the producer contemplated an interstate market. These instances would be almost infinite, as we have seen; but still there would always remain the possibility, and often it would be the case, that the producer contemplated a domestic market. In that case the supervisory power must be executed by the state; and the interminable trouble would be presented that whether the one power or the other should exercise the authority in question would be determined, not by any general or intelligible rule, but by the secret and changeable intention of the producer in each and every act of production. A situation more paralyzing to the state governments, and more provocative of conflicts between the general government and the states, and less likely to have been what the framers of the constitution intended, it would be difficult to imagine.'

In Gibbons v. Ogden, Brown v. Maryland, and other cases often cited, the state laws, which were held inoperative, were instances of direct interference with, or regulations of, interstate or international commerce; yet in Kidd v. Pearson the refusal of a state to allow articles to be manufactured within her borders, even for export, was held not to directly affect external commerce; and state legislation which, in a great variety of ways, affected interstate commerce and persons engaged in it, has been frequently sustained because the interference was not direct.

Contracts, combinations, or conspiracies to control domestic enterprise in manufacture, agriculture, mining, production in all its forms, or to raise or lower prices or wages, might unquestionably tend to restrain external as well as domestic trade, but the restraint would be an indirect result, however inevitable, and whatever its extent, and such result would not necessarily determine the object of the contract, combination, or conspiracy.

Again, all the authorities agree that, in order to vitiate a contract or combination, it is not essential that its result should be a complete monopoly; it is sufficient if it really tends to that end, and to deprive the public of the advantages which flow from free competition. Slight reflection will show that, if the national power extends to all contracts and combinations in manufacture, agriculture, mining, and other productive industries, whose ultimate result may affect external commerce, comparatively little of business operations and affairs would be left for state control.

It was in the light of well-settled principles that the act of July 2, 1890, was framed. Congress did not attempt thereby to assert the power to deal with monopoly directly as such; or to limit and restrict the rights of corporations created by the states or the citizens of the states in the acquisition, control, or disposition of property; or to regulate or prescribe the price or prices at which such property or the products thereof should be sold; or to make criminal the acts of persons in the acquisition and control of property which the states of their residence or creation sanctioned or permitted. Aside from the provisions applicable where congress might exercise municipal power, what the law struck at was combinations, contracts, and conspiracies to monopolize trade and commerce among the several states or with foreign nations; but the contracts and acts of the defendants related exclusively to the acquisition of the Philadelphia refineries and the business of sugar refining in Pennsylvania, and bore no direct relation to commerce between the states or with foreign nations. The object was manifestly private gain in the manufacture of the commodity, but not through the control of interstate or foreign commerce. It is true that the bill alleged that the products of these refineries were sold and distributed among the several states, and that all the companies were engaged in trade or commerce with the several states and with foreign nations; but this was no more than to say that trade and commerce served manufacture to fulfill its function. Sugar was refined for sale, and sales were probably made at Philadelphia for consumption, and undoubtedly for resale by the first purchasers throughout Pennsylvania and other states, and refined sugar was also for warded by the companies to other states for sale. Nevertheless it does not follow that an attempt to monopolize, or the actual monopoly of, the manufacture was an attempt, whether executory or consummated, to monopolize commerce, even though, in order to dispose of the product, the instrumentality of commerce was necessarily invoked. There was nothing in the proofs to indicate any intention to put a restraint upon trade or commerce, and the fact, as we have seen, that trade or commerce might be indirectly affected, was not enough to entitle complainants to a decree. The subject-matter of the sale was shares of manufacturing stock, and the relief sought was the surrender of property which had already passed, and the suppression of the alleged monopoly in manufacture by the restoration of the status quo before the transfers; yet the act of congress only authorized the circuit courts to proceed by way of preventing and restraining violations of the act in respect of contracts, combinations, or conspiracies in restraint of interstate or international trade or commerce.

The circuit court declined, upon the pleadings and proofs, to grant the relief prayed, and dismissed the bill, and we are of opinion that the circuit court of appears did not err in affirming that decree.

Decree affirmed.

---

**Questions:** In 1828, James Madison wrote that the power to regulate interstate commerce "has been understood and used by all commercial and manufacturing Nations as embracing the object of encouraging manufactures." James Madison, "To Joseph Cabell," *in* James Madison, *Writings* 813, 815 (Jack Rakove ed., Library of America, 1999). Why was the Supreme Court in *E.C. Knight* so concerned with conceptually separating trade from manufacturing or production? Who benefitted from the decision? Would Knight apply to a federal statute banning the interstate shipment of goods made using child labor? See *Hammer v. Dagenhart*, 247 U.S. 251 (1918).

## WICKARD, SECRETARY OF AGRICULTURE, ET AL. V. FILBURN

317 U.S. 111 (1942)

* * *

MR. JUSTICE JACKSON delivered the opinion of the Court.

The appellee filed his complaint against the Secretary of Agriculture of the United States, three members of the County Agricultural Conservation Committee for Montgomery County, Ohio, and a member of the State Agricultural Conservation Committee for Ohio. He sought to enjoin enforcement against himself of the marketing penalty imposed by the amendment of May 26, 1941, to the Agricultural Adjustment Act of 1938, upon that part of his 1941 wheat crop which was available for marketing in excess of the marketing quota established for his farm. He also sought a declaratory judgment that the wheat marketing quota provisions of the Act as amended and applicable to him were unconstitutional because not sustainable under the Commerce Clause.

* * *

The appellee for many years past has owned and operated a small farm in Montgomery County, Ohio, maintaining a herd of dairy cattle, selling milk, raising poultry, and selling poultry and eggs. It has been his practice to raise a small acreage of winter wheat, sown in the Fall and harvested in the following July; to sell a portion of the crop; to feed part to poultry and livestock on the farm, some of which is sold; to use some in making flour for home consumption; and to keep the rest for the following seeding. The intended disposition of the crop here involved has not been expressly stated.

In July of 1940, pursuant to the Agricultural Adjustment Act of 1938, as then amended, there were established for the appellee's 1941 crop a wheat acreage allotment of 11.1 acres and a normal yield of 20.1 bushels of wheat an acre. He was given notice of such allotment in July of 1940 before the Fall planting of his 1941 crop of wheat, and again in July of 1941, before it was harvested. He sowed, however, 23 acres, and harvested from his 11.9 acres of excess acreage 239 bushels, which under the terms of the Act as amended on May 26, 1941, constituted farm marketing excess, subject to a penalty of 49 cents a bushel, or $117.11 in all. The appellee has not paid the penalty and he has not postponed or avoided it by storing the excess under regulations of the Secretary of Agriculture, or by delivering it up to the Secretary. The Committee, therefore, refused him a marketing card, which was, under the terms of Regulations promulgated by the Secretary, necessary to protect a buyer from liability to the penalty and upon its protecting lien.

The general scheme of the Agricultural Adjustment Act of 1938 as related to wheat is to control the volume moving in interstate and foreign commerce in order to avoid surpluses and shortages and the consequent abnormally low or high wheat prices and obstructions to commerce. Within prescribed limits and by prescribed standards the Secretary of Agriculture is directed to ascertain and proclaim each year a national acreage allotment for the next crop of wheat, which is then apportioned to the states and their counties, and is eventually broken up into allotments for individual farms. Loans and payments to wheat farmers are authorized in stated circumstances.

* * *

It is urged that under the Commerce Clause of the Constitution, Article I, § 8, clause 3, Congress does not possess the power it has in this instance sought to exercise. The question would merit little consideration since our decision in United States v. Darby, 312 U.S. 100, sustaining the federal power to regulate production of goods for commerce except for the fact that this Act extends federal regulation to production not intended in any part for commerce but wholly for consumption on the farm. The Act includes a definition of 'market' and its derivatives so that as related to wheat in addition to its conventional meaning it also means to dispose of 'by feeding (in any form) to poultry or livestock which, or the products of which, are sold, bartered, or exchanged, or to be so disposed of.' Hence, marketing quotas not only embrace all that may be sold without penalty but also what may be consumed on the premises. Wheat produced on excess acreage is designated as 'available for marketing' as so defined and the penalty is imposed thereon. Penalties do not depend upon whether any part of the wheat either within or without the quota is sold or intended to be sold. The sum of this is that the Federal Government fixes a quota including all that the farmer may harvest for sale or for his own farm needs, and declares that wheat produced on excess acreage may neither be disposed of nor used except upon payment of the penalty or except it is stored as required by the Act or delivered to the Secretary of Agriculture.

Appellee says that this is a regulation of production and consumption of wheat. Such activities are, he urges, beyond the reach of Congressional power under the Commerce Clause, since they are local in character, and their effects upon interstate commerce are at most 'indirect.' In answer the Government argues that the statute regulates neither production nor consumption, but only marketing; and, in the alternative, that if the Act does go beyond the regulation of marketing it is sustainable as a 'necessary and proper' implementation of the power of Congress over interstate commerce.

The Government's concern lest the Act be held to be a regulation of production or consumption rather than of marketing is attributable to a few dicta and decisions of this Court which might be understood to lay it down that activities such as 'production,' 'manufacturing,' and 'mining' are strictly 'local' and, except in special circumstances which are not present here, cannot be regulated under the commerce power because their effects upon interstate commerce are, as matter of law, only 'indirect.' Even today, when this power has been held to have great latitude, there is no decision of this Court that such activities may be regulated where no part of the product is intended for interstate commerce or intermingled with the subjects thereof. We believe that a review of the course of decision under the Commerce Clause will make plain, however, that questions of the power of Congress are not to be decided by reference to any formula which would give controlling force to nomenclature such as 'production' and 'indirect' and foreclose consideration of the actual effects of the activity in question upon interstate commerce.

At the beginning Chief Justice Marshall described the Federal commerce power with a breadth never yet exceeded. Gibbons v. Ogden, 9 Wheat. 1, 194, 195. He made emphatic the embracing and penetrating nature of this power by warning that effective restraints on its exercise must proceed from political rather than from judicial processes. 9 Wheat. at page 197.

For nearly a century, however, decisions of this Court under the Commerce Clause dealt rarely with questions of what Congress might do in the exercise of its granted power under the Clause and almost entirely with the permissibility of state activity which it was claimed discriminated against or burdened interstate commerce. During this period there was perhaps little occasion for the affirmative exercise of the commerce power, and the influence of the Clause on American life and law was a negative one, resulting almost wholly from its operation as a restraint upon the powers of the states. In discussion and decision the point of reference instead of being what was 'necessary and proper' to the exercise by Congress of its granted power, was often some concept of sovereignty thought to be implicit in the status of statehood. Certain activities such as 'production,' 'manufacturing,' and 'mining' were occasionally said to be within the province of state governments and beyond the power of Congress under the Commerce Clause.

It was not until 1887 with the enactment of the Interstate Commerce Act that the interstate commerce power began to exert positive influence in American law and life. This first important federal resort to the commerce power was followed in 1890 by the Sherman Anti-Trust Act and, thereafter, mainly after 1903, by many others. These statutes ushered in new phases of adjudication, which required the Court to approach the interpretation of the Commerce Clause in the light of an actual exercise by Congress of its power thereunder.

When it first dealt with this new legislation, the Court adhered to its earlier pronouncements, and allowed but little scope to the power of Congress. United States v. E. C. Knight Co., 156 U.S. 1. These earlier pronouncements also played an important part in several of the five cases in which this Court later held that Acts of Congress under the Commerce Clause were in excess of its power.

Even while important opinions in this line of restrictive authority were being written, however, other cases called forth broader interpretations of the Commerce Clause destined to supersede the earlier ones, and to bring about a return to the principles first enunciated by Chief Justice Marshall in Gibbons v. Ogden, supra.

* * *

In the Shreveport Rate Cases (Houston, E. & W.T.R. Co. v. United States), 234 U.S. 342, the Court held that railroad rates of an admittedly intrastate character and fixed by authority of the state might, nevertheless, be revised by the Federal Government because of the economic effects which they had upon interstate commerce. The opinion of Mr. Justice Hughes found federal intervention constitutionally authorized because of 'matters having such a close and substantial relation to interstate traffic that the control is essential or appropriate to the security of that traffic, to the efficiency of the interstate service, and to the maintenance of the conditions under which interstate commerce may be conducted upon fair terms and without molestation or hindrance.' 234 U.S. at page 351.

The Court's recognition of the relevance of the economic effects in the application of the Commerce Clause exemplified by this statement has made the mechanical application of legal formulas no longer feasible. Once an economic measure of the reach of the power granted to Congress in the Commerce Clause is accepted, questions of federal power cannot be decided simply by finding the activity in question to be 'production' nor can consideration of its economic effects be foreclosed by calling them 'indirect.' The present Chief Justice has said in summary of the present state of the law: 'The commerce power is not confined in its exercise to the regulation of commerce among the states. It extends to those activities intrastate which so affect interstate commerce, or the exertion of the power of Congress over it, as to make regulation of them appropriate means to the attainment of a legitimate end, the effective execution of the granted power to regulate interstate commerce. * * * The power of Congress over interstate commerce is plenary and complete in itself, may be exercised to its utmost extent, and acknowledges no limitations other than are prescribed in the Constitution. * * * It follows that no form of state activity can constitutionally thwart the regulatory power granted by the commerce clause to Congress. Hence the reach of that power extends to those intrastate activities which in a substantial way interfere with or obstruct the exercise of the granted power.' United States v. Wrightwood Dairy Co., 315 U.S. 110, 119.

Whether the subject of the regulation in question was 'production,' 'consumption,' or 'marketing' is, therefore, not material for purposes of deciding the question of federal power before us. That an activity is of local character may help in a doubtful case to determine whether Congress intended to reach it. The same consideration might help in determining whether in the absence of Congressional action it would be permissible for the state to exert its power on the subject matter, even though in so doing it to some degree affected interstate commerce. But even if appellee's activity be local and though it may not be regarded as commerce, it may still, whatever its nature, be reached by Congress if it exerts a substantial economic effect on interstate commerce and this irrespective of whether such effect is what might at some earlier time have been defined as 'direct' or 'indirect.'

* * *

The wheat industry has been a problem industry for some years. Largely as a result of increased foreign production and import restrictions, annual exports of wheat and flour from the United States during the ten-year period ending in 1940 averaged less than 10 per cent of total production, while during the 1920's they averaged more than 25 per cent. The decline in the export trade has left a large surplus in production which in connection with an abnormally large supply of wheat and other grains in recent years caused congestion in a number of markets; tied up railroad cars; and caused elevators in some instances to turn away grains, and railroads to institute embargoes to prevent further congestion.

Many countries, both importing and exporting, have sought to modify the impact of the world market conditions on their own economy. Importing countries have taken measures to stimulate production and self-sufficiency. The four large exporting countries of Argentina, Australia, Canada, and the United States have all undertaken various programs for the relief of growers. Such measures have been designed in part at least to protect the domestic price received by producers. Such plans have generally evolved towards control by the central government.

In the absence of regulation the price of wheat in the United States would be much affected by world conditions. During 1941 producers who cooperated with the Agricultural Adjustment program received an average price on the farm of about $1.16 a bushel as compared with the world market price of 40 cents a bushel.

* * *

The effect of consumption of homegrown wheat on interstate commerce is due to the fact that it constitutes the most variable factor in the disappearance of the wheat crop. Consumption on the farm where grown appears to vary in an amount greater than 20 per cent of average production. The total amount of wheat consumed as food varies but relatively little, and use as seed is relatively constant.

The maintenance by government regulation of a price for wheat undoubtedly can be accomplished as effectively by sustaining or increasing the demand as by limiting the supply. The effect of the statute before us is to restrict the amount which may be produced for market and the extent as well to which one may forestall resort to the market by producing to meet his own needs. That appellee's own contribution to the demand for wheat may be trivial by itself is not enough to remove him from the scope of federal regulation where, as here, his contribution, taken together with that of many others similarly situated, is far from trivial. National Labor Relations Board v. Fainblatt, 306 U.S. 601, 606, et seq., 307 U.S. 609; United States v. Darby, supra, 312 U.S. at page 123.

It is well established by decisions of this Court that the power to regulate commerce includes the power to regulate the prices at which commodities in that commerce are dealt in and practices affecting such prices. One of the primary purposes of the Act in question was to increase the market price of wheat and to that end to limit the volume thereof that could affect the market. It can hardly be denied that a factor of such volume and variability as home-consumed wheat would have a substantial influence on price and market conditions. This may arise because being in marketable condition such wheat overhangs the market and if induced by rising prices tends to flow into the market and check price increases. But if we assume that it is never marketed, it supplies a need of the man who grew it which would otherwise be reflected by purchases in the open market. Home-grown wheat in this sense competes with wheat in commerce. The stimulation of commerce is a use of the regulatory function quite as definitely as prohibitions or restrictions thereon. This record leaves us in no doubt that Congress may properly have considered that wheat consumed on the farm where grown if wholly outside the scheme of regulation would have a substantial effect in defeating and obstructing its purpose to stimulate trade therein at increased prices.

It is said, however, that this Act, forcing some farmers into the market to buy what they could provide for themselves, is an unfair promotion of the markets and prices of specializing wheat growers. It is of the essence of regulation that it lays a restraining hand on the self-interest of the regulated and that advantages from the regulation commonly fall to others. The conflicts of economic interest between the regulated and those who advantage by it are wisely left under our system to resolution by the Congress under its more flexible and responsible legislative process. Such conflicts rarely lend themselves to judicial determination. And with the wisdom, workability, or fairness, of the plan of regulation we have nothing to do.

* * *

Reversed.

---

**Question:** *Wickard* seems to suggest that there are few limits on the definition of commerce. Did the *Wickard* decision render the Commerce Clause meaningless?

## UNITED STATES V. LOPEZ

514 US 549 (1995)

CHIEF JUSTICE REHNQUIST delivered the opinion of the Court.

In the Gun Free School Zones Act of 1990, Congress made it a federal offense "for any individual knowingly to possess a firearm at a place that the individual knows, or has reasonable cause to believe, is a school zone." 18 U.S.C. § 922(q)(1)(A) (1988 ed., Supp. V). The Act neither regulates a commercial activity nor contains a requirement that the possession be connected in any way to interstate commerce. We hold that the Act exceeds the authority of Congress "[t]o regulate Commerce . . . among the several States . . . ." U. S. Const., Art. I, § 8, cl. 3.

On March 10, 1992, respondent, who was then a 12th grade student, arrived at Edison High School in San Antonio, Texas, carrying a concealed .38 caliber handgun and five bullets. Acting upon an anonymous tip, school authorities confronted respondent, who admitted that he was carrying the weapon. He was arrested and charged under Texas law with firearm possession on school premises. See Tex. Penal Code Ann. § 46.03(a)(1) (Supp. 1994). The next day, the state charges were dismissed after federal agents charged respondent by complaint with violating the Gun Free School Zones Act of 1990. 18 U.S.C. § 922(q)(1)(A) (1988 ed., Supp. V).

A federal grand jury indicted respondent on one count of knowing possession of a firearm at a school zone, in violation of § 922(q). Respondent moved to dismiss his federal indictment on the ground that § 922(q) "is unconstitutional as it is beyond the power of Congress to legislate control over our public schools." The District Court denied the motion, concluding that § 922(q) "is a constitutional exercise of Congress' well defined power to regulate activities in and affecting commerce, and the 'business' of elementary, middle and high schools . . . affects interstate commerce." App. to Pet. for Cert. 55a. Respondent waived his right to a jury trial. The District Court conducted a bench trial, found him guilty of violating

§ 922(q), and sentenced him to six months' imprisonment and two years' supervised release.

On appeal, respondent challenged his conviction based on his claim that § 922(q) exceeded Congress' power to legislate under the Commerce Clause. The Court of Appeals for the Fifth Circuit agreed and reversed respondent's conviction. It held that, in light of what it characterized as insufficient congressional findings and legislative history, "section 922(q), in the full reach of its terms, is invalid as beyond the power of Congress under the Commerce Clause." 2 F. 3d 1342, 1367–1368 (1993). Because of the importance of the issue, we granted certiorari, 511 U. S. ___ (1994), and we now affirm.

We start with first principles. The Constitution creates a Federal Government of enumerated powers. See U. S. Const., Art. I, § 8. As James Madison wrote, "[t]he powers delegated by the proposed Constitution to the federal government are few and defined. Those which are to remain in the State governments are numerous and indefinite." The Federalist No. 45, pp. 292–293 (C. Rossiter ed. 1961). This constitutionally mandated division of authority "was adopted by the Framers to ensure protection of our fundamental liberties." *Gregory* v. *Ashcroft,* 501 U.S. 452, 458 (1991) (internal quotation marks omitted). "Just as the separation and independence of the coordinate branches of the Federal Government serves to prevent the accumulation of excessive power in any one branch, a healthy balance of power between the States and the Federal Government will reduce the risk of tyranny and abuse from either front." *Ibid.*

The Constitution delegates to Congress the power "[t]o regulate Commerce with foreign Nations, and among the several States, and with the Indian Tribes." U. S. Const., Art. I, § 8, cl. 3. The Court, through Chief Justice Marshall, first defined the nature of Congress' commerce power in *Gibbons* v. *Ogden,* 9 Wheat. 1, 189–190 (1824).

* * *

The commerce power "is the power to regulate; that is, to prescribe the rule by which commerce is to be governed. This power, like all others vested in Congress, is complete in itself, may be exercised to its utmost extent, and acknowledges no limitations, other than are prescribed in the constitution." *Id.,* at 196. The *Gibbons* Court, however, acknowledged that limitations on the commerce power are inherent in the very language of the Commerce Clause.

"It is not intended to say that these words comprehend that commerce, which is completely internal, which is carried on between man and man in a State, or between different parts of the same State, and which does not extend to or affect other States. Such a power would be inconvenient, and is certainly unnecessary.

"Comprehensive as the word 'among' is, it may very properly be restricted to that commerce which concerns more States than one. . . . The enumeration presupposes something not enumerated; and that something, if we regard the language or the subject of the sentence, must be the exclusively internal commerce of a State." *Id.*, at 194–195.

* * *

In 1887, Congress enacted the Interstate Commerce Act, 24 Stat. 379, and in 1890, Congress enacted the Sherman Antitrust Act, 26 Stat. 209, as amended, 15 U.S.C. § 1 *et seq.* These laws ushered in a new era of federal regulation under the commerce power. When cases involving these laws first reached this Court, we imported from our negative Commerce Clause cases the approach that Congress could not regulate activities such as "production," "manufacturing," and "mining." See, *e.g., United States* v. *E. C. Knight Co.*, 156 U.S. 1, 12 (1895) ("Commerce succeeds to manufacture, and is not part of it"); *Carter* v. *Carter Coal Co.*, 298 U.S. 238, 304 (1936) ("Mining brings the subject matter of commerce into existence. Commerce disposes of it.").

* * *

In *A. L. A. Schecter Poultry Corp.* v. *United States*, 295 U.S. 495, 550 (1935), the Court struck down regulations that fixed the hours and wages of individuals employed by an intrastate business because the activity being regulated related to interstate commerce only indirectly. In doing so, the Court characterized the distinction between direct and indirect effects of intrastate transactions upon interstate commerce as "a fundamental one, essential to the maintenance of our constitutional system." *Id.*, at 548. Activities that affected interstate commerce directly were within Congress' power; activities that affected interstate commerce indirectly were beyond Congress' reach. *Id.*, at 546. The justification for this formal distinction was rooted in the fear that otherwise "there would be virtually no limit to the federal power and for all practical purposes we should have a completely centralized government." *Id.*, at 548.

Two years later, in the watershed case of *NLRB* v. *Jones & Laughlin Steel Corp.*, 301 U.S. 1 (1937), the Court upheld the National Labor Relations Act against a Commerce Clause challenge, and in the process, departed from the distinction between "direct" and "indirect" effects on interstate commerce. *Id.*, at 36–38 ("The question [of the scope of Congress' power] is necessarily one of degree"). The Court held that intrastate activities that "have such a close and substantial relation to interstate commerce that their control is essential or appropriate to protect that commerce from burdens and obstructions" are within Congress' power to regulate. *Id.*, at 37.

In *United States* v. *Darby*, 312 U.S. 100 (1941), the Court upheld the Fair Labor Standards Act, stating:

"The power of Congress over interstate commerce is not confined to the regulation of commerce among the states. It extends to those activities intrastate which so affect interstate commerce or the exercise of the power of Congress over it as to make regulation of them appropriate means to the attainment of a legitimate end, the exercise of the granted power of Congress to regulate interstate commerce." *Id.*, at 118. * * *

In *Wickard* v. *Filburn*, the Court upheld the application of amendments to the Agricultural Adjustment Act of 1938 to the production and consumption of home grown wheat. 317 U. S., at 128–129. The *Wickard* Court explicitly rejected earlier distinctions between direct and indirect effects on interstate commerce, stating:

"[E]ven if appellee's activity be local and though it may not be regarded as commerce, it may still, whatever its nature, be reached by Congress if it exerts a substantial economic effect on interstate commerce . . .'" *Id.*, at 125.

The *Wickard* Court emphasized that although Filburn's own contribution to the demand for wheat may have been trivial by itself, that was not "enough to remove him from the scope of federal regulation where, as here, his contribution, taken together with that of many others similarly situated, is far from trivial." *Id.*, at 127–128.

*Jones & Laughlin Steel, Darby,* and *Wickard* ushered in an era of Commerce Clause jurisprudence that greatly expanded the previously defined authority of Congress under that Clause. In part, this was a recognition of the great changes that had occurred in the way business was carried on in this country. Enterprises that had once been local or at most regional in nature had become national in scope. But the doctrinal change also reflected a view that earlier Commerce Clause cases artificially had constrained the authority of Congress to regulate interstate commerce.

* * *

We now turn to consider the power of Congress, in the light of this framework, to enact § 922(q). * * * [I]f § 922(q) is to be sustained, it must be . . . as a regulation of an activity that substantially affects interstate commerce.

[W]e have upheld a wide variety of congressional Acts regulating intrastate economic activity where we have concluded that the activity substantially affected interstate commerce. Examples include the regulation of intrastate coal mining; *Hodel, supra,* intrastate extortionate credit transactions, *Perez, supra,* restaurants utilizing substantial interstate supplies, *McClung, supra, inns* and hotels catering to interstate guests, *Heart of Atlanta Motel, supra,* and production and consumption of home grown wheat, *Wickard* v. *Filburn*, 317 U.S. 111 (1942). These examples are by no means exhaustive, but the pattern is clear. Where economic activity substantially affects interstate commerce, legislation regulating that activity will be sustained.

Even *Wickard*, which is perhaps the most far reaching example of Commerce Clause authority over intrastate activity, involved economic activity in a way that the possession of a gun in a school zone does not. . . . .

* * *

The Government's essential contention, *in fine*, is that we may determine here that § 922(q) is valid because possession of a firearm in a local school zone does indeed substantially affect interstate commerce. Brief for United States 17. The Government argues that possession of a firearm in a school zone may result in violent crime and that violent crime can be expected to affect the functioning of the national economy in two ways. First, the costs of violent crime are substantial, and, through the mechanism of insurance, those costs are spread throughout the population. See *United States* v. *Evans*, 928 F. 2d 858, 862 (CA9 1991). Second, violent crime reduces the willingness of individuals to travel to areas within the country that are perceived to be unsafe. Cf. *Heart of Atlanta Motel*, 379 U. S., at 253. The Government also argues that the presence of guns in schools poses a substantial threat to the educational process by threatening the learning environment. A handicapped educational process, in turn, will result in a less productive citizenry. That, in turn, would have an adverse effect on the Nation's economic well being. As a result, the Government argues that Congress could rationally have concluded that § 922(q) substantially affects interstate commerce.

We pause to consider the implications of the Government's arguments. The Government admits, under its "costs of crime" reasoning, that Congress could regulate not only all violent crime, but all activities that might lead to violent crime, regardless of how tenuously they relate to interstate commerce. See Tr. of Oral Arg. 8–9. Similarly, under the Government's "national productivity" reasoning, Congress could regulate any activity that it found was related to the economic productivity of individual citizens: family law (including marriage, divorce, and child custody), for example. Under the theories that the Government presents in support of § 922(q), it is difficult to perceive any limitation on federal power, even in areas such as criminal law enforcement or education where States historically have been sovereign. Thus, if we were to accept the Government's arguments, we are hard pressed to posit any activity by an individual that Congress is without power to regulate.

* * *

The possession of a gun in a local school zone is in no sense an economic activity that might, through repetition elsewhere, substantially affect any sort of interstate commerce. Respondent was a local student at a local school; there is no indication that he had recently moved in interstate commerce, and there is no requirement that his possession of the firearm have any concrete tie to interstate commerce.

To uphold the Government's contentions here, we would have to pile inference upon inference in a manner that would bid fair to convert congressional authority under the Commerce Clause to a general police power of the sort retained by the States. Admittedly, some of our prior cases have taken long steps down that road, giving great deference to congressional action. See *supra*, at 8. The broad language in these opinions has suggested the possibility of additional expansion, but we decline here to proceed any further. To do so would require us to conclude that the Constitution's enumeration of powers does not presuppose something not enumerated, cf. *Gibbons* v. *Ogden*, *supra*, at 195, and that there never will be a distinction between what is truly national and what is truly local, cf. *Jones & Laughlin Steel*, *supra*, at 30. This we are unwilling to do.

For the foregoing reasons the judgment of the Court of Appeals is

*Affirmed.*

JUSTICE STEVENS, dissenting.

* * *

Guns are both articles of commerce and articles that can be used to restrain commerce. Their possession is the consequence, either directly or indirectly, of commercial activity. In my judgment, Congress's power to regulate commerce in firearms includes the power to prohibit possession of guns at any location because of their potentially harmful use; it necessarily follows that Congress may also prohibit their possession in particular markets. The market for the possession of handguns by school age children is, distressingly, substantial. Whether or not the national interest in eliminating that market would have justified federal legislation in 1789, it surely does today.

---

**Questions:** A federal statute authorizes victims of gender-motivated violence to sue their assailants for money damages. Was Congress authorized to enact this legislation under the Commerce Clause? See *United States v. Morrison,* 529 U.S. 598 (2000). Is the economic/noneconomic distinction workable? What about federal regulation of illegal drugs? See *Gonzales v. Raich,* 545 U.S. 1 (2005).

## NATIONAL FEDERATION OF INDEPENDENT BUSINESS V. SEBELIUS

567 U.S. 519 (2012)

[In 2010, Congress enacted the Patient Protection and Affordable Care Act to increase the number of Americans covered by health insurance and decrease the cost of health care. One key provision is the individual mandate, which requires most Americans to maintain "minimum essential" health insurance coverage. 26 U. S. C. § 5000A. For individuals who are not exempt or who do not receive health insurance through an employer or government program, the means of satisfying the requirement is to purchase insurance from a private company. Beginning in 2014, those who do not comply with the mandate had to make a "[s]hared responsibility payment" to the Federal Government. § 5000A(b)(1). The Act provides that this "penalty" will be paid to the Internal Revenue Service with an individual's taxes, and "shall be assessed and collected in the same manner" as tax penalties. §§ 5000A(c), (g)(1). Twenty-six states, several individuals, and the National Federation of Independent Business brought suit in Federal District Court, challenging the constitutionality of the individual mandate.]

* * *

[Chief Justice Roberts concluded for the majority of the Court in Part III–A that the individual mandate is not a valid exercise of Congress's power under the Commerce Clause. The majority considered that the Constitution grants Congress the power to "*regulate* Commerce," which presupposes the existence of commercial activity to be regulated. This Court's precedent reflects that understanding: The Court's cases construing the scope of the commerce power uniformly describe the power as reaching "activity." *E.g., United States* v. *Lopez*, 514 U. S. 549, 560. The individual mandate, however, does not regulate existing commercial activity. It instead compels individuals to *become* active in commerce by purchasing a product, on the ground that their failure to do so affects interstate commerce.

Interpreting the Commerce Clause as permitting Congress to regulate individuals precisely because they are doing nothing would open a new and potentially vast domain to congressional authority. Congress already possesses expansive power to regulate what people do. Upholding the Affordable Care Act under the Commerce Clause would give Congress the same license to regulate what people do not do. The Framers knew the difference between doing something and doing nothing. They gave Congress the power to *regulate* commerce, not to *compel* it. Ignoring that distinction would undermine the principle that the Federal Government is a government of limited and enumerated powers. The individual mandate thus could not be sustained under Congress's power to "regulate Commerce."]

JUSTICE GINSBURG dissenting [on the Commerce Clause issue].

The Commerce Clause, it is widely acknowledged, "was the Framers' response to the central problem that gave rise to the Constitution itself." (citation). Under the Articles of Confederation, the Constitution's precursor, the regulation of commerce was left to the States. This scheme proved unworkable, because the individual States, understandably focused on their own economic interests, often failed to take actions critical to the success of the Nation as a whole. See Vices of the Political System of the United States, in James Madison: Writings 69, 71, ¶ 5 (J. Rakove ed. 1999) (As a result of the "want of concert in matters where common interest requires it," the "national dignity, interest, and revenue [have] suffered.").

What was needed was a "national Government . . . armed with a positive & compleat authority in all cases where uniform measures are necessary." See Letter from James Madison to Edmund Randolph (Apr. 8, 1787), in 9 Papers of James Madison 368, 370 (R. Rutland ed. 1975). See also Letter from George Washington to James Madison (Nov. 30, 1785), in 8 *id.*, at 428, 429 ("We are either a United people, or we are not. If the former, let us, in all matters of general concern act as a nation, which ha[s] national objects to promote, and a national character to support."). The Framers' solution was the Commerce Clause, which, as they perceived it, granted Congress the authority to enact economic legislation "in all Cases for the general Interests of the Union, and also in those Cases to which the States are separately incompetent." 2 Records of the Federal Convention of 1787, pp. 131–132, ¶ 8 (M. Farrand rev. 1966). See also *North American Co.* v. *SEC*, 327 U. S. 686, 705 (1946) ("[The commerce power] is an affirmative power commensurate with the national needs.").The Framers understood that the "general Interests of the Union" could change over time, In ways they could not anticipate. Accordingly, they recognized that the Constitution was of necessity a "great outlin[e]," not a detailed blueprint, see *McCulloch* v. *Maryland*, 4 Wheat. 316, 407 (1819), and that its provisions included broad concepts, to be "explained by the context or by the facts of the case," Letter from James Madison to N. P. Trist (Dec. 1831), in 9 Writings of James Madison 471, 475 (G. Hunt ed. 1910). "Nothing . . . can be more fallacious," Alexander Hamilton emphasized, "than to infer the extent of any power, proper to be lodged in the national government, from . . . its immediate necessities. There ought to be a capacity to provide for future contingencies[,] as they may happen; and as these are illimitable in their nature, it is impossible safely to limit that capacity." The Federalist No. 34, pp. 205, 206 (John Harvard Library ed. 2009). See also *McCulloch*, 4 Wheat., at 415 (The Necessary and Proper Clause is lodged "in a constitution[,] intended to endure for ages to come, and consequently, to be adapted to the various *crises* of human affairs.").

Consistent with the Framers' intent, we have repeatedly emphasized that Congress' authority under the Commerce Clause is dependent upon "practical" considerations, including "actual experience." *Jones & Laughlin Steel Corp.*, 301 U. S., at 41–42; see *Wickard* v. *Filburn*, 317 U. S. 111, 122 (1942); *United States* v. *Lopez*, 514 U. S. 549, 573 (1995) (Kennedy, J., concurring) (emphasizing "the Court's definitive commitment to the practical conception of the commerce power"). See also *North American Co.*, 327 U. S., at 705 ("Commerce itself is an intensely practical matter. To deal with it effectively, Congress must be able to act in terms of economic and financial realities." (citation omitted)). We afford Congress the leeway "to undertake to solve national problems directly and realistically." *American Power & Light Co.* v. *SEC*, 329 U. S. 90, 103 (1946).

Until today, this Court's pragmatic approach to judging whether Congress validly exercised its commerce power was guided by two familiar principles. First, Congress has the power to regulate economic activities "that substantially affect interstate commerce." *Gonzales* v. *Raich*, 545 U. S. 1, 17 (2005). This capacious power extends even to local activities that, viewed in the aggregate, have a substantial impact on interstate commerce. See *ibid.* See also *Wickard*, 317 U. S., at 125 ("[E]ven if appellee's activity be local and though it may not be regarded as commerce, it may still, *whatever its nature,* be reached by Congress if it exerts a substantial economic effect on interstate commerce." (emphasis added)); *Jones & Laughlin Steel Corp.*, 301 U. S., at 37.

Second, we owe a large measure of respect to Congress when it frames and enacts economic and social legislation. See *Raich*, 545 U. S., at 17. See also *Pension Benefit Guaranty Corporation* v. *R. A. Gray & Co.*, 467 U. S. 717, 729 (1984) ("[S]trong deference [is] accorded legislation in the field of national economic policy."); *Hodel* v. *Indiana*, 452 U. S. 314, 326 (1981) ("This [C]ourt will certainly not substitute its judgment for that of Congress unless the relation of the subject to interstate commerce and its effect upon it are clearly non-existent." When appraising such legislation, we ask only (1) whether Congress had a "rational basis" for concluding that the regulated activity substantially affects interstate commerce, and (2) whether there is a "reasonable connection between the regulatory means selected and the asserted ends." *Id.,* at 323–324. See also [additional citations]. In answering these questions, we presume the statute under review is constitutional and may strike it down only on a "plain showing" that Congress

Straightforward application of these principles would require the Court to hold that the minimum coverage provision is proper Commerce Clause legislation. Beyond dispute, Congress had a rational basis for concluding that the uninsured, as a class, substantially affect interstate commerce. Those without insurance consume billions of dollars of health-care products and services each year. Those goods are produced, sold, and delivered largely by national and regional companies who routinely transact business across state lines. The uninsured also cross state lines to receive care. Some have medical emergencies while away from home. Others, when sick, go to a neighboring State that provides better care for those who have not prepaid for care.

Not only do those without insurance consume a large amount of health care each year; critically, as earlier explained, their inability to pay for a significant portion of that consumption drives up market prices, foists costs on other consumers, and reduces market efficiency and stability. Given these far-reaching effects on interstate commerce, the decision to forgo insurance is hardly inconsequential or equivalent to "doing nothing." . . . [I]t is, instead, an economic decision Congress has the authority to address under the Commerce Clause. See also *Wickard,* 317 U. S., at 128 ("It is well established by decisions of this Court that the power to regulate commerce includes the power to regulate the prices at which commodities in that commerce are dealt in and *practices affecting such prices.*" (emphasis added)).

The minimum coverage provision, furthermore, bears a "reasonable connection" to Congress' goal of protecting the health-care market from the disruption caused by individuals who fail to obtain insurance. By requiring those who do not carry insurance to pay a toll, the minimum overage provision gives individuals a strong incentive to insure. This incentive, Congress had good reason to believe, would reduce the number of uninsured and, correspondingly, mitigate the adverse impact the uninsured have on the national health-care market.

Congress also acted reasonably in requiring uninsured individuals, whether sick or healthy, either to obtain insurance or to pay the specified penalty. As earlier observed, because every person is at risk of needing care at any moment, all those who lack insurance, regardless of their current health status, adversely affect the price of health care and health insurance. See *supra,* at 6–7. Moreover, an insurance-purchase requirement limited to those in need of immediate care simply could not work. Insurance companies would either charge these individuals prohibitively expensive premiums, or, if community-rating regulations were in place, close up shop. See also Brief for State of Maryland and 10 Other States et al. as *Amici Curiae* in No. 11–398, p. 28 (hereinafter Maryland Brief) ("No insurance regime can survive if people can opt out when the risk insured against is only a risk, but opt in when the risk materializes.").

[W]here we find that the legislators . . . have a rational basis for finding a chosen regulatory scheme necessary to the protection of commerce, our investigation is at an end." *Katzenbach,* 379 U. S., at 303–304. Congress' enactment of the minimum coverage provision, which addresses a specific interstate problem in a practical, experience-informed manner, easily meets this criterion.

* * *

---

**Questions:** Which of the *NFIB v. Sebelius* opinions, that of the majority or Justice Ginsburg's, more accurately reflects the intent of the founders? Which is more practical? In another part of the same decision, Court upheld the ACA's mandate as a tax. See Chapter 5 below.

# CHAPTER 4

# DORMANT COMMERCE CLAUSE

■ ■ ■

## CONTEXT & SOURCES

Conceptually originating in Justice Johnson's *Gibbons v. Ogden* concurrence, the Dormant Commerce Clause pertains when a state's protectionist law discriminates against another state's business in the absence of a conflicting federal statute. Skeptics of such regulation have called it "death by tariff." This chapter covers a variety of such fact situations with which the Court has dealt and continues to deal.

There have been many judicial and scholarly critiques of the doctrine; for a clear exposition of the Court's approach, see Donald H. Regan, "The Supreme Court and State Protectionism: Making Sense of the Dormant Commerce Principle," 84 *Michigan Law Review* 1091 (1986). Philip M. Tatarowicz, "The Dormant Commerce Clause and State Tax Discrimination: Parceling State Actions Between Permissible and Impermissible Burdens," *The State and Local Tax Symposium Edition* 135 (American Bar Association, 2007) is a thorough dissection of current jurisprudential approaches.

### JUSTICE WILLIAM JOHNSON, CONCURRENCE IN *GIBBONS V. OGDEN*

22 U.S. 1, 222, 232 (1824)

[The majority struck down New York's granting of a steamboat company's monopoly over New York-New Jersey trade, based on the monopoly's conflict with the federal Coasting Act of 1793, which authorized the U.S. government to issue licenses for interstate maritime traffic. The Court ruled that Congress's authority to pass the Coasting Act arose from the Commerce Clause and thus superseded inconsistent state legislation. Justice Johnson went further, considering that the monopoly would have been invalid even without the existence of the statute, since only Congress, and not the states, can regulate interstate commerce.]

* * *

The power of a sovereign state over commerce . . . amounts to nothing more than a power to limit and restrain it at pleasure. And since the power to prescribe the limits to its freedom, necessarily implies the power to determine what shall remain unrestrained, it follows, that the power must be exclusive; it can reside but in one potentate; and hence, the grant of this power carries with it the whole subject, leaving nothing for the State to act upon. . .

It is impossible, with the views which I entertain of the principle on which the commercial privileges of the people of United States, among themselves, rests, to concur in the view which this Court takes of the effect of the coasting license in this cause. I do not regard it as the foundation of the right set up in behalf of the appellant. If there was any one object riding over every other in the adoption of the constitution, it was to keep the commercial intercourse among the States free from all invidious and partial restraints. And I cannot overcome the conviction, that if the licensing act was repealed to-morrow, the rights of the appellant to a reversal of the decision complained of, would be as strong as it is under this license. . .

---

**Questions:** Is Justice Johnson's interpretation of the Commerce Clause practical? How does it set the stage for the Dormant Commerce Clause? When reading the cases in this chapter, think about the Supreme Court's parameters for state involvement in interstate commerce.

## MINNESOTA V. CLOVER LEAF CREAMERY COMPANY

449 U.S. 456 (1981)

JUSTICE BRENNAN delivered the opinion of the Court:

In 1977, the Minnesota Legislature enacted a statute banning the retail sale of milk in plastic nonreturnable, nonrefillable containers, but permitting such sale in other nonreturnable, nonrefillable containers, such as paperboard milk cartons. 1977 Minn.Laws, ch. 268, Minn.Stat. § 116F.21 (1978). Respondents contend that the statute violates the Equal Protection and Commerce Clauses of the Constitution.

* * *

Minnesota's statute does not effect "simple protectionism," but "regulates evenhandedly" by prohibiting all milk retailers from selling their products in plastic, nonreturnable milk containers, without regard to whether the milk, the containers, or the sellers are from outside the State. This statute is therefore unlike statutes discriminating against interstate commerce, which we have consistently struck down. [citing cases preventing states from barring investment advisory services by banks with principal offices out of state, banning the export of natural minnows from the state, and imposing additional costs on out of state apple shippers].

Since the statute does not discriminate between interstate and intrastate commerce, the controlling question is whether the incidental burden imposed on interstate commerce by the Minnesota Act is "clearly excessive in relation to the putative local benefits." Pike v. Bruce Church, Inc., 397 U.S. 137, 142. We conclude that it is not.

The burden imposed on interstate commerce by the statute is relatively minor. Milk products may continue to move freely across the Minnesota border, and since most dairies package their products in more than one type of containers, the inconvenience of having to conform to different packaging requirements in Minnesota and the surrounding States should be slight. See Pacific States Box & Basket Co. v. White, 296 U.S. 176 (1935). Within Minnesota, business will presumably shift from manufacturers of plastic nonreturnable containers to producers of paperboard cartons, refillable bottles, and plastic pouches, but there is no reason to suspect that the gainers will be Minnesota firms, or the losers out-of-state firms. Indeed, two of the three dairies, the sole milk retailer, and the sole milk container producer challenging the statute in this litigation are Minnesota firms.

Pulpwood producers are the only Minnesota industry likely to benefit significantly from the Act at the expense of out-of-state firms. Respondents point out that plastic resin, the raw material used for making plastic nonreturnable milk jugs, is produced entirely by non-Minnesota firms, while pulpwood, used for making paperboard, is a major Minnesota product. Nevertheless, it is clear that respondents exaggerate the degree of burden on out-of-state interests, both because plastics will continue to be used in the production of plastic pouches, plastic returnable bottles, and paperboard itself, and because out-of-state pulpwood producers will presumably absorb some of the business generated by the Act.

Even granting that the out-of-state plastics industry is burdened relatively more heavily than the Minnesota pulpwood industry, we find that this burden is not "clearly excessive" in light of the substantial state interest in promoting conservation of energy and other natural resources and easing solid waste disposal problems, which we have already reviewed in the context of equal protection analysis. . . . We find these local benefits ample to support Minnesota's decision under the Commerce Clause. Moreover, we find that no approach with "a lesser impact on interstate activities," Pike v. Bruce Church, Inc., supra, at 142, is available. Respondents have suggested several alternative statutory schemes, but these alternatives are either more burdensome on commerce than the Act (as, for example, banning all nonreturnables) or less likely to be effective (as, for example, providing incentives for recycling). See Brief for Respondents 32–33.

In Exxon Corp. v. Governor of Maryland, 437 U.S. 117 (1978), we upheld a Maryland statute barring producers and refiners of petroleum products—all of which were out-of-state businesses—from retailing gasoline in the State. We stressed that the Commerce Clause "protects the interstate market, not particular interstate firms, from prohibitive or burdensome regulations." Id., at 127–128 A nondiscriminatory regulation serving substantial state purposes is not invalid simply because it causes some business to shift from a predominantly out-of-state industry to a predominantly in-state industry. Only if the burden on interstate commerce clearly outweighs the State's legitimate purposes does such a regulation violate the Commerce Clause.

The judgment of the Minnesota Supreme Court is

Reversed.

---

**Questions:** Under the Dormant Commerce Clause, does it matter whether a state's motive is protectionist? A state denied a license sought by an out-of-state milk distributor to operate a receiving station just beyond its home state's boundary, on the ground that the new facility would reduce the local supply and result in destructive competition. Constitutional? See *H.P. Hood & Sons v. Du Mond,* 336 U.S. 525 (1949).

## HUGHES V. ALEXANDRIA SCRAP CORPORATION

426 U.S. 794 (1976)

MR. JUSTICE POWELL delivered the opinion of the Court.

This case involves a two-pronged constitutional attack on a recent amendment to one part of a complex Maryland plan for ridding that State of abandoned automobiles. The three-judge District Court agreed with appellee, a Virginia scrap processor that participates in the plan, that the amendment violated the Commerce Clause and denied appellee equal protection of the laws. We disagree on both points.

The 1967 session of the Maryland Legislature commissioned a study to suggest some way to deal with the growing aesthetic problem of abandoned automobiles. The study concluded that the root of the problem was the existence of bottlenecks in the "scrap cycle," the course that a vehicle follows from abandonment to processing into scrap metal for ultimate re-use by steel mills. At its 1969 session, the legislature responded by enacting a comprehensive statute designed to speed up the scrap cycle by using state money both as a carrot and as a stick. The statute is intricate, but its provisions relevant to this case may be sketched briefly.

The legislative study had found that one of the bottlenecks occurred in the junkyards of wrecking companies, which tended to accumulate vehicles for the resale value of their spare parts. The statute's stick designed to clear this bottleneck is a requirement that a Maryland wrecker desiring to keep abandoned vehicles on its premises must obtain a license and pay a recurring fine for any vehicle of a specified age retained for more than a year. The study had identified as another cause of sluggishness in the scrap cycle the low profits earned by wreckers and others for delivering vehicles to scrap processors. The carrot written into the statute to remedy this problem is a "bounty" paid by the State for the destruction, by a processor licensed under the statute, of any vehicle formerly titled in Maryland. When a wrecker licensed under the statute to stockpile vehicles delivers one of them for scrapping its shares the bounty equally with the processor. The processor receives the entire bounty when it destroys a vehicle supplied by someone other than a licensed wrecker.

These penalty and bounty provisions work with elementary laws of economics to speed up the scrap cycle. The penalty for retention of vehicles, plus the prospect of sharing the bounty, work in tandem to encourage licensed wreckers to move vehicles to processors. The bounties to processors on vehicles from unlicensed suppliers also encourage those suppliers to deliver to the processors, because the processors are able to pay higher than normal market prices by sharing the bounties with them.

The Penalty and bounty provisions, however, did not remove another impediment to the smooth functioning of the scrap cycle that was legal rather than economic in origin. This was the possibility of suits for conversion against a processor by owners who might claim that they had not abandoned their vehicles. To meet this problem the statute specified several documents with which a processor could prove clear title to a vehicle, and required that a processor obtain one of these documents from its supplier and submit it to the State as a condition of receiving the bounty. One of the documents, called a "Wrecker's Certificate," can be given only by a wrecker licensed under the statute. It is essentially a clear title that the wrecker secures by following statutory notice procedures at the time it first obtains a vehicle. Suppliers other than licensed wreckers must provide some other document either a properly endorsed certificate of title, a certificate from a police department vesting title in the supplier after statutory notices, or a bill of sale from a police auction.

These documentation requirements, although vital for the protection of processors, are themselves some slight encumbrance upon the free transfer of abandoned vehicles to processors. Apparently in recognition of this fact, and the reduced potential for owners' claims in the case of ancient automobiles, the statute placed vehicles over eight years old and inoperable ("hulks") into a special category. Section 11–1002.2(f)(5) of the statute, as enacted, provided in substance that anyone in possession of a hulk could transfer it to a scrap processor, and the processor could claim a bounty for its destruction, without delivery to the processor or subsequent submission to the State of any documentation of title.

The statute extends its burdens of fines, and its benefits in the form of a share in bounties, only to wreckers that maintain junkyards located in Maryland, and requires a license only of those wreckers. There is no similar residency requirement for scrap processors that wish to obtain a license and participate in the bounty program, and in fact seven of the 16 scrap processors that have participated are located in either Pennsylvania or Virginia. Appellee, a Virginia corporation with a processing plant near the Potomac River in Alexandria, was an original licensee under the Maryland statute. Presumably because of its proximity to the southern Maryland and Washington, D. C., areas, appellee attracted enough Maryland-titled vehicles to its plant to rank third among licensed processors in receipt of bounties through the summer of 1974.

As is apparently the case with most of the licensed processors, virtually all (96%) of the bounty-eligible vehicles processed by appellee during that period were hulks, upon which appellee did not have to demand title documentation from its suppliers in order later to receive the bounty. In the summer of 1974, however, Maryland changed significantly the treatment of hulks by amending § 11–1002.2(f)(5). Under the law as amended it is no longer possible for a licensed scrap processor to receive a bounty on a hulk without submitting title documentation to the State. But the documentation required of a processor whose plant is in Maryland differs from that required of a processor, like appellee, whose plant is not in Maryland. The former need only submit a simple document in which the person who delivered the hulk certified his own right to it and agreed to indemnify the processor for any third-party claims arising from its destruction. Hulk processors long had required such "indemnity agreements" from their hulk suppliers as a matter of industry practice. The effect of the 1974 amendment is to give these agreements legal recognition and to require one when a Maryland processor applies for a bounty on a hulk. The non-Maryland processor, however, cannot submit a simple indemnity agreement. For it, receipt of a bounty on a hulk now depends upon the same documentation specified for abandoned vehicles in general: a certificate of title, a police certificate vesting title, a bill of sale from a police auction, or in the case of licensed wreckers only a Wrecker's Certificate.

* * *

Appellee contended below that the 1974 amendment to § 11–1002.2(f)(5) violated the Commerce Clause by interfering with, or "burdening," the flow of bounty-eligible hulks across state lines, and denied appellee equal protection of the laws by discriminating arbitrarily between it and licensed processors located in Maryland as to the right to claim bounties on hulks by submitting indemnity agreements. The District Court granted summary judgment to appellee on both claims, and enjoined the State of Maryland from giving further effect to that part of the 1974 amendment which restricts the right to obtain bounties based on indemnity agreements to Maryland processors only. D.C., 391 F.Supp. 46. The State appealed . . .

* * *

In this Court appellee relies on the Commerce Clause argument that was adopted by the District Court. The argument starts from the premise, well established by the history of the Commerce Clause, that this Nation is a common market in which state lines cannot be made barriers to the free flow of both raw materials and finished goods in response to the economic laws of supply and demand. See Great A&P Tea Co. v. Cottrell, 424 U.S. 366, 370–371, 96 S.Ct. 923, 927–928, 47 L.Ed.2d 55 (1976). Appellee concedes that until the 1974 amendment the Maryland system operated in conformity with the common-market principle. There was free competition among licensed processors for Maryland hulks from unlicensed suppliers and an unimpeded flow of such hulks out of Maryland to appellee and other non-Maryland processors. The only effect of the bounty was to enhance the value of hulks and thus make it more likely that they would be moved to processing plants.

The practical effect of the amendment, however, was to limit the enhanced price available to unlicensed suppliers to hulks that stayed inside Maryland, thus discouraging such suppliers from taking their hulks out of State for processing. The result was that the movement of hulks in interstate commerce was reduced. Appellee contends that this effect of the 1974 amendment is a "burden" on interstate commerce, the permissibility of which must be determined under the test of Pike v. Bruce Church, Inc., 397 U.S. 137, 142 (1970). The Court there stated that "the extent of the burden that will be tolerated will . . . depend on the nature of the local interest involved, and on whether it could be promoted as well with a lesser impact on interstate activities."

* * *

The District Court accepted appellee's analysis, and concluded that the 1974 amendment failed the Pike Test. First, the court found that the amendment did impose "substantial burdens upon the free flow of interstate commerce." 391 F.Supp., at 62. Moreover, it considered the disadvantage suffered by out-of-state processors to be particularly suspect under previous decisions of this Court, noting that to avoid the disadvantage those processors would have to build new plants inside Maryland to carry on a business which, prior to the amendment, they had pursued efficiently outside the State. See [additional citations]. Maryland's principal argument in support of the amendment was that, by making it difficult for out-of-state processors to claim bounties on hulks delivered by unlicensed suppliers, the amendment tends to reduce the amount of state funds paid for destruction of Maryland-titled hulks abandoned in the States where those processors are located instead of in Maryland. The District Court acknowledged the validity of this interest, but considered the means employed inappropriate under Pike because the same interest could have been furthered, with less impact upon interstate commerce, by amending the statute to condition the bounty upon a hulk's abandonment in Maryland instead of its previous titling there.

This line of reasoning is not without force if its basic premise is accepted. That premise is that every action by a State that has the effect of reducing in some manner the flow of goods in interstate commerce is potentially an impermissible burden. But we are not persuaded that Maryland's action in amending its statute was the kind of action with which the Commerce Clause is concerned.

The situation presented by this statute and the 1974 amendment is quite unlike that found in the cases upon which appellee relies.

* * *

The common thread of all these cases is that the State interfered with the natural functioning of the interstate market either through prohibition or through burdensome regulation. By contrast, Maryland has not sought to prohibit the flow of hulks, or to regulate the conditions under which it may occur. Instead, it has entered into the market itself to bid up their price. There has been an impact upon the interstate flow of hulks only because, since the 1974 amendment, Maryland effectively has made it more lucrative for unlicensed suppliers to dispose of their hulks in Maryland rather than take them outside the State.

* * *

We believe, however, that the novelty of this case is not its presentation of a new form of "burden" upon commerce, but that appellee should characterize Maryland's action as a burden which the Commerce Clause was intended to make suspect. The Clause was designed in part to prevent trade barriers that had undermined efforts of the fledgling States to form a cohesive whole following their victory in the Revolution.

* * *

We do not believe the Commerce Clause was intended to require independent justification for such action. Maryland entered the market for the purpose, agreed by all to be commendable as well as legitimate, of protecting the State's environment. As the means of furthering this purpose, it elected the payment of state funds in the form of bounties to encourage the removal of automobile hulks from Maryland streets and junkyards. It is true that the state money initially was made available to licensed out-of-state processors as well as those located within Maryland, and not until the 1974 amendment was the financial benefit channeled, in practical effect, to domestic processors. But this chronology does not distinguish the case, for Commerce Clause purposes, from one in which a State offered bounties only to domestic processors from the start. Regardless of when the State's largesse is first confined to domestic processors, the effect upon the flow of hulks resting within the State is the same: they will tend to be processed inside the State rather than flowing to foreign processors. But no trade barrier of the type forbidden by the Commerce Clause, and involved in previous cases, impedes their movement out of State. They remain within Maryland in response to market forces, including that exerted by money from the State. Nothing in the purposes animating the Commerce Clause prohibits a State, in the absence of congressional action, from participating in the market and exercising the right to favor its own citizens over others.

[The Court also ruled that the Maryland statute did not violate the Equal Protection Clause].

We hold that the District Court erred in finding the 1974 amendment invalid under either the Commerce Clause or the Equal Protection Clause. Accordingly, its judgment is reversed.

MR. JUSTICE STEVENS, concurring.

The dissent creates the impression that the Court's opinion, which I join without reservation, represents a significant retreat from its settled practice in adjudicating claims that a state program places an unconstitutional burden on interstate commerce. This is not the fact. There is no prior decision of this Court even addressing e critical Commerce Clause issue presented by this case.

It is important to differentiate between commerce which flourishes in a free market and commerce which owes its existence to a state subsidy program. Our cases finding that a state regulation constitutes an impermissible burden on interstate commerce all dealt with restrictions that adversely affected the operation of a free market. This case is unique because the commerce which Maryland has "burdened" is commerce which would not exist if Maryland had not decided to subsidize a portion of the automobile scrap-processing business.

By artificially enhancing the value of certain abandoned hulks, Maryland created a market that did not previously exist. The program which Maryland initiated in 1969 included subsidies for scrapping plants located in Virginia and Pennsylvania as well as for plants located in Maryland. Those subsidies stimulated the movement of abandoned hulks from Maryland to out-of-state scrapping plants and thereby gave rise to the interstate commerce which is at stake in this litigation.

That commerce, which is now said to be burdened, would never have existed if in the first instance Maryland had decided to confine its subsidy to operators of Maryland plants. A failure to create that commerce would have been unobjectionable because the Commerce Clause surely does not impose on the States any obligation to subsidize out-of-state business. Nor, in my judgment, does that Clause inhibit a State's power to experiment with different methods of encouraging local industry. Whether the encouragement takes the form of a cash subsidy, a tax credit, or a special privilege intended to attract investment capital, it should note characterized as a "burden" on commerce. . . .

* * *

This is the first case in which any litigant has asked a federal court to address the question whether a state subsidy constitutes a "burden" on interstate commerce. That fact is significant because there must have been countless situations during the past two centuries in which the several States have experimented with different methods of encouraging local enterprise without providing like encouragement to out-of-state competitors. The absence of any previous challenge to such programs reflects, I believe, a common and correct interpretation of the Commerce Clause as primarily intended (at least when Congress has not spoken) to inhibit the several States' power to create restrictions on the free flow of goods within the national market, rather than to provide the basis for questioning a State's right to experiment with different incentives to business. The District Court's novel interpretation of the "burden" concept represented a departure which, had it been accepted, would impair rather than protect interstate commerce.

---

**Question:** In *Hughes v. Alexandria Scrap,* what if, rather than penalizing out-of-state junk suppliers with additional regulations, the state had used a tax deduction to encourage in-state suppliers?

## CITY OF PHILADELPHIA V. NEW JERSEY

437 U.S. 617 (1978)

MR. JUSTICE STEWART delivered the opinion of the Court.

A New Jersey law prohibits the importation of most "solid or liquid waste which originated or was collected outside the territorial limits of the State . . . ." In this case we are required to decide whether this statutory prohibition violates the Commerce Clause of the United States Constitution.

* * *

As authorized by ch. 363, the Commissioner promulgated regulations permitting four categories of waste to enter the State. Apart from these narrow exceptions, however, New Jersey closed its borders to all waste from other States.

Immediately affected by these developments were the operators of private landfills in New Jersey, and several cities in other States that had agreements with these operators for waste disposal. They brought suit against New Jersey and its Department of Environmental Protection in state court, attacking the statute and regulations on a number of state and federal grounds. In an oral opinion granting the plaintiffs' motion for summary judgment, the trial court declared the law unconstitutional because it discriminated against interstate commerce. The New Jersey Supreme Court consolidated this case with another reaching the same conclusion . . . Hackensack Meadowlands Development Comm'n v. Municipal Sanitary Landfill Auth., 127 N.J.Super. 160, 316 A.2d 711, and reversed, 68 N.J. 451 It found that ch. 363 advanced vital health and environmental objectives with no economic discrimination against, and with little burden upon, interstate commerce, and that the law was therefore permissible under the Commerce Clause of the Constitution. The court also found no congressional intent to preempt ch. 363 by enacting in 1965 the Solid Waste Disposal Act, 79 Stat. 997, 42 U.S.C. § 3251 et seq., as amended by the Resource Recovery Act of 1970, 84 Stat. 1227.

The plaintiffs then appealed to this Court.

* * *

We agree with the New Jersey court that the state law has not been pre-empted by federal legislation. The dispositive question, therefore, is whether the law is constitutionally permissible in light of the Commerce Clause of the Constitution.

* * *

The opinions of the Court through the years have reflected an alertness to the evils of "economic isolation" and protectionism, while at the same time recognizing that incidental burdens on interstate commerce may be unavoidable when a State legislates to safeguard the health and safety of its people. Thus, where simple economic protectionism is effected by state legislation, a virtually per se rule of invalidity has been erected. See, e. g., [citations]. The clearest example of such legislation is a law that overtly blocks the flow of interstate commerce at a State's borders. Cf. Welton v. Missouri, 91 U.S. 275. But where other legislative objectives are credibly advanced and there is no patent discrimination against interstate trade, the Court has adopted a much more flexible approach, the general contours of which were outlined in Pike v. Bruce Church, Inc., 397 U.S. 137, 142:

"Where the statute regulates evenhandedly to effectuate a legitimate local public interest, and its effects on interstate commerce are only incidental, it will be upheld unless the burden imposed on such commerce is clearly excessive in relation to the putative local benefits. . . . If a legitimate local purpose is found, then the question becomes one of degree. And the extent of the burden that will be tolerated will of course depend on the nature of the local interest involved, and on whether it could be promoted as well with a lesser impact on interstate activities."

* * *

The crucial inquiry, therefore, must be directed to determining whether ch. 363 is basically a protectionist measure, or whether it can fairly be viewed as a law directed to legitimate local concerns, with effects upon interstate commerce that are only incidental.

* * *

The state court . . . found that New Jersey's existing landfill sites will be exhausted within a few years; that to go on using these sites or to develop new ones will take a heavy environmental toll, both from pollution and from loss of scarce open lands; that new techniques to divert waste from landfills to other methods of disposal and resource recovery processes are under development, but that these changes will require time; and finally, that "the extension of the lifespan of existing landfills, resulting from the exclusion of out-of-state waste, may be of crucial importance in preventing further virgin wetlands or other undeveloped lands from being devoted to landfill purposes." 68 N.J., at 460–465. Based on these findings, the court concluded that ch. 363 was designed to protect, not the State's economy, but its environment, and that its substantial benefits outweigh its "slight" burden on interstate commerce. Id., at 471–478.

The appellants strenuously contend that ch. 363, "while outwardly cloaked 'in the currently fashionable garb of environmental protection,' . . . is actually no more than a legislative effort to suppress competition and stabilize the cost of solid waste disposal for New Jersey residents . . . ." They cite passages of legislative history suggesting that the problem addressed by ch. 363 is primarily financial: Stemming the flow of out-of-state waste into certain landfill sites will extend their lives, thus delaying the day when New Jersey cities must transport their waste to more distant and expensive sites.

The appellees, on the other hand, deny that ch. 363 was motivated by financial concerns or economic protectionism. In the words of their brief, "[n]o New Jersey commercial interests stand to gain advantage over competitors from outside the state as a result of the ban on dumping out-of-state waste." Noting that New Jersey landfill operators are among the plaintiffs, the appellee's brief argues that "[t]he complaint is not that New

Jersey has forged an economic preference for its own commercial interests, but rather that it has denied a small group of its entrepreneurs an economic opportunity to traffic in waste in order to protect the health, safety and welfare of the citizenry at large."

This dispute about ultimate legislative purpose need not be resolved, because its resolution would not be relevant to the constitutional issue to be decided in this case. Contrary to the evident assumption of the state court and the parties, the evil of protectionism can reside in legislative means as well as legislative ends. Thus, it does not matter whether the ultimate aim of ch. 363 is to reduce the waste disposal costs of New Jersey residents or to save remaining open lands from pollution, for we assume New Jersey has every right to protect its residents' pocketbooks as well as their environment. And it may be assumed as well that New Jersey may pursue those ends by slowing the flow of all waste into the State's remaining landfills, even though interstate commerce may incidentally be affected. But whatever New Jersey's ultimate purpose, it may not be accomplished by discriminating against articles of commerce coming from outside the State unless there is some reason, apart from their origin, to treat them differently. Both on its face and in its plain effect, ch. 363 violates this principle of nondiscrimination.

The Court has consistently found parochial legislation of this kind to be constitutionally invalid, whether the ultimate aim of the legislation was to assure a steady supply of milk by erecting barriers to allegedly ruinous outside competition, Baldwin v. G. A. F. Seelig, Inc., 294 U.S., at 522–524, or to create jobs by keeping industry within the State, Foster-Fountain Packing Co. v. Haydel, 278 U.S. 1, 10, [additional citations]; or to preserve the State's financial resources from depletion by fencing out indigent immigrants, Edwards v. California, 314 U.S. 160. In each of these cases, a presumably legitimate goal was sought to be achieved by the illegitimate means of isolating the State from the national economy.

* * *

The New Jersey law at issue in this case falls squarely within the area that the Commerce Clause puts off limits to state regulation. On its face, it imposes on out-of-state commercial interests the full burden of conserving the State's remaining landfill space. It is true that in our previous cases the scarce natural resource was itself the article of commerce, whereas here the scarce resource and the article of commerce are distinct. But that difference is without consequence. In both instances, the State has overtly moved to slow or freeze the flow of commerce for protectionist reasons. It does not matter that the State has shut the article of commerce inside the State in one case and outside the State in the other. What is crucial is the attempt by one State to isolate itself from a problem common to many by erecting a barrier against the movement of interstate trade.

The appellees argue that not all laws which facially discriminate against out-of-state commerce are forbidden protectionist regulations. In particular, they point to quarantine laws, which this Court has repeatedly upheld even though they appear to single out interstate commerce for special treatment. See [citations]. In the appellees' view, ch. 363 is analogous to such health-protective measures, since it reduces the exposure of New Jersey residents to the allegedly harmful effects of landfill sites.

It is true that certain quarantine laws have not been considered forbidden protectionist measures, even though they were directed against out-of-state commerce. See [citations]. But those quarantine laws banned the importation of articles such as diseased livestock that required destruction as soon as possible because their very movement risked contagion and other evils. Those laws thus did not discriminate against interstate commerce as such, but simply prevented traffic in noxious articles, whatever their origin.

The New Jersey statute is not such a quarantine law. There has been no claim here that the very movement of waste into or through New Jersey endangers health, or that waste must be disposed of as soon and as close to its point of generation as possible. The harms caused by waste are said to arise after its disposal in landfill sites, and at that point, as New Jersey concedes, there is no basis to distinguish out-of-state waste from domestic waste. If one is inherently harmful, so is the other. Yet New Jersey has banned the former while leaving its landfill sites open to the latter. The New Jersey law blocks the importation of waste in an obvious effort to saddle those outside the State with the entire burden of slowing the flow of refuse into New Jersey's remaining landfill sites. That legislative effort is clearly impermissible under the Commerce Clause of the Constitution.

Today, cities in Pennsylvania and New York find it expedient or necessary to send their waste into New Jersey for disposal, and New Jersey claims the right to close its borders to such traffic. Tomorrow, cities in New Jersey may find it expedient or necessary to send their waste into Pennsylvania or New York for disposal, and those States might then claim the right to close their borders. The Commerce Clause will protect New Jersey in the future, just as it protects her neighbors now, from efforts by one State to isolate itself in the stream of interstate commerce from a problem shared by all. The judgment is

Reversed.

MR. JUSTICE REHNQUIST, with whom THE CHIEF JUSTICE joins, dissenting.

A growing problem in our Nation is the sanitary treatment and disposal of solid waste. For many years, solid waste was incinerated. Because of the significant environmental problems attendant on incineration, however, this method of solid waste disposal has declined in use in many localities, including New Jersey. "Sanitary" landfills have replaced incineration as the principal method of disposing of solid waste. In ch. 363 of the 1973 N.J. Laws, the State of New Jersey legislatively recognized the unfortunate fact that landfills also present extremely serious health and safety problems. First, in New Jersey, "virtually all sanitary landfills can be expected to produce leachate, a noxious and highly polluted liquid which is seldom visible and frequently pollutes . . . ground and surface waters." App. 149. The natural decomposition process which occurs in landfills also produces large quantities of methane and thereby presents a significant explosion hazard. Id., at 149, 156–157. Landfills can also generate "health hazards caused by rodents, fires and scavenger birds" and, "needless to say, do not help New Jersey's aesthetic appearance nor New Jersey's noise or water or air pollution problems." Supp.App. 5.

The health and safety hazards associated with landfills present appellees with a currently unsolvable dilemma. Other, hopefully safer, methods of disposing of solid wastes are still in the development stage and cannot presently be used. But appellees obviously cannot completely stop the tide of solid waste that its citizens will produce in the interim. For the moment, therefore, appellees must continue to use sanitary landfills to dispose of New Jersey's own solid waste despite the critical environmental problems thereby created.

The question presented in this case is whether New Jersey must also continue to receive and dispose of solid waste from neighboring States, even though these will inexorably increase the health problems discussed above. The Court answers this question in the affirmative. New Jersey must either prohibit all landfill operations, leaving itself to cast about for a presently nonexistent solution to the serious problem of disposing of the waste generated within its own borders, or it must accept waste from every portion of the United States, thereby multiplying the health and safety problems which would result if it dealt only with such wastes generated within the State. Because past precedents establish that the Commerce Clause does not present appellees with such a Hobson's choice, I dissent.

* * *

The Supreme Court of New Jersey expressly found that ch. 363 was passed "to preserve the health of New Jersey residents by keeping their exposure to solid waste and landfill areas to a minimum." 68 N.J. 451, 473, 348 A.2d 505, 516. The Court points to absolutely no evidence that would contradict this finding by the New Jersey Supreme Court. Because I find no basis for distinguishing the laws under challenge here from our past cases upholding state laws that prohibit the importation of items that could endanger the population of the State, I dissent.

**Questions:** Is the *Philadelphia v. New Jersey* majority's view consistent with *Massachusetts v. E.P.A.'s* affirmation that states possess sovereignty over their natural resources? Would it have made any difference if the waste landfills were publicly owned? In order to facilitate efficient tax collection from non-local businesses, a state requires out-of-state wineries to sell directly to consumers. Does the DCC apply? See *Granholm v. Heald,* 544 U.S. 460 (2005).

# CHAPTER 5

# TAXING AND SPENDING CLAUSE

■ ■ ■

## CONTEXT & SOURCES

In the Constitution's Article I, § 8, para. 1, Congress is given the power "[t]o lay and collect Taxes . . . to pay the Debts and provide for the common Defence and general welfare of the United States." As with the Commerce Clause, this expansion of federal power was subject to an evolution of Supreme Court interpretation in response to the shifting politics of laissez-faire capitalism and regulation. With the Taxing Power, the debate has focused on the question whether a monetary charge was a "tax" (considered constitutional) or a "penalty" (unconstitutional), with the same move from a sharp, formalistic distinction to a more pragmatic blurring of the categories based on specific facts. Also similarly, this dichotomy in approaches has been recently revived in the Affordable Care Act case, *N.F.I.B. v. Sebelius.*

For an overview of the Court's responses to taxation, see Erik M. Jensen, *The Taxing Power: A Reference Guide to the U.S. Constitution* (Praeger, 2005). A critical history of the tax/penalty distinction is provided by Barry Cushman, "NFIB v. Sibelius and the Transformation of the Taxing Power," 89 *Notre Dame Law Review* 133 (2014).

---

**Question:** In "Federalist No. 41," James Madison wrote that the Constitution's critics considered the Taxing and Spending Clause to be "an unlimited commission to exercise every power which may be alleged to be necessary for the common defense or general welfare," but that this view was a "misconstruction." James Madison, "Federalist No. 41," in *The Federalist Papers*, 251, 258–59 (Charles R. Kesler ed., 2003) (1788). Is the Clause a broad or narrow grant of power to Congress?

## BAILEY V. DREXEL FURNITURE COMPANY (THE CHILD LABOR TAX CASE)

259 U.S. 20 (1922)

* * *

MR. CHIEF JUSTICE TAFT delivered the opinion of the Court.

This case presents the question of the constitutional validity of the Child Labor Tax Law. The plaintiff below, the Drexel Furniture Company, is engaged in the manufacture of furniture in the Western district of North Carolina. On September 20, 1921, it received a notice from Bailey, United States collector of internal revenue for the district, that it had been assessed $6,312.79 for having during the taxable year 1919 employed and permitted to work in its factory a boy under 14 years of age, thus incurring the tax of 10 per cent. on its net profits for that year. The company paid the tax under protest, and, after rejection of its claim for a refund, brought this suit. On demurrer to an amended complaint, judgment was entered for the company against the collector for the full amount, with interest. The writ of error is prosecuted by the collector direct from the District Court under section 238 of the Judicial Code (Comp. St. § 1215).

The Child Labor Tax Law is title No. XII of an act entitled 'An act to provide revenue and for other purposes,' approved February 24, 1919, 40 Stat. 1057, 1138 (Comp. St. Ann. Supp. 1919, §§ 6336 7/8 a to 6336 7/8 h). The heading of the title is 'Tax on Employment of Child Labor.' It begins with section 1200 and includes eight sections. Section 1200 is as follows:

'Sec. 1200. That every person (other than a bona fide boys' or girls' canning club recognized by the agricultural department of a state and of the United States) operating (a) any mine or quarry situated in the United States in which children under the age of sixteen years have been employed or permitted to work during any portion of the taxable year; or (b) any mill, cannery, workshop, factory, or manufacturing establishment situated in the United States in which children under the age of fourteen years have been employed or permitted to work, or children between the ages of fourteen and sixteen have been employed or permitted to work more than eight hours in any day or more than six days in any week, or after the hour of seven o'clock post meridian, or before the hour of six o'clock ante meridian, during any portion of the taxable year, shall pay for each taxable year, in addition to all other taxes imposed by law, an excise tax equivalent to 10 per centum of the entire net profits received or accrued for such year from the sale or disposition of the product of such mine, quarry, mill, cannery, workshop, factory, or manufacturing establishment.'

Section 1203 relieves from liability to the tax any one who employs a child, believing him to be of proper age relying on a certificate to this effect issued by persons prescribed by a board consisting of the Secretary of the

Treasury, the Commissioner of Internal Revenue, and the Secretary of Labor, or issued by state authorities. The section also provides in paragraph (b) that—

'The tax imposed by this title shall not be imposed in the case of any person who proves to the satisfaction of the Secretary that the only employment or permission to work which but for this section would subject him to the tax, has been of a child employed or permitted to work under a mistake of fact as to the age of such child and without intention to evade the tax.'

Section 1206 gives authority to the Commissioner of Internal Revenue, or any other person authorized by him 'to enter and inspect at any time any mine, quarry, mill, cannery, workshop, factory or manufacturing establishment.' The Secretary of Labor, or any person whom he authorizes, is given like authority in order to comply with a request of the Commissioner to make such inspection and report the same. Any person who refuses entry or obstructs inspection is made subject to fine or imprisonment or both.

The law is attacked on the ground that it is a regulation of the employment of child labor in the states—an exclusively state function under the federal Constitution and within the reservations of the Tenth Amendment. It is defendant on the ground that it is a mere excise tax levied by the Congress of the United States under its broad power of taxation conferred by section 8, article 1, of the federal Constitution. We must construe the law and interpret the intent and meaning of Congress from the language of the act. The words are to be given their ordinary meaning unless the context shows that they are differently used. Does this law impose a tax with only that incidental restraint and regulation which a tax must inevitably involve? Or does it regulate by the use of the so-called tax as a penalty? If a tax, it is clearly an excise. If it were an excise on a commodity or other thing of value, we might not be permitted under previous decisions of this court to infer solely from its heavy burden that the act intends a prohibition instead of a tax. But this act is more. It provides a heavy exaction for a departure from a detailed and specified course of conduct in business. That course of business is that employers shall employ in mines and quarries, children of an age greater than 16 years; in mills and factories, children of an age greater than 14 years, and shall prevent children of less than 16 years in mills and factories from working more than 8 hours a day or 6 days in the week. If an employer departs from this prescribed course of business, he is to pay to the government one-tenth of his entire net income in the business for a full year. The amount is not to be proportioned in any degree to the extent or frequency of the departures, but is to be paid by the employer in full measure whether he employs 500 children for a year, or employs only one for a day. Moreover, if he does not know the child is within the named age limit, he is not to pay; that is to say, it is only where he knowingly departs from the prescribed course that payment is to be exacted. Scienters are associated with penalties, not with taxes. The employer's factory is to be subject to inspection at any time not only by the taxing officers of the Treasury, the Department normally charged with the collection of taxes, but also by the Secretary of Labor and his subordinates, whose normal function is the advancement and protection of the welfare of the workers. In the light of these features of the act, a court must be blind not to see that the so-called tax is imposed to stop the employment of children within the age limits prescribed. Its prohibitory and regulatory effect and purpose are palpable. All others can see and understand this. How can we properly shut our minds to it?

It is the high duty and function of this court in cases regularly brought to its bar to decline to recognize or enforce seeming laws of Congress, dealing with subjects not intrusted to Congress, but left or committed by the supreme law of the land to the control of the states. We cannot avoid the duty, even though it require us to refuse to give effect to legislation designed to promote the highest good. The good sought in unconstitutional legislation is an insidious feature, because it leads citizens and legislators of good purpose to promote it, without thought of the serious breach it will make in the ark of our covenant, or the harm which will come from breaking down recognized standards. In the maintenance of local self-government, on the one hand, and the national power, on the other, our country has been able to endure and prosper for near a century and a half.

Out of a proper respect for the acts of a co-ordinate branch of the government, this court has gone far to sustain taxing acts as such, even though there has been ground for suspecting, from the weight of the tax, it was intended to destroy its subject. But in the act before us the presumption of validity cannot prevail, because the proof of the contrary is found on the very face of its provisions. Grant the validity of this law, and all that Congress would need to do, hereafter, in seeking to take over to its control any one of the great number of subjects of public interest, jurisdiction of which the states have never parted with, and which are reserved to them by the Tenth Amendment, would be to enact a detailed measure of complete regulation of the subject and enforce it by a so called tax upon departures from it. To give such magic to the word 'tax' would be to break down all constitutional limitation of the powers of Congress and completely wipe out the sovereignty of the states.

The difference between a tax and a penalty is sometimes difficult to define, and yet the consequences of the distinction in the required method of their collection often are important. Where the sovereign enacting the law has power to impose both tax and penalty, the difference between revenue production and mere regulation may be immaterial, but not so when one sovereign can impose a tax only, and the power of regulation rests in another. Taxes are occasionally imposed in the discretion of the Legislature on proper subjects with the primary motive of obtaining revenue from them and with the incidental motive of discouraging them by making their continuance onerous. They do not lose their character as taxes because of the incidental motive. But there comes a time in the extension of the penalizing features of the so-called tax when it loses its character as such and becomes a mere penalty, with the characteristics of regulation and punishment. Such is the case in the law before us. Although Congress does not invalidate the contract of employment or expressly declare that the employment within the mentioned ages is illegal, it does exhibit its intent practically to achieve the latter result by adopting the criteria of wrongdoing and imposing its principal consequence on those who transgress its standard.

The case before us cannot be distinguished from that of Hammer v. Dagenhart, 247 U. S. 251. Congress there enacted a law to prohibit transportation in interstate commerce of goods made at a factory in which there was employment of children within the same ages and for the same number of hours a day and days in a week as are penalized by the act in this case. This court held the law in that case to be void. It said:

'In our view the necessary effect of this act is, by means of a prohibition against the movement in interstate commerce of ordinary commercial commodities, to regulate the hours of labor of children in factories and mines within the states, a purely state authority.'

In the case at the bar, Congress in the name of a tax which on the face of the act is penalty seeks to do the same thing, and the effort must be equally futile.

The analogy of the Dagenhart Case is clear. The congressional power over interstate commerce is, within its proper scope, just as complete and unlimited as the congressional power to tax, and the legislative motive in its exercise is just as free from judicial suspicion and inquiry. Yet when Congress threatened to stop interstate commerce in ordinary and necessary commodities, unobjectionable as subjects of transportation, and to deny the same to the people of a state in order to coerce them into compliance with Congress' regulation of state concerns, the court said this was not in fact regulation of interstate commerce, but rather that of state concerns and was invalid. So here the so-called tax is a penalty to coerce people of a state to act as Congress wishes them to act in respect of a matter completely the business of the state government under the federal Constitution. This case requires as did the Dagenhart Case the application of the principle announced by Chief Justice Marshall in McCulloch v. Maryland, 4 Wheat. 316, 423. 579), in a much-quoted passage: 'Should Congress, in the execution of its powers, adopt measures which are prohibited by the Constitution; or should Congress, under the pretext of executing its powers, pass laws for the accomplishment of objects not intrusted to the government; it would become the painful duty of this tribunal, should a case requiring such a decision come before it, to say that such an act was not the law of the land.'

* * *

For the reasons given, we must hold the Child Labor Tax Law invalid and the judgment of the District Court is

Affirmed.

MR. JUSTICE CLARKE, dissents.

---

**Question:** The majority's holding parallels that of *Hammer v. Dagenhart,* 247 U.S. 251 (1918) (referenced in the Chapter 3 questions), where the Court struck down a federal ban on the shipment of goods produced by child labor, based on the formalistic distinction between trade and production. A federal law imposes an "excise tax" on liquor dealers who violate the alcohol laws of their state. Under the *Bailey* approach, should this law be upheld or struck down under the Taxing and Spending Clause? See *United States v. Constantine,* 296 U.S. 287 (1935).

## SONZINSKY V. UNITED STATES

300 U.S. 506 (1937)

* * *

MR. JUSTICE STONE delivered the opinion of the Court.

The question for decision is whether section 2 of the National Firearms Act of June 26, 1934, c. 757, 48 Stat. 1236, 26 U.S.C. §§ 1132–1132q (26 U.S.C.A. §§ 1132–1132q), which imposes a $200 annual license tax on dealers in firearms, is a constitutional exercise of the legislative power of Congress.

Petitioner was convicted by the District Court for Eastern Illinois on two counts of an indictment, the first charging him with violation of section 2 (26 U.S.C.A. § 1132a), by dealing in firearms without payment of the tax. On appeal the Circuit Court of Appeals set aside the conviction on the second count and affirmed on the first. 86 F.(2d) 486. On petition of the accused we granted certiorari, limited to the question of the constitutional validity of the statute in its application under the first count in the indictment. 300 U.S. 648.

Section 2 of the National Firearms Act (26 U.S.C.A. § 1132a) requires every dealer in firearms to register with the Collector of Internal Revenue in the district where he carries on business, and to pay a special excise tax of $200 a year. Importers or manufacturers are taxed $500 a year. Section 3 (26 U.S.C.A. § 1132b) imposes a tax of $200 on each transfer of a firearm, payable by the transferor, and section 4 (26 U.S.C.A. § 1132c) prescribes regulations for the identification of purchasers. The term 'firearm' is defined by section 1 (26 U.S.C.A. § 1132) as meaning a shotgun or a rifle having a barrel less than eighteen inches in length, or any other weapon, except a pistol or revolver, from which a shot is discharged by an explosive, if capable of being concealed on the person, or a machine gun, and includes a muffler or silencer for any firearm. As the conviction for nonpayment of the tax exacted by section 2 has alone been sustained, it is unnecessary to inquire whether the different tax levied by section 3 and the regulations pertaining to it are valid. Section 16 (26 U.S.C.A. § 1132*o*) declares that the provisions of the act are separable. Each tax is on a different activity and is collectible independently of the other. Full effect may be given to the license tax standing alone, even though all other provisions are invalid. Weller v. New York, 268 U.S. 319; Marshall Field & Co. v. Clark, 143 U.S. 649, 697, [additional citations].

In the exercise of its constitutional power to lay taxes, Congress may select the subjects of taxation, choosing some and omitting others. See Flint v. Stone Tracy Co., 220 U.S. 107; [additional citations]. Its power extends to the imposition of exercise taxes upon the doing of business. See License Tax Cases, 5 Wall. 462, 18 L.Ed. 497; [additional citations]. Petitioner does not deny that Congress may tax his business as a dealer in firearms. He insists that the present levy is not a true tax, but a penalty imposed for the purpose of suppressing traffic in a certain noxious type of firearms, the local regulation of which is reserved to the states because not granted to the national government. To establish its penal and prohibitive character, he relies on the amounts of the tax imposed by section 2 on dealers, manufacturers, and importers, and of the tax imposed by section 3 on each transfer of a 'firearm,' payable by the transferor. The cumulative effect on the distribution of a limited class of firearms, of relatively small value, by the successive imposition of different taxes, one on the business of the importer or manufacturer, another on that of the dealer, and a third on the transfer to a buyer, is said to be prohibitive in effect and to disclose unmistakably the legislative purpose to regulate rather than to tax.

The case is not one where the statute contains regulatory provisions related to a purported tax in such a way as has enabled this Court to say in other cases that the latter is a penalty resorted to as a means of enforcing the regulations. See Child Labor Tax Cases, 259 U.S. 20, [additional citations]. Nor is the subject of the tax described or treated as criminal by the taxing statute. Compare United States v. Constantine, 296 U.S. 287. Here section 2 contains no regulation other than the mere registration provisions, which are obviously supportable as in aid of a revenue purpose. On its face it is only a taxing measure, and we are asked to say that the tax, by virtue of its deterrent effect on the activities taxed, operates as a regulation which is beyond the congressional power.

Every tax is in some measure regulatory. To some extent it interposes an economic impediment to the activity taxed as compared with others not taxed. But a tax is not any the less a tax because it has a regulatory effect, United States v. Doremus, 249 U.S. 86, 93, 94 [additional citations]; and it has long been established that an Act of Congress which on its face purports to be an exercise of the taxing power is not any the less so because the tax is burdensome or tends to restrict or suppress the thing taxed. Veazie Bank v. Fenno, 8 Wall. 533, 548; McCray v. United States, 195 U.S. 27, [additional citations].

Inquiry into the hidden motives which may move Congress to exercise a power constitutionally conferred upon it is beyond the competency of courts. Veazie Bank v. Fenno, supra; [additional citations]. They will not undertake, by collateral inquiry as to the measure of the regulatory effect of a tax, to ascribe to Congress an attempt, under the guise of taxation, to exercise another power denied by the Federal Constitution. McCray v. United States, supra; [additional citation].

Here the annual tax of $200 is productive of some revenue. We are not free to speculate as to the motives which moved Congress to impose it, or as to the extent to which it may operate to restrict the activities taxed. As it is not attended by an offensive regulation, and since it operates as a tax, it is within the national taxing power. Alston v. United States, 274 U.S. 289, 294; [additional citations].

We do not discuss petitioner's contentions which he failed to assign as error below.

Affirmed.

---

**Question:** A federal law imposes a "wagering tax" and registration requirement on bookmakers. The law does not produce any significant revenue. Tax or penalty? See *United States v. Kahriger,* 345 U.S. 22 (1953).

## NATIONAL FEDERATION OF INDEPENDENT BUSINESS V. SEBELIUS

567 U.S. 519 (2012)

Chief Justice Roberts announced the judgment of the Court and delivered the opinion of the Court with respect to Parts I, II, and III–C, an opinion with respect to Part IV, in which Justice Breyer and Justice Kagan join, and an opinion with respect to Parts III–A, III–B, and III–D.

* * *

That is not the end of the matter. Because the Commerce Clause does not support the individual mandate, it is necessary to turn to the Government's second argument: that the mandate may be upheld as within Congress's enumerated power to "lay and collect Taxes." Art. I, § 8, cl. 1.

The Government's tax power argument asks us to view the statute differently than we did in considering its commerce power theory. In making its Commerce Clause argument, the Government defended the mandate as a regulation requiring individuals to purchase health insurance. The Government does not claim that the taxing power allows Congress to issue such a command. Instead, the Government asks us to read the mandate not as ordering individuals to buy insurance, but rather as imposing a tax on those who do not buy that product.

The text of a statute can sometimes have more than one possible meaning. To take a familiar example, a law that reads "no vehicles in the park" might, or might not, ban bicycles in the park. And it is well established that if a statute has two possible meanings, one of which violates the Constitution, courts should adopt the meaning that does not do so. Justice Story said that 180 years ago: "No court ought, unless the terms of an act rendered it unavoidable, to give a construction to it which should involve a violation, however unintentional, of the constitution." Parsons v. Bedford, 3 Pet. 433, 448–449 (1830). Justice Holmes made the same point a century later: "[T]he rule is settled that as between two possible interpretations of a statute, by one of which it would be unconstitutional and by the other valid, our plain duty is to adopt that which will save the Act." Blodgett v. Holden, 275 U. S. 142, 148 (1927) (concurring opinion).

The most straightforward reading of the mandate is that it commands individuals to purchase insurance. After all, it states that individuals "shall" maintain health insurance. 26 U. S. C. § 5000A(a). Congress thought it could enact such a command under the Commerce Clause, and the Government primarily defended the law on that basis. But, for the reasons explained above, the Commerce Clause does not give Congress that power. Under our precedent, it is therefore necessary to ask whether the Government's alternative reading of the statute—that it only imposes a tax on those without insurance—is a reasonable one.

Under the mandate, if an individual does not maintain health insurance, the only consequence is that he must make an additional payment to the IRS when he pays his taxes. See § 5000A(b). That, according to the Government, means the mandate can be regarded as establishing a condition—not owning health insurance—that triggers a tax—the required payment to the IRS. Under that theory, the mandate is not a legal command to buy insurance. Rather, it makes going without insurance just another thing the Government taxes, like buying gasoline or earning income. And if the mandate is in effect just a tax hike on certain taxpayers who do not have health insurance, it may be within Congress's constitutional power to tax.

The question is not whether that is the most natural interpretation of the mandate, but only whether it is a "fairly possible" one. Crowell v. Benson, 285 U. S. 22, 62 (1932). As we have explained, "every reasonable construction must be resorted to, in order to save a statute from unconstitutionality." Hooper v. California, 155 U. S. 648, 657 (1895). The Government asks us to interpret the mandate as imposing a tax, if it would otherwise violate the Constitution. Granting the Act the full measure of deference owed to federal statutes, it can be so read, for the reasons set forth below.

The exaction the Affordable Care Act imposes on those without health insurance looks like a tax in many respects. The "[s]hared responsibility payment," as the statute entitles it, is paid into the Treasury by "taxpayer[s]" when they file their tax returns. 26 U. S. C. § 5000A(b). It does not apply to individuals who do not pay federal income taxes because their household income is less than the filing threshold in the Internal Revenue Code. § 5000A(e)(2). For taxpayers who do owe the payment, its amount is determined by such familiar factors as taxable income, number of dependents, and joint filing status. §§ 5000A(b)(3), (c)(2), (c)(4). The requirement to pay is found in the Internal Revenue Code and enforced by the IRS, which—as we previously explained—must assess and collect it "in the same manner as taxes." Supra, at 13–14. This process yields the essential feature of any tax: it produces at least some revenue for the Government. United States v. Kahriger, 345 U. S. 22, 28, n. 4 (1953). Indeed, the payment is expected to raise about $4 billion per year by 2017. Congressional Budget Office, Payments of Penalties for Being Uninsured Under the Patient Protection and Affordable Care Act (Apr. 30, 2010), in Selected CBO Publications Related to Health Care Legislation, 2009–2010, p. 71 (rev. 2010).

It is of course true that the Act describes the payment as a "penalty," not a "tax." But while that label is fatal to the application of the Anti-Injunction Act, supra, at 12–13, it does not determine whether the payment may be viewed as an exercise of Congress's taxing power. It is up to Congress whether to apply the Anti-Injunction Act to any particular statute, so it makes sense to be guided by Congress's choice of label on that question. That choice does not, however, control whether an exaction is within Congress's constitutional power to tax.

Our precedent reflects this: In 1922, we decided two challenges to the "Child Labor Tax" on the same day. In the first, we held that a suit to enjoin collection of the so-called tax was barred by the Anti-Injunction Act. George, 259 U. S., at 20. Congress knew that suits to obstruct taxes had to await payment under the Anti-Injunction Act; Congress called the child labor tax a tax; Congress therefore intended the Anti-Injunction Act to apply. In the second case, however, we held that the same exaction, although labeled a tax, was not in fact authorized by Congress's taxing power. Drexel Furniture, 259 U. S., at 38. That constitutional question was not controlled by Congress's choice of label.

We have similarly held that exactions not labeled taxes nonetheless were authorized by Congress's power to tax. In the License Tax Cases, for example, we held that federal licenses to sell liquor and lottery tickets—for which the licensee had to pay a fee—could be sustained as exercises of the taxing power. 5 Wall., at 471. And in New York v. United States we upheld as a tax a "surcharge" on out-of-state nuclear waste shipments, a portion of which was paid to the Federal Treasury. 505 U. S., at 171. We thus ask whether the shared responsibility payment falls within Congress's taxing power, "[d]isregarding the designation of the exaction, and viewing its substance and application." United States v. Constantine, 296 U. S. 287, 294 (1935); cf. Quill Corp. v. North Dakota, 504 U. S. 298, 310 (1992) ("[M]agic words or labels" should not "disable an otherwise constitutional levy" (internal quotation marks omitted)); Nelson v. Sears, Roebuck & Co., 312 U. S. 359, 363 (1941) ("In passing on the constitutionality of a tax law, we are concerned only with its practical operation, not its definition or the precise form of descriptive words which may be applied to it" (internal quotation marks omitted)); United States v. Sotelo, 436 U. S. 268, 275 (1978) ("That the funds due are referred to as a 'penalty' . . . does not alter their essential character as taxes").

Our cases confirm this functional approach. For example, in Drexel Furniture, we focused on three practical characteristics of the so-called tax on employing child laborers that convinced us the "tax" was actually a penalty. First, the tax imposed an exceedingly heavy burden—10 percent of a company's net income—on those who employed children, no matter how small their infraction. Second, it imposed that exaction only on those who knowingly employed underage laborers. Such scienter requirements are typical of punitive statutes, because Congress often wishes to punish only those who intentionally break the law. Third, this "tax" was enforced in part by the Department of Labor, an agency responsible for punishing violations of labor laws, not collecting revenue. 259 U. S., at 36–37; see also, e.g., Kurth Ranch, 511 U. S., at 780–782 (considering, inter alia, the amount of the exaction, and the fact that it was imposed for violation of a separate criminal law); Constantine, supra, at 295 (same).

The same analysis here suggests that the shared responsibility payment may for constitutional purposes be considered a tax, not a penalty: First, for most Americans the amount due will be far less than the price of insurance, and, by statute, it can never be more. It may often be a reasonable financial decision to make the payment rather than purchase insurance, unlike the "prohibitory" financial punishment in Drexel Furniture. 259 U. S., at 37. Second, the individual mandate contains no scienter requirement. Third, the payment is collected solely by the IRS through the normal means of taxation—except that the Service is not allowed to use those means most suggestive of a punitive sanction, such as criminal prosecution. See § 5000A(g)(2). The reasons the Court in Drexel Furniture held that what was called a "tax" there was a penalty support the conclusion that what is called a "penalty" here may be viewed as a tax.

None of this is to say that the payment is not intended to affect individual conduct. Although the payment will raise considerable revenue, it is plainly designed to expand health insurance coverage. But taxes that seek to influence conduct are nothing new. Some of our earliest federal taxes sought to deter the purchase of imported manufactured goods in order to foster the growth of domestic industry. See W. Brownlee, Federal Taxation in America 22 (2d ed. 2004); cf. 2 J. Story, Commentaries on the Constitution of the United States § 962, p. 434 (1833) ("the taxing power is often, very often, applied for other purposes, than revenue"). Today, federal and state taxes can compose more than half the retail price of cigarettes, not just to raise more money, but to encourage people to quit smoking. And we have upheld such obviously regulatory measures as taxes on selling marijuana and sawed-off shotguns. See United States v. Sanchez, 340 U. S. 42, 44–45 (1950); Sonzinsky v. United States, 300 U. S. 506, 513 (1937). Indeed, "[e]very tax is in some measure regulatory. To some extent it interposes an economic impediment to the activity taxed as compared with others not taxed." Sonzinsky, supra, at 513. That § 5000A seeks to shape decisions about whether to buy health insurance does not mean that it cannot be a valid exercise of the taxing power.

In distinguishing penalties from taxes, this Court has explained that "if the concept of penalty means anything, it means punishment for an unlawful act or omission." United States v. Reorganized CF&I Fabricators of Utah, Inc., 518 U. S. 213, 224 (1996); see also United States v. La Franca, 282 U. S. 568, 572 (1931) ("[A] penalty, as the word is here used, is an exaction imposed by statute as punishment for an unlawful act"). While the individual mandate clearly aims to induce the purchase of health insurance, it need not be read to declare that failing to do so is unlawful. Neither the Act nor any other law attaches negative legal consequences to not buying health insurance, beyond requiring a payment to the IRS. The Government agrees with that reading, confirming that if someone chooses to pay rather than obtain health insurance, they have fully complied with the law. Brief for United States 60–61; Tr. of Oral Arg. 49–50 (Mar. 26, 2012).

Indeed, it is estimated that four million people each year will choose to pay the IRS rather than buy insurance. See Congressional Budget Office, supra, at 71. We would expect Congress to be troubled by that prospect if such conduct were unlawful. That Congress apparently regards such extensive failure to comply with the mandate as tolerable suggests that Congress did not think it was creating four million outlaws. It suggests instead that the shared responsibility payment merely imposes a tax citizens may lawfully choose to pay in lieu of buying health insurance.

The plaintiffs contend that Congress's choice of language—stating that individuals "shall" obtain insurance or pay a "penalty"—requires reading § 5000A as punishing unlawful conduct, even if that interpretation would ren-der the law unconstitutional. We have rejected a similar argument before. In New York v. United States we examined a statute providing that " '[e]ach State shall be responsible for providing . . . for the disposal of . . . low-level radioactive waste.' " 505 U. S., at 169 (quoting 42 U. S. C. § 2021c(a)(1)(A)). A State that shipped its waste to another State was exposed to surcharges by the receiving State, a portion of which would be paid over to the Federal Government. And a State that did not adhere to the statutory scheme faced "[p]enalties for failure to comply," including increases in the surcharge. § 2021e(e)(2); New York, 505 U. S., at 152–153. New York urged us to read the statute as a federal command that the state legislature enact legislation to dispose of its waste, which would have violated the Constitution. To avoid that outcome, we interpreted the statute to impose only "a series of incentives" for the State to take responsibility for its waste. We then sustained the charge paid to the Federal Government as an exercise of the taxing power. Id., at 169–174. We see no insurmountable obstacle to a similar approach here.

The joint dissenters argue that we cannot uphold § 5000A as a tax because Congress did not "frame" it as such. Post, at 17. In effect, they contend that even if the Constitution permits Congress to do exactly what we interpret this statute to do, the law must be struck down because Congress used the wrong labels. An example may help illustrate why labels should not control here. Suppose Congress enacted a statute providing that every taxpayer who owns a house without energy efficient windows must pay $50 to the IRS. The amount due is adjusted based on factors such as taxable income and joint filing status, and is paid along with the taxpayer's income tax return. Those whose income is below the filing threshold need not pay. The required payment is not called a "tax," a "penalty," or anything else. No one would doubt that this law imposed a tax, and was within Congress's power to tax. That conclusion should not change simply because Congress used the word "penalty" to describe the payment. Interpreting such a law to be a tax would hardly "[i]mpos[e] a tax through judicial legislation." Post, at 25. Rather, it would give practical effect to the Legislature's enactment.

Our precedent demonstrates that Congress had the power to impose the exaction in § 5000A under the taxing power, and that § 5000A need not be read to do more than impose a tax. That is sufficient to sustain it. The "question of the constitutionality of action taken by Congress does not depend on recitals of the power which it undertakes to exercise." Woods v. Cloyd W. Miller Co., 333 U. S. 138, 144 (1948).

* * *

There may, however, be a more fundamental objection to a tax on those who lack health insurance. Even if only a tax, the payment under § 5000A(b) remains a burden that the Federal Government imposes for an omission, not an act. If it is troubling to interpret the Commerce Clause as authorizing Congress to regulate those who abstain from commerce, perhaps it should be similarly troubling to permit Congress to impose a tax for not doing something.

Three considerations allay this concern. First, and most importantly, it is abundantly clear the Constitution does not guarantee that individuals may avoid taxation through inactivity. A capitation, after all, is a tax that everyone must pay simply for existing, and capitations are expressly contemplated by the Constitution. The Court today holds that our Constitution protects us from federal regulation under the Commerce Clause so long as we ab-stain from the regulated activity. But from its creation, the Constitution has made no such promise with respect to taxes. See Letter from Benjamin Franklin to M. Le Roy (Nov. 13, 1789) ("Our new Constitution is now established . . . but in this world nothing can be said to be certain, except death and taxes").

Whether the mandate can be upheld under the Commerce Clause is a question about the scope of federal authority. Its answer depends on whether Congress can exercise what all acknowledge to be the novel course of directing individuals to purchase insurance. Congress's use of the Taxing Clause to encourage buying something is, by contrast, not new. Tax incentives already promote, for example, purchasing homes and professional educations. See 26 U. S. C. §§ 163(h), 25A. Sustaining the mandate as a tax depends only on whether Congress has properly exercised its taxing power to encourage purchasing health insurance, not whether it can. Upholding the individual mandate under the Taxing Clause thus does not recognize any new federal power. It determines that Congress has used an existing one.

Second, Congress's ability to use its taxing power to influence conduct is not without limits. A few of our cases policed these limits aggressively, invalidating punitive exactions obviously designed to regulate behavior otherwise regarded at the time as beyond federal authority. See, e.g., United States v. Butler, 297 U. S. 1 (1936); Drexel Furniture, 259 U. S. 20. More often and more recently we have declined to closely examine the regulatory motive or effect of revenue-raising measures. See Kahriger, 345 U. S., at 27–31 (collecting cases). We have nonetheless maintained that " 'there comes a time in the extension of the penalizing features of the so-called tax when it loses its character as such and becomes a mere penalty with the characteristics of regulation and punishment.' " Kurth Ranch, 511 U. S., at 779 (quoting Drexel Furniture, supra, at 38).

We have already explained that the shared responsibility payment's practical characteristics pass muster as a tax under our narrowest interpretations of the taxing power. Supra, at 35–36. Because the tax at hand is within even those strict limits, we need not here decide the precise point at which an exaction becomes so punitive that the taxing power does not authorize it. It remains true, however, that the " 'power to tax is not the power to destroy while this Court sits.' " Oklahoma Tax Comm'n v. Texas Co., 336 U. S. 342, 364 (1949) (quoting Panhandle Oil Co. v. Mississippi ex rel. Knox, 277 U. S. 218, 223 (1928) (Holmes, J., dissenting)).

Third, although the breadth of Congress's power to tax is greater than its power to regulate commerce, the taxing power does not give Congress the same degree of control over individual behavior. Once we recognize that Congress may regulate a particular decision under the Commerce Clause, the Federal Government can bring its full weight to bear. Congress may simply command individuals to do as it directs. An individual who disobeys may be subjected to criminal sanctions. Those sanctions can include not only fines and imprisonment, but all the attendant consequences of being branded a criminal: deprivation of otherwise protected civil rights, such as the right to bear arms or vote in elections; loss of employment opportunities; social stigma; and severe disabilities in other controversies, such as custody or immigration disputes.

By contrast, Congress's authority under the taxing power is limited to requiring an individual to pay money into the Federal Treasury, no more. If a tax is properly paid, the Government has no power to compel or punish individuals subject to it. We do not make light of the severe burden that taxation—especially taxation motivated by a regulatory purpose—can impose. But imposition of a tax nonetheless leaves an individual with a lawful choice to do or not do a certain act, so long as he is willing to pay a tax levied on that choice.

The Affordable Care Act's requirement that certain individuals pay a financial penalty for not obtaining health insurance may reasonably be characterized as a tax. Because the Constitution permits such a tax, it is not our role to forbid it, or to pass upon its wisdom or fairness.

* * *

JUSTICE SCALIA, JUSTICE KENNEDY, JUSTICE THOMAS, and JUSTICE ALITO, dissenting.

* * *

The Taxing Power

.... The Government contends ... that "the minimum coverage provision is independently authorized by congress's taxing power." Petitioners' Minimum Coverage Brief 52. The phrase "independently authorized" suggests the existence of a creature never hitherto seen in the United States Reports: A penalty for constitutional purposes that is also a tax for constitutional purposes. In all our cases the two are mutually exclusive. The provision challenged under the Constitution is either a penalty or else a tax. Of course in many cases what was a regulatory mandate enforced by a penalty could have been imposed as a tax upon permissible action; or what was imposed as a tax upon permissible action could have been a regulatory mandate enforced by a penalty. But we know of no case, and the Government cites none, in which the imposition was, for constitutional purposes, both. The two are mutually exclusive. Thus, what the Government's caption should have read was "alternatively, the minimum coverage provision is not a mandate-with-penalty but a tax." It is important to bear this in mind in evaluating the tax argument of the Government and of those who support it: The issue is not whether Congress had the power to frame the minimum-coverage provision as a tax, but whether it did so.

In answering that question we must, if "fairly possible," Crowell v. Benson, 285 U. S. 22, 62 (1932), construe the provision to be a tax rather than a mandate-with-penalty, since that would render it constitutional rather than un-constitutional (ut res magis valeat quam pereat). But we cannot rewrite e statute to be what it is not. " ' "[A]lthough this Court will often strain to construe legislation so as to save it against constitutional attack, it must not and will not carry this to the point of perverting the purpose of a statute . . ." or judicially rewriting it.' " Commodity Futures Trading Comm'n v. Schor, 478 U. S. 833, 841 (1986) (quoting Aptheker v. Secretary of State, 378 U. S. 500, 515 (1964), in turn quoting Scales v. United States, 367 U. S. 203, 211 (1961)). In this case, there is simply no way, "without doing violence to the fair meaning of the words used," Grenada County Supervisors v. Brogden, 112 U. S. 261, 269 (1884), to escape what Congress enacted: a mandate that individuals maintain minimum essential coverage, enforced by a penalty.

Our cases establish a clear line between a tax and a penalty: " '[A] tax is an enforced contribution to provide for the support of government; a penalty ... is an exaction imposed by statute as punishment for an unlawful act.' " United States v. Reorganized CF&I Fabricators of Utah, Inc., 518 U. S. 213, 224 (1996) (quoting United States v. La Franca, 282 U. S. 568, 572 (1931)). In a few cases, this Court has held that a "tax" imposed upon private conduct was so onerous as to be in effect a penalty. But we have never held—never—that a penalty imposed for violation of the law was so trivial as to be in effect a tax. We have never held that any exaction imposed for violation of the law is an exercise of Congress' taxing power—even when the statute calls it a tax, much less when (as here) the statute repeatedly calls it a penalty. When an act "adopt[s] the criteria of wrongdoing" and then imposes a monetary penalty as the "principal consequence on those who transgress its standard," it creates a regulatory penalty, not a tax. Child Labor Tax Case, 259 U. S. 20, 38 (1922).

So the question is, quite simply, whether the exaction here is imposed for violation of the law. It unquestionably is. The minimum-coverage provision is found in 26 U. S. C. § 5000A, entitled "Requirement to maintain minimum essential coverage." (Emphasis added.) It commands that every "applicable individual shall . . . ensure that the individual . . . is covered under minimum essential coverage." Ibid. (emphasis added). And the immediately following provision states that, "[i]f . . . an applicable individual . . . fails to meet the requirement of subsection (a) . . . there is hereby imposed . . . a penalty." § 5000A(b) (emphasis added). And several of Congress' legislative "findings" with regard to § 5000A confirm that it sets forth a legal requirement and constitutes the assertion of regulatory power, not mere taxing power. See 42 U. S. C. § 18091(2)(A) ("The requirement regulates activity . . ."); § 18091(2)(C) ("The requirement . . . will add millions of new consumers to the health insurance market . . ."); § 18091(2)(D) ("The requirement achieves near-universal coverage"); § 18091(2)(H) ("The requirement is an essential part of this larger regulation of economic activity, and the absence of the requirement would undercut Federal regulation of the health insurance market"); § 18091(3) ("[T]he Supreme Court of the United States ruled that insurance is interstate commerce subject to Federal regulation").

The Government and those who support its view on the tax point rely on New York v. United States, 505 U. S. 144, to justify reading "shall" to mean "may." The "shall" in that case was contained in an introductory provision—a recital that provided for no legal consequences—which said that "[e]ach State shall be responsible for providing . . . for the disposal of . . . low-level radioactive waste." 42 U. S. C. § 2021c(a)(1)(A). The Court did not hold that "shall" could be construed to mean "may," but rather that this preliminary provision could not impose upon the operative provisions of the Act a mandate that they did not contain: "We . . . decline petitioners' invitation to construe § 2021c(a)(1)(A), alone and in isolation, as a command to the States independent of the remainder of the Act." New York, 505 U. S., at 170. Our opinion then proceeded to "consider each [of the three operative provisions] in turn." Ibid. Here the mandate—the "shall"—is contained not in an inoperative preliminary recital, but in the dispositive operative provision itself. New York provides no support for reading it to be permissive.

Quite separately, the fact that Congress (in its own words) "imposed . . . a penalty," 26 U. S. C. § 5000A(b)(1), for failure to buy insurance is alone sufficient to render that failure unlawful. It is one of the canons of interpretation that a statute that penalizes an act makes it unlawful: "[W]here the statute inflicts a penalty for doing an act, although the act itself is not expressly prohibited, yet to do the act is unlawful, because it cannot be supposed that the Legislature intended that a penalty should be inflicted for a lawful act." Powhatan Steamboat Co. v. Appomattox R. Co., 24 How. 247, 252 (1861). Or in the words of Chancellor Kent: "If a statute inflicts a penalty for doing an act, the penalty implies a prohibition, and the thing is unlawful, though there be no prohibitory words in the statute." 1 J. Kent, Commentaries on American Law 436 (1826).

We never have classified as a tax an exaction imposed for violation of the law, and so too, we never have classified as a tax an exaction described in the legislation itself as a penalty. To be sure, we have sometimes treated as a tax a statutory exaction (imposed for something other than a violation of law) which bore an agnostic label that does not entail the significant constitutional consequences of a penalty—such as "license" (License Tax Cases, 5 Wall. 462 (1867)) or "surcharge" (New York v. United States, supra.). But we have never—never—treated as a tax an exaction which faces up to the critical difference between a tax and a penalty, and explicitly denominates the exaction a "penalty." Eighteen times in § 5000A itself and elsewhere throughout the Act, Congress called the exaction in § 5000A(b) a "penalty."

That § 5000A imposes not a simple tax but a mandate to which a penalty is attached is demonstrated by the fact that some are exempt from the tax who are not exempt from the mandate—a distinction that would make no sense if the mandate were not a mandate. Section 5000A(d) exempts three classes of people from the definition of "applicable individual" subject to the minimum coverage requirement: Those with religious objections or who participate in a "health care sharing ministry," § 5000A(d)(2); those who are "not lawfully present" in the United States, § 5000A(d)(3); and those who are incarcerated, § 5000A(d)(4). Section 5000A(e) then creates a separate set of exemptions, excusing from liability for the penalty certain individuals who are subject to the minimum coverage requirement: Those who cannot afford coverage, § 5000A(e)(1); who earn too little income to require filing a tax return, § 5000A(e)(2); who are members of an Indian tribe, § 5000A(e)(3); who experience only short gaps in coverage, § 5000A(e)(4); and who, in the judgment of the Secretary of Health and Human Services, "have suffered a hardship with respect to the capability to obtain coverage," § 5000A(e)(5). If § 5000A were a tax, these two classes of exemption would make no sense; there being no requirement, all the exemptions would attach to the penalty (renamed tax) alone.

In the face of all these indications of a regulatory requirement accompanied by a penalty, the Solicitor General assures us that "neither the Treasury Department nor the Department of Health and Human Services interprets Section 5000A as imposing a legal obligation," Petitioners' Minimum Coverage Brief 61, and that "[i]f [those subject to the Act] pay the tax penalty, they're in compliance with the law," Tr. of Oral Arg. 50 (Mar. 26, 2012). These self-serving litigating positions are entitled to no weight. What counts is what the statute says, and that is entirely clear. It is worth noting, moreover, that these assurances contradict the Government's position in related litigation. Shortly before the Affordable Care Act was passed, the Commonwealth of Virginia enacted Va. Code Ann. § 38.2–3430.1:1 (Lexis Supp. 2011), which states, "No resident of [the] Commonwealth . . . shall be required to obtain or maintain a policy of individual insurance coverage except as required by a court or the Department of Social Services . . . ." In opposing Virginia's assertion of standing to challenge § 5000A based on this statute, the Government said that "if the minimum coverage provision is unconstitutional, the [Virginia] statute is unnecessary, and if the minimum coverage provision is upheld, the state statute is void under the Supremacy Clause." Brief for Appellant in No. 11–1057 etc. (CA4), p. 29. But it would be void under the Supremacy Clause only if it was contradicted by a federal "require[ment] to obtain or maintain a policy of individual insurance coverage."

Against the mountain of evidence that the minimum coverage requirement is what the statute calls it—a requirement—and that the penalty for its violation is what the statute calls it—a penalty—the Government brings forward the flimsiest of indications to the contrary. It notes that "[t]he minimum coverage provision amends the Internal Revenue Code to provide that a non-exempted individual . . . will owe a monetary penalty, in addition to the income tax itself," and that "[t]he [Internal Revenue Service (IRS)] will assess and collect the penalty in the same manner as assessable penalties under the Internal Revenue Code." Petitioners' Minimum Coverage Brief 53. The manner of collection could perhaps suggest a tax if IRS penalty-collection were unheard-of or rare. It is not. See, e.g., 26 U. S. C. § 527(j) (2006 ed.) (IRS-collectible penalty for failure to make campaign-finance disclosures); § 5761(c) (IRS-collectible penalty for domestic sales of tobacco products labeled for export); § 9707 (IRS-collectible penalty for failure to make required health-insurance premium payments on behalf of mining employees). In Reorganized CF&I Fabricators of Utah, Inc., 518 U. S. 213, we held that an exaction not only enforced by the Commissioner of Internal Revenue but even called a "tax" was in fact a penalty. "[I]f the concept of penalty means anything," we said, "it means punishment for an unlawful act or omission." Id., at 224. See also Lipke v. Lederer, 259 U. S. 557 (1922) (same). Moreover, while the penalty is assessed and collected by the IRS, § 5000A is administered both by that agency and by the Department of Health and Human Services (and also the Secretary of Veteran Affairs), see § 5000A(e)(1)(D), (e)(5), (f)(1)(A)(v), (f)(1)(E) (2006 ed., Supp. IV), which is responsible for defining its substantive scope—a feature that would be quite extraordinary for taxes.

The Government points out that "[t]he amount of the penalty will be calculated as a percentage of household income for federal income tax purposes, subject to a floor and [a] ca[p]," and that individuals who earn so little money that they "are not required to file income tax returns for the taxable year are not subject to the penalty" (though they are, as we discussed earlier, subject to the mandate). Petitioners' Minimum Coverage Brief 12, 53. But varying a penalty according to ability to pay is an utterly familiar practice. See, e.g., 33 U. S. C. § 1319(d) (2006 ed., Supp. IV) ("In determining the amount of a civil penalty the court shall consider . . . the economic impact of the penalty on the violator"); [additional citations].

The last of the feeble arguments in favor of petitioners that we will address is the contention that what this statute repeatedly calls a penalty is in fact a tax because it contains no scienter requirement. The presence of such a requirement suggests a penalty—though one can imagine a tax imposed only on willful action; but the absence of such a requirement does not suggest a tax. Penalties for absolute-liability offenses are commonplace. And where a statute is silent as to scienter, we traditionally presume a mens rea requirement if the statute imposes a "severe penalty." Staples v. United States, 511 U. S. 600, 618 (1994). Since we have an entire jurisprudence addressing when it is that a scienter requirement should be inferred from a penalty, it is quite illogical to suggest that a penalty is not a penalty for want of an express scienter requirement.

And the nail in the coffin is that the mandate and penalty are located in Title I of the Act, its operative core, rather than where a tax would be found—in Title IX, containing the Act's "Revenue Provisions." In sum, "the terms of [the] act rende[r] it unavoidable," Parsons v. Bedford, 3 Pet. 433, 448 (1830), that Congress imposed a regulatory penalty, not a tax.

For all these reasons, to say that the Individual Mandate merely imposes a tax is not to interpret the statute but to rewrite it. Judicial tax-writing is particularly troubling. Taxes have never been popular, see, e.g., Stamp Act of 1765, and in part for that reason, the Constitution requires tax increases to originate in the House of Representatives. See Art. I, § 7, cl. 1. That is to say, they must originate in the legislative body most accountable to the people, where legislators must weigh the need for the tax against the terrible price they might pay at their next election, which is never more than two years off. The Federalist No. 58 "defend[ed] the decision to give the origination power to the House on the ground that the Chamber that is more accountable to the people should have the primary role in raising revenue." United States v. Munoz-Flores, 495 U. S. 385, 395 (1990). We have no doubt that Congress knew precisely what it was doing when it rejected an earlier version of this legislation that imposed a tax instead of a requirement-with-penalty. See Affordable Health Care for America Act, H. R. 3962, 111th Cong., 1st Sess., § 501 (2009); America's Healthy Future Act of 2009, S. 1796, 111th Cong., 1st Sess., § 1301. Imposing a tax through judicial legislation inverts the constitutional scheme, and places the power to tax in the branch of government least accountable to the citizenry.

* * *

---

**Question:** Looking at Justice Roberts's majority opinion and the dissent in *NFIB v. Sebelius,* which is more consistent with previous holdings?



# CHAPTER 6

# PRESIDENT'S FOREIGN AFFAIRS AND MILITARY POWERS

■ ■ ■

## CONTEXT & SOURCES

The Constitution grants the president significant authority over foreign affairs and military operations. Article II, § 1, para. 1 states that "[t]he executive Power is vested" in the president; § 2, para. 1 makes the holder of the office "Commander in Chief" of the military; and § 2, para. 2 grants the president the power to make treaties and appoint ambassadors with Senate approval. Controversies have continually arisen as to the scope of these provisions, so this chapter presents cases in which the Supreme Court has analyzed the extent of presidential authority, as well as Congress's attempt to restrict executive action via the 1973 War Powers Resolution.

The standard survey of presidential foreign relations and military powers is Louis Henkin, *Foreign Affairs and the Constitution* (2d ed., Oxford University Press, 1996). Two of the decisions this chapter covers are studied in Foundation's *Stories* series: H. Jefferson Powell, "The Story of *Curtiss-Wright Export Corporation,*" and Thomas D. Lee & Michael D. Ramsey, "The Story of the *Prize Cases*: Executive Action and Judicial Review in Wartime," *Presidential Power Stories* 195–231; 53–92 (Christopher H. Schroeder & Curtis A. Bradley eds., Foundation Press 2009). *The War Powers Resolution After 30 Years* (Gerald M. Perkins, ed., Novinka Books 2005) studies the background and implementation of this legislative check on the President's authority.

## FOREIGN AFFAIRS POWER

### UNITED STATES V. CURTISS-WRIGHT EXPORT CORPORATION

299 U.S. 304 (1936)

MR. JUSTICE SUTHERLAND delivered the opinion of the Court.

On January 27, 1936, an indictment was returned in the court below, the first count of which charges that appellees, beginning with the 29th day of May, 1934, conspired to sell in the United States certain arms of war, namely, fifteen machine guns, to Bolivia, a country then engaged in armed conflict in the Chaco, in violation of the Joint Resolution of Congress approved May 28, 1934, and the provisions of a proclamation issued on the same day by the President of the United States pursuant to authority conferred by section 1 of the resolution. In pursuance of the conspiracy, the commission of certain overt acts was alleged, details of which need not be stated. The Joint Resolution (chapter 365, 48 Stat. 811) follows: 'Resolved by the Senate and House of Representatives of the United States of America in Congress assembled, That if the President finds that the prohibition of the sale of arms and munitions of war in the United States to those countries now engaged in armed conflict in the Chaco may contribute to the reestablishment of peace between those countries, and if after consultation with the governments of other American Republics and with their cooperation, as well as that of such other governments as he may deem necessary, he makes proclamation to that effect, it shall be unlawful to sell, except under such limitations and exceptions as the President prescribes, any arms or munitions of war in any place in the United States to the countries now engaged in that armed conflict, or to any person, company, or association acting in the interest of either country, until otherwise ordered by the President or by Congress.

'Sec. 2. Whoever sells any arms or munitions of war in violation of section 1 shall, on conviction, be punished by a fine not exceeding $10,000 or by imprisonment not exceeding two years, or both.'

The President's proclamation (48 Stat. 1744, No. 2087), after reciting the terms of the Joint Resolution, declares:

'Now, Therefore, I, Franklin D. Roosevelt, President of the United States of America, acting under and by virtue of the authority conferred in me by the said joint resolution of Congress, do hereby declare and proclaim that I have found that the prohibition of the sale of arms and munitions of war in the United States to those countries now engaged in armed conflict in the Chaco may contribute to the reestablishment of peace between those countries, and that I have consulted with the governments of other American Republics and have been assured of the cooperation of such governments as I have deemed necessary as contemplated by the said joint resolution; and I do hereby admonish all citizens of the United States and every person to abstain from every violation of the provisions of the joint resolution above set forth, hereby made applicable to Bolivia and Paraguay, and I do hereby warn them that all violations of such provisions will be rigorously prosecuted.

'And I do hereby enjoin upon all officers of the United States charged with the execution of the laws thereof, the utmost diligence in preventing violations of the said joint resolution and this my proclamation issued thereunder, and in bringing to trial and punishment any offenders against the same.'

[The District Court refused to indict the defendants on the ground that the joint resolution was an invalid delegation of legislative power from Congress to the President. The defendants appealed directly to the Supreme Court under a provision permitting this procedure when a court's failure to indict was based upon the invalidity or construction of the statute upon which the indictment is founded.]

* * *

It will contribute to the elucidation of the question if we first consider the differences between the powers of the federal government in respect of foreign or external affairs and those in respect of domestic or internal affairs. That there are differences between them, and that these differences are fundamental, may not be doubted.

The two classes of powers are different, both in respect of their origin and their nature. The broad statement that the federal government can exercise no powers except those specifically enumerated in the Constitution, and such implied powers as are necessary and proper to carry into effect the enumerated powers, is categorically true only in respect of our internal affairs. In that field, the primary purpose of the Constitution was to carve from the general mass of legislative powers then possessed by the states such portions as it was thought desirable to vest in the federal government, leaving those not included in the enumeration still in the states. Carter v. Carter Coal Co., 298 U.S. 238, 294,

* * *

As a result of the separation from Great Britain by the colonies, acting as a unit, the powers of external sovereignty passed from the Crown not to the colonies severally, but to the colonies in their collective and corporate capacity as the United States of America.

* * *

It results that the investment of the federal government with the powers of external sovereignty did not depend upon the affirmative grants of the Constitution. The powers to declare and wage war, to conclude peace, to make treaties, to maintain diplomatic relations with other sovereignties, if they had never been mentioned in the Constitution, would have vested in the federal government as necessary concomitants of nationality.

* * *

Not only, as we have shown, is the federal power over external affairs in origin and essential character different from that over internal affairs, but participation in the exercise of the power is significantly limited. In this vast external realm, with its important, complicated, delicate and manifold problems, the President alone has the power to speak or listen as a representative of the nation. He makes treaties with the advice and consent of the Senate; but he alone negotiates. Into the field of negotiation the Senate cannot intrude; and Congress itself is powerless to invade it. As Marshall said in his great argument of March 7, 1800, in the House of Representatives, 'The President is the sole organ of the nation in its external relations, and its sole representative with foreign nations.' Annals, 6th Cong., col. 613. The Senate Committee on Foreign Relations at a very early day in our history (February 15, 1816), reported to the Senate, among other things, as follows:

'The President is the constitutional representative of the United States with regard to foreign nations. He manages our concerns with foreign nations and must necessarily be most competent to determine when, how, and upon what subjects negotiation may be urged with the greatest prospect of success. For his conduct he is responsible to the Constitution. The committee considers this responsibility the surest pledge for the faithful discharge of his duty. They think the interference of the Senate in the direction of foreign negotiations calculated to diminish that responsibility and thereby to impair the best security for the national safety. The nature of transactions with foreign nations, moreover, requires caution and unity of design, and their success frequently depends on secrecy and dispatch.' 8 U.S.Sen.Reports Comm. on Foreign Relations, p. 24.

It is important to bear in mind that we are here dealing not alone with an authority vested in the President by an exertion of legislative power, but with such an authority plus the very delicate, plenary and exclusive power of the President as the sole organ of the federal government in the field of international relations—a power which does not require as a basis for its exercise an act of Congress, but which, of course, like every other governmental power, must be exercised in subordination to the applicable provisions of the Constitution. It is quite apparent that if, in the maintenance of our international relations, embarrassment—perhaps serious embarrassment—is to be avoided and success for our aims achieved, congressional legislation which is to be made effective through negotiation and inquiry within the international field must often accord to the President a degree of discretion and freedom from statutory restriction which would not be admissible were domestic affairs alone involved. Moreover, he, not Congress, has the better opportunity of knowing the conditions which prevail in foreign countries, and especially is this true in time of war. He has his confidential sources of information. He has his agents in the form of diplomatic, consular and other officials. Secrecy in respect of information gathered by them may be highly necessary, and the premature disclosure of it productive of harmful results. Indeed, so clearly is this true that the first President refused to accede to a request to lay before the House of Representatives the instructions, correspondence and documents relating to the negotiation of the Jay Treaty—a refusal the wisdom of which was recognized by the House itself and has never since been doubted. In his reply to the request, President Washington said:

'The nature of foreign negotiations requires caution, and their success must often depend on secrecy; and even when brought to a conclusion a full disclosure of all the measures, demands, or eventual concessions which may have been proposed or contemplated would be extremely impolitic; for this might have a pernicious influence on future negotiations, or produce immediate inconveniences, perhaps danger and mischief, in relation to other powers. The necessity of such caution and secrecy was one cogent reason for vesting the power of making treaties in the President, with the advice and consent of the Senate, the principle on which that body was formed confining it to a small number of members. To admit, then, a right in the House of Representatives to demand and to have as a matter of course all the papers respecting a negotiation with a foreign power would be to establish a dangerous precedent.' 1 Messages and Papers of the Presidents, p. 194.

* * *

When the President is to be authorized by legislation to act in respect of a matter intended to affect a situation in foreign territory, the legislator properly bears in mind the important consideration that the form of the President's action—or, indeed, whether he shall act at all—may well depend, among other things, upon the nature of the confidential information which he has or may thereafter receive, or upon the effect which his action may have upon our foreign relations. This consideration, in connection with what we have already said on the subject discloses the unwisdom of requiring Congress in this field of governmental power to lay down narrowly definite standards by which the President is to be governed.

* * *

In the light of the foregoing observations, it is evident that this court should not be in haste to apply a general rule which will have the effect of condemning legislation like that under review as constituting an unlawful delegation of legislative power. The principles which justify such legislation find overwhelming support in the unbroken legislative practice which has prevailed almost from the inception of the national government to the present day.

* * *

The judgment of the court below must be reversed and the cause remanded for further proceedings in accordance with the foregoing opinion.

---

**Question:** Is the interpretation of the president's foreign affairs power, with congressional approval, in *Curtiss-Wright* consistent with Congress's enumerated powers as set out in Article 1, section 8?

## ZIVOTOFSKY V. KERRY

576 U.S. 1 (2015)

[Petitioner Zivotofsky was born to U.S. citizens living in Jerusalem. Following § 214(d) of the Foreign Relations Authorization Act (2003, his mother asked American Embassy officials to list his place of birth as "Israel" on, inter alia, his passport. Section 214(d) states for "purposes of the registration of birth, certification of nationality, or issuance of a passport of a United States citizen born in the city of Jerusalem, the Secretary shall, upon the request of the citizen or the citizen's legal guardian, record the place of birth as Israel." The Embassy refused to list Zivotofsky's place of birth as "Israel" on his passport, based on the Executive Branch's longstanding position that the United States does not recognize any country as having sovereignty over Jerusalem. Zivotofsky's parents sued on his behalf in federal court to enforce § 214(d). The D. C. Circuit held the statute unconstitutional, concluding that it contradicts the Executive Branch's exclusive power to recognize foreign sovereigns.]

JUSTICE KENNEDY delivered the opinion of the Court.

A delicate subject lies in the background of this case. That subject is Jerusalem. Questions touching upon the history of the ancient city and its present legal and international status are among the most difficult and complex in international affairs. In our constitutional system these matters are committed to the Legislature and the Executive, not the Judiciary. As a result, in this opinion the Court does no more, and must do no more, than note the existence of international debate and tensions respecting Jerusalem. Those matters are for Congress and the President to discuss and consider as they seek to shape the Nation's foreign policies.

The Court addresses two questions to resolve the interbranch dispute now before it. First, it must determine whether the President has the exclusive power to grant formal recognition to a foreign sovereign. Second, if he has that power, the Court must determine whether Congress can command the President and his Secretary of State to issue a formal statement that contradicts the earlier recognition. The statement in question here is a congressional mandate that allows a United States citizen born in Jerusalem to direct the President and Secretary of State, when issuing his passport, to state that his place of birth is "Israel."

* * *

The inference that the President exercises the recognition power is further supported by his additional Article II powers. It is for the President, "by and with the Advice and Consent of the Senate," to "make Treaties, provided two thirds of the Senators present concur." Art. II, § 2, cl. 2. In addition, "he shall nominate, and by and with the Advice and Consent of the Senate, shall appoint Ambassadors" as well as "other public Ministers and Consuls." Ibid.

As a matter of constitutional structure, these additional powers give the President control over recognition decisions. At international law, recognition may be effected by different means, but each means is dependent upon Presidential power. In addition to receiving an ambassador, recognition may occur on "the conclusion of a bilateral treaty," or the "formal initiation of diplomatic relations," including the dispatch of an ambassador. Brownlie 93; see also 1 Moore § 27, at 73. The President has the sole power to negotiate treaties, see United States v. Curtiss-Wright Export Corp., 299 U. S. 304, 319 (1936), and the Senate may not conclude or ratify a treaty without Presidential action. The President, too, nominates the Nation's ambassadors and dispatches other diplomatic agents. Congress may not send an ambassador without his involvement. Beyond that, the President himself has the power to open diplomatic channels simply by engaging in direct diplomacy with foreign heads of state and their ministers. The Constitution thus assigns the President means to effect recognition on his own initiative. Congress, by contrast, has no constitutional power that would enable it to initiate diplomatic relations with a foreign nation. Because these specific Clauses confer the recognition power on the President, the Court need not consider whether or to what extent the Vesting Clause, which provides that the "executive Power" shall be vested in the President, provides further support for the President's action here. Art. II, § 1, cl. 1.

The text and structure of the Constitution grant the President the power to recognize foreign nations and governments. The question then becomes whether that power is exclusive. The various ways in which the President may unilaterally effect recognition—and the lack of any similar power vested in Congress—suggest that it is. So, too, do functional considerations. Put simply, the Nation must have a single policy regarding which governments are legitimate in the eyes of the United States and which are not. Foreign countries need to know, before entering into diplomatic relations or commerce with the United States, whether their ambassadors will be received; whether their officials will be immune from suit in federal court; and whether they may initiate lawsuits here to vindicate their rights. These assurances cannot be equivocal.

* * *

The President's exclusive recognition power encompasses the authority to acknowledge, in a formal sense, the legitimacy of other states and governments, including their territorial bounds. Albeit limited, the exclusive recognition power is essential to the conduct of Presidential duties. The formal act of recognition is an executive power that Congress may not qualify. If the President is to be effective in negotiations over a formal recognition determination, it must be evident to his counterparts abroad that he speaks for the Nation on that precise question.

* * *

The problem with § 214(d), however, lies in how Congress exercised its authority over passports. It was an improper act for Congress to "aggrandiz[e] its power at the expense of another branch" by requiring the President to contradict an earlier recognition determination in an official document issued by the Executive Branch. Freytag v. Commissioner, 501 U. S. 868, 878 (1991). To allow Congress to control the President's communication in the context of a formal recognition determination is to allow Congress to exercise that exclusive power itself. As a result, the statute is unconstitutional.

* * *

The judgment of the Court of Appeals for the District of Columbia Circuit is

Affirmed.

JUSTICE SCALIA, with whom THE CHIEF JUSTICE and JUSTICE ALITO join, dissenting.

* * *

. . . . § 214(d) has nothing to do with recognition. Section 214(d) does not require the Secretary to make a formal declaration about Israel's sovereignty over Jerusalem. And nobody suggests that international custom infers acceptance of sovereignty from the birthplace designation on a passport or birth report, as it does from bilateral treaties or exchanges of ambassadors. Recognition would preclude the United States (as a matter of international law) from later contesting Israeli sovereignty over Jerusalem. But making a notation in a passport or birth report does not encumber the Republic with any international obligations. It leaves the Nation free (so far as international law is concerned) to change its mind in the future. That would be true even if the statute required all passports to list "Israel." But in fact it requires only those passports to list "Israel" for which the citizen (or his guardian) requests "Israel"; all the rest, under the Secretary's policy, list "Jerusalem." It is utterly impossible for this deference to private requests to constitute an act that unequivocally manifests an intention to grant recognition.

* * *

The Court identifies no reason to believe that the United States—or indeed any other country—uses the place-of-birth field in passports and birth reports as a forum for performing the act of recognition. That is why nobody thinks the United States withdraws recognition from Canada when it accommodates a Quebec nationalist's request to have his birthplace recorded as "Montreal."

* * *

The Court protests ... that § 214(d) "directly contradicts" the President's refusal to recognize Israel's sovereignty over Jerusalem. But even if the Constitution empowers the President alone to extend recognition, it nowhere obliges Congress to align its laws with the President's recognition decisions. Because the President and Congress are "perfectly co-ordinate by the terms of their common commission," The Federalist No. 49, p. 314 (C. Rossiter ed. 1961) (Madison), the President's use of the recognition power does not constrain Congress's use of its legislative powers.

* * *

In the end, the Court's decision does not rest on text or history or precedent. It instead comes down to "functional considerations"—principally the Court's perception that the Nation "must speak with one voice" about the status of Jerusalem. Ante, at 11 (ellipsis and internal quotation marks omitted). The vices of this mode of analysis go beyond mere lack of footing in the Constitution. Functionalism of the sort the Court practices today will systematically favor the unitary President over the plural Congress in disputes involving foreign affairs. It is possible that this approach will make for more effective foreign policy, perhaps as effective as that of a monarchy. It is certain that, in the long run, it will erode the structure of separated powers that the People established for the protection of their liberty.

* * *

That is not the chief magistrate under which the American People agreed to live when they adopted the national charter. They believed that "[t]he accumulation of all powers, legislative, executive, and judiciary, in the same hands, ... may justly be pronounced the very definition of tyranny." The Federalist No. 47, p. 301 (Madison). For this reason, they did not entrust either the President or Congress with sole power to adopt uncontradictable policies about any subject—foreign-sovereignty disputes included. They instead gave each political department its own powers, and with that the freedom to contradict the other's policies. Under the Constitution they approved, Congress may require Zivotofsky's passport and birth report to record his birthplace as Israel, even if that requirement clashes with the President's preference for neutrality about the status of Jerusalem.

I dissent.

---

**Question:** How do the Zivotovsky majority and Justice Scalia's differ on the nature of the president's and Congress's powers regarding foreign policy?

## EXECUTIVE AGREEMENTS

In **DAMES & MOORE v. REGAN, 453 U.S. 654 (1981)**, the U.S. Supreme Court addressed an executive agreement relating to the 1979 hostage crisis in Iran. President Ronald Reagan and the Iranian government negotiated a bargain to free the hostages in the U.S. Embassy in exchange for unfreezing Iranian assets then attached in the United States. Upholding the agreement, the Court noted that that releasing attachments had been directly authorized by Congress in the International Emergency Economic Powers Act of 1977, permitting the President to regulate international commerce in response to an "unusual and extraordinary threat." Furthermore, there was a long history of presidents negotiating claims settlements with foreign nations. In light of this express and implied congressional consent, the President did not exceed his powers.

---

**Question:** What is the basis in the U.S. Constitution for the president's authority to enter into executive agreements?

## MILITARY POWER

### THE PRIZE CASES

67 U.S. 635 (1862)

* * *

These were cases in which the vessels named, together with their cargoes, were severally captured and brought in as prizes by public ships of the United States. The libels were filed by the proper District Attorneys, on behalf of the United States and on behalf of the officers and crews of the ships, by which the captures were respectively made. In each case the District Court pronounced a decree of condemnation, from which the claimants took an appeal.

The Amy Warwick was a merchant vessel, and belonged to Richmond. Her registered owners were David and William Currie, Abraham Warwick and George W. Allen, who resided at that place. Previous to her capture she had made a voyage from New York to Richmond, and thence to Rio de Janeiro, Brazil. At the last named port she shipped a cargo of coffee, 5,100 bags, to be delivered at New York, Philadelphia, Baltimore or Richmond, according to the orders which the master would receive at Hampton Roads. She was on her voyage from Rio to Hampton Roads and off Cape Henry when she was captured (July 10th, 1861) by the Quaker City. At the time of the capture the barque was sailing under American colors, and her commander was ignorant of the war. The Quaker City carried her into Boston, where she was libelled as enemy's property. The claimants of the vessel were the persons already named as owners. James Dunlap, Robert Edmonds, John L. Phipps, and Charles Brown claimed the cargo. The claimants in their several answers denied any hostility on their part to the Government or Laws of the United States, averred that the master was ignorant of any blockade, embargo or other interdiction of commerce with the ports of Virginia, and asserted generally that the capture was unlawful.

The Crenshaw was captured by the United States Steamer Star, at the mouth of James River, on the 17th of May, 1861. She was bound for Liverpool with a cargo of tobacco from Richmond, and was owned by David and William Currie, who admitted the existence of an insurrection in Virginia against the Laws and Government of the United States, but averred that they were innocent of it. The claimants of the cargo made similar answers, and all the claimants asserted that they had no such notice of the blockade as rendered the vessel or cargo liable to seizure for leaving the port of Richmond at the time when the voyage was commenced. She was condemned as prize on the ground that she had broken, or was attempting to break, the blockade at the time of her capture.

The Hiawatha was a British barque, and was on her voyage from Richmond to Liverpool with a cargo of tobacco. She left Richmond on the 17th of May, 1861, and was captured in Hampton Roads on the 20th by the Minnesota, and taken to New York. Her owners were Miller, Massman & Co., of Liverpool, who denied her liability to capture and condemnation on the ground that no sufficient notice had been given of the blockade. The claimants of the cargo put their right to restoration upon a similar basis.

The Brilliante was a Mexican schooner, owned by Rafael Preciat and Julian Gual, residents of Campeche. She had on board a cargo of flour, part of which was owned by the owners of the vessel, and part by the Senores Ybana & Donde, who were also Mexican citizens. She had a regular clearance at Campeche for New Orleans, and had made the voyage between those ports. At New Orleans she took in her cargo of flour, part to be delivered at Sisal and part at Campeche, and took a clearance for both those places. On her homeward voyage she anchored in Biloxi Bay, intending to communicate with some vessel of the blockading fleet and get a permit to go to sea, and while so at anchor she was taken by two boats sent off from the Massachusetts. She was carried into Key West, where the legal proceedings against her were prosecuted in the District Court of the United States for the District of Florida.

* * *

MR. JUSTICE GRIER.

* * *

Had the President a right to institute a blockade of ports in possession of persons in armed rebellion against the Government, on the principles of international law, as known and acknowledged among civilized States?

* * *

Neutrals have a right to challenge the existence of a blockade de facto, and also the authority of the party exercising the right to institute it. They have a right to enter the ports of a friendly nation for the purposes of trade and commerce, but are bound to recognize the rights of a belligerent engaged in actual war, to use this mode of coercion, for the purpose of subduing the enemy.

That a blockade de facto actually existed, and was formally declared and notified by the President on the 27th and 30th of April, 1861, is an admitted fact in these cases.

That the President, as the Executive Chief of the Government and Commander-in-chief of the Army and Navy, was the proper person to make such notification, has not been, and cannot be disputed.

The right of prize and capture has its origin in the 'jus belli,' and is governed and adjudged under the law of nations. To legitimate the capture of a neutral vessel or property on the high seas, a war must exist de facto, and the neutral must have knowledge or notice of the intention of one of the parties belligerent to use this mode of coercion against a port, city, or territory, in possession of the other.

Let us enquire whether, at the time this blockade was instituted, a state of war existed which would justify a resort to these means of subduing the hostile force.

War has been well defined to be, 'That state in which a nation prosecutes its right by force.'

The parties belligerent in a public war are independent nations. But it is not necessary to constitute war, that both parties should be acknowledged as independent nations or sovereign States. A war may exist where one of the belligerents, claims sovereign rights as against the

Insurrection against a government may or may not culminate in an organized rebellion, but a civil war always begins by insurrection against the lawful authority of the Government. A civil war is never solemnly declared; it becomes such by its accidents—the number, power, and organization of the persons who originate and carry it on. When the party in rebellion occupy and hold in a hostile manner a certain portion of territory; have declared their independence; have cast off their allegiance; have organized armies; have commenced hostilities against their former sovereign, the world acknowledges them as belligerents, and the contest a war. They claim to be in arms to establish their liberty and independence, in order to become a sovereign State, while the sovereign party treats them as insurgents and rebels who owe allegiance, and who should be punished with death for their treason.

The laws of war, as established among nations, have their foundation in reason, and all tend to mitigate the cruelties and misery produced by the scourge of war. Hence the parties to a civil war usually concede to each other belligerent rights. They exchange prisoners, and adopt the other courtesies and rules common to public or national wars.

'A civil war,' says Vattel, 'breaks the bands of society and government, or at least suspends their force and effect; it produces in the nation two independent parties, who consider each other as enemies, and acknowledge no common judge. Those two parties, therefore, must necessarily be considered as constituting, at least for a time, two separate bodies, two distinct societies. Having no common superior to judge between them, they stand in precisely the same predicament as two nations who engage in a contest and have recourse to arms.

'This being the case, it is very evident that the common laws of war—those maxims of humanity, moderation, and honor—ought to be observed by both parties in every civil war. Should the sovereign conceive he has a right to hang up his prisoners as rebels, the opposite party will make reprisals, &c., &c.; the war will become cruel, horrible, and every day more destructive to the nation.'

As a civil war is never publicly proclaimed, eo nomine, against insurgents, its actual existence is a fact in our domestic history which the Court is bound to notice and to know.

The true test of its existence, as found in the writings of the sages of the common law, may be thus summarily stated: 'When the regular course of justice is interrupted by revolt, rebellion, or insurrection, so that the Courts of Justice cannot be kept open, civil war exists and hostilities may be prosecuted on the same footing as if those opposing the Government were foreign enemies invading the land.'

By the Constitution, Congress alone has the power to declare a national or foreign war. It cannot declare war against a State, or any number of States, by virtue of any clause in the Constitution. The Constitution confers on the President the whole Executive power. He is bound to take care that the laws be faithfully executed. He is Commander-in-chief of the Army and Navy of the United States, and of the militia of the several States when called into the actual service of the United States. He has no power to initiate or declare a war either again t a foreign nation or a domestic State. But by the Acts of Congress of February 28th, 1795, and 3d of March, 1807, he is authorized to called out the militia and use the military and naval forces of the United States in case of invasion by foreign nations, and to suppress insurrection against the government of a State or of the United States.

If a war be made by invasion of a foreign nation, the President is not only authorized but bound to resist force by force. He does not initiate the war, but is bound to accept the challenge without waiting for any special legislative authority. And whether the hostile party be a foreign invader, or States organized in rebellion, it is none the less a war, although the declaration of it be 'unilateral.' Lord Stowell (1 Dodson, 247) observes, 'It is not the less a war on that account, for war may exist without a declaration on either side. It is so laid down by the best writers on the law of nations. A declaration of war by one country only, is not a mere challenge to be accepted or refused at pleasure by the other.

The battles of Palo Alto and Resaca de la Palma had been fought before the passage of the Act of Congress of May 13th, 1846, which recognized 'a state of war as existing by the act of the Republic of Mexico.' This act not only provided for the future prosecution of the war, but was itself a vindication and ratification of the Act of the President in accepting the challenge without a previous formal declaration of war by Congress.

This greatest of civil wars was not gradually developed by popular commotion, tumultuous assemblies, or local unorganized insurrections. However long may have been its previous conception, it nevertheless sprung forth suddenly from the parent brain, a Minerva in the full panoply of war. The President was bound to meet it in the shape it presented itself, without waiting for Congress to baptize it with a name; and no name given to it by him or them could change the fact.

It is not the less a civil war, with belligerent parties in hostile array, because it may be called an 'insurrection' by one side, and the insurgents be considered as rebels or traitors. It is not necessary that the independence of the revolted province or State be acknowledged in order to constitute it a party belligerent in a war according to the law of nations. Foreign nations acknowledge it as war by a declaration of neutrality. The condition of neutrality cannot exist unless there be two belligerent parties. In the case of the Santissima Trinidad, (7 Wheaton, 337,) this Court say: 'The Government of the United States has recognized the existence of a civil war between Spain and her colonies, and has avowed her determination to remain neutral between the parties. Each party is therefore deemed by us a belligerent nation, having, so far as concerns us, the sovereign rights of war.' (See also 3 Binn., 252.)

As soon as the news of the attack on Fort Sumter, and the organization of a government by the seceding States, assuming to act as belligerents, could become known in Europe, to wit, on the 13th of May, 1861, the Queen of England issued her proclamation of neutrality, 'recognizing hostilities as existing between the Government of the United States of American and certain States styling themselves the Confederate States of America.' This was immediately followed by similar declarations or silent acquiescence by other nations.

After such an official recognition by the sovereign, a citizen of a foreign State is estopped to deny the existence of a war with all its consequences as regards neutrals. They cannot ask a Court to affect a technical ignorance of the existence of a war, which all the world acknowledges to be the greatest civil war known in the history of the human race, and thus cripple the arm of the Government and paralyze its power by subtle definitions and ingenious sophisms.

The law of nations is also called the law of nature; it is founded on the common consent as well as the common sense of the world. It contains no such anomalous doctrine as that which this Court are now for the first time desired to pronounce, to wit: That insurgents who have risen in rebellion against their sovereign, expelled her Courts, established a revolutionary government, organized armies, and commenced hostilities, are not enemies because they are traitors; and a war levied on the Government by traitors, in order to dismember and destroy it, is not a war

Whether the President in fulfilling his duties, as Commander-in-chief, in suppressing an insurrection, has met with such armed hostile resistance, and a civil war of such alarming proportions as will compel him to accord to them the character of belligerents, is a question to be decided by him, and this Court must be governed by the decisions and acts of the political department of the Government to which this power was entrusted. 'He must determine what degree of force the crisis demands.' The proclamation of blockade is itself official and conclusive evidence to the Court that a state of war existed which demanded and authorized a recourse to such a measure, under the circumstances peculiar to the case.

* * *

If it were necessary to the technical existence of a war, that it should have a legislative sanction, we find it in almost every act passed at the extraordinary session of the Legislature of 1861, which was wholly employed in enacting laws to enable the Government to prosecute the war with vigor and efficiency. And finally, in 1861, we find Congress 'ex majore cautela' and in anticipation of such astute objections, passing an act 'approving, legalizing, and making valid all the acts, proclamations, and orders of the President, &c., as if they had been issued and done under the previous express authority and direction of the Congress of the United States.' Without admitting that such an act was necessary under the circumstances, it is plain that if the President had in any manner assumed powers which it was necessary should have the authority or sanction of Congress, that on the well known principle of law, 'omnis ratihabitio retrotrahitur et mandato equiparatur,' this ratification has operated to perfectly cure the defect. In the case of Brown vs. United States, (8 Cr., 131, 132, 133,) Mr. Justice Story treats of this subject, and cites numerous authorities to which we may refer to prove this position, and concludes, 'I am perfectly satisfied that no subject can commence hostilities or capture property of an enemy, when the sovereign has prohibited it. But suppose he did, I would ask if the sovereign may not ratify his proceedings, and thus by a retroactive operation give validity to them?'

* * *

The objection made to this act of ratification, that it is ex post facto, and therefore unconstitutional and void, might possibly have some weight on the trial of an indictment in a criminal Court. But precedents from that source cannot be received as authoritative in a tribunal administering public and international law.

On this . . . question therefore we are of the opinion that the President had a right, jure belli, to institute a blockade of ports in possession of the States in rebellion, which neutrals are bound to regard.

* * *

MR. JUSTICE NELSON, dissenting.

* * *

Upon the whole, after the most careful consideration of this case which the pressure of other duties has admitted, I am compelled to the conclusion that no civil war existed between this Government and the States in insurrection till recognized by the Act of Congress 13th of July, 1861; that the President does not possess the power under the Constitution to declare war or recognize its existence within the meaning of the law of nations, which carries with it belligerent rights, and thus change the country and all its citizens from a state of peace to a state of war; that this power belongs exclusively to the Congress of the United States, and, consequently, that the President had no power to set on foot a blockade under the law of nations, and that the capture of the vessel and cargo in this case, and in all cases before us in which the capture occurred before the 13th of July, 1861, for breach of blockade, or as enemies' property, are illegal and void, and that the decrees of condemnation should be reversed and the vessel and cargo restored.

MR. CHIEF JUSTICE TANEY, MR. JUSTICE CATRON and MR. JUSTICE CLIFFORD, concurred in the dissenting opinion of MR. JUSTICE NELSON.

---

**Question:** Due to advances in military technology, formal blockades such as that which precipitated *The Prize Cases* are rarely used in modern warfare. What is the relevance of the decision today?

## WAR POWERS RESOLUTION

50 U.S. Code §§ 1541 et. seq. (1973)

50 U.S. Code § 1541—Purpose and policy

(a) Congressional declaration

It is the purpose of this chapter to fulfill the intent of the framers of the Constitution of the United States and insure that the collective judgment of both the Congress and the President will apply to the introduction of United States Armed Forces into hostilities, or into situations where imminent involvement in hostilities is clearly indicated by the circumstances, and to the continued use of such forces in hostilities or in such situations.

(b) Congressional legislative power under necessary and proper clause

Under article I, section 8, of the Constitution, it is specifically provided that the Congress shall have the power to make all laws necessary and proper for carrying into execution, not only its own powers but also all other powers vested by the Constitution in the Government of the United States, or in any department or officer thereof.

(c) Presidential executive power as Commander-in-Chief; limitation

The constitutional powers of the President as Commander-in-Chief to introduce United States Armed Forces into hostilities, or into situations where imminent involvement in hostilities is clearly indicated by the circumstances, are exercised only pursuant to (1) a declaration of war, (2) specific statutory authorization, or (3) a national emergency created by attack upon the United States, its territories or possessions, or its armed forces.

* * *

50 U.S. Code § 1544. Congressional action

(a) Transmittal of report and referral to Congressional committees; joint request for convening Congress

Each report submitted pursuant to section 1543(a)(1) of this title shall be transmitted to the Speaker of the House of Representatives and to the

President pro tempore of the Senate on the same calendar day. Each report so transmitted shall be referred to the Committee on Foreign Affairs of the House of Representatives and to the Committee on Foreign Relations of the Senate for appropriate action. If, when the report is transmitted, the Congress has adjourned sine die [indefinitely] or has adjourned for any period in excess of three calendar days, the Speaker of the House of Representatives and the President pro tempore of the Senate, if they deem it advisable (or if petitioned by at least 30 percent of the membership of their respective Houses) shall jointly request the President to convene Congress in order that it may consider the report and take appropriate action pursuant to this section.

(b) Termination of use of United States Armed Forces; exceptions; extension period

Within sixty calendar days after a report is submitted or is required to be submitted pursuant to section 1543(a)(1) of this title, whichever is earlier, the President shall terminate any use of United States Armed Forces with respect to which such report was submitted (or required to be submitted), unless the Congress (1) has declared war or has enacted a specific authorization for such use of United States Armed Forces, (2) has extended by law such sixty-day period, or (3) is physically unable to meet as a result of an armed attack upon the United States. Such sixty-day period shall be extended for not more than an additional thirty days if the President determines and certifies to the Congress in writing that unavoidable military necessity respecting the safety of United States Armed Forces requires the continued use of such armed forces in the course of bringing about a prompt removal of such forces.

(c) Concurrent resolution for removal by President of United States Armed Forces

Notwithstanding subsection (b), at any time that United States Armed Forces are engaged in hostilities outside the territory of the United States, its possessions and territories without a declaration of war or specific statutory authorization, such forces shall be removed by the President if the Congress so directs by concurrent resolution.

* * *

---

**Questions:** Does the War Powers Resolution contradict the president's constitutional authority as Commander in Chief?

# CHAPTER 7

# PRESIDENTIAL POWER AND INDIVIDUAL RIGHTS

■ ■ ■

## CONTEXT & SOURCES

This chapter builds on the previous one by examining how the President's foreign affairs and military powers are balanced against individual rights, also protected in the Constitution. The decisions upholding detentions of U.S. citizens based on alleged security risks, and recent selective exclusion of immigrants from certain countries, sparked strong dissents which are also included.

For analyses of two of these cases, see Roger Daniels, *The Japanese American Cases: The Rule of Law in Time of War* (University Press of Kansas, 2013); and Allan A. Ryan, *The 9/11 Terror Cases: Constitutional Challenges in the War Against Terror* (University of Kansas Press, 2015). *The Constitution in Wartime: Beyond Alarmism and Complacency* (Mark Tushnet ed., Duke University Press, 2005) offers a variety of perspectives on the effect of national security risk on constitutional norms.

### KOREMATSU V. UNITED STATES

323 U.S. 214 (1944)

* * *

MR. JUSTICE BLACK delivered the opinion of the Court.

The petitioner, an American citizen of Japanese descent, was convicted in a federal district court for remaining in San Leandro, California, a 'Military Area', contrary to Civilian Exclusion Order No. 34 of the Commanding General of the Western Command, U.S. Army, which directed that after May 9, 1942, all persons of Japanese ancestry should be excluded from that area. No question was raised as to petitioner's loyalty to the United States. The Circuit Court of Appeals affirmed, and the importance of the constitutional question involved caused us to grant certiorari.

It should be noted, to begin with, that all legal restrictions which curtail the civil rights of a single racial group are immediately suspect. That is not to say that all such restrictions are unconstitutional. It is to say that courts must subject them to the most rigid scrutiny. Pressing public necessity may sometimes justify the existence of such restrictions; racial antagonism never can.

In the instant case prosecution of the petitioner was begun by information charging violation of an Act of Congress, of March 21, 1942, 56 Stat. 173, 18 U.S.C.A. § 97a, which provides that

'* * * whoever shall enter, remain in, leave, or commit any act in any military area or military zone prescribed, under the authority of an Executive order of the President, by the Secretary of War, or by any military commander designated by the Secretary of War, contrary to the restrictions applicable to any such area or zone or contrary to the order of the Secretary of War or any such military commander, shall, if it appears that he knew or should have known of the existence and extent of the restrictions or order and that his act was in violation thereof, be guilty of a misdemeanor and upon conviction shall be liable to a fine of not to exceed $5,000 or to imprisonment for not more than one year, or both, for each offense.'

Exclusion Order No. 34, which the petitioner knowingly and admittedly violated was one of a number of military orders and proclamations, all of which were substantially based upon Executive Order No. 9066, 7 Fed.Reg. 1407. That order, issued after we were at war with Japan, declared that 'the successful prosecution of the war requires every possible protection against espionage and against sabotage to national-defense material, national-defense premises, and national-defense utilities. * * *'

One of the series of orders and proclamations, a curfew order, which like the exclusion order here **was** promulgated pursuant to Executive Order 9066, subjected all persons of Japanese ancestry in prescribed West Coast military areas to remain in their residences from 8 p.m. to 6 a.m. As is the case with the exclusion order here, that prior curfew order was designed as a 'protection against espionage and against sabotage.' In Kiyoshi Hirabayashi v. United States, 320 U.S. 81, we sustained a conviction obtained for violation of the curfew order. The Hirabayashi conviction and this one thus rest on the same 1942 Congressional Act and the same basic executive and military orders, all of which orders were aimed at the twin dangers of espionage and sabotage.

The 1942 Act was attacked in the Hirabayashi case as an unconstitutional delegation of power; it was contended that the curfew order and other orders on which it rested were beyond the war powers of the Congress, the military authorities and of the President, as Commander in Chief of the Army; and finally that to apply the curfew order against none but citizens of Japanese ancestry amounted to a constitutionally prohibited discrimination solely on account of race. To these questions, we gave the serious consideration which their importance justified. We upheld the curfew order as an exercise of the power of the government to take steps necessary to prevent espionage and sabotage in an area threatened by Japanese attack.

In the light of the principles we announced in the Hirabayashi case, we are unable to conclude that it was beyond the war power of Congress and the Executive to exclude those of Japanese ancestry from the West Coast war area at the time they did. True, exclusion from the area in which one's home is located is a far greater deprivation than constant confinement to the home from 8 p.m. to 6 a.m. Nothing short of apprehension by the proper military authorities of the gravest imminent danger to the public safety can constitutionally justify either. But exclusion from a threatened area, no less than curfew, has a definite and close relationship to the prevention of espionage and sabotage. The military authorities, charged with the primary responsibility of defending our shores, concluded that curfew provided inadequate protection and ordered exclusion. They did so, as pointed out in our Hirabayashi opinion, in accordance with Congressional authority to the military to say who should, and who should not, remain in the threatened areas.

In this case the petitioner challenges the assumptions upon which we rested our conclusions in the Hirabayashi case. He also urges that by May 1942, when Order No. 34 was promulgated, all danger of Japanese invasion of the West Coast had disappeared. After careful consideration of these contentions we are compelled to reject them.

Here, as in the Hirabayashi case, supra, 320 U.S. at page 99, '* * * we cannot reject as unfounded the judgment of the military authorities and of Congress that there were disloyal members of that population, whose number and strength could not be precisely and quickly ascertained. We cannot say that the war-making branches of the Government did not have ground for believing that in a critical hour such persons could not readily be isolated and separately dealt with, and constituted a menace to the national defense and safety, which demanded that prompt and adequate measures be taken to guard against it.'

Like curfew, exclusion of those of Japanese origin was deemed necessary because of the presence of an unascertained number of disloyal members of the group, most of whom we have no doubt were loyal to this country. It was because we could not reject the finding of the military authorities that it was impossible to bring about an immediate segregation of the disloyal from the loyal that we sustained the validity of the curfew order as applying to the whole group. In the instant case, temporary exclusion of the entire group was rested by the military on the same ground. The judgment that exclusion of the whole group was for the same reason a military imperative answers the contention that the exclusion was in the nature of group punishment based on antagonism to those of Japanese origin. That there were members of the group who retained loyalties to Japan has been confirmed by investigations made subsequent to the exclusion. Approximately five thousand American citizens of Japanese ancestry refused to swear unqualified allegiance to the United States and to renounce allegiance to the Japanese Emperor, and several thousand evacuees requested repatriation to Japan.

We uphold the exclusion order as of the time it was made and when the petitioner violated it. [citations]. In doing so, we are not unmindful of the hardships imposed by it upon a large group of American citizens. [citation]. But hardships are part of war, and war is an aggregation of hardships. All citizens alike, both in and out of uniform, feel the impact of war in greater or lesser measure. Citizenship has its responsibilities as well as its privileges, and in time of war the burden is always heavier. Compulsory exclusion of large groups of citizens from their homes, except under circumstances of direst emergency and peril, is inconsistent with our basic governmental institutions. But when under conditions of modern warfare our shores are threatened by hostile forces, the power to protect must be commensurate with the threatened danger.

* * *

It is said that we are dealing here with the case of imprisonment of a citizen in a concentration camp solely because of his ancestry, without evidence or inquiry concerning his loyalty and good disposition towards the United States. Our task would be simple, our duty clear, were this a case involving the imprisonment of a loyal citizen in a concentration camp because of racial prejudice. Regardless of the true nature of the assembly and relocation centers—and we deem it unjustifiable to call them concentration camps with all the ugly connotations that term implies—we are dealing specifically with nothing but an exclusion order. To cast this case into outlines of racial prejudice, without reference to the real military dangers which were presented, merely confuses the issue. Korematsu was not excluded from the Military Area because of hostility to him or his race. He was excluded because we are at war with the Japanese Empire, because the properly constituted military authorities feared an invasion of our West Coast and felt constrained to take proper security measures, because they decided that the military urgency of the situation demanded that all citizens of Japanese ancestry be segregated from the West Coast temporarily, and finally, because Congress, reposing its confidence in this time of war in our military leaders—as inevitably it must—determined that they should have the power to do just this. There was evidence of disloyalty on the part of some, the military authorities considered that the need for action was great, and time was short. We cannot—by availing ourselves of the calm perspective of hindsight—now say that at that time these actions were unjustified.

Affirmed.

* * *

MR. JUSTICE MURPHY, dissenting.

This exclusion of 'all persons of Japanese ancestry, both alien and non-alien,' from the Pacific Coast area on a plea of military necessity in the absence of martial law ought not to be approved. Such exclusion goes over 'the very brink of constitutional power' and falls into the ugly abyss of racism.

In dealing with matters relating to the prosecution and progress of a war, we must accord great respect and consideration to the judgments of the military authorities who are on the scene and who have full knowledge of the military facts. The scope of their discretion must, as a matter of necessity and common sense, be wide. And their judgments ought not to be overruled lightly by those whose training and duties ill-equip them to deal intelligently with matters so vital to the physical security of the nation.

At the same time, however, it is essential that there be definite limits to military discretion, especially where martial law has not been declared. Individuals must not be left impoverished of their constitutional rights on a plea of military necessity that has neither substance nor support. Thus, like other claims conflicting with the asserted constitutional rights of the individual, the military claim must subject itself to the judicial process of having its reasonableness determined and its conflicts with other interests reconciled. 'What are the allowable limits of military discretion, and whether or not they have been overstepped in a particular case, are judicial questions.' Sterling v. Constantin, 287 U.S. 378.

The judicial test of whether the Government, on a plea of military necessity, can validly deprive an individual of any of his constitutional rights is whether the deprivation is reasonably related to a public danger that is so 'immediate, imminent, and impending' as not to admit of delay and not to permit the intervention of ordinary constitutional processes to alleviate the danger. United States v. Russell, 13 Wall. 623, 627, 628;[additional citations]. Civilian Exclusion Order No. 34, banishing from a prescribed area of the Pacific Coast 'all persons of Japanese ancestry, both alien and non-alien,' clearly does not meet that test. Being an obvious racial discrimination, the order deprives all those within its scope of the equal protection of the laws as guaranteed by the Fifth Amendment. It further deprives these individuals of their constitutional rights to live and work where they will, to establish a home where they choose and to move about freely. In excommunicating them without benefit of hearings, this order also deprives them of all their constitutional rights to procedural due process. Yet no reasonable relation to an 'immediate, imminent, and impending' public danger is evident to support this racial restriction which is one of the most sweeping and complete deprivations of constitutional rights in the history of this nation in the absence of martial law.

It must be conceded that the military and naval situation in the spring of 1942 was such as to generate a very real fear of invasion of the Pacific Coast, accompanied by fears of sabotage and espionage in that area. The military command was therefore justified in adopting all reasonable means necessary to combat these dangers. In adjudging the military action taken in light of the then apparent dangers, we must not erect too high or too meticulous standards; it is necessary only that the action have some reasonable relation to the removal of the dangers of invasion, sabotage and espionage. But the exclusion, either temporarily or permanently, of all persons with Japanese blood in their veins has no such reasonable relation. And that relation is lacking because the exclusion order necessarily must rely for its reasonableness upon the assumption that all persons of Japanese ancestry may have a dangerous tendency to commit sabotage and espionage and to aid our Japanese enemy in other ways. It is difficult to believe that reason, logic or experience could be marshalled in support of such an assumption.

That this forced exclusion was the result in good measure of this erroneous assumption of racial guilt rather than bona fide military necessity is evidenced by the Commanding General's Final Report on the evacuation from the Pacific Coast area. In it he refers to all individuals of Japanese descent as 'subversive,' as belonging to 'an enemy race' whose 'racial strains are undiluted,' and as constituting 'over 112,000 potential enemies . . . at large today' along the Pacific Coast. In support of this blanket condemnation of all persons of Japanese descent, however, no reliable evidence is cited to show that such individuals were generally disloyal, or had generally so conducted themselves in this area as to constitute a special menace to defense installations or war industries, or had otherwise by their behavior furnished reasonable ground for their exclusion as a group.

Justification for the exclusion is sought, instead, mainly upon questionable racial and sociological grounds not ordinarily within the realm of expert military judgment, supplemented by certain semi-military conclusions drawn from an unwarranted use of circumstantial evidence. Individuals of Japanese ancestry are condemned because they are said to be 'a large, unassimilated, tightly knit racial group, bound to an enemy nation by strong ties of race, culture, custom and religion.' They are claimed to be given to 'emperor worshipping ceremonies' and to 'dual citizenship.' Japanese language schools and allegedly pro-Japanese organizations are cited as evidence of possible group disloyalty, together with facts as to certain persons being educated and residing at length in Japan. It is intimated that many of these individuals deliberately resided 'adjacent to strategic points,' thus enabling them 'to carry into execution a tremendous program of sabotage on a mass scale should any considerable number of them have been inclined to do so.' The need for protective custody is also asserted. The report refers without identity to 'numerous incidents of violence' as well as to other admittedly unverified or cumulative incidents. From this, plus certain other events not shown to have been connected with the Japanese Americans, it is concluded that the 'situation was fraught with danger to the Japanese population itself' and that the general public 'was ready to take matters into its own hands.' Finally, it is intimated, though not directly charged or proved, that persons of Japanese ancestry were responsible for three minor isolated shellings and bombings of the Pacific Coast area, as well as for unidentified radio transmissions and night signaling.

The main reasons relied upon by those responsible for the forced evacuation, therefore, do not prove a reasonable relation between the group characteristics of Japanese Americans and the dangers of invasion, sabotage and espionage. The reasons appear, instead, to be largely an accumulation of much of the misinformation, half-truths and insinuations that for years have been directed against Japanese Americans by people with racial and economic prejudices—the same people who have been among the foremost advocates of the evacuation. A military judgment based upon such racial and sociological considerations is not entitled to the great weight ordinarily given the judgments based upon strictly military considerations. Especially is this so when every charge relative to race, religion, culture, geographical location, and legal and economic status has been substantially discredited by independent studies made by experts in these matters.

The military necessity which is essential to the validity of the evacuation order thus resolves itself into a few intimations that certain individuals actively aided the enemy, from which it is inferred that the entire group of Japanese Americans could not be trusted to be or remain loyal to the United States. No one denies, of course, that there were some disloyal persons of Japanese descent on the Pacific Coast who did all in their power to aid their ancestral land. Similar disloyal activities have been engaged in by many persons of German, Italian and even more pioneer stock in our country. But to infer that examples of individual disloyalty prove group disloyalty and justify discriminatory action against the entire group is to deny that under our system of law individual guilt is the sole basis for deprivation of rights. Moreover, this inference, which is at the very heart of the evacuation orders, has been used in support of the abhorrent and despicable treatment of minority groups by the dictatorial tyrannies which this nation is now pledged to destroy. To give constitutional sanction to that inference in this case, however well-intentioned may have been the military command on the Pacific Coast, is to adopt one of the cruelest of the rationales used by our enemies to destroy the dignity of the individual and to encourage and open the door to discriminatory actions against other minority groups in the passions of tomorrow.

* * *

Moreover, there was no adequate proof that the Federal Bureau of Investigation and the military and naval intelligence services did not have the espionage and sabotage situation well in hand during this long period. Nor is there any denial of the fact that not one person of Japanese ancestry was accused or convicted of espionage or sabotage after Pearl Harbor while they were still free, a fact which is some evidence of the loyalty of the vast majority of these individuals and of the effectiveness of the established methods of combatting these evils. It seems incredible that under these circumstances it would have been impossible to hold loyalty hearings for the mere 112,000 persons involved—or at least for the 70,000 American citizens—especially when a large part of this number represented children and elderly men and women. Any inconvenience that may have accompanied an attempt to conform to procedural due process cannot be said to justify violations of constitutional rights of individuals.

I dissent, therefore, from this legalization of racism. Racial discrimination in any form and in any degree has no justifiable part whatever in our democratic way of life. It is unattractive in any setting but it is utterly revolting among a free people who have embraced the principles set forth in the Constitution of the United States. All residents of this nation are kin in some way by blood or culture to a foreign land. Yet they are primarily and necessarily a part of the new and distinct civilization of the United States. They must accordingly be treated at all times as the heirs of the American experiment and as entitled to all the rights and freedoms guaranteed by the Constitution.

---

**Questions:** What was the constitutional basis for the *Korematsu* majority's decision? For the dissent's?

## HAMDI V. RUMSFELD

542 U.S. 507 (2004)

JUSTICE O'CONNOR announced the judgment of the Court and delivered an opinion, in which THE CHIEF JUSTICE, JUSTICE KENNEDY, and JUSTICE BREYER join.

At this difficult time in our Nation's history, we are called upon to consider the legality of the Government's detention of a United States citizen on United States soil as an "enemy combatant" and to address the process that is constitutionally owed to one who seeks to challenge his classification as such. The United States Court of Appeals for the Fourth Circuit held that petitioner's detention was legally authorized and that he was entitled to no further opportunity to challenge his enemy-combatant label. We now vacate and remand. We hold that although Congress authorized the detention of combatants in the narrow circumstances alleged here, due process demands that a citizen held in the United States as an enemy combatant be given a meaningful opportunity to contest the factual basis for that detention before a neutral decisionmaker.

* * *

This case arises out of the detention of a man whom the Government alleges took up arms with the Taliban . . . . His name is Yaser Esam Hamdi. Born an American citizen in Louisiana in 1980, Hamdi moved with his family to Saudi Arabia as a child. By 2001, the parties agree, he resided in Afghanistan. At some point that year, he was seized by members of the Northern Alliance, a coalition of military groups opposed to the Taliban government, and eventually was turned over to the United States military. The Government asserts that it initially detained and interrogated Hamdi in Afghanistan before transferring him to the United States Naval Base in Guantanamo Bay in January 2002. In April 2002, upon learning that Hamdi is an American citizen, authorities transferred him to a naval brig in Norfolk, Virginia, where he remained until a recent transfer to a brig in Charleston, South Carolina. The Government contends that Hamdi is an "enemy combatant," and that this status justifies holding him in the United States indefinitely—without formal charges or proceedings—unless and until it makes the determination that access to counsel or further process is warranted.

[Hearing a habeas corpus petition filed on Hamdi's behalf, the District Court held that Congress's 2001 resolution authorizing the use of force against terrorists authorized indefinite detention of alleged enemy combatants, but that the detainee here was entitled to notice of the charges against him and a neutral hearing in which he could contest the claim that he was an illegal combatant. The Fourth Circuit Court of Appeals rejected this ruling and held that Hamdi was not entitled to any further opportunity to challenge the allegations].

* * *

The capture and detention of lawful combatants and the capture, detention, and trial of unlawful combatants, by "universal agreement and practice," are "important incident[s] of war." Ex parte Quirin, 317 U.S., at 28. The purpose of detention is to prevent captured individuals from returning to the field of battle and taking up arms once again. Naqvi, Doubtful Prisoner-of-War Status, 84 Int'l Rev. Red Cross 571, 572 (2002) ("[C]aptivity in war is 'neither revenge, nor punishment, but solely protective custody, the only purpose of which is to prevent the prisoners of war from further participation in the war' " (quoting decision of Nuremberg Military Tribunal, reprinted in 41 Am. J. Int'l L. 172, 229 (1947).

* * *

Even in cases in which the detention of enemy combatants is legally authorized, there remains the question of what process is constitutionally due to a citizen who disputes his enemy-combatant status. Hamdi argues that he is owed a meaningful and timely hearing and that "extra-judicial detention [that] begins and ends with the submission of an affidavit based on third-hand hearsay" does not comport with the Fifth and Fourteenth Amendments. Brief for Petitioners 16. The Government counters that any more process than was provided below would be both unworkable and "constitutionally intolerable." Brief for Respondents 46.

* * *

We ... hold that a citizen-detainee seeking to challenge his classification as an enemy combatant must receive notice of the factual basis for his classification, and a fair opportunity to rebut the Government's factual assertions before a neutral decisionmaker. See Cleveland Bd. of Ed. v. Loudermill, 470 U.S. 532, 542 (1985) ("An essential principle of due process is that a deprivation of life, liberty, or property 'be preceded by notice and opportunity for hearing appropriate to the nature of the case' " (quoting Mullane v. Central Hanover Bank & Trust Co., 339 U.S. 306, 313 (1950)) [additional citations.]

* * *

We think it unlikely that this basic process will have the dire impact on the central functions of warmaking that the Government forecasts. The parties agree that initial captures on the battlefield need not receive the process we have discussed here; that process is due only when the determination is made to continue to hold those who have been seized. The Government has made clear in its briefing that documentation regarding battlefield detainees already is kept in the ordinary course of military affairs. Brief for Respondents 3–4. Any factfinding imposition created by requiring a knowledgeable affiant to summarize these records to an independent tribunal is a minimal one. Likewise, arguments that military officers ought not have to wage war under the threat of litigation lose much of their steam when factual disputes at enemy-combatant hearings are limited to the alleged combatant's acts. This focus meddles little, if at all, in the strategy or conduct of war, inquiring only into the appropriateness of continuing to detain an individual claimed to have taken up arms against the United States. While we accord the greatest respect and consideration to the judgments of military authorities in matters relating to the actual prosecution of a war, and recognize that the scope of that discretion necessarily is wide, it does not infringe on the core role of the military for the courts to exercise their own time-honored and constitutionally mandated roles of reviewing and resolving claims like those presented here. Cf. Korematsu v. United States, 323 U.S. 214, 233–234 (1944) (Murphy, J., dissenting) ("[L]ike other claims conflicting with the asserted constitutional rights of the individual, the military claim must subject itself to the judicial process of having its reasonableness determined and its conflicts with other interests reconciled") [additional citation.]

In sum, while the full protections that accompany challenges to detentions in other settings may prove unworkable and inappropriate in the enemy-combatant setting, the threats to military operations posed by a basic system of independent review are not so weighty as to trump a citizen's core rights to challenge meaningfully the Government's case and to be heard by an impartial adjudicator.

* * *

The judgment of the United States Court of Appeals for the Fourth Circuit is vacated, and the case is remanded for further proceedings. It is so ordered.

JUSTICE SOUTER, with whom JUSTICE GINSBURG joins, concurring in part, dissenting in part, and concurring in the judgment.

According to Yaser Hamdi's petition for writ of habeas corpus, brought on his behalf by his father, the Government of the United States is detaining him, an American citizen on American soil, with the explanation that he was seized on the field of battle in Afghanistan, having been on the enemy side. It is undisputed that the Government has not charged him with espionage, treason, or any other crime under domestic law. It is likewise undisputed that for one year and nine months, on the basis of an Executive designation of Hamdi as an "enemy combatant," the Government denied him the right to send or receive any communication beyond the prison where he was held and, in particular, denied him access to counsel to represent him. The Government asserts a right to hold Hamdi under these conditions indefinitely, that is, until the Government determines that the United States is no longer threatened by the terrorism exemplified in the attacks of September 11, 2001.

In these proceedings on Hamdi's petition, he seeks to challenge the facts claimed by the Government as the basis for holding him as an enemy combatant. And in this Court he presses the distinct argument that the Government's claim, even if true, would not implicate any authority for holding him that would satisfy 18 U.S.C. § 4001(a) (Non-Detention Act), which bars imprisonment or detention of a citizen "except pursuant to an Act of Congress."

The Government responds that Hamdi's incommunicado imprisonment as an enemy combatant seized on the field of battle falls within the President's power as Commander in Chief under the laws and usages of war, and is in any event authorized by two statutes.

* * *

The plurality does . . . accept the Government's position that if Hamdi's designation as an enemy combatant is correct, his detention (at least as to some period) is authorized by an Act of Congress as required by § 4001(a), that is, by the Authorization for Use of Military Force, 115 Stat. 224 (hereinafter Force Resolution). Ante, at 9–14. Here, I disagree and respectfully dissent. The Government has failed to demonstrate that the Force Resolution authorizes the detention complained of here even on the facts the Government claims. If the Government raises nothing further than the record now shows, the Non-Detention Act entitles Hamdi to be released.

* * *

Under this principle of reading § 4001(a) robustly to require a clear statement of authorization to detain, none of the Government's arguments suffices to justify Hamdi's detention.

* * *

The Government's claim, accepted by the Court, [is] that the terms of the Force Resolution are adequate to authorize detention of an enemy combatant under the circumstances described,3 a claim the Government fails to support sufficiently to satisfy § 4001(a) as read to require a clear statement of authority to detain. Since the Force Resolution was adopted one week after the attacks of September 11, 2001, it naturally speaks with some generality, but its focus is clear, and that is on the use of military power. It is fairly read to authorize the use of armies and weapons, whether against other armies or individual terrorists. But . . . it never so much as uses the word detention, and there is no reason to think Congress might have perceived any need to augment Executive power to deal with dangerous citizens within the United States, given the well-stocked statutory arsenal of defined criminal offenses covering the gamut of actions that a citizen sympathetic to terrorists might commit. See, e.g., 18 U.S.C. § 2339A (material support for various terrorist acts); § 2339B (material support to a foreign terrorist organization); § 2332a (use of a weapon of mass destruction, including conspiracy and attempt); § 2332b(a)(1) (acts of terrorism "transcending national boundaries," including threats, conspiracy, and attempt); 18 U.S.C. A. § 2339C (Supp. 2004) (financing of certain terrorist acts); see also 18 U.S.C. § 3142(e) (pretrial detention). See generally Brief for Janet Reno et al. as Amici Curiae in Rumsfeld v. Padilla, O. T. 2003, No. 03–1027, pp. 14–19, and n. 17 (listing the tools available to the Executive to fight terrorism even without the power the Government claims here); Brief for Louis Henkin et al. as Amici Curiae in Rumsfeld v. Padilla, O. T. 2003, No. 03–1027, p. 23, n. 27.4

Even so, there is one argument for treating the Force Resolution as sufficiently clear to authorize detention of a citizen consistently with § 4001(a). Assuming the argument to be sound, however, the Government is in no position to claim its advantage.

Because the Force Resolution authorizes the use of military force in acts of war by the United States, the argument goes, it is reasonably clear that the military and its Commander in Chief are authorized to deal with enemy belligerents according to the treaties and customs known collectively as the laws of war. Brief for Respondents 20–22; see ante, at 9–14 (accepting this argument). Accordingly, the United States may detain captured enemies, and Ex parte Quirin, 317 U.S. 1 (1942), may perhaps be claimed for the proposition that the American citizenship of such a captive does not as such limit the Government's power to deal with him under the usages of war. Id., at 31, 37–38. Thus, the Government here repeatedly argues that Hamdi's detention amounts to nothing more than customary detention of a captive taken on the field of battle: if the usages of war are fairly authorized by the Force Resolution, Hamdi's detention is authorized for purposes of § 4001(a).

There is no need, however, to address the merits of such an argument in all possible circumstances. For now it is enough to recognize that the Government's stated legal position in its campaign against the Taliban (among whom Hamdi was allegedly captured) is apparently at odds with its claim here to be acting in accordance with customary law of war and hence to be within the terms of the Force Resolution in its detention of Hamdi. In a statement of its legal position cited in its brief, the Government says that "the Geneva Convention applies to the Taliban detainees." Office of the White House Press Secretary, Fact Sheet, Status of Detainees at Guantanamo (Feb. 7, 2002), . . . (available in Clerk of Court's case file) (hereinafter White House Press Release) (cited in Brief for Respondents 24, n. 9). Hamdi presumably is such a detainee, since according to the Government's own account, he was taken bearing arms on the Taliban side of a field of battle in Afghanistan. He would therefore seem to qualify for treatment as a prisoner of war under the Third Geneva Convention, to which the United States is a party. Article 4 of the Geneva Convention (III) Relative to the Treatment of Prisoners of War, Aug. 12, 1949, [1955] 6 U.S. T. 3316, 3320, T. I. A. S. No. 3364.

By holding him incommunicado, however, the Government obviously has not been treating him as a prisoner of war, and in fact the Government claims that no Taliban detainee is entitled to prisoner of war status. See Brief for Respondents 24; White House Press Release. This treatment appears to be a violation of the Geneva Convention provision that even in cases of doubt, captives are entitled to be treated as prisoners of war "until such time as their status has been determined by a competent tribunal." Art. 5, 6 U.S. T., at 3324. The Government answers that the President's determination that Taliban detainees do not qualify as prisoners of war is conclusive as to Hamdi's status and removes any doubt that would trigger application of the Convention's tribunal requirement. See Brief for Respondents 24. But reliance on this categorical pronouncement to settle doubt is apparently at odds with the military regulation, Enemy Prisoners of War, Retained Personnel, Civilian Internees and Other Detainees, Army Reg. 190–8, §§ 1–5, 1–6 (1997), adopted to implement the Geneva Convention, and setting out a detailed procedure for a military tribunal to determine an individual's status.

* * *

Thus, there is reason to question whether the United States is acting in accordance with the laws of war it claims as authority.

Whether, or to what degree, the Government is in fact violating the Geneva Convention and is thus acting outside the customary usages of war are not matters I can resolve at this point. What I can say, though, is that the Government has not made out its claim that in detaining Hamdi in the manner described, it is acting in accord with the laws of war authorized to be applied against citizens by the Force Resolution. I conclude accordingly that the Government has failed to support the position that the Force Resolution authorizes the described detention of Hamdi for purposes of § 4001(a).

* * *

Because I find Hamdi's detention forbidden by § 4001(a) and unauthorized by the Force Resolution, I would not reach any questions of what process he may be due in litigating disputed issues in a proceeding under the habeas statute or prior to the habeas enquiry itself. For me, it suffices that the Government has failed to justify holding him in the absence of a further Act of Congress, criminal charges, a showing that the detention conforms to the laws of war, or a demonstration that § 4001(a) is unconstitutional. I would therefore vacate the judgment of the Court of Appeals and remand for proceedings consistent with this view.

Since this disposition does not command a majority of the Court, however, the need to give practical effect to the conclusions of eight members of the Court rejecting the Government's position calls for me to join with the plurality in ordering remand on terms closest to those I would impose. See Screws v. United States, 325 U.S. 91, 134 (1945) (Rutledge, J., concurring in result). Although I think litigation of Hamdi's status as an enemy combatant is unnecessary, the terms of the plurality's remand will allow Hamdi to offer evidence that he is not an enemy combatant, and he should at the least have the benefit of that opportunity.

* * *

Subject to these qualifications, I join with the plurality in a judgment of the Court vacating the Fourth Circuit's judgment and remanding the case.

---

**Questions:** Are the facts in *Hamdi* distinguishable from those in *Korematsu*? In *Hamdi,* how do the plurality and Justices Souter's and Ginsburg's concurrence/dissent differ over the relevance of Congress's role?

## TRUMP V. HAWAII

585 U.S. 667 (2018)

CHIEF JUSTICE ROBERTS delivered the opinion of the Court.

Under the Immigration and Nationality Act, foreign nationals seeking entry into the United States undergo a vetting process to ensure that they satisfy the numerous requirements for admission. The Act also vests the President with authority to restrict the entry of aliens whenever he finds that their entry "would be detrimental to the interests of the United States." 8 U. S. C. § 1182(f). Relying on that delegation, the President concluded that it was necessary to impose entry restrictions on nationals of countries that do not share adequate information for an informed entry determination, or that otherwise present national security risks. Presidential Proclamation No. 9645, 82 Fed. Reg. 45161 (2017) (Proclamation). The plaintiffs in this litigation, respondents here, challenged the application of those entry restrictions to certain aliens abroad. We now decide whether the President had authority under the Act to issue the Proclamation, and whether the entry policy violates the Establishment Clause of the First Amendment.

Shortly after taking office, President Trump signed Executive Order No. 13769, Protecting the Nation From Foreign Terrorist Entry Into the United States. 82 Fed. Reg. 8977 (2017) (EO–1). EO–1 directed the Secretary of Homeland Security to conduct a review to examine the adequacy of information provided by foreign governments about their nationals seeking to enter the United States. § 3(a). Pending that review, the order suspended for 90 days the entry of foreign nationals from seven countries—Iran, Iraq, Libya, Somalia, Sudan, Syria, and Yemen—that had been previously identified by Congress or prior administrations as posing heightened terrorism risks. § 3(c). The District Court for the Western District of Washington entered a temporary restraining order blocking the entry restrictions, and the Court of Appeals for the Ninth Circuit denied the Government's request to stay that order.

In response, the President revoked EO–1, replacing it with Executive Order No. 13780, which again directed a worldwide review. 82 Fed. Reg. 13209 (2017) (EO–2). Citing investigative burdens on agencies and the need to diminish the risk that dangerous individuals would enter without adequate vetting, EO–2 also temporarily restricted the entry (with case-by-case waivers) of foreign nationals from six of the countries covered by EO–1: Iran, Libya, Somalia, Sudan, Syria, and Yemen. §§ 2(c), 3(a). The order explained that those countries had been selected because each "is a state sponsor of terrorism, has been significantly compromised by terrorist organizations, or contains active conflict zones." § 1(d). The entry restriction was to stay in effect for 90 days, pending completion of the worldwide review.

* * *

On September 24, 2017, after completion of the worldwide review, the President issued the Proclamation before us—Proclamation No. 9645, Enhancing Vetting Capabilities and Processes for Detecting Attempted Entry Into the United States by Terrorists or Other Public-Safety Threats. 82 Fed. Reg. 45161. The Proclamation (as its title indicates) sought to improve vetting procedures by identifying ongoing deficiencies in the information needed to assess whether nationals of particular countries present "public safety threats." § 1(a). To further that purpose, the Proclamation placed entry restrictions on the nationals of eight foreign states whose systems for managing and sharing information about their nationals the President deemed inadequate.

* * *

Invoking his authority under 8 U. S. C. §§ 1182(f) and 1185(a), the President determined that certain entry restrictions were necessary to "prevent the entry of those foreign nationals about whom the United States Government lacks sufficient information"; "elicit improved identity-management and information-sharing protocols and practices from foreign governments"; and otherwise "advance [the] foreign policy, national security, and counterterrorism objectives" of the United States. Proclamation § 1(h). The President explained that these restrictions would be the "most likely to encourage cooperation" while "protect[ing] the United States until such time as improvements occur." Ibid.

The Proclamation imposed a range of restrictions that vary based on the "distinct circumstances" in each of the eight countries. Ibid. For countries that do not cooperate with the United States in identifying security risks (Iran, North Korea, and Syria), the Proclamation suspends entry of all nationals, except for Iranians seeking nonimmigrant student and exchange-visitor visas. §§ 2(b)(ii), (d)(ii), (e)(ii). For countries that have information-sharing deficiencies but are nonetheless "valuable counterterrorism partner[s]" (Chad, Libya, and Yemen), it restricts entry of nationals seeking immigrant visas and nonimmigrant business or tourist visas. §§ 2(a)(i), (c)(i), (g)(i). Because Somalia generally satisfies the baseline standards but was found to present special risk factors, the Proclamation suspends entry of nationals seeking immigrant visas and requires additional scrutiny of nationals seeking nonimmigrant visas. § 2(h)(ii). And for Venezuela, which refuses to cooperate in information sharing but for which alternative means are available to identify its nationals, the Proclamation limits entry only of certain government officials and their family members on nonimmigrant business or tourist visas. § 2(f)(ii).

* * *

Plaintiffs in this case are the State of Hawaii, three individuals (Dr. Ismail Elshikh, John Doe #1, and John Doe #2), and the Muslim Association of Hawaii. The State operates the University of Hawaii system, which recruits students and faculty from the designated countries. The three individual plaintiffs are U. S. citizens or lawful permanent residents who have relatives from Iran, Syria, and Yemen applying for immigrant or nonimmigrant visas. The Association is a nonprofit organization that operates a mosque in Hawaii.

Plaintiffs challenged the Proclamation—except as applied to North Korea and Venezuela—on several grounds. As relevant here, they argued that the Proclamation contravenes provisions in the Immigration and Nationality Act (INA), 66 Stat. 187, as amended. Plaintiffs further claimed that the Proclamation violates the Establishment Clause of the First Amendment, because it was motivated not by concerns pertaining to national security but by animus toward Islam.

The District Court granted a nationwide preliminary injunction barring enforcement of the entry restrictions. The court concluded that the Proclamation violated two provisions of the INA: § 1182(f), because the President did not make sufficient findings that the entry of the covered foreign nationals would be detrimental to the national interest, and § 1152(a)(1)(A), because the policy discriminates against immigrant visa applicants on the basis of nationality. 265 F. Supp. 3d 1140, 1155–1159 (Haw. 2017). The Government requested expedited briefing and sought a stay pending appeal. The Court of Appeals for the Ninth Circuit granted a partial stay, permitting enforcement of the Proclamation with respect to foreign nationals who lack a bona fide relationship with the United States. This Court then stayed the injunction in full pending disposition of the Government's appeal. 583 U. S. ___ (2017).

The Court of Appeals affirmed. The court first held that the Proclamation exceeds the President's authority under § 1182(f). In its view, that provision authorizes only a "temporary" suspension of entry in response to "exigencies" that "Congress would be ill-equipped to address." 878 F. 3d 662, 684, 688 (2017). The court further reasoned that the Proclamation "conflicts with the INA's finely reticulated regulatory scheme" by addressing "matters of immigration already passed upon by Congress." Id., at 685, 690. The Ninth Circuit then turned to § 1152(a)(1)(A) and determined that the entry restrictions also contravene the prohibition on nationality-based discrimination in the issuance of immigrant visas. The court did not reach plaintiffs' Establishment Clause claim.

We granted certiorari.

The Immigration and Nationality Act establishes numerous grounds on which an alien abroad may be inadmissible to the United States and ineligible for a visa. See, e.g., 8 U. S. C. §§ 1182(a)(1) (health-related grounds), (a)(2) (criminal history), (a)(3)(B) (terrorist activities), (a)(3)(C) (foreign policy grounds). Congress has also delegated to the President authority to suspend or restrict the entry of aliens in certain circumstances. The principal source of that authority, § 1182(f), enables the President to "suspend the entry of all aliens or any class of aliens" whenever he "finds" that their entry "would be detrimental to the interests of the United States."

Plaintiffs argue that the Proclamation is not a valid exercise of the President's authority under the INA. In their view, § 1182(f) confers only a residual power to temporarily halt the entry of a discrete group of aliens engaged in harmful conduct. They also assert that the Proclamation violates another provision of the INA—8 U. S. C. § 1152(a)(1)(A)—because it discriminates on the basis of nationality in the issuance of immigrant visas.

By its plain language, § 1182(f) grants the President broad discretion to suspend the entry of aliens into the United States. The President lawfully exercised that discretion based on his findings—following a worldwide, multi-agency review—that entry of the covered aliens would be detrimental to the national interest. And plaintiffs' attempts to identify a conflict with other provisions in the INA, and their appeal to the statute's purposes and legislative history, fail to overcome the clear statutory language.

The text of § 1182(f) states:

"Whenever the President finds that the entry of any aliens or of any class of aliens into the United States would be detrimental to the interests of the United States, he may by proclamation, and for such period as he shall deem necessary, suspend the entry of all aliens or any class of aliens as immigrants or nonimmigrants, or impose on the entry of aliens any restrictions he may deem to be appropriate."

By its terms, § 1182(f) exudes deference to the President in every clause. It entrusts to the President the decisions whether and when to suspend entry ("[w]henever [he] finds that the entry" of aliens "would be detrimental" to the national interest); whose entry to suspend ("all aliens or any class of aliens"); for how long ("for such period as he shall deem necessary"); and on what conditions ("any restrictions he may deem to be appropriate"). It is therefore unsurprising that we have previously observed that § 1182(f) vests the President with "ample power" to impose entry restrictions in addition to those elsewhere enumerated in the INA. Sale, 509 U. S., at 187 (finding it "perfectly clear" that the President could "establish a naval blockade" to prevent illegal migrants from entering the United States); see also Abourezk v. Reagan, 785 F. 2d 1043, 1049, n. 2 (CADC 1986) (describing the "sweeping proclamation power" in § 1182(f) as enabling the President to supplement the other grounds of inadmissibility in the INA).

The Proclamation falls well within this comprehensive delegation. The sole prerequisite set forth in § 1182(f) is that the President "find[ ]" that the entry of the covered aliens "would be detrimental to the interests of the United States." The President has undoubtedly fulfilled that requirement here. He first ordered DHS and other agencies to conduct a comprehensive evaluation of every single country's compliance with the information and risk assessment baseline. The President then issued a Proclamation setting forth extensive findings describing how deficiencies in the practices of select foreign governments—several of which are state sponsors of terrorism—deprive the Government of "sufficient information to assess the risks [those countries' nationals] pose to the United States." Proclamation § 1(h)(i). Based on that review, the President found that it was in the national interest to restrict entry of aliens who could not be vetted with adequate information—both to protect national security and public safety, and to induce improvement by their home countries. The Proclamation therefore "craft[ed] . . . country-specific restrictions that would be most likely to encourage cooperation given each country's distinct circumstances," while securing the Nation "until such time as improvements occur." Ibid.2

* * *

The Proclamation is squarely within the scope of Presidential authority under the INA. Indeed, neither dissent even attempts any serious argument to the contrary, despite the fact that plaintiffs' primary contention below and in their briefing before this Court was that the Proclamation violated the statute.

[The Court held that the Proclamation did not violate the Establishment Clause.]

* * *

For our purposes today, we assume that we may look behind the face of the Proclamation to the extent of applying rational basis review. That standard of review considers whether the entry policy is plausibly related to the Government's stated objective to protect the country and improve vetting processes. See Railroad Retirement Bd. v. Fritz, 449 U. S. 166, 179 (1980). As a result, we may consider plaintiffs' extrinsic evidence, but will uphold the policy so long as it can reasonably be understood to result from a justification independent of unconstitutional grounds.

* * *

[B]ecause there is persuasive evidence that the entry suspension has a legitimate grounding in national security concerns, quite apart from any religious hostility, we must accept that independent justification.

The Proclamation is expressly premised on legitimate purposes: preventing entry of nationals who cannot be adequately vetted and inducing other nations to improve their practices. The text says nothing about religion. Plaintiffs and the dissent nonetheless emphasize that five of the seven nations currently included in the Proclamation have Muslim-majority populations. Yet that fact alone does not support an inference of religious hostility, given that the policy covers just 8% of the world's Muslim population and is limited to countries that were previously designated by Congress or prior administrations as posing national security risks. See 8 U. S. C. § 1187(a)(12)(A) (identifying Syria and state sponsors of terrorism such as Iran as "countr[ies] or area[s] of concern" for purposes of administering the Visa Waiver Program); Dept. of Homeland Security, DHS Announces Further Travel Restrictions for the Visa Waiver Program (Feb. 18, 2016) (designating Libya, Somalia, and Yemen as additional countries of concern); see also Rajah, 544 F. 3d, at 433, n. 3 (describing how nonimmigrant aliens from Iran, Libya, Somalia, Syria, and Yemen were covered by the National Security Entry-Exit Registration System).

The Proclamation, moreover, reflects the results of a worldwide review process undertaken by multiple Cabinet officials and their agencies. Plaintiffs seek to discredit the findings of the review, pointing to deviations from the review's baseline criteria resulting in the inclusion of Somalia and omission of Iraq. But as the Proclamation explains, in each case the determinations were justified by the distinct conditions in each country. Although Somalia generally satisfies the information-sharing component of the baseline criteria, it "stands apart . . . in the degree to which [it] lacks command and control of its territory." Proclamation § 2(h)(i). As for Iraq, the Secretary of Homeland Security determined that entry restrictions were not warranted in light of the close cooperative relationship between the U. S. and Iraqi Governments and the country's key role in combating terrorism in the region. § 1(g). It is, in any event, difficult to see how exempting one of the largest predominantly Muslim countries in the region from coverage under the Proclamation can be cited as evidence of animus toward Muslims.

Finally, the dissent invokes Korematsu v. United States, 323 U. S. 214 (1944). Whatever rhetorical advantage the dissent may see in doing so, Korematsu has nothing to do with this case. The forcible relocation of U. S. citizens to concentration camps, solely and explicitly on the basis of race, is objectively unlawful and outside the scope of Presidential authority. But it is wholly inapt to liken that morally repugnant order to a facially neutral policy denying certain foreign nationals the privilege of admission. See post, at 26–28. The entry suspension is an act that is well within executive authority and could have been taken by any other President—the only question is evaluating the actions of this particular President in promulgating an otherwise valid Proclamation.

* * *

Under these circumstances, the Government has set forth a sufficient national security justification to survive rational basis review. We express no view on the soundness of the policy. We simply hold today that plaintiffs have not demonstrated a likelihood of success on the merits of their constitutional claim.

The judgment of the Court of Appeals is reversed, and the case is remanded for further proceedings consistent with this opinion.

It is so ordered.

JUSTICE SOTOMAYOR, with whom JUSTICE GINSBURG joins, dissenting.

The United States of America is a Nation built upon the promise of religious liberty. Our Founders honored that core promise by embedding the principle of religious neutrality in the First Amendment. The Court's decision today fails to safeguard that fundamental principle. It leaves undisturbed a policy first advertised openly and unequivocally as a "total and complete shutdown of Muslims entering the United States" because the policy now masquerades behind a façade of national-security concerns. . . . . Because that troubling result runs contrary to the Constitution and our precedent, I dissent. * * *

Although the majority briefly recounts a few of the statements and background events that form the basis of plaintiffs' constitutional challenge, ante, at 27–28, that highly abridged account does not tell even half of the story. See Brief for The Roderick & Solange MacArthur Justice Center as Amicus Curiae 5–31 (outlining President Trump's public statements expressing animus toward Islam). The full record paints a far more harrowing picture, from which a reasonable observer would readily conclude that the Proclamation was motivated by hostility and animus toward the Muslim faith.

During his Presidential campaign, then-candidate Donald Trump pledged that, if elected, he would ban Muslims from entering the United States. Specifically, on December 7, 2015, he issued a formal statement "calling for a total and complete shutdown of Muslims entering the United States." App. 119.

* * *

On December 8, 2015, Trump justified his proposal during a television interview by noting that President Franklin D. Roosevelt "did the same thing" with respect to the internment of Japanese Americans during World War II. Id., at 120. * * * In March 2016, he expressed his belief that "Islam hates us. . . . [W]e can't allow people coming into this country who have this hatred of the United States . . . [a]nd of people that are not Muslim." Id., at 120–121. That same month, Trump asserted that "[w]e're having problems with the Muslims, and we're having problems with Muslims coming into the country." Id., at 121. He therefore called for surveillance of mosques in the United States, blaming terrorist attacks on Muslims' lack of "assimilation" and their commitment to "sharia law." Ibid.; id., at 164. A day later, he opined that Muslims "do not respect us at all" and "don't respect a lot of the things that are happening throughout not only our country, but they don't respect other things." Ibid.

As Trump's presidential campaign progressed, he began to describe his policy proposal in slightly different terms. In June 2016, for instance, he characterized the policy proposal as a suspension of immigration from countries "where there's a proven history of terrorism." Id., at 121. He also described the proposal as rooted in the need to stop "importing radical Islamic terrorism to the West through a failed immigration system." Id., at 121–122.

* * *

On January 27, 2017, one week after taking office, President Trump signed Executive Order No. 13769, 82 Fed. Reg. 8977 (2017) (EO–1), entitled "Protecting the Nation From Foreign Terrorist Entry Into the United States."

* * *

On February 3, 2017, the United States District Court for the Western District of Washington enjoined the enforcement of EO–1. See Washington v. Trump, 2017 WL 462040, *3. The Ninth Circuit denied the Government's request to stay that injunction. Washington v. Trump, 847 F. 3d 1151, 1169

(2017) (per curiam). Rather than appeal the Ninth Circuit's decision, the Government declined to continue defending EO–1 in court and instead announced that the President intended to issue a new executive order to replace EO–1.

On March 6, 2017, President Trump issued that new executive order, which, like its predecessor, imposed temporary entry and refugee bans. See Exec. Order No. 13,780, 82 Fed. Reg. 13209 (EO–2). One of the President's senior advisers publicly explained that EO–2 would "have the same basic policy outcome" as EO–1, and that any changes would address "very technical issues that were brought up by the court." App. 127.

* * *

While litigation over EO–2 was ongoing, President Trump repeatedly made statements alluding to a desire to keep Muslims out of the country. For instance, he said at a rally of his supporters that EO–2 was just a "watered down version of the first one" and had been "tailor[ed]" at the behest of "the lawyers." App. 131. He further added that he would prefer "to go back to the first [executive order] and go all the way" and reiterated his belief that it was "very hard" for Muslims to assimilate into Western culture. Id., at 131–132. During a rally in April 2017, President Trump recited the lyrics to a song called "The Snake," a song about a woman who nurses a sick snake back to health but then is attacked by the snake, as a warning about Syrian refugees entering the country. Id., at 132, 163. * * *

In September 2017, President Trump tweeted that "[t]he travel ban into the United States should be far larger, tougher and more specific—but stupidly, that would not be politically correct!" App. 133. Later that month, on September 24, 2017, President Trump issued Presidential Proclamation No. 9645, 82 Fed. Reg. 45161 (2017) (Proclamation), which restricts entry of certain nationals from six Muslim-majority countries.

* * *

Taking all the relevant evidence together, a reasonable observer would conclude that the Proclamation was driven primarily by anti-Muslim animus, rather than by the Government's asserted national-security justifications. Even before being sworn into office, then-candidate Trump stated that "Islam hates us," App. 399, warned that "[w]e're having problems with the Muslims, and we're having problems with Muslims coming into the country," id., at 121, promised to enact a "total and complete shutdown of Muslims entering the United States," id., at 119, and instructed one of his advisers to find a "lega[l]" way to enact a Muslim ban, id., at 125. The President continued to make similar statements well after his inauguration, as detailed above.

Moreover, despite several opportunities to do so, President Trump has never disavowed any of his prior statements about Islam. Instead, he has continued to make remarks that a reasonable observer would view as an unrelenting attack on the Muslim religion and its followers. Given President Trump's failure to correct the reasonable perception of his apparent hostility toward the Islamic faith, it is unsurprising that the President's lawyers have, at every step in the lower courts, failed in their attempts to launder the Proclamation of its discriminatory taint. See United States v. Fordice, 505 U. S. 717, 746–747 (1992) ("[G]iven an initially tainted policy, it is eminently reasonable to make the [Government] bear the risk of nonpersuasion with respect to intent at some future time, both because the [Government] has created the dispute through its own prior unlawful conduct, and because discriminatory intent does tend to persist through time" (citation omitted)). * * *

Ultimately, what began as a policy explicitly "calling for a total and complete shutdown of Muslims entering the United States" has since morphed into a "Proclamation" putatively based on national-security concerns. But this new window dressing cannot conceal an unassailable fact: the words of the President and his advisers create the strong perception that the Proclamation is contaminated by impermissible discriminatory animus against Islam and its followers. * * *

Today's holding is all the more troubling given the stark parallels between the reasoning of this case and that of Korematsu v. United States, 323 U. S. 214 (1944).* * *

Our Constitution demands, and our country deserves, a Judiciary willing to hold the coordinate branches to account when they defy our most sacred legal commitments. Because the Court's decision today has failed in that respect, with profound regret, I dissent.

---

**Questions:** Does the *Hamdi* decision's basis in national security concerns lend support to the *Trump v. Hawaii* majority? How might the cases in this section be used to bolster the argument for indefinite detention of Central American political asylum applicants at the border? How might the dissenting opinions in these cases be used to argue the contrary?

# CHAPTER 8

# JUDICIAL LIMITATIONS ON PRESIDENTIAL POWER

■ ■ ■

## CONTEXT & SOURCES

Under the separation of powers doctrine as developed by the Supreme Court, the judicial branch serves as a check on the executive. Cases establishing this doctrine include rulings on the scope of the president's privilege to keep communications confidential and immunity from civil and criminal liability. With immunity, the result turns on the definition of "official" as opposed to "unofficial conduct."

An examination of the key decision delimiting executive privilege can be found in Christopher H. Schroeder, "The Story of *United States v. Nixon*: The President and the Tapes," *Presidential Power Stories* (Christopher H. Schroeder & Curtis A. Bradley eds., Foundation 2009). In L. Peter Schultz, "The Constitution, The Court, and Presidential Immunity: A Defense of *Nixon v. Fitzgerald,* the author concisely supports the justices' broad definition of official conduct for purposes of civil immunity. Vincent Bugliosi, *No Island of Sanity. Paula Jones v. Bill Clinton: The Supreme Court on Trial* (Ballentine Publishing, 1998) is a critical take on the Court's more limited view of immunity when unofficial conduct is at issue. For a brief but fascinating discussion of the uses of history in determining criminal immunity, see Note, "Article II—Presidential Immunity—State Criminal Investigation—*Trump v. Vance*, 134 *Harvard Law Review* 430 (2020).

## PRIVILEGE

### UNITED STATES V. NIXON

418 U.S. 693 (1974)

* * *

MR. CHIEF JUSTICE BURGER delivered the opinion of the Court.

* * *

On March 1, 1974, a grand jury of the United States District Court for the District of Columbia returned an indictment charging seven named individuals with various offenses, including conspiracy to defraud the United States and to obstruct justice [arising out of the burglary of the Democratic National Committee headquarters inn the Watergate Hotel in 1972]. Although he was not designated as such in the indictment, the grand jury named the President, among others, as an unindicted coconspirator. On April 18, 1974, upon motion of the Special Prosecutor, see n. 8, infra, a subpoena duces tecum [ordering appearance with documents] was issued pursuant to Rule 17(c) to the President by the United States District Court and made returnable on May 2, 1974. This subpoena required the production, in advance of the September 9 trial date, of certain tapes, memoranda, papers, transcripts or other writings relating to certain precisely identified meetings between the President and others. The Special Prosecutor was able to fix the time, place, and persons present at these discussions because the White House daily logs and appointment records had been delivered to him. On April 30, the President publicly released edited transcripts of 43 conversations; portions of 20 conversations subject to subpoena in the present case were included. On May 1, 1974, the President's counsel, filed a 'special appearance' and a motion to quash the subpoena under Rule 17(c). This motion was accompanied by a formal claim of privilege. At a subsequent hearing, further motions to expunge the grand jury's action naming the President as an unindicted coconspirator and for protective orders against the disclosure of that information were filed or raised orally by counsel for the President.

* * *

Having determined that the requirements of Rule 17(c) were satisfied, we turn to the claim that the subpoena should be quashed because it demands 'confidential conversations between a President and his close advisors that it would be inconsistent with the public interest to produce.' App. 48a. The first contention is a broad claim that the separation of powers doctrine precludes judicial review of a President's claim of privilege. The second contention is that if he does not prevail on the claim of absolute privilege, the court should hold as a matter of constitutional law that the privilege prevails over the subpoena duces tecum.

In the performance of assigned constitutional duties each branch of the Government must initially interpret the Constitution, and the interpretation of its powers by any branch is due great respect from the others. The President's counsel, as we have noted, reads the Constitution as providing an absolute privilege of confidentiality for all Presidential communications. Many decisions of this Court, however, have unequivocally reaffirmed the holding of Marbury v. Madison, 1 Cranch, 137 (1803), that '(i)t is emphatically the province and duty of the judicial department to say what the law is.' Id., at 177.

No holding of the Court has defined the scope of judicial power specifically relating to the enforcement of a subpoena for confidential Presidential communications for use in a criminal prosecution, but other exercises of power by the Executive Branch and the Legislative Branch have been found invalid as in conflict with the Constitution. Powell v. McCormack, 395 U.S. 486, 89 (1969); Youngstown, Sheet & Tube Co. v. Sawyer, 343 U.S. 579 (1952). In a series of cases, the Court interpreted the explicit immunity conferred by express provisions of the Constitution on Members of the House and Senate by the Speech or Debate Clause, U.S.Const. Art. I, § 6. Doe v. McMillan, 412 U.S. 306 (1973);[additional citations]. Since this Court has consistently exercised the power to construe and delineate claims arising under express powers, it must follow that the Court has authority to interpret claims with respect to powers alleged to derive from enumerated powers.

Our system of government 'requires that federal courts on occasion interpret the Constitution in a manner at variance with the construction given the document by another branch.' Powell v. McCormack, supra, 395 U.S., at 549. And in Baker v. Carr, 369 U.S., at 211, the Court stated:

'(D)eciding whether a matter has in any measure been committed by the Constitution to another branch of government, or whether the action of that branch exceeds whatever authority has been committed, is itself a delicate exercise in constitutional interpretation, and is a responsibility of this Court as ultimate interpreter of the Constitution.'

Notwithstanding the deference each branch must accord the others, the 'judicial Power of the United States' vested in the federal courts by Art. III, § 1, of the Constitution can no more be shared with the Executive Branch than the Chief Executive, for example, can share with the Judiciary the veto power, or the Congress share with the Judiciary the power to override a Presidential veto. Any other conclusion would be contrary to the basic concept of separation of powers and the checks and balances that flow from the scheme of a tripartite government. The Federalist, No. 47, p. 313 (S. Mittell ed. 1938). We therefore reaffirm that it is the province and duty of this Court 'to say what the law is' with respect to the claim of privilege presented in this case. Marbury v. Madison, supra, 1 Cranch. at 177.

In support of his claim of absolute privilege, the President's counsel urges two grounds, one of which is common to all governments and one of which is peculiar to our system of separation of powers. The first ground is the valid need for protection of communications between high Government officials and those who advise and assist them in the performance of their manifold duties; the importance of this confidentiality is too plain to require further discussion. Human experience teaches that those who expect public dissemination of their remarks may well temper candor with a concern for appearances and for their own interests to the detriment of the decisionmaking process. Whatever the nature of the privilege of confidentiality of Presidential communications in the exercise of Art. II powers, the privilege can be said to derive from the supremacy of each branch within its own assigned area of constitutional duties. Certain powers and privileges flow from the nature of enumerated powers; the protection of the confidentiality of Presidential communications has similar constitutional underpinnings.

The second ground asserted by the President's counsel in support of the claim of absolute privilege rests on the doctrine of separation of powers. Here it is argued that the independence of the Executive Branch within its own sphere, Humphrey's Executor v. United States, 295 U.S. 602, 629–630 (1935); Kilbourn v. Thompson, 103 U.S. 168, 190–191 (1881), insulates a President from a judicial subpoena in an ongoing criminal prosecution, and thereby protects confidential Presidential communications.

However, neither the doctrine of separation of powers, nor the need for confidentiality of high-level communications, without more, can sustain an absolute, unqualified Presidential privilege of immunity from judicial process under all circumstances. The President's need for complete candor and objectivity from advisers calls for great deference from the courts. However, when the privilege depends solely on the broad, undifferentiated claim of public interest in the confidentiality of such conversations, a confrontation with other values arises. Absent a claim of need to protect military, diplomatic, or sensitive national security secrets, we find it difficult to accept the argument that even the very important interest in confidentiality of Presidential communications is significantly diminished by production of such material for in camera inspection with all the protection that a district court will be obliged to provide.

The impediment that an absolute, unqualified privilege would place in the way of the primary constitutional duty of the Judicial Branch to do justice in criminal prosecutions would plainly conflict with the function of the courts under Art. III. In designing the structure of our Government and dividing and allocating the sovereign power among three co-equal branches, the Framers of the Constitution sought to provide a comprehensive system, but the separate powers were not intended to operate with absolute independence.

'While the Constitution diffuses power the better to secure liberty, it also contemplates that practice will integrate the dispersed powers into a workable government. It enjoins upon its branches separateness but interdependence, autonomy but reciprocity.' Youngstown Sheet & Tube Co. v. Sawyer, 343 U.S., at 635 (Jackson, J., concurring).

To read the Art. II powers of the President as providing an absolute privilege as against a subpoena essential to enforcement of criminal statutes on no more than a generalized claim of the public interest in confidentiality of nonmilitary and nondiplomatic discussions would upset the constitutional balance of 'a workable government' and gravely impair the role of the courts under Art. III.

Since we conclude that the legitimate needs of the judicial process may outweigh Presidential privilege, it is necessary to resolve those competing interests in a manner that preserves the essential functions of each branch. The right and indeed the duty to resolve that question does not free the Judiciary from according high respect to the representations made on behalf of the President. United States v. Burr, 25 F.Cas. pp. 187, 190, 191 192 (No. 14,694) (CCVa.1807).

The expectation of a President to the confidentiality of his conversations and correspondence, like the claim of confidentiality of judicial deliberations, for example, has all the values to which we accord deference for the privacy of all citizens and, added to those values, is the necessity for protection of the public interest in candid, objective, and even blunt or harsh opinions in Presidential decisionmaking. A President and those who assist him must be free to explore alternatives in the process of shaping policies and making decisions and to do so in a way many would be unwilling to express except privately. These are the considerations justifying a presumptive privilege for Presidential communications. The privilege is fundamental to the operation of Government and inextricably rooted in the separation of powers under the Constitution. In Nixon v. Sirica, 487 F.2d 700 (1973), the Court of Appeals held that such Presidential communications are 'presumptively privileged,' id., at 717, and this position is accepted by both parties in the present litigation. We agree with Mr. Chief Justice Marshall's observation, therefore, that '(i)n no case of this kind would a court be required to proceed against the president as against an ordinary individual.' United States v. Burr, 25 F.Cas., at 192.

But this presumptive privilege must be considered in light of our historic commitment to the rule of law. This is nowhere more profoundly manifest than in our view that 'the twofold aim (of criminal justice) is that guilt shall not escape or innocence suffer.' Berger v. United States, 295 U.S., at 88. We have elected to employ an adversary system of criminal justice in which the parties contest all issues before a court of law. The need to develop all relevant facts in the adversary system is both fundamental and comprehensive. The ends of criminal justice would be defeated if judgments were to be founded on a partial or speculative presentation of the facts. The very integrity of the judicial system and public confidence in the system depend on full disclosure of all the facts, within the framework of the rules of evidence. To ensure that justice is done, it is imperative to the function of courts that compulsory process be available for the production of evidence needed either by the prosecution or by the defense.

Only recently the Court restated the ancient proposition of law, albeit in the context of a grand jury inquiry rather than a trial,

'that 'the public . . . has a right to every man's evidence,' except for those persons protected by a constitutional, common-law, or statutory privilege, United States v. Bryan, 339 U.S. 323, 331 (1949)); [additional citations].

The privileges referred to by the Court are designed to protect weighty and legitimate competing interests. Thus, the Fifth Amendment to the Constitution provides that no man 'shall be compelled in any criminal case to be a witness against himself.' And, generally, an attorney or a priest may not be required to disclose what has been revealed in professional confidence. These and other interests are recognized in law by privileges against forced disclosure, established in the Constitution, by statute, or at common law. Whatever their origins, these exceptions to the demand for every man's evidence are not lightly created nor expansively construed, for they are in derogation of the search for truth.

In this case the President challenges a subpoena served on him as a third party requiring the production of materials for use in a criminal prosecution; he does so on the claim that he has a privilege against disclosure of confidential communications. He does not place his claim of privilege on the ground they are military or diplomatic secrets. As to these areas of Art. II duties the courts have traditionally shown the utmost deference to Presidential responsibilities. In C. & S. Air Lines v. Waterman S.S. Corp., 333 U.S. 103, 111 (1948), dealing with Presidential authority involving foreign policy considerations, the Court said:

'The President, both as Commander-in-Chief and as the Nation's organ for foreign affairs, has available intelligence services whose reports are not and ought not to be published to the world. It would be intolerable that courts, without the relevant information, should review and perhaps nullify actions of the Executive taken on information properly held secret.'

In United States v. Reynolds, 345 U.S. 1 (1953), dealing with a claimant's demand for evidence in a Tort Claims Act case against the Government, the Court said:

'It may be possible to satisfy the court, from all the circumstances of the case, that there is a reasonable danger that compulsion of the evidence will expose military matters which, in the interest of national security, should not be divulged. When this is the case, the occasion for the privilege is appropriate, and the court should not jeopardize the security which the privilege is meant to protect by insisting upon an examination of the evidence, even by the judge alone, in chambers.' Id., at 10.

No case of the Court, however, has extended this high degree of deference to a President's generalized interest in confidentiality. Nowhere in the Constitution, as we have noted earlier, is there any explicit reference to a privilege of confidentiality, yet to the extent this interest relates to the effective discharge of a President's powers, it is constitutionally based.

The right to the production of all evidence at a criminal trial similarly has constitutional dimensions. The Sixth Amendment explicitly confers upon every defendant in a criminal trial the right 'to be confronted with the witnesses against him' and 'to have compulsory process for obtaining witnesses in his favor. Moreover, the Fifth Amendment also guarantees that no person shall be deprived of liberty without due process of law. It is the manifest duty of the courts to vindicate those guarantees, and to accomplish that it is essential that all relevant and admissible evidence be produced.

In this case we must weigh the importance of the general privilege of confidentiality of Presidential communications in performance of the President's responsibilities against the inroads of such a privilege on the fair administration of criminal justice. The interest in preserving confidentiality is weighty indeed and entitled to great respect. However, we cannot conclude that advisers will be moved to temper the candor of their remarks by the infrequent occasions of disclosure because of the possibility that such conversations will be called for in the context of a criminal prosecution.

On the other hand, the allowance of the privilege to withhold evidence that is demonstrably relevant in a criminal trial would cut deeply into the guarantee of due process of law and gravely impair the basic function of the courts. A President's acknowledged need for confidentiality in the communications of his office is general in nature, whereas the constitutional need for production of relevant evidence in a criminal proceeding is specific and central to the fair adjudication of a particular criminal case in the administration of justice. Without access to specific facts a criminal prosecution may be totally frustrated. The President's broad interest in confidentiality of communications will not be vitiated by disclosure of a limited number of conversations preliminarily shown to have some bearing on the pending criminal cases.

We conclude that when the ground for asserting privilege as to subpoenaed materials sought for use in a criminal trial is based only on the generalized interest in confidentiality, it cannot prevail over the fundamental demands of due process of law in the fair administration of criminal justice. The generalized assertion of privilege must yield to the demonstrated, specific need for evidence in a pending criminal trial.

* * *

Affirmed.

**Questions:** If the burglary at issue had been conducted against a foreign embassy rather than the Democratic National Committee, how might the *US v. Nixon* Court have viewed executive privilege? Survivors of civilians killed in the crash of a military aircraft sued the Air Force and requested the official accident investigation report which included information on secret electronic equipment being tested on the flight, claiming that the report was vital to their case. Does executive privilege apply? See *United States v. Reynolds,* 345 U.S. 1 (1953).

## CIVIL IMMUNITY

### NIXON V. FITZGERALD

457 U.S. 731 (1982)

JUSTICE POWELL delivered the opinion of the Court.

The plaintiff in this lawsuit seeks relief in civil damages from a former President of the United States. The claim rests on actions allegedly taken in the former President's official capacity during his tenure in office. The issue before us is the scope of the immunity possessed by the President of the United States.

In January 1970 the respondent A. Ernest Fitzgerald lost his job as a management analyst with the Department of the Air Force. Fitzgerald's dismissal occurred in the context of a departmental reorganization and reduction in force, in which his job was eliminated. In announcing the reorganization, the Air Force characterized the action as taken to promote economy and efficiency in the Armed Forces. * * *

On November 13, 1968, Fitzgerald appeared before the Subcommittee on Economy in Government of the Joint Economic Committee of the United States Congress. To the evident embarrassment of his superiors in the Department of Defense, Fitzgerald testified that cost-overruns on the C–5A transport plane could approximate $2 billion. He also revealed that unexpected technical difficulties had arisen during the development of the aircraft.

* * *

[Although the president initially suggested that Fitzgerald be reassigned, the White House Staff recommended he be dismissed, and the president agreed.] Absent any offer of alternative federal employment, Fitzgerald complained to the Civil Service Commission. In a letter of January 20, 1970, he alleged that his separation represented unlawful retaliation for his truthful testimony before a congressional Committee.

* * *

[After the U.S. Civil Service Commission rejected Fitzgerald's claim that he was dismissed as retaliation for his testimony, he sued in U.S. District Court, which ruled that the president could not claim absolute immunity, and allowed the matter to proceed to trial. On a collateral appeal to the District of Columbia Circuit Court of Appeals, that court similarly rejected this claimed immunity defense.]

As this Court has not ruled on the scope of immunity available to a President of the United States, we granted certiorari to decide this important issue.

* * *

This Court consistently has recognized that government officials are entitled to some form of immunity from suits for civil damages. In Spalding v. Vilas, 161 U.S. 483 (1896), the Court considered the immunity available to the Postmaster General in a suit for damages based upon his official acts. Drawing upon principles of immunity developed in English cases at common law, the Court concluded that "[t]he interests of the people" required a grant of absolute immunity to public officers. Id., at 498. In the absence of immunity, the Court reasoned, executive officials would hesitate to exercise their discretion in a way "injuriously affect[ing] the claims of particular individuals," id., at 499, even when the public interest required bold and unhesitating action. Considerations of "public policy and convenience" therefore compelled a judicial recognition of immunity from suits arising from official acts.

* * *

This case now presents the claim that the President of the United States is shielded by absolute immunity from civil damages liability. In the case of the President the inquiries into history and policy, though mandated independently by our cases, tend to converge. Because the Presidency did not exist through most of the development of common law, any historical analysis must draw its evidence primarily from our constitutional heritage and structure. Historical inquiry thus merges almost at its inception with the kind of "public policy" analysis appropriately undertaken by a federal court. This inquiry involves policies and principles that may be considered implicit in the nature of the President's office in a system structured to achieve effective government under a constitutionally mandated separation of powers.

* * *

Applying the principles of our cases to claims of this kind, we hold that petitioner, as a former President of the United States, is entitled to absolute immunity from damages liability predicated on his official acts. We consider this immunity a functionally mandated incident of the

President's unique office, rooted in the constitutional tradition of the separation of powers and supported by our history.

* * *

In defining the scope of an official's absolute privilege, this Court has recognized that the sphere of protected action must be related closely to the immunity's justifying purposes. Frequently our decisions have held that an official's absolute immunity should extend only to acts in performance of particular functions of his office. See [citations.] See, e.g., Spalding v. Vilas, 161 U.S., at 498 (privilege extends to all matters "committed by law to [an official's] control or supervision"); Barr v. Matteo, 360 U.S. 564, 575, (1959) (fact "that the action here taken was within the outer perimeter of petitioner's line of duty is enough to render the privilege applicable . . ."); [additional citation.] In view of the special nature of the President's constitutional office and functions, we think it appropriate to recognize absolute Presidential immunity from damages liability for acts within the "outer perimeter" of his official responsibility.

Under the Constitution and laws of the United States the President has discretionary responsibilities in a broad variety of areas, many of them highly sensitive. In many cases it would be difficult to determine which of the President's innumerable "functions" encompassed a particular action. In this case, for example, respondent argues that he was dismissed in retaliation for his testimony to Congress—a violation of 5 U.S.C. § 7211 (1976 ed., Supp.IV) and 18 U.S.C. § 1505. The Air Force, however, has claimed that the underlying reorganization was undertaken to promote efficiency. Assuming that petitioner Nixon ordered the reorganization in which respondent lost his job, an inquiry into the President's motives could not be avoided under the kind of "functional" theory asserted both by respondent and the dissent. Inquiries of this kind could be highly intrusive.

Here respondent argues that petitioner Nixon would have acted outside the outer perimeter of his duties by ordering the discharge of an employee who was lawfully entitled to retain his job in the absence of " 'such cause as will promote the efficiency of the service.' " Brief for Respondent 39, citing 5 U.S.C. § 7512(a). Because Congress has granted this legislative protection, respondent argues, no federal official could, within the outer perimeter of his duties of office, cause Fitzgerald to be dismissed without satisfying this standard in prescribed statutory proceedings.

This construction would subject the President to trial on virtually every allegation that an action was unlawful, or was taken for a forbidden purpose. Adoption of this construction thus would deprive absolute immunity of its intended effect. It clearly is within the President's constitutional and statutory authority to prescribe the manner in which the Secretary will conduct the business of the Air Force. See 10 U.S.C.

§ 8012(b). Because this mandate of office must include the authority to prescribe reorganizations and reductions in force, we conclude that petitioner's alleged wrongful acts lay well within the outer perimeter of his authority.

A rule of absolute immunity for the President will not leave the Nation without sufficient protection against misconduct on the part of the Chief Executive.38 There remains the constitutional remedy of impeachment.39 In addition, there are formal and informal checks on Presidential action that do not apply with equal force to other executive officials. The President is subjected to constant scrutiny by the press. Vigilant oversight by Congress also may serve to deter Presidential abuses of office, as well as to make credible the threat of impeachment.40 Other incentives to avoid misconduct may include a desire to earn reelection, the need to maintain prestige as an element of Presidential influence, and a President's traditional concern for his historical stature.

The existence of alternative remedies and deterrents establishes that absolute immunity will not place the President "above the law."41 For the President, as for judges and prosecutors, absolute immunity merely precludes a particular private remedy for alleged misconduct in order to advance compelling public ends.

For the reasons stated in this opinion, the decision of the Court of Appeals is reversed, and the case is remanded for action consistent with this opinion.

So ordered.

JUSTICE WHITE, with whom JUSTICE BRENNAN, JUSTICE MARSHALL, and JUSTICE BLACKMUN join, dissenting.

* * *

Attaching absolute immunity to the Office of the President, rather than to particular activities that the President might perform, places the President above the law. It is a reversion to the old notion that the King can do no wrong. Until now, this concept had survived in this country only in the form of sovereign immunity. That doctrine forecloses suit against the Government itself and against Government officials, but only when the suit against the latter actually seeks relief against the sovereign. Larson v. Domestic & Foreign Commerce Corp., 337 U.S. 682 (1949). Suit against an officer, however, may be maintained where it seeks specific relief against him for conduct contrary to his statutory authority or to the Constitution. Id., at 698. Now, however, the Court clothes the Office of the President with sovereign immunity, placing it beyond the law.

* * *

Taken at face value, the Court's position that as a matter of constitutional law the President is absolutely immune should mean that he is immune not only from damages actions but also from suits for injunctive relief, criminal prosecutions and, indeed, from any kind of judicial process. But there is no contention that the President is immune from criminal prosecution in the courts under the criminal laws enacted by Congress or by the States for that matter. Nor would such a claim be credible. The Constitution itself provides that impeachment shall not bar "Indictment, Trial, Judgment and Punishment, according to Law." Art. I, § 3, cl. 7. Similarly, our cases indicate that immunity from damages actions carries no protection from criminal prosecution. Supra, at 765–766.

Neither can there be a serious claim that the separation-of-powers doctrine insulates Presidential action from judicial review or insulates the President from judicial process. No argument is made here that the President, whatever his liability for money damages, is not subject to the courts' injunctive powers. See, e.g., [citations]. Petitioner's attempt to draw an analogy to the Speech or Debate Clause, Brief for Petitioner 45, one purpose of which is "to prevent . . . accountability before a possibly hostile judiciary," Gravel v. United States, 408 U.S., at 617, breaks down at just this point. While the Speech or Debate Clause guarantees that "for any Speech or Debate" Congressmen "shall not be questioned in any other Place," and, thus, assures that Congressmen, in their official capacity, shall not be the subject of the courts' injunctive powers, no such protection is afforded the Executive. Indeed, as the cases cited above indicate, it is the rule, not the exception, that executive actions—including those taken at the immediate direction of the President—are subject to judicial review. Regardless of the possibility of money damages against the President, then, the constitutionality of the President's actions or their legality under the applicable statutes can and will be subject to review. Indeed, in this very case, respondent Fitzgerald's dismissal was set aside by the Civil Service Commission as contrary to the applicable regulations issued pursuant to authority granted by Congress.

Nor can private damages actions be distinguished on the ground that such claims would involve the President personally in the litigation in a way not necessitated by suits seeking declaratory or injunctive relief against certain Presidential actions. The President has been held to be subject to judicial process at least since 1807. United States v. Burr, 25 F.Cas. 30 (No. 14,692d) (CC Va.1807) (Marshall, C.J., sitting as Circuit Justice). Burr "squarely ruled that a subpoena may be directed to the President." Nixon v. Sirica, 487 F.2d 700, 709 (1973). Chief Justice Marshall flatly rejected any suggestion that all judicial process, in and of itself, constitutes an unwarranted interference in the Presidency: "The guard, furnished to this high officer, to protect him from being harassed by vexatious and unnecessary subpoenas, is to be looked for in the conduct of a court after those subpoenas have issued; not in any circumstance which is to precede their being issued." 25 F.Cas., at 34 (emphasis added).

This position was recently rearticulated by the Court in United States v. Nixon, 418 U.S., at 706:

"[N]either the doctrine of separation of powers, nor the need for confidentiality . . . without more, can sustain an absolute, unqualified Presidential privilege of immunity from judicial process under all circumstances."

* * *

The wholesale claim that the President is entitled to absolute immunity in all of his actions stands on no firmer ground than did the claim that all Presidential communications are entitled to an absolute privilege, which was rejected in favor of a functional analysis, by a unanimous Court in United States v. Nixon, 418 U.S. 683 (1974). Therefore, whatever may be true of the necessity of such a broad immunity in certain areas of executive responsibility, the only question that must be answered here is whether the dismissal of employees falls within a constitutionally assigned executive function, the performance of which would be substantially impaired by the possibility of a private action for damages. I believe it does not.

* * *

The majority may be correct in its conclusion that "[a] rule of absolute immunity . . . will not leave the Nation without sufficient protection against misconduct on the part of the Chief Executive." Ante, at 757. Such a rule will, however, leave Mr. Fitzgerald without an adequate remedy for the harms that he may have suffered. More importantly, it will leave future plaintiffs without a remedy, regardless of the substantiality of their claims. The remedies in which the Court finds comfort were never designed to afford relief for individual harms. Rather, they were designed as political safety valves. Politics and history, however, are not the domain of the courts; the courts exist to assure each individual that he, as an individual, has enforceable rights

I find it ironic, as well as tragic, that the Court would so casually discard its own role of assuring "the right of every individual to claim the protection of the laws," Marbury v. Madison, 1 Cranch, at 163, in the name of protecting the principle of separation of powers. Accordingly, I dissent.

---

**Question:** How convinced are you that the president's actions in *Nixon v. Fitzgerald* were connected with his official duties?

## CLINTON V. JONES

520 U.S. 681 (1997)

JUSTICE STEVENS delivered the opinion of the Court.

This case raises a constitutional and a prudential question concerning the Office of the President of the United States. Respondent, a private citizen, seeks to recover damages from the current occupant of that office based on actions allegedly taken before his term began. The President submits that in all but the most exceptional cases the Constitution requires federal courts to defer such litigation until his term ends and that, in any event, respect for the office warrants such a stay. Despite the force of the arguments supporting the President's submissions, we conclude that they must be rejected.

Petitioner, William Jefferson Clinton, was elected to the Presidency in 1992, and re-elected in 1996. His term of office expires on January 20, 2001. In 1991 he was the Governor of the State of Arkansas. Respondent, Paula Corbin Jones, is a resident of California. In 1991 she lived in Arkansas, and was an employee of the Arkansas Industrial Development Commission.

On May 6, 1994, she commenced this action in the United States District Court for the Eastern District of Arkansas by filing a complaint naming petitioner and Danny Ferguson, a former Arkansas State Police officer, as defendants. The complaint alleges two federal claims, and two state law claims over which the federal court has jurisdiction because of the diverse citizenship of the parties. As the case comes to us, we are required to assume the truth of the detailed-but as yet untested-factual allegations in the complaint.

Those allegations principally describe events that are said to have occurred on the afternoon of May 8, 1991, during an official conference held at the Excelsior Hotel in Little Rock, Arkansas. The Governor delivered a speech at the conference; respondent-working as a state employee-staffed the registration desk. She alleges that Ferguson persuaded her to leave her desk and to visit the Governor in a business suite at the hotel, where he made "abhorrent" sexual advances that she vehemently rejected. She further claims that her superiors at work subsequently dealt with her in a hostile and rude manner, and changed her duties to punish her for rejecting those advances. Finally, she alleges that after petitioner was elected President, Ferguson defamed her by making a statement to a reporter that implied she had accepted petitioner's alleged overtures, and that various persons authorized to speak for the President publicly branded her a liar by denying that the incident had occurred.

Respondent seeks actual damages of $75,000, and punitive damages of $100,000. Her complaint contains four counts. The first charges that petitioner, acting under color of state law, deprived her of rights protected by the Constitution, in violation of Rev. Stat. § 1979, 42 U.S.C. § 1983. The second charges that petitioner and Ferguson engaged in a conspiracy to violate her federal rights, also actionable under federal law. See Rev. Stat. § 1980, 42 U.S.C. § 1985. The third is a state common law claim for intentional infliction of emotional distress, grounded primarily on the incident at the hotel. The fourth count, also based on state law, is for defamation, embracing both the comments allegedly made to the press by Ferguson and the statements of petitioner's agents. . . . . With the exception of the last charge, which arguably may involve conduct within the outer perimeter of the President's official responsibilities, it is perfectly clear that the alleged misconduct of petitioner was unrelated to any of his official duties as President of the United States and, indeed, occurred before he was elected to that office.

In response to the complaint, petitioner promptly advised the District Court that he intended to file a motion to dismiss on grounds of Presidential immunity, and requested the court to defer all other pleadings and motions until after the immunity issue was resolved, [which request was granted.] Petitioner thereupon filed a motion "to dismiss . . . without prejudice and to toll any statutes of limitation [that may be applicable] until he is no longer President, at which time the plaintiff may refile the instant suit." Record, Doc. No. 17. . . .

[The District Judge denied the motion to dismiss but stayed the trial until the end of Clinton's presidency. On appeal, the Circuit Court upheld the denial of the motion to dismiss, but reversed the stay, stating that "the President . . . is subject to the same laws that apply to all other members of our society."]

* * *

Petitioner's principal submission-that "in all but the most exceptional cases," Brief for Petitioner i, the Constitution affords the President temporary immunity from civil damages litigation arising out of events that occurred before he took office-cannot be sustained on the basis of precedent.

* * *

The principal rationale for affording certain public servants immunity from suits for money damages arising out of their official acts is inapplicable to unofficial conduct. In cases involving prosecutors, legislators, and judges we have repeatedly explained that the immunity serves the public interest in enabling such officials to perform their designated functions effectively without fear that a particular decision may give rise to personal liability.

* * *

That rationale provided the principal basis for our holding that a former President of the United States was "entitled to absolute immunity from damages liability predicated on his official acts," Fitzgerald, 457 U.S., at 749 . . . Our central concern was to avoid rendering the President "unduly cautious in the discharge of his official duties." 457 U.S., at 752, n. 32

This reasoning provides no support for an immunity for unofficial conduct. As we explained in Fitzgerald, "the sphere of protected action must be related closely to the immunity's justifying purposes." Id., at 755. Because of the President's broad responsibilities, we recognized in that case an immunity from damages claims arising out of official acts extending to the "outer perimeter of his authority." Id., at 757. But we have never suggested that the President, or any other official, has an immunity that extends beyond the scope of any action taken in an official capacity. See id., at 759 (Burger, C. J., concurring) (noting that "a President, like Members of Congress, judges, prosecutors, or congressional aides—all having absolute immunity—are not immune for acts outside official duties"); see also id., at 761, n. 4.

* * *

Petitioner's effort to construct an immunity from suit for unofficial acts grounded purely in the identity of his office is unsupported by precedent.

* * *

Petitioner's strongest argument supporting his immunity claim is based on the text and structure of the Constitution. He does not contend that the occupant of the Office of the President is "above the law," in the sense that his conduct is entirely immune from judicial scrutiny. The President argues merely for a postponement of the judicial proceedings that will determine whether he violated any law. His argument is grounded in the character of the office that was created by Article II of the Constitution, and relies on separation of powers principles that have structured our constitutional arrangement since the founding.

* * *

[P]etitioner contends that he occupies a unique office with powers and responsibilities so vast and important that the public interest demands that he devote his undivided time and attention to his public duties. He submits that—given the nature of the office—the doctrine of separation of powers places limits on the authority of the Federal Judiciary to interfere with the Executive Branch that would be transgressed by allowing this action to proceed.

* * *

Petitioner's predictive judgment finds little support in either history or the relatively narrow compass of the issues raised in this particular case. [I] in the more than 200-year history of the Republic, only three sitting Presidents have been subjected to suits for their private actions. If the past is any indicator, it seems unlikely that a deluge of such litigation will ever engulf the Presidency. As for the case at hand, if properly managed by the District Court, it appears to us highly unlikely to occupy any substantial amount of petitioner's time.

* * *

In sum, "[i]t is settled law that the separation-of-powers doctrine does not bar every exercise of jurisdiction over the President of the United States." Fitzgerald, 457 U.S., at 753–754. If the Judiciary may severely burden the Executive Branch by reviewing the legality of the President's official conduct, and if it may direct appropriate process to the President himself, it must follow that the federal courts have power to determine the legality of his unofficial conduct. The burden on the President's time and energy that is a mere by-product of such review surely cannot be considered as onerous as the direct burden imposed by judicial review and the occasional invalidation of his official actions. We therefore hold that the doctrine of separation of powers does not require federal courts to stay all private actions against the President until he leaves office.

* * *

If Congress deems it appropriate to afford the President stronger protection, it may respond with appropriate legislation. As petitioner notes in his brief, Congress has enacted more than one statute providing for the deferral of civil litigation to accommodate important public interests. Brief for Petitioner 34–36. See, e.g., 11 U.S.C. § 362 (litigation against debtor stayed upon filing of bankruptcy petition); Soldiers' and Sailors' Civil Relief Act of 1940, 50 U.S.C.App. §§ 501–525 (provisions governing, inter alia, tolling or stay of civil claims by or against military personnel during course of active duty). If the Constitution embodied the rule that the President advocates, Congress, of course, could not repeal it. But our holding today raises no barrier to a statutory response to these concerns.

The Federal District Court has jurisdiction to decide this case. Like every other citizen who properly invokes that jurisdiction, respondent has a right to an orderly disposition of her claims. Accordingly, the judgment of the Court of Appeals is affirmed.

It is so ordered.

# CRIMINAL IMMUNITY

## TRUMP V. VANCE

591 U.S. 786 (2020)

CHIEF JUSTICE ROBERTS delivered the opinion of the Court.

In our judicial system, "the public has a right to every man's evidence."1 Since the earliest days of the Republic, "every man" has included the President of the United States. Beginning with Jefferson and carrying on through Clinton, Presidents have uniformly testified or produced documents in criminal proceedings when called upon by federal courts. This case involves—so far as we and the parties can tell—the first state criminal subpoena directed to a President. The President contends that the subpoena is unenforceable. We granted certiorari to decide whether Article II and the Supremacy Clause categorically preclude, or require a heightened standard for, the issuance of a state criminal subpoena to a sitting President.

In the summer of 2018, the New York County District Attorney's Office opened an investigation into what it opaquely describes as "business transactions involving multiple individuals whose conduct may have violated state law." Brief for Respondent Vance 2. A year later, the office—acting on behalf of a grand jury—served a subpoena duces tecum (essentially a request to produce evidence) on Mazars USA, LLP, the personal accounting firm of President Donald J. Trump. The subpoena directed Mazars to produce financial records relating to the President and business organizations affiliated with him, including "[t]ax returns and related schedules," from "2011 to the present." App. to Pet. for Cert. 119a.2

[President Trump sought an injunction against enforcement of the subpoena, which the District Court denied. The Court of Appeals agreed with the denial.]

* * *

[The Court reviewed the background of federal courts requiring presidents to comply with subpoenas, including the 1807 Aaron Burr trial and *U.S. v. Nixon*.]

The history surveyed above all involved federal criminal proceedings. Here we are confronted for the first time with a subpoena issued to the President by a local grand jury operating under the supervision of a state court.

* * *

We begin with the question of absolute immunity. No one doubts that Article II guarantees the independence of the Executive Branch. As the head of that branch, the President "occupies a unique position in the constitutional scheme." Nixon v. Fitzgerald, 457 U. S. 731, 749 (1982). His duties, which range from faithfully executing the laws to commanding the Armed Forces, are of unrivaled gravity and breadth. Quite appropriately, those duties come with protections that safeguard the President's ability to perform his vital functions. See, e.g., ibid. (concluding that the President enjoys "absolute immunity from damages liability predicated on his official acts"); U.S. v. Nixon, 418 U. S., 683, 708 (1974) (recognizing that presidential communications are presumptively privileged).

In addition, the Constitution guarantees "the entire independence of the General Government from any control by the respective States." Farmers and Mechanics Sav. Bank of Minneapolis v. Minnesota, 232 U. S. 516, 521 (1914). As we have often repeated, "States have no power . . . to retard, impede, burden, or in any manner control the operations of the constitutional laws enacted by Congress." McCulloch v. Maryland, 4 Wheat. 316, 436 (1819). It follows that States also lack the power to impede the President's execution of those laws.

* * *

The President's primary contention, which the Solicitor General supports, is that complying with state criminal subpoenas would necessarily divert the Chief Executive from his duties. He grounds that concern in Nixon v. Fitzgerald, which recognized a President's "absolute immunity from damages liability predicated on his official acts." 457 U. S., at 749. In explaining the basis for that immunity, this Court observed that the prospect of such liability could "distract a President from his public duties, to the detriment of not only the President and his office but also the Nation that the Presidency was designed to serve." Id., at 753. The President contends that the diversion occasioned by a state criminal subpoena imposes an equally intolerable burden on a President's ability to perform his Article II functions.

But Fitzgerald did not hold that distraction was sufficient to confer absolute immunity. We instead drew a careful analogy to the common law absolute immunity of judges and prosecutors, concluding that a President, like those officials, must "deal fearlessly and impartially with the duties of his office"—not be made "unduly cautious in the discharge of [those] duties" by the prospect of civil liability for official acts. Id., at 751–752, and n. 32 (internal quotation marks omitted). Indeed, we expressly rejected immunity based on distraction alone 15 years later in Clinton v. Jones. There, President Clinton argued that the risk of being "distracted by the need to participate in litigation" entitled a sitting President to absolute immunity from civil liability, not just for official acts, as in Fitzgerald, but for private conduct as well. 520 U. S., at 694, n. 19. We disagreed with that rationale, explaining that the "dominant concern" in Fitzgerald was not mere distraction but the distortion of the Executive's "decisionmaking process" with respect to official acts that would stem from "worry as to the possibility of damages." 520 U. S., at 694, n. 19. The Court recognized that Presidents constantly face myriad demands on their attention, "some private, some political, and some as a result of official duty." Id., at 705, n. 40. But, the Court concluded, "[w]hile such distractions may be vexing to those subjected to them, they do not ordinarily implicate constitutional . . . concerns." Ibid.

The same is true of criminal subpoenas. Just as a "properly managed" civil suit is generally "unlikely to occupy any substantial amount of" a President's time or attention, id., at 702, two centuries of experience confirm that a properly tailored criminal subpoena will not normally hamper the performance of the President's constitutional duties. If anything, we expect that in the mine run of cases, where a President is subpoenaed during a proceeding targeting someone else, as Jefferson was, the burden on a President will ordinarily be lighter than the burden of defending against a civil suit.

The President, however, believes the district attorney is investigating him and his businesses. In such a situation, he contends, the "toll that criminal process . . . exacts from the President is even heavier" than the distraction at issue in Fitzgerald and Clinton, because "criminal litigation" poses unique burdens on the President's time and will generate a "considerable if not overwhelming degree of mental preoccupation." Brief for Petitioner 16–18, 30 (internal quotation marks omitted).

But the President is not seeking immunity from the diversion occasioned by the prospect of future criminal liability. Instead he concedes—consistent with the position of the Department of Justice—that state grand juries are free to investigate a sitting President with an eye toward charging him after the completion of his term. See Reply Brief 19 (citing Memorandum from Randolph D. Moss, Assistant Atty. Gen., Office of Legal Counsel, to the Atty. Gen.: A Sitting President's Amenability to Indictment and Criminal Prosecution, 24 Op. OLC 222, 257, n. 36 (Oct. 16, 2000)). The President's objection therefore must be limited to the additional distraction caused by the subpoena itself. But that argument runs up against the 200 years of precedent establishing that Presidents, and their official communications, are subject to judicial process, see Burr, 25 F. Cas., at 34, even when the President is under investigation, see Nixon, 418 U. S., at 706.

* * *

We next consider whether a state grand jury subpoena seeking a President's private papers must satisfy a heightened need standard. The Solicitor General would require a threshold showing that the evidence sought is "critical" for "specific charging decisions" and that the subpoena is a "last resort," meaning the evidence is "not available from any other source" and is needed "now, rather than at the end of the President's term." Brief for United States as Amicus Curiae 29, 32. * * *

We disagree, for three reasons. First, such a heightened standard would extend protection designed for official documents to the President's private papers.

* * *

Second, neither the Solicitor General nor Justice Alito has established that heightened protection against state subpoenas is necessary for the Executive to fulfill his Article II functions. * * * For if the state subpoena is not issued to manipulate, supra, at 16–17, the documents themselves are not protected, supra, at 18, and the Executive is not impaired, supra, at 12–15, then nothing in Article II or the Supremacy Clause supports holding state subpoenas to a higher standard than their federal counterparts.

Finally, in the absence of a need to protect the Executive, the public interest in fair and effective law enforcement cuts in favor of comprehensive access to evidence.

* * *

A President can raise subpoena-specific constitutional challenges, in either a state or federal forum. As previously noted, he can challenge the subpoena as an attempt to influence the performance of his official duties, in violation of the Supremacy Clause. See supra, at 17. This avenue protects against local political machinations "interposed as an obstacle to the effective operation of a federal constitutional power." United States v. Belmont, 301 U. S. 324, 332 (1937).

We affirm the judgment of the Court of Appeals and remand the case for further proceedings consistent with this opinion. It is so ordered.

JUSTICE ALITO, dissenting.

This case is almost certain to be portrayed as a case about the current President and the current political situation, but the case has a much deeper significance. While the decision will of course have a direct effect on President Trump, what the Court holds today will also affect all future Presidents—which is to say, it will affect the Presidency, and that is a matter of great and lasting importance to the Nation.

* * *

The event that precipitated this case is unprecedented. Respondent Vance, an elected state prosecutor, launched a criminal investigation of a sitting President and obtained a grand jury subpoena for his records. The specific question before us—whether the subpoena may be enforced—cannot be answered adequately without considering the broader question that frames it: whether the Constitution imposes restrictions on a State's deployment of its criminal law enforcement powers against a sitting President. If the Constitution sets no such limits, then a local prosecutor may prosecute a sitting President. And if that is allowed, it follows a fortiori that the subpoena at issue can be enforced. On the other hand, if the Constitution does not permit a State to prosecute a sitting President, the next logical question is whether the Constitution restrains any other prosecutorial or investigative weapons.

* * *

Just as our Constitution balances power against power among the branches of the Federal Government, it also divides power between the Federal Government and the States. The Constitution permitted the States to retain many of the sovereign powers that they previously possessed, see, e.g., Murphy v. National Collegiate Athletic Assn., 584 U. S. ___ (2018), but it gave the Federal Government powers that were deemed essential for the Nation's well-being and, indeed, its survival. And it provided for the Federal Government to be independent of and, within its allotted sphere, supreme over the States. Art. VI, cl. 2. Accordingly, a State may not block or interfere with the lawful work of the National Government.

This was an enduring lesson of Chief Justice Marshall's landmark opinion for the Court in McCulloch v. Maryland, 4 Wheat. 316 (1819). As is well known, the case concerned the attempt by the State of Maryland to regulate and tax the federally chartered Second Bank of the United States. After holding that Congress had the authority to establish the bank, id., at 425, Marshall's opinion went on to conclude that the State could not tax it. Marshall recognized that the States retained the "sovereign" power to tax persons and entities within their jurisdiction, id., at 429, but this power, he explained, "is subordinate to, and may be controlled by the constitution of the United States." Id., at 427. Noting the potency of the taxing power ("[a] right to tax without limit or control, is essentially a power to destroy," id., at 391), he concluded that a State's power to tax had to give way to Congress's authority to charter the bank. In his words, the state power to tax could not be used to "defeat the legitimate operations," id., at 427, of the Federal Government or "to retard, impede, burden, or in any manner control" it, id., at 436. Marshall thus held, not simply that Maryland was barred from assessing a crushing tax that threatened the bank's ability to operate, but that the State could not tax the bank at all.

* * *

Prior cases involving Presidential subpoenas have always applied special, heightened standards. In the Burr trial, Chief Justice Marshall was careful to note that "in no case of this kind would a court be required to proceed against the president as against an ordinary individual," and he held that the subpoena to President Jefferson was permissible only because the prosecutor had shown that the materials sought were "essential to the justice of the [pending criminal] case." United States v. Burr, 25 F. Cas. 187, 192 (No. 14,694) (CC Va. 1807).

In United States v. Nixon, 418 U. S. 683 (1974), where the Watergate Special Prosecutor subpoenaed tape recordings and documents under the control of President Nixon, this Court refused to quash the subpoena because there was a "demonstrated, specific need for [the] evidence in a pending criminal trial." Id., at 713.

* * *

The important point is not that the subpoena in this case should necessarily be governed by the particular tests used in these cases, most of which involved official records that were claimed to be privileged. Rather, the point is that we should not treat this subpoena like an ordinary grand jury subpoena and should not relegate a President to the meager defenses that are available when an ordinary grand jury subpoena is challenged. But that, at bottom, is the effect of the Court's decision.

* * *

The lesson we should take from Marshall's jurisprudence is the lesson of McCulloch—the importance of preventing a State from undermining the lawful exercise of authority conferred by the Constitution on the Federal Government. There is considerable irony in the Court's invocation of Marshall to defend a decision allowing a State's prosecutorial power to run roughshod over the functioning of a branch of the Federal Government.

The Court turns to United States v. Nixon, but that case arose under markedly different circumstances. Because the trial was in federal court, there was no issue of federalism, and the Court refused to order that the subpoena be quashed because of "the demonstrated, specific need for evidence in a pending criminal trial." Id., at 713. In the case now before us, a "demonstrated, specific need" is precisely what is lacking.

This Court's decision in Clinton v. Jones, provides no greater support for today's decision. In that case, as noted, the lawsuit was brought in federal, not state, court, and while the subject of that particular civil suit was embarrassing, the Court addressed the broad question whether a President is immune from civil suits " 'in all but the most exceptional cases.' " Id., at 692. There is no question that a criminal prosecution holds far greater potential for distracting a President and diminishing his ability to carry out his responsibilities than does the average civil suit.

The subpoena at issue here is unprecedented. Never before has a local prosecutor subpoenaed the records of a sitting President. The Court's decision threatens to impair the functioning of the Presidency and provides no real protection against the use of the subpoena power by the Nation's 2,300+ local prosecutors. Respect for the structure of Government created by the Constitution demands greater protection for an institution that is vital to the Nation's safety and well-being.

I therefore respectfully dissent.

---

**Questions:** Does it make a difference that in *Clinton v. Jones* past conduct was at issue, whereas in *Trump v. Vance* some of the documents related to the president's activities while in office? Does it matter that in one case the lawsuit was brought in federal court while the other originated in state court? How is Justice Marshall's legacy relevant to *Trump v. Vance*? In *Trump v. United States,* 603 U.S. 593 (2024), a majority of the Court held that presidential official act immunity extends to criminal prosecution. In the context of President Trump's alleged interference with the 2020 election, the Court remanded the case to a district court for a determination whether the acts in question were "official."

# CHAPTER 9

# ECONOMIC REGULATION

■ ■ ■

## CONTEXT & SOURCES

The Supreme Court's economic jurisprudence has always asked whether the prohibitions in the 5th and 14th Amendments against the deprivation of "life, liberty, or property, without due process of law" applied to the regulation of business. Paralleling the arcs of Commerce and Taxing Clause decisions, the Court moved from the "substantive due process" doctrine, strictly limiting such regulation, to the more deferential "rational basis" test. The cases here can similarly be categorized along a formalism-realism spectrum.

Paul Kens, *Lochner v. New York: Economic Regulation on Trial* (University Press of Kansas, 1998) evaluates the classically formalist decision most associated with substantive due process. In Helen Knowles, *Making Minimum Wage: Elsie Parrish versus the West Coast Hotel Company* (University of Oklahoma Press, 2021), the author explores the historical context and doctrinal arguments behind the Court's move to legal realism in employment cases. For a revisionist view that the justices' New Deal course change was more incremental than has been supposed, see Barry Cushman, *Rethinking the New Deal Court: The Structure of a Constitutional Revolution* (Oxford University Press, 1998).

### LOCHNER V. NEW YORK

198 U.S. 45 (1905)

* * *

This is a writ of error to the County Court of Oneida County, in the State of New York (to which court the record had been remitted), to review the judgment of the Court of Appeal of that State affirming the judgment of the Supreme Court, which itself affirmed the judgment of the County Court, convicting the defendant of a misdemeanor on an indictment under a statute of that State, known, by its short title, as the labor law. . . .The indictment averred that the defendant "wrongfully and unlawfully required and permitted an employee working for him in his biscuit, bread and cake bakery and confectionery establishment, at the city of Utica, in this county, to work more than sixty hours in one week," after having been theretofore convicted of a violation of the same act, and therefore, as averred, he committed the crime or misdemeanor, second offense.

* * *

[Both the intermediate and highest state appellate courts affirmed the conviction.]

MR. JUSTICE PECKHAM, after making the foregoing statement of the facts, delivered the opinion of the court:

The indictment, it will be seen, charges that the plaintiff in error violated the 110th section of article 8, chapter 415, of the Laws of 1897, known as the labor law of the state of New York, in that he wrongfully and unlawfully required and permitted an employee working for him to work more than sixty hours in one week.

* * *

It is not an act merely fixing the number of hours which shall constitute a legal day's work, but an absolute prohibition upon the employer permitting, under any circumstances, more than ten hours' work to be done in his establishment. The employee may desire to earn the extra money which would arise from his working more than the prescribed time, but this statute forbids the employer from permitting the employee to earn it.

The statute necessarily interferes with the right of contract between the employer and employees, concerning the number of hours in which the latter may labor in the bakery of the employer. The general right to make a contract in relation to his business is part of the liberty of the individual protected by the 14th Amendment of the Federal Constitution. *Allgeyer* v. *Louisiana*, 165 U. S. 578. Under that provision no state can deprive any person of life, liberty, or property without due process of law. The right to purchase or to sell labor is part of the liberty protected by this amendment, unless there are circumstances which exclude the right. There are, however, certain powers, existing in the sovereignty of each state in the Union, somewhat vaguely termed police powers, the exact description and limitation of which have not been attempted by the courts. Those powers, broadly stated, and without, at present, any attempt at a more specific limitation, relate to the safety, health, morals, and general welfare of the public. Both property and liberty are held on such reasonable conditions as may be imposed by the governing power of the state in the exercise of those powers, and with such conditions the 14th Amendment was not designed to interfere. *Mugler* v. *Kansas*, 123 U. S. 623; [additional citations].

The state, therefore, has power to prevent the individual from making certain kinds of contracts, and in regard to them the Federal Constitution offers no protection. If the contract be one which the state, in the legitimate exercise of its police power, has the right to prohibit, it is not prevented from prohibiting it by the 14th Amendment. Contracts in violation of a statute, either of the Federal or state government, or a contract to let one's property for immoral purposes, or to do any other unlawful act, could obtain no protection from the Federal Constitution, as coming under the liberty of person or of free contract. Therefore, when the state, by its legislature, in the assumed exercise of its police powers, has passed an act which seriously limits the right to labor or the right of contract in regard to their means of livelihood between persons who are *sui juris* (both employer and employee), it becomes of great importance to determine which shall prevail,—the right of the individual to labor for such time as he may choose, or the right of the state to prevent the individual from laboring, or from entering into any contract to labor, beyond a certain time prescribed by the state.

This court has recognized the existence and upheld the exercise of the police powers of the states in many cases which might fairly be considered as border ones, and it has, in the course of its determination of questions regarding the asserted invalidity of such statutes, on the ground of their violation of the rights secured by the Federal Constitution, been guided by rules of a very liberal nature, the application of which has resulted, in numerous instances, in upholding the validity of state statutes thus assailed. Among the later cases where the state law has been upheld by this court is that of *Holden* v. *Hardy*, 169 U. S. 366. A provision in the act of the legislature of Utah was there under consideration, the act limiting the employment of workmen in all underground mines or workings, to eight hours per day, 'except in cases of emergency, where life or property is in imminent danger.' It also limited the hours of labor in smelting and other institutions for the reduction or refining of ores or metals to eight hours per day, except in like cases of emergency. The act was held to be a valid exercise of the police powers of the state. A review of many of the cases on the subject, decided by this and other courts, is given in the opinion. It was held that the kind of employment, mining, smelting, etc., and the character of the employees in such kinds of labor, were such as to make it reasonable and proper for the state to interfere to prevent the employees from being constrained by the rules laid down by the proprietors in regard to labor. The following citation from the observations of the supreme court of Utah in that case was made by the judge writing the opinion of this court, and approved: 'This law applies only to the classes subjected by their employment to the peculiar conditions and effects attending underground mining and work in smelters, and other works for the reduction and refining of ores. Therefore it is not necessary to discuss or decide whether the legislature can fix the hours of labor in other employments.'

* * *

The latest case decided by this court, involving the police power, is that of *Jacobson* v. *Massachusetts*, decided at this term and reported in 197 U. S. 11, 25. It related to compulsory vaccination, and the law was held vaild as a proper exercise of the police powers with reference to the public health. It was stated in the opinion that it was a case 'of an adult who, for aught that appears, was himself in perfect health and a fit subject of vaccination, and yet, while remaining in the community, refused to obey the statute and the regulation, adopted in execution of its provisions, for the protection of the public health and the public safety, confessedly endangered by the presence of a dangerous disease.' That case is also far from covering the one now before the court.

* * *

It must, of course, be conceded that there is a limit to the valid exercise of the police power by the state. There is no dispute concerning this general proposition. Otherwise the 14th Amendment would have no efficacy and the legislatures of the states would have unbounded power, and it would be enough to say that any piece of legislation was enacted to conserve the morals, the health, or the safety of the people; such legislation would be valid, no matter how absolutely without foundation the claim might be. The claim of the police power would be a mere pretext,—become another and delusive name for the supreme sovereignty of the state to be exercised free from constitutional restraint. This is not contended for. In every case that comes before this court, therefore, where legislation of this character is concerned, and where the protection of the Federal Constitution is sought, the question necessarily arises: Is this a fair, reasonable, and appropriate exercise of the police power of the state, or is it an unreasonable, unnecessary, and arbitrary interference with the right of the individual to his personal liberty, or to enter into those contracts in relation to labor which may seem to him appropriate or necessary for the support of himself and his family? Of course the liberty of contract relating to labor includes both parties to it. The one has as much right to purchase as the other to sell labor. * * *

The question whether this act is valid as a labor law, pure and simple, may be dismissed in a few words. There is no reasonable ground for interfering with the liberty of person or the right of free contract, by determining the hours of labor, in the occupation of a baker. There is no contention that bakers as a class are not equal in intelligence and capacity to men in other trades or manual occupations, or that they are not able to assert their rights and care for themselves without the protecting arm of the state, interfering with their independence of judgment and of action. They are in no sense wards of the state. Viewed in the light of a purely labor law, with no reference whatever to the question of health, we think that a law like the one before us involves neither the safety, the morals, nor the welfare, of the public, and that the interest of the public is not in the slightest degree affected by such an act. The law must be upheld, if at all, as a law pertaining to the health of the individual engaged in the occupation of a baker. It does not affect any other portion of the public than those who are engaged in that occupation. Clean and wholesome bread does not depend upon whether the baker works but ten hours per day or only sixty hours a week. The limitation of the hours of labor does not come within the police power on that ground.

It is a question of which of two powers or rights shall prevail,—the power of the state to legislate or the right of the individual to liberty of person and freedom of contract. The mere assertion that the subject relates, though but in a remote degree, to the public health, does not necessarily render the enactment valid. The act must have a more direct relation, as a means to an end, and the end itself must be appropriate and legitimate, before an act can be held to be valid which interferes with the general right of an individual to be free in his person and in his power to contract in relation to his own labor.

* * *

We think the limit of the police power has been reached and passed in this case. There is, in our judgment, no reasonable foundation for holding this to be necessary or appropriate as a health law to safeguard the public health, or the health of the individuals who are following the trade of a baker. If this statute be valid, and if, therefore, a proper case is made out in which to deny the right of an individual, *sui juris*, as employer or employee, to make contracts for the labor of the latter under the protection of the provisions of the Federal Constitution, there would seem to be no length to which legislation of this nature might not go. The case differs widely, as we have already stated, from the expressions of this court in regard to laws of this nature, as stated in *Holden* v. *Hardy*, 169 U. S. 366, and *Jacobson* v. *Massachusetts*, 197 U. S. 11.

We think that there can be no fair doubt that the trade of a baker, in and of itself, is not an unhealthy one to that degree which would authorize the legislature to interfere with the right to labor, and with the right of free contract on the part of the individual, either as employer or employee In looking through statistics regarding all trades and occupations, it may be true that the trade of a baker does not appear to be as healthy as some other trades, and is also vastly more healthy than still others. To the common understanding the trade of a baker has never been regarded as an unhealthy one. Very likely physicians would not recommend the exercise of that or of any other trade as a remedy for ill health. Some occupations are more healthy than others, but we think there are none which might not come under the power of the legislature to supervise and control the hours of working therein, if the mere fact that the occupation is not absolutely and perfectly healthy is to confer that right upon the legislative department of the government. It might be safely affirmed that almost all occupations more or less affect the health. There must be more than the mere fact of the possible existence of some small amount of unhealthiness to warrant legislative interference with liberty. It is unfortunately true that labor, even in any department, may possibly carry with it the seeds of unhealthiness. But are we all, on that account, at the mercy of legislative majorities? A printer, a tinsmith, a locksmith, a carpenter, a cabinetmaker, a dry goods clerk, a bank's, a lawyer's, or a physician's clerk, or a clerk in almost any kind of business, would all come under the power of the legislature, on this assumption. No trade, no occupation, no mode of earning one's living, could escape this all-pervading power, and the acts of the legislature in limiting the hours of labor in all employments would be valid, although such limitation might seriously cripple the ability of the laborer to support himself and his family. In our large cities there are many buildings into which the sun penetrates for but a short time in each day, and these buildings are occupied by people carrying on the business of bankers, brokers, lawyers, real estate, and many other kinds of business, aided by many clerks, messengers, and other employees. Upon the assumption of the validity of this act under review, it is not possible to say that an act, prohibiting lawyers' or bank clerks, or others, from contracting to labor for their employers more than eight hours a day would be invalid. It might be said that it is unhealthy to work more than that number of hours in an apartment lighted by artificial light during the working hours of the day; that the occupation of the bank clerk, the lawyer's clerk, the real estate clerk, or the broker's clerk, in such offices is therefore unhealthy, and the legislature, in its paternal wisdom, must, therefore, have the right to legislate on the subject of, and to limit, the hours for such labor; and, if it exercises that power, and its validity be questioned, it is sufficient to say, it has reference to the public health; it has reference to the health of the employees condemned to labor day after day in buildings where the sun never shines; it is a health law, and therefore it is valid, and cannot be questioned by the courts.

It is also urged, pursuing the same line of argument, that it is to the interest of the state that its population should be strong and robust, and therefore any legislation which may be said to tend to make people healthy must be valid as health laws, enacted under the police power. If this be a valid argument and a justification for this kind of legislation, it follows that the protection of the Federal Constitution from undue interference with liberty of person and freedom of contract is visionary, wherever the law is sought to be justified as a valid exercise of the police power. Scarcely any law but might find shelter under such assumptions, and conduct, properly so called, as well as contract, would come under the restrictive sway of the legislature. Not only the hours of employees, but the hours of employers, could be regulated, and doctors, lawyers, scientists, all professional men, as well as athletes and artisans, could be forbidden to fatigue their brains and bodies by prolonged hours of exercise, lest the fighting strength of the state be impaired. We mention these extreme cases because the contention is extreme. We do not believe in the soundness of the views which uphold this law. On the contrary, we think that such a law as this, although passed in the assumed exercise of the police power, and as relating to the public health, or the health of the employees named, is not within that power, and is invalid. The act is not, within any fair meaning of the term, a health law, but is an illegal interference with the rights of individuals, both employers and employees, to make contracts regarding labor upon such terms as they may think best, or which they may agree upon with the other parties to such contracts. Statutes of the nature of that under review, limiting the hours in which grown and intelligent men may labor to earn their living, are mere meddlesome interferences with the rights of the individual, and they are not saved from condemnation by the claim that they are passed in the exercise of the police power and upon the subject of the health of the individual whose rights are interfered with, unless there be some fair ground, reasonable in and of itself, to say that there is material danger to the public health, or to the health of the employees, if the hours of labor are not curtailed. If this be not clearly the case, the individuals whose rights are thus made the subject of legislative interference are under the protection of the Federal Constitution regarding their liberty of contract as well as of person; and the legislature of the state has no power to limit their right as proposed in this statute. All that it could properly do has been done by it with regard to the conduct of bakeries, as provided for in the other sections of the act, above set forth. These several sections provide for the inspection of the premises where the bakery is carried on, with regard to furnishing proper wash rooms and water closets, apart from the bake room, also with regard to providing proper drainage, plumbing, and painting; the sections, in addition, provide for the height of the ceiling, the cementing or tiling of floors, where necessary in the opinion of the factory inspector, and for other things of that nature; alterations are also provided for, and are to be made where necessary in the opinion of the inspector, in order to comply with the provisions of the statute. These various sections may be wise and valid regulations, and they certainly go to the full extent of providing for the cleanliness and the healthiness, so far as possible, of the quarters in which bakeries are to be conducted. Adding to all these requirements a prohibition to enter into any contract of labor in a bakery for more than a certain number of hours a week is, in our judgment, so wholly beside the matter of a proper, reasonable, and fair provision as to run counter to that liberty of person and of free contract provided for in the Federal Constitution.

* * *

This interference on the part of the legislatures of the several states with the ordinary trades and occupations of the people seems to be on the increase. In the supreme court of New York, in the case of *People* v. *Beattie*, appellate division, first department, decided in 1904 (96 App. Div. 383), a statute regulating the trade of horseshoeing, and requiring the person practising such trade to be examined, and to obtain a certificate from a board of examiners and file the same with the clerk of the county wherein the person proposes to practise such trade, was held invalid, as an arbitrary interference with personal liberty and private property without due process of law. The attempt was made, unsuccessfully, to justify it as a health law.

* * *

It is impossible for us to shut our eyes to the fact that many of the laws of this character, while passed under what is claimed to be the police power for the purpose of protecting the public health or welfare, are, in reality, passed from other motives. We are justified in saying so when, from the character of the law and the subject upon which it legislates, it is apparent that the public health or welfare bears but the most remote relation to the law. * * *

It is manifest to us that the limitation of the hours of labor as provided for in this section of the statute under which the indictment was found, and the plaintiff in error convicted, has no such direct relation to, and no such substantial effect upon, the health of the employee, as to justify us in regarding the section as really a health law. It seems to us that the real object and purpose were simply to regulate the hours of labor between the master and his employees (all being men, *Sui juris*), in a private business, not dangerous in any degree to morals, or in any real and substantial degree to the health of the employees. Under such circumstances the freedom of master and employee to contract with each other in relation to their employment, and in defining the same, cannot be prohibited or interfered with, without violating the Federal Constitution.

The judgment of the Court of Appeals of New York, as well as that of the Supreme Court and of the County Court of Oneida County, must be reversed and the case remanded to the County Court for further proceedings not inconsistent with this opinion.

*Reversed.*

MR. JUSTICE HOLMES dissenting:

I regret sincerely that I am unable to agree with the judgment in this case, and that I think it my duty to express my dissent.

This case is decided upon an economic theory which a large part of the country does not entertain. If it were a question whether I agreed with that theory, I should desire to study it further and long before making up my mind. But I do not conceive that to be my duty, because I strongly believe that my agreement or disagreement has nothing to do with the right of a majority to embody their opinions in law. It is settled by various decisions of this court that state constitutions and state laws may regulate life in many ways which we as legislators might think as injudicious, or if you like as tyrannical, as this, and which, equally with this, interfere with the liberty to contract. Sunday laws and usury laws are ancient examples. A more modern one is the prohibition of lotteries. The liberty of the citizen to do as he likes so long as he does not interfere with the liberty of others to do the same, which has been a shibboleth for some well-known writers, is interfered with by school laws, by the Post office, by every state or municipal institution which takes his money for purposes thought desirable, whether he likes it or not. The 14th Amendment does not enact Mr. Herbert Spencer's Social Statics. The other day we sustained the Massachusetts vaccination law. *Jacobson* v. *Massachusetts*, 197 U. S. 11,—United States and state statutes and decisions cutting down the liberty to contract by way of combination are familiar to this court. *Northern Securities Co.* v. *United States*, 193 U. S. 197. Two years ago we upheld the prohibition of sales of stock on margins, or for future delivery, in the Constitution of California. *Otis* v. *Parker*, 187 U. S. 606. The decision sustaining an eight-hour law for miners is still recent. *Holden* v. *Hardy*, 169 U. S. 366. Some of these laws embody convictions or prejudices which judges are likely to share. Some may not. But a Constitution is not intended to embody a particular economic theory, whether of paternalism and the organic relation of the citizen to the state or of *laissez faire*. It is made for people of fundamentally differing views, and the accident of our finding certain opinions natural and familiar, or novel, and even shocking, ought not to conclude our judgment upon the question whether statutes embodying them conflict with the Constitution of the United States.

General propositions do not decide concrete cases. The decision will depend on a judgment or intuition more subtle than any articulate major premise. But I think that the proposition just stated, if it is accepted, will carry us far toward the end. Every opinion tends to become a law. I think that the word 'liberty,' in the 14th Amendment, is perverted when it is held to prevent the natural outcome of a dominant opinion, unless it can be said that a rational and fair man necessarily would admit that the statute proposed would infringe fundamental principles as they have been understood by the traditions of our people and our law. It does not need research to show that no such sweeping condemnation can be passed upon the statute before us. A reasonable man might think it a proper measure on the score of health. Men whom I certainly could not pronounce unreasonable would uphold it as a first instalment of a general regulation of the hours of work. Whether in the latter aspect it would be open to the charge of inequality I think it unnecessary to discuss.

---

**Questions:** How did the majority and dissent in *Lochner* differ on the issue of whether the employees were capable of negotiating contracts with the employer on an equal basis? Who benefitted from the Court's striking down the legislation? The District of Columbia had a minimum wage law applying to women in 1923. With *Lochner* as precedent, how would a court rule on this legislation's constitutionality? See *Adkins v. Children's Hospital,* 261 U.S. 525 (1923). Significantly, in *Muller v. Oregon,* 208 U.S. 412 (1908), the justices upheld a state law limiting women's working *hours,* based on physical and social gender distinctions.

## WEST COAST HOTEL V. PARRISH

300 U.S. 379 (1937)

* * *

MR. CHIEF JUSTICE HUGHES delivered the opinion of the Court.

This case presents the question of the constitutional validity of the minimum wage law of the state of Washington.

The act, entitled 'Minimum Wages for Women,' authorizes the fixing of minimum wages for women and minors. Laws 1913 (Washington) c. 174, p. 602, Remington's Rev.Stat.(1932) § 7623 et seq.

* * *

The appellant conducts a hotel. The appellee Elsie Parrish was employed as a chambermaid and (with her husband) brought this suit to recover the difference between the wages paid her and the minimum wage fixed pursuant to the state law. The minimum wage was $14.50 per week of 48 hours. The appellant challenged the act as repugnant to the due process clause of the Fourteenth Amendment of the Constitution of the United States. The Supreme Court of the state, reversing the trial court, sustained the statute and directed judgment for the plaintiffs. Parrish v. West Coast Hotel Co., 185 Wash. 581. The case is here on appeal.

The appellant relies upon the decision of this Court in Adkins v. Children's Hospital, 261 U.S. 525, which held invalid the District of Columbia Minimum Wage Act (40 Stat. 960) which was attacked under the due process clause of the Fifth Amendment. On the argument at bar, counsel for the appellees attempted to distinguish the Adkins Case upon the ground that the appellee was employed in a hotel and that the business of an innkeeper was affected with a public interest. That effort at distinction is obviously futile, as it appears that in one of the cases ruled by the Adkins opinion the employee was a woman employed as an elevator operator in a hotel. Adkins v. Lyons, 261 U.S. 525, at page 542.

* * *

. . .The Supreme Court of Washington has upheld the minimum wage statute of that state. It has decided that the statute is a reasonable exercise of the police power of the state. In reaching that conclusion, the state court has invoked principles long established by this Court in the application of the Fourteenth Amendment. The state court has refused to regard the decision in the Adkins Case as determinative and has pointed to our decisions both before and since that case as justifying its position. We are of the opinion that this ruling of the state court demands on our part a re-examination of the Adkins Case. The importance of the question, in which many states having similar laws are concerned, the close division by which the decision in the Adkins Case was reached, and the economic conditions which have supervened, and in the light of which the reasonableness of the exercise of the protective power of the state must be considered, make it not only appropriate, but we think imperative, that in deciding the present case the subject should receive fresh consideration.

* * *

The principle which must control our decision is not in doubt. The constitutional provision invoked is the due process clause of the Fourteenth Amendment governing the states, as the due process clause invoked in the Adkins Case governed Congress. In each case the violation alleged by those attacking minimum wage regulation for women is deprivation of freedom of contract. What is this freedom? The Constitution does not speak of freedom of contract. It speaks of liberty and prohibits the deprivation of liberty without due process of law. In prohibiting that deprivation, the Constitution does not recognize an absolute and uncontrollable liberty. Liberty in each of its phases has its history and connotation. But the liberty safeguarded is liberty in a social organization which requires the protection of law against the evils which menace the health, safety, morals, and welfare of the people. Liberty under the Constitution is thus necessarily subject to the restraints of due process, and regulation which is reasonable in relation to its subject and is adopted in the interests of the community is due process.

This essential limitation of liberty in general governs freedom of contract in particular. More than twenty-five years ago we set forth the applicable principle in these words, after referring to the cases where the liberty guaranteed by the Fourteenth Amendment had been broadly described.

'But it was recognized in the cases cited, as in many others, that freedom of contract is a qualified, and not an absolute, right. There is no absolute freedom to do as one wills or to contract as one chooses. The guaranty of liberty does not withdraw from legislative supervision that wide department of activity which consists of the making of contracts, or deny to government the power to provide restrictive safeguards. Liberty implies the absence of arbitrary restraint, not immunity from reasonable regulations and prohibitions imposed in the interests of the community.' Chicago, Burlington & Quincy R. Co. v. McGuire, 219 U.S. 549.

This power under the Constitution to restrict freedom of contract has had many illustrations. That it may be exercised in the public interest with respect to contracts between employer and employee is undeniable. Thus statutes have been sustained limiting employment in underground mines and smelters to eight hours a day (Holden v. Hardy, 169 U.S. 366); in requiring redemption in cash of store orders or other evidences of indebtedness issued in the payment of wages (Knoxville Iron Co. v. Harbison, 183 U.S. 13); in forbidding the payment of seamen's wages in advance (Patterson v. The Bark Eudora, 190 U.S. 169); in making it unlawful to contract to pay miners employed at quantity rates upon the basis of screened coal instead of the weight of the coal as originally produced in the mine (McLean v. Arkansas, 211 U.S. 539); in prohibiting contracts limiting liability for injuries to employees (Chicago, Burlington & Quincy R. Co. v. McGuire, supra); in limiting hours of work of employees in manufacturing establishments (Bunting v. Oregon, 243 U.S. 426); and in maintaining workmen's compensation laws (New York Central R. Co. v. White, 243 U.S. 188; Mountain Timber Co. v. Washington, 243 U.S. 219). In dealing with the relation of employer and employed, the Legislature has necessarily a wide field of discretion in order that there may be suitable protection of health and safety, and that peace and good order may be promoted through regulations designed to insure wholesome conditions of work and freedom from oppression. Chicago, Burlington & Quincy R. Co. v. McGuire, supra, 219 U.S. 549, at 570.

The point that has been strongly stressed that adult employees should be deemed competent to make their own contracts was decisively met nearly forty years ago in Holden v. Hardy, supra, where we pointed out the inequality in the footing of the parties. We said (Id., 169 U.S. 366):

'The legislature has also recognized the fact, which the experience of legislators in many states has corroborated, that the proprietors of these establishments and their operatives do not stand upon an equality, and that their interests are, to a certain extent, conflicting. The former naturally desire to obtain as much labor as possible from their employers, while the latter are often induced by the fear of discharge to conform to regulations which their judgment, fairly exercised, would pronounce to be detrimental to their health or strength. In other words, the proprietors lay down the rules, and the laborers are practically constrained to obey them. In such cases self-interest is often an unsafe guide, and the legislature may properly interpose its authority.'

And we added that the fact 'that both parties are of full age, and competent to contract, does not necessarily deprive the state of the power to interfere, where the parties do not stand upon an equality, or where the public heath demands that one party to the contract shall be protected against himself.' 'The state still retains an interest in his welfare, however reckless he may be. The whole is no greater than the sum of all the parts, and when the individual health, safety, and welfare are sacrificed or neglected, the state must suffer.'

It is manifest that this established principle is peculiarly applicable in relation to the employment of women in whose protection the state has a special interest. That phase of the subject received elaborate consideration in Muller v. Oregon (1908) 208 U.S. 412, where the constitutional authority of the state to limit the working hours of women was sustained. We emphasized the consideration that 'woman's physical structure and the performance of maternal functions place her at a disadvantage in the struggle for subsistence' and that her physical well being 'becomes an object of public interest and care in order to preserve the strength and vigor of the race.' We emphasized the need of protecting women against oppression despite her possession of contractual rights. We said that 'though limitations upon personal and contractual rights may be removed by legislation, there is that in her disposition and habits of life which will operate against a full assertion of those rights. She will still be where some legislation to protect her seems necessary to secure a real equality of right.' Hence she was 'properly placed in a class by herself, and legislation designed for her protection may be sustained, even when like legislation is not necessary for men, and could not be sustained.' We concluded that the limitations which the statute there in question 'places upon her contractual powers, upon her right to agree with her employer, as to the time she shall labor' were 'not imposed solely for her benefit, but also largely for the benefit of all.' Again, in Quong Wing v. Kirkendall, 223 U.S. 59, 63, in referring to a differentiation with respect to the employment of women, we said that the Fourteenth Amendment did not interfere with state power by creating a 'fictitious equality.' We referred to recognized classifications on the basis of sex with regard to hours of work and in other matters, and we observed that the particular points at which that difference shall be enforced by legislation were largely in the power of the state. In later rulings this Court sustained the regulation of hours of work of women employees in Riley v. Massachusetts, 232 U.S. 671 (factories), Miller v. Wilson, 236 U.S. 373 (hotels), and Bosley v. McLaughlin, 236 U.S. 385 (hospitals).

* * *

We think that . . . the decision in the Adkins Case was a departure from the true application of the principles governing the regulation by the state of the relation of employer and employed. Those principles have been reenforced by our subsequent decisions. Thus in Radice v. New York, 264 U.S. 292, we sustained the New York statute which restricted the employment of women in restaurants at night. In O'Gorman & Young v. Hartford Fire Insurance Company, 282 U.S. 251, which upheld an act regulating the commissions of insurance agents, we pointed to the presumption of the constitutionality of a statute dealing with a subject within the scope of the police power and to the absence of any factual foundation of record for deciding that the limits of power had been transcended. In Nebbia v. New York, 291 U.S. 502, dealing with the New York statute providing for minimum prices for milk, the general subject of the regulation of the use of private property and of the making of private contracts received an exhaustive examination, and we again declared that if such laws 'have a reasonable relation to a proper legislative purpose, and are neither arbitrary nor discriminatory, the requirements of due process are satisfied'; that 'with the wisdom of the policy adopted, with the adequacy or practicability of the law enacted to forward it, the courts are both incompetent and unauthorized to deal'; that 'times without number we have said that the Legislature is primarily the judge of the necessity of such an enactment, that every possible presumption is in favor of its validity, and that though the court may hold views inconsistent with the wisdom of the law, it may not be annulled unless palpably in excess of legislative power.' Id., 291 U.S. 502, at 537, 538.

With full recognition of the earnestness and vigor which characterize the prevailing opinion in the Adkins Case, we find it impossible to reconcile that ruling with these well-considered declarations. What can be closer to the public interest than the health of women and their protection from unscrupulous and overreaching employers? And if the protection of women is a legitimate end of the exercise of state power, how can it be said that the requirement of the payment of a minimum wage fairly fixed in order to meet the very necessities of existence is not an admissible means to that end? The Legislature of the state was clearly entitled to consider the situation of women in employment, the fact that they are in the class receiving the least pay, that their bargaining power is relatively weak, and that they are the ready victims of those who would take advantage of their necessitous circumstances. The Legislature was entitled to adopt measures to reduce the evils of the 'sweating system,' the exploiting of workers at wages so low as to be insufficient to meet the bare cost of living, thus making their very helplessness the occasion of a most injurious competition. The Legislature had the right to consider that its minimum wage requirements would be an important aid in carrying out its policy of protection. The adoption of similar requirements by many states evidences a deep seated conviction both as to the presence of the evil and as to the means adapted to check it. Legislative response to that conviction cannot be regarded as arbitrary or capricious and that is all we have to decide. Even if the wisdom of the policy be regarded as debatable and its effects uncertain, still the Legislature is entitled to its judgment.

There is an additional and compelling consideration which recent economic experience has brought into a strong light. The exploitation of a class of workers who are in an unequal position with respect to bargaining power and are thus relatively defenseless against the denial of a living wage is not only detrimental to their health and well being, but casts a direct burden for their support upon the community. What these workers lose in wages the taxpayers are called upon to pay. The bare cost of living must be met. We may take judicial notice of the unparalleled demands for relief which arose during the recent period of depression and still continue to an alarming extent despite the degree of economic recovery which has been achieved. It is unnecessary to cite official statistics to establish what is of common knowledge through the length and breadth of the land. While in the instant case no factual brief has been presented, there is no reason to doubt that the state of Washington has encountered the same social problem that is present elsewhere. The community is not bound to provide what is in effect a subsidy for unconscionable employers. The community may direct its law-making power to correct the abuse which springs from their selfish disregard of the public interest. The argument that the legislation in question constitutes an arbitrary discrimination, because it does not extend to men, is unavailing. This Court has frequently held that the legislative authority, acting within its proper field, is not bound to extend its regulation to all cases which it might possibly reach. The Legislature 'is free to recognize degrees of harm and it may confine its restrictions to those classes of cases where the need is deemed to be clearest.' If 'the law presumably hits the evil where it is most felt, it is not to be overthrown because there are other instances to which it might have been applied.' There is no 'doctrinaire requirement' that the legislation should be couched in all embracing terms. Carroll v. Greenwich Insurance Co., 199 U.S. 401, 411, [additional citations]. This familiar principle has repeatedly been applied to legislation which singles out women, and particular classes of women, in the exercise of the state's protective power. Miller v. Wilson, supra, 236 U.S. 373, at 384; [additional citations]. Their relative need in the presence of the evil, no less than the existence of the evil itself, is a matter for the legislative judgment.

Our conclusion is that the case of Adkins v. Children's Hospital, supra, should be, and it is, overruled. The judgment of the Supreme Court of the state of Washington is affirmed.

---

**Question:** In 1955, an Oklahoma statute prohibited opticians from duplicating or replacing eyeglass lenses without a prescription from an ophthalmologist or optometrist (i.e., a doctor). Is the law constitutional after *West Coast Hotel*? See *Williamson v. Lee Optical,* 348 U.S. 483 (1955). As the justices abandoned substantive due process they increasingly upheld legislation under the minimal "rational basis" standard.

## FEDERAL COMMUNICATIONS COMMISSION v. BEACH COMMUNICATIONS

508 U.S. 307 (1993)

* * *

JUSTICE THOMAS delivered the opinion of the Court.

The Cable Communications Policy Act of 1984 (Cable Act), 98 Stat. 2779, amended the Communications Act of 1934, 47 U.S.C. § 151 et seq., to establish a national framework for regulating cable television. One objective of the Cable Act was to set out "franchise procedures and standards which encourage the growth and development of cable systems and which assure that cable systems are responsive to the needs and interests of the local community." § 601(2), 47 U.S.C. § 521(2). To that end, Congress provided for the franchising of cable systems by local governmental authorities, § 621(a), 47 U.S.C. § 541(a), and prohibited any person from operating a cable system without a franchise, subject to certain exceptions, § 621(b), 47 U.S.C. § 541(b). Section 602(7) of the Communications Act, as amended, 47 U. S. C. A. § 522(7) (Supp. 1993), determines the reach of the franchise requirement by defining the operative term "cable system." A cable system means any facility designed to provide video programming to multiple subscribers through "closed transmission paths," but does not include, inter alia,

"a facility that serves only subscribers in 1 or more multiple unit dwellings under common ownership, control, or management, unless such facility or facilities us[e] any public right of way." § 602(7)(B), 47 U. S. C. A. § 522(7)(B) (Supp. 1993).

In part, this provision tracks a regulatory "private cable" exemption previously promulgated by the Federal Communications Commission (FCC or Commission) pursuant to pre-existing authority under the Communications Act. See 47 CFR § 76.5(a) (1984) (exempting from the definition of "cable television system" "any such facility that serves or will serve only subscribers in one or more multiple unit dwellings under common ownership, control, or management"). The earlier regulatory exemption derived in turn from the Commission's first set of cable rules, published in 1965. See Rules re Microwave Served CATV, 38 F. C. C. 683, 741 (1965) (exempting from the definition of "community antenna television system" "any such facility which serves only the residents of one or more apartment dwellings under common ownership, control, or management, and commercial establishments located on the premises of such an apartment house"). The Cable Act narrowed the terms of the regulatory exemption by further excluding from the exemption any closed transmission facilities that use public rights of way.

This case arises out of an FCC proceeding clarifying the agency's interpretation of the term "cable system" as it is used in the Cable Act. See In re Definition of a Cable Television System, 5 F. C. C. Rcd. 7638 (1990). In this proceeding, the Commission addressed the application of the exemption codified in § 602(7)(B) to satellite master antenna television (SMATV) facilities. Unlike a traditional cable television system, which delivers video programming to a large community of subscribers through coaxial cables laid under city streets or along utility lines, an SMATV system typically receives a signal from a satellite through a small satellite dish located on a rooftop and then retransmits the signal by wire to units within a building or complex of buildings. See 5 F. C. C. Rcd., at 7639. The Commission ruled that an SMATV system that serves multiple buildings via a network of interconnected physical transmission lines is a cable system, unless it falls within the § 602(7)(B) exemption. See id., at 7639–7640. Consistent with the plain terms of the statutory exemption, the Commission concluded that such an SMATV system is subject to the franchise requirement if its transmission lines interconnect separately owned and managed buildings or if its lines use or cross any public right of way. See id., at 7641–7642.

Respondents Beach Communications, Inc., Maxtel Limited Partnership, Pacific Cablevision, and Western Cable Communications, Inc.—SMATV operators that would be subject to franchising under the Cable Act as construed by the Commission—petitioned the Court of Appeals for review. The Court of Appeals rejected respondents' statutory challenge to the Commission's interpretation, but a majority of the court found merit in the claim that § 602(7) violates the implied equal protection guarantee of the Due Process Clause. 959 F. 2d 975 (1992). In the absence of what it termed "the predominant rationale for local franchising" (use of public rights of way), the court saw no rational basis "[o]n the record," and was "unable to imagine" any conceivable basis, for distinguishing between those facilities exempted by the statute and those SMATV cable systems that link separately owned and managed buildings. Id., at 987. The court remanded the record and directed the FCC to provide "additional 'legislative facts' " to justify the distinction. Ibid.

A report subsequently filed by the Commission failed to satisfy the Court of Appeals. The Commission stated that it was "unaware of any desirable policy or other considerations . . . that would support the challenged distinctions," other than those offered by a concurring member of the court. App. to Pet. for Cert. 50a. The concurrence had believed it sufficient that Congress could have reasoned that SMATV systems serving separately owned buildings are more similar to traditional cable systems than are facilities serving commonly owned buildings, in terms of the problems presented for consumers and the potential for regulatory benefits. See 959 F. 2d, at 990 (Mikva, C. J., concurring in part and concurring in judgment).

In a second opinion, the majority found this rationale to be "a naked intuition, unsupported by conceivable facts or policies," 965 F. 2d 1103, 1105 (1992), and held that "the Cable Act violates the equal protection component of the Fifth Amendment, insofar as it imposes a discriminatory franchising requirement," id., at 1104. [n.4] The court declared the franchise requirement void to the extent it covers respondents and similarly situated SMATV operators. Id., at 1106.

Because the Court of Appeals held an Act of Congress unconstitutional, we granted certiorari. We now reverse.

Whether embodied in the Fourteenth Amendment or inferred from the Fifth, equal protection is not a license for courts to judge the wisdom, fairness, or logic of legislative choices. In areas of social and economic policy, a statutory classification that neither proceeds along suspect lines nor infringes fundamental constitutional rights must be upheld against equal protection challenge if there is any reasonably conceivable state of facts that could provide a rational basis for the classification. See [citations]. Where there are "plausible reasons" for Congress' action, "our inquiry is at an end." United States Railroad Retirement Bd. v. Fritz, supra, at 179. This standard of review is a paradigm of judicial restraint. "The Constitution presumes that, absent some reason to infer antipathy, even improvident decisions will eventually be rectified by the democratic process and that judicial intervention is generally unwarranted no matter how unwisely we may think a political branch has acted." Vance v. Bradley, 440 U.S. 93, 97 (1979) (footnote omitted).

On rational basis review, a classification in a statute such as the Cable Act comes to us bearing a strong presumption of validity, see Lyng v. Automobile Workers, 485 U.S. 360, 370 (1988), and those attacking the rationality of the legislative classification have the burden "to negative every conceivable basis which might support it," Lehnhausen v. Lake Shore Auto Parts Co., 410 U.S. 356, 364 (1973) (internal quotation marks omitted). See also Hodel v. Indiana, 452 U.S. 314, 331–332 (1981). Moreover, because we never require a legislature to articulate its reasons for enacting a statute, it is entirely irrelevant for constitutional purposes whether the conceived reason for the challenged distinction actually motivated the legislature. United States Railroad Retirement Bd. v. Fritz, supra, at 179. See Flemming v. Nestor, 363 U.S. 603, 612 (1960). Thus, the absence of " 'legislative facts' " explaining the distinction "[o]n the record," 294 U. S. App. D. C., at 389, 959 F. 2d, at 987, has no significance in rational basis analysis. See Nordlinger v. Hahn, 505 U. S. ___, ___ (1992) (slip op., at 13) (equal protection "does not demand for purposes of rational basis review that a legislature or governing decisionmaker actually articulate at any time the purpose or rationale supporting its classification"). In other words, a legislative choice is not subject to courtroom fact finding and may be based on rational speculation unsupported by evidence or empirical data. See Vance v. Bradley, supra, at 111. See also Minnesota v. Clover Leaf Creamery Co., 449 U.S. 456, 464 (1981). " 'Only by faithful adherence to this guiding principle of judicial review of legislation is it possible to preserve to the legislative branch its rightful independence and its ability to function.' " Lehnhausen, supra, at 365 (quoting Carmichael v. Southern Coal & Coke Co., 301 U.S. 495, 510 (1937)).

These restraints on judicial review have added force "where the legislature must necessarily engage in a process of line drawing." United States Railroad Retirement Bd. v. Fritz, 449 U. S., at 179. Defining the class of persons subject to a regulatory requirement—much like classifying governmental beneficiaries—inevitably requires that some persons who have an almost equally strong claim to favored treatment be placed on different sides of the line, and the fact [that] the line might have been drawn differently at some points is a matter for legislative, rather than judicial, consideration." Ibid. (internal quotation marks and citation omitted). The distinction at issue here represents such a line: By excluding from the definition of "cable system" those facilities that serve commonly owned or managed buildings without using public rights of way, § 602(7)(B) delineates the bounds of the regulatory field. Such scope of coverage provisions are unavoidable components of most economic or social legislation. In establishing the franchise requirement, Congress had to draw the line somewhere; it had to choose which facilities to franchise. This necessity renders the precise coordinates of the resulting legislative judgment virtually unreviewable, since the legislature must be allowed leeway to approach a perceived problem incrementally. See, e. g., Williamson v. Lee Optical of Okla., Inc., 348 U.S. 483 (1955):

"The problem of legislative classification is a perennial one, admitting of no doctrinaire definition. Evils in the same field may be of different dimensions and proportions, requiring different remedies. Or so the legislature may think. Or the reform may take one step at a time, addressing itself to the phase of the problem which seems most acute to the legislative mind. The legislature may select one phase of one field and apply a remedy there, neglecting the others. The prohibition of the Equal Protection Clause goes no further than the invidious discrimination." Id., at 489 (citations omitted).

Applying these principles, we conclude that the common ownership distinction is constitutional. There are at least two possible bases for the distinction; either one suffices. First, Congress borrowed § 602(7)(B) from pre-Cable Act regulations, and although the existence of a prior administrative scheme is certainly not necessary to the rationality of the statute, it is plausible that Congress also adopted the FCC's earlier rationale. Under that rationale, common ownership was thought to be indicative of those systems for which the costs of regulation would outweigh the benefits to consumers. Because the number of subscribers was a similar indicator, the Commission also exempted cable facilities that served fewer than 50 subscribers. See 47 CFR § 76.5(a) (1984). In explaining both exemptions, the Commission stated:

"[N]ot all [systems] can be subject to effective regulation with the resources available nor is regulation necessarily needed in every instance. A sensible regulatory program requires that a division between the regulated and unregulated be made in a manner which best conserves regulatory energies and allows the most cost-effective use of available resources. In attempting to make this division, we have focused on subscriber numbers as well as the multiple unit dwelling indicia on the theory that the very small are inefficient to regulate and can safely be ignored in terms of their potential for impact on broadcast service to the public and on multiple unit dwelling facilities on the theory that this effectively establishes certain maximum size limitations." In re Definition of a Cable Television System, 67 F. C. C. 2d 716, 726 (1978).

This regulatory efficiency model, originally suggested by Chief Judge Mikva in his concurring opinion, provides a conceivable basis for the common ownership exemption. A legislator might rationally assume that systems serving only commonly owned or managed buildings without crossing public rights of way would typically be limited in size or would share some other attribute affecting their impact on the welfare of cable viewers such that regulators could "safely ignor[e]" these systems.

Respondents argue that Congress did not intend common ownership to be a surrogate for small size, since Congress simultaneously rejected the FCC's 50-subscriber exemption by omitting it from the Cable Act. Brief for Respondents 22. Whether the posited reason for the challenged distinction actually motivated Congress is "constitutionally irrelevant," United States Railroad Retirement Bd. v. Fritz, supra, at 179 (internal quotation marks omitted), and, in any event, the FCC's explanation indicates that both common ownership and number of subscribers were considered indicia of "very small" cable systems. Respondents also contend that an SMATV operator could increase his subscription base and still qualify for the exemption simply by installing a separate satellite dish on each building served. Brief for Respondents 42. The additional cost of multiple dishes and associated transmission equipment, however, would impose an independent constraint on system size.

Furthermore, small size is only one plausible ownership related factor contributing to consumer welfare. Subscriber influence is another. Where an SMATV system serves a complex of buildings under common ownership or management, individual subscribers could conceivably have greater bargaining power vis a vis the cable operator (even if the number of dwelling units were large), since all the subscribers could negotiate with one voice through the common owner or manager. Such an owner might have substantial leverage, because he could withhold permission to operate the SMATV system on his property. He would also have an incentive to guard the interests of his tenants. Thus, there could be less need to establish regulatory safeguards for subscribers in commonly owned complexes. Respondents acknowledge such possibilities, see id., at 44, and we certainly cannot say that these assumptions would be irrational.

There is a second conceivable basis for the statutory distinction. Suppose competing SMATV operators wish to sell video programming to subscribers in a group of contiguous buildings, such as a single city block, which can be interconnected by wire without crossing a public right of way. If all the buildings belong to one owner or are commonly managed, that owner or manager could freely negotiate a deal for all subscribers on a competitive basis. But if the buildings are separately owned and managed, the first SMATV operator who gains a foothold by signing a contract and installing a satellite dish and associated transmission equipment on one of the buildings would enjoy a powerful cost advantage in competing for the remaining subscribers: he could connect additional buildings for the cost of a few feet of cable, whereas any competitor would have to recover the cost of his own satellite headend facility. Thus, the first operator could charge rates well above his cost and still undercut the competition. This potential for effective monopoly power might theoretically justify regulating the latter class of SMATV systems and not the former.

The Court of Appeals quite evidently believed that the crossing or use of a public right of way is the only conceivable basis upon which Congress could rationally require local franchising of SMATV systems. See 965 F. 2d, at 1105; 959 F. 2d, at 987. As we have indicated, however, there are plausible rationales unrelated to the use of public rights of way for regulating cable facilities serving separately owned and managed buildings. The assumptions underlying these rationales may be erroneous, but the very fact that they are "arguable" is sufficient, on rational basis review, to "immuniz[e]" the congressional choice from constitutional challenge. Vance v. Bradley, 440 U. S., at 112.

The judgment of the Court of Appeals is reversed, and the case is remanded for further proceedings consistent with this opinion.

So ordered.

---

**Questions:** In *FCC v. Beach,* how important was the legislature's actual motivation behind its passage of the statute? After this decision, has rational basis review become so minimal as to be meaningless?

# CHAPTER 10

# THE TAKINGS CLAUSE

■ ■ ■

## CONTEXT & SOURCES

Constitutional land use planning begins with the 5th Amendment's statement that "private property" shall not "be taken for public use, without just compensation." The Takings Clause has been the subject of much litigation on government interference with property, with the Supreme Court cases here addressing the categories of regulatory, physical, and total takings, as well as defining "public use."

The philosophical claims of society and owners underpinning the Takings Clause are elaborated in Bruce A. Ackerman, *Private Property and the Constitution* (Yale University Press, 1978). On Justice Holmes's formulation of the balancing test for regulatory takings, including his interactions with other Court members, see Joseph F. DiMento, "Mining the Archives of *Pennsylvania Coal*: Heaps of Constitutional Mischief, 11 *Journal of Legal History* 396 (1990). Vicki Been, "Lucas v. The Green Machine: Using the Takings Clause to Promote More Efficient Regulation," *Property Stories* (Gerald Korngold & Andrew P. Morriss eds., Foundation, 2d ed. 2009) dissects the ruling that decided when government action constitutes a total taking. For the history and aftermath of the controversial *Kelo* decision, see Guy F. Burnett, *The Safeguard of Liberty and Property: The Supreme Court,* Kelo v. New London, *and the Takings Clause* (Lexington Books, 2016).

## REGULATORY TAKINGS

### PENNSYLVANIA COAL CO. V. MAHON

260 U.S. 393 (1922)

* * *

MR. JUSTICE HOLMES delivered the opinion of the Court.

This is a bill in equity brought by the defendants in error to prevent the Pennsylvania Coal Company from mining under their property in such way as to remove the supports and cause a subsidence of the surface and of their house. The bill sets out a deed executed by the Coal Company in 1878, under which the plaintiffs claim. The deed conveys the surface but in express terms reserves the right to remove all the coal under the same and the grantee takes the premises with the risk and waives all claim for damages that may arise from mining out the coal. But the plaintiffs say that whatever may have been the Coal Company's rights, they were taken away by an Act of Pennsylvania, approved May 27, 1921 (P. L. 1198), commonly known there as the Kohler Act. The Court of Common Pleas found that if not restrained the defendant would cause the damage to prevent which the bill was brought but denied an injunction, holding that the statute if applied to this case would be unconstitutional. On appeal the Supreme Court of the State agreed that the defendant had contract and property rights protected by the Constitution of the United States, but held that the statute was a legitimate exercise of the police power and directed a decree for the plaintiffs, A writ of error was granted bringing the case to this Court.

The statute forbids the mining of anthracite coal in such way as to cause the subsidence of, among other things, any structure used as a human habitation, with certain exceptions, including among them land where the surface is owned by the owner of the underlying coal and is distant more than one hundred and fifty feet from any improved property belonging to any other person. As applied to this case the statute is admitted to destroy previously existing rights of property and contract. The question is whether the police power can be stretched so far.

Government hardly could go on if to some extent values incident to property could not be diminished without paying for every such change in the general law. As long recognized some values are enjoyed under an implied limitation and must yield to the police power. But obviously the implied limitation must have its limits or the contract and due process clauses are gone. One fact for consideration in determining such limits is the extent of the diminution. When it reaches a certain magnitude, in most if not in all cases there must be an exercise of eminent domain and compensation to sustain the act. So the question depends upon the particular facts. The greatest weight is given to the judgment of the legislature but it always is open to interested parties to contend that the legislature has gone beyond its constitutional power.

This is the case of a single private house. No doubt there is a public interest even in this, as there is in every purchase and sale and in all that happens within the commonwealth. Some existing rights may be modified even in such a case. Rideout v. Knox, 148 Mass. 368. But usually in ordinary private affairs the public interest does not warrant much of this kind of interference. A source of damage to such a house is not a public nuisance even if similar damage is inflicted on others in different places. The damage is not common or public. Wesson v. Washburn Iron Co., 13 Allen (Mass.) 96, 103. The extent of the public interest is shown by the statute to be limited, since the statute ordinarily does not apply to land when the surface is owned by the owner of the coal. Furthermore, it is not justified as a protection of personal safety. That could be provided for by notice. Indeed the very foundation of this bill is that the defendant gave timely notice of its intent to mine under the house. On the other hand the extent of the taking is great. It purports to abolish what is recognized in Pennsylvania as an estate in land—a very valuable estate—and what is declared by the Court below to be a contract hitherto binding the plaintiffs. If we were called upon to deal with the plaintiffs' position alone we should think it clear that the statute does not disclose a public interest sufficient to warrant so extensive a destruction of the defendant's constitutionally protected rights.

But the case has been treated as one in which the general validity of the act should be discussed. The Attorney General of the State, the City of Scranton and the representatives of other extensive interests were allowed to take part in the argument below and have submitted their contentions here. It seems, therefore, to be our duty to go farther in the statement of our opinion, in order that it may be known at once, and that further suits should not be brought in vain.

It is our opinion that the act cannot be sustained as an exercise of the police power, so far as it affects the mining of coal under streets or cities in places where the right to mine such coal has been reserved. As said in a Pennsylvania case, 'For practical purposes, the right to coal consists in the right to mine it.' Commonwealth v. Clearview Coal Co., 256 Pa. 328, 331. What makes the right to mine coal valuable is that it can be exercised with profit. To make it commercially impracticable to mine certain coal has very nearly the same effect for constitutional purposes as appropriating or destroying it. This we think that we are warranted in assuming that the statute does.

It is true that in Plymouth Coal Co. v. Pennsylvania, 232 U. S. 531, it was held competent for the legislature to require a pillar of coal to the left along the line of adjoining property, that with the pillar on the other side of the line would be a barrier sufficient for the safety of the employees of either mine in case the other should be abandoned and allowed to fill with water. But that was a requirement for the safety of employees invited into the mine, and secured an average reciprocity of advantage that has been recognized as a justification of various laws.

The rights of the public in a street purchased or laid out by eminent domain are those that it has paid for. If in any case its representatives have been so short sighted as to acquire only surface rights without the right of support we see no more authority for supplying the latter without compensation than there was for taking the right of way in the first place and refusing to pay for it because the public wanted it very much. The protection of private property in the Fifth Amendment presupposes that it is wanted for public use, but provides that it shall not be taken for such use without compensation. A similar assumption is made in the decisions upon the Fourteenth Amendment. Hairston v. Danville & Western Ry. Co., 208 U. S. 598, 605. When this seemingly absolute protection is found to be qualified by the police power, the natural tendency of human nature is to extend the qualification more and more until at last private property disappears. But that cannot be accomplished in this way under the Constitution of the United States.

The general rule at least is that while property may be regulated to a certain extent, if regulation goes too far it will be recognized as a taking. It may be doubted how far exceptional cases, like the blowing up of a house to stop a conflagration, go and if they go beyond the general rule, whether they do not stand as much upon tradition as upon principle. Bowditch v. Boston, 101 U. S. 16. In general it is not plain that a man's misfortunes or necessities will justify his shifting the damages to his neighbor's shoulders. Spade v. Lynn & Boston Ry. Co., 172 Mass. 488. We are in danger of forgetting that a strong public desire to improve the public condition is not enough to warrant achieving the desire by a shorter cut than the constitutional way of paying for the change. As we already have said this is a question of degree—and therefore cannot be disposed of by general propositions. But we regard this as going beyond any of the cases decided by this Court. The late decisions upon laws dealing with the congestion of Washington and New York, caused by the war, dealt with laws intended to meet a temporary emergency and providing for compensation determined to be reasonable by an impartial board. They were to the verge of the law but fell far short of the present act. Block & Hirsh, 256 U. S. 135; [additional citations].

We assume, of course, that the statute was passed upon the conviction that an exigency existed that would warrant it, and we assume that an exigency exists that would warrant the exercise of eminent domain. But the question at bottom is upon whom the loss of the changes desired should fall. So far as private persons or communities have seen fit to take the risk of acquiring only surface rights, we cannot see that the fact that their risk has become a danger warrants the giving to them greater rights than they bought.

Decree reversed.

MR. JUSTICE BRANDEIS dissenting.

The Kohler Act prohibits, under certain conditions, the mining of anthracite coal within the limits of a city in such a manner or to such an extent 'as to cause the * * * subsidence of * * * any dwelling or other structure used as a human habitation, or any factory, store, or other industrial or mercantile establishment in which human labor is employed.' Act Pa. May 27, 1921, § 1 (P. L. 1198). Coal in place is land, and the right of the owner to use his land is not absolute. He may not so use it as to create a public nuisance, and uses, once harmless, may, owing to changed conditions, seriously threaten the public welfare. Whenever they do, the Legislature has power to prohibit such uses without paying compensation; and the power to prohibit extends alike to the manner, the character and the purpose of the use. Are we justified in declaring that the Legislature of Pennsylvania has, in restricting the right to mine anthracite, exercised this power so arbitrarily as to violate the Fourteenth Amendment?

Every restriction upon the use of property imposed in the exercise of the police power deprives the owner of some right theretofore enjoyed, and is, in that sense, an abridgment by the state of rights in property without making compensation. But restriction imposed to protect the public health, safety or morals from dangers threatened is not a taking. The restriction here in question is merely the prohibition of a noxious use. The property so restricted remains in the possession of its owner. The state does not appropriate it or make any use of it. The state merely prevents the owner from making a use which interferes with paramount rights of the public. Whenever the use prohibited ceases to be noxious—as it may because of further change in local or social conditions—the restriction will have to be removed and the owner will again be free to enjoy his property as heretofore.

The restriction upon the use of this property cannot, of course, be lawfully imposed, unless its purpose is to protect the public. But the purpose of a restriction does not cease to be public, because incidentally some private persons may thereby receive gratuitously valuable special benefits. Thus, owners of low buildings may obtain, through statutory restrictions upon the height of neighboring structures, benefits equivalent to an easement of light and air. Welch v. Swasey, 214 U. S. 91. Compare [additional citations]. Furthermore, a restriction, though imposed for a public purpose, will not be lawful, unless the restriction is an appropriate means to the public end. But to keep coal in place is surely an appropriate means of preventing subsidence of the surface; and ordinarily it is the only available means. Restriction upon use does not become inappropriate as a means, merely because it deprives the owner of the only use to which the property can then be profitably put. The liquor and the oleomargarine cases settled that. Mugler v. Kansas, 123 U. S. 623, 668; Powell v. Pennsylvania, 127 U. S. 678, 682. See also [additional citations]. Nor is a restriction imposed through exercise of the police power inappropriate as a means, merely because the same end might be effected through exercise of the power of eminent domain, or otherwise at public expense. Every restriction upon the height of buildings might be secured through acquiring by eminent domain the right of each owner to build above the limiting height; but it is settled that the state need not resort to that power. Compare [additional citations]. If by mining anthracite coal the owner would necessarily unloose poisonous gases, I suppose no one would doubt the power of the state to prevent the mining, without buying his coal fields. And why may not the state, likewise, without paying compensation, prohibit one from digging so deep or excavating so near the surface, as to expose the community to like dangers? In the latter case, as in the former, carrying on the business would be a public nuisance.

It is said that one fact for consideration in determining whether the limits of the police power have been exceeded is the extent of the resulting diminution in value, and that here the restriction destroys existing rights of property and contract. But values are relative. If we are to consider the value of the coal kept in place by the restriction, we should compare it with the value of all other parts of the land. That is, with the value not of the coal alone, but with the value of the whole property. The rights of an owner as against the public are not increased by dividing the interests in his property into surface and subsoil. The sum of the rights in the parts can not be greater than the rights in the whole. The estate of an owner in land is grandiloquently described as extending ab orco usque ad coelum. But I suppose no one would contend that by selling his interest above 100 feet from the surface he could prevent the state from limiting, by the police power, the height of structures in a city. And why should a sale of underground rights bar the state's power? For aught that appears the value of the coal kept in place by the restriction may be negligible as compared with the value of the whole property, or even as compared with that part of it which is represented by the coal remaining in place and which may be extracted despite the statute. Ordinarily a police regulation, general in operation, will not be held void as to a particular property, although proof is offered that owing to conditions peculiar to it the restriction could not reasonably be applied. See [citations]. But even if the particular facts are to govern, the statute should, in my opinion be upheld in this case. For the defendant has failed to adduce any evidence from which it appears that to restrict its mining operations was an unreasonable exercise of the police power. Compare [additional citations]. Where the surface and the coal belong to the same person, self-interest would ordinarily prevent mining to such an extent as to cause a subsidence. It was, doubtless, for this reason that the Legislature, estimating the degrees of danger, deemed statutory restriction unnecessary for the public safety under such conditions.

* * *

A prohibition of mining which causes subsidence of such structures and facilities is obviously enacted for a public purpose; and it seems, likewise, clear that mere notice of intention to mine would not in this connection secure the public safety. Yet it is said that these provisions of the act cannot be sustained as an exercise of the police power where the right to mine such coal has been reserved. The conclusion seems to rest upon the assumption that in order to justify such exercise of the police power there must be 'an average reciprocity of advantage' as between the owner of the property restricted and the rest of the community; and that here such reciprocity is absent. Reciprocity of advantage is an important consideration, and may even be an essential, where the state's power is exercised for the purpose of conferring benefits upon the property of a neighborhood, as in drainage projects (Wurts v. Hoagland, 114 U. S. 606; Fallbrook Irrigation District v. Bradley, 164 U. S. 112); or upon adjoining owners, as by party wall provisions (Jackman v. Rosenbaum Co., 260 U. S. 22, decided October 23, 1922). But where the police power is exercised, not to confer benefits upon property owners but to protect the public from detriment and danger, there is in my opinion, no room for considering reciprocity of advantage. There was no reciprocal advantage to the owner prohibited from using his oil tanks in 248 U. S. 498; his brickyard, in 239 U. S. 394; his livery stable, in 237 U. S. 171; his billiard hall, in 225 U. S. 623; his oleomargarine factory, in 127 U. S. 678; his brewery, in 123 U. S. 623; unless it be the advantage of living and doing business in a civilized community. That reciprocal advantage is given by the act to the coal operators.

---

**Questions:** In *Mahon,* what is the majority's rule for determining whether regulation goes "too far" and becomes a taking? What is the dissent's?

## PENN. CENTRAL TRANSP. CO. V. CITY OF NEW YORK

438 U.S. 104 (1976)

MR. JUSTICE BRENNAN delivered the opinion of the Court.

The question presented is whether a city may, as part of a comprehensive program to preserve historic landmarks and historic districts, place restrictions on the development of individual historic landmarks—in addition to those imposed by applicable zoning ordinances—without effecting a "taking" requiring the payment of "just compensation."

* * *

Over the past 50 years, all 50 States and over 500 municipalities have enacted laws to encourage or require the preservation of buildings and areas with historic or aesthetic importance.

* * *

New York City, responding to similar concerns and acting pursuant to a New York State enabling Act,5 adopted its Landmarks Preservation Law in 1965. See N.Y.C. Admin. Code, ch. 8-A, § 205–1.0 et seq. (1976). The city acted from the conviction that "the standing of [New York City] as a world-wide tourist center and world capital of business, culture and government" would be threatened if legislation were not enacted to protect historic landmarks and neighborhoods from precipitate decisions to destroy or fundamentally alter their character. § 205–1.0(a). The city believed that comprehensive measures to safeguard desirable features of the existing urban fabric would benefit its citizens in a variety of ways: e. g., fostering "civic pride in the beauty and noble accomplishments of the past"; protecting and enhancing "the city's attractions to tourists and visitors"; "support[ing] and stimul[ating] business and industry"; "strengthen[ing] the economy of the city"; and promoting "the use of historic districts, landmarks, interior landmarks and scenic landmarks for the education, pleasure and welfare of the people of the city." § 205–1.0(b).

* * *

This case involves the application of New York City's Landmarks Preservation Law to Grand Central Terminal (Terminal). The Terminal, which is owned by the Penn Central Transportation Co. and its affiliates (Penn Central), is one of New York City's most famous buildings. Opened in 1913, it is regarded not only as providing an ingenious engineering solution to the problems presented by urban railroad stations, but also as a magnificent example of the French beaux-arts style.

* * *

On August 2, 1967, following a public hearing, the [New York City Landmarks Preservation] Commission designated the Terminal a "landmark" and designated the "city tax block" it occupies a "landmark site."16 The Board of Estimate confirmed this action on September 21, 1967.

* * *

Appellants UGP and Penn Central then applied to the Commission for permission to construct an office building atop the Terminal. Two separate plans, both designed by architect Marcel Breuer and both apparently satisfying the terms of the applicable zoning ordinance, were submitted to the Commission for approval. The first, Breuer I, provided for the construction of a 55-story office building, to be cantilevered above the existing facade and to rest on the roof of the Terminal. The second, Breuer II Revised,17 called for tearing down a portion of the Terminal that included the 42d Street facade, stripping off some of the remaining features of the Terminal's facade, and constructing a 53-story office building. The Commission denied a certificate of no exterior effect on September 20, 1968. Appellants then applied for a certificate of "appropriateness" as to both proposals. After four days of hearings at which over 80 witnesses testified, the Commission denied this application as to both proposals.

* * *

[A]ppellants filed suit in New York Supreme Court, Trial Term, claiming, inter alia, that the application of the Landmarks Preservation Law had "taken" their property without just compensation in violation of the Fifth and Fourteenth Amendments and arbitrarily deprived them of their property without due process of law in violation of the Fourteenth Amendment. Appellants sought a declaratory judgment, injunctive relief barring the city from using the Landmarks Law to impede the construction of any structure that might otherwise lawfully be constructed on the Terminal site, [and damages for the "temporary taking" occurring until the restrictions would be lifted].

* * *

[After the litigation proceeded through the state court system,] [t]he New York Court of Appeals . . . summarily rejected any claim that the Landmarks Law had "taken" property without "just compensation," indicating that there could be no "taking" since the law had not transferred control of the property to the city, but only restricted appellants' exploitation of it.

* * *

[I]t will be useful to review the factors that have shaped the jurisprudence of the Fifth Amendment injunction "nor shall private property be taken for public use, without just compensation." The question of what constitutes a "taking" for purposes of the Fifth Amendment has proved to be a problem of considerable difficulty.

* * *

In engaging in these essentially ad hoc, factual inquiries, the Court's decisions have identified several factors that have particular significance. The economic impact of the regulation on the claimant and, particularly, the extent to which the regulation has interfered with distinct investment-backed expectations are, of course, relevant considerations. See [citation.] So, too, is the character of the governmental action. A "taking" may more readily be found when the interference with property can be characterized as a physical invasion by government, . . .than when interference arises from some public program adjusting the benefits and burdens of economic life to promote the common good.

* * *

Pennsylvania Coal Co. v. Mahon, 260 U.S. 393 (1922), is the leading case for the proposition that a state statute that substantially furthers important public policies may so frustrate distinct investment-backed expectations as to amount to a "taking." There the claimant had sold the surface rights to particular parcels of property, but expressly reserved the right to remove the coal thereunder. A Pennsylvania statute, enacted after the transactions, forbade any mining of coal that caused the subsidence of any house, unless the house was the property of the owner of the underlying coal and was more than 150 feet from the improved property of another. Because the statute made it commercially impracticable to mine the coal, id., at 414, and thus had nearly the same effect as the complete destruction of rights claimant had reserved from the owners of the surface land, see id., at 414–415, the Court held that the statute was invalid as effecting a "taking" without just compensation. See also Armstrong v. United States, 364 U.S. 40 (1960) (Government's complete destruction of a materialman's lien in certain property held a "taking"); Hudson Water Co. v. McCarter, 209 U.S. 349, 355 (1908) (if height restriction makes property wholly useless "the rights of property . . . prevail over the other public interest" and compensation is required). See generally Michelman, Property, Utility, and Fairness: Comments on the Ethical Foundations of "Just Compensation" Law, 80 Harv.L.Rev. 1165, 1229–1234 (1967).

* * *

Stated baldly, appellants' position appears to be that the only means of ensuring that selected owners are not singled out to endure financial hardship for no reason is to hold that any restriction imposed on individual landmarks pursuant to the New York City scheme is a "taking" requiring the payment of "just compensation." Agreement with this argument would, of course, invalidate not just New York City's law, but all comparable landmark legislation in the Nation. We find no merit in it.

* * *

It is true, as appellants emphasize, that both historic-district legislation and zoning laws regulate all properties within given physical communities whereas landmark laws apply only to selected parcels. But, contrary to appellants' suggestions, landmark laws are not like discriminatory, or "reverse spot," zoning: that is, a land-use decision which arbitrarily singles out a particular parcel for different, less favorable treatment than the neighboring ones. See 2 A. Rathkopf, The Law of Zoning and Planning 26–4, and n. 6 (4th ed. 1978). In contrast to discriminatory zoning, which is the antithesis of land-use control as part of some comprehensive plan, the New York City law embodies a comprehensive plan to preserve structures of historic or aesthetic interest wherever they might be found in the city,[28] and as noted, over 400 landmarks and 31 historic districts have been designated pursuant to this plan.

* * *

Appellants, moreover, exaggerate the effect of the law on their ability to make use of the air rights above the Terminal in two respects. First, it simply cannot be maintained, on this record, that appellants have been prohibited from occupying any portion of the airspace above the Terminal. While the Commission's actions in denying applications to construct an office building in excess of 50 stories above the Terminal may indicate that it will refuse to issue a certificate of appropriateness for any comparably sized structure, nothing the Commission has said or done suggests an intention to prohibit any construction above the Terminal. The Commission's report emphasized that whether any construction would be allowed depended upon whether the proposed addition "would harmonize in scale, material and character with [the Terminal]." Record 2251. Since appellants have not sought approval for the construction of a smaller structure, we do not know that appellants will be denied any use of any portion of the airspace above the Terminal.

* * *

On this record, we conclude that the application of New York City's Landmarks Law has not effected a "taking" of appellants' property. The restrictions imposed are substantially related to the promotion of the general welfare and not only permit reasonable beneficial use of the landmark site but also afford appellants opportunities further to enhance not only the Terminal site proper but also other properties.

Affirmed.

---

**Question:** How does *Penn Central* clarify the rule for analyzing a potential taking?

## PHYSICAL TAKINGS

### LORETTO V. TELEPROMPTER MANHATTAN CATV CORP.

458 U.S. 419 (1982)

JUSTICE MARSHALL delivered the opinion of the Court.

This case presents the question whether a minor but permanent physical occupation of an owner's property authorized by government constitutes a "taking" of property for which just compensation is due under the Fifth and Fourteenth Amendments of the Constitution. New York law provides that a landlord must permit a cable television company to install its cable facilities upon his property. N.Y.Exec.Law § 828(1) (McKinney Supp. 1981–1982). In this case, the cable installation occupied portions of appellant's roof and the side of her building. The New York Court of Appeals ruled that this appropriation does not amount to a taking. Because we conclude that such a physical occupation of property is a taking, we reverse.

* * *

Appellant Jean Loretto purchased a five-story apartment building located at 303 West 105th Street, New York City, in 1971. The previous owner had granted appellees Teleprompter Corp. and Teleprompter Manhattan CATV (collectively Teleprompter) permission to install a cable on the building and the exclusive privilege of furnishing cable television (CATV) services to the tenants. The New York Court of Appeals described the installation as follows:

"On June 1, 1970 TelePrompter installed a cable slightly less than one-half inch in diameter and of approximately 30 feet in length along the length of the building about 18 inches above the roof top, and directional taps, approximately 4 inches by 4 inches by 4 inches, on the front and rear of the roof. By June 8, 1970 the cable had been extended another 4 to 6 feet and cable had been run from the directional taps to the adjoining building at 305 West 105th Street."

Teleprompter also installed two large silver boxes along the roof cables. The cables are attached by screws or nails penetrating the masonry at approximately two-foot intervals, and other equipment is installed by bolts.

* * *

In Penn Central Transportation Co. v. New York City, the Court surveyed some of the general principles governing the Takings Clause. The Court noted that no "set formula" existed to determine, in all cases, whether compensation is constitutionally due for a government restriction of property. Ordinarily, the Court must engage in "essentially ad hoc, factual inquiries." 438 U.S. 104, 124 (1992). But the inquiry is not standardless. The economic impact of the regulation, especially the degree of interference with investment-backed expectations, is of particular significance. "So, too, is the character of the governmental action. A 'taking' may more readily be found when the interference with property can be characterized as a physical invasion by government, than when interference arises from some public program adjusting the benefits and burdens of economic life to promote the common good." Ibid. (citation omitted).

* * *

As Penn Central affirms, the Court has often upheld substantial regulation of an owner's use of his own property where deemed necessary to promote the public interest. At the same time, we have long considered a physical intrusion by government to be a property restriction of an unusually serious character for purposes of the Takings Clause. Our cases further establish that when the physical intrusion reaches the extreme form of a permanent physical occupation, a taking has occurred. In such a case, "the character of the government action" not only is an important factor in resolving whether the action works a taking but also is determinative.

* * *

More recent cases confirm the distinction between a permanent physical occupation, a physical invasion short of an occupation, and a regulation that merely restricts the use of property. In United States v. Causby, 328 U.S. 256 (1946), the Court ruled that frequent flights immediately above a landowner's property constituted a taking, comparing such overflights to the quintessential form of a taking:

"If, by reason of the frequency and altitude of the flights, respondents could not use this land for any purpose, their loss would be complete. It would be as complete as if the United States had entered upon the surface of the land and taken exclusive possession of it." Id., at 261.

* * *

Penn Central Transportation Co. v. New York City, as noted above, contains one of the most complete discussions of the Takings Clause. The Court explained that resolving whether public action works a taking is ordinarily an ad hoc inquiry in which several factors are particularly significant—the economic impact of the regulation, the extent to which it interferes with investment-backed expectations, and the character of the governmental action. 438 U.S., at 124. The183pinionn does not repudiate the rule that a permanent physical occupation is a government action of such a unique character that it is a taking without regard to other factors that a court might ordinarily examine.

* * *

In short, when the "character of the governmental action," Penn Central, 438 U.S., at 124, is a permanent physical occupation of property, our cases uniformly have found a taking to the extent of the occupation, without regard to whether the action achieves an important public benefit or has only minimal economic impact on the owner.

The historical rule that a permanent physical occupation of another's property is a taking has more than tradition to commend it. Such an appropriation is perhaps the most serious form of invasion of an owner's property interests. To borrow a metaphor, cf. Andrus v. Allard, 444 U.S. 51, 65–66 (1979), the government does not simply take a single "strand" from the "bundle" of property rights: it chops through the bundle, taking a slice of every strand.

* * *

Teleprompter's cable installation on appellant's building constitutes a taking under the traditional test. The installation involved a direct physical attachment of plates, boxes, wires, bolts, and screws to the building, completely occupying space immediately above and upon the roof and along the building's exterior wall.

* * *

Our holding today is very narrow. We affirm the traditional rule that a permanent physical occupation of property is a taking. In such a case, the property owner entertains a historically rooted expectation of compensation, and the character of the invasion is qualitatively more intrusive than perhaps any other category of property regulation. We do not, however, question the equally substantial authority upholding a State's broad power to impose appropriate restrictions upon an owner's use of his property.

* * *

The issue of the amount of compensation that is due' on which we express no opinion, is a matter for the state courts to consider on remand.

The judgment of the New York Court of Appeals is reversed, and the case is remanded for further proceedings not inconsistent with this opinion. It is so ordered.

---

**Question:** How much compensation was likely due in *Loretto*? Following the decision, the Supreme Court significantly expanded the circumstances under which a landowner can claim a physical taking by government. In *Nollan v. California Coastal Commission,* 483 U.S. 825 (1987), the justices ruled that a state agency conditioning a construction permit approval on a property owner's dedicating a public easement has to show an "essential nexus" between the condition and a legitimate public interest. Without this connection a government "exaction" of property in exchange for permission constitutes a Fifth Amendment violation requiring compensation.

# TOTAL TAKINGS

## LUCAS V. SOUTH CAROLINA COASTAL COUNCIL

505 U.S. 1003 (1992)

* * *

SCALIA, J., delivered the opinion of the Court.

In 1986, petitioner David H. Lucas paid $975,000 for two residential lots on the Isle of Palms in Charleston County, South Carolina, on which he intended to build single-family homes. In 1988, however, the South Carolina Legislature enacted the Beachfront Management Act, S.C.Code § 48–39–250 *et seq.* (Supp.1990) (Act), which had the direct effect of barring petitioner from erecting any permanent habitable structures on his two parcels. See § 48–39–290(A). A state trial court found that this prohibition rendered Lucas's parcels "valueless." App. to Pet. for Cert. 37. This case requires us to decide whether the Act's dramatic effect on the economic value of Lucas's lots accomplished a taking of private property under the Fifth and Fourteenth Amendments requiring the payment of "just compensation." U.S. Const., Amdt. 5.

South Carolina's expressed interest in intensively managing development activities in the so-called "coastal zone" dates from 1977 when, in the aftermath of Congress's passage of the federal Coastal Zone Management Act of 1972, 86 Stat. 1280, as amended, 16 U.S.C. § 1451 *et seq.*, the legislature enacted a Coastal Zone Management Act of its own. See S.C.Code § 48–39–10 *et seq.* (1987). In its original form, the South Carolina Act required owners of coastal zone land that qualified as a "critical area" (defined in the legislation to include beaches and immediately adjacent sand dunes, § 48–39–10(J)) to obtain a permit from the newly created South Carolina Coastal Council (respondent here) prior to committing the land to a "use other than the use the critical area was devoted to on [September 28, 1977]." § 48–39–130(A).

In the late 1970's, Lucas and others began extensive residential development of the Isle of Palms, a barrier island situated eastward of the City of Charleston. Toward the close of the development cycle for one residential subdivision known as "Beachwood East," Lucas in 1986 purchased the two lots at issue in this litigation for his own account. No portion of the lots, which were located approximately 300 feet from the beach, qualified as a "critical area" under the 1977 Act; accordingly, at the time Lucas acquired these parcels, he was not legally obliged to obtain a permit from the Council in advance of any development activity. His intention with respect to the lots was to do what the owners of the immediately adjacent parcels had already done: erect single-family residences. He commissioned architectural drawings for this purpose.

The Beachfront Management Act brought Lucas's plans to an abrupt end. Under that 1988 legislation, the Council was directed to establish a "baseline" connecting the landward-most "point[s] of erosion . . . during the past forty years" in the region of the Isle of Palms that includes Lucas's lots. § 48–39–280(A)(2) (Supp.1988). In action not challenged here, the Council fixed this baseline landward of Lucas's parcels. That was significant, for under the Act construction of occupiable improvements was flatly prohibited seaward of a line drawn 20 feet landward of, and parallel to, the baseline, § 48–39–290(A) (Supp.1988). The Act provided no exceptions.

Lucas promptly filed suit in the South Carolina Court of Common Pleas, contending that the Beachfront Management Act's construction bar effected a taking of his property without just compensation. Lucas did not take issue with the validity of the Act as a lawful exercise of South Carolina's police power, but contended that the Act's complete extinguishment of his property's value entitled him to compensation regardless of whether the legislature had acted in furtherance of legitimate police power objectives. Following a bench trial, the court agreed. Among its factual determinations was the finding that "at the time Lucas purchased the two lots, both were zoned for single-family residential construction and . . . there were no restrictions imposed upon such use of the property by either the State of South Carolina, the County of Charleston, or the Town of the Isle of Palms." App. to Pet. for Cert. 36. The trial court further found that the Beachfront Management Act decreed a permanent ban on construction insofar as Lucas's lots were concerned, and that this prohibition "deprive[d] Lucas of any reasonable economic use of the lots, . . . eliminated the unrestricted right of use, and render[ed] them valueless." *Id.*, at 37. The court thus concluded that Lucas's properties had been "taken" by operation of the Act, and it ordered respondent to pay "just compensation" in the amount of $1,232,387.50. *Id.*, at 40.

The Supreme Court of South Carolina reversed. It found dispositive what it described as Lucas's concession "that the Beachfront Management Act [was] properly and validly designed to preserve . . . South Carolina's beaches." 404 S.E.2d 895, 896 (S.C. 1991). Failing an attack on the validity of the statute as such, the court believed itself bound to accept the "uncontested . . . findings" of the South Carolina legislature that new construction in the coastal zone—such as petitioner intended—threatened this public resource. *Id.*, at 898. The Court ruled that when a regulation respecting the use of property is designed "to prevent serious public harm," *id.*, at 899 (citing, *inter alia, Mugler v. Kansas,* 123 U.S. 623 (1887)), no compensation is owing under the Takings Clause regardless of the regulation's effect on the property's value.

* * *

We granted certiorari.

* * *

Prior to Justice Holmes' exposition in *Pennsylvania Coal Co. v. Mahon,* 260 U.S. 393 (1922), it was generally thought that the Takings Clause reached only a "direct appropriation" of property, *Legal Tender Cases,* 12 Wall. 457, 551 (1871), or the functional equivalent of a "practical ouster of [the owner's] possession." *Transportation Co. v. Chicago,* 99 U.S. 635, 642, (1879). See also [citation]. Justice Holmes recognized in *Mahon,* however, that if the protection against physical appropriations of private property was to be meaningfully enforced, the government's power to redefine the range of interests included in the ownership of property was necessarily constrained by constitutional limits. 260 U.S., at 414–415. If, instead, the uses of private property were subject to unbridled, uncompensated qualification under the police power, "the natural tendency of human nature [would be] to extend the qualification more and more until at last private property disappear[ed]." *Id.,* at 415. These considerations gave birth in that case to the oft-cited maxim that, "while property may be regulated to a certain extent, if regulation goes too far it will be recognized as a taking." *Ibid.*

Nevertheless, our decision in *Mahon* offered little insight into when, and under what circumstances, a given regulation would be seen as going "too far" for purposes of the Fifth Amendment. In 70-odd years of succeeding "regulatory takings" jurisprudence, we have generally eschewed any " 'set formula' " for determining how far is too far, preferring to "engag[e] in . . . essentially ad hoc, factual inquiries," *Penn Central Transportation Co. v. New York City,* 438 U.S. 104 (1978). See Epstein, Takings: Descent and Resurrection, 1987 Sup.Ct. Rev. 1, 4. We have, however, described at least two discrete categories of regulatory action as compensable without case-specific inquiry into the public interest advanced in support of the restraint. The first encompasses regulations that compel the property owner to suffer a physical "invasion" of his property. In general (at least with regard to permanent invasions), no matter how minute the intrusion, and no matter how weighty the public purpose behind it, we have required compensation. For example, in *Loretto v. Teleprompter Manhattan CATV Corp.,* 458 U.S. 419 (1982), we determined that New York's law requiring landlords to allow television cable companies to emplace cable facilities in their apartment buildings constituted a taking, *id.,* at 435–440, even though the facilities occupied at most only 11/2 cubic feet of the landlords' property, see *id.,* at 438, n. 16. See also *United States v. Causby,* 328 U.S. 256, 265, and n. 10 (1946) (physical invasions of airspace); cf. *Kaiser Aetna v. United States,* 444 U.S. 164 (1979) (imposition of navigational servitude upon private marina).

The second situation in which we have found categorical treatment appropriate is where regulation denies all economically beneficial or productive use of land. See *Agins v. Tiburon,* 447 U.S., 255, 260 (1980); see also [additional citations]. As we have said on numerous occasions, the Fifth Amendment is violated when land-use regulation "does not substantially advance legitimate state interests *or denies an owner economically viable use of his land.*" *Agins, supra,* 447 U.S., at 260, (citations omitted) (emphasis added).

We have never set forth the justification for this rule. Perhaps it is simply, as Justice Brennan suggested, that total deprivation of beneficial use is, from the landowner's point of view, the equivalent of a physical appropriation. See *San Diego Gas & Electric Co. v. San Diego,* 450 U.S., at 652 (Brennan, J., dissenting). "[F]or what is the land but the profits thereof[?]" 1 E. Coke, Institutes ch. 1, § 1 (1st Am. ed. 1812). Surely, at least, in the extraordinary circumstance when *no* productive or economically beneficial use of land is permitted, it is less realistic to indulge our usual assumption that the legislature is simply "adjusting the benefits and burdens of economic life," *Penn Central Transportation Co.,* 438 U.S., at 124, in a manner that secures an "average reciprocity of advantage" to everyone concerned. *Pennsylvania Coal Co. v. Mahon,* 260 U.S., at 415. And the *functional* basis for permitting the government, by regulation, to affect property values without compensation—that "Government hardly could go on if to some extent values incident to property could not be diminished without paying for every such change in the general law," *id.,* at 413—does not apply to the relatively rare situations where the government has deprived a landowner of all economically beneficial uses.

On the other side of the balance, affirmatively supporting a compensation requirement, is the fact that regulations that leave the owner of land without economically beneficial or productive options for its use—typically, as here, by requiring land to be left substantially in its natural state—carry with them a heightened risk that private property is being pressed into some form of public service under the guise of mitigating serious public harm. See, *e.g., Annicelli v. South Kingstown,* 463 A.2d 133, 140–141 (R.I.1983) (prohibition on construction adjacent to beach justified on twin grounds of safety and "conservation of open space"); *Morris County Land Improvement Co. v. Parsippany-Troy Hills Township,* 40 N.J. 539, 552–553 (1963) (prohibition on filling marshlands imposed in order to preserve region as water detention basin and create wildlife refuge). As Justice Brennan explained: "From the government's point of view, the benefits flowing to the public from preservation of open space through regulation may be equally great as from creating a wildlife refuge through formal condemnation or increasing electricity production through a dam project that floods private property." *San Diego Gas & Elec. Co., supra,* 450 U.S., at 652, at 1304 (Brennan, J., dissenting). The many statutes on the books, both state and federal, that provide for the use of eminent domain to impose servitudes on private scenic lands preventing developmental uses, or to acquire such lands altogether, suggest the practical equivalence in this setting of negative regulation and appropriation. See, *e.g.*, 16 U.S.C. § 410ff–1(a) (authorizing acquisition of "lands, waters, or interests [within Channel Islands National Park] (including but not limited to scenic easements)"); § 460aa–2(a) (authorizing acquisition of "any lands, or lesser interests therein, including mineral interests and scenic easements" within Sawtooth National Recreation Area); §§ 3921–3923 (authorizing acquisition of wetlands); N.C. Gen.Stat. § 113A–38 (1990) (authorizing acquisition of, *inter alia*, " 'scenic easements' " within the North Carolina natural and scenic rivers system); Tenn.Code Ann. §§ 11–15–101–11–15–108 (1987) (authorizing acquisition of "protective easements" and other rights in real property adjacent to State's historic, architectural, archaeological, or cultural resources).

We think, in short, that there are good reasons for our frequently expressed belief that when the owner of real property has been called upon to sacrifice *all* economically beneficial uses in the name of the common good, that is, to leave his property economically idle, he has suffered a taking.

The trial court found Lucas's two beachfront lots to have been rendered valueless by respondent's enforcement of the coastal-zone construction ban. Under Lucas's theory of the case, which rested upon our "no economically viable use" statements, that finding entitled him to compensation. Lucas believed it unnecessary to take issue with either the purposes behind the Beachfront Management Act, or the means chosen by the South Carolina Legislature to effectuate those purposes. The South Carolina Supreme Court, however, thought otherwise. In its view, the Beachfront Management Act was no ordinary enactment, but involved an exercise of South Carolina's "police powers" to mitigate the harm to the public interest that petitioner's use of his land might occasion. 404 S.E.2d, at 899. By neglecting to dispute the findings enumerated in the Act or otherwise to challenge the legislature's purposes, petitioner "concede[d] that the beach/dune area of South Carolina's shores is an extremely valuable public resource; that the erection of new construction, *inter alia*, contributes to the erosion and destruction of this public resource; and that discouraging new construction in close proximity to the beach/dune area is necessary to prevent a great public harm." *Id.*, at 898. In the court's view, these concessions brought petitioner's challenge within a long line of this Court's cases sustaining against Due Process and Takings Clause challenges the State's use of its "police powers" to enjoin a property owner from activities akin to public nuisances. See *Mugler v. Kansas*, 123 U.S. 623 (1887) (law prohibiting manufacture of alcoholic beverages); *Hadacheck v. Sebastian*, 239 U.S. 394 (1915) (law barring operation of brick mill in residential area);

*Miller v. Schoene,* 276 U.S. 272 (1928) (order to destroy diseased cedar trees to prevent infection of nearby orchards); *Goldblatt v. Hempstead,* 369 U.S. 590 (1962) (law effectively preventing continued operation of quarry in residential area).

It is correct that many of our prior opinions have suggested that "harmful or noxious uses" of property may be proscribed by government regulation without the requirement of compensation. For a number of reasons, however, we think the South Carolina Supreme Court was too quick to conclude that that principle decides the present case. The "harmful or noxious uses" principle was the Court's early attempt to describe in theoretical terms why government may, consistent with the Takings Clause, affect property values by regulation without incurring an obligation to compensate—a reality we nowadays acknowledge explicitly with respect to the full scope of the State's police power. See, *e.g., Penn Central Transportation Co.,* 438 U.S., at 125 (where State "reasonably conclude[s] that 'the health, safety, morals, or general welfare' would be promoted by prohibiting particular contemplated uses of land," compensation need not accompany prohibition); see also *Nollan v. California Coastal Commission,* 483 U.S., at 834–835 ("Our cases have not elaborated on the standards for determining what constitutes a 'legitimate state interest[,]' [but] [t]hey have made clear . . . that a broad range of governmental purposes and regulations satisfy these requirements"). We made this very point in *Penn Central Transportation Co.,* where, in the course of sustaining New York City's landmarks preservation program against a takings challenge, we rejected the petitioner's suggestion that *Mugler* and the cases following it were premised on, and thus limited by, some objective conception of "noxiousness":

"[T]he uses in issue in *Hadacheck, Miller,* and *Goldblatt* were perfectly lawful in themselves. They involved no 'blameworthiness, . . . moral wrongdoing or conscious act of dangerous risk-taking which induce[d society] to shift the cost to a pa[rt]icular individual.' Sax, Takings and the Police Power, 74 Yale L.J. 36, 50 (1964). These cases are better understood as resting not on any supposed 'noxious' quality of the prohibited uses but rather on the ground that the restrictions were reasonably related to the implementation of a policy—not unlike historic preservation expected to produce a widespread public benefit and applicable to all similarly situated property." 438 U.S., at 133–134, n. 30.

"Harmful or noxious use" analysis was, in other words, simply the progenitor of our more contemporary statements that "land-use regulation does not effect a taking if it 'substantially advance[s] legitimate state interests'. . . ." *Nollan, supra,* 483 U.S., at 834); see also *Penn Central Transportation Co., supra,* 438 U.S., at 127; *Euclid v. Ambler Realty Co.,* 272 U.S. 365 (1926).

The transition from our early focus on control of "noxious" uses to our contemporary understanding of the broad realm within which government may regulate without compensation was an easy one, since the distinction between "harm-preventing" and "benefit-conferring" regulation is often in the eye of the beholder. It is quite possible, for example, to describe in *either* fashion the ecological, economic, and aesthetic concerns that inspired the South Carolina legislature in the present case. One could say that imposing a servitude on Lucas's land is necessary in order to prevent his use of it from "harming" South Carolina's ecological resources; or, instead, in order to achieve the "benefits" of an ecological preserve. Compare, *e.g., Claridge v. New Hampshire Wetlands Board,* 125 N.H. 745, 752, 485 A.2d 287, 292 (1984) (owner may, without compensation, be barred from filling wetlands because landfilling would deprive adjacent coastal habitats and marine fisheries of ecological support), with, *e.g., Bartlett v. Zoning Comm'n of Old Lyme,* 282 A.2d 907, 910 (Conn. 1971) (owner barred from filling tidal marshland must be compensated, despite municipality's "laudable" goal of "preserv[ing] marshlands from encroachment or destruction"). Whether one or the other of the competing characterizations will come to one's lips in a particular case depends primarily upon one's evaluation of the worth of competing uses of real estate. See Restatement (Second) of Torts § 822, Comment *g,* p. 112 (1979) ("[p]ractically all human activities unless carried on in a wilderness interfere to some extent with others or involve some risk of interference"). A given restraint will be seen as mitigating "harm" to the adjacent parcels or securing a "benefit" for them, depending upon the observer's evaluation of the relative importance of the use that the restraint favors. See Sax, Takings and the Police Power, 74 Yale L.J. 36, 49 (1964) ("[T]he problem [in this area] is not one of noxiousness or harm-creating activity at all; rather it is a problem of inconsistency between perfectly innocent and independently desirable uses"). Whether Lucas's construction of single-family residences on his parcels should be described as bringing "harm" to South Carolina's adjacent ecological resources thus depends principally upon whether the describer believes that the State's use interest in nurturing those resources is so important that *any* competing adjacent use must yield.

When it is understood that "prevention of harmful use" was merely our early formulation of the police power justification necessary to sustain (without compensation) *any* regulatory diminution in value; and that the distinction between regulation that "prevents harmful use" and that which "confers benefits" is difficult, if not impossible, to discern on an objective, value-free basis; it becomes self-evident that noxious-use logic cannot serve as a touchstone to distinguish regulatory "takings" which require compensation—from regulatory deprivations that do not require compensation. *A fortiori* the legislature's recitation of a noxious-use justification cannot be the basis for departing from our categorical rule that total regulatory takings must be compensated. If it were, departure would virtually always be allowed. The South Carolina Supreme Court's approach would essentially nullify *Mahon*'s affirmation of limits to the non compensable exercise of the police power. Our cases provide no support for this: None of them that employed the logic of "harmful use" prevention to sustain a regulation involved an allegation that the regulation wholly eliminated the value of the claimant's land. See *Keystone Bituminous Coal Assn.,* 480 U.S., at 513–514 (REHNQUIST, C.J., dissenting).

Where the State seeks to sustain regulation that deprives land of all economically beneficial use, we think it may resist compensation only if the logically antecedent inquiry into the nature of the owner's estate shows that the proscribed use interests were not part of his title to begin with. This accords, we think, with our "takings" jurisprudence, which has traditionally been guided by the understandings of our citizens regarding the content of, and the State's power over, the "bundle of rights" that they acquire when they obtain title to property. It seems to us that the property owner necessarily expects the uses of his property to be restricted, from time to time, by various measures newly enacted by the State in legitimate exercise of its police powers; "[a]s long recognized, some values are enjoyed under an implied limitation and must yield to the police power." *Pennsylvania Coal Co. v. Mahon,* 260 U.S., at 413. And in the case of personal property, by reason of the State's traditionally high degree of control over commercial dealings, he ought to be aware of the possibility that new regulation might even render his property economically worthless (at least if the property's only economically productive use is sale or manufacture for sale), see *Andrus v. Allard,* 444 U.S. 51, 66–67 (1979) (prohibition on sale of eagle feathers). In the case of land, however, we think the notion pressed by the Council that title is somehow held subject to the "implied limitation" that the State may subsequently eliminate all economically valuable use is inconsistent with the historical compact recorded in the Takings Clause that has become part of our constitutional culture.

Where "permanent physical occupation" of land is concerned, we have refused to allow the government to decree it anew (without compensation), no matter how weighty the asserted "public interests" involved, *Loretto v. Teleprompter Manhattan CATV Corp.,* 458 U.S., at 426,—though we assuredly *would* permit the government to assert a permanent easement that was a pre-existing limitation upon the landowner's title. Compare *Scranton v. Wheeler,* 179 U.S. 141, 163 (1900) (interests of "riparian owner in the submerged lands . . . bordering on a public navigable water" held subject to Government's navigational servitude), with *Kaiser Aetna v. United States,* 444 U.S., at 178–180 (imposition of navigational servitude on marina created and rendered navigable at private expense held to constitute a taking). We believe similar treatment must be accorded confiscatory regulations, *i.e.,* regulations that prohibit all economically beneficial use of land: Any limitation so severe cannot be newly legislated or decreed (without compensation), but must inhere in the title itself, in the restrictions that background principles of the State's law of property and nuisance already place upon land ownership. A law or decree with such an effect must, in other words, do no more than duplicate the result that could have been achieved in the courts by adjacent landowners (or other uniquely affected persons) under the State's law of private nuisance, or by the State under its complementary power to abate nuisances that affect the public generally, or otherwise.

On this analysis, the owner of a lake bed, for example, would not be entitled to compensation when he is denied the requisite permit to engage in a landfilling operation that would have the effect of flooding others' land. Nor the corporate owner of a nuclear generating plant, when it is directed to remove all improvements from its land upon discovery that the plant sits astride an earthquake fault. Such regulatory action may well have the effect of eliminating the land's only economically productive use, but it does not proscribe a productive use that was previously permissible under relevant property and nuisance principles. The use of these properties for what are now expressly prohibited purposes was *always* unlawful, and (subject to other constitutional limitations) it was open to the State at any point to make the implication of those background principles of nuisance and property law explicit. See Michelman, Property, Utility, and Fairness, Comments on the Ethical Foundations of "Just Compensation" Law, 80 Harv.L.Rev. 1165, 1239–1241 (1967). In light of our traditional resort to "existing rules or understandings that stem from an independent source such as state law" to define the range of interests that qualify for protection as "property" under the Fifth (and Fourteenth) amendments, *Board of Regents of State Colleges v. Roth,* 408 U.S. 564, 577 (1972); see, *e.g.,*[citations], this recognition that the Takings Clause does not require compensation when an owner is barred from putting land to a use that is proscribed by those "existing rules or understandings" is surely unexceptional. When, however, a regulation that declares "off-limits" all economically productive or beneficial uses of land goes beyond what the relevant background principles would dictate, compensation must be paid to sustain it.

The "total taking" inquiry we require today will ordinarily entail (as the application of state nuisance law ordinarily entails) analysis of, among other things, the degree of harm to public lands and resources, or adjacent private property, posed by the claimant's proposed activities, see, *e.g.,* Restatement (Second) of Torts §§ 826, 827, the social value of the claimant's activities and their suitability to the locality in question, see, *e.g., id.,* §§ 828(a) and (b), 831, and the relative ease with which the alleged harm can be avoided through measures taken by the claimant and the government (or adjacent private landowners) alike, see, *e.g., id.,* §§ 827(e),

828(c), 830. The fact that a particular use has long been engaged in by similarly situated owners ordinarily imports a lack of any common-law prohibition (though changed circumstances or new knowledge may make what was previously permissible no longer so, see Restatement (Second) of Torts, *supra,* § 827, comment *g*. So also does the fact that other landowners, similarly situated, are permitted to continue the use denied to the claimant.

It seems unlikely that common-law principles would have prevented the erection of any habitable or productive improvements on petitioner's land; they rarely support prohibition of the "essential use" of land, *Curtin v. Benson,* 222 U.S. 78, 86 (1911). The question, however, is one of state law to be dealt with on remand. We emphasize that to win its case South Carolina must do more than proffer the legislature's declaration that the uses Lucas desires are inconsistent with the public interest, or the conclusory assertion that they violate a common-law maxim such as *sic utere tuo ut alienum non laedas* [use your property so as not to injure that of others]. As we have said, a "State, by *ipse dixit,* may not transform private property into public property without compensation. . . ." *Webb's Fabulous Pharmacies, Inc. v. Beckwith,* 449 U.S. 155, 164 (1980). Instead, as it would be required to do if it sought to restrain Lucas in a common-law action for public nuisance, South Carolina must identify background principles of nuisance and property law that prohibit the uses he now intends in the circumstances in which the property is presently found. Only on this showing can the State fairly claim that, in proscribing all such beneficial uses, the Beachfront Management Act is taking nothing.

The judgment is reversed and the cause remanded for proceedings not inconsistent with this opinion. *So ordered.*

---

**Question:** An owner has two adjoining lots near a scenic river. The state restricts development on riverside properties, which would limit building much more on one lot than on the other. Under *Lucas,* can the owner claim a total taking of the more impacted lot without reference to the less impacted one? See *Murr v. Wisconsin,* 137 S.Ct. 1933 (2017).

## PUBLIC USE

### KELO V. NEW LONDON

545 U.S. 469 (2005)

JUSTICE STEVENS delivered the opinion of the Court.

In 2000, the city of New London approved a development plan that, in the words of the Supreme Court of Connecticut, was "projected to create in excess of 1,000 jobs, to increase tax and other revenues, and to revitalize an economically distressed city, including its downtown and waterfront areas." 268 Conn. 1, 5, 843 A. 2d 500, 507 (2004). In assembling the land needed for this project, the city's development agent has purchased property from willing sellers and proposes to use the power of eminent domain to acquire the remainder of the property from unwilling owners in exchange for just compensation. The question presented is whether the city's proposed disposition of this property qualifies as a "public use" within the meaning of the Takings Clause of the Fifth Amendment to the Constitution.

The city of New London (hereinafter City) sits at the junction of the Thames River and the Long Island Sound in southeastern Connecticut. Decades of economic decline led a state agency in 1990 to designate the City a "distressed municipality." * * *

These conditions prompted state and local officials to target New London, and particularly its Fort Trumbull area, for economic revitalization. To this end, respondent New London Development Corporation (NLDC), a private nonprofit entity established some years earlier to assist the City in planning economic development, was reactivated. * * * In February, the pharmaceutical company Pfizer Inc. announced that it would build a $300 million research facility on a site immediately adjacent to Fort Trumbull; local planners hoped that Pfizer would draw new business to the area, thereby serving as a catalyst to the area's rejuvenation. * * * Upon obtaining state-level approval, the NLDC finalized an integrated development plan focused on 90 acres of the Fort Trumbull area.

* * *

The city council approved the plan in January 2000, and designated the NLDC as its development agent in charge of implementation. See Conn. Gen. Stat. § 8–188 (2005). The city council also authorized the NLDC to purchase property or to acquire property by exercising eminent domain in the City's name. § 8–193. The NLDC successfully negotiated the purchase of most of the real estate in the 90-acre area, but its negotiations with petitioners failed. As a consequence, in November 2000, the NLDC initiated the condemnation proceedings that gave rise to this case.

Petitioner Susette Kelo has lived in the Fort Trumbull area since 1997. She has made extensive improvements to her house, which she prizes for its water view. Petitioner Wilhelmina Dery was born in her Fort Trumbull house in 1918 and has lived there her entire life. Her husband Charles (also a petitioner) has lived in the house since they married some 60 years ago. In all, the nine petitioners own 15 properties in Fort Trumbull–4 in parcel 3 of the development plan and 11 in parcel 4A. Ten of the parcels are occupied by the owner or a family member; the other five are held as investment properties. There is no allegation that any of these properties is blighted or otherwise in poor condition; rather, they were condemned only because they happen to be located in the development area.

In December 2000, petitioners brought this action in the New London Superior Court. They claimed, among other things, that the taking of their properties would violate the "public use" restriction in the Fifth Amendment.

* * *

[Although the trial court granted partial relief to the petitioners], the Connecticut Supreme Court held that such economic development qualified as a valid public use under both the Federal and State Constitutions. 268 Conn., at 40, 843 A. 2d, at 527.

* * *

We granted certiorari to determine whether a city's decision to take property for the purpose of economic development satisfies the "public use" requirement of the Fifth Amendment. 542 U.S. ___ (2004).

* * *

The disposition of this case therefore turns on the question whether the City's development plan serves a "public purpose." Without exception, our cases have defined that concept broadly, reflecting our longstanding policy of deference to legislative judgments in this field.

* * *

Those who govern the City were not confronted with the need to remove blight in the Fort Trumbull area, but their determination that the area was sufficiently distressed to justify a program of economic rejuvenation is entitled to our deference. The City has carefully formulated an economic development plan that it believes will provide appreciable benefits to the community, including—but by no means limited to—new jobs and increased tax revenue. * * * Because that plan unquestionably serves a public purpose, the takings challenged here satisfy the public use requirement of the Fifth Amendment.

It is . . . argued that without a bright-line rule nothing would stop a city from transferring citizen A's property to citizen B for the sole reason that citizen B will put the property to a more productive use and thus pay more taxes. Such a one-to-one transfer of property, executed outside the confines of an integrated development plan, is not presented in this case. While such an unusual exercise of government power would certainly raise a suspicion that a private purpose was afoot, the hypothetical cases posited by petitioners can be confronted if and when they arise. They do not warrant the crafting of an artificial restriction on the concept of public use.

* * *

In affirming the City's authority to take petitioners' properties, we do not minimize the hardship that condemnations may entail, notwithstanding the payment of just compensation. We emphasize that nothing in our opinion precludes any State from placing further restrictions on its exercise of the takings power. Indeed, many States already impose "public use" requirements that are stricter than the federal baseline. Some of these requirements have been established as a matter of state constitutional law, while others are expressed in state eminent domain statutes that carefully limit the grounds upon which takings may be exercised. * * * This Court's authority, however, extends only to determining whether the City's proposed condemnations are for a "public use" within the meaning of the Fifth Amendment to the Federal Constitution. Because over a century of our case law interpreting that provision dictates an affirmative answer to that question, we may not grant petitioners the relief that they seek.

The judgment of the Supreme Court of Connecticut is affirmed. It is so ordered.

JUSTICE KENNEDY, concurring.

I join the opinion for the Court and add these further observations.

This Court has declared that a taking should be upheld as consistent with the Public Use Clause, U.S. Const., Amdt. 5., as long as it is "rationally related to a conceivable public purpose." Hawaii Housing Authority v. Midkiff, 467 U.S. 229, 241 (1984); see also Berman v. Parker, 348 U.S. 26 (1954). This deferential standard of review echoes the rational-basis test used to review economic regulation under the Due Process and Equal Protection Clauses, see, e.g., FCC v. Beach Communications, Inc., 508 U.S. 307, 313–314 (1993); Williamson v. Lee Optical of Okla., Inc., 348 U.S. 483 (1955). The determination that a rational-basis standard of review is appropriate does not, however, alter the fact that transfers intended to confer benefits on particular, favored private entities, and with only incidental or pretextual public benefits, are forbidden by the Public Use Clause.

A court applying rational-basis review under the Public Use Clause should strike down a taking that, by a clear showing, is intended to favor a particular private party, with only incidental or pretextual public benefits, just as a court applying rational-basis review under the Equal Protection Clause must strike down a government classification that is clearly intended to injure a particular class of private parties, with only incidental or pretextual public justifications. See Cleburne v. Cleburne Living Center, Inc., 473 U.S. 432, 446–447, 450 (1985); [additional citation.].

* * *

This taking occurred in the context of a comprehensive development plan meant to address a serious city-wide depression, and the projected economic benefits of the project cannot be characterized as de minimus. The identity of most of the private beneficiaries were unknown at the time the city formulated its plans. The city complied with elaborate procedural requirements that facilitate review of the record and inquiry into the city's purposes. In sum, while there may be categories of cases in which the transfers are so suspicious, or the procedures employed so prone to abuse, or the purported benefits are so trivial or implausible, that courts should presume an impermissible private purpose, no such circumstances are present in this case.

* * *

JUSTICE O'CONNOR, with whom THE CHIEF JUSTICE, JUSTICE SCALIA, and JUSTICE THOMAS join, dissenting.

* * *

Today the Court abandons [a] long-held, basic limitation on government power. Under the banner of economic development, all private property is now vulnerable to being taken and transferred to another private owner, so long as it might be upgraded—i.e., given to an owner who will use it in a way that the legislature deems more beneficial to the public—in the process. To reason, as the Court does, that the incidental public benefits resulting from the subsequent ordinary use of private property render economic development takings "for public use" is to wash out any distinction between private and public use of property—and thereby effectively to delete the words "for public use" from the Takings Clause of the Fifth Amendment. Accordingly I respectfully dissent.

* * *

Where is the line between "public" and "private" property use? We give considerable deference to legislatures' determinations about what governmental activities will advantage the public. But were the political branches the sole arbiters of the public-private distinction, the Public Use Clause would amount to little more than hortatory fluff. An external, judicial check on how the public use requirement is interpreted, however limited, is necessary if this constraint on government power is to retain any meaning. See Cincinnati v. Vester, 281 U.S. 439, 446 (1930) ("It is well established that . . . the question [of] what is a public use is a judicial one").

* * *

This case returns us for the first time in over 20 years to the hard question of when a purportedly "public purpose" taking meets the public use requirement. It presents an issue of first impression: Are economic development takings constitutional? I would hold that they are not.

* * *

. . .[T]he Court today significantly expands the meaning of public use. It holds that the sovereign may take private property currently put to ordinary private use, and give it over for new, ordinary private use, so long as the new use is predicted to generate some secondary benefit for the public—such as increased tax revenue, more jobs, maybe even aesthetic pleasure. But nearly any lawful use of real private property can be said to generate some incidental benefit to the public. Thus, if predicted (or even guaranteed) positive side-effects are enough to render transfer from one private party to another constitutional, then the words "for public use" do not realistically exclude any takings, and thus do not exert any constraint on the eminent domain power.

* * *

Finally, in a coda, the Court suggests that property owners should turn to the States, who may or may not choose to impose appropriate limits on economic development takings. This is an abdication of our responsibility. States play many important functions in our system of dual sovereignty, but compensating for our refusal to enforce properly the Federal Constitution (and a provision meant to curtail state action, no less) is not among them.

* * *

Any property may now be taken for the benefit of another private party, but the fallout from this decision will not be random. The beneficiaries are likely to be those citizens with disproportionate influence and power in the political process, including large corporations and development firms. As for the victims, the government now has license to transfer property from those with fewer resources to those with more. The Founders cannot have intended this perverse result. "[T]hat alone is a just government," wrote James Madison, "which impartially secures to every man, whatever is his own." For the National Gazette, Property, (Mar. 29, 1792), reprinted in 14 Papers of James Madison 266 (R. Rutland et al. eds. 1983).

JUSTICE THOMAS, dissenting.

There is no justification . . . for affording almost insurmountable deference to legislative conclusions that a use serves a "public use." To begin with, a court owes no deference to a legislature's judgment concerning the quintessentially legal question of whether the government owns, or the public has a legal right to use, the taken property. Even under the "public purpose" interpretation, moreover, it is most implausible that the Framers intended to defer to legislatures as to what satisfies the Public Use Clause, uniquely among all the express provisions of the Bill of Rights.

* * *

For all these reasons, I would . . . consider returning to the original meaning of the Public Use Clause: that the government may take property only if it actually uses or gives the public a legal right to use the property.

---

**Questions:** How did the *Kelo* majority define "public use" for taking purposes? What does Justice Kennedy's concurrence contribute to the analysis?

# CHAPTER 11

# EQUAL PROTECTION AND RACE

■ ■ ■

## CONTEXT & SOURCES

The 14th Amendment's language prohibits states (and by extension other government levels) from denying "any person within its jurisdiction the equal protection of the laws." The Equal Protection Clause's post-Civil War legislative history manifests the drafters' intent to bar discrimination based on race. This chapter includes decisions illustrating the Supreme Court's move from a narrow to a broader interpretation of the clause, as well as cases applying "strict scrutiny" (highly critical) analysis to laws using racial categories, and those analyzing disparate effects.

Cheryl I. Harris, "The Story of *Plessy v. Ferguson*: The Death and Resurrection of Racial Formalism," *Constitutional Law Stories* (Michael C. Dorf ed. 2009) places the equal protection doctrine within the same historical/philosophical trends as those described in earlier chapters. For a detailed study of the case that reversed *Plessy,* see Robert J. Cottrol, Raymond J. Diamond, & Leland B. Ware, *Brown v. Board of Education: Caste, Culture, and the Constitution* (University Press of Kansas, 2003). The Court's ruling against interracial marriage bans, and its implications, are explored in Peter Wallenstein, *Race, Sex, and the Freedom to Marry: Loving v. Virginia* (University Press of Kansas, 2014). A longtime housing discrimination attorney comprehensively surveys that field in Robert G. Schwemm, "Reflections on Arlington Heights: Fifty Years of Exclusionary Zoning Litigation and Beyond," 57 *UIC Law Review* 389 (2024).

## EQUAL PROTECTION SCOPE

### PLESSY V. FERGUSON

163 U.S. 537 (1896)

* * *

This was a petition for writs of prohibition and certiorari originally filed in the supreme court of the state by Plessy, the plaintiff in error, against the Hon. John H. Ferguson, judge of the criminal district court for the parish of Orleans, and setting forth, in substance, the following facts:

That petitioner was a citizen of the United States and a resident of the state of Louisiana, of mixed descent, in the proportion of seven-eighths Caucasian and one-eighth African blood; that the mixture of colored blood was not discernible in him, and that he was entitled to every recognition, right, privilege, and immunity secured to the citizens of the United States of the white race by its constitution and laws; that on June 7, 1892, he engaged and paid for a first-class passage on the East Louisiana Railway, from New Orleans to Covington, in the same state, and thereupon entered a passenger train, and took possession of a vacant seat in a coach where passengers of the white race were accommodated; that such railroad company was incorporated by the laws of Louisiana as a common carrier, and was not authorized to distinguish between citizens according to their race, but, notwithstanding this, petitioner was required by the conductor, under penalty of ejection from said train and imprisonment, to vacate said coach, and occupy another seat, in a coach assigned by said company for persons not of the white race, and for no other reason than that petitioner was of the colored race; that, upon petitioner's refusal to comply with such order, he was, with the aid of a police officer, forcibly ejected from said coach, and hurried off to, and imprisoned in, the parish jail of New Orleans, and there held to answer a charge made by such officer to the effect that he was guilty of having criminally violated an act of the general assembly of the state, approved July 10, 1890, in such case made and provided.

* * *

The case coming on for hearing before the [Louisiana] supreme court, that court was of opinion that the law under which the prosecution was had was constitutional and denied the relief prayed for by the petitioner (Ex parte Plessy, 45 La. Ann. 80, 11 South. 948); whereupon petitioner prayed for a writ of error from this court, which was allowed by the chief justice of the supreme court of Louisiana.

* * *

MR. JUSTICE BROWN, after stating the facts in the foregoing language, delivered the opinion of the court.

This case turns upon the constitutionality of an act of the general assembly of the state of Louisiana, passed in 1890, providing for separate railway carriages for the white and colored races. Acts 1890, No. 111, p. 152.

The first section of the statute enacts 'that all railway companies carrying passengers in their coaches in this state, shall provide equal but separate accommodations for the white, and colored races, by providing two or more passenger coaches for each passenger train, or by dividing the passenger coaches by a partition so as to secure separate accommodations: provided, that this section shall not be construed to apply to street railroads. No person or persons shall be permitted to occupy seats in coaches, other than the ones assigned to them, on account of the race they belong to.'

* * *

By the second section it was enacted 'that the officers of such passenger trains shall have power and are hereby required to assign each passenger to the coach or compartment used for the race to which such passenger belongs; any passenger insisting on going into a coach or compartment to which by race he does not belong, shall be liable to a fine of twenty-five dollars, or in lieu thereof to imprisonment for a period of not more than twenty days in the parish prison, and any officer of any railroad insisting on assigning a passenger to a coach or compartment other than the one set aside for the race to which said passenger belongs, shall be liable to a fine of twenty-five dollars, or in lieu thereof to imprisonment for a period of not more than twenty days in the parish prison; and should any passenger refuse to occupy the coach or compartment to which he or she is assigned by the officer of such railway, said officer shall have power to refuse to carry such passenger on his train, and for such refusal neither he nor the railway company which he represents shall be liable for damages in any of the courts of this state.'

* * *

The petition for the writ of prohibition averred that petitioner was seven-eighths Caucasian and one-eighth African blood; that the mixture of colored blood was not discernible in him; and that he was entitled to every right, privilege, and immunity secured to citizens of the United States of the white race; and that, upon such theory, he took possession of a vacant seat in a coach where passengers of the white race were accommodated, and was ordered by the conductor to vacate said coach, and take a seat in another, assigned to persons of the colored race, and, having refused to comply with such demand, he was forcibly ejected, with the aid of a police officer, and imprisoned in the parish jail to answer a charge of having violated the above act.

The constitutionality of this act is attacked upon the ground that it conflicts with the thirteenth amendment of the constitution, abolishing slavery, and the fourteenth amendment, which prohibits certain restrictive legislation on the part of the states.

[The Court held that "refusing accommodations to colored people cannot justly be regarded as imposing any badge of slavery or involuntary servitude. . ., but only as involving an ordinary civil injury," and so did not violate the Thirteenth Amendment.]

* * *

By the fourteenth amendment, all persons born or naturalized in the United States, and subject to the jurisdiction thereof, are made citizens of the United States and of the state wherein they reside; and the states are forbidden from making or enforcing any law which shall abridge the privileges or immunities of citizens of the United States, or shall deprive any person of life, liberty, or property without due process of law, or deny to any person within their jurisdiction the equal protection of the laws.

* * *

The object of the amendment was undoubtedly to enforce the absolute equality of the two races before the law, but, in the nature of things, it could not have been intended to abolish distinctions based upon color, or to enforce social, as distinguish d from political, equality, or a commingling of the two races upon terms unsatisfactory to either. Laws permitting, and even requiring, their separation, in places where they are liable to be brought into contact, do not necessarily imply the inferiority of either race to the other, and have been generally, if not universally, recognized as within the competency of the state legislatures in the exercise of their police power. The most common instance of this is connected with the establishment of separate schools for white and colored children, which have been held to be a valid exercise of the legislative power even by courts of states where the political rights of the colored race have been longest and most earnestly enforced.

* * *

So far, then, as a conflict with the fourteenth amendment is concerned, the case reduces itself to the question whether the statute of Louisiana is a reasonable regulation, and with respect to this there must necessarily be a large discretion on the part of the legislature. In determining the question of reasonableness, it is at liberty to act with reference to the established usages, customs, and traditions of the people, and with a view to the promotion of their comfort, and the preservation of the public peace and good order. Gauged by this standard, we cannot say that a law which authorizes or even requires the separation of the two races in public conveyances is unreasonable, or more obnoxious to the fourteenth amendment than the acts of congress requiring separate schools for colored children in the District of Columbia, the constitutionality of which does not seem to have been questioned, or the corresponding acts of state legislatures.

We consider the underlying fallacy of the plaintiff's argument to consist in the assumption that the enforced separation of the two races stamps the colored race with a badge of inferiority. If this be so, it is not by reason of anything found in the act, but solely because the colored race chooses to put that construction upon it. The argument necessarily assumes that if, as has been more than once the case, and is not unlikely to be so again, the colored race should become the dominant power in the state legislature, and should enact a law in precisely similar terms, it would thereby relegate the white race to an inferior position. We imagine that the white race, at least, would not acquiesce in this assumption. The argument also assumes that social prejudices may be overcome by legislation, and that equal rights cannot be secured to the negro except by an enforced commingling of the two races. We cannot accept this proposition. If the two races are to meet upon terms of social equality, it must be the result of natural affinities, a mutual appreciation of each other's merits, and a voluntary consent of individuals. As was said by the court of appeals of New York in People v. Gallagher, 93 N. Y. 438, 448: 'This end can neither be accomplished nor promoted by laws which conflict with the general sentiment of the community upon whom they are designed to operate. When the government, therefore, has secured to each of its citizens equal rights before the law, and equal opportunities for improvement and progress, it has accomplished the end for which it was organized, and performed all of the functions respecting social advantages with which it is endowed.' Legislation is powerless to eradicate racial instincts, or to abolish distinctions based upon physical differences, and the attempt to do so can only result in accentuating the difficulties of the present situation. If the civil and political rights of both races be equal, one cannot be inferior to the other civilly or politically. If one race be inferior to the other socially, the constitution of the United States cannot put them upon the same plane.

* * *

The judgment of the court below is therefore affirmed.

MR. JUSTICE HARLAN dissenting.

* * *

[I]n view of the constitution, in the eye of the law, there is in this country no superior, dominant, ruling class of citizens. There is no caste here. Our constitution is color-blind, and neither knows nor tolerates classes among citizens. In respect of civil rights, all citizens are equal before the law. The humblest is the peer of the most powerful. The law regards man as man, and takes no account of his surroundings or of his color when his civil rights as guaranteed by the supreme law of the land are involved. It is therefore to be regretted that this high tribunal, the final expositor of the fundamental law of the land, has reached the conclusion that it is competent for a state to regulate the enjoyment by citizens of their civil rights solely upon the basis of race.

* * *

I am of opinion that the state of Louisiana is inconsistent with the personal liberty of citizens, white and black, in that state, and hostile to both the spirit and letter of the constitution of the United States. If laws of like character should be enacted in the several states of the Union, the effect would be in the highest degree mischievous. Slavery, as an institution tolerated by law, would, it is true, have disappeared from our country; but there would remain a power in the states, by sinister legislation, to interfere with the full enjoyment of the blessings of freedom, to regulate civil rights, common to all citizens, upon the basis of race, and to place in a condition of legal inferiority a large body of American citizens, now constituting a part of the political community, called the 'People of the United States,' for whom, and by whom through representatives, our government is administered. Such a system is inconsistent with the guaranty given by the constitution to each state of a republican form of government, and may be stricken down by congressional action, or by the courts in the discharge of their solemn duty to maintain the supreme law of the land, anything in the constitution or laws of any state to the contrary notwithstanding.

For the reason stated, I am constrained to withhold my assent from the opinion and judgment of the majority.

---

**Questions:** In *Plessy,* is the Court assuming that conditions in the cars for Black and White travelers are the same? Does it matter? It should be noted that *Plessy* was followed by decades of civil rights activism, documented in Cottrol, et al., *Brown*, cited above. Prior to *Brown*, excerpted next, which reversed "separate but equal" nationwide, federal courts invalidated segregation in specific localities. See, e.g., *Lopez v. Seccombe*, 71 F. Supp. 769 (S.D. Cal. 1944) (San Bernardino, California public recreational facilities); *Mendez v. Westminster*, 161 F.2d 774 (9th Cir. 1947) (Orange County, California public schools).

## BROWN V. BOARD OF EDUCATION

347 U.S. 483 (1954)

* * *

MR. CHIEF JUSTICE WARREN delivered the opinion of the Court.

These cases come to us from the States of Kansas, South Carolina, Virginia, and Delaware. They are premised on different facts and different local conditions, but a common legal question justifies their consideration together in this consolidated opinion.

In each of the cases, minors of the Negro race, through their legal representatives, seek the aid of the courts in obtaining admission to the public schools of their community on a nonsegregated basis. In each instance, they had been denied admission to schools attended by white children under laws requiring or permitting segregation according to race.

This segregation was alleged to deprive the plaintiffs of the equal protection of the laws under the Fourteenth Amendment. In each of the cases other than the Delaware case, a three-judge federal district court denied relief to the plaintiffs on the so-called "separate but equal" doctrine announced by this Court in Plessy v. Ferguson, 163 U.S. 537. Under that doctrine, equality of treatment is accorded when the races are provided substantially equal facilities, even though these facilities be separate. In the Delaware case, the Supreme Court of Delaware adhered to that doctrine, but ordered that the plaintiffs be admitted to the white schools because of their superiority to the Negro schools.

The plaintiffs contend that segregated public schools are not "equal" and cannot be made "equal," and that hence they are deprived of the equal protection of the laws. Because of the obvious importance of the question presented, the Court took jurisdiction. Argument was heard in the 1952 Term, and reargument was heard this Term on certain questions propounded by the Court.

Reargument was largely devoted to the circumstances surrounding the adoption of the Fourteenth Amendment in 1868. It covered exhaustively consideration of the Amendment in Congress, ratification by the states, then-existing practices in racial segregation, and the views of proponents and opponents of the Amendment. This discussion and our own investigation convince us that, although these sources cast some light, it is not enough to resolve the problem with which we are faced. At best, they are inconclusive. The most avid proponents of the post-War Amendments undoubtedly intended them to remove all legal distinctions among "all persons born or naturalized in the United States." Their opponents, just as certainly, were antagonistic to both the letter and the spirit of the Amendments and wished them to have the most limited effect. What others in Congress and the state legislatures had in mind cannot be determined with any degree of certainty.

An additional reason for the inconclusive nature of the Amendment's history with respect to segregated schools is the status of public education at that time. In the South, the movement toward free common schools, supported by general taxation, had not yet taken hold. Education of white children was largely in the hands of private groups. Education of Negroes was almost nonexistent, and practically all of the race were illiterate. In fact, any education of Negroes was forbidden by law in some states. Today, in contrast, many Negroes have achieved outstanding success in the arts and sciences, as well as in the business and professional world. It is true that public school education at the time of the Amendment had advanced further in the North, but the effect of the Amendment on Northern States was generally ignored in the congressional debates. Even in the North, the conditions of public education did not approximate those existing today. The curriculum was usually rudimentary; ungraded schools were common in rural areas; the school term was but three months a year in many states, and compulsory school attendance was virtually unknown. As a consequence, it is not surprising that there should be so little in the history of the Fourteenth Amendment relating to its intended effect on public education.

In the first cases in this Court construing the Fourteenth Amendment, decided shortly after its adoption, the Court interpreted it as proscribing all state-imposed discriminations against the Negro race. The doctrine of "separate but equal" did not make its appearance in this Court until 1896 in the case of Plessy v. Ferguson, supra, involving not education but transportation. American courts have since labored with the doctrine for over half a century. In this Court, there have been six cases involving the "separate but equal" doctrine in the field of public education. In Cumming v. County Board of Education, 175 U.S. 528, and Gong Lum v. Rice, 275 U.S. 78, the validity of the doctrine itself was not challenged. In more recent cases, all on the graduate school level, inequality was found in that specific benefits enjoyed by white students were denied to Negro students of the same educational qualifications. Missouri ex rel. Gaines v. Canada, 305 U.S. 337; Sipuel v. Oklahoma, 332 U.S. 631; Sweatt v. Painter, 339 U.S. 629; McLaurin v. Oklahoma State Regents, 339 U.S. 637. In none of these cases was it necessary to reexamine the doctrine to grant relief to the Negro plaintiff. And in Sweatt v. Painter, supra, the Court expressly reserved decision on the question whether Plessy v. Ferguson should be held inapplicable to public education.

In the instant cases, that question is directly presented. Here, unlike Sweatt v. Painter, there are findings below that the Negro and white schools involved have been equalized, or are being equalized, with respect to buildings, curricula, qualifications and salaries of teachers, and other "tangible" factors. Our decision, therefore, cannot turn on merely a comparison of these tangible factors in the Negro and white schools involved in each of the cases. We must look instead to the effect of segregation itself on public education.

In approaching this problem, we cannot turn the clock back to 1868, when the Amendment was adopted, or even to 1896, when Plessy v. Ferguson was written. We must consider public education in the light of its full development and its present place in American life throughout the Nation. Only in this way can it be determined if segregation in public schools deprives these plaintiffs of the equal protection of the laws.

Today, education is perhaps the most important function of state and local governments. Compulsory school attendance laws and the great expenditures for education both demonstrate our recognition of the importance of education to our democratic society. It is required in the performance of our most basic public responsibilities, even service in the armed forces. It is the very foundation of good citizenship. Today it is a principal instrument in awakening the child to cultural values, in preparing him for later professional training, and in helping him to adjust normally to his environment. In these days, it is doubtful that any child may reasonably be expected to succeed in life if he is denied the opportunity of an education. Such an opportunity, where the state has undertaken to provide it, is a right which must be made available to all on equal terms.

We come then to the question presented: Does segregation of children in public schools solely on the basis of race, even though the physical facilities and other "tangible" factors may be equal, deprive the children of the minority group of equal educational opportunities? We believe that it does.

In Sweatt v. Painter, supra, in finding that a segregated law school for Negroes could not provide them equal educational opportunities, this Court relied in large part on "those qualities which are incapable of objective measurement but which make for greatness in a law school." In McLaurin v. Oklahoma State Regents, supra, the Court, in requiring that a Negro admitted to a white graduate school be treated like all other students, again resorted to intangible considerations: ". . . his ability to study, to engage in discussions and exchange views with other students, and, in general, to learn his profession." Such considerations apply with added force to children in grade and high schools. To separate them from others of similar age and qualifications solely because of their race generates a feeling of inferiority as to their status in the community that may affect their hearts and minds in a way unlikely ever to be undone. The effect of this separation on their educational opportunities was well stated by a finding in the Kansas case by a court which nevertheless felt compelled to rule against the Negro plaintiffs: Segregation of white and colored children in public schools has a detrimental effect upon the colored children. The impact is greater when it has the sanction of the law, for the policy of separating the races is usually interpreted as denoting the inferiority of the negro group. A sense of inferiority affects the motivation of a child to learn. Segregation with the sanction of law, therefore, has a tendency to [retard] the educational and mental development of negro children and to deprive them of some of the benefits they would receive in a racial[ly] integrated school system. Whatever may have been the extent of psychological knowledge at the time of Plessy v. Ferguson, this finding is amply supported by modern authority. Any language in Plessy v. Ferguson contrary to this finding is rejected.

We conclude that, in the field of public education, the doctrine of "separate but equal" has no place. Separate educational facilities are inherently unequal. Therefore, we hold that the plaintiffs and others similarly situated for whom the actions have been brought are, by reason of the segregation complained of, deprived of the equal protection of the laws guaranteed by the Fourteenth Amendment. This disposition makes unnecessary any discussion whether such segregation also violates the Due Process Clause of the Fourteenth Amendment.

* * *

It is so ordered.

---

**Question:** What is the nature of the inequality on which the *Brown* decision focuses?

## STRICT SCRUTINY

### LOVING V. VIRGINIA

388 U.S. 1 (1967)

* * *

MR. CHIEF JUSTICE WARREN delivered the opinion of the Court.

This case presents a constitutional question never addressed by this Court: whether a statutory scheme adopted by the State of Virginia to prevent marriages between persons solely on the basis of racial classifications violates the Equal Protection and Due Process Clauses of the Fourteenth Amendment. For reasons which seem to us to reflect the central meaning of those constitutional commands, we conclude that these statutes cannot stand consistently with the Fourteenth Amendment.

In June 1958, two residents of Virginia, Mildred Jeter, a Negro woman, and Richard Loving, a white man, were married in the District of Columbia pursuant to its laws. Shortly after their marriage, the Lovings returned to Virginia and established their marital abode in Caroline County. At the October Term, 1958, of the Circuit Court of Caroline County, a grand jury issued an indictment charging the Lovings with violating Virginia's ban on interracial marriages. On January 6, 1959, the Lovings pleaded guilty to the charge and were sentenced to one year in jail; however, the trial judge suspended the sentence for a period of 25 years on the condition that the Lovings leave the State and not return to Virginia together for 25 years. He stated in an opinion that:

'Almighty God created the races white, black, yellow, malay and red, and he placed them on separate continents. And but for the interference with his arrangement there would be no cause for such marriages. The fact that he separated the races shows that he did not intend for the races to mix.'

After their convictions, the Lovings took up residence in the District of Columbia. On November 6, 1963, they filed a motion in the state trial court to vacate the judgment and set aside the sentence on the ground that the statutes which they had violated were repugnant to the Fourteenth Amendment. The motion not having been decided by October 28, 1964, the Lovings instituted a class action in the United States District Court for the Eastern District of Virginia requesting that a three-judge court be convened to declare the Virginia anti-miscegenation statutes unconstitutional and to enjoin state officials from enforcing their convictions. On January 22, 1965, the state trial judge denied the motion to vacate the sentences, and the Lovings perfected an appeal to the Supreme Court of Appeals of Virginia. On February 11, 1965, the three-judge District Court continued the case to allow the Lovings to present their constitutional claims to the highest state court.

The Supreme Court of Appeals upheld the constitutionality of the anti-miscegenation statutes and, after modifying the sentence, affirmed the convictions. The Lovings appealed this decision, and we noted probable jurisdiction on December 12, 1966, 385 U.S. 986.

The two statutes under which appellants were convicted and sentenced are part of a comprehensive statutory scheme aimed at prohibiting and punishing interracial marriages. The Lovings were convicted of violating § 20–58 of the Virginia Code:

'Leaving State to evade law.—If any white person and colored person shall go out of this State, for the purpose of being married, and with the intention of returning, and be married out of it, and afterwards return to and reside in it, cohabiting as man and wife, they shall be punished as provided in § 20–59, and the marriage shall be governed by the same law as if it had been solemnized in this State. The fact of their cohabitation here as man and wife shall be evidence of their marriage.'

Section 20–59, which defines the penalty for miscegenation, provides:

'Punishment for marriage.—If any white person intermarry with a colored person, or any colored person intermarry with a white person, he shall be guilty of a felony and shall be punished by confinement in the penitentiary for not less than one nor more than five years.'

Other central provisions in the Virginia statutory scheme are § 20–57, which automatically voids all marriages between 'a white person and a colored person' without any judicial proceeding, and §§ 20–54 and 1–14 which, respectively, define 'white persons' and 'colored persons and Indians' for purposes of the statutory prohibitions. The Lovings have never disputed in the course of this litigation that Mrs. Loving is a 'colored person' or that Mr. Loving is a 'white person' within the meanings given those terms by the Virginia statutes.

Virginia is now one of 16 States which prohibit and punish marriages on the basis of racial classifications. Penalties for miscegenation arose as an incident to slavery and have been common in Virginia since the colonial period. The present statutory scheme dates from the adoption of the Racial Integrity Act of 1924, passed during the period of extreme nativism which followed the end of the First World War. The central features of this Act, and current Virginia law, are the absolute prohibition of a 'white person' marrying other than another 'white person,' a prohibition against issuing marriage licenses until the issuing official is satisfied that the applicants' statements as to their race are correct, certificates of 'racial composition' to be kept by both local and state registrars, and the carrying forward of earlier prohibitions against racial intermarriage.

In upholding the constitutionality of these provisions in the decision below, the Supreme Court of Appeals of Virginia referred to its 1955 decision in Naim v. Naim, 197 Va. 80, 87 S.E.2d 749, as stating the reasons supporting the validity of these laws. In Naim, the state court concluded that the State's legitimate purposes were 'to preserve the racial integrity of its citizens,' and to prevent 'the corruption of blood,' 'a mongrel breed of citizens,' and 'the obliteration of racial pride,' obviously an endorsement of the doctrine of White Supremacy. Id., at 90, 87 S.E.2d, at 756. The court also reasoned that marriage has traditionally been subject to state regulation without federal intervention, and, consequently, the regulation of marriage should be left to exclusive state control by the Tenth Amendment.

While the state court is no doubt correct in asserting that marriage is a social relation subject to the State's police power, Maynard v. Hill, 125 U.S. 190 (1888), the State does not contend in its argument before this Court that its powers to regulate marriage are unlimited notwithstanding the commands of the Fourteenth Amendment. Nor could it do so in light of Meyer v. State of Nebraska, 262 U.S. 390 (1923), and Skinner v. State of Oklahoma, 316 U.S. 535, 62 (1942). Instead, the State argues that the meaning of the Equal Protection Clause, as illuminated by the statements of the Framers, is only that state penal laws containing an interracial element as part of the definition of the offense must apply equally to whites and Negroes in the sense that members of each race are punished to the same degree. Thus, the State contends that, because its miscegenation statutes punish equally both the white and the Negro participants in an interracial marriage, these statutes, despite their reliance on racial classifications do not constitute an invidious discrimination based upon race. The second argument advanced by the State assumes the validity of its equal application theory. The argument is that, if the Equal Protection Clause does not outlaw miscegenation statutes because of their reliance on racial classifications, the question of constitutionality would thus become whether there was any rational basis for a State to treat interracial marriages differently from other marriages. On this question, the State argues, the scientific evidence is substantially in doubt and, consequently, this Court should defer to the wisdom of the state legislature in adopting its policy of discouraging interracial marriages.

Because we reject the notion that the mere 'equal application' of a statute containing racial classifications is enough to remove the classifications from the Fourteenth Amendment's proscription of all invidious racial discriminations, we do not accept the State's contention that these statutes should be upheld if there is any possible basis for concluding that they serve a rational purpose. The mere fact of equal application does not mean that our analysis of these statutes should follow the approach we have taken in cases involving no racial discrimination where the Equal Protection Clause has been arrayed against a statute discriminating between the kinds of advertising which may be displayed on trucks in New York City, Railway Express Agency, Inc. v. People of State of New York, 336 U.S. 106, (1949), or an exemption in Ohio's ad valorem tax for merchandise owned by a non-resident in a storage warehouse, Allied Stores of Ohio, Inc. v. Bowers, 358 U.S. 522 (1959). In these cases, involving distinctions not drawn according to race, the Court has merely asked whether there is any rational foundation for the discriminations, and has deferred to the wisdom of the state legislatures. In the case at bar, however, we deal with statutes containing racial classifications, and the fact of equal application does not immunize the statute from the very heavy burden of justification which the Fourteenth Amendment has traditionally required of state statutes drawn according to race.

The State argues that statements in the Thirty-ninth Congress about the time of the passage of the Fourteenth Amendment indicate that the Framers did not intend the Amendment to make unconstitutional state miscegenation laws. Many of the statements alluded to by the State concern the debates over the Freedmen's Bureau Bill, which President Johnson vetoed, and the Civil Rights Act of 1866, 14 Stat. 27, enacted over his veto. While these statements have some relevance to the intention of Congress in submitting the Fourteenth Amendment, it must be understood that the pertained to the passage of specific statutes and not to the broader, organic purpose of a constitutional amendment. As for the various statements directly concerning the Fourteenth Amendment, we have said in connection with a related problem, that although these historical sources 'cast some light' they are not sufficient to resolve the problem; '(a)t best, they are inconclusive. The most avid proponents of the post-War Amendments undoubtedly intended them to remove all legal distinctions among 'all persons born or naturalized in the United States.' Their opponents, just as certainly, were antagonistic to both the letter and the spirit of the Amendments and wished them to have the most limited effect.' Brown v. Board of Education of Topeka, 347 U.S. 483, 489 (1954). See also

Strauder v. State of West Virginia, 100 U.S. 303, 310 (1880). We have rejected the proposition that the debates in the Thirty-ninth Congress or in the state legislatures which ratified the Fourteenth Amendment supported the theory advanced by the State, that the requirement of equal protection of the laws is satisfied by penal laws defining offenses based on racial classifications so long as white and Negro participants in the offense were similarly punished. McLaughlin v. State of Florida, 379 U.S. 184 (1964).

The State finds support for its 'equal application' theory in the decision of the Court in Pace v. State of Alabama, 106 U.S. 583 (1883). In that case, the Court upheld a conviction under an Alabama statute forbidding adultery or fornication between a white person and a Negro which imposed a greater penalty than that of a statute proscribing similar conduct by members of the same race. The Court reasoned that the statute could not be said to discriminate against Negroes because the punishment for each participant in the offense was the same. However, as recently as the 1964 Term, in rejecting the reasoning of that case, we stated 'Pace represents a limited view of the Equal Protection Clause which has not withstood analysis in the subsequent decisions of this Court.' McLaughlin v. Florida, supra, 379 U.S. at 188. As we there demonstrated, the Equal Protection Clause requires the consideration of whether the classifications drawn by any statute constitute an arbitrary and invidious discrimination. The clear and central purpose of the Fourteenth Amendment was to eliminate all official state sources of invidious racial discrimination in the States. Slaughter-House Cases, 16 Wall. 36, 71 (1873); Strauder v. State of West Virginia, 100 U.S. 303, 307–308 (1880); Ex parte Virginia, 100 U.S. 339, 344–345 (1880); Shelley v. Kraemer, 334 U.S. 1 (1948); Burton v. Wilmington Parking Authority, 365 U.S. 715, (1961).

There can be no question but that Virginia's miscegenation statutes rest solely upon distinctions drawn according to race. The statutes proscribe generally accepted conduct if engaged in by members of different races. Over the years, this Court has consistently repudiated '(d)istinctions between citizens solely because of their ancestry' as being 'odious to a free people whose institutions are founded upon the doctrine of equality.' Hirabayashi v. United States, 320 U.S. 81, 100 (1943). At the very least, the Equal Protection Clause demands that racial classifications, especially suspect in criminal statutes, be subjected to the 'most rigid scrutiny,' Korematsu v. United States, 323 U.S. 214, 216 (1944), and, if they are ever to be upheld, they must be shown to be necessary to the accomplishment of some permissible state objective, independent of the racial discrimination which it was the object of the Fourteenth Amendment to eliminate. Indeed, two members of this Court have already stated that they 'cannot conceive of a valid legislative purpose * * * which makes the color of a person's skin the test of whether his conduct is a criminal offense.' McLaughlin v.

Florida, supra, 379 U.S. at 198 (Stewart, J., joined by Douglas, J., concurring).

There is patently no legitimate overriding purpose independent of invidious racial discrimination which justifies this classification. The fact that Virginia prohibits only interracial marriages involving white persons demonstrates that the racial classifications must stand on their own justification, as measures designed to maintain White Supremacy. We have consistently denied the constitutionality of measures which restrict the rights of citizens on account of race. There can be no doubt that restricting the freedom to marry solely because of racial classifications violates the central meaning of the Equal Protection Clause.

These statutes also deprive the Lovings of liberty without due process of law in violation of the Due Process Clause of the Fourteenth Amendment. The freedom to marry has long been recognized as one of the vital personal rights essential to the orderly pursuit of happiness by free men.

Marriage is one of the 'basic civil rights of man,' fundamental to our very existence and survival. Skinner v. State of Oklahoma, 316 U.S. 535, 541 (1942). See also Maynard v. Hill, 125 U.S. 190 (1888). To deny this fundamental freedom on so unsupportable a basis as the racial classifications embodied in these statutes, classifications so directly subversive of the principle of equality at the heart of the Fourteenth Amendment, is surely to deprive all the State's citizens of liberty without due process of law. The Fourteenth Amendment requires that the freedom of choice to marry not be restricted by invidious racial discriminations. Under our Constitution, the freedom to marry or not marry, a person of another race resides with the individual and cannot be infringed by the State.

These convictions must be reversed. It is so ordered.

---

**Question:** A state family court removed a White woman's child from her custody because she was cohabiting with a Black man. After *Loving,* was this ruling constitutional? See *Palmore v. Sidoti,* 466 U.S. 429 (1984).

# DISPARATE IMPACT

## VILLAGE OF ARLINGTON HEIGHTS V. METROPOLITAN HOUSING DEVELOPMENT CORP.

429 U.S. 252 (1977)

* * *

MR. JUSTICE POWELL delivered the opinion of the Court.

In 1971 respondent Metropolitan Housing Development Corporation (MHDC) applied to petitioner, the Village of Arlington Heights, Ill., for the rezoning of a 15-acre parcel from single-family to multiple-family classification. Using federal financial assistance, MHDC planned to build 190 clustered townhouse units for low- and moderate-income tenants. The Village denied the rezoning request. MHDC, joined by other plaintiffs who are also respondents here, brought suit in the United States District Court for the Northern District of Illinois. They alleged that the denial was racially discriminatory and that it violated, inter alia, the Fourteenth Amendment and the Fair Housing Act of 1968, 82 Stat. 81, 42 U.S.C. § 3601 et seq. Following a bench trial, the District Court entered judgment for the Village, 373 F.Supp. 208 (1974), and respondents appealed. The Court of Appeals for the Seventh Circuit reversed, finding that the "ultimate effect" of the denial was racially discriminatory, and that the refusal to rezone therefore violated the Fourteenth Amendment. 517 F.2d 409 (1975). We granted the Village's petition for certiorari, 423 U.S. 1030 (1975), and now reverse.

Arlington Heights is a suburb of Chicago, located about 26 miles northwest of the downtown Loop area. Most of the land in Arlington Heights is zoned for detached single-family homes, and this is in fact the prevailing land use. The Village experienced substantial growth during the 1960's, but, like other communities in northwest Cook County, its population of racial minority groups remained quite low. According to the 1970 census, only 27 of the Village's 64,000 residents were black.

The Clerics of St. Viator, a religious order (Order), own an 80-acre parcel just east of the center of Arlington Heights. Part of the site is occupied by the Viatorian high school, and part by the Order's three-story novitiate building, which houses dormitories and a Montessori school. Much of the site, however, remains vacant. Since 1959, when the Village first adopted a zoning ordinance, all the land surrounding the Viatorian property has been zoned R–3, a single-family specification with relatively small minimum lot-size requirements. On three sides of the Viatorian land there are single-family homes just across a street; to the east the Viatorian property directly adjoins the backyards of other single-family homes.

The Order decided in 1970 to devote some of its land to low- and moderate-income housing. Investigation revealed that the most expeditious way to build such housing was to work through a nonprofit developer experienced in the use of federal housing subsidies under § 236 of the National Housing Act, 48 Stat. 1246, as added and amended, 12 U.S.C. § 1715z–1.2

MHDC is such a developer. It was organized in 1968 by several prominent Chicago citizens for the purpose of building low- and moderate-income housing throughout the Chicago area. In 1970 MHDC was in the process of building one § 236 development near Arlington Heights and already had provided some federally assisted housing on a smaller scale in other parts of the Chicago area.

After some negotiation, MHDC and the Order entered into a 99-year lease and an accompanying agreement of sale covering a 15-acre site in the southeast corner of the Viatorian property. MHDC became the lessee immediately, but the sale agreement was contingent upon MHDC's securing zoning clearances from the Village and § 236 housing assistance from the Federal Government. If MHDC proved unsuccessful in securing either, both the lease and the contract of sale would lapse. The agreement established a bargain purchase price of $300,000, low enough to comply with federal limitations governing land-acquisition costs for § 236 housing.

MHDC engaged an architect and proceeded with the project, to be known as Lincoln Green. The plans called for 20 two-story buildings with a total of 190 units, each unit having its own private entrance from outside. One hundred of the units would have a single bedroom, thought likely to attract elderly citizens. The remainder would have two, three, or four bedrooms. A large portion of the site would remain open, with shrubs and trees to screen the homes abutting the property to the east.

The planned development did not conform to the Village's zoning ordinance and could not be built unless Arlington Heights rezoned the parcel to R–5, its multiple-family housing classification. Accordingly, MHDC filed with the Village Plan Commission a petition for rezoning, accompanied by supporting materials describing the development and specifying that it would be subsidized under § 236. The materials made clear that one requirement under § 236 is an affirmative marketing plan designed to assure that a subsidized development is racially integrated. MHDC also submitted studies demonstrating the need for housing of this type and analyzing the probable impact of the development. To prepare for the hearings before the Plan Commission and to assure compliance with the Village building code, fire regulations, and related requirements, MHDC consulted with the Village staff for preliminary review of the development. The parties have stipulated that every change recommended during such consultations was incorporated into the plans.

During the spring of 1971, the Plan Commission considered the proposal at a series of three public meetings, which drew large crowds. Although many of those attending were quite vocal and demonstrative in opposition to Lincoln Green, a number of individuals and representatives of community groups spoke in support of rezoning. Some of the comments, both from opponents and supporters, addressed what was referred to as the "social issue" the desirability or undesirability of introducing at this location in Arlington Heights low- and moderate-income housing, housing that would probably be racially integrated.

Many of the opponents, however, focused on the zoning aspects of the petition, stressing two arguments. First, the area always had been zoned single-family, and the neighboring citizens had built or purchased there in reliance on that classification. Rezoning threatened to cause a measurable drop in property value for neighboring sites. Second, the Village's apartment policy, adopted by the Village Board in 1962 and amended in 1970, called for R–5 zoning primarily to serve as a buffer between single-family development and land uses thought incompatible, such as commercial or manufacturing districts. Lincoln Green did not meet this requirement, as it adjoined no commercial or manufacturing district.

At the close of the third meeting, the Plan Commission adopted a motion to recommend to the Village's Board of Trustees that it deny the request. The motion stated: "While the need for low and moderate income housing may exist in Arlington Heights or its environs, the Plan Commission would be derelict in recommending it at the proposed location." Two members voted against the motion and submitted a minority report, stressing that in their view the change to accommodate Lincoln Green represented "good zoning." The Village Board met on September 28, 1971, to consider MHDC's request and the recommendation of the Plan Commission. After a public hearing, the Board denied the rezoning by a 6–1 vote.

The following June MHDC and three Negro individuals filed this lawsuit against the Village, seeking declaratory and injunctive relief. A second nonprofit corporation and an individual of Mexican-American descent intervened as plaintiffs. The trial resulted in a judgment for petitioners. Assuming that MHDC had standing to bring the suit, the District Court held that the petitioners were not motivated by racial discrimination or intent to discriminate against low-income groups when they denied rezoning, but rather by a desire "to protect property values and the integrity of the Village's zoning plan." 373 F.Supp., at 211. The District Court concluded also that the denial would not have a racially discriminatory effect.

A divided Court of Appeals reversed. It first approved the District Court's finding that the defendants were motivated by a concern for the integrity of the zoning plan, rather than by racial discrimination. Deciding whether their refusal to rezone would have discriminatory effects was more complex. The court observed that the refusal would have a disproportionate impact on blacks. Based upon family income, blacks constituted 40% of those Chicago area residents who were eligible to become tenants of Lincoln Green, although they composed a far lower percentage of total area population. The court reasoned, however, that under our decision in James v. Valtierra, 402 U.S. 137 (1971), such a disparity in racial impact alone does not call for strict scrutiny of a municipality's decision that prevents the construction of the low-cost housing.

There was another level to the court's analysis of allegedly discriminatory results. Invoking language from Kennedy Park Homes Assn. v. City of Lackawanna, 436 F.2d 108, 112 (C.A.2 1971), cert. denied, 401 U.S. 1010 (1970), the Court of Appeals ruled that the denial of rezoning must be examined in light of its "historical context and ultimate effect."6 517 F.2d, at 413. Northwest Cook County was enjoying rapid growth in employment opportunities and population, but it continued to exhibit a high degree of residential segregation. The court held that Arlington Heights could not simply ignore this problem. Indeed, it found that the Village had been "exploiting" the situation by allowing itself to become a nearly all white community. Id., at 414. The Village had no other current plans for building low- and moderate-income housing, and no other R–5 parcels in the Village were available to MHDC at an economically feasible price.

Against this background, the Court of Appeals ruled that the denial of the Lincoln Green proposal had racially discriminatory effects and could be tolerated only if it served compelling interests. Neither the buffer policy nor the desire to protect property values met this exacting standard. The court therefore concluded that the denial violated the Equal Protection Clause of the Fourteenth Amendment.

* * *

Our decision last Term in Washington v. Davis, 426 U.S. 229 (1976), made it clear that official action will not be held unconstitutional solely because it results in a racially disproportionate impact. "Disproportionate impact is not irrelevant, but it is not the sole touchstone of an invidious racial discrimination." Id., at 242. Proof of racially discriminatory intent or purpose is required to show a violation of the Equal Protection Clause. Although some contrary indications may be drawn from some of our cases, the holding in Davis reaffirmed a principle well established in a variety of contexts. E. g., Keyes v. School Dist. No. 1, Denver, Colo., 413 U.S. 189, 208 (1973) (schools); Wright v. Rockefeller, 376 U.S. 52, 56–572 (1964) (election districting); Akins v. Texas, 325 U.S. 398, 403–404 (1945) (jury selection).

Davis does not require a plaintiff to prove that the challenged action rested solely on racially discriminatory purposes. Rarely can it be said that a legislature or administrative body operating under a broad mandate made a decision motivated solely by a single concern, or even that a particular purpose was the "dominant" or "primary" one. In fact, it is because legislators and administrators are properly concerned with balancing numerous competing considerations that courts refrain from reviewing the merits of their decisions, absent a showing of arbitrariness or irrationality. But racial discrimination is not just another competing consideration. When there is a proof that a discriminatory purpose has been a motivating factor in the decision, this judicial deference is no longer justified.

Determining whether invidious discriminatory purpose was a motivating factor demands a sensitive inquiry into such circumstantial and direct evidence of intent as may be available. The impact of the official action whether it "bears more heavily on one race than another," Washington v. Davis, supra, 426 U.S., at 242 may provide an important starting point. Sometimes a clear pattern, unexplainable on grounds other than race, emerges from the effect of the state action even when the governing legislation appears neutral on its face. Yick Wo v. Hopkins, 118 U.S. 356 (1886); . . . Gomillion v. Lightfoot, 364 U.S. 339 (1960). The evidentiary inquiry is then relatively easy. But such cases are rare. Absent a pattern as stark as that in Gomillion or Yick Wo, impact alone is not determinative, and the Court must look to other evidence.

The historical background of the decision is one evidentiary source, particularly if it reveals a series of official actions taken for invidious purposes. See [citations]. The specific sequence of events leading up the challenged decision also may shed some light on the decisionmaker's purposes. [citations]. For example, if the property involved here always had been zoned R–5 but suddenly was changed to R–3 when the town learned of MHDC's plans to erect integrated housing, we would have a far different case. Departures from the normal procedural sequence also might afford evidence that improper purposes are playing a role. Substantive departures too may be relevant, particularly if the factors usually considered important by the decisionmaker strongly favor a decision contrary to the one reached.

The legislative or administrative history may be highly relevant, especially where there are contemporary statements by members of the decision-making body, minutes of its meetings, or reports. In some extraordinary instances the members might be called to the stand at trial to testify concerning the purpose of the official action, although even then such testimony frequently will be barred by privilege. See [citations].

The foregoing summary identifies, without purporting to be exhaustive, subjects of proper inquiry in determining whether racially discriminatory intent existed. With these in mind, we now address the case before us.

This case was tried in the District Court and reviewed in the Court of Appeals before our decision in Washington v. Davis, supra. The respondents proceeded on the erroneous theory that the Village's refusal to rezone carried a racially discriminatory effect and was, without more, unconstitutional. But both courts below understood that at least part of their function was to examine the purpose underlying the decision. In making its findings on this issue, the District Court noted that some of the opponents of Lincoln Green who spoke at the various hearings might have been motivated by opposition to minority groups. The court held, however, that the evidence "does not warrant the conclusion that this motivated the defendants." 373 F.Supp., at 211.

* * *

We also have reviewed the evidence. The impact of the Village's decision does arguably bear more heavily on racial minorities. Minorities constitute 18% of the Chicago area population, and 40% of the income groups said to be eligible for Lincoln Green. But there is little about the sequence of events leading up to the decision that would spark suspicion. The area around the Viatorian property has been zoned R–3 since 1959, the year when Arlington Heights first adopted a zoning map. Single-family homes surround the 80-acre site, and the Village is undeniably committed to single-family homes as its dominant residential land use. The rezoning request progressed according to the usual procedures. The Plan Commission even scheduled two additional hearings, at least in part to accommodate MHDC and permit it to supplement its presentation with answers to questions generated at the first hearing.

The statements by the Plan Commission and Village Board members, as reflected in the official minutes, focused almost exclusively on the zoning aspects of the MHDC petition, and the zoning factors on which they relied are not novel criteria in the Village's rezoning decisions. There is no reason to doubt that there has been reliance by some neighboring property owners on the maintenance of single-family zoning in the vicinity. The Village originally adopted its buffer policy long before MHDC entered the picture and has applied the policy too consistently for us to infer discriminatory purpose from its application in this case. Finally, MHDC called one member of the Village Board to the stand at trial. Nothing in her testimony supports an inference of invidious purpose.

In sum, the evidence does not warrant overturning the concurrent findings of both courts below. Respondents simply failed to carry their burden of proving that discriminatory purpose was a motivating factor in the Village's decision. This conclusion ends the constitutional inquiry. The court of Appeals' further finding that the Village's decision carried a discriminatory "ultimate effect" is without independent constitutional significance.

* * *

Reversed and remanded.

---

**Question:** A state constitution disenfranchised voters convicted of certain criminal offences. Research into legislative history revealed a statement that the purpose of the provision was "to establish White supremacy in this state." Constitutional after *Arlington Heights*? See *Hunter v. Underwood,* 471 U.S. 222 (1985). Following Arlington Heights, federal courts were increasingly sympathetic to discriminatory effects claims brought specifically under the Fair Housing Act. See Schwemm, "Reflecting on Arlington Heights," cited above.

# CHAPTER 12

# EQUAL PROTECTION, GENDER, AND EDUCATION

■ ■ ■

## CONTEXT & SOURCES

"Living constitutionalism" interpretive theory has extended 14th Amendment equal protection analysis beyond race to include legislation differentiating by gender and to laws limiting educational opportunities. This chapter shows how the Court has applied, or been reluctant to apply, different levels of constitutional scrutiny in these contexts.

The development of gender discrimination law is traced by Philippa Strum, *On Account of Sex: Ruth Bader Ginsburg and the Making of Gender Equality Law* (University Press of Kansas, 2022). Michael A. Olivas, *No Undocumented Child Left Behind: Plyler v. Doe and the Education of Undocumented Schoolchildren* (NYU Press 2012) studies this case's litigation, implementation, and effect on subsequent policy.

## GENDER

### CRAIG V. BOREN

429 U.S. 190 (1976)

* * *

MR. JUSTICE BRENNAN delivered the opinion of the Court.

The interaction of two sections of an Oklahoma statute, Okla.Stat., Tit. 37, §§ 241 and 245 (1958 and Supp.1976), prohibits the sale of "nonintoxicating" 3.2% beer to males under the age of 21 and to females under the age of 18. The question to be decided is whether such a gender-based differential constitutes a denial to males 18–20 years of age of the equal protection of the laws in violation of the Fourteenth Amendment.

This action was brought in the District Court for the Western District of Oklahoma on December 20, 1972, by appellant Craig, a male then between 18 and 21 years of age, and by appellant Whitener, a licensed vendor of 3.2% beer. The complaint sought declaratory and injunctive relief against enforcement of the gender-based differential on the ground that it constituted invidious discrimination against males 18–20 years of age. A three-judge court convened under 28 U.S.C. § 2281 sustained the constitutionality of the statutory differential and dismissed the action. 399 F.Supp. 1304 (1975). We noted probable jurisdiction of appellants' appeal, 423 U.S. 1047 (1976). We reverse.

* * *

Before 1972, Oklahoma defined the commencement of civil majority at age 18 for females and age 21 for males. Okla.Stat., Tit. 15, § 13 (1972 and Supp.1976). In contrast, females were held criminally responsible as adults at age 18 and males at age 16. Okla.Stat., Tit. 10, § 1101(a) (Supp.1976). After the Court of Appeals for the Tenth Circuit held in 1972, on the authority of Reed v. Reed, 404 U.S. 71 (1971), that the age distinction was unconstitutional for purposes of establishing criminal responsibility as adults, Lamb v. Brown, 456 F.2d 18, the Oklahoma Legislature fixed age 18 as applicable to both males and females. Okla.Stat., Tit. 10, § 1101(a) (Supp.1976). In 1972, 18 also was established as the age of majority for males and females in civil matters, Okla.Stat., Tit. 15, § 13 (1972 and Supp.1976), except that §§ 241 and 245 of the 3.2% beer statute were simultaneously codified to create an exception to the gender-free rule.

Analysis may appropriately begin with the reminder that Reed emphasized that statutory classifications that distinguish between males and females are "subject to scrutiny under the Equal Protection Clause." 404 U.S., at 75. To withstand constitutional challenge, previous cases establish that classifications by gender must serve important governmental objectives and must be substantially related to achievement of those objectives. Thus, in Reed, the objectives of "reducing the workload on probate courts," id., at 76, and "avoiding intrafamily controversy," id., at 77, were deemed of insufficient importance to sustain use of an overt gender criterion in the appointment of administrators of intestate decedents' estates. Decisions following Reed similarly have rejected administrative ease and convenience as sufficiently important objectives to justify gender-based classifications. See, e. g., [citations]. And only two Terms ago, Stanton v. Stanton, 421 U.S. 7 (1975), expressly stating that Reed v. Reed was "controlling," 421 U.S., at 13, held that Reed required invalidation of a Utah differential age-of-majority statute, notwithstanding the statute's coincidence with and furtherance of the State's purpose of fostering "old notions" of role typing and preparing boys for their expected performance in the economic and political worlds. 421 U.S., at 14–15.

Reed v. Reed has also provided the underpinning for decisions that have invalidated statutes employing gender as an inaccurate proxy for other, more germane bases of classification. Hence, "archaic and overbroad" generalizations, Schlesinger v. Ballard, supra, 419 U.S., at 508, concerning the financial position of servicewomen, Frontiero v. Richardson, supra, 411 U.S., at 689 n. 23, and working women, Weinberger v.

Wiesenfeld, 420 U.S. 636, 643 (1975), could not justify use of a gender line in determining eligibility for certain governmental entitlements. Similarly, increasingly outdated misconceptions concerning the role of females in the home rather than in the "marketplace and world of ideas" were rejected as loose-fitting characterizations incapable of supporting state statutory schemes that were premised upon their accuracy. Stanton v. Stanton, supra; Taylor v. Louisiana, 419 U.S. 522, 535 n. 17 (1975). In light of the weak congruence between gender and the characteristic or trait that gender purported to represent, it was necessary that the legislatures choose either to realign their substantive laws in a gender-neutral fashion, or to adopt procedures for identifying those instances where the sex-centered generalization actually comported with fact. See, e. g., [citations].

In this case, too, "Reed, we feel is controlling . . .," Stanton v. Stanton, supra, 421 U.S., at 13. We turn then to the question whether, under Reed, the difference between males and females with respect to the purchase of 3.2% beer warrants the differential in age drawn by the Oklahoma statute. We conclude that it does not.

The District Court recognized that Reed v. Reed was controlling. In applying the teachings of that case, the court found the requisite important governmental objective in the traffic-safety goal proffered by the Oklahoma Attorney General. It then concluded that the statistics introduced by the appellees established that the gender-based distinction was substantially related to achievement of that goal.

We accept for purposes of discussion the District Court's identification of the objective underlying §§ 241 and 245 as the enhancement of traffic safety. Clearly, the protection of public health and safety represents an important function of state and local governments. However, appellees' statistics in our view cannot support the conclusion that the gender-based distinction closely serves to achieve that objective and therefore the distinction cannot under Reed withstand equal protection challenge.

The appellees introduced a variety of statistical surveys. First, an analysis of arrest statistics for 1973 demonstrated that 18–20-year-old male arrests for "driving under the influence" and "drunkenness" substantially exceeded female arrests for that same age period. Similarly, youths aged 17–21 were found to be overrepresented among those killed or injured in traffic accidents, with males again numerically exceeding females in this regard. Third, a random roadside survey in Oklahoma City revealed that young males were more inclined to drive and drink beer than were their female counterparts. Fourth, Federal Bureau of Investigation nationwide statistics exhibited a notable increase in arrests for "driving under the influence." Finally, statistical evidence gathered in other jurisdictions, particularly Minnesota and Michigan, was offered to corroborate Oklahoma's experience by indicating the pervasiveness of youthful participation in motor vehicle accidents following the imbibing of alcohol. Conceding that "the case is not free from doubt," 399 F.Supp., at 1314, the District Court nonetheless concluded that this statistical showing substantiated "a rational basis for the legislative judgment underlying the challenged classification." Id., at 1307.

Even were this statistical evidence accepted as accurate, it nevertheless offers only a weak answer to the equal protection question presented here. The most focused and relevant of the statistical surveys, arrests of 18–20-year-olds for alcohol-related driving offenses, exemplifies the ultimate unpersuasiveness of this evidentiary record. Viewed in terms of the correlation between sex and the actual activity that Oklahoma seeks to regulate driving while under the influence of alcohol the statistics broadly establish that .18% of females and 2% of males in that age group were arrested for that offense. While such a disparity is not trivial in a statistical sense, it hardly can form the basis for employment of a gender line as a classifying device. Certainly if maleness is to serve as a proxy for drinking and driving, a correlation of 2% must be considered an unduly tenuous "fit." Indeed, prior cases have consistently rejected the use of sex as a decisionmaking factor even though the statutes in question certainly rested on far more predictive empirical relationships than this.

Moreover, the statistics exhibit a variety of other shortcomings that seriously impugn their value to equal protection analysis. Setting aside the obvious methodological problems, the surveys do not adequately justify the salient features of Oklahoma's gender-based traffic-safety law. None purports to measure the use and dangerousness of 3.2% beer as opposed to alcohol generally, a detail that is of particular importance since, in light of its low alcohol level, Oklahoma apparently considers the 3.2% beverage to be "nonintoxicating." Okla.Stat., Tit. 37, § 163.1 (1958); see State ex rel. Springer v. Bliss, 185 P.2d 220 (1947). Moreover, many of the studies, while graphically documenting the unfortunate increase in driving while under the influence of alcohol, make no effort to relate their findings to age-sex differentials as involved here. Indeed, the only survey that explicitly centered its attention upon young drivers and their use of beer albeit apparently not of the diluted 3.2% variety reached results that hardly can be viewed as impressive in justifying either a gender or age classification.

There is no reason to belabor this line of analysis. It is unrealistic to expect either members of the judiciary or state officials to be well versed in the rigors of experimental or statistical technique. But this merely illustrates that proving broad sociological propositions by statistics is a dubious business, and one that inevitably is in tension with the normative philosophy that underlies the Equal Protection Clause. Suffice to say that the showing offered by the appellees does not satisfy us that sex represents a legitimate, accurate proxy for the regulation of drinking and driving. In fact, when it is further recognized that Oklahoma's statute prohibits only the selling of 3.2% beer to young males and not their drinking the beverage once acquired (even after purchase by their 18–20-year-old female companions), the relationship between gender and traffic safety becomes far too tenuous to satisfy Reed's requirement that the gender-based difference be substantially related to achievement of the statutory objective.

We hold, therefore, that under Reed, Oklahoma's 3.2% beer statute invidiously discriminates against males 18–20 years of age.

* * *

We conclude that the gender-based differential contained in Okla.Stat., Tit. 37, § 245 (1976 Supp.) constitutes a denial of the equal protection of the laws to males aged 18–20 and reverse the judgment of the District Court.

It is so ordered.

MR. JUSTICE REHNQUIST, dissenting.

The Court's disposition of this case is objectionable on two grounds. First is its conclusion that men challenging a gender-based statute which treats them less favorably than women may invoke a more stringent standard of judicial review than pertains to most other types of classifications. Second is the Court's enunciation of this standard, without citation to any source, as being that "classifications by gender must serve important governmental objectives and must be substantially related to achievement of those objectives." Ante at 197 (emphasis added). The only redeeming feature of the Court's opinion, to my mind, is that it apparently signals a retreat by those who joined the plurality opinion in Frontiero v. Richardson, 411 U.S. 677 (1973), from their view that sex is a "suspect" classification for purposes of equal protection analysis. I think the Oklahoma statute challenged here need pass only the "rational basis" equal protection analysis expounded in cases such as McGowan v. Maryland, 366 U.S. 420 (1961), and Williamson v. Lee Optical Co., 348 U.S. 483 (1955), and I believe that it is constitutional under that analysis.

* * *

The Oklahoma Legislature could have believed that 18–20-year-old males drive substantially more, and tend more often to be intoxicated than their female counterparts; that they prefer beer and admit to drinking and driving at a higher rate than females; and that they suffer traffic injuries out of proportion to the part they make up of the population. Under the appropriate rational-basis test for equal protection, it is neither irrational nor arbitrary to bar them from making purchases of 3.2% beer, which purchases might in many cases be made by a young man who immediately returns to his vehicle with the beverage in his possession. The record does not give any good indication of the true proportion of males in the age group who drink and drive (except that it is no doubt greater than the 2% who are arrested), but whatever it may be I cannot see that the mere purchase right involved could conceivably raise a due process question. There being no violation of either equal protection or due process, the statute should accordingly be upheld.

---

**Questions:** A state nursing college admits only women as students. Constitutional after *Craig v. Boren*? See *Mississippi University for Women v. Hogan,* 458 U.S. 718 (1982). What about the U.S. government's male-only draft registration requirement? See *Rostker v. Goldberg,* 453 U.S. 57 (1981).

## UNITED STATES V. VIRGINIA

518 U.S. 515 (1996)

JUSTICE GINSBURG delivered the opinion of the Court.

Founded in 1839, VMI is today the sole single sex school among Virginia's 15 public institutions of higher learning. VMI's distinctive mission is to produce "citizen soldiers," men prepared for leadership in civilian life and in military service. VMI pursues this mission through pervasive training of a kind not available anywhere else in Virginia. Assigning prime place to character development, VMI uses an "adversative method" modeled on English public schools and once characteristic of military instruction. VMI constantly endeavors to instill physical and mental discipline in its cadets and impart to them a strong moral code. The school's graduates leave VMI with heightened comprehension of their capacity to deal with duress and stress, and a large sense of accomplishment for completing the hazardous course.

* * *

In 1990, prompted by a complaint filed with the Attorney General by a female high school student seeking admission to VMI, the United States sued the Commonwealth of Virginia and VMI, alleging that VMI's exclusively male admission policy violated the Equal Protection Clause of the Fourteenth Amendment.

* * *

The District Court ruled in favor of VMI, however, and rejected the equal protection challenge pressed by the United States.

* * *

The Court of Appeals for the Fourth Circuit disagreed and vacated the District Court's judgment. The appellate court held: "The Commonwealth of Virginia has not. . . advanced any state policy by which it can justify its determination, under an announced policy of diversity, to afford VMI's unique type of program to men and not to women." 976 F. 2d 890, 892 (1992).

* * *

In response to the Fourth Circuit's ruling, Virginia proposed a parallel program for women: Virginia Women's Institute for Leadership (VWIL). The 4 year, state sponsored undergraduate program would be located at Mary Baldwin College, a private liberal arts school for women, and would be open, initially, to about 25 to 30 students. Although VWIL would share VMI's mission—to produce "citizen soldiers"—the VWIL program would differ, as does Mary Baldwin College, from VMI in academic offerings, methods of education, and financial resources.

* * *

Virginia represented that it will provide equal financial support for in state VWIL students and VMI cadets, 852 F. Supp., at 483, and the VMI Foundation agreed to supply a $5.4625 million endowment for the VWIL program, id., at 499. Mary Baldwin's own endowment is about $19 million; VMI's is $131 million. Id., at 503. Mary Baldwin will add $35 million to its endowment based on future commitments; VMI will add $220 million. Ibid. The VMI Alumni Association has developed a network of employers interested in hiring VMI graduates. The Association has agreed to open its network to VWIL graduates, id., at 499, but those graduates will not have the advantage afforded by a VMI degree.

Virginia returned to the District Court seeking approval of its proposed remedial plan, and the court decided the plan met the requirements of the Equal Protection Clause. Id., at 473.

* * *

A divided Court of Appeals affirmed the District Court's judgment. 44 F. 3d 1229 (CA4 1995).

* * *

The cross petitions in this case present two ultimate issues. First, does Virginia's exclusion of women from the educational opportunities provided by VMI—extraordinary opportunities for military training and civilian leadership development—deny to women "capable of all of the individual activities required of VMI cadets," 766 F. Supp., at 1412, the equal protection of the laws guaranteed by the Fourteenth Amendment? Second, if VMI's "unique" situation, id., at 1413—as Virginia's sole single sex public institution of higher education—offends the Constitution's equal protection principle, what is the remedial requirement?

* * *

To summarize the Court's current directions for cases of official classification based on gender: Focusing on the differential treatment or denial of opportunity for which relief is sought, the reviewing court must determine whether the proffered justification is "exceedingly persuasive." The burden of justification is demanding and it rests entirely on the State. See Mississippi Univ. for Women, 458 U. S. 718, 724 (1982). The State must show "at least that the [challenged] classification serves 'important governmental objectives and that the discriminatory means employed' are 'substantially related to the achievement of those objectives.' " Ibid.

* * *

The heightened review standard our precedent establishes does not make sex a proscribed classification. Supposed "inherent differences" are no longer accepted as a ground for race or national origin classifications. See Loving v. Virginia, 388 U.S. 1 (1967). Physical differences between men and women, however, are enduring: "[T]he two sexes are not fungible; a community made up exclusively of one [sex] is different from a community composed of both." Ballard v. United States, 329 U.S. 187, 193 (1946).

* * *

Single sex education affords pedagogical benefits to at least some students, Virginia emphasizes, and that reality is uncontested in this litigation. Similarly, it is not disputed that diversity among public educational institutions can serve the public good. But Virginia has not shown that VMI was established, or has been maintained, with a view to diversifying, by its categorical exclusion of women, educational opportunities within the State. In cases of this genre, our precedent instructs that "benign" justifications proffered in defense of categorical exclusions will not be accepted automatically; a tenable justification must describe actual state purposes, not rationalizations for actions in fact differently grounded.

* * *

Mississippi Univ. for Women is immediately in point. There the State asserted, in justification of its exclusion of men from a nursing school, that it was engaging in "educational affirmative action" by "compensat[ing] for discrimination against women." 458 U. S. at 727 (1982). Undertaking a "searching analysis," id., at 728, the Court found no close resemblance between "the alleged objective" and "the actual purpose underlying the discriminatory classification," id., at 730. Pursuing a similar inquiry here, we reach the same conclusion.

Neither recent nor distant history bears out Virginia's alleged pursuit of diversity through single sex educational options. In 1839, when the State established VMI, a range of educational opportunities for men and women was scarcely contemplated. Higher education at the time was considered dangerous for women; reflecting widely held views about women's proper place, the Nation's first universities and colleges—for example, Harvard in Massachusetts, William and Mary in Virginia—admitted only men. See E. Farello, A History of the Education of Women in the United States 163 (1970). VMI was not at all novel in this respect: In admitting no women, VMI followed the lead of the State's flagship school, the University of Virginia, founded in 1819.

* * *

Virginia describes the current absence of public single sex higher education for women as "an historical anomaly." Brief for Cross Petitioners 30. But the historical record indicates action more deliberate than anomalous: First, protection of women against higher education; next, schools for women far from equal in resources and stature to schools for men; finally, conversion of the separate schools to coeducation.

* * *

In sum, we find no persuasive evidence in this record that VMI's male only admission policy "is in furtherance of a state policy of 'diversity.' " See 976 F. 2d, at 899.

* * *

Virginia next argues that VMI's adversative method of training provides educational benefits that cannot be made available, unmodified, to women. Alterations to accommodate women would necessarily be "radical," so "drastic," Virginia asserts, as to transform, indeed "destroy," VMI's program. See Brief for Cross Petitioners 34–36. Neither sex would be favored by the transformation, Virginia maintains: Men would be deprived of the unique opportunity currently available to them; women would not gain that opportunity because their participation would "eliminat[e] the very aspects of [the] program that distinguish [VMI] from . . . other institutions of higher education in Virginia." Id., at 34 (internal quotation marks omitted).

The notion that admission of women would downgrade VMI's stature, destroy the adversative system and, with it, even the school, is a judgment hardly proved, a prediction hardly different from other "self fulfilling prophec[ies]," see Mississippi Univ. for Women, 458 U. S., at 730, once routinely used to deny rights or opportunities.

* * *

Women's successful entry into the federal military academies, and their participation in the Nation's military forces, indicate that Virginia's fears for the future of VMI may not be solidly grounded. The State's justification for excluding all women from "citizen soldier" training for which some are qualified, in any event, cannot rank as "exceedingly persuasive," as we have explained and applied that standard.

* * *

Virginia, in sum, "has fallen far short of establishing the 'exceedingly persuasive justification,' " Mississippi Univ. for Women, 458 U. S., at 731, that must be the solid base for any gender defined classification.

In the second phase of the litigation, Virginia presented its remedial plan—maintain VMI as a male only college and create VWIL as a separate program for women.

* * *

Virginia chose not to eliminate, but to leave untouched, VMI's exclusionary policy. For women only, however, Virginia proposed a separate program, different in kind from VMI and unequal in tangible and intangible facilities.

* * *

VWIL affords women no opportunity to experience the rigorous military training for which VMI is famed. See 766 F. Supp., at 1413–1414 ("No other school in Virginia or in the United States, public or private, offers the same kind of rigorous military training as is available at VMI."); id., at 1421 (VMI "is known to be the most challenging military school in the United States"). Instead, the VWIL program "deemphasize[s]" military education, 44 F. 3d, at 1234, and uses a "cooperative method" of education "which reinforces self esteem," 852 F. Supp., at 476.

* * *

Virginia maintains that these methodological differences are "justified pedagogically," based on "important differences between men and women in learning and developmental needs," "psychological and sociological differences" Virginia describes as "real" and "not stereotypes." Brief for Respondents 28 (internal quotation marks omitted). The Task Force charged with developing the leadership program for women, drawn from the staff and faculty at Mary Baldwin College, "determined that a military model and, especially VMI's adversative method, would be wholly inappropriate for educating and training most women." 852 F. Supp., at 476 (emphasis added).

* * *

In myriad respects other than military training, VWIL does not qualify as VMI's equal. VWIL's student body, faculty, course offerings, and facilities hardly match VMI's. Nor can the VWIL graduate anticipate the benefits associated with VMI's 157-year history, the school's prestige, and its influential alumni network.

* * *

Virginia, in sum, while maintaining VMI for men only, has failed to provide any "comparable single gender women's institution." Id., at 1241. Instead, the Commonwealth has created a VWIL program fairly appraised as a "pale shadow" of VMI in terms of the range of curricular choices and faculty stature, funding, prestige, alumni support and influence. See id., at 1250 (Phillips, J., dissenting).

* * *

VMI, too, offers an educational opportunity no other Virginia institution provides, and the school's "prestige"—associated with its success in developing "citizen soldiers"—is unequaled. Virginia has closed this facility to its daughters and, instead, has devised for them a "parallel program," with a faculty less impressively credentialed and less well paid, more limited course offerings, fewer opportunities for military training and for scientific specialization.

* * *

Women seeking and fit for a VMI quality education cannot be offered anything less, under the State's obligation to afford them genuinely equal protection.

A prime part of the history of our Constitution, historian Richard Morris recounted, is the story of the extension of constitutional rights and protections to people once ignored or excluded.[21] VMI's story continued as our comprehension of "We the People" expanded. See supra, at 29, n. 16. There is no reason to believe that the admission of women capable of all the activities required of VMI cadets would destroy the Institute rather than enhance its capacity to serve the "more perfect Union."

976 F. 2d 890, affirmed; 44 F. 3d 1229, reversed and remanded. [All notes except 21 omitted].

JUSTICE SCALIA, dissenting.

Much of the Court's opinion is devoted to deprecating the closed mindedness of our forebears with regard to women's education, and even

[21] R. Morris, The Forging of the Union, 1781–1789, p. 193 (1987); see id., at 191, setting out letter to a friend from Massachusetts patriot (later second President) John Adams, on the subject of qualifications for voting in his home state: "[I]t is dangerous to open so fruitful a source of controversy and altercation as would be opened by attempting to alter the qualifications of voters; there will be no end of it. New claims will arise; women will demand a vote; lads from twelve to twenty one will think their rights not enough attended to; and every man who has not a farthing, will demand an equal voice with any other, in all acts of state. It tends to confound and destroy all distinctions, and prostrate all ranks to one common level." Letter from John Adams to James Sullivan (May 26, 1776), in 9 Works of John Adams 378 (C. Adams ed. 1854).

with regard to the treatment of women in areas that have nothing to do with education. Closed minded they were—as every age is, including our own, with regard to matters it cannot guess, because it simply does not consider them debatable. The virtue of a democratic system with a First Amendment is that it readily enables the people, over time, to be persuaded that what they took for granted is not so, and to change their laws accordingly. That system is destroyed if the smug assurances of each age are removed from the democratic process and written into the Constitution. So to counterbalance the Court's criticism of our ancestors, let me say a word in their praise: they left us free to change. The same cannot be said of this most illiberal Court, which has embarked on a course of inscribing one after another of the current preferences of the society (and in some cases only the counter majoritarian preferences of the society's law trained elite) into our Basic Law. Today it enshrines the notion that no substantial educational value is to be served by an all men's military academy—so that the decision by the people of Virginia to maintain such an institution denies equal protection to women who cannot attend that institution but can attend others. Since it is entirely clear that the Constitution of the United States—the old one—takes no sides in this educational debate, I dissent.

I shall devote most of my analysis to evaluating the Court's opinion on the basis of our current equal protection jurisprudence, which regards this Court as free to evaluate everything under the sun by applying one of three tests: "rational basis" scrutiny, intermediate scrutiny, or strict scrutiny. These tests are no more scientific than their names suggest, and a further element of randomness is added by the fact that it is largely up to us which test will be applied in each case. Strict scrutiny, we have said, is reserved for state "classifications based on race or national origin and classifications affecting fundamental rights," Clark v. Jeter, 486 U.S. 456, 461 (1988) (citation omitted). It is my position that the term "fundamental rights" should be limited to "interest[s] traditionally protected by our society," Michael H. v. Gerald D., 491 U.S. 110, 122 (1989) (plurality opinion of Scalia, J.); but the Court has not accepted that view, so that strict scrutiny will be applied to the deprivation of whatever sort of right we consider "fundamental." We have no established criterion for "intermediate scrutiny" either, but essentially apply it when it seems like a good idea to load the dice. So far it has been applied to content neutral restrictions that place an incidental burden on speech, to disabilities attendant to illegitimacy, and to discrimination on the basis of sex. See, e.g., Turner Broadcasting System, Inc. v. FCC, 512 U. S. ___, ___ (1994) (slip op., at 38); Mills v. Habluetzel, 456 U.S. 91, 98–99 (1982); Craig v. Boren, 429 U.S. 190, 197 (1976).

I have no problem with a system of abstract tests such as rational basis, intermediate, and strict scrutiny (though I think we can do better than applying strict scrutiny and intermediate scrutiny whenever we feel like it). Such formulas are essential to evaluating whether the new restrictions that a changing society constantly imposes upon private conduct comport with that "equal protection" our society has always accorded in the past. But in my view the function of this Court is to preserve our society's values regarding (among other things) equal protection, not to revise them; to prevent backsliding from the degree of restriction the Constitution imposed upon democratic government, not to prescribe, on our own authority, progressively higher degrees. For that reason it is my view that, whatever abstract tests we may choose to devise, they cannot supersede—and indeed ought to be crafted so as to reflect—those constant and unbroken national traditions that embody the people's understanding of ambiguous constitutional texts. More specifically, it is my view that "when a practice not expressly prohibited by the text of the Bill of Rights bears the endorsement of a long tradition of open, widespread, and unchallenged use that dates back to the beginning of the Republic, we have no proper basis for striking it down." Rutan v. Republican Party of Ill., 497 U.S. 62, 95 (1990) (Scalia, J., dissenting). The same applies, mutatis mutandis, to a practice asserted to be in violation of the post-Civil War Fourteenth Amendment. See, e.g., Burnham v. Superior Court of Cal., County of Marin, 495 U.S. 604 (1990) (plurality opinion of Scalia, J.) (Due Process Clause); J. E. B. v. Alabama ex rel. T. B., 511 U.S. 127, 156–163 (Scalia, J., dissenting) (Equal Protection Clause); Planned Parenthood of S. E. Pa. v. Casey, 505 U.S. 833, 979–984, 1000–1001 (1992) (Scalia, J., dissenting) (various alleged "penumbras").

* * *

In an odd sort of way, it is precisely VMI's attachment to such old fashioned concepts as manly "honor" that has made it, and the system it represents, the target of those who today succeed in abolishing public single sex education. The record contains a booklet that all first year VMI students (the so called "rats") were required to keep in their possession at all times. Near the end there appears the following period piece, entitled "The Code of a Gentleman":

"Without a strict observance of the fundamental Code of Honor, no man, no matter how 'polished,' can be considered a gentleman. The honor of a gentleman demands the inviolability of his word, and the incorruptibility of his principles. He is the descendant of the knight, the crusader; he is the defender of the defenseless and the champion of justice . . . or he is not a Gentleman.

* * *

I do not know whether the men of VMI lived by this Code; perhaps not. But it is powerfully impressive that a public institution of higher education still in existence sought to have them do so. I do not think any of us, women included, will be better off for its destruction.

---

**Questions:** In *U.S. v. Virginia*, how do Justice Ginsburg's majority opinion and Justice Scalia's dissent employ historical arguments differently? After this case, should the male-only draft be viewed differently?

## EDUCATION

### SAN ANTONIO SCHOOL DISTRICT V. RODRIGUEZ

411 U.S. 1 (1973)

MR. JUSTICE POWELL delivered the opinion of the Court.

This suit attacking the Texas system of financing public education was initiated by Mexican-American parents . . . on behalf of schoolchildren throughout the State who are members of minority groups or who are poor and reside in school districts having a low property tax base. [A District Court panel held that the system was unconstitutional under the Equal Protection Clause of the Fourteenth Amendment and the Supreme Court permitted the State a direct appeal.]

* * *

Recognizing the need for increased state funding to help offset disparities in local spending and to meet Texas' changing educational requirements, the state legislature in the late 1940's undertook a thorough evaluation of public education with an eye toward major reform.

* * *

[The legislature established] the Texas Minimum Foundation School Program. Today, this Program accounts for approximately half of the total educational expenditures in Texas. The Program calls for state and local contributions to a fund earmarked specifically for teacher salaries, operating expenses, and transportation costs. The State, supplying funds from its general revenues, finances approximately 80% of the Program, and the school districts are responsible—as a unit—for providing the remaining 20%. The districts' share, known as the Local Fund Assignment, is apportioned among the school districts under a formula designed to reflect each district's relative taxpaying ability. The Assignment is first divided among Texas' 254 counties pursuant to a complicated economic index that takes into account the relative value of each county's contribution to the State's total income from manufacturing, mining, and agricultural activities. It also considers each county's relative share of all payrolls paid within the State and, to a lesser extent, considers each county's share of all property in the State. Each county's assignment is then divided among its school districts on the basis of each district's share of assessable property within the county. The district, in turn, finances its share of the Assignment out of revenues from local property taxation.

* * *

In the years since this program went into operation in 1949, expenditures for education—from state as well as local sources have increased steadily. Between 1949 and 1967, expenditures increased approximately 500%. In the last decade alone the total public school budget rose from $750 million to.$2.1 billion and these increases have been reflected in consistently rising per pupil expenditures throughout the State. 28 Teacher salaries, by far the largest item in any school's budget, have increased dramatically—the state-supported minimum salary for teachers possessing college degrees has risen from $2,400 to $6,000 over the last 20 years.

The school district in which appellees reside, the Edgewood Independent School District, has been compared throughout this litigation with the Alamo Heights Independent School District. This comparison between the least and most affluent districts in the San Antonio area serves to illustrate the manner in which the dual system of finance operates and to indicate the extent to which substantial disparities exist despite the State's impressive progress in recent years.

* * *

Despite . . . recent increases, substantial interdistrict disparities in school expenditures . . . prevail in San Antonio and in varying degrees throughout the State still exist. And it was these disparities, largely attributable to differences in the amounts of money collected through local property taxation, that led the District Court to conclude that Texas' dual system of public school financing violated the Equal Protection Clause. The District Court held that the Texas system discriminates on the basis of wealth in the manner in which education is provided for its people. 337 F.Supp., at 282. Finding that wealth is a 'suspect' classification and that education is a 'fundamental' interest, the District Court held that the Texas system could be sustained only if the State could show that it was premised upon some compelling state interest. Id., at 282–284. On this issue the court concluded that '(n)ot only are defendants unable to demonstrate compelling state interests . . . they fail even to establish a reasonable basis for these classifications.' Id., at 284.

* * *

The wealth discrimination discovered by the District Court in this case, and by several other courts that have recently struck down school-financing laws in other States, is quite unlike any of the forms of wealth discrimination heretofore reviewed by this Court. Rather than focusing on the unique features of the alleged discrimination, the courts in these cases have virtually assumed their findings of a suspect classification through a simplistic process of analysis: since, under the traditional systems of financing public schools, some poorer people receive less expensive educations than other more affluent people, these systems discriminate on the basis of wealth.

* * *

The individuals, or groups of individuals, who constituted the class discriminated against [on the basis of wealth] in our prior cases shared two distinguishing characteristics: because of their impecunity they were completely unable to pay for some desired benefit, and as a consequence, they sustained an absolute deprivation of a meaningful opportunity to enjoy that benefit. In Griffin v. Illinois, 351 U.S. 12 (1956), and its progeny, the Court invalidated state laws that prevented an indigent criminal defendant from acquiring a transcript, or an adequate substitute for a transcript, for use at several stages of the trial and appeal process. The payment requirements in each case were found to occasion de facto discrimination against those who, because of their indigency, were totally unable to pay for transcripts. And the Court in each case emphasized that no constitutional violation would have been shown if the State had provided some 'adequate substitute' for a full stenographic transcript. [citations.]

[N]either of the two distinguishing characteristics of wealth classifications can be found here. First, in support of their charge that the system discriminates against the 'poor,' appellees have made no effort to demonstrate that it operates to the peculiar disadvantage of any class fairly definable as indigent, or as composed of persons whose incomes are beneath any designated poverty level. Indeed, there is reason to believe that the poorest families are not necessarily clustered in the poorest property districts.

* * *

Second, neither appellees nor the District Court addressed the fact that, unlike each of the foregoing cases, lack of personal resources has not occasioned an absolute deprivation of the desired benefit. The argument here is not that the children in districts having relatively low assessable property values are receiving no public education; rather, it is that they are receiving a poorer quality education than that available to children in districts having more assessable wealth. Apart from the unsettled and disputed question whether the quality of education may be determined by the amount of money expended for it, a sufficient answer to appellees' argument is that, at least where wealth is involved, the Equal Protection Clause does not require absolute equality or precisely equal advantages.

* * *

For these two reasons—the absence of any evidence that the financing system discriminates against any definable category of 'poor' people or that it results in the absolute deprivation of education—the disadvantaged class is not susceptible of identification in traditional terms.

* * *

This brings us, then, to the third way in which the classification scheme might be defined—district wealth discrimination. Since the only correlation indicated by the evidence is between district property wealth and expenditures, it may be argued that discrimination might be found without regard to the individual income characteristics of district residents.

* * *

However described, it is clear that appellees' suit asks this Court to extend its most exacting scrutiny to review a system that allegedly discriminates against a large, diverse, and amorphous class, unified only by the common factor of residence in districts that happen to have less taxable wealth than other districts. The system of alleged discrimination and the class it defines have none of the traditional indicia of suspectness: the class is not saddled with such disabilities, or subjected to such a history of purposeful unequal treatment, or relegated to such a position of political powerlessness as to command extraordinary protection from the majoritarian political process.

We thus conclude that the Texas system does not operate to the peculiar disadvantage of any suspect class. But in recognition of the fact that this Court has never heretofore held that wealth discrimination alone provides an adequate basis for invoking strict scrutiny, appellees have not relied solely on this contention. They also assert that the State's system impermissibly interferes with the exercise of a 'fundamental' right and that accordingly the prior decisions of this Court require the application of the strict standard of judicial review. [citations.] It is this question—whether education is a fundamental right, in the sense that it is among the rights and liberties protected by the Constitution—which has so consumed the attention of courts and commentators in recent years.

* * *

Nothing this Court holds today in any way detracts from our historic dedication to public education. We are in complete agreement with the conclusion of the three-judge panel below that 'the grave significance of education both to the individual and to our society' cannot be doubted. But the importance of a service performed by the State does not determine whether it must be regarded as fundamental for purposes of examination under the Equal Protection Clause.

* * *

It is not the province of this Court to create substantive constitutional rights in the name of guaranteeing equal protection of the laws.

* * *

Education, of course, is not among the rights afforded explicit protection under our Federal Constitution. Nor do we find any basis for saying it is implicitly so protected. As we have said, the undisputed importance of education will not alone cause this Court to depart from the usual standard for reviewing a State's social and economic legislation.

* * *

It should be clear, for the reasons stated above and in accord with the prior decisions of this Court, that this is not a case in which the challenged state action must be subjected to the searching judicial scrutiny reserved for laws that create suspect classifications or impinge upon constitutionally protected rights.

* * *

A century of Supreme Court adjudication under the Equal Protection Clause affirmatively supports the application of the traditional standard of review, which requires only that the State's system be shown to bear some rational relationship to legitimate state purposes. This case represents far more than a challenge to the manner in which Texas provides for the education of its children. We have here nothing lass than a direct attack on the way in which Texas has chosen to raise and disburse state and local tax revenues. We are asked to condemn the State's judgment in conferring on political subdivisions the power to tax local property to supply revenues for local interests. In so doing, appellees would have the Court intrude in an area in which it has traditionally deferred to state legislatures.

* * *

It must be remembered, also, that every claim arising under the Equal Protection Clause has implications for the relationship between national and state power under our federal system. Questions of federalism are always inherent in the process of determining whether a State's laws are to be accorded the traditional presumption of constitutionality, or are to be subjected instead to rigorous judicial scrutiny. . . .[I]t would be difficult to imagine a case having a greater potential impact on our federal system than the one now before us, in which we are urged to abrogate systems of financing public education presently in existence in virtually every State.

The foregoing considerations buttress our conclusion that Texas' system of public school finance is an inappropriate candidate for strict judicial scrutiny. These same considerations are relevant to the determination whether that system, with its conceded imperfections, nevertheless bears some rational relationship to a legitimate state purpose. It is to this question that we next turn our attention.

* * *

In its reliance on state as well as local resources, the Texas system is comparable to the systems employed in virtually every other State. The power to tax local property for educational purposes has been recognized in Texas at least since 1883. When the growth of commercial and industrial centers and accompanying shifts in population began to create disparities in local resources, Texas undertook a program calling for a considerable investment of state funds.

* * *

In sum, to the extent that the Texas system of school financing results in unequal expenditures between children who happen to reside in different districts, we cannot say that such disparities are the product of a system that is so irrational as to be invidiously discriminatory. Texas has acknowledged its shortcomings and has persistently endeavored—not without some success—to ameliorate the differences in levels of expenditures without sacrificing the benefits of local participation. The Texas plan is not the result of hurried, ill-conceived legislation. It certainly is not the product of purposeful discrimination against any group or class. On the contrary, it is rooted in decades of experience in Texas and elsewhere, and in major part is the product of responsible studies by qualified people.

* * *

We are unwilling to assume for ourselves a level of wisdom superior to that of legislators, scholars, and educational authorities in 50 States, especially where the alternatives proposed are only recently conceived and nowhere yet tested. The constitutional standard under the Equal Protection Clause is whether the challenged state action rationally furthers a legitimate state purpose or interest. McGinnis v. Royster, 410 U.S. 263, 270 (1973). We hold that the Texas plan abundantly satisfies this standard.

* * *

The consideration and initiation of fundamental reforms with respect to state taxation and education are matters reserved for the legislative processes of the various States, and we do no violence to the values of federalism and separation of powers by staying our hand. We hardly need add that this Court's action today is not to be viewed as placing its judicial imprimatur on the status quo. The need is apparent for reform in tax systems which may well have relied too long and too heavily on the local property tax. And certainly innovative thinking as to public education, its methods, and its funding is necessary to assure both a higher level of quality and greater uniformity of opportunity. These matters merit the continued attention of the scholars who already have contributed much by their challenges. But the ultimate solutions must come from the lawmakers and from the democractic pressures of those who elect them.

Reversed.

MR. JUSTICE MARSHALL, with whom MR. JUSTICE DOUGLAS concurs, dissenting.

The Court today decides, in effect, that a State may constitutionally vary the quality of education which it offers its children in accordance with the amount of taxable wealth located in the school districts within which they reside. The majority's decision represents an abrupt departure from the mainstream of recent state and federal court decisions concerning the unconstitutionality of state educational financing schemes dependent upon taxable local wealth. More unfortunately, though, the majority's holding can only be seen as a retreat from our historic commitment to equality of educational opportunity and as unsupportable acquiescence in a system which deprives children in their earliest years of the chance to reach their full potential as citizens. The Court does this despite the absence of any substantial justification for a scheme which arbitrarily channels educational resources in accordance with the fortuity of the amount of taxable wealth within each district.

In my judgment, the right of every American to an equal start in life, so far as the provision of a state service as important as education is concerned, is far too vital to permit state discrimination on grounds as tenuous as those presented by this record. Nor can I accept the notion that it is sufficient to remit these appellees to the vagaries of the political process which, contrary to the majority's suggestion, has proved singularly unsuited to the task of providing a remedy for this discrimination. I, for one, am unsatisfied with the hope of an ultimate 'political' solution sometime in the indefinite future while, in the meantime, countless children unjustifiably receive inferior educations that may affect their hearts and minds in a way unlikely ever to be undone.' Brown v. Board of Education, 347 U.S. 483, 494 (1954). I must therefore respectfully dissent.

The Court acknowledges that 'substantial interdistrict disparities in school expenditures' exist in Texas, ante, at 15, and that these disparities are 'largely attributable to differences in the amounts of money collected through local property taxation,' ante, at 16. But instead of closely examining the seriousness of these disparities and the invidiousness of the Texas financing scheme, the Court undertakes an elaborate exploration of the efforts Texas has purportedly made to close the gaps between its districts in terms of levels of district wealth and resulting educational funding. Yet, however praiseworthy Texas' equalizing efforts, the issue in this case is not whether Texas is doing its best to ameliorate the worst features of a discriminatory scheme but, rather, whether the scheme itself is in fact unconstitutionally discriminatory in the face of the Fourteenth Amendment's guarantee of equal protection of the laws. When the Texas financing scheme is taken as a whole, I do not think it can be doubted that it produces a discriminatory impact on substantial numbers of the school age children of the State of Texas.

* * *

[I]t is these stark differences in the treatment of Texas school districts and school children inherent in the Texas financing scheme, not the absolute amount of state aid provided to any particular school district, that are the crux of this case. There can, moreover, be no escaping the conclusion that the local property tax which is dependent upon taxable district property wealth is an essential feature of the Texas scheme for financing public education.

* * *

To begin, I must once more voice my disagreement with the Court's rigidified approach to equal protection analysis. See Dandridge v. Williams, 397 U.S. 471, 519–521 (1970) (dissenting opinion); Richardson v. Belcher, 404 U.S. 78, 90 (1971) (dissenting opinion). The Court apparently seeks to establish today that equal protection cases fall into one of two neat categories which dictate the appropriate standard of review—strict scrutiny or mere rationality. But this Court's decisions in the field of equal protection defy such easy categorization. A principled reading of what this Court has done reveals that it has applied a spectrum of standards in reviewing discrimination allegedly violative of the Equal Protection Clause. This spectrum clearly comprehends variations in the degree of care with which the Court will scrutinize particular classifications, depending, I believe, on the constitutional and societal importance of the interest adversely affected and the recognized invidiousness of the basis upon which the particular classification is drawn. I find in fact that many of the Court's recent decisions embody the very sort of reasoned approach to equal protection analysis for which I previously argued—that is, an approach in which 'concentration (is) placed upon the character of the classification in question, the relative importance to individuals in the class discriminated against of the governmental benefits that they do not receive, and the asserted state interests in support of the classification.' Dandridge v. Williams, supra, 397 U.S., at 520–521 (dissenting opinion).

I therefore cannot accept the majority's labored efforts to demonstrate that fundamental interests, which call for strict scrutiny of the challenged classification, encompass only established rights which we are somehow bound to recognize from the text of the Constitution itself. To be sure, some interests which the Court has deemed to be fundamental for purposes of equal protection analysis are themselves constitutionally protected rights. Thus, discrimination against the guaranteed right of freedom of speech has called for strict judicial scrutiny. See Police Dept. of City of Chicago v. Mosley, 408 U.S. 92 (1972). Further, every citizen's right to travel interstate, although nowhere expressly mentioned in the Constitution, has long been recognized as implicit in the premises underlying that document: the right 'was conceived from the beginning to be a necessary concomitant of the stronger Union the Constitution created.' United States v. Guest, 383 U.S. 745, 758 (1966). See also [citation]. Consequently, the Court has required that a state classification affecting the constitutionally protected right to travel must be 'shown to be necessary to promote a compelling governmental interest.' Shapiro v. Thompson, 394 U.S., at 634. But it will not do to suggest that the 'answer' to whether an interest is fundamental for purposes of equal protection analysis is always determined by whether that interest 'is a right . . . explicitly or implicitly guaranteed by the Constitution,' ante, at 33–34.

I would like to know where the Constitution guarantees the right to procreate, Skinner v. Oklahoma ex rel. Williamson, 316 U.S. 535 (1942), or the right to vote in state elections, e.g., Reynolds v. Sims, 377 U.S. 533 (1964), or the right to an appeal from a criminal conviction, e.g., Griffin v. Illinois, 351 U.S. 12 (1956). These are instances in which, due to the importance of the interests at stake, the Court has displayed a strong concern with the existence of discriminatory state treatment. But the Court has never said or indicated that these are interests which independently enjoy full blown constitutional protection.

* * *

The majority is, of course, correct when it suggests that the process of determining which interests are fundamental is a difficult one. But I do not think the problem is insurmountable. And I certainly do not accept the view that the process need necessarily degenerate into an unprincipled, subjective 'picking-and-choosing' between various interests or that it must involve this Court in creating 'substantive constitutional rights in the name of guaranteeing equal protection of the laws,' ante, at 33. Although not all fundamental interests are constitutionally guaranteed, the determination of which interests are fundamental should be firmly rooted in the text of the Constitution. The task in every case should be to determine the extent to which constitutionally guaranteed rights are dependent on interests not mentioned in the Constitution.

* * *

Procreation is now understood to be important because of its interaction with the established constitutional right of privacy. The exercise of the state franchise is closely tied to basic civil and political rights inherent in the First Amendment. And access to criminal appellate processes enhances the integrity of the range of rights implicit in the Fourteenth Amendment guarantee of due process of law. Only if we closely protect the related interests from state discrimination do we ultimately ensure the integrity of the constitutional guarantee itself. This is the real lesson that must be taken from our previous decisions involving interests deemed to be fundamental.

* * *

In the final analysis, then, the invidious characteristics of the group wealth classification present in this case merely serve to emphasize the need for careful judicial scrutiny of the State's justifications for the resulting interdistrict discrimination in the educational opportunity afforded to the schoolchildren of Texas.

* * *

In my judgment, any substantial degree of scrutiny of the operation of the Texas financing scheme reveals that the State has selected means wholly inappropriate to secure its purported interest in assuring its school districts local fiscal control. At the same time, appellees have pointed out a variety of alternative financing schemes which may serve the State's purported interest in local control as well as, if not better than, the present scheme without the current impairment of the educational opportunity of vast numbers of Texas schoolchildren.

* * *

The Court seeks solace for its action today in the possibility of legislative reform. The Court's suggestions of legislative redress and experimentation will doubtless be of great comfort to the schoolchildren of Texas' disadvantaged districts, but considering the vested interests of wealthy school districts in the preservation of the status quo, they are worth little more. The possibility of legislative action is, in all events, no answer to this Court's duty under the Constitution to eliminate unjustified state discrimination. In this case we have been presented with an instance of such discrimination, in a particularly invidious form, against an individual interest of large constitutional and practical importance. To support the demonstrated discrimination in the provision of educational opportunity the State has offered a justification which, on analysis, takes on at best an ephemeral character. Thus, I believe that the wide disparities in taxable district property wealth inherent in the local property tax element of the Texas financing scheme render that scheme violative of the Equal Protection Clause.

I would therefore affirm the judgment of the District Court.

**Question:** How do the majority opinion and the dissent in *San Antonio School District* differ on the way courts should identify fundamental rights?

## PLYLER V. DOE

457 U.S. 202 (1982)

JUSTICE BRENNAN delivered the opinion of the Court.

The question presented by these cases is whether, consistent with the Equal Protection Clause of the Fourteenth Amendment, Texas may deny to undocumented school-age children the free public education that it provides to children who are citizens of the United States or legally admitted aliens.

* * *

In May 1975, the Texas Legislature revised its education laws to withhold from local school districts any state funds for the education of children who were not "legally admitted" into the United States. The 1975 revision also authorized local school districts to deny enrollment in their public schools to children not "legally admitted" to the country. Tex.Educ.Code Ann. § 21.031 (Vernon Supp.1981). These cases involve constitutional challenges to those provisions.

This is a class action [for injunctive relief], filed in the United States District Court for the Eastern District of Texas in September 1977, on behalf of certain school-age children of Mexican origin residing in Smith County, Tex., who could not establish that they had been legally admitted into the United States. The action complained of the exclusion of plaintiff children from the public schools of the Tyler Independent School District. [The District Court enjoined the provisions' enforcement and the Fifth Circuit Court of Appeals upheld the decision.]

* * *

The . . . question is whether the Equal Protection Clause has been violated by the refusal of the State of Texas to reimburse local school boards for the education of children who cannot demonstrate that their presence within the United States is lawful, or by the imposition by those school boards of the burden of tuition on those children.

* * *

Sheer incapability or lax enforcement of the laws barring entry into this country, coupled with the failure to establish an effective bar to the employment of undocumented aliens, has resulted in the creation of a substantial "shadow population" of illegal migrants—numbering in the millions—within our borders. This situation raises the specter of a permanent caste of undocumented resident aliens, encouraged by some to remain here as a source of cheap labor, but nevertheless denied the benefits that our society makes available to citizens and lawful residents. The existence of such an underclass presents most difficult problems for a Nation that prides itself on adherence to principles of equality under law.

The children who are plaintiffs in these cases are special members of this underclass. Persuasive arguments support the view that a State may withhold its beneficence from those whose very presence within the United States is the product of their own unlawful conduct.

* * *

[B]ut the children who are plaintiffs in these cases "can affect neither their parents' conduct nor their own status." Trimble v. Gordon, 430 U.S. 762, 770 (1977). Even if the State found it expedient to control the conduct of adults by acting against their children, legislation directing the onus of a parent's misconduct against his children does not comport with fundamental conceptions of justice.

* * *

We reject the claim that "illegal aliens" are a "suspect class." No case in which we have attempted to define a suspect class . . . has addressed the status of persons unlawfully in our country. Unlike most of the classifications that we have recognized as suspect, entry into this class, by virtue of entry into this country, is the product of voluntary action. . . . Of course, undocumented status is not irrelevant to any proper legislative goal. Nor is undocumented status an absolutely immutable characteristic since it is the product of conscious, indeed unlawful, action. But § 21.031 is directed against children, and imposes its discriminatory burden on the basis of a legal characteristic over which children can have little control. It is thus difficult to conceive of a rational justification for penalizing these children for their presence within the United States. . . .

Public education is not a "right" granted to individuals by the Constitution. San Antonio Independent School Dist. v. Rodriguez, 411 U.S. 1, 35 (1973). But neither is it merely some governmental "benefit" indistinguishable from other forms of social welfare legislation. Both the importance of education in maintaining our basic institutions, and the lasting impact of its deprivation on the life of the child, mark the distinction.

* * *

In addition, education provides the basic tools by which individuals might lead economically productive lives to the benefit of us all. In sum, education has a fundamental role in maintaining the fabric of our society. We cannot ignore the significant social costs borne by our Nation when select groups are denied the means to absorb the values and skills upon which our social order rests.

* * *

[M]ore is involved in these cases than the abstract question whether § 21.031 discriminates against a suspect class, or whether education is a fundamental right. Section 21.031 imposes a lifetime hardship on a discrete class of children not accountable for their disabling status.

* * *

In determining the rationality of § 21.031, we may appropriately take into account its costs to the Nation and to the innocent children who are its victims. In light of these countervailing costs, the discrimination contained in § 21.031 can hardly be considered rational unless it furthers some substantial goal of the State.

* * *

First, appellants appear to suggest that the State may seek to protect itself from an influx of illegal immigrants. While a State might have an interest in mitigating the potentially harsh economic effects of sudden shifts in population, § 21.031 hardly offers an effective method of dealing with an urgent demographic or economic problem. There is no evidence in the record suggesting that illegal entrants impose any significant burden on the State's economy. To the contrary, the available evidence suggests that illegal aliens underutilize public services, while contributing their labor to the local economy and tax money to the state fisc. [citations.] The dominant incentive for illegal entry into the State of Texas is the availability of employment; few if any illegal immigrants come to this country, or presumably to the State of Texas, in order to avail themselves of a free education.

* * *

Second, . . . appellants suggest that undocumented children are appropriately singled out for exclusion because of the special burdens they impose on the State's ability to provide high-quality public education.

* * *

In terms of educational cost and need, however, undocumented children are "basically indistinguishable" from legally resident alien children.

Finally, appellants suggest that undocumented children are appropriately singled out because their unlawful presence within the United States renders them less likely than other children to remain within the boundaries of the State, and to put their education to productive social or political use within the State. Even assuming that such an interest is legitimate, it is an interest that is most difficult to quantify. The State has no assurance that any child, citizen or not, will employ the education provided by the State within the confines of the State's borders. In any event, the record is clear that many of the undocumented children disabled by this classification will remain in this country indefinitely, and that some will become lawful residents or citizens of the United States. It is difficult to understand precisely what the State hopes to achieve by promoting the creation and perpetuation of a subclass of illiterates within our boundaries, surely adding to the problems and costs of unemployment, welfare, and crime. It is thus clear that whatever savings might be achieved by denying these children an education, they are wholly insubstantial in light of the costs involved to these children, the State, and the Nation.

If the State is to deny a discrete group of innocent children the free public education that it offers to other children residing within its borders, that denial must be justified by a showing that it furthers some substantial state interest. No such showing was made here. Accordingly, the judgment of the Court of Appeals in each of these cases is

Affirmed.

CHIEF JUSTICE BURGER, with whom JUSTICE WHITE, JUSTICE REHNQUIST, and JUSTICE O'CONNOR join, dissenting.

The dispositive issue in these cases, simply put, is whether, for purposes of allocating its finite resources, a state has a legitimate reason to differentiate between persons who are lawfully within the state and those who are unlawfully there. The distinction the State of Texas has drawn—based not only upon its own legitimate interests but on classifications established by the Federal Government in its immigration laws and policies—is not unconstitutional.

The Court acknowledges that, except in those cases when state classifications disadvantage a *"suspect class" or impinge upon a "fundamental right," the Equal Protection Clause permits a* state "substantial latitude" in distinguishing between different groups of persons. Moreover, the Court expressly—and correctly—rejects any suggestion that illegal aliens are a suspect class, or that education is a fundamental right. Yet by patching together bits and pieces of what might be termed quasi-suspect-class and quasi-fundamental-rights analysis, the Court spins out a theory custom-tailored to the facts of these cases.

In the end, we are told little more than that the level of scrutiny employed to strike down the Texas law applies only when illegal alien children are deprived of a public education . . . If ever a court was guilty of an unabashedly result-oriented approach, this case is a prime example.

* * *

Once it is conceded—as the Court does—that illegal aliens are not a suspect class, and that education is not a fundamental right, our inquiry should focus on and be limited to whether the legislative classification at issue bears a rational relationship to a legitimate state purpose. [citation.]

* * *

[I]t simply is not "irrational" for a state to conclude that it does not have the same responsibility to provide benefits for persons whose very presence in the state and this country is illegal as it does to provide for persons lawfully present.

---

**Questions:** How does the *Plyler* majority distinguish *San Antonio*? A state law authorizes school districts to charge families in districts that have chosen not to consolidate with neighboring districts an extra fee to bus students to school. Should *Plyler* apply to this situation? See *Kadrmas v. Dickinson Public Schools,* 487 U.S. 450 (1988).

# CHAPTER 13

# FIRST AMENDMENT

■ ■ ■

## CONTEXT & SOURCES

The Constitution's First Amendment states that "Congress shall make no law . . . abridging the freedom of speech, or of the press . . . ." This right is a core principle of U.S. constitutional jurisprudence, and its scope leads many law schools to offer it as a course unto itself. Cases in this chapter concern the "incitement" standard for speech regulation; conduct that can be considered speech; press confidentiality; zoning issues; and electronic media.

For a comprehensive collection of perspectives on free speech, conduct, and the media see *First Amendment Anthology* (Donald Lively, et al., eds., Anderson Publishing Company, 1994). Conduct as speech is analyzed through a detailed study in Robert Justin Goldstein, *Flag Burning and Free Speech: The Case of Texas v. Johnson* (University Press of Kansas, 2000). Alan E. Garfield, "The Mischief of *Cohen v. Cowles Media Co.,"* 35 *Georgia Law Review* 1087 (2001) sharply critiques this decision for its chilling effect on journalism. In Felicia Witt and Brian Scher, "Does the Supreme Court Extend the Definition of Obscenity To 'I Know It When I Hear It?': *Sable Communications of California, Inc. v. FCC,* 109 S.Ct. 2829 (1989)," 7 *University of Miami Entertainment and Sports Law Review* 90 (1989), the authors raise unresolved questions about definitions and legislative deference.

## INCITEMENT STANDARD

### SCHENCK V. UNITED STATES

249 U.S. 47 (1919)

* * *

MR. JUSTICE HOLMES delivered the opinion of the Court.

This is an indictment in three counts. The first charges a conspiracy to violate the Espionage Act of June 15, 1917, c. 30, tit. 1, § 3, 40 Stat. 217, 219 (Comp. St. 1918, § 10212c), by causing and attempting to cause insubordination, &c., in the military and naval forces of the United States, and to obstruct the recruiting and enlistment service of the United States, when the United States was at war with the German Empire, to-wit, that the defendant willfully conspired to have printed and circulated to men who had been called and accepted for military service under the Act of May 18, 1917, c. 15, 40 Stat. 76 (Comp. St. 1918, §§ 2044a–2044k), a document set forth and alleged to be calculated to cause such insubordination and obstruction. The count alleges overt acts in pursuance of the conspiracy, ending in the distribution of the document set forth. The second count alleges a conspiracy to commit an offense against the United States, to-wit, to use the mails for the transmission of matter declared to be non-mailable by title 12, § 2, of the Act of June 15, 1917 (Comp. St. 1918, § 10401b), to-wit, the above mentioned document, with an averment of the same overt acts. The third count charges an unlawful use of the mails for the transmission of the same matter and otherwise as above. The defendants were found guilty on all the counts. They set up the First Amendment to the Constitution forbidding Congress to make any law abridging the freedom of speech, or of the press . . .

It is argued that the evidence, if admissible, was not sufficient to prove that the defendant Schenck was concerned in sending the documents. According to the testimony Schenck said he was general secretary of the Socialist party and had charge of the Socialist headquarters from which the documents were sent. He identified a book found there as the minutes of the Executive Committee of the party. The book showed a resolution of August 13, 1917, that 15,000 leaflets should be printed on the other side of one of them in use, to be mailed to men who had passed exemption boards, and for distribution. Schenck personally attended to the printing. On August 20 the general secretary's report said 'Obtained new leaflets from printer and started work addressing envelopes' &c.; and there was a resolve that Comrade Schenck be allowed $125 for sending leaflets through the mail. He said that he had about fifteen or sixteen thousand printed. There were files of the circular in question in the inner office which he said were printed on the other side of the one sided circular and were there for distribution. Other copies were proved to have been sent through the mails to drafted men. Without going into confirmatory details that were proved, no reasonable man could doubt that the defendant Schenck was largely instrumental in sending the circulars about. As to the defendant Baer there was evidence that she was a member of the Executive Board and that the minutes of its transactions were hers. The argument as to the sufficiency of the evidence that the defendants conspired to send the documents only impairs the seriousness of the real defence.

* * *

The document in question, upon its first printed side, recited the first section of the Thirteenth Amendment, said that the idea embodied in it was violated by the conscription act and that a conscript is little better than a convict. In impassioned language it intimated that conscription was despotism in its worst form and a monstrous wrong against humanity in the interest of Wall Street's chosen few. It said, 'Do not submit to intimidation,' but in form at least confined itself to peaceful measures such as a petition for the repeal of the act. The other and later printed side of the sheet was headed 'Assert Your Rights.' It stated reasons for alleging that any one violated the Constitution when he refused to recognize 'your right to assert your opposition to the draft,' and went on, 'If you do not assert and support your rights, you are helping to deny or disparage rights which it is the solemn duty of all citizens and residents of the United States to retain.' It described the arguments on the other side as coming from cunning politicians and a mercenary capitalist press, and even silent consent to the conscription law as helping to support an infamous conspiracy. It denied the power to send our citizens away to foreign shores to shoot up the people of other lands, and added that words could not express the condemnation such cold-blooded ruthlessness deserves, &c., &c., winding up, 'You must do your share to maintain, support and uphold the rights of the people of this country.' Of course the document would not have been sent unless it had been intended to have some effect, and we do not see what effect it could be expected to have upon persons subject to the draft except to influence them to obstruct the carrying of it out. The defendants do not deny that the jury might find against them on this point.

But it is said, suppose that that was the tendency of this circular, it is protected by the First Amendment to the Constitution. Two of the strongest expressions are said to be quoted respectively from well-known public men. It well may be that the prohibition of laws abridging the freedom of speech is not confined to previous restraints, although to prevent them may have been the main purpose, as intimated in Patterson v. Colorado, 205 U. S. 454, 462. We admit that in many places and in ordinary times the defendants in saying all that was said in the circular would have been within their constitutional rights. But the character of every act depends upon the circumstances in which it is done. Aikens v. Wisconsin, 195 U. S. 194, 205, 206. The most stringent protection of free speech would not protect a man in falsely shouting fire in a theatre and causing a panic. It does not even protect a man from an injunction against uttering words that may have all the effect of force. Gompers v. Buck's Stove & Range Co., 221 U. S. 418, 439. The question in every case is whether the words used are used in such circumstances and are of such a nature as to create a clear and present danger that they will bring about the substantive evils that Congress has a right to prevent. It is a question of proximity and degree. When a nation is at war many things that might be said in time of peace are such a hindrance to its effort that their utterance will not be endured so long as men fight and that no Court could regard them as protected by any constitutional right. It seems to be admitted that if an actual obstruction of the recruiting service were proved, liability for words that produced that effect might be enforced. The statute of 1917 in section 4

(Comp. St. 1918, § 10212d) punishes conspiracies to obstruct as well as actual obstruction. If the act, (speaking, or circulating a paper,) its tendency and the intent with which it is done are the same, we perceive no ground for saying that success alone warrants making the act a crime. Goldman v. United States, 245 U. S. 474, 477.

* * *

Judgments affirmed.

---

**Questions:** In his concurring opinion in *Whitney v. California,* 274 U.S. 357 (1927), Justice Louis Brandeis clarified Justice Holmes's incitement standard in *Schenck*: "To justify suppression of free speech there must be reasonable ground to believe that serious evil will result if free speech is practiced. There must be reasonable ground to believe that the evil apprehended is imminent." How should this test be applied to draft card burning as part of an antiwar protest? See *United States v. O'Brien,* 391 U.S. 367 (1968). Sleeping in a public park as a protest? See *Clark v. Community for Creative Non-Violence,* 468 U.S. 288 (1984).

## SPEECH AS CONDUCT

### TEXAS V. JOHNSON

491 U.S. 397 (1989)

JUSTICE BRENNAN delivered the opinion of the Court.

After publicly burning an American flag as a means of political protest, Gregory Lee Johnson was convicted of desecrating a flag in violation of Texas law. This case presents the question whether his conviction is consistent with the First Amendment. We hold that it is not.

While the Republican National Convention was taking place in Dallas in 1984, respondent Johnson participated in a political demonstration dubbed the "Republican War Chest Tour." As explained in literature distributed by the demonstrators a d in speeches made by them, the purpose of this event was to protest the policies of the Reagan administration and of certain Dallas-based corporations. The demonstrators marched through the Dallas streets, chanting political slogans and stopping at several corporate locations to stage "die-ins" intended to dramatize the consequences of nuclear war. On several occasions they spray-painted the walls of buildings and overturned potted plants, but Johnson himself took no part in such activities. He did, however, accept an American flag handed to him by a fellow protestor who had taken it from a flagpole outside one of the targeted buildings.

The demonstration ended in front of Dallas City Hall, where Johnson unfurled the American flag, doused it with kerosene, and set it on fire. While the flag burned, the protestors chanted: "America, the red, white, and blue, we spit on you." After the demonstrators dispersed, a witness to the flag burning collected the flag's remains and buried them in his backyard. No one was physically injured or threatened with injury, though several witnesses testified that they had been seriously offended by the flag burning.

Of the approximately 100 demonstrators, Johnson alone was charged with a crime. The only criminal offense with which he was charged was the desecration of a venerated object in violation of Tex.Penal Code Ann. § 42.09(a)(3) (1989). After a trial, he was convicted, sentenced to one year in prison, and fined $2,000. The Court of Appeals for the Fifth District of Texas at Dallas affirmed Johnson's conviction, 706 S.W.2d 120 (1986), but the Texas Court of Criminal Appeals reversed, 755 S.W.2d 92 (1988), holding that the State could not, consistent with the First Amendment, punish Johnson for burning the flag in these circumstances.

* * *

We granted certiorari . . ., and now affirm.

* * *

The First Amendment literally forbids the abridgment only of "speech," but we have long recognized that its protection does not end at the spoken or written word. While we have rejected "the view that an apparently limitless variety of conduct can be labeled 'speech' whenever the person engaging in the conduct intends thereby to express an idea," *United States v. O'Brien, supra,* at 376, we have acknowledged that conduct may be "sufficiently imbued with elements of communication to fall within the scope of the First and Fourteenth Amendments," *Spence v. Washington,* 418 U.S. 405, 409 (1974).

In deciding whether particular conduct possesses sufficient communicative elements to bring the First Amendment into play, we have asked whether "[a]n intent to convey a particularized message was present, and [whether] the likelihood was great that the message would be understood by those who viewed it." 418 U.S., at 410–411. Hence, we have recognized the expressive nature of students' wearing of black armbands to protest American military involvement in Vietnam, *Tinker v. Des Moines Independent Community School Dist.,* 393 U.S. 503, 505 (1969); of a sit-in by blacks in a "whites only" area to protest segregation, *Brown v. Louisiana,* 383 U.S. 131 (1966); of the wearing of American military uniforms in a dramatic presentation criticizing American involvement in Vietnam, *Schacht v. United States,* 398 U.S. 58 (1970); and of picketing about a wide variety of causes, see, *e.g., Food Employees v. Logan Valley Plaza, Inc.,* 391 U.S. 308, 313–314 (1968); [additional citation.].

Especially pertinent to this case are our decisions recognizing the communicative nature of conduct relating to flags. Attaching a peace sign to the flag, *Spence, supra,* at 409–410; refusing to salute the flag, *West Virginia Board of Education v. Barnette,* 319 U.S. 624, 632; (1943); and displaying a red flag, *Stromberg v. California,* 283 U.S. 359, 368–369 (1931), we have held, all may find shelter under the First Amendment.

* * *

The government generally has a freer hand in restricting expressive conduct than it has in restricting the written or spoken word. See *O'Brien,* 391 U.S. at 376–377; [additional citations.]

* * *

[A]lthough we have recognized that where " 'speech' and 'nonspeech' elements are combined in the same course of conduct, a sufficiently important governmental interest in regulating the nonspeech element can justify incidental limitations on First Amendment freedoms," *O'Brien, supra,* at 376, we have limited the applicability of *O'Brien*'s relatively lenient standard to those cases in which "the governmental interest is unrelated to the suppression of free expression." *Id.,* at 377.

* * *

In order to decide whether *O'Brien*'s test applies here, therefore, we must decide whether Texas has asserted an interest in support of Johnson's conviction that is unrelated to the suppression of expression. If we find that an interest asserted by the State is simply not implicated on the facts before us, we need not ask whether *O'Brien*'s test applies. See *Spence, supra,* at 414, n. 8. The State offers two separate interests to justify this conviction: preventing breaches of the peace and preserving the flag as a symbol of nationhood and national unity. We hold that the first interest is not implicated on this record and that the second is related to the suppression of expression.

Texas claims that its interest in preventing breaches of the peace justifies Johnson's conviction for flag desecration. However, no disturbance of the peace actually occurred or threatened to occur because of Johnson's burning of the flag. Although the State stresses the disruptive behavior of the protestors during their march toward City Hall, Brief for Petitioner 34–36, it admits that "no actual breach of the peace occurred at the time of the flagburning or in response to the flagburning." *Id.,* at 34. The State's emphasis on the protestors' disorderly actions prior to arriving at City Hall is not only somewhat surprising given that no charges were brought on the basis of this conduct, but it also fails to show that a disturbance of the peace was a likely reaction to *Johnson's* conduct. The only evidence offered by the State at trial to show the reaction to Johnson's actions was the testimony of several persons who had been seriously offended by the flag burning. *Id.*, at 6–7.

The State's position, therefore, amounts to a claim that an audience that takes serious offense at particular expression is necessarily likely to disturb the peace and that the expression may be prohibited on this basis. Our precedents do not countenance such a presumption. On the contrary, they recognize that a principal "function of free speech under our system of government is to invite dispute. It may indeed best serve its high purpose when it induces a condition of unrest, creates dissatisfaction with conditions as they are, or even stirs people to anger." [citations.]

* * *

Nor does Johnson's expressive conduct fall within that small class of "fighting words" that are "likely to provoke the average person to retaliation, and thereby cause a breach of the peace." *Chaplinsky v. New Hampshire,* 315 U.S. 568, 574, (1942). No reasonable onlooker would have regarded Johnson's generalized expression of dissatisfaction with the policies of the Federal Government as a direct personal insult or an invitation to exchange fisticuffs. See [citations.]

We thus conclude that the State's interest in maintaining order is not implicated on these facts. The State need not worry that our holding will disable it from preserving the peace . . . [In]fact, Texas already has a statute specifically prohibiting breaches of the peace, Tex.Penal Code Ann. § 42.01 (1989), which tends to confirm that Texas need not punish this flag desecration in order to keep the peace.

* * *

It remains to consider whether the State's interest in preserving the flag as a symbol of nationhood and national unity justifies Johnson's conviction.

* * *

[T]he State's claim is that it has an interest in preserving the flag as a symbol of *nationhood* and *national unity,* a symbol with a determinate range of meanings. Brief for Petitioner 20–24. According to Texas, if one physically treats the flag in a way that would tend to cast doubt on either the idea that nationhood and national unity are the flag's referents or that national unity actually exists, the message conveyed thereby is a harmful one and therefore may be prohibited.

If there is a bedrock principle underlying the First Amendment, it is that the government may not prohibit the expression of an idea simply because society finds the idea itself offensive or disagreeable. See, *e.g., Hustler Magazine, Inc. v. Falwell,* 485 U.S., at 55–56; [additional citations.]

We have not recognized an exception to this principle even where our flag has been involved. In *Street v. New York,* 394 U.S. 576, (1969), we held that a State may not criminally punish a person for uttering words critical of the flag. Rejecting the argument that the conviction could be sustained on the ground that Street had "failed to show the respect for our national symbol which may properly be demanded of every citizen," we concluded that "the constitutionally guaranteed 'freedom to be intellectually . . . diverse or even contrary,' and the 'right to differ as to things that touch the heart of the existing order,' encompass the freedom to express publicly one's opinions about our flag, including those opinions which are defiant or contemptuous." *Id.,* at 593. Nor may the government, we have held, compel conduct that would evince respect for the flag. "To sustain the compulsory flag salute we are required to say that a Bill of Rights which guards the individual's right to speak his own mind, left it open to public authorities to compel him to utter what is not in his mind." *Id.,* at 634.

* * *

In short, nothing in our precedents suggests that a State may foster its own view of the flag by prohibiting expressive conduct relating to it. To bring its argument outside our precedents, Texas attempts to convince us that even if its interest in preserving the flag's symbolic role does not allow it to prohibit words or some expressive conduct critical of the flag, it does permit it to forbid the outright destruction of the flag. The State's argument cannot depend here on the distinction between written or spoken words and nonverbal conduct. That distinction, we have shown, is of no moment where the nonverbal conduct is expressive, as it is here, and where the regulation of that conduct is related to expression, as it is here.

* * *

We never before have held that the Government may ensure that a symbol be used to express only one view of that symbol or its referents.

* * *

We are fortified in today's conclusion by our conviction that forbidding criminal punishment for conduct such as Johnson's will not endanger the special role played by our flag or the feelings it inspires.

* * *

We are tempted to say, in fact, that the flag's deservedly cherished place in our community will be strengthened, not weakened, by our holding today. Our decision is a reaffirmation of the principles of freedom and inclusiveness that the flag best reflects, and of the conviction that our toleration of criticism such as Johnson's is a sign and source of our strength. Indeed, one of the proudest images of our flag, the one immortalized in our own national anthem, is of the bombardment it survived at Fort McHenry. It is the Nation's resilience, not its rigidity, that Texas sees reflected in the flag—and it is that resilience that we reassert today.

The way to preserve the flag's special role is not to punish those who feel differently about these matters. It is to persuade them that they are wrong. "To courageous, self-reliant men, with confidence in the power of free and fearless reasoning applied through the processes of popular government, no danger flowing from speech can be deemed clear and present, unless the incidence of the evil apprehended is so imminent that it may befall before there is opportunity for full discussion. If there be time to expose through discussion the falsehood and fallacies, to avert the evil by the processes of education, the remedy to be applied is more speech, not enforced silence." *Whitney v. California,* 274 U.S. 357, 377 (1927) (Brandeis, J., concurring). And, precisely because it is our flag that is involved, one response to the flag burner may exploit the uniquely persuasive power of the flag itself. We can imagine no more appropriate response to burning a flag than waving one's own, no better way to counter a flag burner's message than by saluting the flag that burns, no surer means of preserving the dignity even of the flag that burned than by—as one witness here did—according its remains a respectful burial. We do not consecrate the flag by punishing its desecration, for in doing so we dilute the freedom that this cherished emblem represents.

Johnson was convicted for engaging in expressive conduct. The State's interest in preventing breaches of the peace does not support his conviction because Johnson's conduct did not threaten to disturb the peace. Nor does the State's interest in preserving the flag as a symbol of nationhood and national unity justify his criminal conviction for engaging in political expression. The judgment of the Texas Court of Criminal Appeals is therefore

*Affirmed.*

* * *

JUSTICE STEVENS, dissenting.

As the Court analyzes this case, it presents the question whether the State of Texas, or indeed the Federal Government, has the power to prohibit the public desecration of the American flag. The question is unique. In my judgment rules that apply to a host of other symbols, such as state flags, armbands, or various privately promoted emblems of political or commercial identity, are not necessarily controlling. Even if flag burning could be considered just another species of symbolic speech under the logical application of the rules that the Court has developed in its interpretation of the First Amendment in other contexts, this case has an intangible dimension that makes those rules inapplicable.

A country's flag is a symbol of more than "nationhood and national unity." . . .It also signifies the ideas that characterize the society that has chosen that emblem as well as the special history that has animated the growth and power of those ideas. The fleurs-de-lis and the tricolor both symbolized "nationhood and national unity," but they had vastly different meanings. The message conveyed by some flags—the swastika, for example—may survive long after it has outlived its usefulness as a symbol of regimented unity in a particular nation.

* * *

The value of the flag as a symbol cannot be measured. Even so, I have no doubt that the interest in preserving that value for the future is both significant and legitimate. Conceivably that value will be enhanced by the Court's conclusion that our national commitment to free expression is so strong that even the United States as ultimate guarantor of that freedom is without power to prohibit the desecration of its unique symbol. But I am unpersuaded. The creation of a federal right to post bulletin boards and graffiti on the Washington Monument might enlarge the market for free expression, but at a cost I would not pay. Similarly, in my considered judgment, sanctioning the public desecration of the flag will tarnish its value—both for those who cherish the ideas for which it waves and for those who desire to don the robes of martyrdom by burning it. That tarnish is not justified by the trivial burden on free expression occasioned by requiring that an available, alternative mode of expression including uttering words critical of the flag, see *Street v. New York,* 394 U.S. 576, 89 (1969)—be employed.

* * *

The content of respondent's message has no relevance whatsoever to the case. The concept of "desecration" does not turn on the substance of the message the actor intends to convey, but rather on whether those who view the *act* will take serious offense. Accordingly, one intending to convey a message of respect for the flag by burning it in a public square might nonetheless be guilty of desecration if he knows that others perhaps simply because they misperceive the intended message—will be seriously offended. Indeed, even if the actor knows that all possible witnesses will understand that he intends to send a message of respect, he might still be guilty of desecration if he also knows that this understanding does not lessen the offense taken by some of those witnesses. Thus, this is not a case in which the fact that "it is the speaker's opinion that gives offense" provides a special "reason for according it constitutional protection," *FCC v. Pacifica Foundation,* 438 U.S. 726 (1978) (plurality opinion). The case has nothing to do with "disagreeable ideas," see *ante,* at 409. It involves disagreeable conduct that, in my opinion, diminishes the value of an important national asset.

The Court is therefore quite wrong in blandly asserting that respondent "was prosecuted for his expression of dissatisfaction with the policies of this country, expression situated at the core of our First Amendment values." Respondent was prosecuted because of the method he chose to express his dissatisfaction with those policies. Had he chosen to spray-paint or perhaps convey with a motion picture projector—his message of dissatisfaction on the facade of the Lincoln Memorial, there would be no question about the power of the Government to prohibit his means of expression. The prohibition would be supported by the legitimate interest in preserving the quality of an important national asset. Though the asset at stake in this case is intangible, given its unique value, the same interest supports a prohibition on the desecration of the American flag.

The ideas of liberty and equality have been an irresistible force in motivating leaders like Patrick Henry, Susan B. Anthony, and Abraham Lincoln, schoolteachers like Nathan Hale and Booker T. Washington, the Philippine Scouts who fought at Bataan, and the soldiers who scaled the bluff at Omaha Beach. If those ideas are worth fighting for—and our history demonstrates that they are—it cannot be true that the flag that uniquely symbolizes their power is not itself worthy of protection from unnecessary desecration.

I respectfully dissent.

---

**Questions:** Why does the majority in *Texas v. Johnson* focus on disturbing the peace while the dissent emphasizes traditional values? Is flag-burning any different than other examples of conduct the majority cites, like protesting with black armbands, or civil rights sit-ins?

## PRESS CONFIDENTIALITY

### COHEN V. COWLES MEDIA COMPANY

501 U.S. 663 (1991)

JUSTICE WHITE delivered the opinion of the Court.

The question before us is whether the First Amendment prohibits a plaintiff from recovering damages, under state promissory estoppel law, for a newspaper's breach of a promise of confidentiality given to the plaintiff in exchange for information. We hold that it does not.

During the closing days of the 1982 Minnesota gubernatorial race, Dan Cohen, an active Republican associated with Wheelock Whitney's Independent-Republican gubernatorial campaign, approached reporters from the St. Paul Pioneer Press Dispatch (Pioneer Press) and the Minneapolis Star and Tribune (Star Tribune) and offered to provide documents relating to a candidate in the upcoming election. Cohen made clear to the reporters that he would provide the information only if he was given a promise of confidentiality. Reporters from both papers promised to keep Cohen's identity anonymous and Cohen turned over copies of two public court records concerning Marlene Johnson, the Democratic-Farmer-Labor candidate for Lieutenant Governor. The first record indicated that Johnson had been charged in 1969 with three counts of unlawful assembly, and the second that she had been convicted in 1970 of petit theft. Both newspapers interviewed Johnson for her explanation and one reporter tracked down the person who had found the records for Cohen. As it turned out, the unlawful assembly charges arose out of Johnson's participation in a protest of an alleged failure to hire minority workers on municipal construction projects and the charges were eventually dismissed. The petit theft conviction was for leaving a store without paying for $6.00 worth of sewing materials. The incident apparently occurred at a time during which Johnson was emotionally distraught, and the conviction was later vacated.

After consultation and debate, the editorial staffs of the two newspapers independently decided to publish Cohen's name as part of their stories concerning Johnson. In their stories, both papers identified Cohen as the source of the court records, indicated his connection to the Whitney campaign, and included denials by Whitney campaign officials of any role in the matter. The same day the stories appeared, Cohen was fired by his employer.

Cohen sued respondents, the publishers of the Pioneer Press and Star Tribune, in Minnesota state court, alleging fraudulent misrepresentation and breach of contract. [The trial court awarded damages, but that decision was reversed by the Minnesota Supreme Court, which concluded that enforcing the confidentiality promise based on Cohen's reliance on it, i.e. applying the doctrine of promissory estoppel, would violate defendants' First Amendment rights.]

We granted certiorari to consider the First Amendment implications of this case.

* * *

This case [is controlled] by the . . .line of decisions holding that generally applicable laws do not offend the First Amendment simply because their enforcement against the press has incidental effects on its ability to gather and report the news. As the cases relied on by respondents recognize, the truthful information sought to be published must have been lawfully acquired. The press may not with impunity break and enter an office or dwelling to gather news. Neither does the First Amendment relieve a newspaper reporter of the obligation shared by all citizens to respond to a grand jury subpoena and answer questions relevant to a criminal investigation, even though the reporter might be required to reveal a confidential source. Branzburg v. Hayes, 408 U.S. 665 (1972). The press, like others interested in publishing, may not publish copyrighted material without obeying the copyright laws. See Zacchini v. Scripps-Howard Broadcasting Co., 433 U.S. 562, 576–579, (1977). Similarly, the media must obey the National Labor Relations Act, Associated Press v. NLRB, 301 U.S. 103 (1937), and the Fair Labor Standards Act, Oklahoma Press Publishing Co. v. Walling, 327 U.S. 186, 192–193 (1946); may not restrain trade in violation of the antitrust laws, Associated Press v. United States, 326 U.S. 1, (1945); Citizen Publishing Co. v. United States, 394 U.S. 131, 139, (1969); and must pay non-discriminatory taxes. Murdock v. Pennsylvania, 319 U.S. 105, 112, (1943); [additional citation.]

* * *

There can be little doubt that the Minnesota doctrine of promissory estoppel is a law of general applicability. It does not target or single out the press. Rather, in so far as we are advised, the doctrine is generally applicable to the daily transactions of all the citizens of Minnesota. The First Amendment does not forbid its application to the press.

* * *

Respondents and amici argue that permitting Cohen to maintain a cause of action for promissory estoppel will inhibit truthful reporting because news organizations will have legal incentives not to disclose a confidential source's identity even when that person's identity is itself newsworthy. . . . But if this is the case, it is no more than the incidental, and constitutionally insignificant, consequence of applying to the press a generally applicable law that requires those who make certain kinds of promises to keep them.

* * *

[P]erhaps the State Constitution may be construed to shield the press from a promissory estoppel cause of action such as this one. These are matters for the Minnesota Supreme Court to address and resolve in the first instance on remand. Accordingly, the judgment of the Minnesota Supreme Court is reversed, and the case is remanded for further proceedings not inconsistent with this opinion.

So ordered.

JUSTICE SOUTER, with whom JUSTICE MARSHALL, JUSTICE BLACKMUN and JUSTICE O'CONNOR join, dissenting.

* * *

The importance of [the] public interest is integral to the balance that should be struck in this case. There can be no doubt that the fact of Cohen's identity expanded the universe of information relevant to the choice faced by Minnesota voters in that State's 1982 gubernatorial election, the publication of which was thus of the sort quintessentially subject to strict First Amendment protection. See, *e.g., Eu v. San Francisco County Democratic Central Committee,* 489 U.S. 214, 223, (1989). The propriety of his leak to respondents could be taken to reflect on his character, which in turn could be taken to reflect on the character of the candidate who had retained him as an adviser. An election could turn on just such a factor; if it should, I am ready to assume that it would be to the greater public good, at least over the long run.

This is not to say that the breach of such a promise of confidentiality could never give rise to liability. One can conceive of situations in which the injured party is a private individual, whose identity is of less public concern than that of the petitioner; liability there might not be constitutionally prohibited.

* * *

Because I believe the State's interest in enforcing a newspaper's promise of confidentiality insufficient to outweigh the interest in unfettered publication of the information revealed in this case, I respectfully dissent.

---

**Question:** Does the First Amendment prevent a lawsuit for a Fourth Amendment violation by a homeowner against police officers who brought reporters with them on a "media ride-along" to photograph the execution of an arrest warrant? See *Wilson v. Layne,* 526 U.S. 603 (1999).

## FIRST AMENDMENT & ZONING

### RENTON V. PLAYTIME THEATRES, INC.

475 U.S. 41 (1986)

REHNQUIST, J., delivered the opinion of the Court.

This case involves a constitutional challenge to a zoning ordinance, enacted by appellant city of Renton, Washington, that prohibits adult motion picture theaters from locating within 1,000 feet of any residential zone, single- or multiple-family dwelling, church, park, or school. Appellees, Playtime Theatres, Inc., and Sea-First Properties, Inc., filed an action in the United States District Court for the Western District of Washington seeking a declaratory judgment that the Renton ordinance violated the First and Fourteenth Amendments and a permanent injunction against its enforcement. The District Court ruled in favor of Renton and denied the permanent injunction, but the Court of Appeals for the Ninth Circuit reversed and remanded for reconsideration. We noted probable jurisdiction, and now reverse the judgment of the Ninth Circuit.

* * *

In April 1981, acting on the basis of the Planning and Development Committee's recommendation, the [Renton] City Council enacted Ordinance No. 3526. The ordinance prohibited any "adult motion picture theater" from locating within 1,000 feet of any residential zone, single- or multiple-family dwelling, church, or park, and within one mile of any school. App. to Juris. Statement 79a. The term "adult motion picture theater" was defined as "[a]n enclosed building used for presenting motion picture films, video cassettes, cable television, or any other such visual media, distinguished or characteri[zed] by an emphasis on matter depicting, describing or relating to 'specified sexual activities' or 'specified anatomical areas' . . . for observation by patrons therein." *Id.*, at 78a.

In early 1982, respondents acquired two existing theaters in downtown Renton, with the intention of using them to exhibit feature-length adult films. The theaters were located within the area proscribed by Ordinance No. 3526. [Playtime requested an injunction against the ordinance, which the District Court denied. The Ninth Circuit Court of Appeals reversed, holding that the ordinance constituted a substantial restriction on First Amendment interests, and granted the injunction.]

* * *

The ordinance is . . . properly analyzed as a form of time, place, and manner regulation.

* * *

[T]ime, place, and manner regulations are acceptable so long as they are designed to serve a substantial governmental interest and do not unreasonably limit alternative avenues of communication. See *Clark v. Community for Creative Non-Violence,* 468 U.S. 288, 293, (1984); [additional citations.]

* * *

[T]he Renton ordinance is aimed not at the *content* of the films shown at "adult motion picture theatres," but rather at the *secondary effects* of such theaters on the surrounding community.

* * *

The appropriate inquiry in this case, then, is whether the Renton ordinance is designed to serve a substantial governmental interest and allows for reasonable alternative avenues of communication. See [citations.] It is clear that the ordinance meets such a standard. As a majority of this Court recognized in *Young v. American Mini Theatres,* a city's "interest in attempting to preserve the quality of urban life is one that must be accorded high respect." 427 U.S., 50, 71 (1976) (plurality opinion); see *id.,* at 80 (POWELL, J., concurring) ("Nor is there doubt that the interests furthered by this ordinance are both important and substantial"). Exactly the same vital governmental interests are at stake here.

* * *

We also find no constitutional defect in the method chosen by Renton to further its substantial interests. Cities may regulate adult theaters by dispersing them, as in Detroit, or by effectively concentrating them, as in Renton. "It is not our function to appraise the wisdom of [the city's] decision to require adult theaters to be separated rather than concentrated in the same areas. . . . [T]he city must be allowed a reasonable opportunity to experiment with solutions to admittedly serious problems." *American Mini Theatres,* 427 U.S., at 71. Moreover, the Renton ordinance is "narrowly tailored" to affect only that category of theaters shown to produce the unwanted secondary effects, thus avoiding the flaw that proved fatal to the regulations in [citations.]

* * *

Finally, turning to the question whether the Renton ordinance allows for reasonable alternative avenues of communication, we note that the ordinance leaves some 520 acres, or more than five percent of the entire land area of Renton, open to use as adult theater sites.

In sum, we find that the Renton ordinance represents a valid governmental response to the "admittedly serious problems" created by adult theaters. See id. at 71. Renton has not used "the power to zone as a pretext for suppressing expression," *id.,* at 849 (POWELL, J., concurring), but rather has sought to make some areas available for adult theaters and their patrons, while at the same time preserving the quality of life in the community at large by preventing those theaters from locating in other areas. This, after all, is the essence of zoning. Here, as in *American Mini Theatres,* the city has enacted a zoning ordinance that meets these goals while also satisfying the dictates of the First Amendment. The judgment of the Court of Appeals is therefore

*Reversed.*

JUSTICE BRENNAN, with whom JUSTICE MARSHALL joins, dissenting.

Renton's zoning ordinance selectively imposes limitations on the location of a movie theater based exclusively on the content of the films shown there. The constitutionality of the ordinance is therefore not correctly analyzed under standards applied to content-neutral time, place, and manner restrictions. But even assuming that the ordinance may fairly be characterized as content neutral, it is plainly unconstitutional under the standards established by the decisions of this Court. Although the Court's analysis is limited to cases involving "businesses that purvey sexually explicit materials," *ante,* at 49, and n. 2, and thus does not affect our holdings in cases involving state regulation of other kinds of speech, I dissent.

"[A] constitutionally permissible time, place, or manner restriction may not be based upon either the content or subject matter of speech." *Consolidated Edison Co. v. Public Service Comm'n of N.Y.,* 447 U.S. 530, 536, (1980). The Court asserts that the ordinance is "aimed not at the *content* of the films shown at 'adult motion picture theatres,' but rather at the *secondary effects* of such theaters on the surrounding community," *ante,* at 47 (emphasis in original), and thus is simply a time, place, and manner regulation. This analysis is misguided.

The fact that adult movie theaters may cause harmful "secondary" land-use effects may arguably give Renton a compelling reason to regulate such establishments; it does not mean, however, that such regulations are content neutral. Because the ordinance imposes special restrictions on certain kinds of speech on the basis of *content,* I cannot simply accept, as the Court does, Renton's claim that the ordinance was not designed to suppress the content of adult movies. "[W]hen regulation is based on the content of speech, governmental action must be scrutinized more carefully to ensure that communication has not been prohibited 'merely because public officials disapprove the speaker's views.' " *Consolidated Edison Co., supra,* at 536. . . . In this case, both the language of the ordinance and its dubious legislative history belie the Court's conclusion that "the city's pursuit of its zoning interests here was unrelated to the suppression of free expression." *Ante,* at 48.

The ordinance discriminates on its face against certain forms of speech based on content. Movie theaters specializing in "adult motion pictures" may not be located within 1,000 feet of any residential zone, single- or multiple-family dwelling, church, park, or school. Other motion picture theaters, and other forms of "adult entertainment," such as bars, massage parlors, and adult bookstores, are not subject to the same restrictions. This selective treatment strongly suggests that Renton was interested not in controlling the "secondary effects" associated with adult businesses, but in discriminating against adult theaters based on the content of the films they exhibit. The Court ignores this discriminatory treatment, declaring that Renton is free "to address the potential problems created by one particular kind of adult business," *ante,* at 52–53, and to amend the ordinance in the future to include other adult enterprises. *Ante,* at 53 (citing *Williamson v. Lee Optical Co.,* 348 U.S. 483, 488–489 (1955)). However, because of the

First Amendment interests at stake here, this one-step-at-a-time analysis is wholly inappropriate.

* * *

Despite the evidence in the record, the Court reasons that the fact "[t]hat respondents must fend for themselves in the real estate market, on an equal footing with other prospective purchasers and lessees, does not give rise to a First Amendment violation." *Ante,* at 54. However, respondents are not on equal footing with other prospective purchasers and lessees, but must conduct business under severe restrictions not imposed upon other establishments. The Court also argues that the First Amendment does not compel "the government to ensure that adult theaters, or any other kinds of speech-related businesses for that matter, will be able to obtain sites at bargain prices." *Ibid.* However, respondents do not ask Renton to guarantee low-price sites for their businesses, but seek only a reasonable opportunity to operate adult theaters in the city. By denying them this opportunity, Renton can effectively ban a form of protected speech from its borders. The ordinance "greatly restrict[s] access to . . . lawful speech," *American Mini Theatres, supra,* 427 U.S., at 71, n. 35 (plurality opinion), and is plainly unconstitutional.

---

**Question:** Under *Renton,* should a District of Columbia ordinance banning signs within 500 feet of a foreign embassy that would tend to bring the foreign government into "public odium" or "disrepute," but would not interfere with access or security, be considered constitutional? See *Boos v. Barry,* 485 U.S. 312 (1988).

## ELECTRONIC MEDIA

### SABLE COMMUNICATIONS V. FEDERAL COMMUNICATIONS COMMISSION

492 U.S. 115 (1989)

JUSTICE WHITE delivered the opinion of the Court.

The issue before us is the constitutionality of § 223(b) of the Communications Act of 1934. 47 U.S.C. § 223(b) (1982 ed., Supp. V). The statute, as amended in 1988, imposes an outright ban on indecent as well as obscene interstate commercial telephone messages. The District Court upheld the prohibition against obscene interstate telephone communications for commercial purposes, but enjoined the enforcement of the statute insofar as it applied to indecent messages. We affirm the District Court in both respects.

In 1983, Sable Communications, Inc., a Los Angeles-based affiliate of Carlin Communications, Inc., began offering sexually oriented prerecorded telephone messages (popularly known as "dial-a-porn") through the Pacific Bell telephone network. In order to provide the messages, Sable arranged with Pacific Bell to use special telephone lines, designed to handle large volumes of calls simultaneously. Those who called the adult message number were charged a special fee. The fee was collected by Pacific Bell and divided between the phone company and the message provider. Callers outside the Los Angeles metropolitan area could reach the number by means of a long-distance toll call to the Los Angeles area code.

In 1988, Sable brought suit in District Court seeking declaratory and injunctive relief against enforcement of the recently amended § 223(b). The 1988 amendments to the statute imposed a blanket prohibition on indecent as well as obscene interstate commercial telephone messages. Sable brought this action to enjoin the Federal Communications Commission (FCC) and the Justice Department from initiating any criminal investigation or prosecution, civil action or administrative proceeding under the statute. Sable also sought a declaratory judgment, challenging the indecency and the obscenity provisions of the amended § 223(b) as unconstitutional, chiefly under the First and Fourteenth Amendments to the Constitution.

The District Court found that a concrete controversy existed and that Sable met the irreparable injury requirement for issuance of a preliminary injunction under *Elrod v. Burns,* 427 U.S. 347, 373, (1976). 692 F.Supp. 1208, 1209 (C.D.Cal.1988). The District Court denied Sable's request for a preliminary injunction against enforcement of the statute's ban on obscene telephone messages, rejecting the argument that the statute was unconstitutional because it created a national standard of obscenity. The District Court, however, struck down the "indecent speech" provision of § 223(b), holding that in this respect the statute was overbroad and unconstitutional and that this result was consistent with *FCC v. Pacifica Foundation,* 438 U.S. 726 (1978). "While the government unquestionably has a legitimate interest in, *e.g.,* protecting children from exposure to indecent dial-a-porn messages, § 223(b) is not narrowly drawn to achieve any such purpose. Its flat-out ban of indecent speech is contrary to the First Amendment." 692 F.Supp., at 1209. Therefore, the court issued a preliminary injunction prohibiting enforcement of § 223(b) with respect to any communication alleged to be "indecent."

We noted probable jurisdiction on Sable's appeal of the obscenity ruling (No. 88–515); we also noted probable jurisdiction on the federal parties' cross-appeal of the preliminary injunction holding the statute unconstitutional with respect to its ban on indecent speech.

While dial-a-porn services are a creature of this decade, the medium, in its brief history, has been the subject of much litigation and the object of a series of attempts at regulation. The first litigation involving dial-a-porn was brought under 82 Stat. 112, 47 U.S.C. § 223, which proscribed knowingly "permitting a telephone under [one's] control" to be used to make "any comment, request, suggestion or proposal which is obscene, lewd, lascivious, filthy, or indecent." However, the FCC concluded in an administrative action that the existing law did not cover dial-a-porn. *In re Application for Review of Complaint Filed by Peter F. Cohalan,* FCC File No. E–83–14 (memorandum opinions and orders adopted May 13, 1983).

In reaction to that FCC determination, Congress made its first effort explicitly to address "dial-a-porn" when it added a subsection 223(b) to the 1934 Communications Act. The provision, which was the predecessor to the amendment at issue in this case, pertained directly to sexually oriented commercial telephone messages and sought to restrict the access of minors to dial-a-porn. The relevant provision of the Act, Federal Communications Commission Authorization Act of 1983, Pub.L. 98–214, § 8(b), 97 Stat. 1470, made it a crime to use telephone facilities to make "obscene or indecent" interstate telephone communications "for commercial purposes to any person under eighteen years of age or to any other person without that person's consent." 47 U.S.C. § 223(b)(1)(A) (1982 ed., Supp. V). The statute criminalized commercial transmission of sexually oriented communications to minors and required the FCC to promulgate regulations laying out the means by which dial-a-porn sponsors could screen out underaged callers. § 223(b)(2). The enactment provided that it would be a defense to prosecution that the defendant restricted access to adults only, in accordance with procedures established by the FCC. The statute did not criminalize sexually oriented messages to adults, whether the messages were obscene or indecent.

The FCC initially promulgated regulations that would have established a defense to message providers operating only between the hours of 9 p.m. and 8 a.m. eastern time (time channeling) and to providers requiring payment by credit card (screening) before transmission of the dial-a-porn message. Restrictions on Obscene or Indecent Telephone Message Services, 47 CFR § 64.201 (1988). In *Carlin Communications, Inc. v. FCC,* 749 F.2d 113 (1984) *(Carlin I),* the Court of Appeals for the Second Circuit set aside the time channeling regulations and remanded to the FCC to examine other alternatives, concluding that the operating hours requirement was "both overinclusive and underinclusive" because it denied "access to adults between certain hours, but not to youths who can easily pick up a private or public telephone and call dial-a-porn during the remaining hours." *Id.,* at 121. The Court of Appeals did not reach the constitutionality of the underlying legislation.

In 1985, the FCC promulgated new regulations which continued to permit credit card payment as a defense to prosecution. Instead of time restrictions, however, the Commission added a defense based on use of access codes (user identification codes). Thus, it would be a defense to prosecution under § 223(b) if the defendant, before transmission of the message, restricted customer access by requiring either payment by credit card or authorization by access or identification code. 50 Fed.Reg. 42699, 42705 (1985). The regulations required each dial-a-porn vendor to develop an identification code data base and implementation scheme. Callers would be required to provide an access number for identification (or a credit card) before receiving the message. The access code would be received through the mail after the message provider reviewed the application and concluded through a written age ascertainment procedure that the applicant was at least 18 years of age. The FCC rejected a proposal for "exchange blocking" which would block or screen telephone numbers at the customer's premises or at the telephone company offices. In *Carlin Communications, Inc. v. FCC,* 787 F.2d 846 (C.A.2 1986) *(Carlin II),* the Court of Appeals set aside the new regulations because of the FCC's failure adequately to consider customer premises blocking. Again, the constitutionality of the underlying legislation was not addressed.

The FCC then promulgated a third set of regulations, which again rejected customer premises blocking but added to the prior defenses of credit card payment and access code use a third defense: message scrambling. 52 Fed.Reg. 17760 (1987). Under this system, providers would scramble the message, which would then be unintelligible without the use of a descrambler, the sale of which would be limited to adults. On January 15, 1988, in *Carlin Communications, Inc. v. FCC,* 837 F.2d 546 *(Carlin III),* cert. denied, 488 U.S. 924, 109 (1988), the Court of Appeals for the Second Circuit held that the new regulations, which made access codes, along with credit card payments and scrambled messages, defenses to prosecution under § 223(b) for dial-a-porn providers, were supported by the evidence, had been properly arrived at, and were a "feasible and effective way to serve" the "compelling state interest" in protecting minors, 837 F.2d, at 555; but the Court directed the FCC to reopen proceedings if a less restrictive technology became available. The Court of Appeals, however, this time reaching the constitutionality of the statute, invalidated § 223(b) insofar as it sought to apply to nonobscene speech. *Id.,* at 560, 561.

Thereafter, in April 1988, Congress amended § 223(b) of the Communications Act to prohibit indecent as well as obscene interstate commercial telephone communications directed to any person regardless of age. The amended statute, which took effect on July 1, 1988, also eliminated the requirement that the FCC promulgate regulations for restricting access to minors since a total ban was imposed on dial-a-porn, making it illegal for adults, as well as children, to have access to the sexually explicit messages, Pub.L. 100–297, 102 Stat. 424. It was this version of the statute that was in effect when Sable commenced this action.

In the ruling at issue in No. 88–515, the District Court upheld § 223(b)'s prohibition of obscene telephone messages as constitutional. We agree with that judgment. In contrast to the prohibition on indecent communications, there is no constitutional barrier to the ban on obscene dial-a-porn recordings. We have repeatedly held that the protection of the First Amendment does not extend to obscene speech. See, *e.g., Paris Adult Theatre I v. Slaton,* 413 U.S. 49, 69 (1973). The cases before § today do not require us to decide what is obscene or what is indecent but rather to determine whether Congress is empowered to prohibit transmission of obscene telephonic communications.

In its facial challenge to the statute, Sable argues that the legislation creates an impermissible national standard of obscenity, and that it places message senders in a "double bind" by compelling them to tailor all their messages to the least tolerant community.

We do not read § 223(b) as contravening the "contemporary community standards" requirement of *Miller v. California,* 413 U.S. 15 (1973). Section 223(b) no more establishes a "national standard" of obscenity than do federal statutes prohibiting the mailing of obscene materials, 18 U.S.C. § 1461, see *Hamling v. United States,* 418 U.S. 87 (1974), or the broadcasting of obscene messages, 18 U.S.C. § 1464. In *United States v. Reidel,* 402 U.S. 351 (1971), we said that Congress could prohibit the use of the mails for commercial distribution of materials properly classifiable as obscene, even though those materials were being distributed to willing adults who stated that they were adults. Similarly, we hold today that there is no constitutional stricture against Congress' prohibiting the interstate transmission of obscene commercial telephone recordings.

We stated in *United States v. 12 200-ft. Reels of Film,* 413 U.S. 123 (1973), that the *Miller* standards, including the "contemporary community standards" formulation, apply to federal legislation. As we have said before, the fact that "distributors of allegedly obscene materials may be subjected to varying community standards in the various federal judicial districts into which they transmit the materials does not render a federal statute unconstitutional because of the failure of application of uniform national standards of obscenity." *Hamling v. United States, supra,* 418 U.S., at 106.

Furthermore, Sable is free to tailor its messages, on a selective basis, if it so chooses, to the communities it chooses to serve. While Sable may be forced to incur some costs in developing and implementing a system for screening the locale of incoming calls, there is no constitutional impediment to enacting a law which may impose such costs on a medium electing to provide these messages. Whether Sable chooses to hire operators to determine the source of the calls or engages with the telephone company to arrange for the screening and blocking of out-of-area calls or finds another means for providing messages compatible with community standards is a decision for the message provider to make. There is no constitutional barrier under *Miller* to prohibiting communications that are obscene in some communities under local standards even though they are not obscene in others. If Sable's audience is comprised of different communities with different local standards, Sable ultimately bears the burden of complying with the prohibition on obscene messages.

In No. 88–525, the District Court concluded that while the Government has a legitimate interest in protecting children from exposure to indecent dial-a-porn messages, § 223(b) was not sufficiently narrowly drawn to serve that purpose and thus violated the First Amendment. We agree.

Sexual expression which is indecent but not obscene is protected by the First Amendment; and the federal parties do not submit that the sale of such materials to adults could be criminalized solely because they are indecent. The Government may, however, regulate the content of constitutionally protected speech in order to promote a compelling interest if it chooses the least restrictive means to further the articulated interest. We have recognized that there is a compelling interest in protecting the physical and psychological well-being of minors. This interest extends to shielding minors from the influence of literature that is not obscene by adult standards. *Ginsberg v. New York,* 390 U.S. 629, 639–640 (1968); *New York v. Ferber,* 458 U.S. 747, 756–757 (1982). The Government may serve this legitimate interest, but to withstand constitutional scrutiny, "it must do so by narrowly drawn regulations designed to serve those interests without unnecessarily interfering with First Amendment freedoms. *Hynes v. Mayor of Oradell,* 425 U.S. [610], at 620 (1976) [additional citations]. It is not enough to show that the Government's ends are compelling; the means must be carefully tailored to achieve those ends.

In *Butler v. Michigan,* 352 U.S. 380, (1957), a unanimous Court reversed a conviction under a statute which made it an offense to make available to the general public materials found to have a potentially harmful influence on minors. The Court found the law to be insufficiently tailored since it denied adults their free speech rights by allowing them to read only what was acceptable for children. As Justice Frankfurter said in that case, "[s]urely this is to burn the house to roast the pig." *Id.,* at 383. In our judgment, this case, like *Butler,* presents us with "legislation not reasonably restricted to the evil with which it is said to deal." *Ibid.*

In attempting to justify the complete ban and criminalization of the indecent commercial telephone communications with adults as well as minors, the federal parties rely on *FCC v. Pacifica Foundation,* 438 U.S.

726 (1978), a case in which the Court considered whether the FCC has the power to regulate a radio broadcast that is indecent but not obscene. In an emphatically narrow holding, the *Pacifica* Court concluded that special treatment of indecent broadcasting was justified.

*Pacifica* is readily distinguishable from these cases, most obviously because it did not involve a total ban on broadcasting indecent material. The FCC rule was not " 'intended to place an absolute prohibition on the broadcast of this type of language, but rather sought to channel it to times of day when children most likely would not be exposed to it.' " *Pacifica, supra,* at 733, quoting *Pacifica Foundation,* 59 F.C.C.2d 892 (1976). The issue of a total ban was not before the Court. 438 U.S., at 750, n. 28.

The *Pacifica* opinion also relied on the "unique" attributes of broadcasting, noting that broadcasting is "uniquely pervasive," can intrude on the privacy of the home without prior warning as to program content, and is "uniquely accessible to children, even those too young to read." *Id.,* at 748–749. The private commercial telephone communications at issue here are substantially different from the public radio broadcast at issue in *Pacifica.* In contrast to public displays, unsolicited mailings and other means of expression which the recipient has no meaningful opportunity to avoid, the dial-it medium requires the listener to take affirmative steps to receive the communication. There is no "captive audience" problem here; callers will generally not be unwilling listeners. The context of dial-in services, where a caller seeks and is willing to pay for the communication, is manifestly different from a situation in which a listener does not want the received message. Placing a telephone call is not the same as turning on a radio and being taken by surprise by an indecent message. Unlike an unexpected outburst on a radio broadcast, the message received by one who places a call to a dial-a-porn service is not so invasive or surprising that it prevents an unwilling listener from avoiding exposure to it.

The Court in *Pacifica* was careful "to emphasize the narrowness of [its] holding." *Id.,* at 750. As we did in *Bolger v. Youngs Drug Products Corp.,* 463 U.S. 60, 103 (1983), we distinguish *Pacifica* from the cases before us and reiterate that "the government may not 'reduce the adult population . . . to . . . only what is fit for children.' " 463 U.S., at 73. The federal parties nevertheless argue that the total ban on indecent commercial telephone communications is justified because nothing less could prevent children from gaining access to such messages. We find the argument quite unpersuasive. The FCC, after lengthy proceedings, determined that its credit card, access code, and scrambling rules were a satisfactory solution to the problem of keeping indecent dial-a-porn messages out of the reach of minors. The Court of Appeals, after careful consideration, agreed that these rules represented a "feasible and effective" way to serve the Government's compelling interest in protecting children. 837 F.2d, at 555.

The federal parties now insist that the rules would not be effective enough—that enterprising youngsters could and would evade the rules and gain access to communications from which they should be shielded. There is no evidence in the record before us to that effect, nor could there be since the FCC's implementation of § 223(b) prior to its 1988 amendment has never been tested over time. In this respect, the federal parties assert that in amending § 223(b) in 1988, Congress expressed its view that there was not a sufficiently effective way to protect minors short of the total ban that it enacted. The federal parties claim that we must give deference to that judgment.

* * *

Beyond the fact that whatever deference is due legislative findings would not foreclose our independent judgment of the facts bearing on an issue of constitutional law, our answer is that the congressional record contains no legislative findings that would justify us in concluding that there is no constitutionally acceptable less restrictive means, short of a total ban, to achieve the Government's interest in protecting minors.

There is no doubt Congress enacted a total ban on both obscene and indecent telephone communications. But aside from conclusory statements during the debates by proponents of the bill, as well as similar assertions in hearings on a substantially identical bill the year before, H.R. 1786, that under the FCC regulations minors could still have access to dial-a-porn messages, the congressional record presented to us contains no evidence as to *how* effective or ineffective the FCC's most recent regulations were or might prove to be.

* * *

For all we know from this record, the FCC's technological approach to restricting dial-a-porn messages to adults who seek them would be extremely effective, and only a few of the most enterprising and disobedient young people would manage to secure access to such messages. If this is the case, it seems to us that § 223(b) is not a narrowly tailored effort to serve the compelling interest of preventing minors from being exposed to indecent telephone messages. Under our precedents, § 223(b), in its present form, has the invalid effect of limiting the content of adult telephone conversations to that which is suitable for children to hear. . . .

Because the statute's denial of adult access to telephone messages which are indecent but not obscene far exceeds that which is necessary to limit the access of minors to such messages, we hold that the ban does not survive constitutional scrutiny.

Accordingly, we affirm the judgment of the District Court in Nos. 88–515 and 88–525.

*It is so ordered.*

---

**Question:** The 1996 Telecommunications Act, a federal statute, required cable TV operators to scramble sexually explicit channels or limit transmission of such material to late hours when children would be less likely to watch. Constitutional after *Sable*? See *United States v. Playboy Entertainment Group,* 529 U.S. 803 (2000).

# CHAPTER 14

# FOURTH AMENDMENT

■ ■ ■

## CONTEXT & SOURCES

The Fourth Amendment protects "[t]he right of the people to be secure in their persons, houses, papers, and effects, against unreasonable searches and seizures . . . ." This provision is one of the major sources of what is now considered the privacy right, although privacy is not expressly mentioned in the Constitution. Like the First Amendment, the Fourth is often the focus of a specific law school course, such as criminal procedure. Included here are cases on law enforcement's electronic listening to criminal suspects, the adequacy of search warrants, and detentions at the U.S.-Mexico border.

For a useful survey of Fourth Amendment jurisprudence and the increasing variety of ways contemporary violations can occur, see Stephen J. Schulhofer, *More Essential Than Ever: The Fourth Amendment in the Twenty-First Century* (Oxford, 2012). Louis Brandeis and Samuel Warren laid the philosophical foundation for Brandeis's *Olmstead* dissent and the later *Katz* majority in their famous article, "The Right to Privacy," 4 *Harvard Law Review* 193 (1890). The Supreme Court's attempt to clarify "unreasonable searches and seizures" in *U.S. v. Leon* is critically analyzed in Craig M. Bradley, "The 'Good Faith Exception' Cases: Reasonable Exercises in Futility," 60 *Indiana Law Journal* 287 (1985). Peter L. Reich, *The Law of the United States-Mexico Border: A Casebook*, ch. 3 (Carolina Academic Press, 2017) provides commentary on a range of border detention cases, including *U.S. v. Cortez*.

## PRIVACY

### OLMSTEAD V. UNITED STATES

27 U.S. 438 (1928)

* * *

MR. CHIEF JUSTICE TAFT delivered the opinion of the Court.

These cases are here by certiorari from the Circuit Court of Appeals for the Ninth Circuit. 19 F.(2d) 842, 53 A. L. R. 1472, and 19 F.(2d) 850. The petition in No. 493 Was filed August 30, 1927; in Nos. 532 and 533,

September 9, 1927. They were granted with the distinct limitation that the hearing should be confined to the single question whether the use of evidence of private telephone conversations between the defendants and others, intercepted by means of wire tapping, amounted to a violation of the Fourth and Fifth Amendments. 276 U. S. 609.

The petitioners were convicted in the District Court for the Western District of Washington of a conspiracy to violate the National Prohibition Act (27 USCA) by unlawfully possessing, transporting and importing intoxicating liquors and maintaining nuisances, and by selling intoxicating liquors. Seventy-two others, in addition to the petitioners, were indicted. Some were not apprehended, some were acquitted, and others pleaded guilty.

The evidence in the records discloses a conspiracy of amazing magnitude to import, possess, and sell liquor unlawfully. It involved the employment of not less than 50 persons, of two sea-going vessels for the transportation of liquor to British Columbia, of smaller vessels for coastwise transportation to the state of Washington, the purchase and use of a branch beyond the suburban limits of Seattle, with a large underground cache for storage and a number of smaller caches in that city, the maintenance of a central office manned with operators, and the employment of executives, salesmen, deliverymen dispatchers, scouts, bookkeepers, collectors, and an attorney. In a bad month sales amounted to $176,000; the aggregate for a year must have exceeded $2,000,000.

Olmstead was the leading conspirator and the general manager of the business. He made a contribution of $10,000 to the capital; 11 others contributed $1,000 each. The profits were divided, one-half to Olmstead and the remainder to the other 11. Of the several offices in Seattle, the chief one was in a large office building. In this there were three telephones on three different lines. There were telephones in an office of the manager in his own home, at the homes of his associates, and at other places in the city. Communication was had frequently with Vancouver, British Columbia. Times were fixed for the deliveries of the 'stuff' to places along Puget Sound near Seattle, and from there the liquor was removed and deposited in the caches already referred to. One of the chief men was always on duty at the main office to receive orders by the telephones and to direct their filling by a corps of men stationed in another room-the 'bull pen.' The call numbers of the telephones were given to those known to be likely customers. At times the sales amounted to 200 cases of liquor per day.

The information which led to the discovery of the conspiracy and its nature and extent was largely obtained by intercepting messages on the telephones of the conspirators by four federal prohibition officers. Small wires were inserted along the ordinary telephone wires from the residences of four of the petitioners and those leading from the chief office. The insertions were made without trespass upon any property of the defendants. They were made in the basement of the large office building. The taps from house lines were made in the streets near the houses.

The gathering of evidence continued for many months. Conversations of the conspirators, of which refreshing stenographic notes were currently made, were testified to by the government witnesses. They revealed the large business transactions of the partners and their subordinates. Men at the wires heard the orders given for liquor by customers and the acceptances; they became auditors of the conversations between the partners. All this disclosed the conspiracy charged in the indictment. Many of the intercepted conversations were not merely reports, but parts of the criminal acts. The evidence also disclosed the difficulties to which the conspirators were subjected, the reported news of the capture of vessels, the arrest of their men, and the seizure of cases of liquor in garages and other places. It showed the dealing by Olmstead, the chief conspirator, with members of the Seattle police, the messages to them which secured the release of arrested members of the conspiracy, and also direct promises to officers of payments as soon as opportunity offered.

The Fourth Amendment provides:

'The right of the people to be secure in their persons, houses, papers, and effects, against unreasonable searches and seizures, shall not be violated, and no warrants shall issue, but upon probable cause, supported by oath or affirmation, and particularly describing the place to be searched, and the persons or things to be seized.'

And the Fifth:

'No person * * * shall be compelled in any criminal case to be a witness against himself.' It will be helpful to consider the chief cases in this court which bear upon the construction of these amendments.

* * *

... Ex parte Jackson, 96 U. S. 727, 733 held that the Fourth Amendment as a principle of protection was applicable to sealed letters and packages in the mail, and that, consistently with it, such matter could only be opened and examined upon warrants issued on oath or affirmation particularly describing the thing to be seized.

* * *

There is no room in the present case for applying the Fifth Amendment, unless the Fourth Amendment was first violated. There was no evidence of compulsion to induce the defendants to talk over their many telephones. They were continually and voluntarily transacting business without knowledge of the interception. Our consideration must be confined to the Fourth Amendment.

* * *

The well-known historical purpose of the Fourth Amendment, directed against general warrants and writs of assistance, was to prevent the use of governmental force to search a man's house, his person, his papers, and his effects, and to prevent their seizure against his will. This phase of the misuse of governmental power of compulsion is the emphasis of the opinion of the court in the Boyd Case. This appears, too, in the Weeks Case, in the Silverthorne Case, and in the Amos Case.

* * *

The amendment itself shows that the search is to be of material things-the person, the house, his papers, or his effects. The description of the warrant necessary to make the proceeding lawful is that it must specify the place to be searched and the person or things to be seized.

* * *

The Fourth Amendment may have proper application to a sealed letter in the mail, because of the constitutional provision for the Post office Department and the relations between the government and those who pay to secure protection of their sealed letters. See Revised Statutes, §§ 3978 to 3988, whereby Congress monopolizes the carriage of letters and excludes from that business everyone else, and section 3929 (39 USCA § 259), which forbids any postmaster or other person to open any letter not addressed to himself. It is plainly within the words of the amendment to say that the unlawful rifling by a government agent of a sealed letter is a search and seizure of the sender's papers of effects. The letter is a paper, an effect, and in the custody of a government that forbids carriage, except under its protection.

The United States takes no such care of telegraph or telephone messages as of mailed sealed letters. The amendment does not forbid what was done here. There was no searching. There was no seizure. The evidence was secured by the use of the sense of hearing and that only. There was no entry of the houses or offices of the defendants.

By the invention of the telephone 50 years ago, and its application for the purpose of extending communications, one can talk with another at a far distant place.

The language of the amendment cannot be extended and expanded to include telephone wires, reaching to the whole world from the defendant's house or office. The intervening wires are not part of his house or office, any more than are the highways along which they are stretched.

This court, in Carroll v. United States, 267 U. S. 132, 149, declared:

'The Fourth Amendment is to be construed in the light of what was deemed an unreasonable search and seizure when it was adopted, and in a manner which will conserve public interests, as well as the interest and rights of individual citizens.'

* * *

Congress may, of course, protect the secrecy of telephone messages by making them, when intercepted, inadmissible in evidence in federal criminal trials, by direct legislation, and thus depart from the common law of evidence. But the courts may not adopt such a policy by attributing an enlarged and unusual meaning to the Fourth Amendment. The reasonable view is that one who installs in his house a telephone instrument with connecting wires intends to project his voice to those quite outside, and that the wires beyond his house, and messages while passing over them, are not within the protection of the Fourth Amendment. Here those who intercepted the projected voices were not in the house of either party to the conversation.

Neither the cases we have cited nor any of the many federal decisions brought to our attention hold the Fourth Amendment to have been violated as against a defendant, unless there has been an official search and seizure of his person or such a seizure of his papers or his tangible material effects or an actual physical invasion of his house 'or curtilage' for the purpose of making a seizure.

We think, therefore, that the wire tapping here disclosed did not amount to a search or seizure within the meaning of the Fourth Amendment.

* * *

Affirmed.

MR. JUSTICE BRANDEIS (dissenting).

The defendants were convicted of conspiring to violate the National Prohibition Act (27 USCA). Before any of the persons now charged had been arrested or indicted, the telephones by means of which they habitually communicated with one another and with others had been tapped by federal officers. To this end, a lineman of long experience in wire tapping was employed, on behalf of the government and at its expense. He tapped eight telephones, some in the homes of the persons charged, some in their offices. Acting on behalf of the government and in their official capacity, at least six other prohibition agents listened over the tapped wires and reported the messages taken. Their operations extended over a period of nearly five months. The typewritten record of the notes of conversations overheard occupies 775 typewritten pages. By objections seasonably made and persistently renewed, the defendants objected to the admission of the evidence obtained by wire tapping, on the ground that the government's wire tapping constituted an unreasonable search and seizure, in violation of the Fourth Amendment, and that the use as evidence of the conversations overheard compelled the defendants to be witnesses against themselves, in violation of the Fifth Amendment.

The government makes no attempt to defend the methods employed by its officers. Indeed, it concedes that, if wire tapping can be deemed a search and seizure within the Fourth Amendment, such wire tapping as was practiced in the case at bar was an unreasonable search and seizure, and that the evidence thus obtained was inadmissible. But it relies on the language of the amendment, and it claims that the protection given thereby cannot properly be held to include a telephone conversation.

'We must never forget,' said Mr. Chief Justice Marshall in McCulloch v. Maryland, 4 Wheat. 316, 'that it is a Constitution we are expounding.' Since then this court has repeatedly sustained the exercise of power by Congress, under various clauses of that instrument, over objects of which the fathers could not have dreamed. See Pensacola Telegraph Co. v. Western Union Telegraph Co., 96 U. S. 1, [additional citations]. We have likewise held that general limitations on the powers of government, like those embodied in the due process clauses of the Fifth and Fourteenth Amendments, do not forbid the United States or the states from meeting modern conditions by regulations which 'a century ago, or even half a century ago, probably would have been rejected as arbitrary and oppressive.' Village of Euclid v. Ambler Realty Co., 272 U. S. 365, 387. Clauses guaranteeing to the individual protection against specific abuses of power, must have a similar capacity of adaptation to a changing world.

* * *

When the Fourth and Fifth Amendments were adopted, 'the form that evil had theretofore taken' had been necessarily simple. Force and violence were then the only means known to man by which a government could directly effect self-incrimination. It could compel the individual to testify-a compulsion effected, if need be, by torture. It could secure possession of his papers and other articles incident to his private life-a seizure effected, if need be, by breaking and entry. Protection against such invasion of 'the sanctities of a man's home and the privacies of life' was provided in the Fourth and Fifth Amendments by specific language. Boyd v. United States, 116 U. S. 616, 630. But 'time works changes, brings into existence new conditions and purposes.' Subtler and more far-reaching means of invading privacy have become available to the government. Discovery and invention have made it possible for the government, by means far more effective than stretching upon the rack, to obtain disclosure in court of what is whispered in the closet.

Moreover, 'in the application of a Constitution, our contemplation cannot be only of what has been, but of what may be.' The progress of science in furnishing the government with means of espionage is not likely to stop with wire tapping. Ways may some day be developed by which the government, without removing papers from secret drawers, can reproduce them in court, and by which it will be enabled to expose to a jury the most intimate occurrences of the home. Advances in the psychic and related sciences may bring means of exploring unexpressed beliefs, thoughts and emotions.

* * *

In Ex parte Jackson, 96 U. S. 727, 24, it was held that a sealed letter intrusted to the mail is protected by the amendments. The mail is a public service furnished by the government. The telephone is a public service furnished by its authority. There is, in essence, no difference between the sealed letter and the private telephone message.

* * *

The evil incident to invasion of the privacy of the telephone is far greater than that involved in tampering with the mails. Whenever a telephone line is tapped, the privacy of the persons at both ends of the line is invaded, and all conversations between them upon any subject, and although proper, confidential, and privileged, may be overheard. Moreover, the tapping of one man's telephone line involves the tapping of the telephone of every other person whom he may call, or who may call him. As a means of espionage, writs of assistance and general warrants are but puny instruments of tyranny and oppression when compared with wire tapping.

Time and again this court, in giving effect to the principle underlying the Fourth Amendment, has refused to place an unduly literal construction upon it . . . . Decisions of this court . . .have settled these things. Unjustified search and seizure violates the Fourth Amendment, whatever the character of the paper; whether the paper when taken by the federal officers was in the home, in an office, or elsewhere; whether the taking was effected by force, by fraud, or in the orderly process of a court's procedure. From these decisions, it follows necessarily that the amendment is violated by the officer's reading the paper without a physical seizure, without his even touching it, and that use, in any criminal proceeding, of the contents of the paper so examined-as where they are testified to by a federal officer who thus saw the document or where, through knowledge so obtained, a copy has been procured elsewhere-any such use constitutes a violation of the Fifth Amendment.

* * *

Applying to the Fourth and Fifth Amendments the established rule of construction, the defendants' objections to the evidence obtained by wire tapping must, in my opinion, be sustained. It is, of course, immaterial where the physical connection with the telephone wires leading into the defendants' premises was made. And it is also immaterial that the intrusion was in aid of law enforcement. Experience should teach us to be most on our guard to protect liberty when the government's purposes are beneficent. Men born to freedom are naturally alert to repel invasion of their liberty by evil-minded rulers. The greatest dangers to liberty lurk in insidious encroachment by men of zeal, well-meaning but without understanding.

* * *

Decency, security, and liberty alike demand that government officials shall be subjected to the same rules of conduct that are commands to the citizen. In a government of laws, existence of the government will be imperiled if it fails to observe the law scrupulously. Our government is the potent, the omnipresent teacher. For good or for ill, it teaches the whole people by its example. Crime is contagious. If the government becomes a lawbreaker, it breeds contempt for law; it invites every man to become a law unto himself; it invites anarchy. To declare that in the administration of the criminal law the end justifies the means-to declare that the government may commit crimes in order to secure the conviction of a private criminal-would bring terrible retribution. Against that pernicious doctrine this court should resolutely set its face.

---

**Question:** Instead of tapping a suspect's phone, officers place a microphone on the outer wall of a private office. Constitutional under Olmstead? See *Goldman v. United States,* 316 U.S. 129 (1942).

## KATZ V. UNITED STATES

389 U.S. 347 (1967)

* * *

MR. JUSTICE STEWART delivered the opinion of the Court.

The petitioner was convicted in the District Court for the Southern District of California under an eight-count indictment charging him with transmitting wagering information by telephone from Los Angeles to Miami and Boston in violation of a federal statute. At trial the Government was permitted, over the petitioner's objection, to introduce evidence of the petitioner's end of telephone conversations, overheard by FBI agents who had attached an electronic listening and recording device to the outside of the public telephone booth from which he had placed his calls. In affirming his conviction, the Court of Appeals rejected the contention that the recordings had been obtained in violation of the Fourth Amendment, because '(t)here was no physical entrance into the area occupied by, (the petitioner). We granted certiorari in order to consider the constitutional questions thus presented.

* * *

The petitioner has strenuously argued that the booth was a 'constitutionally protected area.' The Government has maintained with equal vigor that it was not. But this effort to decide whether or not a given 'area,' viewed in the abstract, is 'constitutionally protected' deflects attention from the problem presented by this case. For the Fourth Amendment protects people, not places. What a person knowingly exposes to the public, even in his own home or office, is not a subject of Fourth Amendment protection. See Lewis v. United States, 385 U.S. 206, 210, 87; United States v. Lee, 274 U.S. 559, 563. But what he seeks to preserve as private, even in an area accessible to the public, may be constitutionally protected. See Rios v. United States, 364 U.S. 253.

The Government stresses the fact that the telephone booth from which the petitioner made his calls was constructed partly of glass, so that he was as visible after he entered it as he would have been if he had remained outside. But what he sought to exclude when he entered the booth was not the intruding eye—it was the uninvited ear. He did not shed his right to do so simply because he made his calls from a place where he might be seen. No less than an individual in a business office, in a friend's apartment, or in a taxicab, a person in a telephone booth may rely upon the protection of the Fourth Amendment. One who occupies it, shuts the door behind him, and pays the toll that permits him to place a call is surely entitled to assume that the words he utters into the mouthpiece will not be broadcast to the world. To read the Constitution more narrowly is to ignore the vital role that the public telephone has come to play in private communication.

The Government contends, however, that the activities of its agents in this case should not be tested by Fourth Amendment requirements, for the surveillance technique they employed involved no physical penetration of the telephone booth from which the petitioner placed his calls. It is true that the absence of such penetration was at one time thought to foreclose further Fourth Amendment inquiry, Olmstead v. United States, 277 U.S. 438, 457, 464, 466; Goldman v. United States, 316 U.S. 129, 134–136, for that Amendment was thought to limit only searches and seizures of tangible property. But '(t)he premise that property interests control the right of the Government to search and seize has been discredited.' Warden, Md. Penitentiary v. Hayden, 387 U.S. 294, 304. Thus, although a closely divided Court supposed in Olmstead that surveillance without any trespass and without the seizure of any material object fell outside the ambit of the

Constitution, we have since departed from the narrow view on which that decision rested. Indeed, we have expressly held that the Fourth Amendment governs not only the seizure of tangible items, but extends as well to the recording of oral statements overheard without any 'technical trespass under * * * local property law.' Silverman v. United States, 365 U.S. 505, 511. Once this much is acknowledged, and once it is recognized that the Fourth Amendment protects people and not simply 'areas'—against unreasonable searches and seizures it becomes clear that the reach of that Amendment cannot turn upon the presence or absence of a physical intrusion into any given enclosure.

We conclude that the underpinnings of Olmstead and Goldman have been so eroded by our subsequent decisions that the 'trespass' doctrine there enunciated can no longer be regarded as controlling. The Government's activities in electronically listening to and recording the petitioner's words violated the privacy upon which he justifiably relied while using the telephone booth and thus constituted a 'search and seizure' within the meaning of the Fourth Amendment. The fact that the electronic device employed to achieve that end did not happen to penetrate the wall of the booth can have no constitutional significance.

The question remaining for decision, then, is whether the search and seizure conducted in this case complied with constitutional standards. In that regard, the Government's position is that its agents acted in an entirely defensible manner: They did not begin their electronic surveillance until investigation of the petitioner's activities had established a strong probability that he was using the telephone in question to transmit gambling information to persons in other States, in violation of federal law. Moreover, the surveillance was limited, both in scope and in duration, to the specific purpose of establishing the contents of the petitioner's unlawful telephonic communications. The agents confined their surveillance to the brief periods during which he used the telephone booth, and they took great care to overhear only the conversations of the petitioner himself.

Accepting this account of the Government's actions as accurate, it is clear that this surveillance was so narrowly circumscribed that a duly authorized magistrate, properly notified of the need for such investigation, specifically informed of the basis on which it was to proceed, and clearly apprised of the precise intrusion it would entail, could constitutionally have authorized, with appropriate safeguards, the very limited search and seizure that the Government asserts in fact took place.

* * *

The Government urges that, because its agents relied upon the decisions in Olmstead and Goldman, and because they did no more here than they might properly have done with prior judicial sanction, we should retroactively validate their conduct. That we cannot do. It is apparent that the agents in this case acted with restraint. Yet the inescapable fact is that this restraint was imposed by the agents themselves, not by a judicial officer. They were not required, before commencing the search, to present their estimate of probable cause for detached scrutiny by a neutral magistrate. They were not compelled, during the conduct of the search itself, to observe precise limits established in advance by a specific court order. Nor were they directed, after the search had been completed, to notify the authorizing magistrate in detail of all that had been seized. In the absence of such safeguards, this Court has never sustained a search upon the sole ground that officers reasonably expected to find evidence of a particular crime and voluntarily confined their activities to the least intrusive means consistent with that end. Searches conducted without warrants have been held unlawful 'notwithstanding facts unquestionably showing probable cause,' Agnello v. United States, 269 U.S. 20, 33, for the Constitution requires 'that the deliberate, impartial judgment of a judicial officer * * * be interposed between the citizen and the police * * *.' Wong Sun v. United States, 371 U.S. 471, 481–482. 'Over and again this Court has emphasized that the mandate of the (Fourth) Amendment requires adherence to judicial processes,' United States v. Jeffers, 342 U.S. 48, 51, and that searches conducted outside the judicial process, without prior approval by judge or magistrate, are per se unreasonable under the Fourth Amendment—subject only to a few specifically established and well-delineated exceptions.

It is difficult to imagine how any of those exceptions could ever apply to the sort of search and seizure involved in this case. Even electronic surveillance substantially contemporaneous with an individual's arrest could hardly be deemed an 'incident' of that arrest. Nor could the use of electronic surveillance without prior authorization be justified on grounds of 'hot pursuit.' And, of course, the very nature of electronic surveillance precludes its use pursuant to the suspect's consent.

The Government . . . argues that surveillance of a telephone booth should be exempted from the usual requirement of advance authorization by a magistrate upon a showing of probable cause. We cannot agree.

* * *

[B]ypassing a neutral predetermination of the scope of a search leaves individuals secure from Fourth Amendment violations 'only in the discretion of the police.' Id., at 97.

These considerations do not vanish when the search in question is transferred from the setting of a home, an office, or a hotel room to that of a telephone booth. Wherever a man may be, he is entitled to know that he will remain free from unreasonable searches and seizures. The government agents here ignored 'the procedure of antecedent justification * * * that is central to the Fourth Amendment,' 24 a procedure that we hold to be a constitutional precondition of the kind of electronic surveillance involved in this case. Because the surveillance here failed to meet that condition, and because it led to the petitioner's conviction, the judgment must be reversed.

It is so ordered. Judgment reversed.

MR. JUSTICE BLACK, dissenting.

If I could agree with the Court that eavesdropping carried on by electronic means (equivalent to wiretapping) constitutes a 'search' or 'seizure,' I would be happy to join the Court's opinion.

* * *

My basic objection is twofold: (1) I do not believe that the words of the Amendment will bear the meaning given them by today's decision, and (2) I do not believe that it is the proper role of this Court to rewrite the Amendment in order 'to bring it into harmony with the times' and thus reach a result that many people believe to be desirable.

* * *

The first clause [of the Fourth Amendment] protects 'persons, houses, papers, and effects, against unreasonable searches and seizures * * *.' These words connote the idea of tangible things with size, form, and weight, things capable of being searched, seized, or both. The second clause of the Amendment still further establishes its Framers' purpose to limit its protection to tangible things by providing that no warrants shall issue but those 'particularly describing the place to be searched, and the persons or things to be seized.' A conversation overheard by eavesdropping, whether by plain snooping or wiretapping, is not tangible and, under the normally accepted meanings of the words, can neither be searched nor seized. In addition the language of the second clause indicates that the Amendment refers not only to something tangible so it can be seized but to something already in existence so it can be described. Yet the Court's interpretation would have the Amendment apply to overhearing future conversations which by their very nature are nonexistent until they take place. How can one 'describe' a future conversation, and, if one cannot, how can a magistrate issue a warrant to eavesdrop one in the future? It is argued that information showing what is expected to be said is sufficient to limit the boundaries of what later can be admitted into evidence; but does such general information really meet the specific language of the Amendment which says 'particularly describing'? Rather than using language in a completely artificial way, I must conclude that the Fourth Amendment simply does not apply to eavesdropping.

Tapping telephone wires, of course, was an unknown possibility at the time the Fourth Amendment was adopted. But eavesdropping (and wiretapping is nothing more than eavesdropping by telephone) was, as even the majority opinion in Berger, supra, recognized, 'an ancient practice which at common law was condemned as a nuisance. IV Blackstone, Commentaries § 168. In those days the eavesdropper listened by naked ear under the eaves of houses or their windows, or beyond their walls seeking out private discourse.' 388 U.S., at 45, There can be no doubt that the Framers were aware of this practice, and if they had desired to outlaw or restrict the use of evidence obtained by eavesdropping, I believe that they would have used the appropriate language to do so in the Fourth Amendment. They certainly would not have left such a task to the ingenuity of language-stretching judges. No one, it seems to me, can read the debates on the Bill of Rights without reaching the conclusion that its Framers and critics well knew the meaning of the words they used, what they would be understood to mean by others, their scope and their limitations. Under these circumstances it strikes me as a charge against their scholarship, their common sense and their candor to give to the Fourth Amendment's language the eavesdropping meaning the Court imputes to it today.

I do not deny that common sense requires and that this Court often has said that the Bill of Rights' safeguards should be given a liberal construction. This principle, however, does not justify construing the search and seizure amendment as applying to eavesdropping or the 'seizure' of conversations. The Fourth Amendment was aimed directly at the abhorred practice of breaking in, ransacking and searching homes and other buildings and seizing people's personal belongings without warrants issued by magistrates. The Amendment deserves, and this Court has given it, a liberal construction in order to protect against warrantless searches of buildings and seizures of tangible personal effects. But until today this Court has refused to say that eavesdropping comes within the ambit of Fourth Amendment restrictions. See, e.g., Olmstead v. United States, 277 U.S. 438 (1928), and Goldman v. United States, 316 U.S. 129, 62 (1942).

* * *

Since I see no way in which the words of the Fourth Amendment can be construed to apply to eavesdropping, that closes the matter for me. . . .I will not distort the words of the Amendment in order to 'keep the Constitution up to date' or 'to bring it into harmony with the times.' It was never meant that this Court have such power, which in effect would make us a continuously functioning constitutional convention.

With this decision the Court has completed, I hope, its rewriting of the Fourth Amendment, which started only recently when the Court began referring incessantly to the Fourth Amendment not so much as a law against unreasonable searches and seizures as one to protect an individual's privacy. By clever word juggling the Court finds it plausible to argue that language aimed specifically at searches and seizures of things that can be searched and seized may, to protect privacy, be applied to eavesdropped evidence of conversations that can neither be searched nor seized. Few things happen to an individual that do not affect his privacy in one way or another. Thus, by arbitrarily substituting the Court's language, designed to protect privacy, for the Constitution's language, designed to protect against unreasonable searches and seizures, the Court has made the Fourth Amendment its vehicle for holding all laws violative of the Constitution which offend the Court's broadest concept of privacy. As I said in Griswold v. State of Connecticut, 381 U.S. 479, 85, 'The Court talks about a constitutional 'right of privacy' as though there is some constitutional provision or provisions forbidding any law ever to be passed which might abridge the 'privacy' of individuals. But there is not.' (Dissenting opinion, at 508.) I made clear in that dissent my fear of the dangers involved when this Court uses the 'broad, abstract and ambiguous concept' of 'privacy' as a 'comprehensive substitute for the Fourth Amendment's guarantee against 'unreasonable searches and seizures."' (See generally dissenting opinion, at 507–527)

The Fourth Amendment protects privacy only to the extent that it prohibits unreasonable searches and seizures of 'persons, houses, papers, and effects.' No general right is created by the Amendment so as to give this Court the unlimited power to hold unconstitutional everything which affects privacy. Certainly the Framers, well acquainted as they were with the excesses of governmental power, did not intend to grant this Court such omnipotent lawmaking authority as that. The history of governments proves that it is dangerous to freedom to repose such powers in courts.

For these reasons I respectfully dissent.

---

**Questions:** Why does the *Katz* majority revise the *Olmstead* doctrine? How do the majority and dissent differ regarding the right of privacy?

## WARRANT ADEQUACY

### UNITED STATES V. LEON

468 U.S. 897 (1984)

JUSTICE WHITE delivered the opinion of the Court.

This case presents the question whether the Fourth Amendment exclusionary rule should be modified so as not to bar the use in the prosecution's case in chief of evidence obtained by officers acting in reasonable reliance on a search warrant issued by a detached and neutral magistrate but ultimately found to be unsupported by probable cause. To resolve this question, we must consider once again the tension between the sometimes competing goals of, on the one hand, deterring official misconduct and removing inducements to unreasonable invasions of privacy and, on the other, establishing procedures under which criminal defendants are "acquitted or convicted on the basis of all the evidence which exposes the truth." Alderman v. United States, 394 U.S. 165, 175 (1969).

In August 1981, a confidential informant of unproven reliability informed an officer of the Burbank Police Department that two persons known to him as "Armando" and "Patsy" were selling large quantities of cocaine and methaqualone from their residence at 620 Price Drive in Burbank, Cal. The informant also indicated that he had witnessed a sale of methaqualone by "Patsy" at the residence approximately five months earlier and had observed at that time a shoebox containing a large amount of cash that belonged to "Patsy." He further declared that "Armando" and "Patsy" generally kept only small quantities of drugs at their residence and stored the remainder at another location in Burbank.

On the basis of this information, the Burbank police initiated an extensive investigation focusing first on the Price Drive residence and later on two other residences as well. Cars parked at the Price Drive residence were determined to belong to respondents Armando Sanchez, who had previously been arrested for possession of marihuana, and Patsy Stewart, who had no criminal record. During the course of the investigation, officers observed an automobile belonging to respondent Ricardo Del Castillo, who had previously been arrested for possession of 50 pounds of marihuana, arrive at the Price Drive residence. The driver of that car entered the house, exited shortly thereafter carrying a small paper sack, and drove away. A check of Del Castillo's probation records led the officers to respondent Alberto Leon, whose telephone number Del Castillo had listed as his employer's. Leon had been arrested in 1980 on drug charges, and a companion had informed the police at that time that Leon was heavily involved in the importation of drugs into this country. Before the current investigation began, the Burbank officers had learned that an informant had told a Glendale police officer that Leon stored a large quantity of methaqualone at his residence in Glendale. During the course of this investigation, the Burbank officers learned that Leon was living at 716 South Sunset Canyon in Burbank.

Subsequently, the officers observed several persons, at least one of whom had prior drug involvement, arriving at the Price Drive residence and leaving with small packages; observed a variety of other material activity at the two residences as well as at a condominium at 7902 Via Magdalena; and witnessed a variety of relevant activity involving respondents' automobiles. The officers also observed respondents Sanchez and Stewart board separate flights for Miami. The pair later returned to Los Angeles together, consented to a search of their luggage that revealed only a small amount of marihuana, and left the airport. Based on these and other observations summarized in the affidavit, App. 34, Officer Cyril Rombach of the Burbank Police Department, an experienced and well-trained narcotics investigator, prepared an application for a warrant to search 620 Price Drive, 716 South Sunset Canyon, 7902 Via Magdalena, and automobiles registered to each of the respondents for an extensive list of items believed to be related to respondents' drug-trafficking activities. Officer Rombach's extensive application was reviewed by several Deputy District Attorneys.

A facially valid search warrant was issued in September 1981 by a State Superior Court Judge. The ensuing searches produced large quantities of drugs at the Via Magdalena and Sunset Canyon addresses and a small quantity at the Price Drive residence. Other evidence was discovered at each of the residences and in Stewart's and Del Castillo's automobiles. Respondents were indicted by a grand jury in the District Court for the Central District of California and charged with conspiracy to possess and distribute cocaine and a variety of substantive counts.

The respondents then filed motions to suppress the evidence seized pursuant to the warrant. The District Court held an evidentiary hearing and, while recognizing that the case was a close one, granted the motions to suppress in part. . . . In response to a request from the Government, the court made clear that Officer Rombach had acted in good faith, but it rejected the Government's suggestion that the exclusionary rule should not apply where evidence is seized in reasonable, good-faith reliance on a search warrant.

[T]he Court of Appeals for the Ninth Circuit affirmed. The Court of Appeals first concluded that Officer Rombach's affidavit could not establish probable cause to search the Price Drive residence. To the extent that the affidavit set forth facts demonstrating the basis of the informant's knowledge of criminal activity, the information included was fatally stale. The affidavit, moreover, failed to establish the informant's credibility. Accordingly, the Court of Appeals concluded that the information provided by the informant was inadequate ... The officers' independent investigation neither cured the staleness nor corroborated the details of the informant's declarations. The Court of Appeals then considered whether the affidavit formed a proper basis for the search of the Sunset Canyon residence. In its view, the affidavit included no facts indicating the basis for the informants' statements concerning respondent Leon's criminal activities and was devoid of information establishing the informants' reliability. Because these deficiencies had not been cured by the police investigation, the District Court properly suppressed the fruits of the search. The Court of Appeals refused the Government's invitation to recognize a good-faith exception to the Fourth Amendment exclusionary rule. App. to Pet. for Cert. 4a.

The Government's petition for certiorari expressly declined to seek review of the lower courts' determinations that the search warrant was unsupported by probable cause and presented only the question "[w]hether the Fourth Amendment exclusionary rule should be modified so as not to bar the admission of evidence seized in reasonable, good-faith reliance on a search warrant that is subsequently held to be defective." We granted certiorari to consider the propriety of such a modification. 463 U.S. 1206 (1983). Although it undoubtedly is within our power to consider the question whether probable cause existed under the "totality of the circumstances" test announced last Term in Illinois v. Gates, 462 U.S. 213 (1983), that question has not been briefed or argued; and it is also within our authority, which we choose to exercise, to take the case as it comes to us, accepting the Court of Appeals' conclusion that probable cause was lacking under the prevailing legal standards. See this Court's Rule 21.1(a).

We have concluded that, in the Fourth Amendment context, the exclusionary rule can be modified somewhat without jeopardizing its ability to perform its intended functions. Accordingly, we reverse the judgment of the Court of Appeals.

* * *

The Fourth Amendment contains no provision expressly precluding the use of evidence obtained in violation of its commands, and an examination of its origin and purposes makes clear that the use of fruits of a past unlawful search or seizure "work[s] no new Fourth Amendment wrong." United States v. Calandra, 414 U.S. 338, 354 (1974). The wrong condemned by the Amendment is "fully accomplished" by the unlawful search or seizure itself, ibid., and the exclusionary rule is neither intended nor able to "cure the invasion of the defendant's rights which he has already suffered." Stone v. Powell, supra, 428 U.S., at 540 (WHITE, J., dissenting). The rule thus operates as "a judicially created remedy designed to safeguard Fourth Amendment rights generally through its deterrent effect, rather than a personal constitutional right of the party aggrieved." United States v. Calandra, supra, 414 U.S., at 348.

Whether the exclusionary sanction is appropriately imposed in a particular case, our decisions make clear, is "an issue separate from the question whether the Fourth Amendment rights of the party seeking to invoke the rule were violated by police conduct." Illinois v. Gates, supra, 426 U.S., at 223. Only the former question is currently before us, and it must be resolved by weighing the costs and benefits of preventing the use in the prosecution's case in chief of inherently trustworthy tangible evidence obtained in reliance on a search warrant issued by a detached and neutral magistrate that ultimately is found to be defective.

The substantial social costs exacted by the exclusionary rule for the vindication of Fourth Amendment rights have long been a source of concern. "Our cases have consistently recognized that unbending application of the exclusionary sanction to enforce ideals of governmental rectitude would impede unacceptably the truth-finding functions of judge and jury." United States v. Payner, 447 U.S. 727, 734 (1980). An objectionable collateral consequence of this interference with the criminal justice system's truth-finding function is that some guilty defendants may go free or receive reduced sentences as a result of favorable plea bargains. Particularly when law enforcement officers have acted in objective good faith or their transgressions have been minor, the magnitude of the benefit conferred on such guilty defendants offends basic concepts of the criminal justice system. Stone v. Powell, 428 U.S., at 490. Indiscriminate application of the exclusionary rule, therefore, may well "generat[e] disrespect for the law and administration of justice." Id., at 491. Accordingly, "[a]s with any remedial device, the application of the rule has been restricted to those areas where its remedial objectives are thought most efficaciously served." United States v. Calandra, supra, 414 U.S., at 348, 94 S.Ct., at 670; see [citations.]

Close attention to those remedial objectives has characterized our recent decisions concerning the scope of the Fourth Amendment exclusionary rule. The Court has, to be sure, not seriously questioned, "in the absence of a more efficacious sanction, the continued application of the rule to suppress evidence from the [prosecution's] case where a Fourth Amendment violation has been substantial and deliberate. . . ." Franks v. Delaware, 438 U.S. 154, 171 (1978). Nevertheless, the balancing approach that has evolved in various contexts—including criminal trials—"forcefully suggest[s] that the exclusionary rule be more generally modified to permit the introduction of evidence obtained in the reasonable good-faith belief that a search or seizure was in accord with the Fourth Amendment." Illinois v. Gates, 462 U.S., at 255 (WHITE, J., concurring in judgment).

* * *

When considering the use of evidence obtained in violation of the Fourth Amendment in the prosecution's case in chief, moreover, we have declined to adopt a per se or "but for" rule that would render inadmissible any evidence that came to light through a chain of causation that began with an illegal arrest. Brown v. Illinois, 422 U.S. 590 (1975). We also have held that a witness' testimony may be admitted even when his identity was discovered in an unconstitutional search. United States v. Ceccolini, 435 U.S. 268 (1978). The perception underlying these decisions—that the connection between police misconduct and evidence of crime may be sufficiently attenuated to permit the use of that evidence at trial—is a product of considerations relating to the exclusionary rule and the constitutional principles it is designed to protect. Dunaway v. New York, 442 U.S. 200 (1979). In short, the "dissipation of the taint" concept that the Court has applied in deciding whether exclusion is appropriate in a particular case "attempts to mark the point at which the detrimental consequences of illegal police action become so attenuated that the deterrent effect of the exclusionary rule no longer justifies its cost." Brown v. Illinois, supra, 422 U.S., at 609 (POWELL, J., concurring in part). Not surprisingly in view of this purpose, an assessment of the flagrancy of the police misconduct constitutes an important step in the calculus. [citations.]

* * *

As yet, we have not recognized any form of good-faith exception to the Fourth Amendment exclusionary rule. But the balancing approach that has evolved during the years of experience with the rule provides strong support for the modification currently urged upon us. As we discuss below, our evaluation of the costs and benefits of suppressing reliable physical evidence seized by officers reasonably relying on a warrant issued by a detached and neutral magistrate leads to the conclusion that such evidence should be admissible in the prosecution's case in chief.

Because a search warrant "provides the detached scrutiny of a neutral magistrate, which is a more reliable safeguard against improper searches than the hurried judgment of a law enforcement officer 'engaged in the often competitive enterprise of ferreting out crime,'" United States v. Chadwick, 433 U.S. 1 (1977), we have expressed a strong preference for warrants and declared that "in a doubtful or marginal case a search under a warrant may be sustainable where without one it would fall." United States v. Ventresca, 380 U.S. 102, 106 (1965). Reasonable minds frequently may differ on the question whether a particular affidavit establishes probable cause, and we have thus concluded that the preference for warrants is most appropriately effectuated by according "great deference" to a magistrate's determination. Spinelli v. United States, 393 U.S., at 419.

Deference to the magistrate, however, is not boundless. It is clear, first, that the deference accorded to a magistrate's finding of probable cause does not preclude inquiry into the knowing or reckless falsity of the affidavit on which that determination was based. Franks v. Delaware, 438 U.S. 154 (1978). Second, the courts must also insist that the magistrate purport to "perform his 'neutral and detached' function and not serve merely as a rubber stamp for the police." Aguilar v. Texas, supra, 378 U.S., at 111. A magistrate failing to "manifest that neutrality and detachment demanded of a judicial officer when presented with a warrant application" and who acts instead as "an adjunct law enforcement officer" cannot provide valid authorization for an otherwise unconstitutional search. Lo-Ji Sales, Inc. v. New York, 442 U.S. 319, 326–327 (1979). Third, reviewing courts will not defer to a warrant based on an affidavit that does not "provide the magistrate with a substantial basis for determining the existence of probable cause." Illinois v. Gates, 462 U.S., at 239, 103. "Sufficient information must be presented to the magistrate to allow that official to determine probable cause; his action cannot be a mere ratification of the bare conclusions of others." Ibid. See [citations.] Even if the warrant application was supported by more than a "bare bones" affidavit, a reviewing court may properly conclude that, notwithstanding the deference that magistrates deserve, the warrant was invalid because the magistrate's probable-cause determination reflected an improper analysis of the totality of the circumstances, Illinois v. Gates, supra, 462 U.S., at 238–239, or because the form of the warrant was improper in some respect.

Only in the first of these three situations, however, has the Court set forth a rationale for suppressing evidence obtained pursuant to a search warrant; in the other areas, it has simply excluded such evidence without considering whether Fourth Amendment interests will be advanced. To the extent that proponents of exclusion rely on its behavioral effects on judges and magistrates in these areas, their reliance is misplaced. First, the exclusionary rule is designed to deter police misconduct rather than to punish the errors of judges and magistrates. Second, there exists no evidence suggesting that judges and magistrates are inclined to ignore or subvert the Fourth Amendment or that lawlessness among these actors requires application of the extreme sanction of exclusion.

Third, and most important, we discern no basis, and are offered none, for believing that exclusion of evidence seized pursuant to a warrant will have a significant deterrent effect on the issuing judge or magistrate. Many of the factors that indicate that the exclusionary rule cannot provide an effective "special" or "general" deterrent for individual offending law enforcement officers apply as well to judges or magistrates. And, to the extent that the rule is thought to operate as a "systemic" deterrent on a wider audience, it clearly can have no such effect on individuals empowered to issue search warrants. Judges and magistrates are not adjuncts to the law enforcement team; as neutral judicial officers, they have no stake in the outcome of particular criminal prosecutions. The threat of exclusion thus cannot be expected significantly to deter them. Imposition of the exclusionary sanction is not necessary meaningfully to inform judicial officers of their errors, and we cannot conclude that admitting evidence obtained pursuant to a warrant while at the same time declaring that the warrant was somehow defective will in any way reduce judicial officers' professional incentives to comply with the Fourth Amendment, encourage them to repeat their mistakes, or lead to the granting of all colorable warrant requests.

If exclusion of evidence obtained pursuant to a subsequently invalidated warrant is to have any deterrent effect, therefore, it must alter the behavior of individual law enforcement officers or the policies of their departments. One could argue that applying the exclusionary rule in cases where the police failed to demonstrate probable cause in the warrant application deters future inadequate presentations or "magistrate shopping" and thus promotes the ends of the Fourth Amendment. Suppressing evidence obtained pursuant to a technically defective warrant supported by probable cause also might encourage officers to scrutinize more closely the form of the warrant and to point out suspected judicial errors. We find such arguments speculative and conclude that suppression of evidence obtained pursuant to a warrant should be ordered only on a case-by-case basis and only in those unusual cases in which exclusion will further the purposes of the exclusionary rule.

We have frequently questioned whether the exclusionary rule can have any deterrent effect when the offending officers acted in the objectively reasonable belief that their conduct did not violate the Fourth Amendment. "No empirical researcher, proponent or opponent of the rule, has yet been able to establish with any assurance whether the rule has a deterrent effect. . . ." United States v. Janis, 428 U.S., at 452, n. 22. But even assuming that the rule effectively deters some police misconduct and provides incentives for the law enforcement profession as a whole to conduct itself in accord with the Fourth Amendment, it cannot be expected, and should not be applied, to deter objectively reasonable law enforcement activity.

* * *

Suppression therefore remains an appropriate remedy if the magistrate or judge in issuing a warrant was misled by information in an affidavit that the affiant knew was false or would have known was false except for his reckless disregard of the truth. Franks v. Delaware, 438 U.S. 154 (1978). The exception we recognize today will also not apply in cases where the issuing magistrate wholly abandoned his judicial role in the manner condemned in Lo-Ji Sales, Inc. v. New York, 442 U.S. 319 (1979); in such circumstances, no reasonably well trained officer should rely on the warrant. Nor would an officer manifest objective good faith in relying on a warrant based on an affidavit "so lacking in indicia of probable cause as to render official belief in its existence entirely unreasonable." Brown v. Illinois, 422 U.S., at 610–611 (POWELL, J., concurring in part); see Illinois v. Gates, supra, 462 U.S., at 263–264 (WHITE, J., concurring in the judgment). Finally, depending on the circumstances of the particular case, a warrant may be so facially deficient—i.e., in failing to particularize the place to be searched or the things to be seized—that the executing officers cannot reasonably presume it to be valid.

* * *

In the absence of an allegation that the magistrate abandoned his detached and neutral role, suppression is appropriate only if the officers were dishonest or reckless in preparing their affidavit or could not have harbored an objectively reasonable belief in the existence of probable cause.

Only respondent Leon has contended that no reasonably well trained police officer could have believed that there existed probable cause to search his house; significantly, the other respondents advance no comparable argument. Officer Rombach's application for a warrant clearly was supported by much more than a "bare bones" affidavit. The affidavit related the results of an extensive investigation and, as the opinions of the divided panel of the Court of Appeals make clear, provided evidence sufficient to create disagreement among thoughtful and competent judges as to the existence of probable cause. Under these circumstances, the officers' reliance on the magistrate's determination of probable cause was objectively reasonable, and application of the extreme sanction of exclusion is inappropriate.

Accordingly, the judgment of the Court of Appeals is

Reversed.

JUSTICE BRENNAN, with whom JUSTICE MARSHALL joins, dissenting.

[I]n case after case, I have witnessed the Court's gradual but determined strangulation of the [exclusionary] rule. It now appears that the Court's victory over the Fourth Amendment is complete. That today's decisions represent the piece de resistance of the Court's past efforts cannot be doubted, for today the Court sanctions the use in the prosecution's case in chief of illegally obtained evidence against the individual whose rights have been violated—a result that had previously been thought to be foreclosed.

The Court seeks to justify this result on the ground that the "costs" of adhering to the exclusionary rule in cases like those before us exceed the "benefits." But the language of deterrence and of cost/benefit analysis, if used indiscriminately, can have a narcotic effect. It creates an illusion of technical precision and ineluctability. It suggests that not only constitutional principle but also empirical data support the majority's result. When the Court's analysis is examined carefully, however, it is clear that we have not been treated to an honest assessment of the merits of the exclusionary rule, but have instead been drawn into a curious world where the "costs" of excluding illegally obtained evidence loom to exaggerated heights and where the "benefits" of such exclusion are made to disappear with a mere wave of the hand.

The majority ignores the fundamental constitutional importance of what is at stake here. While the machinery of law enforcement and indeed the nature of crime itself have changed dramatically since the Fourth Amendment became part of the Nation's fundamental law in 1791, what the Framers understood then remains true today—that the task of combating crime and convicting the guilty will in every era seem of such critical and pressing concern that we may be lured by the temptations of expediency into forsaking our commitment to protecting individual liberty and privacy. It was for that very reason that the Framers of the Bill of Rights insisted that law enforcement efforts be permanently and unambiguously restricted in order to preserve personal freedoms.

* * *

At the outset, the Court suggests that society has been asked to pay a high price—in terms either of setting guilty persons free or of impeding the proper functioning of trials—as a result of excluding relevant physical evidence in cases where the police, in conducting searches and seizing evidence, have made only an "objectively reasonable" mistake concerning the constitutionality of their actions. See ante, at 907–908. But what evidence is there to support such a claim?

Significantly, the Court points to none, and, indeed, as the Court acknowledges, see ante, at 907–908, n. 6, recent studies have demonstrated that the "costs" of the exclusionary rule calculated in terms of dropped prosecutions and lost convictions are quite low. Contrary to the claims of the rule's critics that exclusion leads to "the release of countless guilty criminals," Bivens v. Six Unknown Federal Narcotics Agents, 403 U.S. 388, 416 (1971) (BURGER, C.J., dissenting), these studies have demonstrated that federal and state prosecutors very rarely drop cases because of potential search and seizure problems.

* * *

What then supports the Court's insistence that this evidence be admitted? Apparently, the Court's only answer is that even though the costs of exclusion are not very substantial, the potential deterrent effect in these circumstances is so marginal that exclusion cannot be justified. The key to the Court's conclusion in this respect is its belief that the prospective deterrent effect of the exclusionary rule operates only in those situations in which police officers, when deciding whether to go forward with some particular search, have reason to know that their planned conduct will violate the requirements of the Fourth Amendment. . . . If these officers in fact understand (or reasonably should understand because the law is well settled) that their proposed conduct will offend the Fourth Amendment and that, consequently, any evidence they seize will be suppressed in court, they will refrain from conducting the planned search. In those circumstances, the incentive system created by the exclusionary rule will have the hoped-for deterrent effect. But in situations where police officers reasonably (but mistakenly) believe that their planned conduct satisfies Fourth Amendment requirements—presumably either (a) because they are acting on the basis of an apparently valid warrant, or (b) because their conduct is only later determined to be invalid as a result of a subsequent change in the law or the resolution of an unsettled question of law—then such officers will have no reason to refrain from conducting the search and the exclusionary rule will have no effect.

* * *

The flaw in the Court's argument, however, is that its logic captures only one comparatively minor element of the generally acknowledged deterrent purposes of the exclusionary rule. To be sure, the rule operates to some extent to deter future misconduct by individual officers who have had evidence suppressed in their own cases. But what the Court overlooks is that the deterrence rationale for the rule is not designed to be, nor should it be thought of as, a form of "punishment" of individual police officers for their failures to obey the restraints imposed by the Fourth Amendment. See United States v. Peltier, 422 U.S., at 556–557 (BRENNAN, J., dissenting). Instead, the chief deterrent function of the rule is its tendency to promote institutional compliance with Fourth Amendment requirements on the part of law enforcement agencies generally. Thus, as the Court has previously recognized, "over the long term, [the] demonstration [provided by the exclusionary rule] that our society attaches serious consequences to violation of constitutional rights is thought to encourage those who formulate law enforcement policies, and the officers who implement them, to incorporate Fourth Amendment ideals into their value system." Stone v. Powell, 428 U.S., at 492. It is only through such an institutionwide mechanism that information concerning Fourth Amendment standards can be effectively communicated to rank-and-file officers.

If the overall educational effect of the exclusionary rule is considered, application of the rule to even those situations in which individual police officers have acted on the basis of a reasonable but mistaken belief that their conduct was authorized can still be expected to have a considerable long-term deterrent effect. If evidence is consistently excluded in these circumstances, police departments will surely be prompted to instruct their officers to devote greater care and attention to providing sufficient information to establish probable cause when applying for a warrant, and to review with some attention the form of the warrant that they have been issued, rather than automatically assuming that whatever document the magistrate has signed will necessarily comport with Fourth Amendment requirements.

After today's decisions, however, that institutional incentive will be lost. Indeed, the Court's "reasonable mistake" exception to the exclusionary rule will tend to put a premium on police ignorance of the law. Armed with the assurance provided by today's decisions that evidence will always be admissible whenever an officer has "reasonably" relied upon a warrant, police departments will be encouraged to train officers that if a warrant has simply been signed, it is reasonable, without more, to rely on it. Since in close cases there will no longer be any incentive to err on the side of constitutional behavior, police would have every reason to adopt a "let's-wait-until-it's-decided" approach in situations in which there is a question about a warrant's validity or the basis for its issuance.

Although the Court brushes these concerns aside, a host of grave consequences can be expected to result from its decision to carve this new exception out of the exclusionary rule. A chief consequence of today's decisions will be to convey a clear and unambiguous message to magistrates that their decisions to issue warrants are now insulated from subsequent judicial review. Creation of this new exception for good-faith reliance upon a warrant implicitly tells magistrates that they need not take much care in reviewing warrant applications, since their mistakes will from now on have virtually no consequence: If their decision to issue a warrant was correct, the evidence will be admitted; if their decision was incorrect but the police relied in good faith on the warrant, the evidence will also be admitted. Inevitably, the care and attention devoted to such an inconsequential chore will dwindle

* * *

Moreover, the good-faith exception will encourage police to provide only the bare minimum of information in future warrant applications. The police will now know that if they can secure a warrant, so long as the circumstances of its issuance are not "entirely unreasonable," ante, at 923, all police conduct pursuant to that warrant will be protected from further judicial review. The clear incentive that operated in the past to establish probable cause adequately because reviewing courts would examine the magistrate's judgment carefully, see, e.g., [citations] has now been so completely vitiated that the police need only show that it was not "entirely unreasonable" under the circumstances of a particular case for them to believe that the warrant they were issued was valid. See ante, at 923. The long-run effect unquestionably will be to undermine the integrity of the warrant process.

* * *

When the public, as it quite properly has done in the past as well as in the present, demands that those in government increase their efforts to combat crime, it is all too easy for those government officials to seek expedient solutions. In contrast to such costly and difficult measures as building more prisons, improving law enforcement methods, or hiring more prosecutors and judges to relieve the overburdened court systems in the country's metropolitan areas, the relaxation of Fourth Amendment standards seems a tempting, costless means of meeting the public's demand for better law enforcement. In the long run, however, we as a society pay a heavy price for such expediency, because as Justice Jackson observed, the rights guaranteed in the Fourth Amendment "are not mere second-class rights but belong in the catalog of indispensable freedoms." Brinegar v. United States, 338 U.S. 160, 180 (1949) (dissenting opinion).

Once lost, such rights are difficult to recover. There is hope, however, that in time this or some later Court will restore these precious freedoms to their rightful place as a primary protection for our citizens against overreaching officialdom.

I dissent.

---

**Questions:** What if a judge issues an open-ended warrant that leaves the determination of the items to be seized within the discretion of the officials conducting the search? See *Lo-Ji Sales v. New York,* 442 U.S. 319 (1979). Constitutional under *Leon*? A police officer applies for a warrant with an itemized list of sought items, which the magistrate sees, but the warrant as issued fails to include the items. Constitutional? See *Groh v. Ramirez,* 540 U.S. 551 (2004).

## BORDER SEARCHES

### UNITED STATES V. CORTEZ

449 U.S. 411 (1981)

* * *

CHIEF JUSTICE BURGER delivered the opinion of the Court.

We granted certiorari, to consider whether objective facts and circumstantial evidence suggesting that a particular vehicle is involved in criminal activity may provide a sufficient basis to justify an investigative stop of that vehicle.

Late in 1976, Border Patrol officers patrolling a sparsely populated section of southern central Arizona found human footprints in the desert. In time, other sets of similar footprints were discovered in the same area. From these sets of footprints, it was deduced that, on a number of occasions, groups of from 8 to 20 persons had walked north from the Mexican border, across 30 miles of desert and mountains, over a fairly well-defined path, to an isolated point on Highway 86, an east-west road running roughly parallel to the Mexican border.

Officers observed that one recurring shoeprint bore a distinctive and repetitive V-shaped or chevron design. Because the officers knew from recorded experience that the area through which the groups passed was heavily trafficked by aliens illegally entering the country from Mexico, they surmised that a person, to whom they gave the case-name "Chevron," was guiding aliens illegally into the United States over the path marked by the tracks to a point where they could be picked up by a vehicle.

The tracks led into or over obstacles that would have been avoided in daylight. From this, the officers deduced that "Chevron" probably led his groups across the border and to the pickup point at night. Moreover, based upon the times when they had discovered the distinctive sets of tracks, they concluded that "Chevron" generally traveled during or near weekends and on nights when the weather was clear.

Their tracking disclosed that when "Chevron's" groups came within 50 to 75 yards of Highway 86, they turned right and walked eastward, parallel to the road. Then, approximately at highway milepost 122, the tracks would turn north and disappear at the road. From this pattern, the officers concluded that the aliens very likely were picked up by a vehicle probably one approaching from the east, for after a long overland march the group was most likely to walk parallel to the highway *toward* the approaching vehicle. The officers also concluded that, after the pickup, the vehicle probably returned to the east, because it was unlikely that the group would be walking away from its ultimate destination.

On the Sunday night of January 30–31, 1977, Officers Gray and Evans, two Border Patrolmen who had been pursuing the investigation of "Chevron," were on duty in the Casa Grande area. The latest set of observed "Chevron" tracks had been made on Saturday night, January 15–16. January 30–31 was the first clear night after three days of rain. For these reasons, Gray and Evans decided there was a strong possibility that "Chevron" would lead aliens from the border to the highway that night.

The officers assumed that, if "Chevron" did conduct a group that night, he would not leave Mexico until after dark, that is, about 6 p. m. They knew from their experience that groups of this sort, traveling on foot, cover about two and a half to three miles an hour. Thus, the 30-mile journey would take from 8 to 12 hours. From this, the officers calculated that "Chevron" and his group would arrive at Highway 86 somewhere between 2 a. m. and 6 a. m. on January 31.

About 1 a. m., Gray and Evans parked their patrol car on an elevated location about 100 feet off Highway 86 at milepost 149, a point some 27 miles east of milepost 122. From their vantage point, the officers could observe the Altar Valley, an adjoining territory they had been assigned to watch that night, and they also could see vehicles passing on Highway 86. They estimated that it would take approximately one hour and a half for a vehicle to make a round trip from their vantage point to milepost 122. Working on the hypothesis that the pickup vehicle approached milepost 122 from the east and thereafter returned to its starting point, they focused upon vehicles that passed them from the east and, after about one hour and a half, passed them returning to the east.

Because "Chevron" appeared to lead groups of between 8 and 20 aliens at a time, the officers deduced that the pickup vehicle would be one that was capable of carrying that large a group without arousing suspicion. For this reason, and because they knew that certain types of vehicles were commonly used for smuggling sizable groups of aliens, they decided to limit their attention to vans, pickup trucks, other small trucks, campers, motor homes, and similar vehicles.

Traffic on Highway 86 at milepost 149 was normal on the night of the officers' surveillance. In the 5-hour period between 1 a. m. and 6 a. m., 15 to 20 vehicles passed the officers heading west, toward milepost 122. Only two of them—both pickup trucks with camper shells—were of the kind that the officers had concluded "Chevron" would likely use if he was to carry aliens that night. One, a distinctively colored pickup truck with a camper shell, passed for the first time at 4:30 a. m. Officer Gray was able to see and record only a partial license number, "GN 88_." At 6:12 a. m., almost exactly the estimated one hour and a half later, a vehicle looking like this same pickup passed them again, this time heading east.

The officers followed the pickup and were satisfied from its license plate, "GN 8804" that it was the same vehicle that had passed at 4:30 a. m. At that point, they flashed their police lights and intercepted the vehicle. Respondent Jesus Cortez was the driver and owner of the pickup; respondent Pedro Hernandez-Loera was sitting in the passenger's seat. Hernandez-Loera was wearing shoes with soles matching the distinctive "chevron" shoeprint.

The officers identified themselves and told Cortez they were conducting an immigration check. They asked if he was carrying any passengers in the camper. Cortez told them he had picked up some hitchhikers, and he proceeded to open the back of the camper. In the camper, there were six illegal aliens. The officers then arrested the respondents.

Cortez and Hernandez-Loera were charged with six counts of transporting illegal aliens in violation of 8 U.S.C. § 1324(a). By pretrial motion, they sought to suppress the evidence obtained by Officers Gray and Evans as a result of stopping their vehicle. They argued that the officers did not have adequate cause to make the investigative stop. The District Court denied the motion. A jury found the respondents guilty as charged. They were sentenced to concurrent prison terms of five years on each of six counts. In addition, Hernandez-Loera was fined $12,000.

[T]he Court of Appeals for the Ninth Circuit reversed, holding that the officers lacked a sufficient basis to justify the stop of the pickup. 595 F.2d 505 (1979). That court recognized that *United States v. Brignoni-Ponce*, 422 U.S. 873 (1975), provides a standard governing investigative stops of the kind involved in this case, stating:

"The quantum of cause necessary in . . . cases [like this one] was established . . . in *United States v. Brignoni-Ponce* . . . '[O]fficers on roving patrol may stop vehicles only if they are aware of specific articulable facts, together with rational inferences from those facts, that reasonably warrant suspicion that the vehicles contain aliens who may be illegally in the country.' " 595 F.2d, at 507 (quoting *United States v. Brignoni-Ponce, supra*, at 884) (citations omitted).

The court also recognized that "the ultimate question on appeal is whether the trial judge's finding that founded suspicion was present here was clearly erroneous." 595 F.2d, at 507. Here, because, in the view of the facts of the two judges constituting the majority, "[t]he officers did not have a valid basis for singling out the Cortez vehicle," *id.*, at 508, and because the circumstances admitted "far too many innocent inferences to make the officers' suspicions reasonably warranted," *ibid.*, the panel concluded that the stop of Cortez' vehicle was a violation of the respondents' rights under the Fourth Amendment. In dissent, Judge Chambers was persuaded that *Brignoni-Ponce* recognized the validity of permitting an officer to assess the facts in light of his past experience.

The Fourth Amendment applies to seizures of the person, including brief investigatory stops such as the stop of the vehicle here. *Reid v. Georgia*, 448 U.S. 438, 440, (1980); *United States v. Brignoni-Ponce*, 422 U.S., *supra*, at 878 (1969) . . . *Terry v. Ohio*, 392 U.S. 1, 16–19 (1968). An investigatory stop must be justified by some objective manifestation that the person stopped is, or is about to be, engaged in criminal activity. *Brown v. Texas*, 443 U.S. 47 (1979) [additional citations].

Courts have used a variety of terms to capture the elusive concept of what cause is sufficient to authorize police to stop a person. Terms like "articulable reasons" and "founded suspicion" are not self-defining; they fall short of providing clear guidance dispositive of the myriad factual situations that arise. But the essence of all that has been written is that the totality of the circumstances—the whole picture—must be taken into account. Based upon that whole picture the detaining officers must have a particularized and objective basis for suspecting the particular person stopped of criminal activity. See, *e. g., Brown v. Texas, supra*, 443 U.S., at 51; *United States v. Brignoni-Ponce, supra*, 422 U.S., at 884.

The idea that an assessment of the whole picture must yield a particularized suspicion contains two elements, each of which must be present before a stop is permissible. First, the assessment must be based upon all the circumstances. The analysis proceeds with various objective observations, information from police reports, if such are available, and consideration of the modes or patterns of operation of certain kinds of lawbreakers. From these data, a trained officer draws inferences and makes deductions inferences and deductions that might well elude an untrained person.

The process does not deal with hard certainties, but with probabilities. Long before the law of probabilities was articulated as such, practical people formulated certain common sense conclusions about human behavior; jurors as factfinders are permitted to do the same—and so are law enforcement officers. Finally, the evidence thus collected must be seen and weighed not in terms of library analysis by scholars, but as understood by those versed in the field of law enforcement.

The second element contained in the idea that an assessment of the whole picture must yield a particularized suspicion is the concept that the process just described must raise a suspicion that the particular individual being stopped is engaged in wrongdoing. Chief Justice Warren, speaking for the Court in *Terry v. Ohio, supra,* said that, "[t]his demand for specificity in the information upon which police action is predicated is *the central teaching of this Court's Fourth Amendment jurisprudence.*" *Id.*, 392 U.S., at 21, (emphasis added). . . .

This case portrays at once both the enormous difficulties of patrolling a 2,000-mile open border and the patient skills needed by those charged with halting illegal entry into this country. It implicates all of the principles just discussed especially the imperative of recognizing that, when used by trained law enforcement officers, objective facts, meaningless to the untrained, can be combined with permissible deductions from such facts to form a legitimate basis for suspicion of a particular person and for action on that suspicion. We see here the kind of police work often suggested by judges and scholars as examples of appropriate and reasonable means of law enforcement. Here, fact on fact and clue on clue afforded a basis for the deductions and inferences that brought the officers to focus on "Chevron."

Of critical importance, the officers knew that the area was a crossing point for illegal aliens. They knew that it was common practice for persons to lead aliens through the desert from the border to Highway 86, where they could—by prearrangement—be picked up by a vehicle. Moreover, based upon clues they had discovered in the 2-month period prior to the events at issue here, they believed that one such guide, whom they designated "Chevron," had a particular pattern of operations.

By piecing together the information at their disposal, the officers tentatively concluded that there was a reasonable likelihood that "Chevron" would attempt to lead a group of aliens on the night of Sunday, January 30–31. Someone with chevron-soled shoes had led several groups of aliens in the previous two months, yet it had been two weeks since the latest crossing. "Chevron," they deduced, was therefore due reasonably soon. "Chevron" tended to travel on clear weekend nights. Because it had rained on the Friday and Saturday nights of the weekend involved here,

Sunday was the only clear night of that weekend; the officers surmised it was therefore a likely night for a trip.

Once they had focused on that night, the officers drew upon other objective facts known to them to deduce a time frame within which "Chevron" and the aliens were likely to arrive. From what they knew of the practice of those who smuggle aliens, including what they knew of "Chevron's" previous activities, they deduced that the border crossing and journey through the desert would probably be at night. They knew the time when sunset would occur at the point of the border crossing; they knew about how long the trip would take. They were thus able to deduce that "Chevron" would likely arrive at the pickup point on Highway 86 in the time frame between 2 a. m. and 6 a. m.

From objective facts, the officers also deduced the probable point on the highway—milepost 122—at which "Chevron" would likely rendezvous with a pickup vehicle. They deduced from the direction taken by the sets of "Chevron" footprints they had earlier discovered that the pickup vehicle would approach the aliens from, and return with them to, a point east of milepost 122. They therefore staked out a position east of milepost 122 (at milepost 149) and watched for vehicles that passed them going west and then, approximately one and a half hours later, passed them again, this time going east.

From what they had observed about the previous groups guided by the person with "chevron" shoes, they deduced that "Chevron" would lead a group of 8 to 20 aliens. They therefore focused their attention on enclosed vehicles of that passenger capacity.

The analysis produced by Officers Gray and Evans can be summarized as follows: if, on the night upon which they believed "Chevron" was likely to travel, sometime between 2 a. m. and 6 a. m., a large enclosed vehicle was seen to make an east-west-east round trip to and from a deserted point (milepost 122) on a deserted road (Highway 86), the officers would stop the vehicle on the return trip. In a 4-hour period the officers observed only one vehicle meeting that description. And it is not surprising that when they stopped the vehicle on its return trip it contained "Chevron" and several illegal aliens.

The limited purpose of the stop in this case was to question the occupants of the vehicle about their citizenship and immigration status and the reasons for the round trip in a short timespan in a virtually deserted area. No search of the camper or any of its occupants occurred until after respondent Cortez voluntarily opened the back door of the camper; thus, only the stop, not the search is at issue here. The intrusion upon privacy associated with this stop was limited and was "reasonably related in scope to the justification for [its] initiation," *Terry v. Ohio*, 392 U.S., at 29.

We have recently held that stops by the Border Patrol may be justified under circumstances less than those constituting probable cause for arrest or search. *United States v. Brignoni-Ponce*, 422 U.S., at 880. Thus, the test is not whether Officers Gray and Evans had probable cause to conclude that the vehicle they stopped would contain "Chevron" and a group of illegal aliens. Rather the question is whether, based upon the whole picture, they, as experienced Border Patrol officers, could reasonably surmise that the particular vehicle they stopped was engaged in criminal activity. On this record, they could so conclude.

*Reversed.*

---

**Questions:** Should Fourth Amendment protections be stronger depending on how far from the border an investigative stop occurs? Seventy miles from the Mexico-U.S. border, a truck with Mexican license plates is speeding north, making erratic lane changes. Is an investigative stop by border patrol agents constitutional following *Cortez*? See *United States v. Valdez-Vega,* 738 F.3d 1074 (9th Cir. 2013).

# CHAPTER 15

# STATE CONSTITUTIONAL LAW—PARALLELS TO U.S. CONSTITUTIONAL LAW

■ ■ ■

## CONTEXT & SOURCES

Just as the U.S. Supreme Court has shaped understanding of the U.S. Constitution, state supreme courts have interpreted their own constitutions as sources of law. Some of these decisions parallel the U.S. Supreme Court's framing of the issues, albeit often with different results. Other holdings view state constitutions as creating entirely new rights. Scholars disagree about whether these offshoots of the principles of liberty and equality are beneficial or have created a confusing legal patchwork that undermines uniform enforcement. In this chapter, state cases parallel, or elaborate on, federal jurisprudence on takings, school financing, undocumented children's rights, and the First Amendment.

For a comprehensive overview of state constitutional history, structure, and interpretation, see Robert F. Williams, *The Law of American State Constitutions* (Oxford University Press, 2009) In Kathleen M. Trafford, "City of Norwood v. Horney—Much More Than Eminent Domain: A Forceful Affirmation of the Independent Authority of the Ohio Constitution and the Court's Power to Enforce It," 48 *Akron Law Review* 34 (2015), the author explains how this decision both parallels and goes beyond the U.S. Supreme Court's *Kelo* holding. Peter L. Reich, "Three Lessons I Learned from Cruz Reynoso," 39 *Chicanx-Latinx Law Review* 71 (2023) provides a personal perspective on Justice Reynoso's expansion of *Plyler* in *Darces v. Woods*.

## TAKINGS

### CITY OF NORWOOD V. HORNEY

853 N.E. 2d 1115 (Ohio 2006)

* * *

In case Nos. 2005–1210 and 2005–1211, we decide the constitutionality of a municipality's taking of an individual's property by eminent domain and transferring the property to a private entity for redevelopment. In doing so, we must balance two competing interests of great import in American democracy: the individual's rights in the possession and security of property and the sovereign's power to take private property for the benefit of the community. In case Nos. 2005–0227 and 2005–0228, we determine the constitutionality of the provision in R.C. 163.19 prohibiting a court from enjoining the taking and using of property appropriated by the government and transferred to a private party for redevelopment, after the compensation for the property has been deposited with the court but prior to appellate review of the taking.

Our consideration does not take place in a vacuum. We recognize that eminent domain engenders great debate. Its use, though necessary, is fraught with great economic, social, and legal implications for the individual and the community. See, generally, Keasha Broussard, Social Consequences of Eminent Domain: Urban Revitalization Against the Backdrop of the Takings Clause (2000), 24 Law & Psychology Rev. 99.

Appropriation cases often represent more than a battle over a plot of cold sod in a farmland pasture or the plat of municipal land on which a building sits. For the individual property owner, the appropriation is not simply the seizure of a house. It is the taking of a home-the place where ancestors toiled, where families were raised, where memories were made. Fittingly, appropriations are scrutinized by the people and debated in their institutions.

In reviewing an appropriation similar to that at issue here, a sharply divided United States Supreme Court recently upheld the taking over a federal Fifth Amendment challenge mounted by individual property owners. Kelo v. New London (2005), 545 U.S. 469. Although it determined that the Federal Constitution did not prohibit the takings, the court acknowledged that property owners might find redress in the states' courts and legislatures, which remain free to restrict such takings pursuant to state laws and constitutions.

In response to that invitation in Kelo, Ohio's General Assembly unanimously enacted 2005 Am.Sub. S.B. No. 167. The legislature expressly noted in the Act its belief that as a result of Kelo, "the interpretation and use of the state's eminent domain law could be expanded to allow the taking of private property that is not within a blighted area, ultimately resulting in ownership of that property being vested in another private person in violation of Sections 1 and 19 of Article I, Ohio Constitution." Section 4(A), 2005 Am.Sub.S.B. No. 167. The Act created a task force to study the use and application of eminent domain in Ohio and imposed "a moratorium on any takings of this nature by any public body until further legislative remedies may be considered." Id.

We now turn to the cases pending before us, which raise social and legal issues similar to those in Kelo.

The appellants' property was appropriated by the city of Norwood after the city determined that the appellants' neighborhood was a "deteriorating area," as that term is defined in the provisions governing appropriations in the Codified Ordinances of the City of Norwood ("Norwood Code"). Although we have held that a city may take a slum, blighted, or deteriorated property for redevelopment, State ex rel. Bruestle v. Rich (1953) 110 N.E.2d 778, and suggested that the taking is proper even when the city transfers the appropriated property to a private party for redevelopment, AAAA Ents., Inc. v. River Place Community Urban Redevelopment Corp. (1990) 553 N.E.2d 597, we have never been asked whether a city may appropriate property that the city determines is in an area that may deteriorate in the future.

[After the city filed complaints against the appellants to appropriate their properties, the trial court concluded that there was no showing that Norwood abused its discretion in finding that the neighborhood was a "deteriorating area."]

We hold that although economic factors may be considered in determining whether private property may be appropriated, the fact that the appropriation would provide an economic benefit to the government and community, standing alone, does not satisfy the public-use requirement of Section 19, Article I of the Ohio Constitution.

We also hold that the void-for-vagueness doctrine applies to statutes that regulate the use of eminent-domain powers. Courts shall apply heightened scrutiny when reviewing statutes that regulate the use of eminent-domain powers. Applying that standard, we hold that Norwood's use of "deteriorating area" as a standard for appropriation is void for vagueness. We further hold that the use of the term "deteriorating area" as a standard for a taking is unconstitutional because the term inherently incorporates speculation as to the future condition of the property to be appropriated rather than the condition of the property at the time of the taking.

Finally, we hold that the provision in R.C. 163.19 that prohibits a court from enjoining the taking and using of property appropriated by the government after the compensation for the property has been deposited with the court but prior to appellate review of the taking violates the separation-of-powers doctrine and is therefore unconstitutional. We further hold that the unconstitutional portion of R.C. 163.19 can be severed from the rest of the statute, and, accordingly, the remainder of the statute remains in effect.

* * *

Judgments reversed.

---

**Question:** In *Norwood,* does the court make clear at what point a "deteriorating" area immunized from taking turns into a "blighted" area subject to taking?

## SCHOOL FINANCING

### SERRANO V. PRIEST (SERRANO II)

18 Cal.3d 728 (1976)

* * *

SULLIVAN, J.

The instant proceeding, which involves a constitutional challenge to the California public school financing system, is before us for the second time. * * *

We—along with the trial court and the parties—think it is clear that Rodriguez undercuts our decision in Serrano I to the extent that we held the California public school financing system (if proved to be as alleged) to be invalid as in violation of the equal protection clause of the Fourteenth Amendment to the United States Constitution. However, . . . our decision in Serrano I was based not only on the provisions of the federal Constitution but on the provisions of our own state Constitution as well.

* * *

As Serrano I makes clear, . . .our state equal protection provisions, while "substantially the equivalent of" the guarantees contained in the Fourteenth Amendment to the United States Constitution, are possessed of an independent vitality which, in a given case, may demand an analysis different from that which would obtain if only the federal standard were applicable. We have recently stated in a related context: "[I]n the area of fundamental civil liberties—which includes . . . all protections of the California Declaration of Rights—we sit as a court of last resort, subject only to the qualification that our interpretations may not restrict the guarantees accorded the national citizenry under the federal charter. In such constitutional adjudication, our first referent is California law and the full panoply of rights Californians have come to expect as their due. Accordingly, decisions of the United States Supreme Court defining fundamental rights are persuasive authority to be afforded respectful consideration, but are to be followed by California courts only when they provide no less individual protection than is guaranteed by California law." (People v. Longwill (1975) 14 Cal. 3d 943, 951).

Thus, the fact that a majority of the United States Supreme Court have now chosen to contract the area of active and critical analysis under the strict scrutiny test for federal constitutional purposes can have no effect upon the existing construction and application afforded our own constitutional provisions. Nor can the additional fact—if it be a fact—that certain of the high court's former decisions (which may have been relied upon by us in Serrano I) may not be expected to thrive in the shadow of Rodriguez cause us to withdraw from the principles we there announced on state as well as federal grounds.

For these reasons then, we now adhere to our determinations, made in Serrano I, that for the reasons there stated and for purposes of assessing our state public school financing system in light of our state constitutional provisions guaranteeing equal protection of the laws discrimination in educational opportunity on the basis of district wealth involves a suspect classification, and (2) education is a fundamental interest. Because the school financing system here in question has been shown by substantial and convincing evidence produced at trial to involve a suspect classification (insofar as this system, like the former one, draws distinctions on the basis of district wealth), and because that classification affects the fundamental interest of the students of this state in education, we have no difficulty in concluding today, as we concluded in Serrano I, that the school financing system before us must be examined under our state constitutional provisions with that strict and searching scrutiny appropriate to such a case.

We conclude that the holding of the trial court is grounded solidly and soundly on our earlier decision in Serrano I wherein we determined among other things that the California public school financing system, failing to withstand "strict scrutiny," denied plaintiffs the equal protection of the laws under the relevant provisions of our state Constitution. We therefore confirm that our decision in Serrano I was based not only on the equal protection provisions of the federal Constitution but also on such provisions of our state Constitution . . .

We observe that the trial court so deemed it and properly adhered to the law set forth in our earlier opinion in assessing for state constitutional purposes the same financing system . . . Since such system before the court was shown on substantial evidence to involve a suspect classification (based on district wealth) and to touch upon the fundamental interest of education, the trial court properly followed Serrano I in subjecting it to the "strict scrutiny" test under which the state has the burden of establishing that the classification in question is necessary to achieve a compelling state interest. Applying this test, the court properly determined on findings supported by substantial evidence that the state had failed to bear its burden and that the financing system before it was invalid as denying equal protection of the laws as guaranteed by the California Constitution.

The judgment is affirmed.

CLARK, J.

I dissent.

Our schools serve nearly 5 million students, spending over $5 billion. (1973–1974, Cal. Public Schs. Selected Stats., pp. 84–85, tables IV–1 B, IV–2 B.) fn. 1 . . .

Approximately half our schools' budget of $5 billion comes from local real property tax. Eliminating this resource would be unfair to our youth, jeopardizing the quality of their education. It is questionable whether raising an additional $2 1/2 billion through other taxes is politically feasible. The answer lies with the legislative and executive branches of state government.* * *

I conclude that we cannot have absolute equality of opportunity in school funding—and perhaps not in any other sector of governmental activity. The absolute equality demanded by today's majority opinion is particularly unobtainable if fiscal responsibility and local control—both compelling interests—shall be preserved. While California's present system for school financing may be less than perfect and although it departs from total equality, the minor departure is justified and the system should be upheld.

---

**Questions:** The Texas Constitution requires that the state legislature "establish and make suitable provision for the support and maintenance of an efficient system of free public schools." Does a 700 to 1 ratio in the amount of assessed property value between the richest and poorest district violate this standard? Is *Serrano II* helpful in answering this question, even though California state cases are not binding on other states? See *Edgewood Independent School District v. Kirby,* 777 S.W.2d 391 (Tex. 1989).

## UNDOCUMENTED CHILDREN'S RIGHTS

### DARCES V. WOODS

384 Cal. 3d 871 (1984)

* * *

REYNOSO, J.

May the state disadvantage citizen children eligible for governmental assistance on the basis that they live with their brothers and sisters who are undocumented aliens? We hold that the equal protection clause of the California Constitution does not permit that disparate treatment.

Bernadette Obando Darces is an undocumented alien and working mother whose income is insufficient to meet the subsistence needs of her six children, three of whom are native-born citizens. Her three older children Marisol, Pablo and Carlos are ineligible for assistance under the Aid to Families With Dependent Children (AFDC) program because of their undocumented immigration status. However, her three younger children Larry, Jorge and Guido as citizens are eligible to be, and were in fact recipients of an AFDC grant at the time this litigation was instituted.

This case concerns a decision by defendant Marion Woods, as director of the State Department of Social Services (DSS), reducing the grant received by Ms. Darces for the benefit of her three citizen children. In particular we consider the validity, under state and federal law, of administrative regulations which authorize DSS to assume that Ms. Darces' total income is available only to the citizen children without taking into account the fact that a portion of her earned income must of necessity be allocated to meet the needs of her other children.

* * *

We . . . take up appellant's constitutional contention that the challenged practice penalizes her eligible children solely on the basis of their status as siblings of undocumented aliens in violation of equal protection under the state and federal Constitutions.

The guarantees of equal protection embodied in the Fourteenth Amendment of the United States Constitution and article I, section 7 of the California Constitution "compel[ ] recognition of the proposition that persons similarly situated with respect to the legitimate purpose of the law receive like treatment." (Purdy & Fitzpatrick v. State of Calif. (1969) 71 Cal. 2d 566; Reed v. Reed (1971) 404 U.S. 71, 75–76). "This principle, of course, does not preclude the state from drawing any distinctions between different groups of individuals, but does require that, at a minimum, classifications which are created bear a rational relationship to a legitimate public purpose." (In re King (1971) 3 Cal. 3d 226, 232). However, this deferential standard is inapplicable " 'in cases involving "suspect classifications" or touching on "fundamental interests" . . . .' " (Ibid.) In such cases "the state bears the burden of establishing not only that it has a compelling interest which justifies the law but that distinctions drawn by the law are necessary to further its purpose." (Westbrook v. Mihaly (1970) 2 Cal. 3d 765, 784–785.)

Most recently the United States Supreme Court, in Plyler v. Doe, supra, 457 U.S. 202, 216, reviewed its decisions applying the familiar two-tier equal protection analysis and set out the circumstances which require a more stringent standard of review than the traditional "fair relationship to a legitimate public purpose" (ibid.) standard: "[W]e would not be faithful to our obligations under the Fourteenth Amendment if we applied so deferential a standard to every classification. The Equal Protection Clause was intended as a restriction on state legislative action inconsistent with elemental constitutional premises. Thus we have treated as presumptively invidious those classifications that disadvantage a 'suspect class,' or that impinge upon the exercise of a 'fundamental right.' With respect to such classifications, it is appropriate to enforce the mandate of equal protection by requiring the State to demonstrate that its classification has been precisely tailored to serve a compelling governmental interests." (Id. at pp. 216–217).

A. Standard of Review

We begin our analysis with the task of choosing the standard of review appropriate for the evaluation of appellant's equal protection contention.

1. Nature of classification

Preliminarily, we consider the nature of the classification created by respondent. Respondent's regulations provide for the exclusion of individuals from the FBU in a variety of contexts. Respondent's implementation of his department's eligibility requirements (which include EAS exclusionary provisions) creates two classes of AFDC-eligible children: those who reside with ineligible persons, and those who do not. As earlier noted, ineligible persons may nevertheless qualify for inclusion in the FBU as "essential persons" under section 11203 of the Welfare and Institutions Code. Appellant's three older children, however, cannot under any circumstances be included in the FBU because of their undocumented status. This brings us to the particular exclusion with which we are here concerned. The application of the statutorily mandated exclusion for undocumented aliens, as implemented by respondent's regulations, creates a subclass within the previously identified class of eligibles residing with ineligibles namely, AFDC-eligible children who reside with persons who are ineligible because of their undocumented status.

Appellant does not argue that her undocumented children have a constitutional right to receive welfare benefits. Rather, she contends that although the challenged classification turns upon the status of the undocumented children, in practical effect it operates to deprive the eligible siblings of the full benefits to which they are entitled while granting full benefits to those eligible children who do not reside with undocumented aliens. Our focus, then, is on discrimination (in the provision of AFDC benefits) against eligible children who, through no fault of their own, must live in the same home as their undocumented siblings. The Legislature, having chosen to extend AFDC benefits to eligible children, then denies them, in part or whole, to a small class of eligible children solely on the basis of their familial relationship and residency with undocumented aliens.

This case thus comes before us in an unusual posture in that it is the rights of citizens ¶ not undocumented aliens that are implicated. This situation is not unlike cases involving illegitimate children wherein the challenged classification is dependent upon the marital status of the parents but operates in effect to deprive children of their rights. The United States Supreme Court has consistently struck down legislation which discriminates against illegitimate children, reasoning that it is "illogical and unjust" to deprive a child "simply because its natural father has not married its mother." (Gomez v. Perez (1973) 409 U.S. 535, 538; see also [additional citations]. We should be similarly hostile to legislative classifications which deprive eligible children of governmental beneficence simply because they are brothers or sisters of undocumented aliens. The fact that the children in the above-cited cases can be readily identified in a word—illegitimates—while it is more difficult to find a convenient label to describe the affected class in this case should not obscure the fundamental principle that when the Legislature differentiates between similarly situated persons, it must comport with the equal protection guarantees of the Constitution.

Appellant correctly points out that the line drawn by respondent between AFDC-eligible children who live with undocumented siblings and eligible children who do not is clearly irrelevant to the goals and objectives of the AFDC program. The members of both classes are similarly situated with respect to the legitimate purpose of the AFDC program the relief of eligible, needy children. All are needy, and meet the statutory criteria for assistance, and yet, one class of children is singled out for unequal treatment solely on the basis of the undocumented status of their family members a factor unrelated to dependency, and over which they have no control. [7] Thus, if this classification is to be sustained, the state must justify the lines it has drawn among similarly situated persons.

2. Strict scrutiny is the appropriate standard of review.

The question, then, is whether the state need show only that its classification is reasonably related to a legitimate governmental objective or whether it must comply with the mandate of the more stringent equal protection test by demonstrating "that its classification has been precisely tailored to serve a compelling governmental interest." (Plyler, supra, 457 U.S. at p. 217.) As we have already noted, this court must employ the latter, "active and critical analysis" in cases involving "suspect classifications" or touching on "fundamental interests." (Serrano v. Priest, supra, 18 Cal. 3d 728, 761 (Serrano II), quoting from Serrano I, supra, 5 Cal.3d at p. 597.) We find ourselves unable to agree with respondent's two principle contentions.

Respondent first contends that because this case involves legislation and regulation in the economic and social welfare area, it must be governed by Dandridge v. Williams (1970) 397 U.S. 471, and other cases employing the rational basis test. (See, e.g., [additional citations].) As will appear, respondent's reliance on Dandridge and its progeny is misplaced to the extent that none of the above-cited cases involved even a colorable claim of discrimination. Dandridge itself notes that a statutory classification does not violate equal protection if it is both "rationally based and free from invidious discrimination." (397 U.S. at p. 487)

In Dandridge the high court sustained a state statute, which imposed a maximum grant available to welfare recipients regardless of family size, against a claim of violation of equal protection. Recipients with large families whose standard of need exceeded the maximum grant contended that their families were disadvantaged in relation to small needy families. In rejecting the claim, the court acknowledged the "dramatically real difference" between state regulation of business and welfare assistance, which "involves the most basic economic needs of impoverished human beings," but nonetheless applied the rational basis constitutional standard of review. (397 U.S. at p. 485.) The court concluded that "[i]n the area of economics and social welfare, a State does not violate the Equal Protection Clause merely because the classifications made by its laws are imperfect. If the classification has some 'reasonable basis,' it does not offend the Constitution simply because the classification 'is not made with mathematical nicety or because in practice it results in some inequality.' [Citation.]" (397 U.S. at p. 485.)

Appellant in the instant case does not challenge the mathematical imperfections with which the state allocates welfare benefits. Of course, "[t]here is no question that States have considerable latitude in allocating their AFDC resources, since each State is free to set its own standard of need . . . ." (King v. Smith, supra, 392 U.S. 309, 318.) Appellant complains, though, that once the state establishes standards of need it cannot create two classes of eligible children, one of which is singled out for unequal treatment on the basis of factors unrelated to the objectives of the statutory and regulatory scheme. Appellant contends that the state has drawn distinctions between otherwise eligible children and that the classification is presumptively invidious as it discriminates against a discrete and powerless minority namely, eligible children who reside with undocumented siblings.

Respondent next contends that appellant's three younger children are not members of a suspect class because it is their siblings' trait rather than their own which is the basis of the differential treatment. He urges that it would be a "novel approach to equal protection" to hold that the traits of the undocumented children place their siblings in a suspect classification. In this regard, respondent argues that because the class affected by the challenged practice is comprised of citizens and documented aliens, the Supreme Court's recent decision in Plyler v. Doe, supra, 457 U.S. 202, involving discrimination against undocumented aliens, is inapposite. While we agree that the holding in Plyler is not squarely applicable here, we think that the high court's analysis and reasoning is especially pertinent.

The Supreme Court in Plyler held that a Texas statute denying undocumented children free public school education violated equal protection. The threshold question before the court was whether undocumented aliens were "persons" within the meaning of the Fourteenth Amendment. In a 1971 decision the high court had declared that "[a]liens as a class are a prime example of a 'discrete and insular' minority." (Graham v. Richardson (1971) 403 U.S. 365, 372.) Graham held discrimination against resident aliens "inherently suspect and ... therefore subject to strict judicial scrutiny" (ibid.) regardless of "whether or not a fundamental right is impaired" (id., at p. 376). In Plyler, the court held that undocumented aliens "may claim the benefit of the Fourteenth Amendment" (457 U.S. at p. 215; cf. Cabral v. State Bd. of Control (1980) 112 Cal. App. 3d 1012), but it perfunctorily dismissed in a footnote the contention that undocumented aliens are a suspect class (457 U.S. at p. 219, fn. 19 cf. id. at p. 235, fn. 3, conc. opn. by Blackmun, J.). Nor was strict scrutiny warranted because education was involved, the court held, since education is not a fundamental right. (Id., at p. 223, citing San Antonio v. Rodriguez (1973) 411 U.S. 1, 28–39.)

Nevertheless, the high court concluded in Plyler that heightened judicial scrutiny was required because "more is involved in these cases than the abstract question whether [the statute] discriminates against a suspect class, or whether education is a fundamental right. [The statute] imposes a lifetime hardship on a discrete class of children not accountable for their disabling status." (457 U.S. at p. 223).

* * *

The primary underpinning of Plyler that innocent children cannot be explicitly disadvantaged on the basis of their status of birth unquestionably applies to the instant case. In both cases the classifying trait is one over which the children have no control: the undocumented status of a family member who in coming to this country, albeit illegally, placed the children in their disadvantaged position. Justice Brennan, writing for the majority in Plyler, reasoned that the Texas statute could not pass constitutional muster because it "direct[ed] the onus of a parent's misconduct against his children" who "are present in this country through no fault of their own." (457 U.S. at pp. 220, 226.) Similarly, a recent federal district court decision held that the state cannot "victimize the citizen child or a lawfully resident child and deprive it of [day care services] ... based solely on his mother's [undocumented] status ...." (Ruiz v. Blum, supra, 549 F. Supp. 871, 877.) As Justice Powell noted, concurring in Plyler, these holdings "find support in decisions of this Court with respect to the status of illegitimates. In Weber v. Aetna Casualty & Surety Co., 406 U.S. 164, 175 (1972), we said: '[V]isiting . . . condemnation on the head of an infant' for the misdeeds of the parents is illogical, unjust, and 'contrary to the basic concept of our system that legal burdens should bear some relationship to individual responsibility or wrongdoing.' [¶] In these cases, the State of Texas effectively denies to the school-age children of illegal aliens the opportunity to attend the free public schools that the State makes available to all residents. They are excluded only because of a status resulting from the violation by parents or guardians of our immigration laws and the fact that they remain in our country unlawfully. The respondent children are innocent in this respect. They can 'affect neither their parents' conduct nor their own status.' Trimble v. Gordon, 430 U.S. 762, 770 (1977)." (457 U.S. at p. 238, conc. opn. by Powell, J.)

In the present case, appellant's citizen children are denied welfare benefits although, like the children in Plyler, they are "innocent" with respect to their parents' violation of the immigration laws. We cannot agree with respondent's position that Plyler is distinguishable because it involved education. We note that the court did not have to ground its holding upon a finding that education is a "fundamental right." (Cf. Serrano II, supra, 18 Cal. 3d 728.) Indeed, Justice Powell's concurring opinion suggests that the court's decision in Plyler is applicable in the welfare context: "If the resident children of illegal aliens were denied welfare assistance, made available by government to all other children who qualify, this also in my opinion would be an impermissible penalizing of children because of their parents' status." (457 U.S. at p. 239, fn. 3.) We conclude that heightened judicial scrutiny is warranted in this case.

What is the standard for such heightened judicial scrutiny? Our state equal protection clause is "possessed of an independent vitality" from the Fourteenth Amendment. (Serrano II, supra, 18 Cal. 3d 728, 764.). We hold that the challenged practice in this case should be reviewed under the strict scrutiny test.

In holding that strict scrutiny is warranted indeed compelled in this case, we do so in recognition that constitutional safeguards can be preserved only by rejecting a rigid, categorical approach to equal protection. It would be truly incongruous to hold that appellant's alien children are entitled to heightened protection but not their brothers and sisters who live in the same home and suffer the same disadvantage.

We have thus far emphasized the reason appellant's children constitute a discrete minority their inability to control their parents' conduct. Equally crucial to our holding is the fact that appellant's citizen children are classified on the basis of an immutable trait they cannot forsake their birth into an undocumented family. They are "saddled with [the same] disabilities [and] subjected to [the same] history of purposeful unequal treatment" as their brothers and mother. (San Antonio School District v. Rodriguez, supra, 411 U.S. 1, 28.) Indeed, the challenged classification touches upon two traits that have been historically disfavored national origin and ancestry. (See, e.g., Hernandez v. Texas (1954) 347 U.S. 475 [national origin]; Takahashi v. Fish Game Comm. (1948) 334 U.S. 410 [origin and ancestry]; Oyama v. California (1948) 332 U.S. 633 [same]; Yick Wo v. Hopkins (1886) 118 U.S. 356 [race, alienage, national origin].) As in these lineage cases, appellant's children are classified on the basis of an immutable trait and are relegated to an inferior status into which they are locked by accident of birth. For all of the foregoing reasons, the classification in the present case must be strictly scrutinized.

B. No Compelling State Interest in Classification

We now reach the point in our analysis where respondent must show a compelling state interest that is furthered by the classification he has drawn. Respondent fails to discharge his burden of proof under this test. He identifies only fiscal concerns, and argues that the state can ill-afford to take into account the needs of undocumented aliens. Preservation of the fisc is an insufficient justification. The high court in Plyler rejected a similar contention, noting that "a concern for the preservation of resources standing alone can hardly justify the classification used in allocating those resources. [Citation.] The state must do more than justify its classification with a concise expression of an intention to discriminate. [Citation.]" (457 U.S. at p. 227.)

We have thus concluded that the classification created by appellant's practice of excluding undocumented aliens from the FBU is invidiously discriminatory, as applied to families like appellant's, and violates the equal protection rights of eligible children in such families. We therefore hold that, under our state Constitution, undocumented aliens, who would otherwise be eligible for AFDC but for their immigration status, must be included in the family budget unit for purposes of calculating the grant amount in those limited cases where the failure to do so would result in a reduction in, or denial of the maximum aid payable benefits to which the eligible persons, United States citizens or lawfully resident aliens, are entitled.

* * *

The judgment is reversed.

---

**Question:** The *Darces v. Woods* opinion refers to *Plyler v. Doe,* which is not precedent because it is based on the U.S. rather than the California Constitution, and involved education rather than benefits. Why does the court think *Plyler* is relevant?

# FIRST AMENDMENT & ZONING

## STATE V. STUMMER

194 P.3d 1043 (Ariz. 2008)

* * *

BERCH, VICE CHIEF JUSTICE.

Petitioners Hubert August Stummer and Dennis Allen Lumm were charged with violating Arizona Revised Statutes ("A.R.S.") section 13–1422 (2005), which forbids adult bookstores from remaining open during certain early morning hours. We have been asked to determine whether the hours of operation provision of § 13–1422 violates the free speech provision of the Arizona Constitution.

Petitioners operate adult-oriented businesses in Phoenix that sell sexually explicit books and magazines. They were charged with violating A.R.S. § 13–1422(A), which requires adult bookstores to close for fifty-three hours each week: from 1:00 a.m. to 8:00 a.m. Monday through Saturday, and from 1:00 a.m. to noon on Sunday. * * *

Petitioners moved to dismiss the charges, citing *Empress Adult Video Bookstore v. City of Tucson*, 59 P.3d 814, 823–24 (App. 2002), which held the hours of operation provision in § 13–1422(A) unconstitutional. Bound by *Empress*, the superior court granted the motion. The State appealed, arguing that *Empress* was wrongly decided.

A different panel of the court of appeals agreed and reversed. *State v. Stummer*, 171 P.3d 1229, 1236 (App. 2007). We granted review to resolve the conflict between *Empress* and the court of appeals opinion in this case. We have jurisdiction pursuant to Article 6, Section 5(3) of the Arizona Constitution, A.R.S. § 13–4033(A)(1) (2001), and Arizona Rule of Criminal Procedure 31.19.

* * *

The Arizona Legislature enacted A.R.S. § 13–1422 in response to complaints from citizens and local businesses that "adult" businesses were causing negative effects, including increased prostitution and sexually oriented litter, in the surrounding communities. *See* 1998 Ariz. Sess. Laws, ch. 296, S 4 (2d Reg. Sess.). These negative effects were alleged to be more prevalent during the early morning hours and the proponents therefore urged the legislature to restrict the operating hours of these businesses to reduce the problems.

* * *

These negative effects are byproducts or "secondary effects" of speech. The legislature purportedly designed § 13–1422(A) to suppress these secondary effects, not to suppress the speech itself. Although such regulations necessarily affect speech, restrictions on secondary effects have received less exacting scrutiny under the Federal Constitution than have laws designed to directly curtail speech. *See City of Renton v. Playtime Theatres, Inc.*, 475 U.S. 41, 47–48, (1986). We must decide what level of scrutiny Arizona courts should apply when determining the constitutionality, under Article 2, Section 6 of the Arizona Constitution, of content-based secondary effects regulations. We review the constitutionality of statutes de novo. *State, v. Hansen*, 160 P.3d 166, 168 (2007).

The issue presented in this case is not . . . whether § 13–1422 violates the First Amendment to the United States Constitution, but rather whether it passes muster under Article 2, Section 6 of the Arizona Constitution. Both the First Amendment and Article 2, Section 6 protect speech from abridgment by the government. The First Amendment does so by restraining government interference with speech rights. It provides that "Congress shall make no law . . . abridging the freedom of speech, or of the press." U.S. Const. amend. I. Arizona's free speech provision, in contrast, guarantees each individual's right to speak freely. It states that "[e]very person may freely speak, write, and publish on all subjects, being responsible for the abuse of that right." Ariz. Const. art. 2, § 6.

* * *

The encompassing text of Article 2, Section 6 indicates the Arizona framers' intent to rigorously protect freedom of speech. *See Mountain States Tel. Tel. Co. v. Ariz. Corp. Cornm'n*, 773 P.2d 455, 459–60 (1989). In addressing censorship, we have said that the words of Arizona's free speech provision "are too plain for equivocation. The right of every person to freely speak, write and publish may not be limited." *Id.* at 355, [citation.]

* * *

We have also stated that Article 2, Section 6 has "greater scope than the first amendment." *Mountain States*, 773 P.2d at 459. This is not a case, however, in which we need to determine the boundaries of Arizona's free speech provision. The State does not argue that the books and magazines in Petitioners' bookstores are obscene. Thus in selling those materials, Petitioners are engaging in protected speech under Article 2, Section 6. We need only decide whether and to what extent the State may curtail this protected speech in order to reduce secondary effects.

* * *

In *Empress*, the court of appeals [required] that the regulation "affect as *little as possible* the ability of the sender and receiver to communicate." 59 P.3d at 821 (quoting *Mountain States*, 773 P.2d at 463) (emphasis added). The court of appeals thus effectively adopted a "least restrictive means" standard. *See id.* at 59, ¶ 21, 59 P.3d at 823. Applying this standard, the court concluded that § 13–1422 violated the Arizona Constitution because closing adult businesses for at least seven hours a day was not the least restrictive means of addressing the secondary effects of adult businesses. *Id.*

The booksellers here urge that we adopt the *Empress* standard. We conclude, however, that such a standard is not appropriate for judging the constitutionality of secondary effects regulations. When a regulation is content based, but directed at addressing the secondary effects of speech, the legislative choice is entitled to more deference than the strict scrutiny test permits. The government may have a substantial interest in addressing certain secondary effects of speech, see *Renton*, 475 U.S. at 50, and applying strict scrutiny may effectively preclude regulations designed to prohibit such effects.

The State urges us instead to apply the federal intermediate scrutiny standard articulated by the Supreme Court in *Renton* and *Alameda Books* . . ., and the court of appeals panel in this case. We decline to strictly apply the federal test because it is inconsistent with the broad protection of speech afforded by the Arizona Constitution. Because Arizona's speech provision safeguards the right to speak freely on all topics, our test must more closely scrutinize laws that single out speech for regulation based on its disfavored content. We thus turn to the question of the appropriate test for determining the constitutionality, under Article 2, Section 6, of secondary effects regulations.

The appropriate test for measuring the constitutionality of content-based secondary effects regulations must vindicate the constitutional right to free speech, yet accommodate the government's interest in protecting the public health, safety, and welfare. The test has two phases. First, to qualify for intermediate scrutiny, the State must demonstrate that a content-based regulation is directed at ameliorating secondary effects, not at suppressing protected speech. Second, to survive intermediate scrutiny, the State must show that, in addressing the secondary effects, the regulation does not sweep too broadly.

In the first phase, the challenger must demonstrate that the challenged provision interferes with the right to freely speak, write, or publish. Once the challenger has shown that a content-based or content-correlated regulation affects free expression, the State bears the burden of demonstrating that the enacting body had a reasonable basis for believing that the speech singled out for regulation created secondary effects different from or greater than the effects of speech generally, *see City of Cincinnati v. Discovery Network Inc.*, 507 U.S. 410, 430, (1993), and that the challenged regulation was designed to suppress those secondary effects, not to suppress the speech itself . . .

The State may carry that burden by demonstrating to the court that, on the basis of the evidence before it, the enacting body might reasonably believe that the regulated speech created negative secondary effects greater than those created by speech generally and that the regulation would address those effects. *See Alameda Books*, 535 U.S. at 438, (Kennedy, J., concurring). If the State meets this burden of showing that the legislative body enacted the challenged regulation to respond to secondary effects rather than disfavored speech, we will address the challenged regulation under a form of intermediate scrutiny.

In the second phase of the inquiry for determining the constitutionality of a content-based secondary effects regulation, the court must examine whether the regulation protects substantial government interests and whether it significantly reduces pact on secondary effects secondary effects without unduly interfering with protected speech. The deference afforded at the first phase, in which the court determines whether intermediate scrutiny applies, does not extend to the second phase, in which the court assesses the effects of the challenged law. For the regulation to survive, its proponent must show that the government has a substantial interest, that the regulation significantly furthers that interest, and that the challenged regulation does not unduly burden speech. To establish or disprove these prongs, the challenger and the proponent of the regulation may bring forth pre- and post-enactment evidence.

In applying the phase-two test, the court must first assess the importance of the government's asserted interest. Regulations designed to reduce crime, protect children, or safeguard constitutional rights, for example, may justify some infringement on speech rights. *See* [citations]. Lesser concerns, such as the abatement of mere litter or governmental convenience, will not justify suppression of speech. *See* [citations].

If the government advances a substantial interest, the court must then determine whether the regulation significantly furthers that interest. A court may find this prong satisfied if the regulation substantially reduces or has a significant ameliorative impact of secondary effects. In this analysis, the court must consider the likelihood that the regulation will achieve its intended result. For example, the court may consider how much sex-related crime occurs during the hours of forced closure. The answer to this inquiry may elucidate whether the regulation is designed to significantly reduce such negative secondary effects and thus whether it may achieve its intended result.

In addressing whether the regulation significantly furthers a substantial government interest, the State need not prove that a particular bookstore generates secondary effects, nor should the court focus solely on the challenging parties' bookstores. Because A.R.S. § 13–1422 applies statewide, the government need only show that, collectively, adult bookstores cause more than de minimis negative secondary effects and that the regulation is designed to significantly reduce such effects.

Finally, the third prong—whether the regulation unduly burdens speech—may be satisfied by establishing that the government's substantial interest would be less effectively achieved without the regulation and ample alternative means of communication exist. Although the test does not require the least restrictive means possible, the proponent must show a close fit or nexus between the ends sought and the means employed for achieving those ends.

In analyzing the facts of this case under the first phase of Arizona's secondary effects test, we conclude that the Petitioners have established that their protected speech is burdened by a content-based regulation. The State, in turn, has met its burden of demonstrating that the hours provision of § 13–1422 was designed to curb the secondary effects of speech, not to prohibit the speech itself. The State adduced evidence that the legislature reasonably believed that adult businesses encourage criminal activity and sexually oriented litter, that these effects were worse in the nighttime hours, and that the statute at issue would ameliorate those effects. We therefore turn to the second phase of the inquiry, application of the three-part test: whether the government's interests are substantial, whether the regulation significantly furthers those interests, and whether the regulation unduly burdens speech.

In the second phase, the court must first assess the significance of the government's interests. The existence of mere litter is not by itself sufficiently important to permit a substantial restriction on speech. As we stated in *New Times*, "minor matters of public inconvenience or annoyance cannot be transformed into substantive evils of sufficient weight to warrant the curtailment of liberty of expression." 519 P.2d at 174. Combating criminal activity such as prostitution and public indecency, however, is a substantial governmental interest. We therefore move to the second and third prongs of the phase-two analysis.

As to the second prong, whether the statute significantly furthers the government's interest, the record is devoid of evidence that secondary effects are greater during the hours of forced closure. The record reflects only two pieces of evidence on this point. One was the testimony of a representative of the City of Phoenix who testified that the city could *not* show a relationship between the hours of operation and the incidence of crime. The other was a study from Glendale, Colorado, finding that *fewer* police calls or incidents arose from a particular adult business during the late night hours than during other times. Neither piece of evidence supports the assertion that the effects are greater during the hours of forced closure. Without such a showing, the State may have difficulty establishing that closure is an appropriate remedy—that is, that this statute significantly furthers the government's interest in reducing secondary effects. The government must establish that, during their early morning operation, adult bookstores disproportionately cause negative secondary effects and that these negative effects are or will be significantly lessened by closure during those hours.

* * *

Finally, regarding the third prong, the State has not shown that any substantial interests would be achieved less effectively without the bookstores' closure for fifty-three hours each week. The record also does not contain evidence regarding the availability of alternative channels of communication during the hours of closure.

In short, because this case was decided on motion to dismiss. . . . no court below has had the opportunity to apply the test we formulate today for evaluating the constitutionality of content-based secondary effects regulations, we conclude that all parties should have the opportunity to present additional evidence supporting their positions, and the trial court should have the opportunity to apply the test for constitutionality detailed above. We therefore remand this case to the superior court for further proceedings consistent with this opinion.

We vacate the opinion of the court of appeals and remand this case to the trial court.

---

**Question:** If the Arizona Supreme Court in *Stummer* is basing its decision on whether the regulation at issue was aimed at "secondary effects" of speech like criminal activity, why does it matter whether the Arizona Constitution's freedom of speech provision is broader than that in the U.S. Constitution?

## WARRANT ADEQUACY

### STATE V. KOIVU

272 P.3d 483 (Idaho 2012)

* * *

EISMANN, J.

This is an appeal asking that we overrule *State v. Guzman,* 842 P.2d 660 (1992), and hold that the *Leon* good-faith exception to the exclusionary rule applies to violations of Article I, section 17, of the Idaho Constitution. Because the State has not shown any ground for doing so, we decline to overrule that case and affirm the order of the district court suppressing evidence obtained incident to an arrest pursuant to a wrongly issued warrant.

Randy Koivu (Defendant) was charged with the crime of possession of methamphetamine in Boundary County. He was found guilty of that crime, and on January 6, 2004, the district court sentenced him to five years in the custody of the Idaho Board of Correction, with three years fixed and two years indeterminate. The court suspended that sentence and placed Defendant on probation for four years. The terms of probation included that Defendant pay a fine of $500.00, court costs of $88.50, public defender reimbursement of $300.00, and restitution of $100.00. Defendant later violated the terms of his probation, and on November 1, 2005, the court entered an order revoking his probation and committing him to the custody of the Idaho Board of Correction. Defendant was released from prison on July 2, 2009.

* * *

On March 5, 2010, two sheriff deputies in neighboring Bonner County lawfully stopped a car for speeding. Defendant was the driver of the car. In running a background check of Defendant, the officers were informed that there was a warrant for his arrest out of Boundary County, [which was later dismissed there for failure to include a court order requiring him to pay a fine]. Reasonably relying upon the validity of the warrant, the deputies arrested Defendant and transported him to the Bonner County jail. Defendant was arrested only because of the warrant; he could not have been arrested for speeding. While searching Defendant at the jail, a baggie of methamphetamine was discovered near his feet.

. . .the district court in the Bonner County case issued an order suppressing the methamphetamine. The State then timely appealed.

* * *

Article I, section 17, of the Idaho Constitution provides, "The right of the people to be secure in their persons, houses, papers and effects against unreasonable searches and seizures shall not be violated; and no warrant shall issue without probable cause shown by affidavit, particularly describing the place to be searched and the person or thing to be seized." The Idaho Constitution does not specify the remedy for a violation of this provision, nor does the Fourth Amendment to the Constitution of the United States.

* * *

In *Weeks v. United States,* 232 U.S. 383, (1914), the United States Supreme Court held for the first time that evidence wrongfully seized by the federal government in violation of a criminal defendant's Fourth Amendment rights could not be used as evidence in the ensuing criminal prosecution. The Court stated that if evidence seized in violation of a defendant's Fourth Amendment rights could be used against him in a criminal prosecution, the protection of the Fourth Amendment would be of no value and it might as well be stricken from the Constitution.

* * *

In *United States v. Leon,* 468 U.S. 897, (1984), the Court adopted what became known as the *Leon* "good-faith" exception to the exclusionary rule under the Fourth Amendment. In *Leon,* the police had seized evidence acting in reasonable reliance on a search warrant, but the warrant was later determined to have been issued without probable cause. The Court held that the exclusionary rule would not apply to evidence obtained in objectively reasonable reliance on a subsequently invalidated search warrant. *Id.* at 922. The Court also held that "the exclusionary rule is designed to deter police misconduct rather than to punish the errors of judges and magistrates." *Id.* at 916.

* * *

The Court has since expanded the good-faith exception to include a search conducted in reasonable reliance upon a subsequently invalidated statute because legislators, like judges, are not the focus of the rule, *Illinois v. Krull,* 480 U.S. 340 (1987); an arrest in reasonable reliance upon information that the arrestee had an outstanding warrant, where the warrant had been quashed but the court clerk had failed to notify the sheriff's office, because applying the exclusionary rule would not deter mistakes made by court employees, *Arizona v. Evans,* 514 U.S. 1 (1995); an arrest in reasonable reliance upon the existence of an outstanding arrest warrant where the officer did not know that the warrant had been recalled due to the negligent failure of a sheriff's employee to update the computer database, *Herring v. United States,* 555 U.S. 135 (2009); and to a search conducted in objectively reasonable reliance upon binding judicial precedent that was later overruled, *Davis v. United States,* 131 S.Ct. 2419 (2011).

[The court then discussed Idaho cases applying the exclusionary rule.]

In *Guzman,* the police had obtained evidence pursuant to a search warrant that was later declared invalid because the supporting affidavit alleged only conclusory statements of fact., 842 P.2d at 663. The trial court applied the good-faith exception under *Leon* and refused to suppress the evidence. 842 P.2d at 661. This Court declined to apply the good-faith exception to the exclusionary rule under Article I, section 17, of the Idaho Constitution. However, a majority did not agree upon the reasons for doing so. . . .Later, a unanimous Court stated that the Court had rejected applying the *Leon* good-faith exception to Article I, section 17, and that the *Guzman* decision would be applied retroactively to all cases that had not become final when *Guzman* was issued. *State v. Josephson* 852 P.2d 1387, 1392 (1993).

The State now asks us to revisit the *Leon* good-faith exception and overrule *Guzman*. . . .

The State also asserts that "[a] review of the authority relied upon by the *Guzman* plurality does not support its analysis or results." It argues that "those cases clearly show that Idaho's exclusionary rule is co-extensive with the exclusionary rule as adopted and applied by the United States Supreme Court." . . .There is absolutely nothing in . . . any other authority relied upon by the *Guzman* Court that commits this Court to construe or apply Article I, section 17, in the same manner as the United States Supreme Court construes or applies the Fourth Amendment. " 'The Fourth Amendment and art. 1, § 17 are designed to protect a person's legitimate expectation of privacy, which "society is prepared to recognize as reasonable".' The similarity of language and purpose, however, does not require this Court to follow United States Supreme Court precedent in interpreting our own constitution." *State v. Donato* 20 P.3d 5, 7 (2001). "Long gone are the days when state courts will blindly apply United States Supreme Court interpretation and methodology when in the process of interpreting their own constitutions." *Id.*

The exclusionary rule is a judicially created remedy for searches and seizures that violate the Constitution. As shown above, courts have disagreed over the years as to whether there should be any remedy for such constitutional violations and, if so, whether it should focus upon redressing the wrong committed against the victim of the unconstitutional search or seizure or only upon deterring future violations of such constitutional rights by law enforcement officials. The holding in *Guzman* was that evidence obtained from a defendant pursuant to a warrant will not be admissible in the defendant's criminal trial if the warrant was issued without probable cause in violation of the Constitution. That holding is not manifestly wrong. It is identical to the holding in *State v. Arregui* (Idaho 1927) and is consistent with the holdings of other courts, including the United States Supreme Court. *Aguilar v. Texas,* 378 U.S. 108 (1964).

The State contends that "[t]he second flaw of Guzman is its contention that the *Leon* good-faith exception to the exclusionary rule is inimical to the values of exclusion unrelated to police deterrence." The State then argues why the *Leon* Court was right and the *Guzman* plurality was wrong. It also asserts that application of the exclusionary rule here would not deter police misconduct because the officers involved simply did what they were required to do—execute an arrest warrant.

This Court's rejection of the *Leon* good-faith exception in *Guzman* was supported by an independent exclusionary rule announced eighty-five years ago in *Arregui*. In *Arregui,* there was no claim of law enforcement misconduct. The officers relied upon the validity of a search warrant that was later held to be invalid due to the lack of a showing of probable cause in the affidavit upon which the warrant was issued. Likewise, in *State v. Oropeza* 545 P.2d 475 (1976), evidence was suppressed for the same reason. When *Guzman* was decided, "Idaho had clearly developed an exclusionary rule as a constitutionally mandated remedy for illegal searches and seizures in addition to other purposes behind the rule such as recognizing the exclusionary rule as a deterrent for police misconduct." *Donato* 20 P.3d at 8. In some instances, we have construed Article I, section 17, to provide greater protection than is provided by the United States Supreme Court's construction of the Fourth Amendment. "[W]e provided greater protection to Idaho citizens based on the uniqueness of our state, our Constitution, and our long-standing jurisprudence." *Id.* To overrule *Guzman* and hold that the exclusionary rule's sole purpose is to deter police misconduct, we would also have to overrule *Arregui,* which adopted the exclusionary rule in Idaho in a case in which there was no police misconduct. The State has not pointed to anything in the record showing that during the last eighty-five years *Arregui* has proved to be unwise or unjust. We therefore uphold the district court's order holding that the methamphetamine is not admissible into evidence because the Defendant's arrest pursuant to an invalid warrant of attachment violated his rights under Article I, section 17, of the Idaho Constitution.

We affirm the order of the district court excluding the methamphetamine.

---

**Question:** Under *Koivu,* officers' good faith in an invalid warrant, even when there is no police misconduct, does not prevent the exclusion of evidence. Is the good faith exception to the exclusionary rule dead in Idaho state courts?

# CHAPTER 16

# STATE CONSTITUTIONAL LAW—POSITIVE RIGHTS

■ ■ ■

## CONTEXT & SOURCES

The U.S. Constitution expressly refers to negative rights, so for example the government cannot *abridge* free speech, or *deny* equal protection of the laws. But many state constitutions guarantee affirmative, or positive rights going beyond a structural parallel to the federal system. The downside of this approach is that state legislatures or voters can typically change their governing documents far more easily than can the nation as a whole through the U.S. Constitution's amendment process. Here, decisions discuss state constitutional rights to a civil jury trial, hunt and fish, receive welfare benefits, have criminal trials translated, and attend criminal prosecutions as a victim.

Jeffrey M. Shaman, *Equality and Liberty in the Golden Age of State Constitutional Law* (Oxford 2008) is an accessible survey of affirmative rights. For a deep dive into the history of Delaware's independent constitutional right to a civil jury trial behind *McCool v. Gehret*, see Randy J. Holland, "State Jury Trials and Federalism: Constitutionalizing Common Law Concepts," 38 *Valparaiso University Law Review* 373 (2004). The application of the California Constitution's interpreter provision in *People v. Aguilar* is discussed in Peter L. Reich, "Three Lessons I Learned from Cruz Reynoso," 39 *Chicanx-Latinx Law Review* 71 (2023).

### MCCOOL V. GEHRET

657 A.2d 269 (Del. 1995)

* * *

HOLLAND, JUSTICE:

This is an appeal from the Superior Court. In their original complaint, the plaintiffs-appellants, Paul and Tammera McCool (the "McCools") alleged medical negligence by the defendant-appellee, John Gehret, M.D. ("Dr. Gehret"), and certain other health care providers. The complaint was amended to allege tortious interference by Dr. Gehret with the plaintiffs' medical expert witness, Robert Dein, M.D. ("Dr. Dein"). Over the plaintiffs' objection, the Superior Court granted Dr. Gehret's motion to sever the trial of the McCools' claim for medical malpractice from the trial of their claim for tortious interference.

A jury trial was held on the medical malpractice claim only, beginning on January 18, 1994. The jury returned a verdict in favor of Dr. Gehret on January 26, 1994. On February 3, 1994, the plaintiffs filed a motion for a mistrial or, in the alternative, a new trial.

On April 20, 1994, a one-day bench trial was held regarding the tortious interference claim. This bench trial was held before a different Superior Court judge than the one who had presided at the malpractice trial.

* * *

The McCools contend that forcing them to proceed with a bench trial on their tortious interference claim, despite their objection, violated their Delaware Constitutional right to have a trial by jury in that civil proceeding. The historical origins of the right to trial by jury which is provided for in the Delaware Constitution was reviewed by this Court in *Claudio v. State,* Del.Supr., 585 A.2d 1278 (1991). In *Claudio,* this Court noted that when Delaware adopted its Constitution in 1792, notwithstanding the ratification of the first ten amendments or federal Bill of Rights in 1791, it did not create "a mirror image of the United States Constitution" with regard to trial by jury. *Id.* at 1289.

When the Delaware Constitution of 1792 was adopted, the right to trial by jury set forth in the federal Bill of Rights as the Sixth and Seventh Amendments to the United States Constitution was only a protection against action by the federal government. *Barron v. Mayor of Baltimore,* 32 U.S. (7 Pet.) 243, (1833). Following the adoption of the Fourteenth Amendment to the United States Constitution, the Sixth Amendment right to trial by jury in *criminal* proceedings has been deemed to have been incorporated by the Due Process clause and now also provides protection against state action. *Duncan v. Louisiana,* 391 U.S. 145 (1968). Nevertheless, the United States Supreme Court has not held that the Seventh Amendment's guarantee of jury trials in *civil* proceedings was made applicable to the states by the incorporation doctrine with the adoption of the Fourteenth Amendment to the United States Constitution. [Citations].

Accordingly, the right to a jury trial in civil proceedings has always been and remains exclusively protected by provisions in the Delaware Constitution. Delaware adopted its first Constitution in 1776, which provided, in pertinent part:

The common law of England, as well as so much of the statute law as have been heretofore adopted in practice in this state, shall remain in force, unless they shall be altered by a future law of the Legislature; such parts only excepted as are repugnant to the rights and privileges contained in this constitution and the declaration of rights, c. agreed to by this convention.

Del. Const. of 1776, art. 25, 1 Del. C. at 118. Delaware also adopted its own Declaration of Rights in 1776, which guaranteed the right to trial by jury to all citizens of the State of Delaware and included a statement "[t]hat trial by jury of facts where they arise is one of the greatest securities of the lives, liberties and estates of the people." Declaration of Rights and Fundamental Rules of the Delaware State § 13 (1776), 1 Del. C. at 110.

When Delaware adopted its next Constitution in 1792, its citizens were guaranteed the right to trial by jury "as heretofore." See Claudio v. State, 585 A.2d at 1298. Consequently, since its inception in 1776, the Delaware Constitution has afforded its citizens the right to trial by jury in both criminal and civil proceedings. In doing so, the Delaware Constitution has expressly preserved all of the fundamental features of the jury system as they existed at common law. Id. See also Nance v. Rees, 161 A.2d 795 (1960).

In 1727, Delaware adopted An Act of Privilege to a Free Man, which provided:

That no free man within this government shall be taken or imprisoned, or disseized of his freehold or liberties, or be outlawed or exiled, or other ways hurt, damnified or destroyed, nor to be tried or condemned but by the lawful judgment of his twelve equals, or by the laws of England, and of this government.

1 *Laws of the State of Delaware* 119 (1797).

A *sine qua non* of that common law jurisprudence is the principle that either party shall have the right to demand a jury trial upon an issue of fact in an action at law. As previously noted, the 1776 Delaware *Declaration of Rights,* which was preserved by the "heretofore" text in the 1792 Constitution, referred to the right to trial by jury regarding factual issues as "one of the greatest securities of the lives, liberties and estates of the people." Similarly, in a letter to Pierre S. DuPont, Thomas Jefferson described the fact finding function of jurors as:

> the very essence of a Republic. . . . We of the United States . . . think experience has proved it safer for the mass of individuals composing the society to reserve to themselves personally the exercise of all rightful powers to which they are competent. . . .

Hence, with us, the people . . . being competent to judge of the facts occurring in ordinary life, . . . have retained the functions of judges of facts under the name of jurors. . . .

I believe . . . that action by the citizens, in person in affairs within their reach and competence, and in all others by representatives chosen immediately and removable by themselves, constitutes the essence of a Republic. . . .

Letter from Thomas Jefferson to Pierre S. DuPont (April 4, 1816), *in* 4 *Annals of America* 414 (Encyclopedia Britannica 1976) (emphasis added). *See* 2 J. Kendall Few, *In Defense of Trial by Jury* 456 (1993).

In 1855, the Delaware General Assembly enacted a statute that purportedly allowed judges to decide issues of fact without a jury in actions at law, with the agreement of all the parties. 11 Del. Laws, ch. 270. Nevertheless, because the Delaware Constitution preserved the right to trial by jury as "heretofore," Delaware judges took the position that, absent constitutional amendment, the General Assembly could not alter the right by statute. *See* 3 *Debates and Proceedings of the Constitutional Convention of the State of Delaware* 1730 (Milford Chronicle Publishing Co. 1958) (hereinafter "*Constitutional Debates*"). Therefore, notwithstanding the enactment of the 1855 statute by the General Assembly, Delaware judges remained reluctant to decide issues of fact in an action at law because they concluded that the Delaware Constitution required a jury to decide such questions. *Id. Compare Seymour v. Swart,* Okl.Supr., 695 P.2d 509 (1985) (similarly interpreting Oklahoma Constitution).

When the present Delaware Constitution was rewritten in 1897, the General Assembly included several significant provisions regarding the right to trial by jury. Article I of the 1897 Delaware Constitution was denominated for the first time as the "Bill of Rights." Section 4 of that article provided for the right to trial by jury as "heretofore." Article IV, Section 19 was a new addition in the 1897 Constitution and provided: "Judges shall not charge juries with respect to matters of fact, but may state the questions of fact in issue and declare the law." Del. Const. art. IV, § 19. The reason given during the Constitutional debates for the adoption of Section 19 was to ensure "that Judges shall confine themselves to their business, which is to adjudge the law and leave juries to determine the facts." 3 *Constitutional Debates* at 1730. *See Storey v. Camper,* Del.Supr., 401 A.2d 458, 463 n. 4 (1979).

That same "heretofore" right had been set forth in all of Delaware's preceding Constitutions since 1792. *See Hopkins v. Justice of the Peace Court No. 1,* Del.Super., 342 A.2d 243, 245–46 (1975).

In *Storey v. Camper* (Del. 1979), this Court characterized Section 19 as perpetuating Delaware's commitment to trial by jury in civil actions at law with regard to issues of fact. *Storey v. Camper,* 401 A.2d at 462–65. In examining when a trial judge may set aside a jury verdict, this Court described Delaware's long history of commitment to trial by jury. *Id.* We explained that Section 19 reaffirmed Delaware's commitment to the common law principles regarding trial by jury:

> In the policy of the law of this state, declared by the courts in numberless decisions, the jury is the sole judge of the facts of a case, and so jealous is the law of this policy that by express provision of the Constitution the court is forbidden to touch upon the facts of the case in its charge to the jury. *Id.* at 462.

In 1897, another new section was added to Article IV of Delaware's Constitution. Article IV, Section 20 provides that, "[i]n civil causes where matters of fact are at issue, if the parties agree, such matters of fact shall be tried by the court, and judgment rendered upon their decision thereon as upon a verdict by a jury." Del. Const. art. IV, § 20. According to the Constitutional debates, the purpose of the new Section was to address the concerns of Delaware's jurists about the constitutionality of the 1855 statutory authorization for litigants to waive a trial by jury in an action at law on an issue of fact.

* * *

In this case the McCools specifically demanded a jury trial on their medical malpractice claim and their tortious interference claim. When the jury that heard their medical malpractice claim was discharged, the McCools agreed to waive their right to a jury trial regarding their tortious interference claim only because the original trial judge offered to decide the remaining claim as a bench trial. The record contains the following statement by the McCools' attorney to the second trial judge:

"For practical reasons, the [medical malpractice] trial went a bit longer than we expected. Because of the two-week period of the jury panel, [the original trial judge] explained to us that it did not appear we would be able to get the same jury.

Discussing this in chambers as well as I think in the courtroom, . . . [the original trial judge] proposed [to personally hear] this count . . . [as] a bench trial, [the] benefit being, again, that even though we don't have the jury, at least we have a judge who did have the benefit of hearing all the testimony, . . ."

When the original trial judge subsequently declined to hear the tortious interference claim, the McCools objected to proceeding with a bench trial before another judge. Their attorney advised the second judge:

"Based on our understanding that the matter would be heard on the bench trial before [the original trial judge], my clients and I agreed to have it heard that way rather than [by] jury trial. [I] just want to go on record that is their position. They still are opposed to . . . the assignment of your honor."

Although a party has no right to insist on a bench trial before a particular judge, the record reflects that the McCools' waiver of their right to a jury trial was, in fact, permitted to be premised upon such a condition. The McCools only waived their right to a jury trial on the condition that the bench trial would be held before the original judge who had heard the medical malpractice claim and was familiar with much of the evidence relevant to the tortious interference claim. When the original trial judge, who had induced the McCools to waive their right to a jury trial, refused to hear their tortious interference claim, the condition upon which the McCools' waiver had been predicated ceased to exist. [Citations].

This Court has recognized that the right to a trial by jury, as guaranteed by the Delaware Constitution, may be relinquished pursuant to a valid waiver. *Graham v. State Farm Mut. Auto. Ins. Co.,* 565 A.2d at 912. Under the circumstances presented in this case, however, the McCools could not be forced to proceed with a bench trial before a second judge, in the absence of an unconditional waiver of their fundamental right to a trial by jury. *Id. See Federal Deposit Ins. Corp. v. Cafritz,* 770 F.Supp. 28, 30 (D.D.C. 1991). Consequently, the bench trial of the tortious interference claim that proceeded, without the McCools' express and unconditional waiver of a jury trial, violated Article IV, Section 20 and Article I, Section 4 of the Delaware Constitution.

The judgments of the Superior Court that were entered in favor of Dr. Gehret with respect to the McCools' claims for medical malpractice and tortious interference are REVERSED. This matter is remanded to the Superior Court, where the President Judge should assign it for a new trial in accordance with this opinion. Super.Ct.Civ.R. 40.

---

**Questions:** In *McCool*, why is it important to the plaintiffs that their case be heard by a jury? Would this concern be transferable to other types of cases?

## CABOT V. THOMAS

514 A.2d 1034 (Vt. 1986)

* * *

ALLEN, CHIEF JUSTICE.

This is an appeal by defendants from a superior court order permanently enjoining them from "hunting, shooting, trapping, or entering upon" plaintiffs' marshlands beyond the normal low water line of Charcoal Creek. We modify the order and affirm it as modified.

The material facts in this case are undisputed. Plaintiffs and their immediate predecessors in title have owned a tract of marshland of approximately 360 acres near West Swanton, Vermont since 1933. Charcoal Creek borders the western portion of their marsh. The creek, so-called, is actually an inlet from Lake Champlain. At its source, the creek connects through a narrow opening to the lake. It ultimately arrives at a dead end in a wooded area.

Although the level of Charcoal Creek is subject to periodic fluctuations, the parties agree it has a definite low water line along plaintiffs' marsh at 93.055 feet above mean sea level. At this low water line the marsh owners have since 1949 posted signs proclaiming: "No Hunting, Shooting, or Trapping."

On October 3, 1979, the water level was 95.36 feet above sea level. Thus, it rose well above the low water line and covered a portion of plaintiffs' land beyond the signs. An area of the marsh designated Jake Nokes Slough was inundated at that time. During drier seasons this slough was soft mud and bog and was separated from Charcoal Creek by a ridge of land.

Defendants entered Jake Nokes Slough from Lake Champlain by way of Charcoal Creek in a sixteen-foot flat bottom boat on October 3, 1979. They were aware of the plaintiffs' signs and of having passed beyond the signs, as they had done previously. Intending to hunt ducks, defendants stopped their boat in a weed bed two hundred yards to the inland side of the signs. The bottom of the boat rested in the mud at a point where the water was approximately five or six inches deep.

A police officer told the defendants they were hunting on private posted land. When they announced their intent to continue hunting there, the officer cited them for criminal trespass and poaching. Based on these facts, plaintiffs then sought and received the injunction which is the subject of this appeal.

As a definite low water line exists along Charcoal Creek, plaintiffs' ownership extends to that line. State v. Cain, 236 A.2d 501, 505 (1967); Hazen v. Perkins, 105 A. 249, 251 (1918). Defendants contend, however, that notwithstanding private ownership of the underlying lands, the public enjoys the right to hunt from boats on the waters overlying plaintiffs' marsh to the ordinary high water line.

Essentially, defendants and amicus curiae, the Vermont Agency of Environmental Conservation, argue that the public has a navigational easement across the waters overlying plaintiffs' land between the ordinary low and high water lines, and that this easement permits recreational uses as well. Among the recreational uses the public enjoys as of right, according to defendants and amicus curiae, are hunting and fowling.

Marshland adjoining Charcoal Creek has been the locus in quo of trespass actions between landowners and hunters since before the turn of the century. Hunters and marsh owners have pressed their respective claims of right with remarkable persistence.

In the late 1890's, W.G. Payne, an earlier landowner along this same creek, commenced a trespass action against Watson Gould, a hunter.[1] Eventually, in Payne v. Gould, 52 A. 421 (1902), the hunter prevailed because the owner had not sufficiently enclosed his land. This Court concluded that Gould was simply exercising his state constitutional right to hunt on "lands not enclosed." 52 A. at 422.

Subsequent landowners, including the immediate predecessor in title of plaintiffs Cabot, sought court sanction of their destruction of a hunting guide's duck blinds which they alleged were situated in their marsh. Although the case came before this Court on a collateral matter, the primary focus of the underlying dispute was the western boundary of the privately owned marshland along Charcoal Creek. See Cabot v. Hemingway, 58 A.2d 823, 823–24 (1948). At that time, the Court indicated in dictum that establishing the westerly boundary would determine if the duck blinds in question could properly have been maintained where they had been placed. 58 A.2d at 823. In 1949, a Franklin County court determined that the marsh's western boundary was the low water line along the creek at 93.055 feet above mean sea level. The owners of the marsh thereafter moved their signs to that line and have maintained them there ever since.

As was earlier intimated, recent duck hunters have been more inventive: they assert a public right of recreational use, including hunting, on the waters of Lake Champlain and its inlet creeks all the way to the normal high water line without regard to the ownership of the underlying land. . . .

The questions raised in this case and in prior Charcoal Creek controversies lie at the crosscurrents of two important concerns: the individual's desire for private enjoyment of privately owned land and the public's wish for sporting access to the forests, fields, and waterways of this state. These are concerns that have long been in conflict.

In the colonial period, residents of the New Hampshire grants (what was later to be Vermont) were well aware of the history of abuses that had occurred in England under authority of fish and game laws:

> They were then smarting under the oppression and inequalities of the English system under which individual development among the common people was impeded and often prevented, and the rights and enjoyments of the many were subjected to the pleasure of a favored few. Among the instrumentalities used to bring about this undesirable condition of life, were the iniquitous fish and game laws of England, enacted by the ruling class for their own enjoyment, and which led to a system under which the catching of

> a fish or the killing of a rabbit was deemed of more consequence than the happiness, liberty or life of a human being. New England Trout & Salmon Club v. Mather, 35 A. 323, 328 (1896) (Thompson, J., dissenting).

One response to the sometimes conflicting concerns of the individual and the larger group of society was Chapter II, Section 39 of the Vermont Constitution of 1777. Now found at Chapter II, Section 67, this provision guarantees to the public the "liberty," subject to legislative regulation, to hunt and fish in certain places:

> The inhabitants of this State shall have liberty in seasonable times, to hunt and fowl on the lands they hold, and on other lands not enclosed, and in like manner to fish in all boatable and other waters (not private property) under proper regulations, to be made and provided by the General Assembly.

Section 67 is an accommodation of competing goals. It offers a general delineation of not only the respective rights of landowners and sportsmen but also the authority of government to regulate those rights in the context of hunting and fishing.

Understanding Section 67 requires a knowledge of the common law which it altered. English law, as we received it, treated hunting on privately owned land as a personal privilege of the landowner. See, e.g., Sterling v. Jackson, 69 Mich. 488, 497 (1888) ("[s]ince every person has the right of exclusive dominion as to the lawful use of the soil owned by him, no man can hunt or sport upon another's land but by consent of the owner").

Waterways overlying private property were not in every instance entirely private, however. Tidal waters could not be privately owned. See Mather, supra, 68 Vt. at 342, 35 A. at 324. Although an individual could own inland lakes and rivers, the public could use them for navigational purposes if the waterways were susceptible to use for commercial passage and transportation. Id. at 342–43, 35 A. at 324. Thus, the common law recognized a "public easement" for navigation on such waters. Id. at 347, 35 A. at 326.

This public right of passage did not initially include a right to fish or hunt on nontidal waterways. The right of fishery was personal to the owner of the underlying land. See 1 R. Clark, Waters and Water Rights 182 (1967). Also personal to the landowner was the right to hunt and fowl on those overlying waters. See, e.g., [citations].

Chapter II, Section 67 extended rights to citizens which the common law had not recognized. . . . It recognized rights to hunt and fish, given certain circumstances, in what had previously been the landowner's private domain.

In New England Trout & Salmon Club v. Mather, supra, this Court, focusing on the right to fish, reasoned that the constitutional provision at issue does more than just recognize a right to fish in boatable waters under appropriate legislative regulation; it also:

> affords the test by which to determine over what waters the State has jurisdiction de jure, thus, "and in like manner to fish in all boatable and other waters (not private property) under proper regulations to be hereafter made and provided by the General Assembly." Thus was jurisdiction expressly reserved to the State over boatable waters and waters not private property. . . . Hence, unless the waters in question are boatable, they are not public, but private, and the State has no jurisdiction over them. Mather, supra, 35 A. at 326. . . By imposing the boatability requirement, Section 67 also limits the State's authority to enforce and regulate an easement across waters overlying an individual's private land. In this way, Section 67 incorporates protections for landowners as well as for those who fish.

Mather's reasoning in the context of fishing applies equally to Section 67's hunting provision. By virtue of Section 67, the State has authority to permit and regulate public hunting on private property, but only when that land is not enclosed.

If landowners fail to take adequate measures to enclose their lands, then individuals who hunt there without first seeking permission would not normally be trespassers. Payne v. Gould, supra, 52 A. at 422. We believe that the presence of water, whether boatable or nonboatable, is irrelevant for purposes of Section 67's right to hunt on nonenclosed, privately owned land. By attaching "boatable waters" and "lands not enclosed" limitations on the respective rights of fishing and hunting, the Vermont Constitution has designated those points beyond which private property becomes inviolate for fishing and hunting purposes nonboatability for the former and enclosure for the latter. Development of the common law must, of course, accommodate these constitutional principles.

* * *

Nothing in Section 67 suggests that its framers intended that boatability would be the standard for hunting either from boats or while standing in water. Indeed, since the provision uses a single standard for "hunting and fowling," applying a separate standard for hunting waterfowl would comport neither with common logic nor with normal use of language. Accordingly, we conclude that the appropriate inquiry in the present case is whether the private lands were enclosed. Such a disparate treatment of hunters and fishers is rational since hunting is normally more dangerous to and intrusive of the landowner's interests.

* * *

The court did not stop there, however. It also enjoined "entering upon the lands of [p]laintiffs, by boat or otherwise, at any point behind their boundary line or as marked by [p]laintiffs' posters. . . ." We cannot find support in the court's findings for such a broad injunction. This portion of the court's order plainly implicates the boatability aspects of the common law's navigational easement and Section 67's guarantee to those who fish. The sole basis for this part of the superior court's injunction appears to be the nonboatability of the water at that point where defendants' boat was resting in the mud on October 3, 1979. Water level on a single day will not normally support a finding of boatability or nonboatability for a body of water subject to seasonal fluctuations. See Mather, supra, 35 A. at 326 ("if [the lake's or stream's] periods of high water ordinarily continue a sufficient length of time to make it useful as a highway, it is subject to the public easement"). Nor, logically, can an injunction affecting a large area rest on a finding merely that a single point in that area is nonboatable.

We accordingly affirm the superior court's injunction order as it pertains to hunting, shooting, or trapping, and we strike that portion of the order which prohibits entering by boat upon the waters overlying plaintiffs' land.

---

**Question:** At issue in *Cabot* are rights to hunt and to fish. Some states differentiate these rights: In California there is a state constitutional right to fish, but not to hunt. Can these rights be distinguished in terms of their effects on private property?

## TUCKER V. TOIA

371 N.E.2d 449 (N.Y. 1977)

* * *

GABRIELLI, J.

The Commissioner of the State Department of Social Services appeals directly to this court . . . from a judgment of the Supreme Court . . . declaring section 15 of chapter 76 of the Laws of 1976 to be unconstitutional, and enjoining its implementation and enforcement. We affirm the judgment appealed from, on the ground that the challenged section constitutes a substantive violation of section 1 of article XVII of the New York State Constitution.

New York residents under the age of 21 who are in need of public assistance normally receive aid through either the Federally subsidized Aid to Families with Dependent Children Program (AFDC), or the State's broad Home Relief Program. The determination of which program is applicable in a particular instance is based on whether the needy individual under 21 is residing with either a parent or a legally responsible relative. If he is residing with such a person, he is eligible for AFDC, but not home relief, whereas if he is not residing with such a person, entitlement to benefits stems from the home relief program and not AFDC.

Section 15 of chapter 76 of the Laws of 1976 amended subdivision (a) of section 158 of the Social Services Law, the section which determines eligibility for home relief. As amended, the statute provides that home relief is not to be provided to a person under the age of 21 who does not live with a parent or legally responsible relative, unless and until the applicant commences a support proceeding against any such parent or relative and an order of disposition is obtained in that support proceeding. Prior to the enactment of section 15, no such limitation was imposed upon a needy young person's right to public assistance. Rather, the public welfare authorities were subrogated to whatever right the recipient might have to support from a parent or responsible relative (see Social Services Law, sec. 101 et. seq.; Family Ct. Act, sec. 415). Under that system, a person under the age of 21, whether or not residing with a parent or responsible relative, was entitled to public assistance upon proof of need, regardless of existence of a parent or responsible relative, and it was left to the State to seek to recoup its welfare expenditures via a support proceeding against any such parent or relative. This is the method which was used in both AFDC and home relief cases prior to adoption of the section under attack and it is of interest to note that it is the method still used in AFDC cases.

Plaintiffs in this action are three individuals under the age of 21 who are not living with a parent or responsible relative, and are thus eligible only for home relief, not for AFDC. They are concededly needy and, prior to the effective date of section 15, they would have been and were entitled to home relief, having met all requisite criteria.

One of the plaintiffs was 18 years old at the time this action was commenced. His father had abandoned his mother before plaintiff's birth, and his whereabouts are unknown. Until 1976, the son had lived with his mother, and was receiving an AFDC grant. His mother was then committed to a State hospital due to mental illness and, as a result, the son became ineligible for AFDC. Although he ultimately obtained a final disposition in a support proceeding against his mother in an attempt to satisfy section 15, he was denied home relief on the ground that he had not obtained a final disposition in a support proceeding against his missing father. * * *

Standing uncontroverted is the accepted fact and reality that in each of these cases in order to obtain the required "disposition" it would take from several weeks to several months, during which time no public assistance would be available to these needy young people . . . In certain areas of the State even greater delays are normal, and, in fact, it has been estimated that in New York City it will often take from 10 to 12 months to obtain a "disposition" in such a support proceeding. Under the challenged statute, the plaintiffs and others in similar situations are, of course, denied any public assistance during this period, although they meet all criteria for measuring need, solely on the basis of their failure to obtain a disposition. Since they do meet the need criteria, and are thus a fortiori unable to support themselves without public aid, one must wonder how they are to survive this period of waiting for an overcrowded Family Court system to process their often quite futile support petitions.

In New York State, the provision for assistance to the needy is not a matter of legislative grace; rather it is specifically mandated by our Constitution. Section I of article XVII of the New York State Constitution declares: "The aid, care and support of the needy are public concerns and shall be provided by the state and by such of its subdivisions, and in such manner and by such means, as the legislature may from time to time determine." This provision was adopted in 1938, in the aftermath of the great depression, and was intended to serve two functions: First, it was felt to be necessary to sustain from constitutional attack the social welfare programs first created by the State during that period [citation]; and second, it was intended as an expression of the existence of a positive duty upon the State to aid the needy.

The legislative history of the Constitutional Convention of 1938 is indicative of a clear intent that State aid to the needy was deemed to be a fundamental part of the social contract. For example, the report of the Committee on Public Welfare, the group which drafted what became section 1 of article XVII of our Constitution, specifically states that one purpose of the amendment was to "recognized the responsibility of the State for the aid, care and support of persons in need" (Revised Record of the Constitutional Convention of the State of New York, vol. II, p. 1084 [1938]).* * *

In view of this legislative history, as well as the mandatory language of the provision itself, it is clear that section 1 of article XVII imposes upon the State an affirmative duty to aid the needy . . . Although our Constitution provides the Legislature with discretion in determining the amount of aid, and in classifying recipients and defining the term "needy," it unequivocally prevents the Legislature from simply refusing to aid those whom it has classified as needy. Such a definite constitutional mandate cannot be ignored or easily evaded in either its letter or its spirit (see [citations]).

We find that section 15 of chapter 76 of the Laws of 1976 is unconstitutional in that it contravenes the letter and spirit of section 1 of article XVII of the Constitution. The effect of the questioned statute is plain: it would effectively deny public assistance to persons under the age of 21 who are concededly needy, often through no fault of their own, who meet all the criteria developed by the Legislature for determining need, solely on the ground that they have not obtained a final disposition in a support proceeding. Certainly, the statute is in furtherance of a valid State objective, for it is intended to prevent unnecessary welfare expenditures by placing the burden of supporting persons under 21 upon their legally responsible relatives. This valid purpose, however, cannot be achieved by methods which ignore the realities of the needy's plight and the State's affirmative obligation to aid all its needy.

* * *

May the Legislature deny all aid to certain individuals who are admittedly needy, solely on the basis of criteria having nothing to do with need? Today, we hold that it may not. As the chairman of the Constitutional Convention's Committee on Social Welfare indicated, although the Legislature is given great discretion in this area, it cannot simply "shirk its responsibility which . . . is as fundamental as any responsibility of government." (Revised Record of the Constitutional Convention, vol. III, p. 2126 [1938]).

---

**Question:** Compare the constitutional welfare provision in New York, upon which the *Tucker* court relies, and that in Montana, which states: "The legislature shall provide such economic assistance and social and rehabilitative services as may be necessary for those inhabitants who, by reasons of age, infirmities, or misfortune, may have need for the aid of society." Should application of the latter to the question of mandatory aid yield a different result? See *Butte Community Union v. Lewis,* 712 P.2d 1309 (Mont. 1986).

## PEOPLE V. AGUILAR

35 Cal. 3d 785 (1984)

* * *

REYNOSO, J.

The right of a criminal defendant to an interpreter is based on the fundamental notion that no person should be subjected to a Kafkaesque trial which may result in the loss of freedom and liberty. We granted hearing in this case to determine the scope of interpreter assistance which article I, section 14 of the California Constitution requires be afforded a non-English speaking criminal defendant. The trial court properly appointed an interpreter for the accused, Marcello Mata Aguilar, after observing him and speaking with him at his arraignment. That interpreter, however, became unavailable to the defendant during the testimony of two Spanish speaking prosecution witnesses. Mata Aguilar was convicted by the jury and he challenges that conviction.

Defendant's central contention on appeal is that the trial court's interference with his exclusive access to the interpreter throughout the proceedings deprived him of a constitutional right.

We hold that article I, section 14, requires that when an interpreter is appointed for a non-English speaking accused, the accused has a constitutional right to the assistance of the interpreter throughout the entire proceeding. Accordingly, we find constitutional error in the proceedings below.

How the Problem Arose

On July 21, 1981, an altercation occurred between two farmworkers employed by Alfred Orosco Ramirez, a Sutter County labor contractor. The two employees, Jose Chaidez and Marcello Mata Aguilar both lived at the nearby labor camp. As the argument between the two Spanish speaking employees became heated, a crowd of fellow employees gathered. The argument escalated into a physical confrontation. Chaidez, the ultimate victim in this case, was the aggressor. The small crowd, which included Chaidez' son, Jose Aurelio Chaidez, witnessed the events; several persons unsuccessfully attempted to intervene.

Chaidez, who was heavier and taller than Mata Aguilar, delivered several blows to the defendant which caused him to be knocked down. Chaidez then picked up a large stick approximately 30 inches long and threatened and yelled at defendant. Frightened and in pain, defendant got up and retreated to his nearby sleeping quarters where he retrieved his rifle which he kept loaded. Defendant emerged from the building and advanced toward Chaidez. As Chaidez dropped the large stick, defendant fired a single shot.

The police arrived shortly thereafter. They ascertained that Chaidez was dead. Police Detective Wilbur Terry located defendant and took him to the sheriff's department to be interviewed. During the interview, Detective Terry learned that defendant could neither read or write Spanish, his native language, nor could he read or write English. He could speak only broken English. After being advised of his constitutional rights, defendant agreed to give the detective a statement. On August 19, 1981, defendant was charged with murder in violation of Penal Code section 187 and use of a firearm within the meaning of Penal Code section 12022.5.

At defendant's jury trial, the court appointed an interpreter for him. However, his interpreter was "borrowed" by the court to function as a witness interpreter for the benefit of the court and jury when Jose Aurelio Chaidez and Alfred Orosco Ramirez, two prosecution witnesses, were called to testify against him. Chaidez was the first witness for the prosecution. Because he was Spanish speaking, the prosecution suggested that he would need "the interpreter." Defense counsel, without consulting defendant, acquiesced in the "borrowing" of the interpreter. Chaidez, the only eyewitness other than defendant, testified about the verbal argument that preceded the physical altercation, the actions of his father and defendant prior to the shooting of his father, and defendant's conduct after the shooting. Orosco Ramirez was the last witness called by the prosecution. The court again directed that defendant's interpreter assist the witness in testifying against him. Counsel, again without consulting defendant, acquiesced in this suggestion. Although defense counsel cross-examined Chaidez, no cross-examination of Orosco Ramirez was conducted.

2. The Solution: Constitutional Right to an Interpreter Throughout the Proceedings

a. *The Parameters of the Right*

Article I, section 14 of the California Constitution was amended in 1974 by vote of the electorate to provide that "[a] person unable to understand English who is charged with a crime has a right to an interpreter *throughout the proceedings.*" (Italics added.) The trial court correctly appointed an interpreter for Mata Aguilar, thus complying with the portion of the Constitution which guarantees that an interpreter be provided. However, the trial court failed to follow the last three words of the constitutional provision "throughout the proceedings" when it deprived Mata Aguilar of that right by using his interpreter to translate for the prosecution's witnesses. California's Constitution does not provide a half measure of protection. Rather, it requires that when an interpreter is appointed for a criminal defendant, that interpreter must be provided to aid the accused during the whole course of the proceedings.

Interpreters play three different but essential roles in criminal proceedings: "They make the questioning of a non-English-speaking witness possible; they facilitate the non-English-speaking defendant's understanding of the colloquy between the attorneys, the witness, and the judge; and they enable the non-English speaking defendant and his English-speaking attorney to communicate . . . an interpreter performing the first service will be called a 'witness interpreter,' one performing the second service, a 'proceedings interpreter,' and one performing the third service a 'defense interpreter.' " (Chang & Araujo, *Interpreters for the Defense: Due Process for the Non-English-Speaking Defendant* (1975) 63 Cal.L.Rev. 801, 802; hereinafter cited as Chang & Araujo.) While the three roles are interrelated they are distinct.

The defendant's right to understand the instructions and rulings of the judge, the questions and objections of defense counsel and the prosecution, as well as the testimony of the witnesses is a continuous one. At moments crucial to the defense when evidentiary rulings and jury instructions are given by the court, when damaging testimony is being introduced the non-English speaking defendant who is denied the assistance of an interpreter, is unable to communicate with the court or with counsel and is unable to understand and participate in the proceedings which hold the key to freedom. Thus, the "borrowing" of the interpreter, the accused's only means of communicating with defense counsel and understanding the proceedings, was a denial of a constitutional right.

Our conclusion finds support in recent Court of Appeal rulings. *People* v. *Chavez* (1981) 124 Cal. App. 3d 215, held that a non-English speaking criminal defendant had been denied his constitutional right to receive interpreter assistance throughout the proceedings. The defendant was wholly without an interpreter during portions of the preliminary proceedings dealing with his competence to stand trial. In *Chavez,* defense counsel acted as an interpreter when Chavez was arraigned (*Id.,* at p. 221); a court-appointed official interpreter was provided for the entry of the plea (*Id.,* at pp. 222–223); and an unofficial interpreter was provided for part of the sentencing process. The Court of Appeal noted that prior to the 1974 amendment of article I, section 14, an interpreter was only required wherever it was "necessary" as a matter of due process. (See *People* v. *Annett* (1967) 251 Cal. App. 2d 858, 861–862.) The court went on to note, however, that "Article I, Section 14, now grants a non-English-speaking defendant the distinct right to an interpreter 'throughout the proceedings.' " (*People* v. *Chavez, supra,* 124 Cal. App.3d at p. 221.) Accordingly, the court found constitutional error in the trial court proceedings.

Recently, in *People* v. *Menchaca* (1983) 146 Cal. App. 3d 1019, the Court of Appeal found, "nothing short of a sworn interpreter at defendant's elbow," will satisfy the article I, section 14 guarantee to an interpreter throughout the proceedings. (*Id.* at p. 1025.) That case involved a Spanish speaking criminal defendant who was illiterate and neither spoke nor understood English. Like defendant Mata Aguilar, Menchaca was initially provided with an interpreter but the interpreter was removed during the testimony of a prosecution witness.

In concluding that a constitutional error had occurred, the *Menchaca* court took judicial notice that when an interpreter is utilized at trial, the interpreter and the witness speak to each other at relatively close range. The court stated, "Under such circumstances, it cannot be assumed a defendant clearly hears and understands the question and answer exchange in Spanish." (*Id.* at p. 1024.) The court observed that even if the defendant could understand the *answers* of the witness, it was not established that the defendant understood the testimony because, "[w]ithout a clear understanding of the *questions,* such testimony is essentially meaningless." (*Ibid.,* italics added.) Finally, the court mentioned that when acting as a witness interpreter, the same interpreter could not provide the defendant with translation of other integral parts of the proceedings, such as the open-court colloquy between bench and counsel and the rulings of the court. (*Id.* at p. 1025.) These concerns, of course, are equally applicable to the case at bench.

We find persuasive discussion in federal case law. One such case addresses the issue of interpreter assistance principally in terms of the right of confrontation under the Sixth Amendment of the United States Constitution. In *U.S.* ex. rel. *Negron* v. *New York* (2d Cir.1970) 434 F.2d 386, the appellate court found constitutional error in the failure of the trial court to provide a Spanish speaking defendant with an interpreter notwithstanding the fact that a prosecution interpreter provided the accused with periodic summaries of the proceedings. "The least we can require is that a court, put on notice of a defendant's severe language difficulty, make unmistakably clear to him that he has a right to have a competent translator to assist him, at state expense if need be, *throughout his trial.*" (*Id.* at pp. 390–391, italics added.) There, the defendant was unable to communicate with his counsel without the use of an interpreter. The single interpreter provided by the court was used primarily to interpret the testimony of the Spanish speaking witnesses for the court and jury. Negron's contacts with counsel through the interpreter were few. The concern of the district court in *Negron* is instructive: "[i]n order to afford Negron his right to confrontation, it was necessary under the circumstances that he be provided with a simultaneous translation of what was being said for the purpose of communicating with his attorney to enable the latter to effectively cross-examine those English-speaking witnesses to test their credibility, their memory and their accuracy of observation in light of Negron's version of the facts." (310 F. Supp. 1304, 1307 (E.D.N.Y.) affd., 434 F.2d 386.)

In affirming the granting of Negron's habeas corpus petition, the Second Circuit went beyond the right of confrontation, ". . . the right that was denied Negron seems to us even more consequential than the right of confrontation. Considerations of fairness, the integrity of the fact-finding process, and the potency of our adversary system of justice forbid that the state should prosecute a defendant who is not present at his own trial, [citation omitted], . . . [a]nd it is equally imperative that every criminal defendant if the right to be present is to have meaning possess 'sufficient present ability to consult with his lawyer with a reasonable degree of rational understanding.' " (434 F.2d at p. 389.)

The Judicial Council has recognized that under circumstances like that at bench the appointment of more than a single interpreter is warranted. "An interpreter is needed . . . if a party is unable to understand and speak English sufficiently to comprehend the proceedings and to assist counsel in the conduct of the case. Separate interpreters may be needed for each non-English speaking party. An additional interpreter may be needed to interpret witness testimony for the court." (Standards of Judicial Administration, section 18(a), appended to Cal. Rules of Court). Two interpreters were required in this case.

Compelling reasons exist for the appointment of more than one interpreter: "[It] is nearly impossible for one interpreter to translate the testimony of a witness while simultaneously translating and listening to the discussions between defendant and counsel. It is in these circumstances that a defense interpreter is most needed to ensure adequate representation by the defendant's counsel." (Chang & Araujo, at pp. 821–822.) Requiring two interpreters in cases such as the one before us has additional benefits to the criminal justice system because "it is difficult for an interpreter who has worked closely with the defendant and his counsel in the preparation of the defense from the pretrial stage to translate the court proceedings impartially. Finally, a separate defense interpreter would serve to ensure the accuracy of the proceedings and witness interpreters." (*Id.*, at p. 822.)

Without an interpreter, the trial is reduced to "a babble of voices" to the defendant. (*U.S.* ex rel. *Negron* v. *New York, supra,* 434 F.2d 386, at p. 388.) Sensitivity toward language difficulties is the hallmark of our multilingual state. This sensitivity has been appropriately elevated to constitutional proportions when the state, through the criminal process, places the life and liberty of the non-English speaker in jeopardy.

b. *The Waiver*

A reversal is required unless the defendant waived the constitutional right we have described. Was there a valid waiver? We reject the People's contention that consent of defense counsel to the use of Mata Aguilar's interpreter to translate testimony for the benefit of the jury and the court amounted to a waiver of the article I, section 14 right.

There is no indication in the record that defendant voluntarily and intelligently waived his constitutional right. Although prior to 1974, appointment of an interpreter could be waived by failure to request one, this is no longer the case. "The right to an interpreter having since been guaranteed in the Constitution, it may not validly be waived without an 'affirmative showing,' on the record, of waiver which was 'intelligent and voluntary' on the part of the affected defendant." (*People* v. *Chavez, supra,* 124 Cal. App. 3d 215, 227.) We agree and thus we hold that a personal waiver by the defendant was required. The mere acquiescence by counsel did not waive the right to interpreter assistance.

Further, the record does not support a conclusion that defendant knew he had a right to an interpreter throughout the proceedings. The issue of knowledge of the right to an interpreter was addressed by the Second Circuit in *Negron,* in which the court stated, "Simply to recall the classic definition of a waiver 'an intentional relinquishment or abandonment of a known right,' Johnson v. Zerbst, 304 U.S. 458 (1938) is a sufficient answer to the government's suggestion that Negron waived any fundamental right by his passive acquiescence in the grinding of the judicial machinery and his failure to affirmatively assert the right. For all that appears, Negron, who was clearly unaccustomed to asserting 'personal rights' against the authority of the judicial arm of the state, may well not have had the slightest notion that he had any 'rights' or any 'privilege' to assert them." (434 F.2d at p. 390.) Similarly, Mata Aguilar's inaction in demanding his personal right did not result in a waiver.

There is no indication in the record that defendant made a voluntary and intentional waiver. An exchange took place entirely in English between the court, the prosecutor, the interpreter, and defense counsel. The defendant was excluded. This conversation, being a "babble of voices" to the defendant, cannot be held to amount to a waiver by him of his right to an interpreter.

In the ethnic richness of California, a multiplicity of languages has been nurtured. Historically, many peoples speaking diverse tongues have formed large portions of our population. The people of this state, through the clear and express terms of their Constitution, require that all persons tried in a California court understand what is happening about them, for them, and against them. Who would have it otherwise?

The judgment is reversed.

BIRD, C.J., KAUS, J., BROUSSARD, J., and GRODIN, J., concurred.

---

**Question:** The *Aguilar* court finds support for its holding in federal constitutional law. In what way is the right to an interpreter more strongly anchored in California constitutional law than at the federal level?

## STATE V. DAMATO-KUSHEL

173 A.3d 357 (Conn. 2017)

* * *

PALMER, J.

This case is before us on a writ of error. The plaintiff in error claims that the trial court improperly precluded him, either personally or through his attorney, from attending plea negotiations and other discussions involving the court, the state's attorney and defense counsel during in-chambers, pretrial disposition conferences in the criminal prosecution of Kyle Damato-Kushel, which is now pending in the judicial district of Fairfield. In that criminal case, Damato-Kushel is charged with various offenses arising out of her alleged sexual misconduct involving the plaintiff in error commencing when Damato-Kushel was a teacher's aide in the school system of the town of Stratford and when the plaintiff in error was a fourteen year old student attending a school in that town. The plaintiff in error claims that the trial court's ruling barring his attendance at the pretrial disposition conferences violated his right as a victim "to attend the trial and all other court proceedings the accused has the right to attend" under article first, § 8, of the Connecticut constitution, as amended by articles seventeen and twenty-nine of the amendments (Conn. Const., amend. XXIX [b] [5]). The defendants in error, Damato-Kushel and the Superior Court, judicial district of Fairfield, maintain that the trial court correctly determined that such conferences, when they are conducted in chambers and off the record, do not constitute "court proceedings the accused has the right to attend" within the meaning of amendment XXIX (b) (5) and, therefore, that the court properly precluded the plaintiff in error from attending them. We agree with the defendants in error and, accordingly, dismiss the writ of error.

The following facts and procedural history are undisputed. On the basis of allegations lodged by the plaintiff in error, Damato-Kushel was arrested and charged with sexual assault in the second degree, risk of injury to a child, sexual assault in the fourth degree, and tampering with a witness. Shortly thereafter, Attorney James Clark of the Victim Rights Center of Connecticut, Inc., filed an appearance in the criminal case on behalf of the plaintiff in error.

At Damato-Kushel's arraignment, her counsel noted that Clark had filed an appearance in the case and advised the court that he objected to Clark's presence at any pretrial disposition conferences held in chambers. The court sustained the objection, explaining that amendment XXIX (b) (5) allows a victim to attend only those court proceedings that the defendant has a right to attend, and concluding that, because a defendant has no right to attend in-chambers, "judicial [pretrial]" conferences—generally, only his or her attorney attends such conferences—a victim also has no right to attend those conferences.

* * *

Thereafter, the plaintiff in error brought this writ of error against the defendants in error, claiming that the trial court's ruling barring him from all future, in-chambers, pretrial disposition conferences violated his rights under amendment XXIX (b) (5).

* * *

In this court, the plaintiff in error renews his contention in the trial court that in-chambers, pretrial disposition conferences are court proceedings that the accused—and thus the victim—have a right to attend under amendment XXIX (b) (5).

* * *

The plaintiff in error contends that the trial court improperly excluded his attorney from in-chambers, pretrial disposition conferences at which the presiding judge, the state's attorney and Damato-Kushel's counsel engaged in plea negotiations, in violation of his "right to attend the trial and all other court proceedings the accused has the right to attend," as guaranteed by amendment XXIX (b) (5). The defendants in error maintain that the trial court properly concluded that a victim's right to attend does not include off-the-record, in-chambers disposition conferences both because such conferences are not "court proceedings" and because the defendant has no right to attend them.

Amendment XXIX (b) (5) of the Connecticut constitution provides in relevant part that, "[i]n all criminal prosecutions, a victim shall have the right to attend the trial and all other court proceedings the accused has the right to attend, unless such person is to testify and the court determines that such person's testimony would be materially affected if such person hears other testimony." With respect to the contention of the defendants in error that the plaintiff in error has no right to attend the pretrial conferences at issue because they are not "court proceedings," as that term is used in amendment XXIX (b) (5), the term appears twice in the victim's rights amendment; see Conn. Const., amend. XXIX (b) (5); see also Conn. Const., amend. XXIX (b) (4) ("the right to notification of court proceedings"); but the term is not defined in the state constitution, in our statutes, or in any case of this court or the Appellate Court. At the time of the amendment, however, Black's Law Dictionary defined "proceeding" as, inter alia, "[a]n act [that] is done by the authority or direction of the court, agency, or tribunal, express or implied" and noted that it "may be used to describe any act done by authority of a court of law." Black's Law Dictionary (6th Ed. 1990) p. 1204. The modifier "court" therefore might reasonably distinguish proceedings undertaken pursuant to the authority of a court of law, such as disposition conferences, from those undertaken by an agency or other tribunal. On the other hand, "court proceedings" also may reasonably be construed to limit the "act[s] done by authority of a court of law"; id.; to those taking place within the physical bounds of a courtroom, as opposed to those acts, like the execution of a bench warrant, undertaken elsewhere. See Webster's Ninth New Collegiate Dictionary (1987) p. 299 ("court" may be "a place for the administration of justice").

* * *

The text of amendment XXIX (b) makes clear that a victim's right to attend such conferences is wholly contingent on the defendant's right of attendance. See Conn. Const., amend. XXIX (b) (5). This court has previously determined, however, in State v. Lopez 497 A.2d 390 (1985), that a defendant possesses no such right under our rules of practice. In that case, the defendant, Jose Lopez, claimed that the trial court improperly had excluded him from "a secret pretrial conference between the court, the [s]tate's [a]ttorney, and [defense counsel]," in which plea negotiations were conducted. (Internal quotation marks omitted.) Id., 348. We rejected Lopez' claim, explaining that, "[a]lthough there may have been a disposition conference from which [Lopez] was excluded, under our established rules of practice neither [Lopez] nor the public is entitled to attend such a proceeding. In fact, under Practice Book §§ [39–1 and 39–2], the [state] is not permitted to engage in plea negotiations directly with a defendant who is represented by counsel, except with defense counsel's permission. [See Practice Book §§ 39–1 and 39–2]; [s]ee also Practice Book § [39–14]. Furthermore, Practice Book § [44–7] does not include the disposition conference or plea negotiations among the specifically enumerated situations [in which] a criminal defendant has the right to be present." (Footnotes added and omitted.) State v. Lopez, supra, 349–50. Thus, Lopez—and, indeed, Practice Book § 44–7 itself—leaves no doubt that a defendant has no right to attend a disposition conference under our rules of practice. Moreover, the plaintiff in error makes no claim that he has a statutory or constitutional right independent of the victim's rights amendment to attend such a conference.

* * *

By contrast, a victim's right to participate meaningfully in the plea bargaining process is safeguarded by other provisions of the victim's rights amendment—in particular, "the right to communicate with the prosecution" under amendment XXIX (b) (6), "the right to make a statement to the court" regarding any plea agreement prior to its acceptance under amendment XXIX (b) (7), and the broader, more encompassing right under amendment XXIX (b) "to be treated with fairness and respect throughout the criminal justice process." Conn. Const., amend. XXIX (b) (1); see, e.g., State v. Thomas, 296 Conn. 375, 390 n.11, 995 A.2d 65 (2010) (legislature sought to give victims " 'true role' " in plea bargaining process by giving victim right to be heard prior to acceptance of plea); S. Welling, "Victim Participation in Plea Bargains," 65 Wash. U. L.Q. 301, 355 (1987) (arguing that victim's right to participate in plea bargains "is best defined as a right to be heard by the trial judge before the plea bargain is accepted"). To the extent that the plaintiff in error suggests that state's attorneys cannot be relied on to adequately communicate the information necessary for a victim to comment on the appropriateness of any plea bargain, we reject that assertion. We have every reason to believe that state's attorneys will fully discharge their constitutional, statutory, and professional responsibilities to victims; see Conn. Const., amend. XXIX (b); General Statutes § 54–91c; see also A.B.A., Criminal Justice Standards for the Prosecution Function (4th Ed. 2015) standard 3–3.4 (i); and that, in the unlikely case of a willful failure to do so, such misconduct will not be taken lightly. See, e.g., Attorney Grievance Commission v. Smith, 109 A.3d 1184 (2015) (prosecutor sanctioned for violating Maryland Lawyer's Rules of Professional Conduct by repeatedly and willfully failing to communicate with victim).

We note, finally, that considerations of public policy—as primarily reflected in court rules and practices, all of which are consistent with constitutional requirements—support our determination that a victim's right of attendance under amendment XXIX (b) (5) does not extend to off-the-record, in-chambers disposition conferences. For better or for worse, plea bargaining involving the court, the state and the defendant has become an important tool for the efficient and orderly disposition of our criminal court dockets. See, e.g., State v. Elson, 91 A.3d 862 (2014) (documenting "our state's extremely heavy reliance on plea bargaining in resolving criminal cases"); State v. Revelo, 775 A.2d 260 ("[w]hatever might be the situation in an ideal world, the fact is that the guilty plea and the often concomitant plea bargain are important components of [the] criminal justice system" [internal quotation marks omitted]), cert. denied, 534 U.S. 1052 (2001). Moreover, although many jurisdictions forbid or strictly limit judicial participation in plea conferences, practice and policy in Connecticut recognize that judges may play a valuable role in facilitating plea negotiations. See State v. Revelo, supra, 508 n.25 ("[i]t is a common practice in this state for the presiding criminal judge to conduct plea negotiations with the parties"); J. Turner, "Judicial Participation in Plea Negotiations: A Comparative View," 54 Am. J. Comp. L. 199, 201, 214 (2006) (explaining that, unlike judges in many states, Connecticut judges "are actively involved in the negotiations as moderators and comment not only on the ultimate sentence acceptable to the court, but also on the merits of the case," and arguing that such "[a]ctive judicial participation" in plea negotiations may be "a better way to promote accuracy and fairness in plea bargaining"). We agree with the defendants in error that the likelihood of defense counsel being willing to engage candidly with the state's attorney and the presiding judge during plea discussions would be greatly diminished by the presence of the victim or the victim's representative at such conferences. In such circumstances, the judicial role in plea negotiations will be sharply reduced in contravention of our established public policy.

We therefore conclude that in-chambers, off-the-record disposition conferences between the prosecuting attorney, defense counsel, and the presiding judge are not "court proceedings the accused has the right to attend" under amendment XXIX (b) (5). Consequently, neither the victim nor his authorized representative has a right to attend them.

The writ of error is dismissed.

---

**Questions:** Are society's interests in allowing criminal defendants and victims to attend court proceedings the same? Does the *Damato-Kushel* court acknowledge the different situations of these stakeholders?

# CHAPTER 17

# STATUTORY INTERPRETATION

■ ■ ■

## CONTEXT & SOURCES

The balance of this casebook is devoted to the interpretation of statutes. Unlike constitutions, which are general outlines of governance structure, statutes are focused on specific topics that legislatures desire to regulate. As well, constitutions are far more difficult to change, while legislation can be more easily revised, often in response to judicial review holding it unconstitutional or unclear. This chapter covers the two major interpretive approaches—plain meaning and legislative intent—as well as the role of technical sources like dictionaries.

James Willard Hurst, *Dealing with Statutes* (Columbia University Press, 1982), concisely introduces the topic. For a judicial perspective, including comments on the judge's own decisions, see Robert A. Katzmann, *Judging Statutes* (Oxford University Press, 2016). The classic explanation of the "plain meaning rule," is Oliver Wendell Holmes, Jr., "The Theory of Legal Interpretation," *Collected Legal Papers* 203–209 (Peter Smith, 1952) (1920). A key case on the "purposive" approach is detailed in Philip P. Frickey and William N. Eskridge, Jr., "The Story of *Steelworkers v. Weber*: Statutory Text, Spirit, and Practical Reasoning," *Statutory Interpretation Stories* 92–125 (William N. Eskridge, Jr., & Philip P. Frickey, eds., Foundation, 2011).

## PLAIN MEANING RULE

### MCBOYLE V. UNITED STATES

283 U.S. 25 (1931)

* * *

MR. JUSTICE HOLMES delivered the opinion of the Court.

The petitioner was convicted of transporting from Ottawa, Illinois, to Guymon, Oklahoma, an airplane that he knew to have been stolen, and was sentenced to serve three years' imprisonment and to pay a fine of $2,000. The judgment was affirmed by the Circuit Court of Appeals for the Tenth Circuit. 43 F.(2d) 273. A writ of certiorari was granted by this Court on the question whether the National Motor Vehicle Theft Act applies to aircraft. Act of October 29, 1919, c. 89, 41 Stat. 324, U. S. Code, title 18, § 408 (18 USCA § 408). That Act provides: 'Sec. 2. That when used in this Act: (a) The term 'motor vehicle' shall include an automobile, automobile truck, automobile wagon, motor cycle, or any other self-propelled vehicle not designed for running on rails. * * * Sec. 3. That whoever shall transport or cause to be transported in interstate or foreign commerce a motor vehicle, knowing the same to have been stolen, shall be punished by a fine of not more than $5,000, or by imprisonment of not more than five years, or both.'

Section 2 defines the motor vehicles of which the transportation in interstate commerce is punished in Section 3. The question is the meaning of the word 'vehicle' in the phrase 'any other self-propelled vehicle not designed for running on rails.' No doubt etymologically it is possible to use the word to signify a conveyance working on land, water or air, and sometimes legislation extends the use in that direction, e. g., land and air, water being separately provided for, in the Tariff Act, September 21, 1922, c. 356, § 401(b), 42 Stat. 858, 948 (19 USCA § 231(b). But in everyday speech 'vehicle' calls up the picture of a thing moving on land. Thus in Rev. St. § 4 (1 USCA § 4) intended, the Government suggests, rather to enlarge than to restrict the definition, vehicle includes every contrivance capable of being used 'as a means of transportation on land.' And this is repeated, expressly excluding aircraft, in the Tariff Act, June 17, 1930, c. 497, § 401(b), 46 Stat. 590, 708 (19 USCA § 1401). So here, the phrase under discussion calls up the popular picture. For after including automobile truck, automobile wagon and motor cycle, the words 'any other self-propelled vehicle not designed for running on rails' still indicate that a vehicle in the popular sense, that is a vehicle running on land is the theme. It is a vehicle that runs, not something, not commonly called a vehicle, that flies. Airplanes were well known in 1919 when this statute was passed, but it is admitted that they were not mentioned in the reports or in the debates in Congress. It is impossible to read words that so carefully enumerate the different forms of motor vehicles and have no reference of any kind to aircraft, as including airplanes under a term that usage more and more precisely confines to a different class. The counsel for the petitioner have shown that the phraseology of the statute as to motor vehicles follows that of earlier statutes of Connecticut, Delaware, Ohio, Michigan and Missouri, not to mention the late Regulations of Traffic for the District of Columbia, title 6, c. 9, § 242, none of which can be supposed to leave the earth.

Although it is not likely that a criminal will carefully consider the text of the law before he murders or steals, it is reasonable that a fair warning should be given to the world in language that the common world will understand, of what the law intends to do if a certain line is passed. To make the warning fair, so far as possible the line should be clear. When a rule of conduct is laid down in words that evoke in the common mind only the pleture [image] of vehicles moving on land, the statute should not be extended to aircraft simply because it may seem to us that a similar policy applies, or upon the speculation that if the legislature had thought of it, very likely the picture of vehicles moving on land, the United States v. Bhagat Singh Thind, 261 U. S. 204, 209.

Judgment reversed.

---

**Question:** In *McBoyle,* which exemplifies the "plain meaning rule" of interpretation, why do you think the trial court and the 10th Circuit departed from applying the statute literally?

# LEGISLATIVE INTENT

## UNITED STEELWORKERS OF AMERICA V. WEBER

443 U.S. 193 (1979)

* * *

MR. JUSTICE BRENNAN delivered the opinion of the Court.

Challenged here is the legality of an affirmative action plan collectively bargained by an employer and a union—that reserves for black employees 50% of the openings in an in-plant craft-training program until the percentage of black craft-workers in the plant is commensurate with the percentage of blacks in the local labor force. The question for decision is whether Congress, in Title VII of the Civil Rights Act of 1964, 78 Stat., 253, as amended, 42 U.S.C. § 2000e *et seq.*, left employers and unions in the private sector free to take such race-conscious steps to eliminate manifest racial imbalances in traditionally segregated job categories. We hold that Title VII does not prohibit such race-conscious affirmative action plans.

In 1974, petitioner United Steelworkers of America (USWA) and petitioner Kaiser Aluminum & Chemical Corp. (Kaiser) entered into a master collective-bargaining agreement covering terms and conditions of employment at 15 Kaiser plants. The agreement contained, *inter alia,* an affirmative action plan designed to eliminate conspicuous racial imbalances in Kaiser's then almost exclusively white craft-work forces. Black craft-hiring goals were set for each Kaiser plant equal to the percentage of blacks in the respective local labor forces. To enable plants to meet these goals, on-the-job training programs were established to teach unskilled production workers—black and white—the skills necessary to become craftworkers. The plan reserved for black employees 50% of the openings in these newly created in-plant training programs.

This case arose from the operation of the plan at Kaiser's plant in Gramercy, La. Until 1974, Kaiser hired as craftworkers for that plant only persons who had had prior craft experience. Because blacks had long been excluded from craft unions, few were able to present such credentials. As a consequence, prior to 1974 only 1.83% (5 out of 273) of the skilled craftworkers at the Gramercy plant were black, even though the work force in the Gramercy area was approximately 39% black.

Pursuant to the national agreement Kaiser altered its craft-hiring practice in the Gramercy plant. Rather than hiring already trained outsiders, Kaiser established a training program to train its production workers to fill craft openings. Selection of craft trainees was made on the basis of seniority, with the proviso that at least 50% of the new trainees were to be black until the percentage of black skilled craftworkers in the Gramercy plant approximated the percentage of blacks in the local labor force. See 415 F.Supp. 761, 764.

During 1974, the first year of the operation of the Kaiser-USWA affirmative action plan, 13 craft trainees were selected from Gramercy's production work force. Of these, seven were black and six white. The most senior black selected into the program had less seniority than several white production workers whose bids for admission were rejected. Thereafter one of those white production workers, respondent Brian Weber (hereafter respondent), instituted this class action in the United States District Court for the Eastern District of Louisiana.

The complaint alleged that the filling of craft trainee positions at the Gramercy plant pursuant to the affirmative action program had resulted in junior black employees' receiving training in preference to senior white employees, thus discriminating against respondent and other similarly situated white employees in violation of §§ 703(a) and (d) of Title VII. The District Court held that the plan violated Title VII, entered a judgment in favor of the plaintiff class, and granted a permanent injunction prohibiting Kaiser and the USWA "from denying plaintiffs, Brian F. Weber and all other members of the class, access to on-the-job training programs on the basis of race." App. 171. A divided panel of the Court of Appeals for the Fifth Circuit affirmed, holding that all employment preferences based upon race, including those preferences incidental to bona fide affirmative action plans, violated Title VII's prohibition against racial discrimination in employment. 563 F.2d 216 (1977). We granted certiorari. 439 U.S. 1045. We reverse.

We emphasize at the outset the narrowness of our inquiry. Since the Kaiser-USWA plan does not involve state action, this case does not present an alleged violation of the Equal Protection Clause of the Fourteenth Amendment. Further, since the Kaiser-USWA plan was adopted voluntarily, we are not concerned with what Title VII requires or with what a court might order to remedy a past proved violation of the Act. The only question before us is the narrow statutory issue of whether Title VII *forbids* private employers and unions from voluntarily agreeing upon bona fide affirmative action plans that accord racial preferences in the manner and for the purpose provided in the Kaiser-USWA plan. That question was expressly left open in *McDonald v. Santa Fe Trail Transp. Co.*, 427 U.S. 273, 281 n. 8 (1976), which held, in a case not involving affirmative action, that Title VII protects whites as well as blacks from certain forms of racial discrimination.

Respondent argues that Congress intended in Title VII to prohibit all race-conscious affirmative action plans. Respondent's argument rests upon a literal interpretation of §§ 703(a) and (d) of the Act. Those sections make it unlawful to "discriminate . . . because of . . . race" in hiring and in the selection of apprentices for training programs. Since, the argument runs, *McDonald v. Sante Fe Trail Transp. Co., supra,* settled that Title VII forbids discrimination against whites as well as blacks, and since the Kaiser-USWA affirmative action plan operates to discriminate against white employees solely because they are white, it follows that the Kaiser-USWA plan violates Title VII.

Respondent's argument is not without force. But it overlooks the significance of the fact that the Kaiser-USWA plan is an affirmative action plan voluntarily adopted by private parties to eliminate traditional patterns of racial segregation. In this context respondent's reliance upon a literal construction of §§ 703(a) and (d) and upon *McDonald* is misplaced. See *McDonald v. Sante Fe Trail Transp. Co., supra,* at 281 n. 8. It is a "familiar rule that a thing may be within the letter of the statute and yet not within the statute, because not within its spirit nor within the intention of its makers." *Holy Trinity Church v. United States,* 143 U.S. 457, 459 (1892). The prohibition against racial discrimination in §§ 703(a) and (d) of Title VII must therefore be read against the background of the legislative history of Title VII and the historical context from which the Act arose. See [citations.] Examination of those sources makes clear that an interpretation of the sections that forbade all race-conscious affirmative action would "bring about an end completely at variance with the purpose of the statute" and must be rejected. [citations.]

Congress' primary concern in enacting the prohibition against racial discrimination in Title VII of the Civil Rights Act of 1964 was with "the plight of the Negro in our economy." 110 Cong.Rec. 6548 (1964) (remarks of Sen. Humphrey). Before 1964, blacks were largely relegated to "unskilled and semi-skilled jobs." *Ibid.* (remarks of Sen. Humphrey); *id.*, at 7204 (remarks of Sen. Clark); *id.*, at 7379–7380 (remarks of Sen. Kennedy). Because of automation the number of such jobs was rapidly decreasing. See *id.*, at 6548 (remarks of Sen. Humphrey); *id.*, at 7204 (remarks of Sen. Clark). As a consequence, "the relative position of the Negro worker [was] steadily worsening. In 1947 the nonwhite unemployment rate was only 64 percent higher than the white rate; in 1962 it was 124 percent higher." *Id.*, at 6547 (remarks of Sen. Humphrey). See also *id.*, at 7204 (remarks of Sen. Clark). Congress considered this a serious social problem. As Senator Clark told the Senate:

"The rate of Negro unemployment has gone up consistently as compared with white unemployment for the past 15 years. This is a social malaise and a social situation which we should not tolerate. That is one of the principal reasons why the bill should pass." *Id.*, at 7220.

Congress feared that the goals of the Civil Rights Act—the integration of blacks into the mainstream of American society could not be achieved unless this trend were reversed. And Congress recognized that that would not be possible unless blacks were able to secure jobs "which have a future." *Id.*, at 7204 (remarks of Sen. Clark). See also *id.*, at 7379–7380 (remarks of Sen. Kennedy). As Senator Humphrey explained to the Senate:

"What good does it do a Negro to be able to eat in a fine restaurant if he cannot afford to pay the bill? What good does it do him to be accepted in a hotel that is too expensive for his modest income? How can a Negro child be motivated to take full advantage of integrated educational facilities if he has no hope of getting a job where he can use that education?" *Id.*, at 6547.

"Without a job, one cannot afford public convenience and accommodations. Income from employment may be necessary to further a man's education, or that of his children. If his children have no hope of getting a good job, what will motivate them to take advantage of educational opportunities?" *Id.*, at 6552.

These remarks echoed President Kennedy's original message to Congress upon the introduction of the Civil Rights Act in 1963.

"There is little value in a Negro's obtaining the right to be admitted to hotels and restaurants if he has no cash in his pocket and no job." 109 Cong.Rec. at 11159.

Accordingly, it was clear to Congress that "[t]he crux of the problem [was] to open employment opportunities for Negroes in occupations which have been traditionally closed to them," 10 Cong.Rec. 6548 (1964) (remarks of Sen. Humphrey), and it was to this problem that Title VII's prohibition against racial discrimination in employment was primarily addressed.

It plainly appears from the House Report accompanying the Civil Rights Act that Congress did not intend wholly to prohibit private and voluntary affirmative action efforts as one method of solving this problem. The Report provides:

"No bill can or should lay claim to eliminating all of the causes and consequences of racial and other types of discrimination against minorities. There is reason to believe, however, that national leadership provided by the enactment of Federal legislation dealing with the most troublesome problems *will create an atmosphere conducive to voluntary or local resolution of other forms of discrimination.*" H.R.Rep. No. 914, 88th Cong., 1st Sess., pt. 1, p. 18 (1963); U.S.Code Cong. & Admin.News 1964, pp. 2355, 2393. (Emphasis supplied.)

Given this legislative history, we cannot agree with respondent that Congress intended to prohibit the private sector from taking effective steps to accomplish the goal that Congress designed Title VII to achieve. The very statutory words intended as a spur or catalyst to cause "employers and unions to self-examine and to self-evaluate their employment practices and to endeavor to eliminate, so far as possible, the last vestiges of an unfortunate and ignominious page in this country's history," *Albemarle Paper Co. v. Moody*, 422 U.S. 405, 418 (1975), cannot be interpreted as an absolute prohibition against all private, voluntary, race-conscious affirmative action efforts to hasten the elimination of such vestiges. It would be ironic indeed if a law triggered by a Nation's concern over centuries of racial injustice and intended to improve the lot of those who had "been excluded from the American dream for so long," 110 Cong.Rec. 6552 (1964) (remarks of Sen. Humphrey), constituted the first legislative prohibition of all voluntary, private, race-conscious efforts to abolish traditional patterns of racial segregation and hierarchy.

Our conclusion is further reinforced by examination of the language and legislative history of § 703(j) of Title VII. Opponents of Title VII raised two related arguments against the bill. First, they argued that the Act would be interpreted to *require* employers with racially imbalanced work forces to grant preferential treatment to racial minorities in order to integrate. Second, they argued that employers with racially imbalanced work forces would grant preferential treatment to racial minorities, even if not required to do so by the Act. See 110 Cong.Rec. 8618–8619 (1964) (remarks of Sen. Sparkman). Had Congress meant to prohibit all race-conscious affirmative action, as respondent urges, it easily could have answered both objections by providing that Title VII would not require or *permit* racially preferential integration efforts. But Congress did not choose such a course. Rather, Congress added § 703(j) which addresses only the first objection. The section provides that nothing contained in Title VII "shall be interpreted to *require* any employer . . . to grant preferential treatment . . . to any group because of the race . . . of such . . . group on account of" a *de facto* racial imbalance in the employer's work force. The section does *not* state that "nothing in Title VII shall be interpreted to *permit*" voluntary affirmative efforts to correct racial imbalances. The natural inference is that Congress chose not to forbid all voluntary race-conscious affirmative action.

The reasons for this choice are evident from the legislative record. Title VII could not have been enacted into law without substantial support from legislators in both Houses who traditionally resisted federal regulation of private business. Those legislators demanded as a price for their support that "management prerogatives, and union freedoms . . . be left undisturbed to the greatest extent possible." H.R.Rep. No. 914, 88th Cong., 1st Sess., pt. 2, p. 29 (1963), U.S.Code Cong. & Admin.News 1964, p. 2391. Section 703(j) was proposed by Senator Dirksen to allay any fears that the Act might be interpreted in such a way as to upset this compromise. The section was designed to prevent § 703 of Title VII from being interpreted in such a way as to lead to undue "Federal Government interference with private businesses because of some Federal employee's ideas about racial balance or racial imbalance." 110 Cong.Rec. 14314 (1964) (remarks of Sen. Miller). See also *id.*, at 9881 (remarks of Sen. Allott); *id.*, at 10520 (remarks of Sen. Carlson); *id.*, at 11471 (remarks of Sen. Javits); *id.*, at 12817 (remarks of Sen. Dirksen). Clearly, a prohibition against all voluntary, race-conscious, affirmative action efforts would disserve these ends. Such a prohibition would augment the powers of the Federal Government and diminish traditional management prerogatives while at the same time impeding attainment of the ultimate statutory goals. In view of this legislative history and in view of Congress' desire to avoid undue federal regulation of private businesses, use of the word "require" rather than the phrase "require or permit" in § 703(j) fortifies the conclusion that Congress did not intend to limit traditional business freedom to such a degree as to prohibit all voluntary, race-conscious affirmative action.

We therefore hold that Title VII's prohibition in §§ 703(a) and (d) against racial discrimination does not condemn all private, voluntary, race-conscious affirmative action plans.

We need not today define in detail the line of demarcation between permissible and impermissible affirmative action plans. It suffices to hold that the challenged Kaiser-USWA affirmative action plan falls on the permissible side of the line. The purposes of the plan mirror those of the statute. Both were designed to break down old patterns of racial segregation and hierarchy. Both were structured to "open employment opportunities for Negroes in occupations which have been traditionally closed to them." 110 Cong.Rec. 6548 (1964) (remarks of Sen. Humphrey).

At the same time, the plan does not unnecessarily trammel the interests of the white employees. The plan does not require the discharge of white workers and their replacement with new black hirees. Cf. *McDonald v. Santa Fe Trail Transp. Co.*, 427 U.S. 273, (1976). Nor does the plan create an absolute bar to the advancement of white employees;

half of those trained in the program will be white. Moreover, the plan is a temporary measure; it is not intended to maintain racial balance, but simply to eliminate a manifest racial imbalance. Preferential selection of craft trainees at the Gramercy plant will end as soon as the percentage of black skilled craftworkers in the Gramercy plant approximates the percentage of blacks in the local labor force. See 415 F.Supp., at 763.

We conclude, therefore, that the adoption of the Kaiser-USWA plan for the Gramercy plant falls within the area of discretion left by Title VII to the private sector voluntarily to adopt affirmative action plans designed to eliminate conspicuous racial imbalance in traditionally segregated job categories. Accordingly, the judgment of the Court of Appeals for the Fifth Circuit is

*Reversed.*

MR. JUSTICE BLACKMUN, concurring.

* * *

I . . . think it significant that, while the Court's opinion does not foreclose other forms of affirmative action, the Kaiser program it approves is a moderate one. The opinion notes that the program does not afford an absolute preference for blacks, and that it ends when the racial composition of Kaiser's craft workforce matches the racial composition of the local population. It thus operates as a temporary tool for remedying past discrimination without attempting to "maintain" a previously achieved balance. *See University of California Regents v. Bakke,* 438 U. S. 265, 438 U. S. 342 n. 17 (1978) (opinion of BRENNAN, WHITE, MARSHALL, and BLACKMUN, JJ.). Because the duration of the program is finite, it perhaps will end even before the "stage of maturity when action along this line is no longer necessary." *Id.* at 438 U. S. 403 (opinion of BLACKMUN, J.). And if the Court has misperceived the political will, it has the assurance that, because the question is statutory, Congress may set a different course if it so chooses.

The jobs in question here include those of carpenter, electrician, general repairman, insulator, machinist, and painter. App. 165. The sources cited *ante* at 443 U. S. 198 n. 1, establish, for example, that, although 11.7% of the United States population in 1970 was black, the percentage of blacks among the membership of carpenters' unions in 1972 was only 3.7%. For painters, the percentage was 4.9, and for electricians, 2.6. U.S. Commission on Civil Rights, The Challenge Ahead: Equal Opportunity in Referral Unions 274, 281 (1976). Kaiser's Director of Equal Opportunity Affairs testified that, as a result of discrimination in employment and training opportunity, blacks were underrepresented in skilled crafts "in every industry in the United States, and in every area of the United States." App. 90. While the parties dispute the cause of the relative underrepresentation of blacks in Kaiser's craft workforce, the Court of Appeals indicated that it thought "the general lack of skills among available blacks" was responsible. 563 F.2d 216, 224 n. 13. There can be little doubt that any lack of skill has its roots in purposeful discrimination of the past, including segregated and inferior trade schools for blacks in Louisiana, U.S. Commission on Civil Rights, 50 States Report 209 (1961); traditionally all-white craft unions in that State, including the electrical workers and the plumbers, *id.* at 208; union nepotism, *Asbestos Workers v. Vogler,* 407 F.2d 1047 (CA5 1969); and segregated apprenticeship programs, F. Marshall & V. Briggs, The Negro and Apprenticeship 27 (1967).

MR. JUSTICE REHNQUIST, with whom THE CHIEF JUSTICE joins, dissenting.

In a very real sense, the Court's opinion is ahead of its time: it could more appropriately have been handed down five years from now, in 1984, a year coinciding with the title of a book from which the Court's opinion borrows, perhaps subconsciously, at least one idea. Orwell describes in his book a governmental official of Oceania, one of the three great world powers, denouncing the current enemy, Eurasia, to an assembled crowd:

"It was almost impossible to listen to him without being first convinced and then maddened. . . . The speech had been proceeding for perhaps twenty minutes when a messenger hurried onto the platform and a scrap of paper was slipped into the speaker's hand. He unrolled and read it without pausing in his speech. Nothing altered in his voice or manner, or in the content of what he was saying, but suddenly the names were different. Without words said, a wave of understanding rippled through the crowd. Oceania was at war with Eastasia! . . . The banners and posters with which the square was decorated were all wrong! . . .

"[T]he speaker had switched from one line to the other actually in mid-sentence, not only without a pause, but without even breaking the syntax." G. Orwell, Nineteen Eighty-Four 181–182 (1949).

Today's decision represents an equally dramatic and equally unremarked switch in this Court's interpretation of Title VII.

The operative sections of Title VII prohibit racial discrimination in employment *simpliciter*. Taken in its normal meaning and as understood by all Members of Congress who spoke to the issue during the legislative debates, see *infra,* at 231–251, this language prohibits a covered employer from considering race when making an employment decision, whether the race be black or white. Several years ago, however, a United States District Court held that "the dismissal of white employees charged with misappropriating company property while not dismissing a similarly charged Negro employee does not raise a claim upon which Title VII relief may be granted." *McDonald v. Santa Fe Trail Transp. Co.,* 427 U.S. 273 (1976). This Court unanimously reversed, concluding from the "uncontradicted legislative history" that "[T]itle VII prohibits racial discrimination against the white petitioners in this case upon the same standards as would be applicable were they Negroes . . . ." *Id.*, at 280.

We have never wavered in our understanding that Title VII "prohibits *all* racial discrimination in employment, without exception for any group of particular employees." *Id.*, at 283, at 2580 (emphasis in original). In *Griggs v. Duke Power Co.*, 401 U.S. 424, 431, (1971), our first occasion to interpret Title VII, a unanimous Court observed that "[d]iscriminatory preference, for any group, minority or majority, is precisely and only what Congress has proscribed." And in our most recent discussion of the issue, we uttered words seemingly dispositive of this case: "It is clear beyond cavil that the obligation imposed by Title VII is to provide an equal opportunity for *each* applicant regardless of race, without regard to whether members of the applicant's race are already proportionately represented in the work force." *Furnco Construction Corp. v. Waters,* 438 U.S. 567, 579, (1978) (emphasis in original).

Today, however, the Court behaves much like the Orwellian speaker earlier described, as if it had been handed a note indicating that Title VII would lead to a result unacceptable to the Court if interpreted here as it was in our prior decisions. Accordingly, without even a break in syntax, the Court rejects "a literal construction of § 703(a)" in favor of newly discovered "legislative history," which leads it to a conclusion directly contrary to that compelled by the "uncontradicted legislative history" unearthed in *McDonald* and our other prior decisions. Now we are told that the legislative history of Title VII shows that employers are free to discriminate on the basis of race: an employer may, in the Court's words, "trammel the interests of the white employees" in favor of black employees in order to eliminate "racial imbalance." *Ante,* at 208. Our earlier interpretations of Title VII, like the banners and posters decorating the square in Oceania, were all wrong.

As if this were not enough to make a reasonable observer question this Court's adherence to the oft-stated principle that our duty is to construe rather than rewrite legislation, *United States v. Rutherford,* 442 U.S. 544, 555, (1979), the Court also seizes upon § 703(j) of Title VII as an independent, or at least partially independent, basis for its holding. Totally ignoring the wording of that section, which is obviously addressed to those charged with the responsibility of interpreting the law rather than those who are subject to its proscriptions, and totally ignoring the months of legislative debates preceding the section's introduction and passage, which demonstrate clearly that it was enacted to prevent precisely what occurred in this case, the Court infers from § 703(j) that "Congress chose not to forbid all voluntary race-conscious affirmative action." *Ante,* at 206.

Thus, by a *tour de force* reminiscent not of jurists such as Hale, Holmes, and Hughes, but of escape artists such as Houdini, the Court eludes clear statutory language, "uncontradicted" legislative history and uniform precedent in concluding that employers are, after all, permitted to consider race in making employment decisions. It may be that one or more of the principal sponsors of Title VII would have preferred to see a provision allowing preferential treatment of minorities written into the bill. Such a provision, however, would have to have been expressly or impliedly excepted from Title VII's explicit prohibition on all racial discrimination in employment. There is no such exception in the Act. And a reading of the legislative debates concerning Title VII, in which proponents and opponents alike uniformly denounced discrimination in favor of, as well as discrimination against, Negroes, demonstrates clearly that any legislator harboring an unspoken desire for such a provision could not possibly have succeeded in enacting it into law.

* * *

When H.R. 7152 reached the House floor, the opening speech in support of its passage was delivered by Representative Celler, Chairman of the House Judiciary Committee and the Congressman responsible for introducing the legislation. A portion of that speech responded to criticism "seriously misrepresent[ing] what the bill would do and grossly distort[ing] its effects":

"[T]he charge has been made that the Equal Employment Opportunity Commission to be established by title VII of the bill would have the power to prevent a business from employing and promoting the people it wished, and that a 'Federal inspector' could then order the hiring and promotion only of employees of certain races or religious groups. This description of the bill is entirely wrong. . . .

"Even [a] court could not order that any preference be given to any particular race, religion or other group, but would be limited to ordering an end of discrimination. The statement that a Federal inspector could order the employment and promotion only of members of a specific racial or religious group is therefore patently erroneous.

". . . The Bill would do no more than prevent . . . employers from discriminating against *or in favor* of workers because of their race, religion, or national origin.

* * *

There is perhaps no device more destructive to the notion of equality than the *numerus clausus*—the quota. Whether described as "benign discrimination" or "affirmative action," the racial quota is nonetheless a creator of castes, a two-edged sword that must demean one in order to prefer another. In passing Title VII, Congress outlawed *all* racial discrimination, recognizing that no discrimination based on race is benign, that no action disadvantaging a person because of his color is affirmative. With today's holding, the Court introduces into Title VII a tolerance for the very evil that the law was intended to eradicate, without offering even a clue as to what the limits on that tolerance may be. We are told simply that Kaiser's racially discriminatory admission quota "falls on the permissible side of the line." *Ante,* at 208. By going not merely *beyond,* but directly *against* Title VII's language and legislative history, the Court has sown the wind. Later courts will face the impossible task of reaping the whirlwind.

---

**Question:** In *Steelworkers,* both the majority and dissent look for the purpose of the statute in its legislative history. Why do their opinions differ so markedly?

## TECHNICAL TOOLS

### TANIGUCHI V. KAN PACIFIC SAIPAN LTD.

566 U.S. 560 (2012)

JUSTICE ALITO delivered the opinion of the Court.

The costs that may be awarded to prevailing parties in lawsuits brought in federal court are set forth in 28 U. S. C. § 1920. The Court Interpreters Act amended that statute to include "compensation of interpreters." § 1920(6); see also § 7, 92 Stat. 2044. The question presented in this case is whether "compensation of interpreters" covers the cost of translating documents. Because the ordinary meaning of the word "interpreter" is a person who translates orally from one language to another, we hold that "compensation of interpreters" is limited to the cost of oral translation and does not include the cost of document translation.

This case arises from a personal injury action brought by petitioner Kouichi Taniguchi, a professional baseball player in Japan, against respondent Kan Pacific Saipan, Ltd., the owner of a resort in the Northern Mariana Islands. Petitioner was injured when his leg broke through a wooden deck during a tour of respondent's resort property. Initially, petitioner said that he needed no medical attention, but two weeks later, he informed respondent that he had suffered cuts, bruises, and torn ligaments from the accident. Due to these alleged injuries, he claimed damages for medical expenses and for lost income from contracts he was unable to honor. After discovery concluded, both parties moved for summary judgment. The United States District Court for the Northern Mariana Islands granted respondent's motion on the ground that petitioner offered no evidence that respondent knew of the defective deck or otherwise failed to exercise reasonable care.

In preparing its defense, respondent paid to have various documents translated from Japanese to English. After the District Court granted summary judgment in respondent's favor, respondent submitted a bill for those costs. Over petitioner's objection, the District Court awarded the costs to respondent as "compensation of interpreters" under § 1920(6). Explaining that interpreter services "cannot be separated into 'translation' and 'interpretation,' " App. to Pet. for Cert. 25a, the court held that costs for document translation "fal[l] within the meaning of 'compensation of an interpreter,' " *ibid.* Finding that it was necessary for respondent to have the documents translated in order to depose petitioner, the court concluded that the translation services were properly taxed as costs.

The United States Court of Appeals for the Ninth Circuit affirmed both the District Court's grant of summary judgment and its award of costs. The court rejected petitioner's argument that the cost of document translation services is not recoverable as "compensation of interpreters." The court explained that "the word 'interpreter' can reasonably encompass a 'translator,' both according to the dictionary definition and common usage of these terms, which does not always draw precise distinctions between foreign language interpretations involving live speech versus written documents." 633 F. 3d 1218, 1221 (2011). "More importantly," the court stressed, this construction of the statute "is more compatible with Rule 54 of the Federal Rules of Civil Procedure, which includes a decided preference for the award of costs to the prevailing party." *Ibid.* The court thus concluded that "the prevailing party should be awarded costs for services required to interpret either live speech or written documents into a familiar language, so long as interpretation of the items is necessary to the litigation." *Id.*, at 1221–1222.

Because there is a split among the Courts of Appeals on this issue, we granted certiorari.

Although the taxation of costs was not allowed at common law, it was the practice of federal courts in the early years to award costs in the same manner as the courts of the relevant forum State. *Alyeska Pipeline Service Co.* v. *Wilderness Society*, 421 U. S. 240, 247–248 (1975). In 1793, Congress enacted a statute that authorized the awarding of certain costs to prevailing parties based on state law:

"That there be allowed and taxed in the supreme, circuit and district courts of the United States, in favour of the parties obtaining judgments therein, such compensation for their travel and attendance, and for at tornies and counsellors' fees . . . as are allowed in the supreme or superior courts of the respective states." Act of Mar. 1, 1793, § 4, 1 Stat. 333.

Although twice reenacted, this provision expired in 1799. *Alyeska Pipeline*, *supra*, at 248, n. 19; *Crawford Fitting Co.* v. *J. T. Gibbons, Inc.*, 482 U. S. 437, 439 (1987). Yet even in the absence of express legislative authorization, the practice of referring to state rules for the taxation of costs persisted. See *Alyeska Pipeline*, 421 U. S., at 250.

Not until 1853 did Congress enact legislation specifying the costs allowable in federal court. *Id.*, at 251. The impetus for a uniform federal rule was largely the consequence of two developments. First, a "great diversity in practice among the courts" had emerged. *Ibid.* Second, "losing litigants were being unfairly saddled with exorbitant fees for the victor's attorney." *Ibid.* Against this backdrop, Congress passed the 1853 Fee Act, which we have described as a "far-reaching Act specifying in detail the nature and amount of the taxable items of cost in the federal courts." *Id.*, at 251–252. The substance of this Act was transmitted through the Revised Statutes of 1874 and the Judicial Code of 1911 to the Revised Code of 1948, where it was codified, "without any apparent intent to change the controlling rules," as 28 U. S. C. § 1920. 421 U. S., at 255.

Federal Rule of Civil Procedure 54(d) gives courts the discretion to award costs to prevailing parties. That Rule provides in relevant part: "Unless a federal statute, these rules, or a court order provides otherwise, costs—other than attorney's fees—should be allowed to the prevailing party." Rule 54(d)(1). We have held that "§ 1920 defines the term 'costs' as used in Rule 54(d)." *Crawford Fitting*, 482 U. S., at 441. In so doing, we rejected the view that "the discretion granted by Rule 54(d) is a separate source of power to tax as costs expenses not enumerated in § 1920." *Ibid.*

As originally configured, § 1920 contained five categories of taxable costs: (1) "[f]ees of the clerk and marshal"; (2) "[f]ees of the court reporter for all or any part of the stenographic transcript necessarily obtained for use in the case"; (3) "[f]ees and disbursements for printing and witnesses"; (4) "[f]ees for exemplification and copies of papers necessarily obtained for use in the case"; and (5) "[d]ocket fees under section 1923 of this title." 62 Stat. 955. In 1978, Congress enacted the Court Interpreters Act, which amended § 1920 to add a sixth category: "Compensation of court appointed experts, compensation of interpreters, and salaries, fees, expenses, and costs of special interpretation services under section 1828 of this title." 28 U. S. C. § 1920(6); see also § 7, 92 Stat. 2044. We are concerned here with this sixth category, specifically the item of taxable costs identified as "compensation of interpreters."

To determine whether the item "compensation of interpreters" includes costs for document translation, we must look to the meaning of "interpreter." That term is not defined in the Court Interpreters Act or in any other relevant statutory provision. When a term goes undefined in a statute, we give the term its ordinary meaning. *Asgrow Seed Co.* v. *Winterboer*, 513 U. S. 179, 187 (1995). The question here is: What is the ordinary meaning of "interpreter"?

Many dictionaries in use when Congress enacted the Court Interpreters Act in 1978 defined "interpreter" as one who translates spoken, as opposed to written, language. The American Heritage Dictionary, for instance, defined the term as "[o]ne who translates orally from one language into another." American Heritage Dictionary 685 (1978). The Scribner-Bantam English Dictionary defined the related word "interpret" as "to translate orally." Scribner- Bantam English Dictionary 476 (1977). Similarly, the Random House Dictionary defined the intransitive form of "interpret" as "to translate what is *said* in a foreign language." Random House Dictionary of the English Language 744 (1973) (emphasis added). And, notably, the Oxford English Dictionary defined "interpreter" as "[o]ne who translates languages," but then divided that definition into two senses: "a. [a] translator of books or writings," which it designated as obsolete, and "b. [o]ne who translates the communications of persons speaking different languages; *spec.* one whose office it is to do so orally in the presence of the persons; a dragoman." 5 Oxford English Dictionary 416 (1933); see also Concise Oxford Dictionary of Current English 566 (6th ed. 1976) ("One who interprets; one whose office it is to translate the words of persons speaking different languages, esp. orally in their presence"); Chambers Twentieth Century Dictionary 686 (1973) ("one who translates orally for the benefit of two or more parties speaking different languages: . . . a translator (*obs.*)").

Pre-1978 legal dictionaries also generally defined the words "interpreter" and "interpret" in terms of oral translation. The then-current edition of Black's Law Dictionary, for example, defined "interpreter" as "[a] person sworn at a trial to interpret the evidence of a foreigner . . . to the court," and it defined "interpret" in relevant part as "to translate orally from one tongue to another." Black's Law Dictionary 954, 953 (rev. 4th ed. 1968); see also W. Anderson, A Dictionary of Law 565 (1888) ("One who translates the testimony of witnesses speaking a foreign tongue, for the benefit of the court and jury"); 1 B. Abbott, Dictionary of Terms and Phrases Used in American or English Jurisprudence 639 (1878) ("one who restates the testimony of a witness testifying in a foreign tongue, to the court and jury, in their language"). But see Ballentine's Law Dictionary 655, 654 (3d ed. 1969) (defining "interpreter" as "[o]ne who interprets, particularly one who interprets words written or spoken in a foreign language," and "interpret" as "to translate from a foreign language").

Against these authorities, respondent relies almost exclusively on Webster's Third New International Dictionary (hereinafter Webster's Third). The version of that dictionary in print when Congress enacted the Court Interpreters Act defined "interpreter" as "one that translates; *esp*: a person who translates orally for parties conversing in different tongues." Webster's Third 1182 (1976). The sense divider *esp* (for especially) indicates that the most common meaning of the term is one "who translates orally," but that meaning is subsumed within the more general definition "one that translates." See 12,000 Words: A Supplement to Webster's Third 15a (1986) (explaining that *esp* "is used to introduce the most common meaning included in the more general preceding definition"). For respondent, the general definition suffices to establish that the term "interpreter" ordinarily includes persons who translate the written word. Explaining that "the word 'interpreter' can reasonably encompass a 'translator,' " the Court of Appeals reached the same conclusion. 633 F. 3d, at 1221. We disagree.

That a definition is broad enough to encompass one sense of a word does not establish that the word is *ordinarily* understood in that sense. See *Mallard* v. *United States Dist. Court for Southern Dist. of Iowa*, 490 U. S. 296, 301 (1989) (relying on the "most common meaning" and the "ordinary and natural signification" of the word "request," even though it may sometimes "double for 'demand' or 'command' "). The fact that the definition of "interpreter" in Webster's Third has a sense divider denoting the most common usage suggests that other usages, although acceptable, might not be common or ordinary. It is telling that all the dictionaries cited above defined "interpreter" at the time of the statute's enactment as including persons who translate orally, but only a handful defined the word broadly enough to encompass translators of written material. See *supra,* at 5–7. Although the Oxford English Dictionary, one of the most authoritative on the English language, recognized that "interpreter" *can* mean one who translates writings, it expressly designated that meaning as obsolete. See *supra,* at 6. Were the meaning of "interpreter" that respondent advocates truly common or ordinary, we would expect to see more support for that meaning. We certainly would not expect to see it designated as obsolete in the Oxford English Dictionary. Any definition of a word that is absent from many dictionaries and is deemed obsolete in others is hardly a common or ordinary meaning.

Based on our survey of the relevant dictionaries, we conclude that the ordinary or common meaning of "interpreter" does not include those who translate writings. Instead, we find that an interpreter is normally understood as one who translates orally from one language to another. This sense of the word is far more natural. As the Seventh Circuit put it: "Robert Fagles made famous translations into English of the *Iliad*, the *Odyssey*, and the *Aeneid*, but no one would refer to him as an English-language 'interpreter' of these works." *Extra Equipamentos E Exportação Ltda.* v. *Case Corp.*, 541 F. 3d 719, 727 (2008).

To be sure, the word "interpreter" can encompass per sons who translate documents, but because that is not the ordinary meaning of the word, it does not control unless the context in which the word appears indicates that it does. Nothing in the Court Interpreters Act or in § 1920, however, even hints that Congress intended to go beyond the ordinary meaning of "interpreter" and to embrace the broadest possible meaning that the definition of the word can bear.

If anything, the statutory context suggests the opposite: that the word "interpreter" applies only to those who translate orally. As previously mentioned, Congress enacted § 1920(6) as part of the Court Interpreters Act. The main provision of that Act is § 2(a), codified in 28 U. S. C. §§ 1827 and 1828. See 92 Stat. 2040–2042. Particularly relevant here is § 1827. As it now reads, that statute provides for the establishment of "a program to facilitate the use of certified and otherwise qualified interpreters in judicial proceedings instituted by the United States." § 1827(a). Subsection (d) directs courts to use an interpreter in any criminal or civil action instituted by the United States if a party or witness "speaks only or primarily a language other than the English language" or "suffers from a hearing impairment" "so as to inhibit such party's comprehension of the proceedings or communication with counsel or the presiding judicial officer, or so as to inhibit such witness' comprehension of questions and the presentation of such testimony." § 1827(d)(1). As originally enacted, subsection (k) mandated that the "interpretation provided by certified interpreters . . . shall be in the consecutive mode except that the presiding judicial officer . . . may authorize a simultaneous or summary interpretation." § 1827(k) (1976 ed., Supp. II); see also 92 Stat. 2042. In its current form, subsection (k) provides that interpretation "shall be in the simultaneous mode for any party . . . and in the consecutive mode for witnesses," unless the court directs otherwise. The simultaneous, consecutive, and summary modes are all methods of oral interpretation and have nothing to do with the translation of writings. Taken together, these provisions are a strong contextual clue that Congress was dealing only with oral translation in the Court Interpreters Act and that it intended to use the term "interpreter" throughout the Act in its ordinary sense as someone who translates the spoken word. As we have said before, it is a "normal rule of statutory construction that 'identical words used in different parts of the same act are intended to have the same meaning." *Gustafson* v. *Alloyd Co.,* 513 U. S. 561, 570 (1995).

The references to technical terminology in the Court Interpreters Act further suggest that Congress used "in terpreter" in a technical sense, and it is therefore significant that relevant professional literature draws a line between "interpreters," who "are used for oral conversations," and "translators," who "are used for written communications." Zazueta, *supra* n. 4, at 477; see also M. Frankenthaler, Skills for Bilingual Legal Personnel 67 (1982) ("While the translator deals with the written word, the interpreter is concerned with the spoken language"); Brislin, Introduction, in Translation: Applications and Research 1 (R. Brislin ed. 1976) (explaining that when both terms are used together, translation "refers to the processing [of] written input, and interpretation to the processing of oral input" (emphasis deleted)); J. Herbert, Interpreter's Handbook 1 (2d ed. 1952) ("In the present-day jargon of international organisations, the words translate, translations, translator are used when the immediate result of the work is a written text; and the words interpret, interpreter, interpretation when it is a speech delivered orally"). That Congress specified "interpreters" but not "translators" is yet another signal that it intended to limit § 1920(6) to the costs of oral, instead of written, translation.

In sum, both the ordinary and technical meanings of "interpreter," as well as the statutory context in which the word is found, lead to the conclusion that § 1920(6) does not apply to translators of written materials.

No other rule of construction compels us to depart from the ordinary meaning of "interpreter." The Court of Appeals reasoned that a broader meaning is "more compatible with Rule 54 of the Federal Rules of Civil Procedure, which includes a decided preference for the award of costs to the prevailing party." 633 F. 3d, at 1221. But we have never held that Rule 54(d) creates a presumption of statutory construction in favor of the broadest possible reading of the costs enumerated in § 1920. To the contrary, we have made clear that the "discretion granted by Rule 54(d) is not a power to evade" the specific categories of costs set forth by Congress. *Crawford Fitting*, 482 U. S., at 442. "Rather," we have said, "it is solely a power to decline to tax, as costs, the items enumerated in § 1920." *Ibid.* Rule 54(d) thus provides no sound basis for casting aside the ordinary meaning of the various items enumerated in the costs statute, including the ordinary meaning of "interpreter."

Our decision is in keeping with the narrow scope of taxable costs. "Although 'costs' has an everyday meaning synonymous with 'expenses,' the concept of taxable costs under Rule 54(d) is more limited and represents those expenses, including, for example, court fees, that a court will assess against a litigant." 10 C. Wright, A. Miller, & M. Kane, Federal Practice and Procedure § 2666, pp. 202–203 (3d ed. 1998) (hereinafter Wright & Miller). Taxable costs are limited to relatively minor, incidental expenses as is evident from § 1920, which lists such items as clerk fees, court reporter fees, expenses for printing and witnesses, expenses for exemplification and copies, docket fees, and compensation of court-appointed experts. Indeed, "the assessment of costs most often is merely a clerical matter that can be done by the court clerk." *Hairline Creations, Inc.* v. *Kefalas*, 664 F. 2d 652, 656 (CA7 1981). Taxable costs are a fraction of the nontaxable expenses borne by litigants for attorneys, experts, consultants, and investigators. It comes as little surprise, therefore, that "costs almost always amount to less than the successful litigant's total expenses in connection with a lawsuit." 10 Wright & Miller § 2666, at 203. Because taxable costs are limited by statute and are modest in scope, we see no compelling reason to stretch the ordinary meaning of the cost items Congress authorized in § 1920.

As for respondent's extratextual arguments, they are more properly directed at Congress. Respondent contends that documentary evidence is no less important than testimonial evidence and that it would be anomalous to require the losing party to cover translation costs for spoken words but not for written words. Brief for Respondent 20. Respondent also observes that some translation tasks are not entirely oral or entirely written. *Id.*, at 20–24. One task, called " 'sight translation,' " involves the oral translation of a document. *Id.*, at 21. Another task involves the written translation of speech. *Ibid.* And a third task, called " 'document comparison,' " involves comparing documents in the source and target language to verify that the two are identical. *Id.*, at 21–22. Respondent argues that a narrow definition cannot account for these variations and that a bright-line definition of "interpreter" as someone who translates spoken and written words would avoid complication and provide a simple, administrable rule for district courts.

Neither of these arguments convinces us that Congress must have intended to dispense with the ordinary meaning of "interpreter" in § 1920(6). First, Congress might have distinguished between oral and written translation out of a concern that requiring losing parties to bear the potentially sizable costs of translating discovery documents, as opposed to the more limited costs of oral testimony, could be too burdensome and possibly unfair, especially for litigants with limited means. Cf. *Fleischmann Distilling Corp.* v. *Maier Brewing Co.*, 386 U. S. 714, 718 (1967) (noting the argument "that since litigation is at best uncertain one should not be penalized for merely defending or prosecuting a lawsuit, and that the poor might be unjustly discouraged from instituting actions to vindicate their rights if the penalty for losing included the fees of their opponents' counsel"). Congress might also have concluded that a document translator is more akin to an expert or consultant retained by a party to decipher documentary evidence—like, for instance, a forensic accountant—than to an interpreter whose real-time oral translation services are necessary for communication between litigants, witnesses, and the court.

Second, respondent has not shown that any of the hybrid translation/ interpretation tasks to which it points actually arise with overwhelming frequency or that the problem of drawing the line between taxable and nontaxable costs in such cases will vex the trial courts. It certainly has not shown that any such problems will be more troublesome than the task of sifting through translated discovery documents to ascertain which can be taxed as necessary to the litigation. In any event, the present case does not present a hybrid situation; it involves purely written translation, which falls outside the tasks performed by an "interpreter" as that term is ordinarily understood.

Because the ordinary meaning of "interpreter" is someone who translates orally from one language to another, we hold that the category "compensation of interpreters" in § 1920(6) does not include costs for document translation. We therefore vacate the judgment of the United States Court of Appeals for the Ninth Circuit and remand the case for further proceedings consistent with this opinion.

It is so ordered.

JUSTICE GINSBURG, with whom JUSTICE BREYER and JUSTICE SOTOMAYOR join, dissenting.

To be comprehended by the parties, the witnesses, and the court, expression in foreign languages must be translated into English. Congress therefore provided, in 28 U. S. C. § 1920(6), that the prevailing party may recoup compensation paid to "interpreters." The word "interpreters," the Court emphasizes, commonly refers to translators of oral speech. *Ante*, at 5–6. But as the Court acknowledges, *ante*, at 7, and n. 2, "interpreters" is more than occasionally used to encompass those who translate written speech as well. See Webster's Third New International Dictionary of the English Language 1182 (1976) (hereinafter Webster's) (defining "interpreter" as "one that translates; *esp*: a person who translates orally for parties conversing in different tongues"); Black's Law Dictionary 895 (9th ed. 2009) (defining "interpreter" as a "person who translates, esp. orally, from one language to another"); Ballentine's Law Dictionary 655 (3d ed. 1969) (defining "interpreter" as "[o]ne who interprets, particularly one who interprets words written or spoken in a foreign language").

In short, employing the word "interpreters" to include translators of written as well as oral speech, if not "the most common usage," *ante*, at 8, is at least an "acceptable" usage, *ibid*. Moreover, the word "interpret" is generally understood to mean "to explain or tell the meaning of: translate into intelligible or familiar language or terms," while "translate" commonly means "to turn into one's own or another language." Webster's 1182, 2429. See also Random House Dictionary of the English Language 744, 1505 (1973) (defining the transitive verb "interpret" as, *inter alia*, "to translate," and "translate" as "to turn (something written or spoken) from one language into another").

Notably, several federal district court decisions refer to translators of written documents as "interpreters." *E.g., United States* v. *Prado-Cervantez*, No. 11–40044–11, 2011 WL 4691934, *3 (Kan., Oct. 6, 2011) ("Standby counsel should also be prepared to arrange for interpreters to interpret or translate documents when necessary for defendant."); *Mendoza* v. *Ring*, No. 07–3114, 2008 WL 2959848, *2 (CD Ill., July 30, 2008) ("The interpreter is also directed to translate filings by the plaintiff from Spanish to English. The original and translated versions will be docketed."). So do a number of state statutes. *E.g.,* Cal. Govt. Code Ann.

§ 26806(a) (West 2008) ("[T]he clerk of the court may employ as many foreign language interpreters as may be necessary . . . to translate documents intended for filing in any civil or criminal action . . . .").

Most federal courts of appeals confronted with the question have held that costs may be awarded under § 1920(6) for the translation of documents necessary to, or in preparation for, litigation. Compare [citations] (all holding that costs for document translation are covered by § 1920(6)), with *Extra Equipamentos E Exportação Ltda.* v. *Case Corp.*, 541 F. 3d 719, 727–728 (CA7 2008) (costs for document translation are not covered by § 1920(6)). See also [citations]; *Quy* v. *Air Am., Inc.*, 667 F. 2d 1059, 1065 (CADC 1981) (allowing "translation costs" under § 1920(6)).

In practice, federal trial courts have awarded document translation costs in cases spanning several decades. See, *e.g.*, *Raffold Process Corp.* v. *Castanea Paper Co.*, 25 F. Supp. 593, 594 (WD Pa. 1938). Before the Court Interpreters Act added § 1920(6) to the taxation of costs statute in 1978, district courts awarded costs for document translation under § 1920(4), which allowed taxation of "[f]ees for exemplification and copies of papers," 28 U. S. C. § 1920(4) (1976 ed.), or under § 1920's predecessor, 28 U. S. C. § 830 (1925 ed.). See, *e.g.*, *Bennett Chemical Co.* v. *Atlantic Commodities, Ltd.*, 24 F. R. D. 200, 204 (SDNY 1959) (§ 1920(4)); *Raffold Process Corp.*, 25 F. Supp., at 594 (§ 830). Pre-1978, district courts also awarded costs for oral translation of witness testimony. See, *e.g.*, *Kaiser Industries Corp.* v. *McLouth Steel Corp.*, 50 F. R. D. 5, 11 (ED Mich. 1970). Nothing in the Court Interpreters Act, a measure intended to expand access to interpretation services, indicates a design to eliminate the availability of costs awards for document translation. See S. Rep. No. 95–569, p. 4 (1977) (hereinafter S. Rep.) ("The committee . . . feels the time has come to provide by statute for the provision of and access to qualified certified interpreters, for a broader spectrum of people than the present law allows."). Post-1978, rulings awarding document translation costs under § 1920(6) indicate the courts' understanding both that the term "interpreter" can readily encompass oral and written translation, and that Congress did not otherwise instruct. I agree that context should guide the determination whether § 1920(b) is most sensibly read to encompass persons who translate documents. See *ante*, at 8–9. But the context key for me is the practice of federal courts both before and after § 1920(6)'s enactment.

The purpose of translation, after all, is to make relevant foreign-language communication accessible to the litigants and the court. See S. Rep., at 1 (The Court Interpreters Act is intended "to insure that all participants in our Federal courts can meaningfully take part."). Documentary evidence in a foreign language, no less than oral statements, must be translated to equip the parties to present their case clearly and the court to decide the merits intelligently. See, *e.g.*, *United States* v. *Mosquera*, 816 F. Supp. 168, 175 (EDNY 1993) ("For a non-English speaking [party] to stand equal with others before the court requires translation [of relevant documents].”); *Lockett* v. *Hellenic Sea Transports, Ltd.*, 60 F. R. D. 469, 473 (ED Pa. 1973) (“To be understood by counsel for plaintiffs and defendant, as well as for use at trial, the [ship's] deck log had to be translated [from Greek] into the English language.”). And it is not extraordinary that what documents say, more than what witnesses testify, may make or break a case.

Distinguishing written from oral translation for cost-award purposes, moreover, is an endeavor all the more dubious, for, as the Court acknowledges, *ante*, at 13, some translation tasks do not fall neatly into one category or the other. An interpreter, for example, may be called upon to “sight translate” a written document, *i.e.*, to convey a written foreign-language document's content orally in English. R. González, V. Vásquez, & H. Mikkelson, Fundamentals of Court Interpretation: Theory, Policy and Practice 401 (1991) (hereinafter González). In-court sight translation, Taniguchi concedes, counts as “interpretation,” even though it does not involve translating verbal expression. Tr. of Oral Arg. 10. Yet an interpreter's preparation for in-court sight translation by translating a written document in advance, Taniguchi maintains, does not count as “interpretation.” *Ibid.* But if the interpreter then reads the prepared written translation aloud in court, that task, in Taniguchi's view, can be charged as “interpretation,” *id.*, at 11, even though the reading involves no translation of foreign-language expression—written *or* oral—at all.

Similarly hard to categorize is the common court-interpreter task of listening to a recording in a foreign language, transcribing it, then translating it into English. See González 439. Although this task involves oral foreign-language communication, it does not, Taniguchi contends, qualify as “interpretation,” because it involves “the luxury of multiple playbacks of the tape and the leisure to consult extrinsic linguistic sources.” Reply Brief for Petitioner 9 (internal quotation marks omitted). But sight translation—which Taniguchi concedes may be charged as “interpretation”—may sometimes involve similarly careful linguistic analysis of a written document in advance of a court proceeding. Davis & Hewitt, Lessons in Administering Justice: What Judges Need to Know about the Requirements, Role, and Professional Responsibilities of the Court Interpreter, 1 Harv. Latino L. Rev. 121, 131 (1994).

Taniguchi warns that translation costs can be exorbitant and burdensome to police. Reply Brief 19–22; Tr. of Oral Arg. 20–21. The Court expresses a similar concern. *Ante*, at 13–14. Current practice in awarding translation costs, however, has shown that district judges are up to the task of confining awards to translation services necessary to present or defeat a claim. See [citations].

In short, § 1920(6)'s prescription on "interpreters" is not so clear as to leave no room for interpretation. Given the purpose served by translation and the practice prevailing in district courts, *supra*, at 3, there is no good reason to exclude from taxable costs payments for placing written words within the grasp of parties, jurors, and judges. I would therefore affirm the judgment of the Ninth Circuit.

---

**Question:** Both the majority and dissent in *Taniguchi* refer to dictionaries to assist their interpretations. Why does Justice Ginsburg cite to many judicial decisions as well?

# CHAPTER 18

# ADMINISTRATIVE LAW

■ ■ ■

## CONTEXT & SOURCES

Administrative law has become a major feature of regulation since the late 1800s and particularly after the New Deal of the 1930s, which inaugurated a series of new agencies. Uniformity in proceedings is ensured by the 1946 Administrative Procedure Act (APA), 5 U.S.C. § 551 et seq. In contrast with courts, the APA allows less formal procedures and relaxed restrictions on the admission of evidence. The cases presented here concern judicial deference to agencies, rulemaking, and explanations for decisions.

Blake Emerson, *The Public's Law: Origins and Architecture of Progressive Democracy* (Oxford, 2019) thoughtfully probes the theories and politics that gave birth to U.S. regulation. The importance of the *Chevron* case and the Supreme Court's evolving interpretation of deference are detailed in Thomas W. Merrill, *The* Chevron *Doctrine: Its Rise and Fall, and the Future of the Administrative State* (Harvard, 2022). For an analysis of the Court's views on agency explanations for policy changes, see Jerome A. Barron, "FCC v. Fox Television Stations and the FCC's New Fleeting Expletive Policy," 62 *Federal Communications Law Journal* 567 (2010).

## DEFERENCE

### CHEVRON USA, INC. V. NATIONAL RESOURCES DEFENSE COUNCIL

467 U.S. 837 (1984)

* * *

JUSTICE STEVENS delivered the opinion of the Court.

In the Clean Air Act Amendments of 1977, Pub.L. 95–95, 91 Stat. 685, Congress enacted certain requirements applicable to States that had not achieved the national air quality standards established by the Environmental Protection Agency (EPA) pursuant to earlier legislation. The amended Clean Air Act required these "nonattainment" States to establish a permit program regulating "new or modified major stationary sources" of air pollution. Generally, a permit may not be issued for a new or modified major stationary source unless several stringent conditions are met. The EPA regulation promulgated to implement this permit requirement allows a State to adopt a plantwide definition of the term "stationary source." Under this definition, an existing plant that contains several pollution-emitting devices may install or modify one piece of equipment without meeting the permit conditions if the alteration will not increase the total emissions from the plant. The question presented by these cases is whether EPA's decision to allow States to treat all of the pollution-emitting devices within the same industrial grouping as though they were encased within a single "bubble" is based on a reasonable construction of the statutory term "stationary source."

The EPA regulations containing the plantwide definition of the term stationary source were promulgated on October 14, 1981. 46 Fed.Reg. 50766. Respondents filed a timely petition for review in the United States Court of Appeals for the District of Columbia Circuit pursuant to 42 U.S.C. § 7607(b)(1). The Court of Appeals set aside the regulations. National Resources Defense Council, Inc. v. Gorsuch, 685 F.2d 718 (1982).

The court observed that the relevant part of the amended Clean Air Act "does not explicitly define what Congress envisioned as a 'stationary source, to which the permit program . . . should apply," and further stated that the precise issue was not "squarely addressed in the legislative history." 685 F.2d, at 723. In light of its conclusion that the legislative history bearing on the question was "at best contradictory," it reasoned that "the purposes of the nonattainment program should guide our decision here." 685 F.2d, at 726, n. 39. Based on two of its precedents concerning the applicability of the bubble concept to certain Clean Air Act programs, the court stated that the bubble concept was "mandatory" in programs designed merely to maintain existing air quality, but held that it was "inappropriate" in programs enacted to improve air quality. 685 F.2d, at 726. Since the purpose of the permit program—its "raison d'etre," in the court's view—was to improve air quality, the court held that the bubble concept was inapplicable in these cases under its prior precedents. Ibid. It therefore set aside the regulations embodying the bubble concept as contrary to law. We granted certiorari to review that judgment, and we now reverse.

The basic legal error of the Court of Appeals was to adopt a static judicial definition of the term "stationary source" when it had decided that Congress itself had not commanded that definition.

* * *

"The power of an administrative agency to administer a congressionally created . . . program necessarily requires the formulation of policy and the making of rules to fill any gap left, implicitly or explicitly, by Congress." Morton v. Ruiz, 415 U.S. 199, 231, (1974). If Congress has explicitly left a gap for the agency to fill, there is an express delegation of authority to the agency to elucidate a specific provision of the statute by regulation. Such legislative regulations are given controlling weight unless they are arbitrary, capricious, or manifestly contrary to the statute. Sometimes the legislative delegation to an agency on a particular question is implicit rather than explicit. In such a case, a court may not substitute its own construction of a statutory provision for a reasonable interpretation made by the administrator of an agency.

We have long recognized that considerable weight should be accorded to an executive department's construction of a statutory scheme it is entrusted to administer, and the principle of deference to administrative interpretations.

* * *

". . . If [the agency's] choice represents a reasonable accommodation of conflicting policies that were committed to the agency's care by the statute, we should not disturb it unless it appears from the statute or its legislative history that the accommodation is not one that Congress would have sanctioned." United States v. Shimer, 367 U.S. 374, 382 (1961) [additional citation.]

In light of these well-settled principles it is clear that the Court of Appeals misconceived the nature of its role in reviewing the regulations at issue. Once it determined, after its own examination of the legislation, that Congress did not actually have an intent regarding the applicability of the bubble concept to the permit program, the question before it was not whether in its view the concept is "inappropriate" in the general context of a program designed to improve air quality, but whether the Administrator's view that it is appropriate in the context of this particular program is a reasonable one. Based on the examination of the legislation and its history which follows, we agree with the Court of Appeals that Congress did not have a specific intention on the applicability of the bubble concept in these cases, and conclude that the EPA's use of that concept here is a reasonable policy choice for the agency to make.

In the 1950's and the 1960's Congress enacted a series of statutes designed to encourage and to assist the States in curtailing air pollution. See generally Train v. Natural Resources Defense Council, Inc., 421 U.S. 60, 63–64 (1975). The Clean Air Amendments of 1970, Pub.L. 91–604, 84 Stat. 1676, "sharply increased federal authority and responsibility in the continuing effort to combat air pollution," 421 U.S., at 64, but continued to assign "primary responsibility for assuring air quality" to the several States, 84 Stat. 1678. Section 109 of the 1970 Amendments directed the EPA to promulgate National Ambient Air Quality Standards (NAAQS's) and § 110 directed the States to develop plans (SIP's) to implement the standards within specified deadlines. In addition, § 111 provided that major new sources of pollution would be required to conform to technology-based performance standards; the EPA was directed to publish a list of categories of sources of pollution and to establish new source performance standards (NSPS) for each. Section 111(e) prohibited the operation of any new source in violation of a performance standard.

* * *

Nonattainment

The 1970 legislation provided for the attainment of primary NAAQS's by 1975. In many areas of the country, particularly the most industrialized States, the statutory goals were not attained. In 1976, the 94th Congress was confronted with this fundamental problem, as well as many others respecting pollution control. As always in this area, the legislative struggle was basically between interests seeking strict schemes to reduce pollution rapidly to eliminate its social costs and interests advancing the economic concern that strict schemes would retard industrial development with attendant social costs. The 94th Congress, confronting these competing interests, was unable to agree on what response was in the public interest: legislative proposals to deal with nonattainment failed to command the necessary consensus.

* * *

The Clean Air Act Amendments of 1977 are a lengthy, detailed, technical, complex, and comprehensive response to a major social issue. A small portion of the statute—91 Stat. 745–751 (Part D of Title I of the amended Act, 42 U.S.C. §§ 7501–7508)—expressly deals with nonattainment areas. The focal point of this controversy is one phrase in that portion of the Amendments.

* * *

Most significantly for our purposes, the statute provided that each plan shall

"(6) require permits for the construction and operation of new or modified major stationary sources in accordance with section 173. . . ." Id., 747.

Before issuing a permit, § 173 requires (1) the state agency to determine that there will be sufficient emissions reductions in the region to offset the emissions from the new source and also to allow for reasonable further progress toward attainment, or that the increased emissions will not exceed an allowance for growth established pursuant to § 172(b)(5); (2) the applicant to certify that his other sources in the State are in compliance with the SIP, (3) the agency to determine that the applicable SIP is otherwise being implemented, and (4) the proposed source to comply with the lowest achievable emission rate (LAER).

* * *

The legislative history of the portion of the 1977 Amendments dealing with nonattainment areas does not contain any specific comment on the "bubble concept" or the question whether a plantwide definition of a stationary source is permissible under the permit program. It does, however, plainly disclose that in the permit program Congress sought to accommodate the conflict between the economic interest in permitting capital improvements to continue and the environmental interest in improving air quality. Indeed, the House Committee Report identified the economic interest as one of the "two main purposes" of this section of the bill.

* * *

In 1981 a new administration took office and initiated a "Government-wide reexamination of regulatory burdens and complexities." 46 Fed.Reg. 16281. In the context of that review, the EPA reevaluated the various arguments that had been advanced in connection with the proper definition of the term "source" and concluded that the term should be given the same definition in both nonattainment areas and PSD areas.

In explaining its conclusion, the EPA first noted that the definitional issue was not squarely addressed in either the statute or its legislative history and therefore that the issue involved an agency "judgment as how to best carry out the Act." Ibid. It then set forth several reasons for concluding that the plantwide definition was more appropriate. It pointed out that the dual definition "can act as a disincentive to new investment and modernization by discouraging modifications to existing facilities" and "can actually retard progress in air pollution control by discouraging replacement of older, dirtier processes or pieces of equipment with new, cleaner ones." Ibid. Moreover, the new definition "would simplify EPA's rules by using the same definition of 'source' for PSD, nonattainment new source review and the construction moratorium. This reduces confusion and inconsistency." Ibid. Finally, the agency explained that additional requirements that remained in place would accomplish the fundamental purposes of achieving attainment with NAAQS's as expeditiously as possible. These conclusions were expressed in a proposed rulemaking in August 1981 that was formally promulgated in October. See id., at 50766.

Legislative History

* * *

We find that the legislative history as a whole is silent on the precise issue before us. It is, however, consistent with the view that the EPA should have broad discretion in implementing the policies of the 1977 Amendments.

More importantly, that history plainly identifies the policy concerns that motivated the enactment; the plantwide definition is fully consistent with one of those concerns—the allowance of reasonable economic growth—and, whether or not we believe it most effectively implements the other, we must recognize that the EPA has advanced a reasonable explanation for its conclusion that the regulations serve the environmental objectives as well. See supra, at 857–859, and n. 29. Indeed, its reasoning is supported by the public record developed in the rulemaking process, as well as by certain private studies.

* * *

Policy

The arguments over policy that are advanced in the parties' briefs create the impression that respondents are now waging in a judicial forum a specific policy battle which they ultimately lost in the agency and in the 32 jurisdictions opting for the "bubble concept," but one which was never waged in the Congress. Such policy arguments are more properly addressed to legislators or administrators, not to judges.

In these cases, the Administrator's interpretation represents a reasonable accommodation of manifestly competing interests and is entitled to deference: the regulatory scheme is technical and complex, the agency considered the matter in a detailed and reasoned fashion, and the decision involves reconciling conflicting policies. Congress intended to accommodate both interests, but did not do so itself on the level of specificity presented by these cases. Perhaps that body consciously desired the Administrator to strike the balance at this level, thinking that those with great expertise and charged with responsibility for administering the provision would be in a better position to do so; perhaps it simply did not consider the question at this level; and perhaps Congress was unable to forge a coalition on either side of the question, and those on each side decided to take their chances with the scheme devised by the agency. For judicial purposes, it matters not which of these things occurred.

Judges are not experts in the field, and are not part of either political branch of the Government. Courts must, in some cases, reconcile competing political interests, but not on the basis of the judges' personal policy preferences. In contrast, an agency to which Congress has delegated policy-making responsibilities may, within the limits of that delegation, properly rely upon the incumbent administration's views of wise policy to inform its judgments. While agencies are not directly accountable to the people, the Chief Executive is, and it is entirely appropriate for this political branch of the Government to make such policy choices—resolving the competing interests which Congress itself either inadvertently did not resolve, or intentionally left to be resolved by the agency charged with the administration of the statute in light of everyday realities.

When a challenge to an agency construction of a statutory provision, fairly conceptualized, really centers on the wisdom of the agency's policy, rather than whether it Is A reasonable choice within a gap left open by Congress, the challenge must fail. In such a case, federal judges—who have no constituency—have a duty to respect legitimate policy choices made by those who do. The responsibilities for assessing the wisdom of such policy choices and resolving the struggle between competing views of the public interest are not judicial ones: "Our Constitution vests such responsibilities in the political branches." TVA v. Hill, 437 U.S. 153, 195, (1978).

We hold that the EPA's definition of the term "source" is a permissible construction of the statute which seeks to accommodate progress in reducing air pollution with economic growth. "The Regulations which the Administrator has adopted provide what the agency could allowably view as . . . [an] effective reconciliation of these twofold ends. . . ." United States v. Shimer, 367 U.S., at 383.

The judgment of the Court of Appeals is reversed. It is so ordered.

---

**Question:** Why did the Supreme Court agree with the Court of Appeals's finding that Congress did not consider "bubbling," but disagreed with that court's conclusion that the policy was unconstitutional?

## LOPER BRIGHT ENTERPRISES V. GINA RAIMONDO

144 S.Ct. 2244 (2024)

* * *

CHIEF JUSTICE ROBERTS delivered the opinion of the Court.

Since our decision in *Chevron U. S. A. Inc.* v. *Natural Resources Defense Council, Inc.*, 467 U.S. 837 (1984), we have sometimes required courts to defer to "permissible" agency interpretations of the statutes those agencies administer—even when a reviewing court reads the statute differently. In these cases we consider whether that doctrine should be overruled.

I

Our *Chevron* doctrine requires courts to use a two-step framework to interpret statutes administered by federal agencies. After determining that a case satisfies the various preconditions we have set for *Chevron* to apply, a reviewing court must first assess "whether Congress has directly spoken to the precise question at issue." *Id.*, at 842. If, and only if, congressional intent is "clear," that is the end of the inquiry. *Ibid.* But if the court determines that "the statute is silent or ambiguous with respect to the specific issue" at hand, the court must, at *Chevron*'s second step, defer to the agency's interpretation if it "is based on a permissible construction of the statute." *Id.*, at 843. The reviewing courts in each of the cases before us applied *Chevron*'s framework to resolve in favor of the Government challenges to the same agency rule.

A

Before 1976, unregulated foreign vessels dominated fishing in the international waters off the U. S. coast, which began just 12 nautical miles offshore. See, *e.g.*, S. Rep. No. 94–459, pp. 2–3 (1975). Recognizing the resultant overfishing and the need for sound management of fishery resources, Congress enacted the Magnuson-Stevens Fishery Conservation and Management Act (MSA). See 90 Stat. 331 (codified as amended at 16 U. S. C. § 1801 *et seq.*). The MSA and subsequent amendments extended the jurisdiction of the United States to 200 nautical miles beyond the U. S. territorial sea and claimed "exclusive fishery management authority over all fish" within that area, known as the "exclusive economic zone." § 1811(a); see Presidential Proclamation No. 5030, 3 CFR 22 (1983 Comp.); §§ 101, 102, 90 Stat. 336. The National Marine Fisheries Service (NMFS) administers the MSA under a delegation from the Secretary of Commerce.

The MSA established eight regional fishery management councils composed of representatives from the coastal States, fishery stakeholders, and NMFS. See 16 U. S. C. §§ 1852(a), (b). The councils develop fishery management plans, which NMFS approves and promulgates as final regulations. See §§ 1852(h), 1854(a). In service of the statute's fishery conservation and management goals, see § 1851(a), the MSA requires that certain provisions—such as "a mechanism for specifying annual catch limits . . . at a level such that overfishing does not occur," § 1853(a)(15)—be included in these plans, see § 1853(a). The plans may also include additional discretionary provisions. See § 1853(b). For example, plans may "prohibit, limit, condition, or require the use of specified types and quantities of fishing gear, fishing vessels, or equipment," § 1853(b)(4); "reserve a portion of the allowable biological catch of the fishery for use in scientific research," § 1853(b)(11); and "prescribe such other measures, requirements, or conditions and restrictions as are determined to be necessary and appropriate for the conservation and management of the fishery," § 1853(b)(14).

Relevant here, a plan may also require that "one or more observers be carried on board" domestic vessels "for the purpose of collecting data necessary for the conservation and management of the fishery." § 1853(b)(8). The MSA specifies three groups that must cover costs associated with observers: (1) foreign fishing vessels operating within the exclusive economic zone (which *must* carry observers), see §§ 1821(h)(1)(A), (h)(4), (h)(6); (2) vessels participating in certain limited access privilege programs, which impose quotas permitting fishermen to harvest only specific quantities of a fishery's total allowable catch, see §§ 1802(26), 1853a(c)(1)(H), (e)(2), 1854(d)(2); and (3) vessels within the jurisdiction of the North Pacific Council, where many of the largest and most successful commercial fishing enterprises in the Nation operate, see § 1862(a). In the latter two cases, the MSA expressly caps the relevant fees at two or three percent of the value of fish harvested on the vessels. See §§ 1854(d)(2)(B), 1862(b)(2)(E). And in general, it authorizes the Secretary to impose "sanctions" when "any payment required for observer services provided to or contracted by an owner or operator . . . has not been paid." § 1858(g)(1)(D).

The MSA does not contain similar terms addressing whether Atlantic herring fishermen may be required to bear costs associated with any observers a plan may mandate. And at one point, NMFS fully funded the observer coverage the New England Fishery Management Council required in its plan for the Atlantic herring fishery. See 79 Fed. Reg. 8792 (2014). In 2013, however, the council proposed amending its fishery management plans to empower it to require fishermen to pay for observers if federal funding became unavailable. Several years later, NMFS promulgated a rule approving the amendment. See 85 Fed. Reg. 7414 (2020).

With respect to the Atlantic herring fishery, the Rule created an industry funded program that aims to ensure observer coverage on 50 percent of trips undertaken by vessels with certain types of permits. Under that program, vessel representatives must "declare into" a fishery before beginning a trip by notifying NMFS of the trip and announcing the species the vessel intends to harvest. If NMFS determines that an observer is required, but declines to assign a Government-paid one, the vessel must contract with and pay for a Government-certified third-party observer. NMFS estimated that the cost of such an observer would be up to $710 per day, reducing annual returns to the vessel owner by up to 20 percent. See *id.*, at 7417–7418.

B

Petitioners Loper Bright Enterprises, Inc., H&L Axelsson, Inc., Lund Marr Trawlers LLC, and Scombrus One LLC are family businesses that operate in the Atlantic herring fishery. In February 2020, they challenged the Rule under the MSA, 16 U. S. C. § 1855(f), which incorporates the Administrative Procedure Act (APA), 5 U. S. C. § 551 *et seq.* In relevant part, they argued that the MSA does not authorize NMFS to mandate that they pay for observers required by a fishery management plan. The District Court granted summary judgment to the Government. It concluded that the MSA authorized the Rule, but noted that even if these petitioners' "arguments were enough to raise an ambiguity in the statutory text," deference to the agency's interpretation would be warranted under *Chevron*. 544 F. Supp. 3d 82, 107 (DC 2021).

A divided panel of the D. C. Circuit affirmed. See 45 F. 4th 359 (2022). The majority addressed various provisions of the MSA and concluded that it was not "wholly unambiguous" whether NMFS may require Atlantic herring fishermen to pay for observers. *Id.*, at 366. Because there remained "some question" as to Congress's intent, *id.*, at 369, the court proceeded to *Chevron*'s second step and deferred to the agency's interpretation as a "reasonable" construction of the MSA, 45 F. 4th, at 370. In dissent, Judge Walker concluded that Congress's silence on industry funded observers for the Atlantic herring fishery—coupled with the express provision for such observers in other fisheries and on foreign vessels—unambiguously indicated that NMFS lacked the authority to "require [Atlantic herring] fishermen to pay the wages of at-sea monitors." *Id.*, at 375.

[The Court then discussed a related First Circuit decision raising the same issues under the MSA, and granted certiorari as to both cases.]

II

A

Article III of the Constitution assigns to the Federal Judiciary the responsibility and power to adjudicate "Cases" and "Controversies"—concrete disputes with consequences for the parties involved. The Framers appreciated that the laws judges would necessarily apply in resolving those disputes would not always be clear. Cognizant of the limits of human language and foresight, they anticipated that "[a]ll new laws, though penned with the greatest technical skill, and passed on the fullest and most mature deliberation," would be "more or less obscure and equivocal, until their meaning" was settled "by a series of particular discussions and adjudications." The Federalist No. 37, p. 236 (J. Cooke ed. 1961) (J. Madison).

The Framers also envisioned that the final "interpretation of the laws" would be "the proper and peculiar province of the courts." *Id.*, No. 78, at 525 (A. Hamilton). Unlike the political branches, the courts would by design exercise "neither Force nor Will, but merely judgment." *Id.*, at 523. To ensure the "steady, upright and impartial administration of the laws," the Framers structured the Constitution to allow judges to exercise that judgment independent of influence from the political branches. *Id.*, at 522; see *id.*, at 522–524; *Stern* v. *Marshall*, 564 U.S. 462, 484 (2011).

This Court embraced the Framers' understanding of the judicial function early on. In the foundational decision of *Marbury* v. *Madison*, Chief Justice Marshall famously declared that "[i]t is emphatically the province and duty of the judicial department to say what the law is." 1 Cranch 137, 177 (1803). And in the following decades, the Court understood "interpret[ing] the laws, in the last resort," to be a "solemn duty" of the Judiciary. *United States* v. *Dickson*, 15 Pet. 141, 162 (1841) (Story, J., for the Court). When the meaning of a statute was at issue, the judicial role was to "interpret the act of Congress, in order to ascertain the rights of the parties." *Decatur* v. *Paulding*, 14 Pet. 497, 515 (1840).

The Court also recognized from the outset, though, that exercising independent judgment often included according due respect to Executive Branch interpretations of federal statutes. For example, in *Edwards' Lessee* v. *Darby*, 12 Wheat. 206 (1827), the Court explained that "[i]n the construction of a doubtful and ambiguous law, the contemporaneous construction of those who were called upon to act under the law, and were appointed to carry its provisions into effect, is entitled to very great respect." *Id.*, at 210; see also *United States* v. *Vowell*, 5 Cranch 368, 372 (1809) (Marshall, C. J., for the Court).

* * *

The Court also gave "the most respectful consideration" to Executive Branch interpretations simply because "[t]he officers concerned [were] usually able men, and masters of the subject," who were "[n]ot unfrequently . . . the draftsmen of the laws they [were] afterwards called upon to interpret." *United States* v. *Moore*, 95 U.S. 760, 763 (1878).

"Respect," though, was just that. The views of the Executive Branch could inform the judgment of the Judiciary, but did not supersede it. Whatever respect an Executive Branch interpretation was due, a judge "certainly would not be bound to adopt the construction given by the head of a department." *Decatur*, 14 Pet., at 515; see also *Burnet* v. *Chicago Portrait Co.*, 285 U.S. 1, 16 (1932). Otherwise, judicial judgment would not be independent at all. As Justice Story put it, "in cases where [a court's] own judgment . . . differ[ed] from that of other high functionaries," the court was "not at liberty to surrender, or to waive it." *Dickson*, 15 Pet., at 162.

B

The New Deal ushered in a "rapid expansion of the administrative process." *United States* v. *Morton Salt Co.*, 338 U.S. 632, 644 (1950). But as new agencies with new powers proliferated, the Court continued to adhere to the traditional understanding that questions of law were for courts to decide, exercising independent judgment.

During this period, the Court often treated agency determinations of *fact* as binding on the courts, provided that there was "evidence to support the findings." *St. Joseph Stock Yards Co.* v. *United States*, 298 U.S. 38, 51 (1936).

* * *

But the Court did not extend similar deference to agency resolutions of questions of *law*. It instead made clear, repeatedly, that "[t]he interpretation of the meaning of statutes, as applied to justiciable controversies," was "exclusively a judicial function." *United States* v. *American Trucking Assns., Inc.*, 310 U.S. 534, 544 (1940) . . . . It also continued to note, as it long had, that the informed judgment of the Executive Branch—especially in the form of an interpretation issued contemporaneously with the enactment of the statute—could be entitled to "great weight." *American Trucking Assns.*, 310 U. S., at 549.

Perhaps most notably along those lines, in *Skidmore* v. *Swift & Co.*, 323 U.S. 134 (1944), the Court explained that the "interpretations and opinions" of the relevant agency, "made in pursuance of official duty" and "based upon . . . specialized experience," "constitute[d] a body of experience and informed judgment to which courts and litigants [could] properly resort for guidance," even on legal questions. *Id.*, at 139–140. "The weight of such a judgment in a particular case," the Court observed, would "depend upon the thoroughness evident in its consideration, the validity of its reasoning, its consistency with earlier and later pronouncements, and all those factors which give it power to persuade, if lacking power to control." *Id.*, at 140.

* * *

C

Congress in 1946 enacted the APA "as a check upon administrators whose zeal might otherwise have carried them to excesses not contemplated in legislation creating their offices." *Morton Salt*, 338 U. S., at 644. It was the culmination of a "comprehensive rethinking of the place of administrative agencies in a regime of separate and divided powers." *Bowen* v. *Michigan Academy of Family Physicians*, 476 U.S. 667, 670–671 (1986).

In addition to prescribing procedures for agency action, the APA delineates the basic contours of judicial review of such action. As relevant here, Section 706 directs that "[t]o the extent necessary to decision and when presented, the reviewing court shall decide all relevant questions of law, interpret constitutional and statutory provisions, and determine the meaning or applicability of the terms of an agency action." 5 U. S. C. § 706. It further requires courts to "hold unlawful and set aside agency action, findings, and conclusions found to be . . . not in accordance with law." § 706(2)(A).

The APA thus codifies for agency cases the unremarkable, yet elemental proposition reflected by judicial practice dating back to *Marbury*: that courts decide legal questions by applying their own judgment. It specifies that courts, not agencies, will decide "*all* relevant questions of law" arising on review of agency action, § 706 (emphasis added)—even those involving ambiguous laws—and set aside any such action inconsistent with the law as they interpret it. And it prescribes no deferential standard for courts to employ in answering those legal questions. That omission is telling, because Section 706 *does* mandate that judicial review of agency policymaking and factfinding be deferential. See § 706(2)(A) (agency action to be set aside if "arbitrary, capricious, [or] an abuse of discretion"); § 706(2)(E) (agency factfinding in formal proceedings to be set aside if "unsupported by substantial evidence").

In a statute designed to "serve as the fundamental charter of the administrative state," *Kisor* v. *Wilkie*, 588 U.S. 558, 580 (2019) (plurality opinion) (internal quotation marks omitted), Congress surely would have articulated a similarly deferential standard applicable to questions of law had it intended to depart from the settled pre-APA understanding that deciding such questions was "exclusively a judicial function," *American Trucking Assns.*, 310 U. S., at 544. But nothing in the APA hints at such a dramatic departure. On the contrary, by directing courts to "interpret constitutional and statutory provisions" without differentiating between the two, Section 706 makes clear that agency interpretations of statutes—like agency interpretations of the Constitution—are *not* entitled to deference. Under the APA, it thus "remains the responsibility of the court to decide whether the law means what the agency says." *Perez* v. *Mortgage Bankers Assn.*, 575 U.S. 92, 109 (2015) (Scalia, J., concurring in judgment).

The text of the APA means what it says. And a look at its history if anything only underscores that plain meaning. According to both the House and Senate Reports on the legislation, Section 706 "provide[d] that questions of law are for courts *rather than agencies* to decide in the last analysis." H. R. Rep. No. 1980, 79th Cong., 2d Sess., 44 (1946) (emphasis added); accord, S. Rep. No. 752, 79th Cong., 1st Sess., 28 (1945). Some of the legislation's most prominent supporters articulated the same view. See 92 Cong. Rec. 5654 (1946) (statement of Rep. Walter); P. McCarran, Improving "Administrative Justice": Hearings and Evidence; Scope of Judicial Review, 32 A. B. A. J. 827, 831 (1946). Even the Department of Justice—an agency with every incentive to endorse a view of the APA favorable to the Executive Branch—opined after its enactment that Section 706 merely "restate[d] the present law as to the scope of judicial review." Dept. of Justice, Attorney General's Manual on the Administrative Procedure Act 108 (1947); see also *Kisor*, 588 U. S., at 582 (plurality opinion) (same). That "present law," as we have described, adhered to the traditional conception of the judicial function. See *supra*, at 9–13.

A. B. A. J. 434, 516 (1947).

* * *

The APA, in short, incorporates the traditional understanding of the judicial function, under which courts must exercise independent judgment in determining the meaning of statutory provisions. In exercising such judgment, though, courts may as they have from the start—seek aid from the interpretations of those responsible for implementing particular statutes. Such interpretations "constitute a body of experience and informed judgment to which courts and litigants may properly resort for guidance" consistent with the APA. *Skidmore*, 323 U. S., at 140. And interpretations issued contemporaneously with the statute at issue, and which have remained consistent over time, may be especially useful in determining the statute's meaning. See *ibid.*; *American Trucking Assns.*, 310 U. S., at 549.

In a case involving an agency, of course, the statute's meaning may well be that the agency is authorized to exercise a degree of discretion. Congress has often enacted such statutes. For example, some statutes "expressly delegate[ ]" to an agency the authority to give meaning to a particular statutory term. *Batterton* v. *Francis*, 432 U.S. 416, 425 (1977) (emphasis deleted). Others empower an agency to prescribe rules to "fill up the details" of a statutory scheme, *Wayman* v. *Southard*, 10 Wheat. 1, 43 (1825), or to regulate subject to the limits imposed by a term or phrase that "leaves agencies with flexibility," *Michigan* v. *EPA*, 576 U.S. 743, 752 (2015), such as "appropriate" or "reasonable."

When the best reading of a statute is that it delegates discretionary authority to an agency, the role of the reviewing court under the APA is, as always, to independently interpret the statute and effectuate the will of Congress subject to constitutional limits. The court fulfills that role by recognizing constitutional delegations, "fix[ing] the boundaries of [the] delegated authority," H. Monaghan, *Marbury* and the Administrative State, 83 Colum. L. Rev. 1, 27 (1983), and ensuring the agency has engaged in " 'reasoned decisionmaking' " within those boundaries, *Michigan*, 576 U. S., at 750 . . . By doing so, a court upholds the traditional conception of the judicial function that the APA adopts.

III

The deference that *Chevron* requires of courts reviewing agency action cannot be squared with the APA.

A

In the decades between the enactment of the APA and this Court's decision in *Chevron*, courts generally continued to review agency interpretations of the statutes they administer by independently examining each statute to determine its meaning. Cf. T. Merrill, Judicial Deference to Executive Precedent, 101 Yale L. J. 969, 972–975 (1992). As an early proponent (and later critic) of *Chevron* recounted, courts during this period thus identified delegations of discretionary authority to agencies on a "statute-by-statute basis." A. Scalia, Judicial Deference to Administrative Interpretations of Law, 1989 Duke L. J. 511, 516.

*Chevron*, decided in 1984 by a bare quorum of six Justices, triggered a marked departure from the traditional approach. The question in the case was whether an EPA regulation "allow[ing] States to treat all of the pollution-emitting devices within the same industrial grouping as though they were encased within a single 'bubble' " was consistent with the term "stationary source" as used in the Clean Air Act. 467 U. S., at 840. To answer that question of statutory interpretation, the Court articulated and employed a now familiar two-step approach broadly applicable to review of agency action.

The first step was to discern "whether Congress ha[d] directly spoken to the precise question at issue." *Id.*, at 842. The Court explained that "[i]f the intent of Congress is clear, that is the end of the matter," *ibid.*, and courts were therefore to "reject administrative constructions which are contrary to clear congressional intent," *id.*, at 843, n. 9. To discern such intent, the Court noted, a reviewing court was to "employ traditional tools of statutory construction." *Ibid.*

Without mentioning the APA, or acknowledging any doctrinal shift, the Court articulated a second step applicable when "Congress ha[d] not directly addressed the precise question at issue." *Id.*, at 843. In such a case—that is, a case in which "the statute [was] silent or ambiguous with respect to the specific issue" at hand—a reviewing court could not "simply impose its own construction on the statute, as would be necessary in the absence of an administrative interpretation." *Ibid.* (footnote omitted). A court instead had to set aside the traditional interpretive tools and defer to the agency if it had offered "a permissible construction of the statute," *ibid.*, even if not "the reading the court would have reached if the question initially had arisen in a judicial proceeding," *ibid.*, n. 11. That directive was justified, according to the Court, by the understanding that administering statutes "requires the formulation of policy" to fill statutory "gap[s]"; by the long judicial tradition of according "considerable weight" to Executive Branch interpretations; and by a host of other considerations, including the complexity of the regulatory scheme, EPA's "detailed and reasoned" consideration, the policy-laden nature of the judgment supposedly required, and the agency's indirect accountability to the people through the President. *Id.*, at 843, 844, and n. 14, 865.

Employing this new test, the Court concluded that Congress had not addressed the question at issue with the necessary "level of specificity" and that EPA's interpretation was "entitled to deference." *Id.*, at 865. It did not matter *why* Congress, as the Court saw it, had not squarely addressed the question, see *ibid.*, or that "the agency ha[d] from time to time changed its interpretation," *id.*, at 863. The latest EPA interpretation was a permissible reading of the Clean Air Act, so under the Court's new rule, that reading controlled.

Initially, *Chevron* "seemed destined to obscurity." T. Merrill, The Story of *Chevron*: The Making of an Accidental Landmark, 66 Admin. L. Rev.

253, 276 (2014). The Court did not at first treat it as the watershed decision it was fated to become; it was hardly cited in cases involving statutory questions of agency authority. See *ibid.* But within a few years, both this Court and the courts of appeals were routinely invoking its two-step framework as the governing standard in such cases. See *id.*, at 276–277. As the Court did so, it revisited the doctrine's justifications. Eventually, the Court decided that *Chevron* rested on "a presumption that Congress, when it left ambiguity in a statute meant for implementation by an agency, understood that the ambiguity would be resolved, first and foremost, by the agency, and desired the agency (rather than the courts) to possess whatever degree of discretion the ambiguity allows." *Smiley* v. *Citibank (South Dakota), N. A.*, 517 U.S. 735, 740–741 (1996); see also [citations].

B

Neither *Chevron* nor any subsequent decision of this Court attempted to reconcile its framework with the APA. The "law of deference" that this Court has built on the foundation laid in *Chevron* has instead been "[h]eedless of the original design" of the APA. *Perez*, 575 U. S., at 109 (Scalia, J., concurring in judgment).

*Chevron* defies the command of the APA that "the reviewing court"—not the agency whose action it reviews—is to "decide *all* relevant questions of law" and "interpret . . . statutory provisions." § 706 (emphasis added). It requires a court to *ignore*, not follow, "the reading the court would have reached" had it exercised its independent judgment as required by the APA. *Chevron*, 467 U. S., at 843, n. 11. And although exercising independent judgment is consistent with the "respect" historically given to Executive Branch interpretations, see, *e.g.*, *Edwards' Lessee*, 12 Wheat., at 210; *Skidmore*, 323 U. S., at 140, *Chevron* insists on much more. It demands that courts mechanically afford *binding* deference to agency interpretations, including those that have been inconsistent over time. See 467 U. S., at 863. Still worse, it forces courts to do so even when a pre-existing judicial precedent holds that the statute means something else—unless the prior court happened to also say that the statute is "unambiguous." *Brand X*, 545 U. S., at 982. That regime is the antithesis of the time honored approach the APA prescribes. In fretting over the prospect of "allow[ing]" a judicial interpretation of a statute "to override an agency's" in a dispute before a court, *ibid.*, *Chevron* turns the statutory scheme for judicial review of agency action upside down.

*Chevron* cannot be reconciled with the APA, as the Government and the dissent contend, by presuming that statutory ambiguities are implicit delegations to agencies. See Brief for Respondents in No. 22–1219, pp. 13, 37–38; *post*, at 4–15 (opinion of Kagan, J.). Presumptions have their place in statutory interpretation, but only to the extent that they approximate reality. *Chevron*'s presumption does not, because "[a]n ambiguity is simply not a delegation of law-interpreting power. *Chevron* confuses the two." C. Sunstein, Interpreting Statutes in the Regulatory State, 103 Harv. L. Rev. 405, 445 (1989). As *Chevron* itself noted, ambiguities may result from an inability on the part of Congress to squarely answer the question at hand, or from a failure to even "consider the question" with the requisite precision. 467 U. S., at 865. In neither case does an ambiguity necessarily reflect a congressional intent that an agency, as opposed to a court, resolve the resulting interpretive question. And many or perhaps most statutory ambiguities may be unintentional. As the Framers recognized, ambiguities will inevitably follow from "the complexity of objects, . . . the imperfection of the human faculties," and the simple fact that "no language is so copious as to supply words and phrases for every complex idea." The Federalist No. 37, at 236.

Courts, after all, routinely confront statutory ambiguities in cases having nothing to do with *Chevron*—cases that do not involve agency interpretations or delegations of authority. Of course, when faced with a statutory ambiguity in such a case, the ambiguity is not a delegation to anybody, and a court is not somehow relieved of its obligation to independently interpret the statute. Courts in that situation do not throw up their hands because "Congress's instructions have" supposedly "run out," leaving a statutory "gap." *Post*, at 2 (opinion of Kagan, J.). Courts instead understand that such statutes, no matter how impenetrable, do—in fact, must—have a single, best meaning. That is the whole point of having written statutes; "every statute's meaning is fixed at the time of enactment." *Wisconsin Central Ltd.* v. *United States*, 585 U.S. 274, 284 (2018). So instead of declaring a particular party's reading "permissible" in such a case, courts use every tool at their disposal to determine the best reading of the statute and resolve the ambiguity.

In an agency case as in any other, though, even if some judges might (or might not) consider the statute ambiguous, there is a best reading all the same—"the reading the court would have reached" if no agency were involved. *Chevron*, 467 U. S., at 843, n. 11. It therefore makes no sense to speak of a "permissible" interpretation that is not the one the court, after applying all relevant interpretive tools, concludes is best. In the business of statutory interpretation, if it is not the best, it is not permissible.

Perhaps most fundamentally, *Chevron*'s presumption is misguided because agencies have no special competence in resolving statutory ambiguities. Courts do. The Framers, as noted, anticipated that courts would often confront statutory ambiguities and expected that courts would resolve them by exercising independent legal judgment. And even *Chevron* itself reaffirmed that "[t]he judiciary is the final authority on issues of statutory construction" and recognized that "in the absence of an administrative interpretation," it is "necessary" for a court to "impose its own construction on the statute." *Id.*, at 843, and n. 9. *Chevron* gravely erred, though, in concluding that the inquiry is fundamentally different just because an administrative interpretation is in play. The very point of the traditional tools of statutory construction—the tools courts use every day—is to resolve statutory ambiguities. That is no less true when the ambiguity is about the scope of an agency's own power—perhaps the occasion on which abdication in favor of the agency is *least* appropriate.

The Government responds that Congress must generally intend for agencies to resolve statutory ambiguities because agencies have subject matter expertise regarding the statutes they administer; because deferring to agencies purportedly promotes the uniform construction of federal law; and because resolving statutory ambiguities can involve policymaking best left to political actors, rather than courts. See Brief for Respondents in No. 22–1219, pp. 16–19. The dissent offers more of the same. See *post*, at 9–14. But none of these considerations justifies *Chevron*'s sweeping presumption of congressional intent.

Beginning with expertise, we recently noted that interpretive issues arising in connection with a regulatory scheme often "may fall more naturally into a judge's bailiwick" than an agency's. *Kisor*, 588 U. S., at 578 (opinion of the Court). We thus observed that "[w]hen the agency has no comparative expertise in resolving a regulatory ambiguity, Congress presumably would not grant it that authority." *Ibid. Chevron*'s broad rule of deference, though, demands that courts presume just the opposite. Under that rule, ambiguities of all stripes trigger deference. Indeed, the Government and, seemingly, the dissent continue to defend the proposition that *Chevron* applies even in cases having little to do with an agency's technical subject matter expertise. See Brief for Respondents in No. 22–1219, p. 17; *post*, at 10.

But even when an ambiguity happens to implicate a technical matter, it does not follow that Congress has taken the power to authoritatively interpret the statute from the courts and given it to the agency. Congress expects courts to handle technical statutory questions. "[M]any statutory cases" call upon "courts [to] interpret the mass of technical detail that is the ordinary diet of the law," *Egelhoff* v. *Egelhoff*, 532 U.S. 141, 161 (2001) (Breyer, J., dissenting), and courts did so without issue in agency cases before *Chevron*, see *post*, at 30 (Gorsuch, J., concurring). Courts, after all, do not decide such questions blindly. The parties and *amici* in such cases are steeped in the subject matter, and reviewing courts have the benefit of their perspectives. In an agency case in particular, the court will go about its task with the agency's "body of experience and informed judgment," among other information, at its disposal. *Skidmore*, 323 U. S., at 140. And although an agency's interpretation of a statute "cannot bind a court," it may be especially informative "to the extent it rests on factual premises within [the agency's] expertise." *Bureau of Alcohol, Tobacco and Firearms* v. *FLRA*, 464 U.S. 89, 98, n. 8 (1983). Such expertise has always been one of the factors which may give an Executive Branch interpretation particular "power to persuade, if lacking power to control." *Skidmore*, 323 U. S., at 140; see, *e.g.*, [citations].

For those reasons, delegating ultimate interpretive authority to agencies is simply not necessary to ensure that the resolution of statutory ambiguities is well informed by subject matter expertise. The better presumption is therefore that Congress expects courts to do their ordinary job of interpreting statutes, with due respect for the views of the Executive Branch. And to the extent that Congress and the Executive Branch may disagree with how the courts have performed that job in a particular case, they are of course always free to act by revising the statute.

Nor does a desire for the uniform construction of federal law justify *Chevron*. Given inconsistencies in how judges apply *Chevron*, see *infra*, at 30–33, it is unclear how much the doctrine as a whole (as opposed to its highly deferential second step) actually promotes such uniformity. In any event, there is little value in imposing a uniform interpretation of a statute if that interpretation is wrong. We see no reason to presume that Congress prefers uniformity for uniformity's sake over the correct interpretation of the laws it enacts.

The view that interpretation of ambiguous statutory provisions amounts to policymaking suited for political actors rather than courts is especially mistaken, for it rests on a profound misconception of the judicial role. It is reasonable to assume that Congress intends to leave policymaking to political actors. But resolution of statutory ambiguities involves legal interpretation. That task does not suddenly become policymaking just because a court has an "agency to fall back on." *Kisor*, 588 U. S., at 575 (opinion of the Court). Courts interpret statutes, no matter the context, based on the traditional tools of statutory construction, not individual policy preferences. Indeed, the Framers crafted the Constitution to ensure that federal judges could exercise judgment free from the influence of the political branches. See The Federalist, No. 78, at 522–525. They were to construe the law with "[c]lear heads . . . and honest hearts," not with an eye to policy preferences that had not made it into the statute. 1 Works of James Wilson 363 (J. Andrews ed. 1896).

That is not to say that Congress cannot or does not confer discretionary authority on agencies. Congress may do so, subject to constitutional limits, and it often has. But to stay out of discretionary policymaking left to the political branches, judges need only fulfill their obligations under the APA to independently identify and respect such delegations of authority, police the outer statutory boundaries of those delegations, and ensure that agencies exercise their discretion consistent with the APA. By forcing courts to instead pretend that ambiguities are necessarily delegations,

*Chevron* does not prevent judges from making policy. It prevents them from judging.

In truth, *Chevron*'s justifying presumption is, as Members of this Court have often recognized, a fiction. See *Buffington* v. *McDonough*, 598 U. S. ___, ___ (2022) (Gorsuch, J., dissenting from denial of certiorari) (slip op., at 11); *Cuozzo*, 579 U. S., at 286 (Thomas, J., concurring); Scalia, 1989 Duke L. J., at 517; see also *post*, at 15 (opinion of Kagan, J.). So we have spent the better part of four decades imposing one limitation on *Chevron* after another, pruning its presumption on the understanding that "where it is in doubt that Congress actually intended to delegate particular interpretive authority to an agency, *Chevron* is 'inapplicable.'" *United States* v. *Mead Corp.*, 533 U.S. 218, 230 (2001); see also [additional citation].

Consider the many refinements we have made in an effort to match *Chevron*'s presumption to reality. We have said that *Chevron* applies only "when it appears that Congress delegated authority to the agency generally to make rules carrying the force of law, and that the agency interpretation claiming deference was promulgated in the exercise of that authority." *Mead*, 533 U. S., at 226–227. In practice, that threshold requirement—sometimes called *Chevron* "step zero"—largely limits *Chevron* to "the fruits of notice-and-comment rulemaking or formal adjudication." 533 U. S., at 230. But even when those processes are used, deference is still not warranted "where the regulation is 'procedurally defective'—that is, where the agency errs by failing to follow the correct procedures in issuing the regulation." *Encino Motorcars, LLC* v. *Navarro*, 579 U.S. 211, 220 (2016).

Even where those procedural hurdles are cleared, substantive ones remain. Most notably, *Chevron* does not apply if the question at issue is one of "deep 'economic and political significance.'" *King* v. *Burwell*, 576 U.S. 473, 486 (2015). We have instead expected Congress to delegate such authority "expressly" if at all, *ibid.*, for "[e]xtraordinary grants of regulatory authority are rarely accomplished through 'modest words,' 'vague terms,' or 'subtle device[s],'" *West Virginia* v. *EPA*, 597 U.S. 697, 723 (2022). Nor have we applied *Chevron* to agency interpretations of judicial review provisions, see *Adams Fruit Co.*, 494 U. S., at 649–650, or to statutory schemes not administered by the agency seeking deference, see *Epic Systems Corp.* v. *Lewis*, 584 U.S. 497, 519–520 (2018).

* * *

This Court, for its part, has not deferred to an agency interpretation under *Chevron* since 2016. See *Cuozzo*, 579 U. S., at 280 . . . But *Chevron* remains on the books. So litigants must continue to wrestle with it, and lower courts—bound by even our crumbling precedents, see *Agostini* v. *Felton*, 521 U.S. 203, 238 (1997)—understandably continue to apply it.

The experience of the last 40 years has thus done little to rehabilitate *Chevron*. It has only made clear that *Chevron*'s fictional presumption of congressional intent was always unmoored from the APA's demand that courts exercise independent judgment in construing statutes administered by agencies. At best, our intricate *Chevron* doctrine has been nothing more than a distraction from the question that matters: Does the statute authorize the challenged agency action? And at worst, it has required courts to violate the APA by yielding to an agency the express responsibility, vested in "the reviewing *court*," to "decide all relevant questions of law" and "interpret . . . statutory provisions." § 706 (emphasis added).

IV

The only question left is whether *stare decisis*, the doctrine governing judicial adherence to precedent, requires us to persist in the *Chevron* project. It does not. *Stare decisis* is not an "inexorable command," *Payne* v. *Tennessee*, 501 U.S. 808, 828 (1991), and the *stare decisis* considerations most relevant here—"the quality of [the precedent's] reasoning, the workability of the rule it established, . . . and reliance on the decision," *Knick* v. *Township of Scott*, 588 U.S. 180, 203 (2019)—all weigh in favor of letting *Chevron* go.

*Chevron* has proved to be fundamentally misguided. Despite reshaping judicial review of agency action, neither it nor any case of ours applying it grappled with the APA—the statute that lays out how such review works. Its flaws were nonetheless apparent from the start, prompting this Court to revise its foundations and continually limit its application.

* * *

Experience has also shown that *Chevron* is unworkable. The defining feature of its framework is the identification of statutory ambiguity, which requires deference at the doctrine's second step. But the concept of ambiguity has always evaded meaningful definition. . . . .

We are no closer to an answer to that question than we were four decades ago. " '[A]mbiguity' is a term that may have different meanings for different judges." *Exxon Mobil Corp.* v. *Allapattah Services, Inc.*, 545 U.S. 546, 572 (2005) (Stevens, J., dissenting). One judge might see ambiguity everywhere; another might never encounter it.

* * *

A rule of law that is so wholly "in the eye of the beholder," *Exxon Mobil Corp.*, 545 U. S., at 572 (Stevens, J., dissenting), invites different results in like cases and is therefore "arbitrary in practice," *Gulfstream Aerospace Corp.* v. *Mayacamas Corp.*, 485 U.S. 271, 283 (1988). Such an impressionistic and malleable concept "cannot stand as an every-day test for allocating" interpretive authority between courts and agencies. *Swift & Co.* v. *Wickham*, 382 U.S. 111, 125 (1965).

* * *

Four decades after its inception, *Chevron* has thus become an impediment, rather than an aid, to accomplishing the basic judicial task of "say[ing] what the law is." *Marbury*, 1 Cranch, at 177. And its continuing import is far from clear. Courts have often declined to engage with the doctrine, saying it makes no difference. See n. 7, *supra*. And as noted, we have avoided deferring under *Chevron* since 2016. That trend is nothing new; for decades, we have often declined to invoke *Chevron* even in those cases where it might appear to be applicable. . . . At this point, all that remains of *Chevron* is a decaying husk with bold pretensions.

Nor has *Chevron* been the sort of " 'stable background' rule" that fosters meaningful reliance. *Post*, at 8, n. 1 (opinion of Kagan, J.) Given our constant tinkering with and eventual turn away from *Chevron*, and its inconsistent application by the lower courts, it instead is hard to see how anyone—Congress included—could reasonably expect a court to rely on *Chevron* in any particular case. And even if it were possible to predict accurately when courts will apply *Chevron*, the doctrine "does not provide 'a clear or easily applicable standard, so arguments for reliance based on its clarity are misplaced.' " *Janus*, 585 U. S., at 927. To plan on *Chevron* yielding a particular result is to gamble not only that the doctrine will be invoked, but also that it will produce readily foreseeable outcomes and the stability that comes with them. History has proved neither bet to be a winning proposition.

Rather than safeguarding reliance interests, *Chevron* affirmatively destroys them. Under *Chevron*, a statutory ambiguity, no matter why it is there, becomes a license authorizing an agency to change positions as much as it likes, with "[u]nexplained inconsistency" being "at most . . . a reason for holding an interpretation to be . . . arbitrary and capricious." *Brand X*, 545 U. S., at 981. But statutory ambiguity, as we have explained, is not a reliable indicator of actual delegation of discretionary authority to agencies. *Chevron* thus allows agencies to change course even when Congress has given them no power to do so. By its sheer breadth, *Chevron* fosters unwarranted instability in the law, leaving those attempting to plan around agency action in an eternal fog of uncertainty.

* * *

*Chevron* was a judicial invention that required judges to disregard their statutory duties. And the only way to "ensure that the law will not merely change erratically, but will develop in a principled and intelligible fashion," *Vasquez* v. *Hillery*, 474 U.S. 254, 265 (1986), is for us to leave *Chevron* behind.

By doing so, however, we do not call into question prior cases that relied on the *Chevron* framework. The holdings of those cases that specific agency actions are lawful—including the Clean Air Act holding of *Chevron* itself—are still subject to statutory *stare decisis* despite our change in interpretive methodology. See *CBOCS West, Inc.* v. *Humphries,* 553 U.S. 442, 457 (2008). Mere reliance on *Chevron* cannot constitute a " 'special justification' " for overruling such a holding, because to say a precedent relied on *Chevron* is, at best, "just an argument that the precedent was wrongly decided." *Halliburton Co.* v. *Erica P. John Fund, Inc.*, 573 U.S. 258, 266 (2014). That is not enough to justify overruling a statutory precedent.

* * *

*Chevron* is overruled. Courts must exercise their independent judgment in deciding whether an agency has acted within its statutory authority, as the APA requires. Careful attention to the judgment of the Executive Branch may help inform that inquiry. And when a particular statute delegates authority to an agency consistent with constitutional limits, courts must respect the delegation, while ensuring that the agency acts within it. But courts need not and under the APA may not defer to an agency interpretation of the law simply because a statute is ambiguous.

Because the D. C. and First Circuits relied on *Chevron* in deciding whether to uphold the Rule, their judgments are vacated, and the cases are remanded for further proceedings consistent with this opinion.

It is so ordered.

---

**Questions:** How convincing is the Court's justification for overruling the deferential *Chevron* standard of review? Is less judicial deference to agencies practical?

## RULEMAKING

### CHOCOLATE MFRS. ASS'N V. BLOCK

755 F.2d 1098 (4th Cir. 1985)

* * *

SPROUSE, CIRCUIT JUDGE:

Chocolate Manufacturers Association (CMA) appeals from the decision of the district court denying it relief from a rule promulgated by the Food and Nutrition Service (FNS) of the United States Department of Agriculture (USDA or Department). CMA protests that part of the rule that prohibits the use of chocolate flavored milk in the federally funded Special

Supplemental Food Program for Women, Infants and Children (WIC Program). Holding that the Department's proposed rulemaking did not provide adequate notice that the elimination of flavored milk would be considered in the rulemaking procedure, we reverse.

* * *

The WIC Program was established by Congress in 1972 to assist pregnant, postpartum, and breastfeeding women, infants and young children from families with inadequate income whose physical and mental health is in danger because of inadequate nutrition or health care. Under the program, the Department designs food packages reflecting the different nutritional needs of women, infants, and children and provides cash grants to state or local agencies, which distribute cash or vouchers to qualifying individuals in accordance with Departmental regulations as to the type and quantity of food. 42 U.S.C. § 1786 (a) (1982).

In 1975 Congress revised and extended the WIC Program through fiscal year 1978 and, for the first time, defined the "supplemental foods" which the program was established to provide. The term

"shall mean those foods containing nutrients known to be lacking in the diets of populations at nutritional risk and, in particular, those foods and food products containing high-quality protein, iron, calcium, vitamin A, and vitamin C. . . . The contents of the food package shall be made available in such a manner as to provide flexibility, taking into account medical and nutritional objectives and cultural eating patterns." 42 U.S.C. § 1786(b)(14) (1982).

Pursuant to this statutory definition, the Department promulgated new regulations specifying the contents of WIC Program food packages. These regulations specified that flavored milk was an acceptable substitute for fluid whole milk in the food packages for women and children, but not infants. This regulation formalized the Department's practice of permitting the substitution of flavored milk, a practice observed in the WIC Program since its inception in 1973 as well as in several of the other food programs administered by the Department. 42 U.S.C. § 1786(b)(14) (1982).

In 1978 Congress, in extending the WIC Program through fiscal year 1982, redefined the term "supplemental foods" to mean

"those foods containing nutrients determined by nutritional research to be lacking in the diets of pregnant, breastfeeding, and postpartum women, infants, and children, as prescribed by the Secretary. State agencies may, with the approval of the Secretary, substitute different foods providing the nutritional equivalent of foods prescribed by the Secretary, to allow for different cultural eating patterns." 42 U.S.C. § 1786(b)(14) (1982).

Congress stated further:

"The Secretary shall prescribe by regulation supplemental foods to be made available in the program under this section. To the degree possible, the Secretary shall assure that the fat, sugar, and salt content of the prescribed foods is appropriate." 42 U.S.C. § 1786 (f)(12) (1982).

To comply with this statutory redefinition, the Department moved to redraft its regulations specifying the WIC Program food packages. In doing so it relied upon information collected during an extensive investigative effort which had begun in 1977. In June 1977 the Department held public hearings in seven cities and elicited testimony on the structure and administration of the WIC Program. The Department invited many interested and informed parties to attend these hearings—the governor and chief health officer of every state, the House Education and Labor Committee, the Senate Select Committee on Nutrition Evaluation, state WIC coordinators, industry representatives, and professional and advocacy groups. In addition to information gathered at the public hearings, the Department received periodic reports from the National Advisory Council on Maternal, Infant, and Fetal Nutrition, as well as recommendations from a Food Package Advisory Panel convened in October 1978.

Using this information as well as its own research as a basis, the Department in November 1979 published for comment the proposed rule at issue in this case. 44 Fed.Reg. 69254 (1979). Along with the proposed rule, the Department published a preamble discussing the general purpose of the rule and acknowledging the congressional directive that the Department design food packages containing the requisite nutritional value and appropriate levels of fat, sugar, and salt. *Id.* at 69254. Discussing the issue of sugar at length, it noted, for example, that continued inclusion of high sugar cereals may be "contrary to nutrition education principles and may lead to unsound eating practices." *Id.* at 69263. It also noted that high sugar foods are more expensive than foods with lower sugar content, and that allowing them would be "inconsistent with the goal of teaching participants economical food buying patterns." *Id.*

The rule proposed a maximum sugar content specifically for authorized cereals. The preamble also contained a discussion of the sugar content in juice, but the Department did not propose to reduce the allowable amount of sugar in juice because of technical problems involved in any reduction. Neither the rule nor the preamble discussed sugar in relation to flavoring in milk. Under the proposed rule, the food packages for women and children without special dietary needs included milk that could be "flavored or unflavored." *Id.*

The notice allowed sixty days for comment and specifically invited comment on the entire scope of the proposed rules: "The public is invited to submit written comments in favor of or in objection to the proposed regulations or to make recommendations for alternatives not considered in the proposed regulations." *Id.* at 69255. Over 1,000 comments were received from state and local agencies, congressional offices, interest groups, and WIC Program participants and others. Seventy-eight commenters, mostly local WIC administrators, recommended that the agency delete flavored milk from the list of approved supplemental foods.

In promulgating the final rule, the Department, responding to these public comments, deleted flavored milk from the list, explaining:

"In the previous regulations, women and children were allowed to receive flavored or unflavored milk. No change in this provision was proposed by the Department. However, 78 commenters requested the deletion of flavored milk from the food packages since flavored milk has a higher sugar content than unflavored milk. They indicated that providing flavored milk contradicts nutrition education and the Department's proposal to limit sugar in the food packages. Furthermore, flavored milk is more expensive than unflavored milk. The Department agrees with these concerns. There are significant differences in the sugar content of fluid whole milk and low fat chocolate milk. Fluid whole milk supplies 12.0 grams of carbohydrate per cup compared to 27.3 grams of carbohydrate per cup provided by low fat chocolate milk. If we assume that the major portion of carbohydrate in milk is in the form of simple sugar, fluid whole milk contains 4.9% sugar contrasted with 10.9% sugar in low fat chocolate milk. Therefore, to reinforce nutrition education, for consistency with the Department's philosophy about sugar in the food packages, and to maintain food package costs at economic levels, the Department is deleting flavored milk from the food packages for women and children. Although the deletion of flavored milk was not proposed, the comments and the Department's policy on sugar validate this change." 45 Fed.Reg. 74854, 74865–66 (1980).

After the final rule was issued, CMA petitioned the Department to reopen the rulemaking to allow it to comment, maintaining that it had been misled into believing that the deletion of flavored milk would not be considered. In a letter to CMA dated November 18, 1981, the Department indicated that it would reopen the issue of flavored milk for "further public comments" and would request "rationale both supporting and opposing the disallowance of flavored milk in the WIC Program." It subsequently reversed this position, however, and declined to reopen the rulemaking procedure.

On this appeal, CMA contends first that the Department did not provide notice that the disallowance of flavored milk would be considered, and second that the Department gave no reasoned justification for changing its position about the nutritional value of chocolate in the food distributed under its authority.

* * *

The requirement of notice and a fair opportunity to be heard is basic to administrative law. *See* 1 K. Davis, *Administrative Law Treatise* § 6.1 at 450 (2d ed. 1978). Our single chore is to determine if the Department's notice provided interested persons, including CMA, with that opportunity. We must decide whether inclusion of flavored milk in the allowable food packages under the proposed rule should have alerted interested persons that the Department might reverse its position and exclude flavored milk if adverse comments recommended its deletion from the program.

Section 4 of the Administrative Procedure Act (APA) requires that the notice in the Federal Register of a proposed rulemaking contain "either the terms or substance of the proposed rule or a description of the subjects and issues involved." 5 U.S.C. § 553(b)(3) (1982). The purpose of the notice-and-comment procedure is both "to allow the agency to benefit from the experience and input of the parties who file comments . . . and to see to it that the agency maintains a flexible and open-minded attitude towards its own rules." *National Tour Brokers Ass'n v. United States,* 591 F.2d 896, 902 (D.C. Cir. 1978). The notice-and-comment procedure encourages public participation in the administrative process and educates the agency, thereby helping to ensure informed agency decisionmaking. *Spartan Radiocasting Co. v. FCC,* 619 F.2d 314, 321 (4th Cir. 1980); *BASF Wyandotte Corp. v. Costle,* 598 F.2d 637, 642 (1st Cir. 1979), *cert. denied,* 444 U.S. 10964 (1980).

The Department's published notice here consisted of the proposed rule and a preamble discussing the negative effect of high sugar content in general and specifically in relation to some foods such as cereals and juices, but it did not mention high sugar content in flavored milk. The proposed rule eliminated certain foods with high sugar content but specifically authorized flavored milk as part of the permissible diet. In a discussion characterized by pointed identification of foods with high sugar content, flavored milk was conspicuous by its exclusion. If after comments the agency had adopted without change the proposed rule as its final rule, there could have been no possible objection to the adequacy of notice. The public was fully notified as to what the Department considered to be a healthy and adequate diet for its target group. The final rule, however, dramatically altered the proposed rule, changing for the first time the milk content of the diet by deleting flavored milk. The agency concedes that the elimination of flavored milk by the final rule is a complete reversal from its treatment in the proposed rule, but it explains that the reversal was caused by the comments received from 78 interested parties—primarily professional administrators of the WIC Program.

This presents then not the simple question of whether the notice of a proposed rule adequately informs the public of its intent, but rather the question of how to judge the adequacy of the notice when the proposal it describes is replaced by a final rule which reaches a conclusion exactly opposite to that proposed, on the basis of comments received from parties representing only a single view of a controversy. In reviewing the propriety of such agency action, we are not constrained by the same degree of deference we afford most agency determinations. "Though our review of an agency's final decision is relatively narrow, we must be strict in reviewing an agency's compliance with procedural rules." *BASF Wyandotte Corp. v. Costle,* 598 F.2d at 641; *see also Weyerhauser Co. v. Costle,* 590 F.2d 1011, 1025–28 (D.C. Cir. 1978) (whereas a court defers to an agency's technical judgments, it is less hesitant to reject the agency's interpretation of statutes, and in reviewing an agency's procedural integrity, the court relies on its own independent judgment). "The question of adequacy of notice where a proposed rule is changed after comment . . . requires careful consideration on a case-by-case basis." *BASF,* 598 F.2d at 642.

* * *

There is no question that an agency may promulgate a final rule that differs in some particulars from its proposal. Otherwise the agency "can learn from the comments on its proposals only at the peril of starting a new procedural round of commentary." *International Harvester Co. v. Ruckelshaus,* 478 F.2d 615, 632 n. 51 (D.C. Cir. 1973). An agency, however, does not have carte blanche to establish a rule contrary to its original proposal simply because it receives suggestions to alter it during the comment period. An interested party must have been alerted by the notice to the possibility of the changes eventually adopted from the comments. *Wagner Electric Corporation v. Volpe,* 466 F.2d 1013, 1019 (3rd Cir. 1972).

* * *

The test devised by the First Circuit for determining adequacy of notice of a change in a proposed rule occurring after comments appears to us to be sound: notice is adequate if the changes in the original plan "are in character with the original scheme," and the final rule is a "logical outgrowth" of the notice and comments already given. *See, e.g., BASF Wyandotte Corp. v. Costle,* 598 F.2d 637, 642 (1st Cir. 1979), *cert. denied,* 444 U.S. 1096 (1980); *South Terminal Corp. v. EPA,* 504 F.2d 646, 659 (1st Cir. 1974). Other circuits also have adopted some form of the "logical outgrowth" test. *See, e.g., Sierra Club v. Costle,* 657 F.2d 298, 352 (D.C. Cir. 1981) (logical outgrowth of the notice and comments); *Taylor Diving Salvage Co. v. Dept. of Labor,* 599 F.2d 622, 626 (5th Cir. 1979) (logical outgrowth of the standard originally proposed). Stated differently, if the final rule materially alters the issues involved in the rulemaking or, as stated in *Rowell v. Andrus,* 631 F.2d 699, 702 n. 2 (10th Cir. 1980), if the final rule "substantially departs from the terms or substance of the proposed rule," the notice is inadequate.

There can be no doubt that the final rule in the instant case was the "outgrowth" of the original rule proposed by the agency, but the question of whether the change in it was in character with the original scheme and whether it was a "*logical* outgrowth" is not easy to answer. In resolving this difficult issue, we recognize that, although helpful, verbal formulations are not omnipotent talismans, and we agree that in the final analysis each case "must turn on how well the notice that the agency gave serves the policies underlying the notice requirement." *Small Refiner Lead Phase-Down Task Force v. EPA,* 705 F.2d 506, 547 (D.C. Cir. 1983). Under either view, we do not feel that CMA was fairly treated or that the administrative rulemaking process was well served by the drastic alteration of the rule without an opportunity for CMA to be heard.

It is apparent that for many years the Department of Agriculture has permitted the use of chocolate in some form in the food distribution programs that it administers. The only time the Department has proposed to remove chocolate in any form from its programs was in April 1978 when it sought to characterize chocolate as a candy and remove it from the School Lunch Program. That proposal was withdrawn after CMA commented, supporting chocolate as a part of the diet. Chocolate flavored milk has been a permissible part of the WIC Program diet since its inception and there have been no proposals for its removal until the present controversy.

The Department sponsored commendable information-gathering proceedings prior to publishing its proposed rule. Together with its own research, the information gathered in the pre-publication information solicitations formed the basis for the proposed rule. Most of the same information was presented to Congress prior to enactment of the 1978 statute that precipitated the 1979 rulemaking here in controversy. The National Advisory Council on Maternal, Infant, and Fetal Nutrition provided information and advice. Regional council meetings were open to the public and held in diverse areas of the country. Department of Agriculture personnel attended a number of regional, state, and local meetings and gathered opinions concerning possible changes in the food packages. The agency also gathered a food package advisory panel of experts seeking their recommendations. Food packages were designed based on the information and advice gleaned from these sources. In all of these activities setting out and discussing food packages, including the proposed rule and its preamble, the Department never suggested that flavored milk be removed from the WIC Program.

The published preamble to the proposed rule consisted of twelve pages in the Federal Register discussing in detail factors that would be considered in making the final rule. Two pages were devoted to a general discussion of nutrients, including protein, iron, calcium, vitamin A, vitamin C, folic acid, zinc, and fiber, and the dangers of overconsumption of sugar, fat, and salt. The preamble discussed some foods containing these ingredients and foods posing specific problems. It did not discuss flavored milk.

In the next eight pages of the preamble, the nutrition content of food packages was discussed—under the general headings of "cereal" and "juice" for infants; and "eggs," "milk," "cheese," "peanut butter and mature dried beans and peas," "juice," "additional foods," "cereals," "iron," "sugar," "whole grain cereals," "highly fortified cereals," and "artificial flavors and colors" for women and children. The only reference to milk concerned the correct quantity to be provided to children, *i.e.*, 24 quarts per month instead of 28 quarts. Although there was considerable discussion of the sugar content of juice and cereal, there was none concerning flavored milk. Likewise, there was considerable discussion of artificial flavor and color in cereal but none concerning flavored milk. The only reference to flavored milk was in the two-page discussion of the individual food packages, which noted that the proposed rule would permit the milk to be flavored or unflavored. The proposed rule which followed the preamble expressly noted that flavored or unflavored milk was permitted in the individual food packages for women and children without special dietary needs.

At the time the proposed rulemaking was published, neither CMA nor the public in general could have had any indication from the history of either the WIC Program or any other food distribution programs that flavored milk was not part of the acceptable diet for women and children without special dietary needs. The discussion in the preamble to the proposed rule was very detailed and identified specific foods which the agency was examining for excess sugar. This specificity, together with total silence concerning any suggestion of eliminating flavored milk, strongly indicated that flavored milk was not at issue. The proposed rule positively and unqualifiedly approved the continued use of flavored milk. Under the specific circumstances of this case, it cannot be said that the ultimate changes in the proposed rule were in character with the original scheme or a logical outgrowth of the notice. We can well accept that, in general, an approval of a practice in a proposed rule may properly alert interested parties that the practice may be disapproved in the final rule in the event of adverse comments. The total effect of the history of the use of flavored milk, the preamble discussion, and the proposed rule, however, could have led interested persons only to conclude that a change in flavored milk would not be considered. Although ultimately their comments may well have been futile, CMA and other interested persons at least should have had the opportunity to make them. We believe that there was insufficient notice that the deletion of flavored milk from the WIC Program would be considered if adverse comments were received and, therefore, that affected parties did not receive a fair opportunity to contribute to the administrative rulemaking process. That process was ill-served by the misleading or inadequate notice concerning the permissibility of chocolate flavored milk in the WIC Program and "does not serve the policy underlying the notice requirement."

The judgment of the district court is therefore reversed, and the case is remanded to the administrative agency with instructions to reopen the comment period and thereby afford interested parties a fair opportunity to comment on the proposed changes in the rule.

REVERSED AND REMANDED WITH INSTRUCTIONS.

---

**Questions:** Would *Chocolate Mfgrs.* have been decided differently following *Loper Bright*? What if the U.S. Department of Labor proposed a rule extending minimum and overtime pay to most "companionship workers," but then issued a final rule exempting them from coverage? See *Long Island Care at Home, Ltd. v. Coke,* 551 U.S. 158 (2007).

## EXPLANATIONS FOR DECISIONS

### FEDERAL COMMUNICATIONS COMMISSION v. FOX TELEVISION STATIONS, INC.

556 U.S. 502 (2009)

* * *

JUSTICE SCALIA delivered the opinion of the Court, except as to Part III–E.

Federal law prohibits the broadcasting of "any . . . indecent . . . language," 18 U. S. C. § 1464, which includes expletives referring to sexual or excretory activity or organs, see *FCC* v. *Pacifica Foundation*, 438 U. S. 726 (1978). This case concerns the adequacy of the Federal Communications Commission's explanation of its decision that this sometimes forbids the broadcasting of indecent expletives even when the offensive words are not repeated.

Statutory and Regulatory Background

The Communications Act of 1934, 48 Stat. 1064, 47 U. S. C. § 151 *et seq.* (2000 ed. and Supp. V), established a system of limited-term broadcast licenses subject to various "conditions" designed "to maintain the control of the United States over all the channels of radio transmission," § 301 (2000 ed.). Twenty-seven years ago we said that "[a] licensed broadcaster is granted the free and exclusive use of a limited and valuable part of the public domain; when he accepts that franchise it is burdened by enforceable public obligations." *CBS, Inc.* v. *FCC*, 453 U. S. 367, 395 (1981).

One of the burdens that licensees shoulder is the indecency ban—the statutory proscription against "utter[ing] any obscene, indecent, or profane language by means of radio communication," 18 U. S. C. § 1464—which Congress has instructed the Commission to enforce between the hours of 6 a.m. and 10 p.m. Public Telecommunications Act of 1992, § 16(a), 106 Stat.

954, note following 47 U. S. C. § 303. Congress has given the Commission various means of enforcing the indecency ban, including civil fines, see § 503(b)(1), and license revocations or the denial of license renewals, see §§ 309(k), 312(a)(6).

The Commission first invoked the statutory ban on indecent broadcasts in 1975, declaring a daytime broadcast of George Carlin's "Filthy Words" monologue actionably indecent. *Pacifica Foundation*, 56 F. C. C. 2d 94. At that time, the Commission announced the definition of indecent speech that it uses to this day, prohibiting "language that describes, in terms patently offensive as measured by contemporary community standards for the broadcast medium, sexual or excretory activities or organs, at times of the day when there is a reasonable risk that children may be in the audience." *Id.*, at 98.

In *FCC* v. *Pacifica Foundation, supra*, we upheld the Commission's order against statutory and constitutional challenge. We rejected the broadcasters' argument that the statutory proscription applied only to speech appealing to the prurient interest, noting that "the normal definition of 'indecent' merely refers to nonconformance with accepted standards of morality." *Id.*, at 740. And we held that the First Amendment allowed Carlin's monologue to be banned in light of the "uniquely pervasive presence" of the medium and the fact that broadcast programming is "uniquely accessible to children." *Id.*, at 748–749.

In the ensuing years, the Commission took a cautious, but gradually expanding, approach to enforcing the statutory prohibition against indecent broadcasts.

* * *

In 2004, the Commission took one step further by declaring for the first time that a nonliteral (expletive) use of the F- and S-Words could be actionably indecent, even when the word is used only once. The first order to this effect dealt with an NBC broadcast of the Golden Globe Awards, in which the performer Bono commented, " 'This is really, really, f* * *ing brilliant.' " *In re Complaints Against Various Broadcast Licensees Regarding Their Airing of the "Golden Globe Awards" Program,* 19 FCC Rcd. 4975, 4976, n. 4 (2004) *(Golden Globes Order).*

* * *

The Commission first declared that Bono's use of the F-Word fell within its indecency definition, even though the word was used as an intensifier rather than a literal descriptor. "[G]iven the core meaning of the 'F-Word,' " it said, "any use of that word . . . inherently has a sexual connotation." *Id.*, at 4978, ¶ 8. The Commission determined, moreover, that the broadcast was "patently offensive" because the F-Word "is one of the most vulgar, graphic and explicit descriptions of sexual activity in the

English language," because "[i]ts use invariably invokes a coarse sexual image," and because Bono's use of the word was entirely "shocking and gratuitous." *Id.*, at 4979, ¶ 9.

The Commission observed that categorically exempting such language from enforcement actions would "likely lead to more widespread use." *Ibid.* Commission action was necessary to "safeguard the well-being of the nation's children from the most objectionable, most offensive language." *Ibid.* The order noted that technological advances have made it far easier to delete ("bleep out") a "single and gratuitous use of a vulgar expletive," without adulterating the content of a broadcast. *Id.*, at 4980, ¶ 11.

* * *

The Present Case

This case concerns utterances in two live broadcasts aired by Fox Television Stations, Inc., and its affiliates prior to the Commission's *Golden Globes Order*. The first occurred during the 2002 Billboard Music Awards, when the singer Cher exclaimed, "I've also had critics for the last 40 years saying that I was on my way out every year. Right. So f* * * 'em." Brief for Petitioners 9. The second involved a segment of the 2003 Billboard Music Awards, during the presentation of an award by Nicole Richie and Paris Hilton, principals in a Fox television series called "The Simple Life." Ms. Hilton began their interchange by reminding Ms. Richie to "watch the bad language," but Ms. Richie proceeded to ask the audience, "Why do they even call it 'The Simple Life?' Have you ever tried to get cow s* * * out of a Prada purse? It's not so f* * *ing simple." *Id.*, at 9–10. Following each of these broadcasts, the Commission received numerous complaints from parents whose children were exposed to the language.

On March 15, 2006, the Commission released Notices of Apparent Liability for a number of broadcasts that the Commission deemed actionably indecent, including the two described above. *In re Complaints Regarding Various Television Broadcasts Between February 2, 2002 and March 8, 2005,* 21FCC Rcd. 2664 (2006). Multiple parties petitioned the Court of Appeals for the Second Circuit for judicial review of the order, asserting a variety of constitutional and statutory challenges. Since the order had declined to impose sanctions, the Commission had not previously given the broadcasters an opportunity to respond to the indecency charges. It therefore requested and obtained from the Court of Appeals a voluntary remand so that the parties could air their objections. 489 F. 3d 444, 453 (2007). The Commission's order on remand upheld the indecency findings for the broadcasts described above. See *In re Complaints Regarding Various Television Broadcasts Between February 2, 2002, and March 8, 2005*, 21FCC Rcd. 13299 (2006) *(Remand Order)*.

The order first explained that both broadcasts fell comfortably within the subject-matter scope of the Commission's indecency test because the 2003 broadcast involved a literal description of excrement and both broadcasts invoked the "F-Word," which inherently has a sexual connotation. *Id.*, at 13304, ¶ 16, 13323, ¶ 58. The order next determined that the broadcasts were patently offensive under community standards for the medium. Both broadcasts, it noted, involved entirely gratuitous uses of "one of the most vulgar, graphic, and explicit words for sexual activity in the English language." *Id.*, at 13305, ¶ 17, 13324, ¶ 59. It found Ms. Richie's use of the "F-Word" and her "explicit description of the handling of excrement" to be "vulgar and shocking," as well as to constitute "pandering," after Ms. Hilton had playfully warned her to " 'watch the bad language.' " *Id.*, at 13305, ¶ 17. And it found Cher's statement patently offensive in part because she metaphorically suggested a sexual act as a means of expressing hostility to her critics. *Id.*, at 13324, ¶ 60. The order relied upon the "critically important" context of the utterances, *id.*, at 13304, ¶ 15, noting that they were aired during prime-time awards shows "designed to draw a large nationwide audience that could be expected to include many children interested in seeing their favorite music stars," *id.*, at 13305, ¶ 18, 13324, ¶ 59. Indeed, approximately 2.5 million minors witnessed each of the broadcasts. *Id.*, at 13306, ¶ 18, 13326, ¶ 65.

The order asserted that both broadcasts under review would have been actionably indecent under the staff rulings and Commission dicta in effect prior to the *Golden Globes Order*—the 2003 broadcast because it involved a literal description of excrement, rather than a mere expletive, because it used more than one offensive word, and because it was planned, 21 FCC Rcd., at 13307, ¶ 22; and the 2002 broadcast because Cher used the F-Word not as a mere intensifier, but as a description of the sexual act to express hostility to her critics, *id.*, at 13324, ¶ 60. The order stated, however, that the pre-*Golden Globes* regime of immunity for isolated indecent expletives rested only upon staff rulings and Commission dicta, and that the Commission itself had never held "that the isolated use of an expletive . . . was not indecent or could not be indecent," 21 FCC Rcd., at 13307, ¶ 21. In any event, the order made clear, the *Golden Globes Order* eliminated any doubt that fleeting expletives could be actionably indecent, 21 FCC Rcd., at 13308, ¶ 23, 13325, ¶ 61, and the Commission disavowed the bureau-level decisions and its own dicta that had said otherwise, *id.*, at 13306–13307, ¶¶ 20, 21. Under the new policy, a lack of repetition "weigh[s] against a finding of indecency," *id.*, at 13325, ¶ 61, but is not a safe harbor.

The order explained that the Commission's prior "strict dichotomy between 'expletives' and 'descriptions or depictions of sexual or excretory functions' is artificial and does not make sense in light of the fact that an 'expletive's' power to offend derives from its sexual or excretory meaning." *Id.*, at 13308, ¶ 23. In the Commission's view, "granting an automatic exemption for 'isolated or fleeting' expletives unfairly forces viewers (including children)" to take " 'the first blow' " and would allow broadcasters "to air expletives at all hours of a day so long as they did so one at a time." *Id.*, at 13309, ¶ 25. Although the Commission determined that Fox encouraged the offensive language by using suggestive scripting in the 2003 broadcast, and unreasonably failed to take adequate precautions in both broadcasts, *id.*, at 13311–13314, ¶¶ 31–37, the order again declined to impose any forfeiture or other sanction for either of the broadcasts, *id.*, at 13321, ¶ 53, 13326, ¶ 66.

Fox returned to the Second Circuit for review of the *Remand Order*, and various intervenors including CBS, NBC, and ABC joined the action. The Court of Appeals reversed the agency's orders, finding the Commission's reasoning inadequate under the Administrative Procedure Act.489 F. 3d 444. The majority was "skeptical that the Commission [could] provide a reasoned explanation for its 'fleeting expletive' regime that would pass constitutional muster," but it declined to reach the constitutional question. *Id.*, at 462. Judge Leval dissented, *id.*, at 467. We granted certiorari.

Analysis

A. Governing Principles

The Administrative Procedure Act, 5 U. S. C. § 551 *et seq.*, which sets forth the full extent of judicial authority to review executive agency action for procedural correctness, see *Vermont Yankee Nuclear Power Corp.* v. *Natural Resources Defense Council, Inc.*, 435 U. S. 519, 545–549 (1978), permits (insofar as relevant here) the setting aside of agency action that is "arbitrary" or "capricious," 5 U. S. C. § 706(2)(A). Under what we have called this "narrow" standard of review, we insist that an agency "examine the relevant data and articulate a satisfactory explanation for its action." *Motor Vehicle Mfrs. Assn. of United States, Inc.* v. *State Farm Mut. Automobile Ins. Co.*, 463 U. S. 29, 43 (1983). We have made clear, however, that "a court is not to substitute its judgment for that of the agency," *ibid.*, and should "uphold a decision of less than ideal clarity if the agency's path may reasonably be discerned," *Bowman Transp., Inc.* v. *Arkansas-Best Freight System, Inc.*, 419 U. S. 281, 286 (1974).

* * *

We find no basis in the Administrative Procedure Act or in our opinions for a requirement that all agency change be subjected to more searching review. The Act mentions no such heightened standard. And our opinion in *State Farm* neither held nor implied that every agency action representing a policy change must be justified by reasons more substantial than those required to adopt a policy in the first instance. That case, which involved the rescission of a prior regulation, said only that such action requires "a reasoned analysis for the change beyond that which may be required when an agency *does not act* in the first instance." 463 U. S., at 42 (emphasis added). Treating failures to act and rescissions of prior action differently for purposes of the standard of review makes good sense, and has basis in the text of the statute, which likewise treats the two separately. It instructs a reviewing court to "compel agency action unlawfully withheld or unreasonably delayed," and to "hold unlawful and set aside agency action, findings, and conclusions found to be [among other things] . . . arbitrary [or] capricious," § 706(2)(A). The statute makes no distinction, however, between initial agency action and subsequent agency action undoing or revising that action.

To be sure, the requirement that an agency provide reasoned explanation for its action would ordinarily demand that it display awareness that it *is* changing position. An agency may not, for example, depart from a prior policy *sub silentio* or simply disregard rules that are still on the books. See *United States* v. *Nixon*, 418 U. S. 683, 696 (1974). And of course the agency must show that there are good reasons for the new policy. But it need not demonstrate to a court's satisfaction that the reasons for the new policy are *better* than the reasons for the old one; it suffices that the new policy is permissible under the statute, that there are good reasons for it, and that the agency *believes* it to be better, which the conscious change of course adequately indicates. This means that the agency need not always provide a more detailed justification than what would suffice for a new policy created on a blank slate. Sometimes it must—when, for example, its new policy rests upon factual findings that contradict those which underlay its prior policy; or when its prior policy has engendered serious reliance interests that must be taken into account. *Smiley* v. *Citibank (South Dakota), N. A.*, 517 U. S. 735, 742 (1996). It would be arbitrary or capricious to ignore such matters. In such cases it is not that further justification is demanded by the mere fact of policy change; but that a reasoned explanation is needed for disregarding facts and circumstances that underlay or were engendered by the prior policy.

* * *

B. Application to This Case

Judged under the above described standards, the Commission's new enforcement policy and its order finding the broadcasts actionably indecent were neither arbitrary nor capricious. First, the Commission forthrightly acknowledged that its recent actions have broken new ground, taking account of inconsistent "prior Commission and staff action" and explicitly disavowing them as "no longer good law." *Golden Globes Order,* 19 FCC Rcd., at 4980, ¶ 12. To be sure, the (superfluous) explanation in its *Remand Order* of why the Cher broadcast would even have violated its earlier policy may not be entirely convincing. But that unnecessary detour is irrelevant.

There is no doubt that the Commission knew it was making a change. That is why it declined to assess penalties; and it relied on the *Golden Globes Order* as removing any lingering doubt. *Remand Order*, 21 FCC Rcd., at 13308, ¶ 23, 13325, ¶ 61.

Moreover, the agency's reasons for expanding the scope of its enforcement activity were entirely rational. It was certainly reasonable to determine that it made no sense to distinguish between literal and nonliteral uses of offensive words, requiring repetitive use to render only the latter indecent. As the Commission said with regard to expletive use of the F-Word, "the word's power to insult and offend derives from its sexual meaning." *Id.*, at 13323, ¶ 58. And the Commission's decision to look at the patent offensiveness of even isolated uses of sexual and excretory words fits with the context-based approach we sanctioned in *Pacifica*, 438 U. S., at 750. Even isolated utterances can be made in "pander[ing,] . . . vulgar and shocking" manners, *Remand Order*,21 FCC Rcd., at 13305, ¶ 17, and can constitute harmful " 'first blow[s]' " to children, *id.*, at 13309, ¶ 25. It is surely rational (if not inescapable) to believe that a safe harbor for single words would "likely lead to more widespread use of the offensive language," *Golden Globes Order, supra,* at 4979, ¶ 9.

When confronting other requests for *per se* rules governing its enforcement of the indecency prohibition, the Commission has declined to create safe harbors for particular types of broadcasts. See *In re Pacifica Foundation, Inc.*, 2 FCC Rcd., at 2699, ¶ 12 (repudiating the view that the Commission's enforcement power was limited to "deliberate, repetitive use of the seven words actually contained in the George Carlin monologue"); *In re Infinity Broadcasting Corp. of Pa.*, 3 FCC Rcd., at 932, ¶ 17 ("reject[ing] an approach that would hold that if a work has merit, it is *per se* not indecent"). The Commission could rationally decide it needed to step away from its old regime where nonrepetitive use of an expletive was *per se* nonactionable because that was "at odds with the Commission's overall enforcement policy." *Remand Order, supra,* at 13308, ¶ 23.

The fact that technological advances have made it easier for broadcasters to bleep out offending words further supports the Commission's stepped-up enforcement policy. *Golden Globes Order, supra,* at 4980, ¶ 11. And the agency's decision not to impose any forfeiture or other sanction precludes any argument that it is arbitrarily punishing parties without notice of the potential consequences of their action.

* * *

The Second Circuit believed that children today "likely hear this language far more often from other sources than they did in the 1970's when the Commission first began sanctioning indecent speech," and that this cuts against more stringent regulation of broadcasts. 489 F. 3d, at 461. Assuming the premise is true (for this point the Second Circuit did not demand empirical evidence) the conclusion does not necessarily follow. The Commission could reasonably conclude that the pervasiveness of foul language, and the coarsening of public entertainment in other media such as cable, justify more stringent regulation of broadcast programs so as to give conscientious parents a relatively safe haven for their children. In the end, the Second Circuit and the broadcasters quibble with the Commission's policy choices and not with the explanation it has given. We decline to "substitute [our] judgment for that of the agency," *State Farm*, 463 U. S., at 43, and we find the Commission's orders neither arbitrary nor capricious.

[The Court noted that the Court of Appeals did not rule on the constitutionality of the Commission's orders under the First Amendment, so that it would be inappropriate for the Supreme Court to address the issue without a lower court opinion to review.]

The judgment of the United States Court of Appeals for the Second Circuit is reversed, and the case is remanded for further proceedings consistent with this opinion.

JUSTICE STEVENS, dissenting.

. . . I think it important to emphasize two flaws in the Court's reasoning. Apparently assuming that the Federal Communications Commission's (FCC or Commission) rulemaking authority is a species of executive power, the Court espouses the novel proposition that the Commission need not explain its decision to discard a longstanding rule in favor of a dramatically different approach to regulation. See *ante*, at 10–11. Moreover, the Court incorrectly assumes that our decision in *FCC* v. *Pacifica Foundation*, 438 U. S. 726 (1978), decided that the word "indecent," as used in 18 U. S. C. § 1464, permits the FCC to punish the broadcast of *any* expletive that has a sexual or excretory origin. *Pacifica* was not so sweeping, and the Commission's changed view of its statutory mandate certainly would have been rejected if presented to the Court at the time. . . . Even if the words that concern the Court in this case *sometimes* retain their sexual or excretory meaning, there are surely countless instances in which they are used in a manner unrelated to their origin. These words may not be polite, but that does not mean they are necessarily "indecent" under § 1464.

* * *

. . . I would affirm the judgment of the Court of Appeals.

---

**Questions:** How would *Loper Bright* have affected the *FCC v. Fox* majority? If an agency alters a rule upon which the public has relied but does not explain the reason for the change, should the courts still defer to the agency's interpretation? See *Encino Motorcars v. Navarro,* 579 U.S. 211 (2016).

# CHAPTER 19

# ENVIRONMENTAL LAW—NATIONAL ENVIRONMENTAL POLICY ACT

■ ■ ■

## CONTEXT & SOURCES

Environmental law comprises the statutory and decisional regime regulating the human relationship with the natural environment, broadly defined. Modern environmental law began with the National Environmental Policy Act of 1969 (NEPA), 42 U.S.C. § 4321 et seq., which requires agencies pursuing "major federal actions" to determine if these will "significantly" affect the "quality of the human environment;" what impacts will ensue; whether there will be unavoidable adverse effects; and possible alternatives. Such studies, or environmental impact statements (EIS), have the twin goals of improving decision-making and providing public access to information regarding the project. NEPA has become a model for equivalent state-level statutes, which often have broader application. The cases here cover the threshold for determining significance of an environmental harm, as well as the scope and content required for an EIS.

The background and major developments in environmental law, including the key role of NEPA, are chronicled in Richard J. Lazarus, *The Making of Environmental Law* (2d ed., University of Chicago Press, 2023). For the statute's focus on tangible harm see Jeffrey P. Groy and Frederick P. Johnston, Jr., "NEPA and the Development of an 'Impact Cognization' Standard: *Metropolitan Edison Co. v. People Against Nuclear Energy*," 26 *Journal of Urban and Contemporary Law* 157 (1984). Tracey Colton Green, "Providing for the Common Defense Versus the General Welfare: The Conflicts between National Security and National Environmental Policy," 6 *South Carolina Environmental Law Journal* 138 (1997) explores the balance struck in the *Catholic Action* ruling. A sharp critique of *Robertson*'s undemanding view of the EIS is provided by Jennifer R. Bartlit, "An Adequate EIS under NEPA: Deference to CEQ; Merely Conceptual Listing of Mitigation Leads Us to a Merely Conceptual National Environmental Policy," 31 *Natural Resources Journal* 653 (1991).

# SIGNIFICANT IMPACT THRESHOLD

## HANLY V. MITCHELL

460 F.2d 640 (2d. Cir.), *cert. denied* 409 U.S. 990 (1972)

* * *

FEINBERG, CIRCUIT JUDGE:

This case raises important issues under the National Environmental Policy Act of 1969, 42 U.S.C. § 4331 et seq., a statute whose meaning is more uncertain than most, not merely because it is relatively new, but also because of the generality of its phrasing. Thus the Act recognizes "the profound influences of . . . high-density urbanization . . . [and] the critical importance of restoring and maintaining environmental quality to the overall welfare and development of man," and declares it the "continuing responsibility of the Federal Government to use all practical means . . . to . . . assure for all Americans safe, healthful, productive and esthetically and culturally pleasing surroundings." To achieve that and similar objectives, the Act sets up a system of procedures for federal agencies to follow in making decisions that might have an impact on the environment. The basic issue before us is whether the Act was complied with in the planning for a nine-story federal jail in back of the United States Court House in Manhattan, just across the street from two large apartment buildings. Plaintiffs, who include some owners of these apartments, allege that defendants violated the Act. Excavation on the project began in mid-February 1972, and a short time later plaintiffs sought a preliminary injunction in the United States District Court for the Southern District of New York against further construction work. On March 17, 1972, Judge Charles H. Tenney denied the injunction. Since the matter was urgent, we expedited the appeal. Because we believe that defendants have failed to comply adequately with the Act, we reverse in part the order of the district court.

* * *

Plaintiffs seek to enjoin defendants from proceeding further with excavation and construction of both buildings and also pray for money damages. This appeal, however, concerns only the denial of preliminary injunctive relief. The theory of plaintiffs' complaint is that defendants were required by the National Environmental Policy Act to take certain preliminary steps before beginning excavation and construction and that they did not do so. Judge Tenney held that the General Services Administration (GSA) had considered "all of the environmental factors relevant to the construction of the Annex," and that GSA's conclusion that the Annex "will not have a significant adverse impact on the environment" was "not arbitrary, capricious, an abuse of discretion or otherwise not in accordance with the law." Judge Tenney further concluded that plaintiffs did not demonstrate a likelihood of success on the merits or irreparable harm if the injunction was not issued and that the balance of equities rested with defendants. From those rulings plaintiffs appeal.

* * *

Plaintiffs properly disclaim any attempt to argue before us the merits of the proposed building project. They concede that the question on appeal is not whether the proposed buildings adjoining this Court House should be built, but whether the requirements of the National Environmental Policy Act have been met. In their complaint and in the district court, plaintiffs' main argument was that defendants have not complied with section 102(2)(C) of the Act, 42 U.S.C. § 4332(2)(C), which provides:

"The Congress authorizes and directs that, to the fullest extent possible: (1) the policies, regulations, and public laws of the United States shall be interpreted and administered in accordance with the policies set forth in this chapter, and (2) all agencies of the Federal Government shall—

* * *

> (C) include in every recommendation or report on proposals for legislation and *other major Federal actions significantly affecting the quality of the human environment,* a detailed statement by the responsible official on—
>
> > (i) the environmental impact of the proposed action,
> >
> > (ii) any adverse environmental effects which cannot be avoided should the proposal be implemented,
> >
> > (iii) alternatives to the proposed action . . . ."

There is no doubt that the Act contemplates some agency action that does not require an impact statement because the action is minor and has so little effect on the environment as to be insignificant. See [citations]. There is, however, a further question of statutory construction. Plaintiffs argue that if a federal action is "major," as defendants now concede this one is, it must have a "significant" effect on the environment and call for an impact statement. Defendants claim that the term "major Federal action" refers to the cost of the project, the amount of planning that preceded it, and the time required to complete it, but does not refer to the impact of the project on the environment. We agree with defendants that the two concepts are different and that the responsible federal agency has the authority to make its own threshold determination as to each in deciding whether an impact statement is necessary.

* * *

GSA's entire determination regarding the Courthouse Annex—including both office building and jail—is found principally in a memorandum dated February 23, 1971, of George M. Paduano, who was then Regional Director of the Public Buildings Service of GSA, and, according to defendants, the proper official to make such a decision under GSA's regulations. [Document reproduced].

* * *

This document is terse, to say the least. Nonetheless, for the purpose of supporting GSA's determination that the proposed office building portion of the Courthouse Annex will have "no adverse effects on the environment," we believe, as did the district judge, that the document is sufficient. True, the memorandum fails to mention aesthetic and architectural considerations, but in a neighborhood such as this with public buildings of wildly varying architecture, we cannot say that failure to mention explicitly such considerations is a vital flaw. Further, as [an additional] memorandum makes clear, see note 5 *supra,* "The building will house 357 people, most of whom are already employed in the same general area."

* * *

The proposed jail, however, stands on a different footing. The Paduano memorandum does adequately discuss problems of water, heat, sewage and garbage. But those considerations apply to virtually any building. The memorandum contains no hard look at the peculiar environmental impact of squeezing a jail into a narrow area directly across the street from two large apartment houses. Indeed, there is not even a word about those apartment houses or the others located nearby. If GSA were planning a missile base on that site, a compact discussion of sewage, garbage, water and heat would hardly be adequate. Additional factors would have to be considered, and the same principle holds true here. Plaintiffs claim that the living environment of all the families in this area will be adversely affected by the presence of the jail and by the fears of "riots and disturbances" so generated. In particular, plaintiffs argue that the city prison formerly located at Sixth Avenue and Eighth Street has been vacated because the noise of the inmates, their demonstrations, and the beckoning and signaling between them and their visitors caused disturbances in the neighborhood. The Paduano memorandum contains no hint that such possible disturbances were considered. Nor is there any mention of the potential dangers of housing an out-patient treatment center in this area. Moreover, even as to more routine considerations, there is a conspicuous absence of a thoughtful discussion of possible traffic and parking problems caused by trucks delivering food and supplies, vans taking prisoners to and from the Eastern District and New Jersey courts, the need for parking space for prison personnel, and the need to accommodate those visiting the prisoners, whether lawyers or family.

Defendants argue to us that these are not "environmental considerations, as they are defined in" the Act and that the injuries plaintiffs envision are speculative at best. As to the latter point, it may be that some of plaintiffs' fears are vague and speculative, but clearly all of them are not and the "responsible official" of GSA has apparently never considered any of them. As to defendants' argument that plaintiffs' concerns are irrelevant under the Act, this assertion, characterized most charitably, is simply incorrect. The National Environmental Policy Act contains no exhaustive list of so-called "environmental considerations," but without question its aims extend beyond sewage and garbage and even beyond water and air pollution. *See* [citations]. The Act must be construed to include protection of the quality of life for city residents. Noise, traffic, overburdened mass transportation systems, crime, congestion and even availability of drugs all affect the urban "environment" and are surely results of the "profound influences of . . . high-density urbanization [and] industrial expansion." Section 101(a) of the Act, 42 U.S.C. § 4331(a). Thus, plaintiffs do raise many "environmental considerations" that should not be ignored. We believe the record in this case indicates that, as to the proposed jail, they were.

* * *

We hasten to point out that we do not suggest plaintiffs are correct in claiming that the jail requires a section 102(2)(C) impact statement. The area in back of the Court House may not be a residential area in the usual sense and the entire Courthouse Annex may actually be an improvement in the area—jail and all. Also, GSA is obviously not required to give the same weight to plaintiffs' concerns as plaintiffs do. But the essential point is that GSA must actually consider them. See generally[citations].

* * *

Accordingly, we affirm in part and reverse in part the district court order denying a preliminary injunction and remand the case for further consideration. Plaintiffs are entitled to a preliminary injunction against further construction of the proposed jail until such time as GSA has made a proper determination under section 102(2)(C), taking account of all relevant factors, of whether the proposed jail significantly affects the quality of the human environment.

* * *

---

**Question:** The *Hanly* opinion holds that "quality of life" concerns such as noise and traffic may affect the environment sufficiently to require an agency to consider them when deciding whether to issue an impact statement under NEPA. Should these effects include the physical deterioration of a traditional urban center that loses customer loyalties to a new suburban shopping complex? On this issue under California's broader version of NEPA, the California Environmental Quality Act (CEQA), see *Citizens Ass'n for Sensible Development of Bishop Area v. County of Inyo,* 172 Cal. App. 3d 151 (1985).

## METROPOLITAN EDISON V. PEOPLE AGAINST NUCLEAR ENERGY

460 U.S. 766 (1983)

* * *

JUSTICE REHNQUIST delivered the opinion of the Court.

The issue in these cases is whether petitioner Nuclear Regulatory Commission (NRC) complied with the National Environmental Policy Act, 42 U.S.C. § 4321 *et seq.* (NEPA), when it considered whether to permit petitioner Metropolitan Edison Co. to resume operation of the Three Mile Island Unit 1 nuclear power plant (TMI-1). The Court of Appeals for the District of Columbia Circuit held that the NRC improperly failed to consider whether the risk of an accident at TMI-1 might cause harm to the psychological health and community well-being of residents of the surrounding area. 678 F.2d 222 (CADC 1982). We reverse.

Metropolitan owns two nuclear power plants at Three Mile Island near Harrisburg, Pennsylvania. Both of these plants were licensed by the NRC after extensive proceedings, which included preparation of Environmental Impact Statements (EIS). On March 28, 1979, TMI-1 was not operating; it had been shut down for refueling. TMI-2 was operating, and it suffered a serious accident that damaged the reactor. Although, as it turned out, no dangerous radiation was released, the accident caused widespread concern. The Governor of Pennsylvania recommended an evacuation of all pregnant women and small children, and many area residents did leave their homes for several days.

After the accident, the NRC ordered Metropolitan to keep TMI-1 shut down until it had an opportunity to determine whether the plant could be operated safely. 44 Fed.Reg. 40461 (1979). The NRC then published a notice of hearing specifying several safety related issues for consideration. 10 N.R.C. 141 (1979). The notice stated that the Commission had not determined whether to consider psychological harm or other indirect effects of the accident or of renewed operation of TMI-1. It invited interested parties to submit briefs on this issue. *Id.,* at 148.

Petitioner People Against Nuclear Energy (PANE), intervened and responded to this invitation. PANE is an association of residents of the Harrisburg area who are opposed to further operation of either TMI reactor. PANE contended that restarting TMI-1 would cause both severe psychological health damage to persons living in the vicinity, and serious damage to the stability, cohesiveness, and well-being of the neighboring communities.

The NRC decided not to take evidence concerning PANE's contentions. *Metropolitan Edison Co.,* 12 N.R.C. 607 (1980); *Metropolitan Edison Co.,* 14 N.R.C. 593 (1981). PANE filed a petition for review in the Court of Appeals, contending that both NEPA and the Atomic Energy Act, 42 U.S.C. § 2011 *et seq.,* require the NRC to address its contentions. Metropolitan intervened on the side of the NRC.

The Court of Appeals concluded that the Atomic Energy Act does not require the NRC to address PANE's contentions. 678 F.2d, at 249–253. It did find, however, that NEPA requires the NRC to evaluate "the potential psychological health effects of operating" TMI-1 which have arisen since the original EIS was prepared. *Id.,* at 235. It also held that, if the NRC finds that significant new circumstances or information exist on this subject, it shall prepare a "supplemental [EIS] which considers not only the effects on psychological health but also effects on the well being of the communities surrounding Three Mile Island." *Id.,* at 235–236. We granted certiorari.

All the parties agree that effects on human health can be cognizable under NEPA, and that human health may include psychological health. The Court of Appeals thought these propositions were enough to complete a syllogism that disposes of the case: NEPA requires agencies to consider effects on health. An effect on psychological health is an effect on health. Therefore, NEPA requires agencies to consider the effects on psychological health asserted by PANE. See 678 F.2d, at 228. PANE, using similar reasoning, contends that because the psychological health damage to its members would be caused by a change in the environment (renewed operation of TMI-1), NEPA requires the NRC to consider that damage. See Brief for Respondent 23. Although these arguments are appealing at first glance, we believe they skip over an essential step in the analysis. They do not consider the closeness of the relationship between the change in the environment and the "effect" at issue.

* * *

To paraphrase the statutory language in light of the facts of this case, where an agency action significantly affects the quality of the human environment, the agency must evaluate the "environmental impact" and any unavoidable adverse environmental effects of its proposal. The theme of § 102 is sounded by the adjective "environmental": NEPA does not require the agency to assess *every* impact or effect of its proposed action, but only the impact or effect on the environment. If we were to seize the word "environmental" out of its context and give it the broadest possible definition, the words "adverse environmental effects" might embrace virtually any consequence of a governmental action that some one thought "adverse." But we think the context of the statute shows that Congress was talking about the physical environment—the world around us, so to speak. NEPA was designed to promote human welfare by alerting governmental actors to the effect of their proposed actions on the physical environment.

The statements of two principal sponsors of NEPA, explaining to their colleagues the Conference Report that was ultimately enacted, illustrate this point: "What is involved [in NEPA] is a declaration that we do not intend as a government or as a people to initiate actions which endanger the continued existence or the health of mankind: That *we will not intentionally initiate actions which do irreparable damage to the air, land and water* which support life on earth." 115 Cong.Rec. 40416 (1969) (Remarks of Sen. Jackson) (emphasis supplied).

"[W]e can now move forward *to preserve and enhance our air, aquatic, and terrestrial environments* . . . to carry out the policies and goals set forth in the bill to provide each citizen of this great country a healthful environment." 115 Cong.Rec. 40924 (1969) (Remarks of Rep. Dingell) (emphasis supplied).

Thus, although NEPA states its goals in sweeping terms of human health and welfare, these goals are *ends* that Congress has chosen to pursue by *means* of protecting the physical environment.

To determine whether § 102 requires consideration of a particular effect, we must look at the relationship between that effect and the change in the physical environment caused by the major federal action at issue. For example, if the Department of Health and Human Services were to implement extremely stringent requirements for hospitals and nursing homes receiving federal funds, many perfectly adequate hospitals and homes might be forced out of existence. The remaining facilities might be so limited or so expensive that many ill people would be unable to afford medical care and would suffer severe health damage. Nonetheless, NEPA would not require the Department to prepare an EIS evaluating that health damage because it would not be proximately related to a change in the physical environment.

Some effects that are "caused by" a change in the physical environment in the sense of "but for" causation, will nonetheless not fall within § 102 because the causal chain is too attenuated. For example, residents of the Harrisburg area have relatives in other parts of the country. Renewed operation of TMI-1 may well cause psychological health problems for these people. They may suffer "anxiety, tension and fear, a sense of helplessness," and accompanying physical disorders, n. 2, *supra,* because of the risk that their relatives may be harmed in a nuclear accident. However, this harm is simply too remote from the physical environment to justify requiring the

NRC to evaluate the psychological health damage to these people that may be caused by renewed operation of TMI-1.

Our understanding of the congressional concerns that led to the enactment of NEPA suggests that the terms "environmental effect" and "environmental impact" in § 102 be read to include a requirement of a reasonably close causal relationship between a change in the physical environment and the effect at issue. This requirement is like the familiar doctrine of proximate cause from tort law. See generally W. Prosser, Law of Torts ch. 7 (4th ed. 1971). The issue before us, then, is how to give content to this requirement. This is a question of first impression in this Court.

The federal action that affects the environment in this case is permitting renewed operation of TMI-1. The direct effects on the environment of this action include release of low-level radiation, increased fog in the Harrisburg area (caused by operation of the plant's cooling towers), and the release of warm water into the Susquehanna River. The NRC has considered each of these effects in its EIS, and again in the EIA. See J.A. 51–58. Another effect of renewed operation is a risk of a nuclear accident. The NRC has also considered this effect. See J.A. 58–60.

PANE argues that the psychological health damage it alleges "will flow directly from the risk of [a nuclear] accident." Brief for Respondent 23. But a *risk* of an accident is not an effect on the physical environment. A risk is, by definition, unrealized in the physical world. In a causal chain from renewed operation of TMI-1 to psychological health damage, the element of risk and its perception by PANE's members are necessary middle links. We believe that the element of risk lengthens the causal chain beyond the reach of NEPA.

Risk is a pervasive element of modern life; to say more would belabor the obvious. Many of the risks we face are generated by modern technology, which brings both the possibility of major accidents and opportunities for tremendous achievements. Medical experts apparently agree that risk can generate stress in human beings, which in turn may rise to the level of serious health damage. For this reason among many others, the question whether the gains from any technological advance are worth its attendant risks may be an important public policy issue. Nonetheless, it is quite different from the question whether the same gains are worth a given level of alteration of our physical environment or depletion of our natural resources. The latter question rather than the former is the central concern of NEPA.

* * *

If contentions of psychological health damage caused by risk were cognizable under NEPA, agencies would, at the very least, be obliged to expend considerable resources developing psychiatric expertise that is not otherwise relevant to their congressionally assigned functions. The available resources may be spread so thin that agencies are unable adequately to pursue protection of the physical environment and natural resources. As we said in another context in *United States v. Dow,* 357 U.S. 17, 25, (1958), "[w]e cannot attribute to Congress the intention to . . . open the door to such obvious incongruities and undesirable possibilities."

* * *

We do not mean to denigrate the fears of PANE's members, or to suggest that the psychological health damage they fear could not, in fact, occur. Nonetheless, it is difficult for us to see the differences between someone who dislikes a government decision so much that he suffers anxiety and stress, someone who fears the effects of that decision so much that he suffers similar anxiety and stress, and someone who suffers anxiety and stress that "flow directly," Brief for Respondent 23, from the risks associated with the same decision. It would be extraordinarily difficult for agencies to differentiate between "genuine" claims of psychological health damage and claims that are grounded solely in disagreement with a democratically adopted policy. Until Congress provides a more explicit statutory instruction than NEPA now contains, we do not think agencies are obliged to undertake the inquiry. See *Maryland National Capital Park & Planning Commission v. Postal Service,* 487 F.2d 1029, 1037 (CA DC 1973).

* * *

For these reasons, we hold that the NRC need not consider PANE's contentions. NEPA does not require agencies to evaluate the effects of risk, *qua* risk. The judgment of the Court of Appeals is reversed, and the case is remanded with instructions to dismiss the petition for review.

*It is so ordered.*

JUSTICE BRENNAN, concurring.

I join the opinion of the Court. There can be no doubt that psychological injuries are cognizable under NEPA. See *ante,* at 771. As the Court points out, however, the particular psychological injury alleged in this case did not arise, for example, out of the direct sensory impact of a change in the physical environment, cf. *Chelsea Neighborhood Associations v. United States Postal Service,* 516 F.2d 378, 388 (CA2 1975), but out of a perception of risk. *Ante,* at 775. In light of the history and policies underlying NEPA, I agree with the Court that this crucial distinction "lengthens the causal chain beyond the reach" of the statute. *Ibid.*

**Questions:** Does *Metropolitan Edison* hold that psychological harm cannot constitute a "significant impact" under NEPA? How does Justice Brennan's concurrence clarify this point?

# SCOPE OF EIS

## WEINBERGER V. CATHOLIC ACTION OF HAWAII

454 U.S. 139 (1981)

* * *

JUSTICE REHNQUIST delivered the opinion of the Court.

The Court of Appeals for the Ninth Circuit held that § 102(2)(C) of the National Environmental Policy Act of 1969 (NEPA), 83 Stat. 853, 42 U.S.C. § 4332(2)(C), requires the Navy to prepare and release to the public a "Hypothetical Environmental Impact Statement" with regard to the operation of a facility capable of storing nuclear weapons. *Catholic Action of Hawaii/Peace Education Project v. Brown*, 643 F.2d 569, 572 (1980). Because we conclude that the "Hypothetical Environmental Impact Statement" is a creature of judicial cloth, not legislative cloth, and that it is not mandated by any of the statutory or regulatory provisions upon which the Court of Appeals relied, we reverse its decision.

The facts relevant to our decision are not seriously controverted. Pursuant to a decision by the Navy to transfer ammunition and weapons stored at various locations on the island of Oahu, Hawaii, to the West Loch branch of the Lualualei Naval Magazine, the Navy prepared an Environmental Impact Assessment (EIA) concerning how the plan would affect the environment. The assessment concluded that the necessary construction of 48 earth-covered magazines and associated structures would have no significant environmental impact, and therefore no Environmental Impact Statement (EIS) was prepared at the construction stage. Construction contracts were let in March 1977 and in April 1978. Construction of the West Loch facilities has been completed and the magazines are now in use. It is stipulated that the magazines are capable of storing nuclear weapons. Because the information is classified for national security reasons, the Navy's regulations forbid it either to admit or to deny that nuclear weapons are actually stored at West Loch.

In 1978, the Navy prepared a Candidate Environmental Impact Statement (CEIS). This CEIS deals generally with the environmental hazards associated with the storage, handling, and transportation of nuclear weapons, but does not refer to any specific site or storage facility. It concludes that no significant hazards to the environment are present.

In March 1978, respondents brought this action seeking an injunction against the building of the new facilities at West Loch until an EIS had been filed. Their principal complaint was that the Navy's EIA had ignored the enhanced risk of a nuclear accident resulting from West Loch's proximity to three nearby air facilities, the effects of such an accident on the population and environment of Hawaii, and the effects of radiation from the storage of nuclear weapons in a populated area. The United States District Court for the District of Hawaii concluded that the "construction and use of the storage facilities at West Loch is a major federal action" within the meaning of § 102(2)(C). 468 F.Supp. 190, 193 (1979). But given certain national security provisions of the Atomic Energy Act, 42 U.S.C. § 2011 *et seq.* (1976 ed. and Supp.IV), and the Navy's own regulations concerning nuclear weapons, the District Court concluded that petitioners had complied with NEPA "to the fullest extent possible." 468 F.Supp., at 193. We find it unnecessary to reach the question posed by the District Court's reliance on the security provisions of the Atomic Energy Act, since respondents have made no showing in this case that the Navy has failed to comply, or even need comply, with NEPA's requirements regarding the preparation and public disclosure of an EIS.

Section 102(2)(C) of NEPA, 42 U.S.C. § 4332(2)(C), provides that, "to the fullest extent possible," all federal agencies shall "include in every recommendation or report on proposals for legislation and other major Federal actions significantly affecting the quality of the human environment, a detailed statement" discussing, *inter alia,* the environmental impact of the proposed action and possible alternatives. Section 102(2)(C) also requires that the EIS be made available to the President, the Council on Environmental Quality (CEQ), and the public, subject to the provisions of the Freedom of Information Act (FOIA), 5 U.S.C. § 552 (1976 ed. and Supp.V).

We have previously noted: "The thrust of § 102(2)(C) is . . . that environmental concerns be integrated into the very process of agency decisionmaking. The 'detailed statement' it requires is the outward sign that environmental values and consequences have been considered during the planning stage of agency actions." *Andrus v. Sierra Club*, 442 U.S. 347, 350, (1979). Section 102(2)(C) thus serves twin aims. The first is to inject environmental considerations into the federal agency's decisionmaking process by requiring the agency to prepare an EIS. The second aim is to inform the public that the agency has considered environmental concerns in its decisionmaking process. Through the disclosure of an EIS, the public is made aware that the agency has taken environmental considerations into account. Public disclosure of the EIS is expressly governed by FOIA. 42 U.S.C. § 4332(2)(C).

The decisionmaking and public disclosure goals of § 102(2)(C), though certainly compatible, are not necessarily coextensive. Thus, § 102(2)(C) contemplates that in a given situation a federal agency might have to include environmental considerations in its decisionmaking process, yet withhold public disclosure of any NEPA documents, in whole or in part, under the authority of an FOIA exemption. That the decisionmaking and disclosure requirements of NEPA are not coextensive has been recognized by the Department of Defense's regulations, both at the time the West Loch facility was constructed and today.

In an apparent attempt to balance what it considered to be the disclosure requirements of NEPA with national security interests, the Court of Appeals concluded that petitioners could prepare and disclose an EIS that would assess the impact of the storage of nuclear weapons at West Loch without revealing specific information regarding the number and type of nuclear weapons to be stored at the facility. 643 F.2d, at 572. The EIS could hypothesize, but not concede, that the facility will be used for the purpose for which it has been made capable. *Ibid.* But in inventing the "Hypothetical Environmental Impact Statement," the Court of Appeals departed from the express intent of Congress manifested by the explicit language in § 102(2)(C). That language provides that public disclosure of the EIS shall be governed by FOIA. As we concluded in *EPA v. Mink*, 410 U.S. 73, 80, (1973), FOIA was intended by Congress to balance the public's need for access to official information with the Government's need for confidentiality. Of the nine exemptions in Subsection (b) of FOIA, we think two are relevant in determining whether the Navy must release an EIS. Exemption 3, 5 U.S.C. § 552(b)(3), which authorizes the withholding of documents "specifically exempted from disclosure by statute," arguably exempts the publication of an EIS under the Atomic Energy Act. But we find it unnecessary to decide this question, because to us it is clear that Exemption 1, 5 U.S.C. § 552(b)(1), is applicable.

Exemption 1 exempts from disclosure matters that are "(A) specifically authorized under criteria established by an Executive order to be kept secret in the interest of national defense or foreign policy and (B) are in fact properly classified pursuant to such Executive order." Executive Order No. 12065, 3 CFR 190 (1978–1979 Comp.), confers upon specified officials the power to classify information if its release would pose a threat to national security. Virtually all information relating to the storage of nuclear weapons is classified. Thus, any material properly classified pursuant to Executive Order No. 120656 is exempt from disclosure under Exemption 1, and therefore is exempt from the public disclosure requirements of NEPA.

Congress has thus effected a balance between the needs of the public for access to documents prepared by a federal agency and the necessity of nondisclosure or secrecy. The Court of Appeals in this case should have accepted the balance struck by Congress, rather than engrafting onto the statutory language unique concepts of its own making. By requiring the Navy to prepare a "hypothetical" EIS, the Court of Appeals required the production of a document that would not exist save for what that court thought to be NEPA's public disclosure requirements. But NEPA's public disclosure requirements are expressly governed by FOIA. In *NLRB v. Sears, Roebuck & Co.*, 421 U.S. 132, 161–162, (1975), we held that FOIA "does not compel agencies to write opinions in cases in which they would not otherwise be required to do so. It only requires disclosure of certain documents which the law requires the agency to prepare or which the agency has decided for its own reasons to create." See *Forsham v. Harris,* 445 U.S. 169, 185–186, (1980); *Kissinger v. Reporters Committee,* 445 U.S. 136, 152, (1980). It follows that if the Navy would not be required by FOIA to release an EIS were one already prepared, it is obviously not required to prepare a "hypothetical" EIS nowhere mentioned in NEPA.

Since the public disclosure requirements of NEPA are governed by FOIA, it is clear that Congress intended that the public's interest in ensuring that federal agencies comply with NEPA must give way to the Government's need to preserve military secrets. In the instant case, an EIS concerning a proposal to store nuclear weapons at West Loch need not be disclosed. As we indicated earlier, whether or not nuclear weapons are stored at West Loch is classified information exempt from disclosure to the public under Exemption 1.

If the Navy proposes to store nuclear weapons at West Loch, the Department of Defense's regulations can fairly be read to require that an EIS be prepared solely for internal purposes, even though such a document cannot be disclosed to the public. The Navy must consider environmental consequences in its decisionmaking process, even if it is unable to meet NEPA's public disclosure goals by virtue of FOIA Exemption 1.

It does not follow, however, that the Navy is required to prepare an EIS in this case. The Navy is not required to prepare an EIS regarding the hazards of storing nuclear weapons at West Loch simply because the facility is "nuclear capable." As we held in *Kleppe v. Sierra Club,* 427 U.S. 390, 405–406, (1976), an EIS need not be prepared simply because a project is *contemplated,* but only when the project is *proposed.* To say that the West Loch facility is "nuclear capable" is to say little more than that the Navy has contemplated the possibility that nuclear weapons, of whatever variety, may at some time be stored here. It is the proposal to *store* nuclear weapons at West Loch that triggers the Navy's obligation to prepare an EIS. Due to national security reasons, however, the Navy can neither admit nor deny that it proposes to store nuclear weapons at West Loch. In this case, therefore, it has not been and cannot be established that the Navy has proposed the only action that would require the preparation of an EIS dealing with the environmental consequences of nuclear weapons storage at West Loch.

Ultimately, whether or not the Navy has complied with NEPA "to the fullest extent possible" is beyond judicial scrutiny in this case. In other circumstances, we have held that "public policy forbids the maintenance of any suit in a court of justice, the trial of which would inevitably lead to the disclosure of matters which the law itself regards as confidential, and respecting which it will not allow the confidence to be violated." *Totten v. United States*, 92 U.S. 105, 107, (1876). See *United States v. Reynolds*, 345 U.S. 1, 73 (1953). We confront a similar situation in the instant case.

The decision of the Court of Appeals for the Ninth Circuit is reversed, and the case is remanded with instructions to reinstate the judgment of dismissal entered by the District Court.

*It is so ordered.*

JUSTICE BLACKMUN, with whom JUSTICE BRENNAN joins, concurring in the judgment.

The law to be applied in this case is relatively simple and straightforward. If the Navy proposes to engage in a major action that will have a significant environmental effect, it must prepare an environmental impact statement (EIS) addressing the consequences of the proposed activity. If disclosing the contents, or even the existence, of the EIS will reveal properly classified materials, the Navy need not publish the document. If nonclassified data is segregable and properly disclosable under Executive Order No. 12065, it must be released to the public.

* * *

---

**Questions:** After *Weinberger,* should a U.S. Navy sonar training exercise potentially harming marine mammals be interrupted pending the preparation of an EIS? Should an EIS be required? Should it be disclosed to the public? See *Winter v. NRDC,* 555 U.S. 7 (2008).

## CONTENT OF EIS

### ROBERTSON V. METHOW VALLEY CITIZENS COUNCIL

490 U.S. 332 (1989)

* * *

JUSTICE STEVENS delivered the opinion of the Court. * * *

Sandy Butte is a 6,000-foot mountain located in the Okanogan National Forest in Okanogan County, Washington. At present Sandy Butte, like the Methow Valley it overlooks, is an unspoiled, sparsely populated area that the District Court characterized as "pristine." App. to Pet. for Cert. 20a. In 1968, Congress established the North Cascades National Park and directed the Secretaries of the Interior and Agriculture to agree on the designation of areas within, and adjacent to, the park for public uses, including ski areas. 82 Stat. 926, 930, 16 U.S.C. §§ 90, 90d–3. A 1970 study conducted by the Forest Service pursuant to this congressional directive identified Sandy Butte as having the highest potential of any site in the State of Washington for development as a major downhill ski resort. App. to Pet. for Cert. 23a.

In 1978, Methow Recreation, Inc. (MRI), applied for a special use permit to develop and operate its proposed "Early Winters Ski Resort" on Sandy Butte and an 1,165-acre parcel of land it had acquired adjacent to the National Forest. The proposed development would make use of approximately 3,900 acres of Sandy Butte; would entice visitors to travel long distances to stay at the resort for several days at a time; and would stimulate extensive commercial and residential growth in the vicinity to accommodate both vacationers and staff.

In response to MRI's application, the Forest Service, in cooperation with state and county officials, prepared an EIS known as the Early Winters Alpine Winter Sports Study (Early Winters Study or Study).

* * *

The Early Winters Study is a printed document containing almost 150 pages of text and 12 appendices. . . . The Study considered the effect of . . . development on water resources, soil, wildlife, air quality, vegetation, and visual quality, as well as land use and transportation in the Methow Valley, probable demographic shifts, the economic market for skiing and other summer and winter recreational activities in the Valley, and the energy requirements for the ski area and related developments. The Study's discussion of possible impacts was not limited to on-site effects, but also, as required by Council on Environmental Quality (CEQ) regulations, see 40 CFR § 1502.16(b) (1987), addressed "off-site impacts that each alternative might have on community facilities, socio-economic and other environmental conditions in the Upper Methow Valley." Early Winters Study 1. As to off-site effects, the Study explained that "due to the uncertainty of where other public and private lands may become developed," it is difficult to evaluate off-site impacts, *id.*, at 76, and thus the document's analysis is necessarily "not site-specific," *id.*, at 1. Finally, the Study outlined certain steps that might be taken to mitigate adverse effects, both on Sandy Butte and in the neighboring Methow Valley, but indicated that these proposed steps are merely conceptual and "will be made more specific as part of the design and implementation stages of the planning process." *Id.*, at 14. [Discussion of non-wildlife impacts in the Study and the Court's analysis has been deleted].

In a comment in response to the draft EIS, the Washington Department of Game voiced a special concern about potential losses to the State's largest migratory deer herd, which uses the Methow Valley as a critical winter range and as its migration route. *Id.*, at Appendix D (letter of November 18, 1982). The state agency estimated that the total population of mule deer in the area most likely to be affected was "better than 30,000 animals" and that "the ultimate impact on the Methow deer herd could exceed a 50 percent reduction in numbers." *Ibid.* The agency asserted that "Okanogan County residents place a great deal of importance on the area's deer herd." *Ibid.* In addition, it explained that hunters had "harvested" 3,247 deer in the Methow Valley area in 1981, and that, since in 1980 hunters on average spent $1,980 for each deer killed in Washington, they had contributed over $6 million to the State's economy in 1981. Because the deer harvest is apparently proportional to the size of the herd, the state agency predicted that "Washington business can expect to lose over $3 million annually from reduced recreational opportunity." *Ibid.* The Forest Service's own analysis of the impact on the deer herd was more modest. It first concluded that the actual operation of the ski hill would have only a "minor" direct impact on the herd, but then recognized that the off-site effect of the development "would noticeably reduce numbers of deer in the Methow [Valley] with any alternative." *Id.,* at 76. Although its estimate indicated a possible 15 percent decrease in the size of the herd, it summarized the State's contrary view in the text of the EIS, and stressed that off-site effects are difficult to estimate due to uncertainty concerning private development. *Ibid.*

[T]he EIS also described both on-site and off-site mitigation measures. Among possible on-site mitigation possibilities, the Study recommended locating runs, ski lifts, and roads so as to minimize interference with wildlife, restricting access to selected roads during fawning season, and further examination of the effect of the development on mule deer migration routes. Off-site options discussed in the Study included the use of zoning and tax incentives to limit development on deer winter range and migration routes, encouragement of conservation easements, and acquisition and management by local government of critical tracts of land.

* * *

Ultimately, the Early Winters Study recommended the issuance of a permit for development at the second highest level considered a 16-lift ski area able to accommodate 8,200 skiers at one time. On July 5, 1984, the Regional Forester decided to issue a special use permit as recommended by the Study. App. to Pet. for Cert. 63a. In his decision, the Regional Forester found that no major adverse effects would result directly from the federal action, but that secondary effects could include . . . a reduction of mule deer winter range. *Id.,* at 67a. He therefore directed the supervisor of the Okanogan National Forest, both independently and in cooperation with local officials, to identify and implement certain mitigating measures. *Id.,* at 67a–70a.

* * *

Thereafter, respondents brought this action under the Administrative Procedure Act, 5 U.S.C. §§ 701–706, to obtain judicial review of the Forest Service's decision. . . . . After a trial, the Magistrate filed a comprehensive written opinion and concluded that the EIS was adequate. App. to Pet. for Cert. 20a. Specifically, he found that the EIS had adequately disclosed the adverse impacts on the mule deer herd . . . and that there was no duty to prepare a "worst case analysis" because the relevant information essential to a reasoned decision was available. *Id.*, at 39a–44a.

* * *

Concluding that the Early Winters Study was inadequate as a matter of law, the Court of Appeals reversed. *Methow Valley Citizens Council v. Regional Forester,* 833 F.2d 810 (CA9 1987). The court held that the Forest Service could not rely on " 'the implementation of mitigation measures' " to support its conclusion that the impact on the mule deer would be minor, "since not only has the effectiveness of these mitigation measures not yet been assessed, but the mitigation measures themselves have yet to be developed." *Id.,* at 817. It then added that if the agency had difficulty obtaining adequate information to make a reasoned assessment of the environmental impact on the herd, it had a duty to make a so-called "worst case analysis." Such an analysis is " 'formulated on the basis of available information, using reasonable projections of the worst possible consequences of a proposed action.' *Save our Ecosystems* [*v. Clark,*] 747 F.2d [1240], at 1244–45 (CA9 1984) (quoting 46 Fed.Reg. 18032 (1981))." *Ibid.* [After discussing air quality] it concluded that "an EIS must include a thorough discussion of measures to mitigate the adverse environmental impacts of a proposed action." 833 F.2d, at 819.

* * *

The statutory requirement that a federal agency contemplating a major action prepare such an environmental impact statement serves NEPA's "action-forcing" purpose in two important respects. See *Baltimore Gas & Electric Co. v. Natural Resources Defense Council, Inc.,* 462 U.S. 87, 97, (1983); *Weinberger v. Catholic Action of Hawaii/Peace Education Project,* 454 U.S. 139, 143, (1981). It ensures that the agency, in reaching its decision, will have available, and will carefully consider, detailed information concerning significant environmental impacts; it also guarantees that the relevant information will be made available to the larger audience that may also play a role in both the decisionmaking process and the implementation of that decision.

* * *

The sweeping policy goals announced in § 101 of NEPA are thus realized through a set of "action-forcing" procedures that require that agencies take a " 'hard look' at environmental consequences," *Kleppe v.*

*Sierra Club,* 427 U.S. 390, 410, n. 21 (1976), and that provide for broad dissemination of relevant environmental information. Although these procedures are almost certain to affect the agency's substantive decision, it is now well settled that NEPA itself does not mandate particular results, but simply prescribes the necessary process. See [citations]. If the adverse environmental effects of the proposed action are adequately identified and evaluated, the agency is not constrained by NEPA from deciding that other values outweigh the environmental costs. See [citations]. In this case, for example, it would not have violated NEPA if the Forest Service, after complying with the Act's procedural prerequisites, had decided that the benefits to be derived from downhill skiing at Sandy Butte justified the issuance of a special use permit, notwithstanding the loss of 15 percent, 50 percent, or even 100 percent of the mule deer herd. Other statutes may impose substantive environmental obligations on federal agencies, but NEPA merely prohibits uninformed—rather than unwise—agency action.

[The Court then held that the Court of Appeals was wrong in requiring the Forest Service to formulate mitigation measures: NEPA did not require the EIS to include a fully developed plan to detail what steps will be taken to mitigate adverse environmental impacts.]

The Court of Appeals also concluded that the Forest Service had an obligation to make a "worst case analysis" if it could not make a reasoned assessment of the impact of the Early Winters project on the mule deer herd. Such a "worst case analysis" was required at one time by CEQ regulations, but those regulations have since been amended. Moreover, although the prior regulations may well have expressed a permissible application of NEPA, the Act itself does not mandate that uncertainty in predicting environmental harms be addressed exclusively in this manner. Accordingly, we conclude that the Court of Appeals also erred in requiring the "worst case" study.

In 1977, President Carter directed that CEQ promulgate binding regulations implementing the procedural provisions of NEPA. Exec. Order No. 11991, CFR 123 (1977 Comp.). Pursuant to this Presidential order, CEQ promulgated implementing regulations. Under § 1502.22 of these regulations—a provision which became known as the "worst case requirement"—CEQ provided that if certain information relevant to the agency's evaluation of the proposed action is either unavailable or too costly to obtain, the agency must include in the EIS a "worst case analysis and an indication of the probability or improbability of its occurrence." 40 CFR § 1502.22 (1985). In 1986, however, CEQ replaced the "worst case" requirement with a requirement that federal agencies, in the face of unavailable information concerning a reasonably foreseeable significant environmental consequence, prepare "a summary of existing credible scientific evidence which is relevant to evaluating the . . . adverse impacts" and prepare an "evaluation of such impacts based upon theoretical approaches or research methods generally accepted in the scientific community." 40 CFR § 1502.22(b) (1987). The amended regulation thus "retains the duty to describe the consequences of a remote, but potentially severe impact, but grounds the duty in evaluation of scientific opinion rather than in the framework of a conjectural 'worst case analysis.' " 50 Fed.Reg. 32237 (1985).

* * *

In *Andrus v. Sierra Club,* 442 U.S., at 358, we held that CEQ regulations are entitled to substantial deference. In that case we recognized that although less deference may be in order in some cases in which the " 'administrative guidelines' " conflict " 'with earlier pronouncements of the agency,' " *ibid.* (quoting *General Electric Co. v. Gilbert,* 429 U.S. 125, 143, (1976)), substantial deference is nonetheless appropriate if there appears to have been good reason for the change, 442 U.S., at 358. Here, the amendment only came after the prior regulation had been subjected to considerable criticism. Moreover, the amendment was designed to better serve the twin functions of an EIS—requiring agencies to take a "hard look" at the consequences of the proposed action and providing important information to other groups and individuals. CEQ explained that by requiring that an EIS focus on reasonably foreseeable impacts, the new regulation "will generate information and discussion on those consequences of greatest concern to the public and of greatest relevance to the agency's decision," 50 Fed.Reg. 32237 (1985), rather than distorting the decisionmaking process by overemphasizing highly speculative harms, 51 Fed.Reg. 15624–15625 (1986); 50 Fed.Reg. 32236 (1985). In light of this well-considered basis for the change, the new regulation is entitled to substantial deference. Accordingly, the Court of Appeals erred in concluding that the Early Winters Study is inadequate because it failed to include a "worst case analysis."

* * *

The judgment of the Court of Appeals is accordingly reversed, and the case is remanded for further proceedings consistent with this opinion.

*It is so ordered.*

---

**Questions:** Did the Supreme Court's *Robertson* decision eliminate meaningful review of environmental impact statements? The case was decided following *Chevron v. NRDC,* which prescribed a deferential court approach to administrative agencies (see Chapter 18). Would the result have been different under the *Loper Bright* standard of deference?

# CHAPTER 20

# ENVIRONMENTAL LAW—ENDANGERED SPECIES AND PUBLIC LANDS

■ ■ ■

## CONTEXT & SOURCES

One important and sometimes controversial, environmental statute is the Endangered Species Act of 1973 (ESA), 16 U.S.C. 1531, et seq., which protects fish, wildlife, and plant species found to be "endangered" from harm. Department of the Interior regulations define "harm" as including "significant habitat modification or degradation" that "impairs essential behavioral patterns." Implementation of the ESA has brought the statute into conflict with other concerns, such as economic development and foreign policy. Cases are included on the ESA's mandatory nature, the meaning of its language, and its role in international disputes. The last decision in this chapter demonstrates that, aside from the ESA, the reservation of public lands as national monuments can also impliedly protect endangered species.

The first Supreme Court holding to apply the ESA is dramatically presented in Kenneth M. Murchison, *The Snail Darter Case: TVA versus the Endangered Species Act* (University Press of Kansas, 2007). In Victoria F. Nourse, "Decision Theory and *Babbitt v. Sweet Home*: Skepticism About Norms Discretion, and the Virtues of Purposivism, 57 *St. Louis University Law Journal* 909 (2013), the Court's overly theoretical approach to the ESA is critiqued. Peter L. Reich, "The Historical, Comparative, and Convergence Trifecta in International Water Law: A Mexico-U.S. Example," 43 *Environmental Law Reporter* 10509 (2013) discusses the extraterritorial limits of the ESA and of NEPA. For insight into the protection of species on public lands through a doctrine developed for Native American water law, see James Spitzenberger, "Expansion of the Reservation of Water Rights Doctrine: *Cappaert v. United States,* 426 U.S. 128 (1976), 56 *Nebraska Law Review* 410 (1977).

# ESA AS MANDATORY

## TENNESSEE VALLEY AUTHORITY V. HILL

437 U.S. 153 (1978)

* * *

MR. CHIEF JUSTICE BURGER delivered the opinion of the Court.

The questions presented in this case are (a) whether the Endangered Species Act of 1973 requires a court to enjoin the operation of a virtually completed federal dam—which had been authorized prior to 1973—when, pursuant to authority vested in him by Congress, the Secretary of the Interior has determined that operation of the dam would eradicate an endangered species; and (b) whether continued congressional appropriations for the dam after 1973 constituted an implied repeal of the Endangered Species Act, at least as to the particular dam.

* * *

In this area of the Little Tennessee River the Tennessee Valley Authority, a wholly owned public corporation o the United States, began constructing the Tellico Dam and Reservoir Project in 1967, shortly after Congress appropriated initial funds for its development. Tellico is a multipurpose regional development project designed principally to stimulate shoreline development, generate sufficient electric current to heat 20,000 homes, and provide flatwater recreation and flood control, as well as improve economic conditions in "an area characterized by underutilization of human resources and outmigration of young people." Hearings on Public Works for Power and Energy Research Appropriation Bill, 1977, before a Subcommittee of the House Committee on Appropriations, 94th Cong., 2d Sess., pt. 5, p. 261 (1976). Of particular relevance to this case is one aspect of the project, a dam which TVA determined to place on the Little Tennessee, a short distance from where the river's waters meet with the Big Tennessee. When fully operational, the dam would impound water covering some 16,500 acres—much of which represents valuable and productive farmland—thereby converting the river's shallow, fast-flowing waters into a deep reservoir over 30 miles in length.

The Tellico Dam has never opened, however, despite the fact that construction has been virtually completed and the dam is essentially ready for operation. Although Congress has appropriated monies for Tellico every year since 1967, progress was delayed, and ultimately stopped, by a tangle of lawsuits and administrative proceedings.

* * *

[In 1973], a discovery was made in the waters of the Little Tennessee which would profoundly affect the Tellico Project. Exploring the area around Coytee Springs, which is about seven miles from the mouth of the river, [an ichthyologist] found a previously unknown species of perch, the snail darter, or *Percina (Imostoma) tanasi*. This three-inch, tannish-colored fish, whose numbers are estimated to be in the range of 10,000 to 15,000, would soon engage the attention of environmentalists, the TVA, the Department of the Interior, the Congress of the United States, and ultimately the federal courts . . .

Until recently the finding of a new species of animal life would hardly generate a cause celebre. This is particularly so in the case of darters, of which there are approximately 130 known species, 8 to 10 of these having been identified only in the last five years. The moving force behind the snail darter's sudden fame came some four months after its discovery, when the Congress passed the Endangered Species Act of 1973 (Act), 87 Stat. 884, 16 U.S.C. § 1531 *et seq.* (1976 ed.). This legislation, among other things, authorizes the Secretary of the Interior to declare species of animal life "endangered" and to identify the "critical habitat" of these creatures. When a species or its habitat is so listed, the following portion of the Act—relevant here—becomes effective:

"The Secretary [of the Interior] shall review other programs administered by him and utilize such programs in furtherance of the purposes of this chapter. All other Federal departments and agencies shall, in consultation with and with the assistance of the Secretary, utilize their authorities in furtherance of the purposes of this chapter by carrying out programs for the conservation of endangered species and threatened species listed pursuant to section 1533 of this title and *by taking such action necessary to insure that actions authorized, funded, or carried out by them do not jeopardize the continued existence of such endangered species and threatened species or result in the destruction or modification of habitat of such species* which is determined by the Secretary, after consultation as appropriate with the affected States, to be critical." 16 U.S.C. § 1536 (1976 ed.) (emphasis added).

* * *

[Upon a lawsuit by respondents to enjoin the dam's construction, a U.S. District Court refused to issue an injunction, both because Congress continued to appropriate funds for the dam knowing of the snail darter, and because the dam was almost complete. The Sixth Circuit Court of Appeals reversed, and the Supreme Court granted certiorari.]

We begin with the premise that operation of the Tellico Dam will either eradicate the known population of snail darters or destroy their critical habitat. Petitioner does not now seriously dispute this fact. In any event, under § 4(a)(1) of the Act, 87 Stat. 886, 16 U.S.C. § 1533(a)(1) (1976 ed.), the Secretary of the Interior is vested with exclusive authority to determine whether a species such as the snail darter is "endangered" or "threatened" and to ascertain the factors which have led to such a precarious existence. By § 4(d) Congress has authorized—indeed commanded—the Secretary to "issue such regulations as he deems necessary and advisable to provide for the conservation of such species." 16 U.S.C. § 1533(d) (1976 ed.). As we have seen, the Secretary promulgated regulations which declared the snail darter an endangered species whose critical habitat would be destroyed by creation of the Tellico Dam. Doubtless petitioner would prefer not to have these regulations on the books, but there is no suggestion that the Secretary exceeded his authority or abused his discretion in issuing the regulations. Indeed, no judicial review of the Secretary's determinations has ever been sought and hence the validity of his actions are not open to review in this Court.

Starting from the above premise, two questions are presented: (a) Would TVA be in violation of the Act if it completed and operated the Tellico Dam as planned? (b) If TVA's actions would offend the Act, is an injunction the appropriate remedy for the violation? For the reasons stated hereinafter, we hold that both questions must be answered in the affirmative.

It may seem curious to some that the survival of a relatively small number of three-inch fish among all the countless millions of species extant would require the permanent halting of a virtually completed dam for which Congress has expended more than $100 million. The paradox is not minimized by the fact that Congress continued to appropriate large sums of public money for the project, even after congressional Appropriations Committees were apprised of its apparent impact upon the survival of the snail darter. We conclude, however, that the explicit provisions of the Endangered Species Act require precisely that result.

One would be hard pressed to find a statutory provision whose terms were any plainer than those in § 7 of the Endangered Species Act. Its very words affirmatively command all federal agencies "to *insure* that actions *authorized, funded,* or *carried out* by them do not *jeopardize* the continued existence" of an endangered species or "*result* in the destruction or modification of habitat of such species . . . ." 16 U.S.C. § 1536 (1976 ed.). (Emphasis added.) This language admits of no exception.

* * *

Concededly, this view of the Act will produce results requiring the sacrifice of the anticipated benefits of the project and of many millions of dollars in public funds. But examination of the language, history, and structure of the legislation under review here indicates beyond doubt that Congress intended endangered species to be afforded the highest of priorities.

* * *

[The Court reviewed the ESA's legislative history.]

It is against this legislative background that we must measure TVA's claim that the Act was not intended to stop operation of a project which, like Tellico Dam, was near completion when an endangered species was discovered in its path. While there is no discussion in the legislative history of precisely this problem, the totality of congressional action makes it abundantly clear that the result we reach today is wholly in accord with both the words of the statute and the intent of Congress. The plain intent of Congress in enacting this statute was to halt and reverse the trend toward species extinction, whatever the cost. This is reflected not only in the stated policies of the Act, but in literally every section of the statute. All persons, including federal agencies, are specifically instructed not to "take" endangered species, meaning that no one is "to harass, harm,] pursue, hunt, shoot, wound, kill, trap, capture, or collect" such life forms. 16 U.S.C. §§ 1532(14), 1538(a)(1)(B) (1976 ed.). Agencies in particular are directed by §§ 2(c) and 3(2) of the Act to "use . . . *all methods* and procedures which are necessary" to preserve endangered species. 16 U.S.C. §§ 1531(c), 1532(2) (emphasis added) (1976 ed.). In addition, the legislative history undergirding § 7 reveals an explicit congressional decision to require agencies to afford first priority to the declared national policy of saving endangered species. The pointed omission of the type of qualifying language previously included in endangered species legislation reveals a conscious decision by Congress to give endangered species priority over the "primary missions" of federal agencies.

It is not for us to speculate, much less act, on whether Congress would have altered it stance had the specific events of this case been anticipated. In any event, we discern no hint in the deliberations of Congress relating to the 1973 Act that would compel a different result than we reach here. Indeed, the repeated expressions of congressional concern over what it saw as the potentially enormous danger presented by the eradication of *any* endangered species suggest how the balance would have been struck had the issue been presented to Congress in 1973.

* * *

The plain language of the Act, buttressed by its legislative history, shows clearly that Congress viewed the value of endangered species as "incalculable." Quite obviously, it would be difficult for a court to balance the loss of a sum certain—even $100 million against a congressionally declared "incalculable" value, even assuming we had the power to engage in such a weighing process, which we emphatically do not.

In passing the Endangered Species Act of 1973, Congress was also aware of certain instances in which exceptions to the statute's broad sweep would be necessary. Thus, § 10, 16 U.S.C. § 1539 (1976 ed.), creates a number of limited "hardship exemptions," none of which would even remotely apply to the Tellico Project [pre-ESA contracts regarding endangered species the canceling of which would cause undue economic hardship or interfere with subsistence livelihood].

* * *

There is nothing in the appropriations measures, as passed, which states that the Tellico Project was to be completed irrespective of the requirements of the Endangered Species Act. These appropriations, in fact, represented relatively minor components of the lump-sum amounts for the *entire* TVA budget. To find a repeal of the Endangered Species Act under these circumstances would surely do violence to the " 'cardinal rule . . . that repeals by implication are not favored.' " *Morton v. Mancari,* 417 U.S. 535, 549 (1974).

* * *

Having determined that there is an irreconcilable conflict between operation of the Tellico Dam and the explicit provisions of § 7 of the Endangered Species Act, we must now consider what remedy, if any, is appropriate.

* * *

Our system of government is . . . a tripartite one, with each branch having certain defined functions delegated to it by the Constitution. While "[i]t is emphatically the province and duty of the judicial department to say what the law is," *Marbury v. Madison,* 1 Cranch 137, 177, 2 L.Ed. 60 (1803), it is equally—and emphatically—the exclusive province of the Congress not only to formulate legislative policies and mandate programs and projects, but also to establish their relative priority for the Nation. Once Congress, exercising its delegated powers, has decided the order of priorities in a given area, it is for the Executive to administer the laws and for the courts to enforce them when enforcement is sought.

Here we are urged to view the Endangered Species Act "reasonably," and hence shape a remedy "that accords with some modicum of common sense and the public weal." *Post,* at 196. But is that our function? We have no expert knowledge on the subject of endangered species, much less do we have a mandate from the people to strike a balance of equities on the side of the Tellico Dam. Congress has spoken in the plainest of words, making it abundantly clear that the balance has been struck in favor of affording endangered species the highest of priorities, thereby adopting a policy which it described as "institutionalized caution."

Our individual appraisal of the wisdom or unwisdom of a particular course consciously selected by the Congress is to be put aside in the process of interpreting a statute. Once the meaning of an enactment is discerned and its constitutionality determined, the judicial process comes to an end. We do not sit as a committee of review, nor are we vested with the power of veto. The lines ascribed to Sir Thomas More by Robert Bolt are not without relevance here:

"The law, Roper, the law. I know what's legal, not what's right. And I'll stick to what's legal. . . . I'm *not* God. The currents and eddies of right and wrong, which you find such plain-sailing, I can't navigate, I'm no voyager. But in the thickets of the law, oh there I'm a forester. . . . What would you do? Cut a great road through the law to get after the Devil? . . . And when the last law was down, and the Devil turned round on you—where would you hide, Roper, the laws all being flat? . . . This country's planted thick with laws from coast to coast—Man's laws, not God's—and if you cut them down . . . d'you really think you could stand upright in the winds that would blow then? . . . Yes, I'd give the Devil benefit of law, for my own safety's sake." R. Bolt, A Man for All Seasons, Act I, p. 147 (Three Plays, Heinemann ed. 1967).

We agree with the Court of Appeals that in our constitutional system the commitment to the separation of powers is too fundamental for us to pre-empt congressional action by judicially decreeing what accords with "common sense and the public weal." Our Constitution vests such responsibilities in the political branches.

*Affirmed.*

MR. JUSTICE POWELL, with whom MR. JUSTICE BLACKMUN joins, dissenting.

The Court today holds that § 7 of the Endangered Species Act requires a federal court, for the purpose of protecting an endangered species or its habitat, to enjoin permanently the operation of any federal project, whether completed or substantially completed. This decision casts a long shadow over the operation of even the most important projects, serving vital needs of society and national defense, whenever it is determined that continued operation would threaten extinction of an endangered species or its habitat. This result is said to be required by the "plain intent of Congress" as well as by the language of the statute.

In my view § 7 cannot reasonably be interpreted as applying to a project that is completed or substantially completed when its threat to an endangered species is discovered. Nor can I believe that Congress could have intended this Act to produce the "absurd result"—in the words of the District Court—of this case. If it were clear from the language of the Act and its legislative history that Congress intended to authorize this result, this Court would be compelled to enforce it. It is not our province to rectify policy or political judgments by the Legislative Branch, however egregiously they may disserve the public interest. But where the statutory language and legislative history, as in this case, need not be construed to reach such a result, I view it as the duty of this Court to adopt a permissible construction that accords with some modicum of common sense and the public weal.

* * *

Today the Court, like the Court of Appeals below, adopts a reading of § 7 of the Act that gives it a retroactive effect and disregards 12 years of consistently expressed congressional intent to complete the Tellico Project. With all due respect, I view this result as an extreme example of a literalist construction, not required by the language of the Act and adopted without regard to its manifest purpose. Moreover, it ignores established canons of statutory construction.

The starting point in statutory construction is, of course, the language of § 7 itself. *Blue Chip Stamps v. Manor Drug Stores,* 421 U.S. 723, 756, (1975) (POWELL, J., concurring). I agree that it can be viewed as a textbook example of fuzzy language, which can be read according to the "eye of the beholder." The critical words direct all federal agencies to take "such action [as may be] necessary to insure that actions authorized, funded, or carried out by them do not jeopardize the continued existence of . . . endangered species . . . or result in the destruction or modification of [a critical] habitat of such species . . . ." Respondents—as did the Sixth Circuit—read these words as sweepingly as possible to include all "actions" that any federal agency ever may take with respect to any federal project, whether completed or not.

The Court today embraces this sweeping construction. *Ante,* at 184–188. Under the Court's reasoning, the Act covers every existing federal installation, including great hydroelectric projects and reservoirs, every river and harbor project, and every national defense installation—however essential to the Nation's economic health and safety. The "actions" that an agency would be prohibited from "carrying out" would include the continued operation of such projects or any change necessary to preserve their continued usefulness. The only precondition, according to respondents, to thus destroying the usefulness of even the most important federal project in our country would be a finding by the Secretary of the Interior that a continuation of the project would threaten the survival or critical habitat of a newly discovered species of water spider or amoeba.

I have little doubt that Congress will amend the Endangered Species Act to prevent the grave consequences made possible by today's decision. Few, if any, Members of that body will wish to defend an interpretation of the Act that requires the waste of at least $53 million, . . . and denies the people of the Tennessee Valley area the benefits of the reservoir that Congress intended to confer. There will be little sentiment to leave this dam standing before an empty reservoir, serving no purpose other than a conversation piece for incredulous tourists.

But more far reaching than the adverse effect on the people of this economically depressed area is the continuing threat to the operation of every federal project, no matter how important to the Nation. If Congress acts expeditiously, as may be anticipated, the Court's decision probably will have no lasting adverse consequences. But I had not thought it to be the province of this Court to force Congress into otherwise unnecessary action by interpreting a statute to produce a result no one intended.

---

**Questions:** Why does the *TVA v. Hill* majority interpret the Endangered Species Act using the plain meaning rule, while the dissent applies the purposive rule? If the dissent considers its position correct, why does it nevertheless call for the ESA to be amended?

## ESA LANGUAGE DEFINITIONS

### BABBITT V. SWEET HOME CHAPTER OF COMMUNITIES FOR A GREAT OREGON

515 U.S. 687 (1995)

* * *

JUSTICE STEVENS delivered the opinion of the Court.

Section 9(a)(1) of the Endangered Species Act provides the following protection for endangered species:

"Except as provided in sections 1535(g)(2) and 1539 of this title, with respect to any endangered species of fish or wildlife listed pursuant to section 1533 of this title it is unlawful for any person subject to the jurisdiction of the United States to—

. . . . .

"(B) take any such species within the United States or the territorial sea of the United States[.]" 16 U.S.C. § 1538(a)(1).

Section 3(19) of the Act defines the statutory term "take":

"The term 'take' means to harass, harm, pursue, hunt, shoot, wound, kill, trap, capture, or collect, or to attempt to engage in any such conduct." 16 U.S.C. § 1532(19).

The Act does not further define the terms it uses to define "take." The Interior Department regulations that implement the statute, however, define the statutory term "harm":

"*Harm* in the definition of 'take' in the Act means an act which actually kills or injures wildlife. Such act may include significant habitat modification or degradation where it actually kills or injures wildlife by significantly impairing essential behavioral patterns, including breeding, feeding, or sheltering." 50 CFR § 17.3 (1994). . . .

A limitation on the § 9 "take" prohibition appears in § 10(a)(1)(B) of the Act, which Congress added by amendment in 1982. That section authorizes the Secretary to grant a permit for any taking otherwise prohibited by § 9(a)(1)(B) "if such taking is incidental to, and not the purpose of, the carrying out of an otherwise lawful activity." 16 U.S.C. § 1539(a)(1)(B).

* * *

Respondents in this action are small landowners, logging companies, and families dependent on the forest products industries in the Pacific Northwest and in the Southeast, and organizations that represent their interests. They brought this declaratory judgment action against petitioners, the Secretary of the Interior and the Director of the Fish and Wildlife Service, in the United States District Court for the District of Columbia to challenge the statutory validity of the Secretary's regulation defining "harm," particularly the inclusion of habitat modification and degradation in the definition. Respondents challenged the regulation on its face. Their complaint alleged that application of the "harm" regulation to the red cockaded woodpecker, an endangered species, and the northern spotted owl, a threatened species, had injured them economically. App. 17–23.

* * *

[The District Court rejected respondents' arguments, finding that Congress intended the word "take" to include habitat modification. Holding that "harm" was limited to the direct application of force, the Court of Appeals for the D.C. Circuit reversed. The Supreme Court granted certiorari.]

Because this case was decided on motions for summary judgment, we may appropriately make certain factual assumptions in order to frame the legal issue. First, we assume respondents have no desire to harm either the red cockaded woodpecker or the spotted owl; they merely wish to continue logging activities that would be entirely proper if not prohibited by the ESA. On the other hand, we must assume *arguendo* that those activities will have the effect, even though unintended, of detrimentally changing the natural habitat of both listed species and that, as a consequence, members of those species will be killed or injured. Under respondents' view of the law, the Secretary's only means of forestalling that grave result—even when the actor knows it is certain to occur—is to use his § 5 authority to purchase the lands on which the survival of the species depends. The Secretary, on the other hand, submits that the § 9 prohibition on takings, which Congress defined to include "harm," places on respondents a duty to avoid harm that habitat alteration will cause the birds unless respondents first obtain a permit pursuant to § 10.

The text of the Act provides three reasons for concluding that the Secretary's interpretation is reasonable. First, an ordinary understanding of the word "harm" supports it. The dictionary definition of the verb form of "harm" is "to cause hurt or damage to: injure." Webster's Third New International Dictionary 1034 (1966). In the context of the ESA, that definition naturally encompasses habitat modification that results in actual injury or death to members of an endangered or threatened species.

Respondents argue that the Secretary should have limited the purview of "harm" to direct applications of force against protected species, but the dictionary definition does not include the word "directly" or suggest in any way that only direct or willful action that leads to injury constitutes "harm." Moreover, unless the statutory term "harm" encompasses indirect as well as direct injuries, the word has no meaning that does not duplicate the meaning of other words that § 3 uses to define "take." A reluctance to treat statutory terms as surplusage supports the reasonableness of the Secretary's interpretation. See, *e.g.*, *Mackey* v. *Lanier Collection Agency & Service, Inc.*, 486 U.S. 825, 837, and n. 11 (1988).

Second, the broad purpose of the ESA supports the Secretary's decision to extend protection against activities that cause the precise harms Congress enacted the statute to avoid. In *TVA* v. *Hill*, 437 U.S. 153 (1978), we described the Act as "the most comprehensive legislation for the preservation of endangered species ever enacted by any nation." *Id.*, at 180. Whereas predecessor statutes enacted in 1966 and 1969 had not contained any sweeping prohibition against the taking of endangered species except on federal lands, see *id.*, at 175, the 1973 Act applied to all land in the United States and to the Nation's territorial seas. As stated in § 2 of the Act, among its central purposes is "to provide a means whereby the ecosystems upon which endangered species and threatened species depend may be conserved . . . ." 16 U.S.C. § 1531(b).

In *Hill*, we construed § 7 as precluding the completion of the Tellico Dam because of its predicted impact on the survival of the snail darter. See 437 U. S., at 193. Both our holding and the language in our opinion stressed the importance of the statutory policy. "The plain intent of Congress in enacting this statute," we recognized, "was to halt and reverse the trend toward species extinction, whatever the cost. This is reflected not only in the stated policies of the Act, but in literally every section of the statute." *Id.*, at 184. Although the § 9 "take" prohibition was not at issue in *Hill*, we took note of that prohibition, placing particular emphasis on the

Secretary's inclusion of habitat modification in his definition of "harm." In light of that provision for habitat protection, we could "not understand how TVA intends to operate Tellico Dam without 'harming' the snail darter." *Id.*, at 184, n. 30. Congress' intent to provide comprehensive protection for endangered and threatened species supports the permissibility of the Secretary's "harm" regulation.

* * *

[Respondents] ask us to invalidate the Secretary's understanding of "harm" in every circumstance, even when an actor knows that an activity, such as draining a pond, would actually result in the extinction of a listed species by destroying its habitat. Given Congress' clear expression of the ESA's broad purpose to protect endangered and threatened wildlife, the Secretary's definition of "harm" is reasonable.

Third, the fact that Congress in 1982 authorized the Secretary to issue permits for takings that § 9(a)(1)(B) would otherwise prohibit, "if such taking is incidental to, and not the purpose of, the carrying out of an otherwise lawful activity," 16 U.S.C. § 1539(a)(1)(B), strongly suggests that Congress understood § 9(a)(1)(B) to prohibit indirect as well as deliberate takings. Cf. *NLRB* v. *Bell Aerospace Co. of Textron, Inc.*, 416 U.S. 267, 274–275 (1974). The permit process requires the applicant to prepare a "conservation plan" that specifies how he intends to "minimize and mitigate" the "impact" of his activity on endangered and threatened species, 16 U.S.C. § 1539(a)(2)(A), making clear that Congress had in mind foreseeable rather than merely accidental effects on listed species. No one could seriously request an "incidental" take permit to avert § 9 liability for direct, deliberate action against a member of an endangered or threatened species, but respondents would read "harm" so narrowly that the permit procedure would have little more than that absurd purpose. . . . Congress' addition of the § 10 permit provision supports the Secretary's conclusion that activities not intended to harm an endangered species, such as habitat modification, may constitute unlawful takings under the ESA unless the Secretary permits them.

* * *

We need not decide whether the statutory definition of "take" compels the Secretary's interpretation of "harm," because our conclusions that Congress did not unambiguously manifest its intent to adopt respondents' view and that the Secretary's interpretation is reasonable suffice to decide this case. See generally *Chevron U. S. A. Inc.* v. *Natural Resources Defense Council, Inc.*, 467 U.S. 837(1984). The latitude the ESA gives the Secretary in enforcing the statute, together with the degree of regulatory expertise necessary to its enforcement, establishes that we owe some degree of deference to the Secretary's reasonable interpretation. See Breyer, Judicial Review of Questions of Law and Policy, 38 Admin. L. Rev. 363, 373 (1986).

Our conclusion that the Secretary's definition of "harm" rests on a permissible construction of the ESA gains further support from the legislative history of the statute. The Committee Reports accompanying the bills that became the ESA do not specifically discuss the meaning of "harm," but they make clear that Congress intended "take" to apply broadly to cover indirect as well as purposeful actions. The Senate Report stressed that " '[t]ake' is defined . . . in the broadest possible manner to include every conceivable way in which a person can 'take' or attempt to 'take' any fish or wildlife." S. Rep. No. 93–307, p. 7 (1973). The House Report stated that "the broadest possible terms" were used to define restrictions on takings. H. R. Rep. No. 93–412, p. 15 (1973). The House Report underscored the breadth of the "take" definition by noting that it included "harassment, *whether intentional or not.*" *Id.*, at 11 (emphasis added). The Report explained that the definition "would allow, for example, the Secretary to regulate or prohibit the activities of birdwatchers where the effect of those activities might disturb the birds and make it difficult for them to hatch or raise their young." *Ibid.*

* * *

When it enacted the ESA, Congress delegated broad administrative and interpretive power to the Secretary. See 16 U.S.C. §§ 1533 1540(f). The task of defining and listing endangered and threatened species requires an expertise and attention to detail that exceeds the normal province of Congress. Fashioning appropriate standards for issuing permits under § 10 for takings that would otherwise violate § 9 necessarily requires the exercise of broad discretion. The proper interpretation of a term such as "harm" involves a complex policy choice. When Congress has entrusted the Secretary with broad discretion, we are especially reluctant to substitute our views of wise policy for his. See *Chevron*, 467 U. S., at 865–866. In this case, that reluctance accords with our conclusion, based on the text, structure, and legislative history of the ESA, that the Secretary reasonably construed the intent of Congress when he defined "harm" to include "significant habitat modification or degradation that actually kills or injures wildlife."

In the elaboration and enforcement of the ESA, the Secretary and all persons who must comply with the law will confront difficult questions of proximity and degree; for, as all recognize, the Act encompasses a vast range of economic and social enterprises and endeavors. These questions must be addressed in the usual course of the law, through case by case resolution and adjudication.

The judgment of the Court of Appeals is reversed.

*It is so ordered.*

JUSTICE SCALIA, with whom THE CHIEF JUSTICE and JUSTICE THOMAS join, dissenting.

I think it unmistakably clear that the legislation at issue here (1) forbade the hunting and killing of endangered animals, and (2) provided federal lands and federal funds *for the acquisition of private lands,* to preserve the habitat of endangered animals. The Court's holding that the hunting and killing prohibition incidentally preserves habitat on private lands imposes unfairness to the point of financial ruin-not just upon the rich, but upon the simplest farmer who finds his land conscripted to national zoological use. I respectfully dissent.

* * *

In my view petitioners must lose—the regulation must fall even under the test of *Chevron U. S. A. Inc.* v. *Natural Resources Defense Council, Inc.,* 467 U. S. 837, 843 (1984), so I shall assume that the Court is correct to apply *Chevron.* See *ante,* at 703–704, and n. 18.

The regulation has three features which, for reasons I shall discuss at length below, do not comport with the statute. First, it interprets the statute to prohibit habitat modification that is no more than the cause-in-fact of death or injury to wildlife. *Any* "significant habitat modification" that in fact produces that result by "impairing essential behavioral patterns" is made unlawful, regardless of whether that result is intended or even foreseeable, and no matter how long the chain of causality between modification and injury. See, *e. g., Palila* v. *Hawaii Dept. of Land and Natural Resources,* 852 F.2d 1106, 1108–1109 (CA9 1988) *(Palila II)* (sheep grazing constituted "taking" of palila birds, since although sheep do not destroy full-grown mamane trees, they do destroy mamane seedlings, which will not grow to full-grown trees, on which the palila feeds and nests). See also Davison, Alteration of Wildlife Habitat as a Prohibited Taking under the Endangered Species Act, 10 J. Land Use & Envtl. L. 155, 190 (1995) (regulation requires only causation-in-fact).

Second, the regulation does not require an "act": The Secretary's officially stated position is that an *omission* will do. The previous version of the regulation made this explicit. See 40 Fed. Reg. 44412, 44416 (1975) (" 'Harm' in the definition of 'take' in the Act means an act or omission which actually kills or injures wildlife . . ."). When the regulation was modified in 1981 the phrase "or omission" was taken out, but only because (as the final publication of the rule advised) "the [Fish and Wildlife] Service feels that 'act' is inclusive of either commissions or omissions which would be prohibited by section [1538(a)(1)(B)]." 46 Fed. Reg. 54748, 54750 (1981). In their brief here petitioners agree that the regulation covers omissions, see Brief for Petitioners 47 (although they argue that "[a]n 'omission' constitutes an 'act' . . . only if there is a legal duty to act"), *ibid.*

The third and most important unlawful feature of the regulation is that it encompasses injury inflicted, not only upon individual animals, but upon populations of the protected species. "Injury" in the regulation includes "significantly impairing essential behavioral patterns, including *breeding,"* 50 CFR § 17.3 (1994) (emphasis added). Impairment of breeding does not "injure" living creatures; it prevents them from propagating, thus "injuring" *a population* of animals which would otherwise have maintained or increased its numbers. What the face of the regulation shows, the Secretary's official pronouncements confirm. The Final Redefinition of "Harm" accompanying publication of the regulation said that "harm" is not limited to "direct physical injury to an individual member of the wildlife species," 46 Fed. Reg. 54748 (1981), and refers to "injury *to a population," id.*, at 54749 (emphasis added). See also *Palila II, supra,* at 1108; Davison, *supra,* at 190, and n. 177, 195; M. Bean, The Evolution of National Wildlife Law 344 (1983).

*None* of these three features of the regulation can be found in the statutory provisions supposed to authorize it. The term "harm" in § 1532(19) has no legal force of its own. An indictment or civil complaint that charged the defendant with "harming" an animal protected under the Act would be dismissed as defective, for the only *operative* term in the statute is to "take." If "take" were not elsewhere defined in the Act, none could dispute what it means, for the term is as old as the law itself. To "take," when applied to wild animals, means to reduce those animals, by killing or capturing, to human control. See, *e.* g., 11 Oxford English Dictionary (1933) ("Take . . . To catch, capture (a wild beast, bird, fish, etc.)"); Webster's New International Dictionary of the English Language (2d ed. 1949) (take defined as "to catch or capture by trapping, snaring, etc., or as prey"); *Geer* v. *Connecticut,* 161 U. S. 519, 523 (1896) (" '[A]ll the animals which can be taken upon the earth, in the sea, or in the air, that is to say, wild animals, belong to those who take them' ") (quoting the Digest of Justinian); 2 W. Blackstone, Commentaries 411 (1766) ("Every man . . . has an equal right of pursuing and taking to his own use all such creatures as are *ferae naturae").* This is just the sense in which "take" is used elsewhere in federal legislation and treaty. See, *e.* g., Migratory Bird Treaty Act, 16 U. S. C. § 703 (1988 ed., Supp. V) (no person may "pursue, hunt, take, capture, kill, [or] attempt to take, capture, or kill" any migratory bird); Agreement on the Conservation of Polar Bears, Nov. 15, 1973, Art. I, 27 U. S. T. 3918, 3921, T. 1. A. S. No. 8409 (defining "taking" as "hunting, killing and capturing"). And that meaning fits neatly with the rest of § 1538(a)(1), which makes it unlawful not only to take protected species, but also to import or export them, § 1538(a)(1)(A); to possess, sell, deliver, carry, transport, or ship any taken species, § 1538(a)(1)(D); and to transport, sell, or offer to sell them in interstate or foreign commerce, §§ 1538(a)(1)(E), (F). The taking prohibition, in other words, is only part of the regulatory plan of § 1538(a)(1), which covers all the stages of the process by which protected wildlife is reduced to man's dominion and made the object of profit. It is obvious that "take" in this sense—a term of art deeply embedded in the statutory and common law concerning wildlife-describes a class of acts (not omissions) done directly and intentionally (not indirectly and by accident) to particular animals (not populations of animals).

* * *

To define "harm" as an act or omission that, however remotely, "actually kills or injures" a population of wildlife through habitat modification is to choose a meaning that makes nonsense of the word that "harm" defines—requiring us to accept that a farmer who tills his field and causes erosion that makes silt run into a nearby river which depletes oxygen and thereby "impairs [the] breeding" of protected fish has "taken" or "attempted to take" the fish. It should take the strongest evidence to make us believe that Congress has defined a term in a manner repugnant to its ordinary and traditional sense.

* * *

The Endangered Species Act is a carefully considered piece of legislation that forbids all persons to hunt or harm endangered animals, but places upon the public at large, rather than upon fortuitously accountable individual landowners, the cost of preserving the habitat of endangered species. There is neither textual support for, nor even evidence of congressional consideration of, the radically different disposition contained in the regulation that the Court sustains. For these reasons, I respectfully dissent.

---

**Question:** Both the majority and the dissent in *Babbitt* appear to be using a version of the plain meaning rule. Why do they arrive at different results?

## ESA EXTRATERRITORIALITY

### DEFENDERS OF WILDLIFE V. NORTON

257 F. Supp. 2d 53 (D.D.C. 2003)

* * *

*MEMORANDUM*

ROBERTSON, DISTRICT JUDGE.

This lawsuit, brought by four American and four Mexican environmental groups, alleges violations of the Endangered Species Act

(ESA) by the Bureau of Reclamation (Reclamation), the Fish and Wildlife Service (FWS), and the National Marine Fisheries Service (NMFS), in connection with Reclamation's management of the lower Colorado River. . . . . [Plaintiffs claim that defendants] failed to satisfy the consultation requirements of the ESA with regard to protected species in the Colorado River Delta in Mexico. Both parties have moved for summary judgment. For the reasons set forth below, defendants' motion will be granted.

Background

I. Development of the lower Colorado and the "Law of the River"

The Colorado River flows approximately 1,400 miles from the Rocky Mountains southwest to the Gulf of California in Mexico, dropping more than 12,000 feet and draining portions of seven states along the way. Updating of Hoover Dam Documents (1978), Administrative Record (AR) Bureau of Reclamation (BOR) Part I at 1. Prior to human development, water volume varied widely from season to season and from year to year, so that the river continually deposited new sediments, shifted its channel, and created and destroyed habitat. Plants and animals adapted to these extremes and developed distinct communities in flood plains, in marshes, and in the river itself. Final Biological Opinion (Apr. 30, 1997), AR FWS F–316 at 74–81.

In the late 1800's, developers began using the Colorado River for large scale irrigation projects. By 1920, California's users were diverting nearly all water from the river in times of low flow. AR BOR Part I at 1–3. Worried that California would claim appropriative rights before their own populations could put the water to use, upstream states pushed for a formal agreement to divide river waters equitably. The resulting Colorado River Compact of 1922 allocated 7.5 million acre-feet to the "upper basin" states (Colorado, Wyoming, Utah, and New Mexico) and 7.5 million acre-feet to the "lower basin" states (California, Arizona, and Nevada). Colorado River Compact of 1922, Art. 111(a), AR BOR Part I at 4.

States and local communities also lobbied the federal government to build dams, in order to foster additional growth and protect already developed areas from unpredictable flooding. In 1928, Congress passed the Boulder Canyon Project Act, approving the Colorado River Compact and authorizing construction of the Hoover Dam. AR BOR Part I at 5. The Hoover Dam, when it was completed in 1935, inundated miles of riparian habitat, blocked high flows in spring and early summer, and trapped massive amounts of sediment in the Lake Mead reservoir. The dam released, not only a smaller volume of water, but consistently cold and clear water. The result was significant changes in fish habitats. AR FWS F–316 at 81–90. Over the following fifteen years, two more major dams, four irrigation canals, and several smaller facilities were constructed, further changing river flows and fragmenting habitats. *Id.*

In 1944, the federal government signed a treaty with Mexico guaranteeing that country 1.5 million acre-feet of water per year from the Colorado (up to 1.7 million acre-feet in flood years) and allocating to Mexico any other waters arriving at Mexican points of diversion or at the Southerly International Border between the two countries. Treaty Between the United States of America & Mexico, Art. 10(b), 15(e), AR BOR Part I at 1–30. Mexico then built and completed in 1950 the Morelos Dam near the intersecting boundaries of Arizona, California, and Baja California to divert its water for use in the Mexicali and San Luis Valleys.

A few years later, Arizona filed suit to resolve continuing disputes over the apportionment of water among the lower basin states. After a decade of litigation, the Supreme Court held that the Secretary of the Interior is bound by the Colorado River Compact, *Arizona v. California,* 373 U.S. 546 (1963), and enjoined the federal government from releasing water (other than that needed to satisfy the Mexican Treaty) except in accordance with the order of priority established by Congress: (1) river regulation, improvement of navigation, and flood control; (2) irrigation and domestic uses; and (3) power. *Arizona v. California,* 376 U.S. 340, 341–42, (1964). The injunction also affirmed the statutory apportionment of mainstream waters among the three lower basin states. *Id.*

The Bureau of Reclamation, which built and/or operates all of the American dams in the lower basin and serves as custodian of the river for the Secretary of the Interior, is responsible for delivering water to the lower basin states and to Mexico in accordance with the Compact, the Treaty, the Supreme Court injunction, and contracts with recipients. After all those obligations are fulfilled, little if any water actually reaches the Gulf of California in a normal year. River flows generally reach the delta only in years of flooding, although, in the 1980's, even those sporadic amounts helped to restore significant habitat.

II. Reclamation's endangered species consultation

A. Initial consultation—from 1995 to 1997

Section 7(a)(2) of the Endangered Species Act directs federal agencies to consult with the Secretary of the Interior to "insure that any action authorized, funded, or carried out by such agency . . . is not likely to jeopardize the continued existence of any endangered species or threatened species or result in the destruction or adverse modification of [designated] critical habitat." 16 U.S.C. § 1536(a)(2). Reclamation began consulting with FWS on new projects in the early 1980s, AR FWS F–316, at 120–22 (listing prior consultations). Until 1995, however, it had never evaluated the impacts of its routine, ongoing operations on listed species and critical habitats along the lower Colorado. In that year, Reclamation began an evaluation of its ongoing operations and initiated negotiations with the three lower basin states and other interested parties over a comprehensive, long-term Multi-Species Conservation Plan (MSCP). AR FWS F–316 at 157.

Regulations issued under § 7(a)(2) require consultations for "all actions in which there is discretionary Federal involvement or control," 50 C.F.R. § 402.03, and govern the consultation process. The consulting agency first prepares a Biological Assessment to evaluate the effects of its action on listed species in the "action area," which is defined as "all areas to be affected directly or indirectly by the Federal action and not merely the immediate area involved in the action." *Id.* § 402.02. If the agency concludes that a listed species may be affected by its action, it must then formally consult with FWS (for land species) or NMFS (for marine species). 16 U.S.C. § 1536(a)(2); 50 C.F.R. § 402.14. The appropriate service (FWS or NMFS) must then issue its own Biological Opinion as to whether the action is likely to jeopardize the species and, if so, propose "reasonable and prudent alternatives" to the agency's proposal. 16 U.S.C. § 1536(b)(3)(A). If no such alternatives are available, or if the agency rejects the recommendation of FWS or NMFS, the agency must obtain an exemption from a cabinet-level Endangered Species Committee to proceed with its original plan. *Id.* § 1536(e)(3), (g).

Reclamation initially defined the action area for its lower Colorado River operations as extending from Lake Mead to the Southerly International Border. It then analyzed the effect of its operations on protected species within that action area over the next five years, or until the MSCP was adopted, whichever came first. Description of Operations, Maintenance, and Sensitive Species of the Lower Colorado River at 11 (Dec.1995), AR FWS S–8. In response to the draft Biological Assessment, however, FWS directed Reclamation to analyze impacts on *Mexican* populations of the Yuma Clapper Rail, the Southwestern Willow Flycatcher, and the Desert Pupfish, and to seek consultation with NMFS with regard to two marine species in the Gulf of California—the Totoaba Bass and Vaquita Harbor Porpoise—because they were found "in Mexico within the project area or . . . within the area of effects from the action under consultation." AR BOR Part III Sec. 2; *see also* AR BOR Part III Sec. 14 at 5 (requesting further analysis concerning Mexican species).

Complying with the FWS directive, Reclamation's Final Biological Assessment analyzed the effects of its operations and maintenance activities on endangered and threatened species in both the United States and parts of Mexico. Final Biological Assessment (Aug.1996), AR FWS S–13 at 9–11, 191–95. Reclamation described its discretionary operations and its nondiscretionary operations, *id.* at 72–75, and found that its discretionary operations would have no effect on the Vaquita Harbor Porpoise and Desert Pupfish, and that the Yuma Clapper Rail was not likely to be adversely affected. *Id.* at 191–95. Among the species that Reclamation concluded might be affected by its discretionary operations were the Totoaba Bass and Southwestern Willow Flycatcher, the former of which was classified as endemic to Mexico and the latter classified as a migrant species. *Id.* at 122, 195. Reclamation requested formal consultation for the Flycatcher. As for the Totoaba Bass, however, Reclamation concluded that no formal consultation was required because, lacking any discretion over water deliveries to or within Mexico, Reclamation had virtually no ability to reverse conditions in the Colorado River delta. *Id.* at 198.5

FWS and NMFS then made their own determinations. NMFS concluded that the Vaquita Harbor Porpoise was not likely to be adversely affected by Reclamation's lower Colorado River operations, AR BOR Part III Sec. 18 at 1–3; AR BOR Part III Sec. 23 at l, and that no formal consultation was required on the Totoaba Bass, because "the United States, and therefore Reclamation, has no authority or discretion over the flow of water to the Colorado River delta as a result of the Mexican Water Treaty of 1944 and the 1964 Supreme Court decision that enjoined Reclamation from releasing excess water to Mexico beyond that called for in the Treaty." AR BOR Part III Sec. 23 at 1–2. FWS wrote a Biological Opinion on the non-marine species, concluding that Reclamation's operations within the next five years could jeopardize, among other species, the Southwestern Willow Flycatcher, but not the Yuma Clapper Rail. Final Biological Opinion (Apr.1997), AR FWS at F–316 at 151; Apr. 30, 1997 FWS Mem. to BOR, AR FWS at F–316. It found that the risk to the Southwestern Willow Flycatcher was not in Mexico, but in the United States, because of Reclamation's plans to flood 1,000 acres of habitat at Lake Mead. AR FWS F–316 at 140–41. FWS's final recommendation was that Reclamation purchase 1,400 acres of replacement habitat for the Flycatcher. *Id.* at 160.

B. Reinitiated consultation in 2002

Plaintiffs Defenders of Wildlife and Southwest Center for Biological Diversity have been actively involved in Reclamation's endangered species consultation and in the negotiations over the Multi-Species Conservation Plan (MSCP) from very early in the process. Both groups accepted positions on the MSCP steering committee, both threatened to sue Reclamation in March 1996 if it did not formalize its consultation FWS, and both submitted numerous comments on the various agencies' draft documents.

* * *

[T]he Southwest Center and Defenders of Wildlife waited nearly three years after the issuance of the Final Biological Opinion before bringing this suit. Plaintiffs say that they attempted to have the Multi-Species Conservation Plan address Mexican species, but, after other participants rejected their efforts, they resigned their positions on the MSCP steering committee. After Reclamation rejected their efforts to secure some other form of commitment to address Mexican species, they began recruiting other plaintiffs to join them in this lawsuit. Snape Declaration, ¶¶ 14–28; Hogan Declaration ¶¶ 13–29. They gave formal notice of their intent to sue and filed this action in June 2000.

In May 2002, Reclamation informed the Court that it had reinitiated consultation with FWS concerning its lower Colorado River operations and maintenance activities through April 30, 2005, or until the MSCP is completed. Based on updated wildlife studies and on some of the positive effects of Reclamation's conservation efforts, FWS's supplemental Biological Opinion concluded that its operations are not likely to jeopardize the continued existence of the Southwestern Willow Flycatcher or Yuma Clapper Rail (among other species not in dispute in this case). Def.'s Not. of Reinitiation and Completion of Consultation, Ex. 2, Biological Opinion (April 30, 2002) at 23. The supplemental Biological Assessment issued by Reclamation incorporates the same distinctions between discretionary and nondiscretionary activities and covers the same ongoing Colorado River operations save for new conservation actions and the Yuma Desalting Plant, which is not expected to become operational by April 2005. Def.'s Not. of Reinitiation and Completion of Consultation, Ex. 1, Biological Assessment (March 26, 2002). Neither Reclamation's supplemental Biological Assessment nor FWS's Biological Opinion systematically discusses the effects on all of the Mexican species that were covered in the previous round of consultation from 1995 to 1997.

Analysis

Contrary to the plaintiffs' assertion that the defendants did not consider protected species in the delta, the agencies did analyze the effects on the Totoaba Bass, Vaquita, Desert Pupfish (species found in Mexico), and on the Yuma Clapper Rail (found both in the United States and Mexico) in the consultation that led to the 1996 Biological Assessment and Biological Opinion, *see supra* pp. 59–60. However, the analysis with respect to all of these species was not supplemented in Reclamation's reinitiated consultation with FWS in April 2002, except for the Southwestern Willow Flycatcher and Yuma Clapper Rail, and both the reinitiated consultation and the previous one in 1995–1997 defined the action area for analysis as Lake Mead to the Southerly International Border and examined the effects on species primarily in the parts of Mexico that received river flows subject to Reclamation's discretionary control. Thus, the issue presented here is whether Reclamation's duty of consultation under the ESA extends to operations affecting extra-territorial species in parts of the delta that are downstream from river flows over which Reclamation has no discretionary control.

* * *

IV. Endangered Species Act Consultation

Under § 7(a)(2) of the Endangered Species Act:

> *Each Federal agency shall, in consultation with and with the assistance of the Secretary, insure that any action authorized, funded, or carried out by such agency* (hereinafter in this section referred to as an "agency action") *is not likely to jeopardize the continued existence of any endangered species or threatened species or result in the destruction or adverse modification of habitat of such species* which is determined by the Secretary, after consultation as appropriate with affected States, to be critical, unless such agency has been granted an exemption for such action by the Committee pursuant to subsection (h) of this section . . . .

16 U.S.C. § 1536(a)(2)(emphasis added). There is a general presumption against extraterritorial application of American statutes in the absence of an "affirmative intention of the Congress clearly expressed" to extend their scope to extraterritorial conduct, *EEOC v. Arabian American Oil Co.,* 499 U.S. 244, 248 (1991); *Foley Bros. v. Filardo,* 336 U.S. 281 (1949). The presumption is inapplicable, however, to federal agency actions within the United States that have extraterritorial effects:

"By definition, an extraterritorial application of a statute involves the regulation of conduct beyond U.S. borders. Even where the significant effects of the regulated conduct are felt outside U.S. borders, the statute itself does not present a problem of extraterritoriality, so long as the conduct which Congress seeks to regulate occurs largely within the United States."

*Environmental Defense Fund v. Massey,* 986 F.2d 528, 531 (D.C.Cir.1993); *see also Gushi Bros. Co. v. Bank of Guam,* 28 F.3d 1535, 1538 (9th Cir.1994)("Questions involving the reach of Congress' prescriptive jurisdiction are not implicated when the conduct sought to be regulated occurs inside the United States."). Defendants present no substantive argument to the contrary.

Defendants argue, however . . . that, even if Reclamation's actions have extraterritorial effects on the protected species in the delta, the consultation requirements of Section 7(a)(2) have no application to non-discretionary actions. Under 50 C.F.R. § 402.03, a facially valid regulation that plaintiffs are in no position to challenge, "Section 7 [of the ESA] and the requirements of this Part apply to all actions in which there is *discretionary* Federal involvement or control." (Emphasis added). No other court in this Circuit appears to have ruled on the question of whether 50 C.F.R. § 402.03 limits the Section 7(a)(2) consultation duty. Other Circuits have found a limitation upon an agency's duty of consultation when the agency has no control of a third party's action that may threaten a protected species, either because of a contract, between the government and the third party that leaves no discretion for the agency to protect the listed species, or because of other statutes or regulations that narrowly define what the agency can do with respect to a particular action. *Sierra Club v. Babbitt,* 65 F.3d 1502, 1509–11 (9th Cir.1995)(consultation not required for Reclamation's approval of logging road project because right-of-way agreement with timber company left no discretion to deny permit to protect endangered species); *Strahan v. Linnon,* 967 F.Supp. 581, 607–08 (D.Mass.1997)(Coast Guard's issuance of Certifications of Documentation and Inspection to vessels, which is based on strict statutory criteria leaving no discretion to protect endangered species, does not trigger § 7(a)(2) consultation requirement), *aff'd,* 1998 WL 1085817, at 3 [additional citations.]

* * *

[But in] *Tenn. Valley Auth. v. Hill,* 437 U.S. 153, 173 (1978), the famous snail darter case, the Supreme Court held that the construction of a dam, even if it was well under way prior to the passage of § 7(a)(2), triggered the duty to consult because § 7(a)(2) "admits of no exception," aside from the "hardship exemptions" specified in statute. That holding somewhat counsels against construing 50 C.F.R. § 402.03 to limit the defendants' duty to consult on agency actions affecting species in the delta, but the Supreme Court was not considering a situation in which an agency has no discretionary control over a proposed action, and 50 C.F.R. § 402.03 did not exist when the Court ruled.

Plaintiffs urge that characterizing the dispute in terms of "discretionary" and "nondiscretionary" is, at this point, only theory, and that the agency should not be heard to argue that it lacks discretion until it has commenced consultation and actually determined whether there are "reasonable and prudent alternatives" to the proposed agency action. Plaintiffs insist that, as long as there are measures that can be taken to protect the endangered species, such as the acquisition of substitute habitat, Reclamation retains discretion in its management of the lower Colorado River. That argument, however, is itself merely theoretical. Substitute habitat is obviously not an alternative for the Totoaba Bass. The record contains no suggestion of a way, with or without consultation, for Reclamation to ensure that more water reaches the listed species in the delta. The formulas established by the Law of the River strictly limit Reclamation's authority to release additional waters to Mexico, and Section 7(a)(2) of the ESA does not loosen those limitations or expand Reclamation's authority. *Arizona v. California,* 376 U.S. 340, 341–42, (1964). *See generally Platte River Whooping Crane Critical Habitat Maintenance Trust v. FERC,* 962 F.2d 27, 33–34 (D.C.Cir.1992)("[Section 7] directs agencies to 'utilize their authorities' to carry out the ESA's objectives; it does not *expand* the powers conferred on an agency . . . .")

(emphasis in original). Plaintiffs do not suggest that Reclamation has any control over water after it reaches Mexican points of diversion.

Plaintiffs' final suggestion is that Reclamation retains some discretionary ability to handle "river regulation, improvement of navigation, and flood control" in a way that indirectly releases excess water to Mexico. After a review of the parties' recent supplemental memoranda, that suggestion must be rejected. Reclamation does not have the discretion to manipulate water delivery in the United States in order to create excess releases for the delta. Plaintiffs characterize Reclamation's recent decision to grant "additional deliveries of water" requested by three agricultural districts in California as proof of the agency's discretion over the release of lower Colorado River waters. Reclamation's water deliveries in California do not have any bearing on whether the agency can release more water *to Mexico,* however. The water in question, moreover, was not surplus or a bonus to the agricultural districts. The deliveries had a string attached—a statement of intent to seek "repayment" through reduced diversions of water in the future if it turned out, after Reclamation completed its yearly accounting of water diversions and return flows, that the districts had actually received more water than they were due. Defs.' Resp. to Pls.' Notice of Filing at 4–6.

The Secretary of Interior's recent decision to suspend the "excess" water that California has previously received also has no bearing on Reclamation's water releases to Mexico. The Secretary's decision is solely an exercise of discretion with respect to the total 7.5 million-acre feet of water (4.4 million-acre feet of which is allotted to California) allocated by the Boulder Canyon Project Act to the three lower basin states of Nevada, Arizona, and California. In previous years, when the lower basin states of Nevada and Arizona did not use all of their respective allotments, California received the "surplus," which gave the state more than its share of 4.4 million-acre feet of water. Defs.' Resp. to Pls.' Notice of Filing at 6–7. However, the lower basin states have now started to use more of their allotments, so that less "surplus" water is available for California. *Id.* Reclamation has been pushing California to reduce its use to the 4.4 million-acre feet allotment. This effort, however, does not cast doubt on Reclamation's position that it cannot interpret the Law of the River in a way that will divert or somehow "indirectly result" in excess flows to Mexico.

The parties have not addressed the question of deference to the agency's interpretation of the Law of the River . . . Acknowledging such deference in this case may give rise to a concern that agencies will increasingly rely on 50 C.F.R. § 402.03 to avoid ESA consultation duties, but it seems unlikely that any case will present facts that more clearly make any agency's actions nondiscretionary than this one: a Supreme Court injunction, an international treaty, federal statutes, and contracts between the government and water users that account for every acre foot of lower Colorado River water.

Conclusion

For the foregoing reasons, plaintiffs' motion for summary judgment will be denied and defendants' cross-motion for summary judgment will be granted.

* * *

---

**Question:** How does *Defenders of Wildlife* demonstrate the limits of statutory interpretation as a way of resolving cases?

# SPECIES ON PUBLIC LANDS

## CAPPAERT V. UNITED STATES

426 U.S. 128 (1976)

* * *

MR. CHIEF JUSTICE BURGER delivered the opinion of the Court.

The question presented in this litigation is whether the reservation of Devil's Hole as a national monument reserved federal water rights in unappropriated water.

Devil's Hole is a deep limestone cavern in Nevada. Approximately 50 feet below the opening of the cavern is a pool 65 feet long, 10 feet wide, and at least 200 feet deep, although its actual depth is unknown. The pool is a remnant of the prehistoric Death Valley Lake System and is situated on land owned by the United States since the Treaty of Guadalupe Hidalgo in 1848, 9 Stat. 922. By the Proclamation of January 17, 1952, President Truman withdrew from the public domain a 40-acre tract of land surrounding Devil's Hole, making it a detached component of the Death Valley National Monument. Proclamation No. 2961, 3 CFR 147 (1949–1953 Comp.). The Proclamation was issued under the American Antiquities Preservation Act, 34 Stat. 225, 16 U.S.C. § 431, which authorizes the President to declare as national monuments "objects of historic or scientific interest that are situated upon the lands owned or controlled by the Government of the United States . . . ."

The 1952 Proclamation notes that Death Valley was set aside as a national monument "for the preservation of the unusual features of scenic, scientific, and educational interest therein contained." The Proclamation also notes that Devil's Hole is near Death Valley and contains a "remarkable underground pool." Additional preambulary statements in the

Proclamation explain why Devil's Hole was being added to the Death Valley National Monument:

* * *

"WHEREAS the geologic evidence that this subterranean pool is an integral part of the hydrographic history of the Death Valley region is further confirmed by the presence in this pool of a peculiar race of desert fish, and zoologists have demonstrated that this race of fish, which is found nowhere else in the world, evolved only after the gradual drying up of the Death Valley Lake System isolated this fish population from the original ancestral stock that in Pleistocene times was common to the entire region; and

"WHEREAS the said pool is of such outstanding scientific importance that it should be given special protection, and such protection can be best afforded by making the said forty-acre tract containing the pool a part of the said monument . . . ."

The Proclamation provides that Devil's Hole should be supervised, managed, and directed by the National Park Service, Department of the Interior. Devil's Hole is fenced off, and only limited access is allowed by the Park Service.

The Cappaert petitioners own a 12,000-acre ranch near Devil's Hole, 4,000 acres of which are used for growing Bermuda grass, alfalfa, wheat, and barley; 1,700 to 1,800 head of cattle are grazed. The ranch represents an investment of more than $7 million; it employs more than 80 people with an annual payroll of more than $340,000.

In 1968 the Cappaerts began pumping groundwater on their ranch on land 21/2 miles from Devil's Hole; they were the first to appropriate groundwater. The groundwater comes from an underground basin or aquifer which is also the source of the water in Devil's Hole. After the Cappaerts began pumping from the wells near Devil's Hole, which they do from March to October, the summer water level of the pool in Devil's Hole began to decrease. Since 1962 the level of water in Devil's Hole has been measured with reference to a copper washer installed on one of the walls of the hole by the United States Geological Survey. Until 1968, the water level, with seasonable variations, had been stable at 1.2 feet below the copper marker. In 1969 the water level in Devil's Hole was 2.3 feet below the copper washer; in 1970, 3.17 feet; in 1971, 3.48 feet; and, in 1972, 3.93 feet.

When the water is at the lowest levels, a large portion of a rock shelf in Devil's Hole is above water. However, when the water level is at 3.0 feet below the marker or higher, most of the rock shelf is below water, enabling algae to grow on it. This in turn enables the desert fish (Cyprinodon diaolis, commonly known as Devil's Hole pupfish), referred to in President

Truman's Proclamation, to spawn in the spring. As the rock shelf becomes exposed, the spawning area is decreased, reducing the ability of the fish to spawn in sufficient quantities to prevent extinction.

* * *

In August 1971 the United States, . . . sought an injunction in the United States District Court for the District of Nevada to limit, except for domestic purposes, the Cappaerts' pumping from six specific wells and from specific locations near Devil's Hole. The complaint alleged that the United States, in establishing Devil's Hole as part of Death Valley National Monument, reserved the unappropriated waters appurtenant to the land to the extent necessary for the requirements and purposes of the reservation.

* * *

On June 5, 1973, the District Court, by Chief Judge Roger D. Foley, entered a preliminary injunction limiting pumping from designated wells so as to return the level of Devil's Hole to not more than 3.0 feet below the marker. Detailed findings of fact were made and the District Judge then appointed a Special Master to establish specific pumping limits for the wells and to monitor the level of the water at Devil's Hole. The District Court found that the water from certain of the wells was hydrologically connected to Devil's Hole, that the Cappaerts were pumping heavily from those wells, and that that pumping had lowered the water level in Devil's Hole.

* * *

The District Court further found that if the injunction did not issue "there is grave danger that the Devil's Hole pupfish may be destroyed, resulting in irreparable injury to the United States." 375 F.Supp., 456, 460 (1974).

The District Court then held that in establishing Devil's Hole as a national monument, the President reserved appurtenant, unappropriated waters necessary to the purpose of the reservation; the purpose included preservation of the pool and the pupfish in it.

* * *

The Court of Appeals for the Ninth Circuit affirmed, 508 F.2d 313 (1974), in a thorough opinion by Senior District Judge Gus J. Solomon, sitting by designation, holding that the implied-reservation-of-water doctrine applied to groundwater as well as to surface water.

* * *

We granted certiorari to consider the scope of the implied-reservation-of- water-rights doctrine. We affirm.

Reserved-Water-Rights Doctrine

This Court has long held that when the Federal Government withdraws its land from the public domain and reserves it for a federal purpose, the Government, by implication, reserves appurtenant water then unappropriated to the extent needed to accomplish the purpose of the reservation. In so doing the United States acquires a reserved right in unappropriated water which vests on the date of the reservation and is superior to the rights of future appropriators. Reservation of water rights is empowered by the Commerce Clause, Art. I, § 8, which permits federal regulation of navigable streams, and the Property Clause, Art. IV, § 3, which permits federal regulation of federal lands.

* * *

In determining whether there is a federally reserved water right implicit in a federal reservation of public land, the issue is whether the Government intended to reserve unappropriated and thus available water. Intent is inferred if the previously unappropriated waters are necessary to accomplish the purposes for which the reservation was created. See, E. g., Arizona v. California, supra, 373 U.S. 546, 599–601 (1963); Winters v. United States, 207 U.S. 564, 576 (1908). Both the District Court and the Court of Appeals held that the 1952 Proclamation expressed an intention to reserve unappropriated water, and we agree. The Proclamation discussed the pool in Devil's Hole in four of the five preambles and recited that the "pool . . . should be given special protection." Since a pool is a body of water, the protection contemplated is meaningful only if the water remains; the water right reserved by the 1952 Proclamation was thus explicit, not implied.

* * *

The implied-reservation-of-water-rights doctrine, however, reserves only that amount of water necessary to fulfill the purpose of the reservation, no more. Arizona v. California, supra, 373 U.S., at 600–601. the purpose of reserving Devil's Hole Monument is preservation of the pool. Devil's Hole was reserved "for the preservation of the unusual features of scenic, scientific, and educational interest." The Proclamation notes that the pool contains "a peculiar race of desert fish . . . which is found nowhere else in the world" and that the "pool is of . . . outstanding scientific importance . . . ." The pool need only be preserved, consistent with the intention expressed in the Proclamation, to the extent necessary to preserve its scientific interest. The fish are one of the features of scientific interest. The preamble noting the scientific interest of the pool follows the preamble describing the fish as unique; the Proclamation must be read in its entirety. Thus, as the District Court has correctly determined, the level of the pool may be permitted to drop to the extent that the drop does not impair the scientific value of the pool as the natural habitat of the species sought to be preserved. The District Court thus tailored its injunction, very appropriately, to minimal need, curtailing pumping only to the extent necessary to preserve an adequate water level at Devil's Hole, thus implementing the stated objectives of the Proclamation.

* * *

Groundwater

No cases of this Court have applied the doctrine of implied reservation of water rights to groundwater. Nevada argues that the implied-reservation doctrine is limited to surface water. Here, however, the water in the pool is surface water. The federal water rights were being depleted because, as the evidence showed, the "(g)roundwater and surface water are physically interrelated as integral parts of the hydrologic cycle." C. Corker, Groundwater Law, Management and Administration, National Water Commission Legal Study No. 6, p. xxiv (1971). Here the Cappaerts are causing the water level in Devil's Hole to drop by their heavy pumping. See Corker, supra; see also Water Policies for the Future Final Report to the President and to the Congress of the United States by the National Water Commission 233 (1973). . . . Thus, since the implied-reservation-of-water-rights doctrine is based on the necessity of water for the purpose of the federal reservation, we hold that the United States can protect its water from subsequent diversion, whether the diversion is of surface or groundwater.

[The Court went on to rule that federal water rights were superior to any arising under state law.]

We hold, therefore, that as of 1952 when the United States reserved Devil's Hole, it acquired by reservation water rights in unappropriated appurtenant water sufficient to maintain the level of the pool to preserve its scientific value and thereby implement Proclamation No. 2961. Accordingly, the judgment of the Court of Appeals is

Affirmed.

---

**Questions:** Since the *Cappaert* Court finds that the 1952 Proclamation explicitly created a federal water right, why did the justices go on to apply the implied reservation doctrine as well? If Congress creates a national forest (as distinguished from a national monument) for purposes of timber harvesting and watershed control, is there an implied reservation of water sufficient to protect wildlife? See *United States v. New Mexico,* 438 U.S. 696 (1978).

# CHAPTER 21

# IMMIGRATION LAW—PLENARY POWER AND IMMIGRANT STATUS

■ ■ ■

## CONTEXT & SOURCES

The federal government has more direct control over states and individuals regarding immigration than with regard to any other area of law. Article I, § 8, para. 4 grants Congress the power "[t]o establish a Uniform Rule of Naturalization," and the Supreme Court has repeatedly held that the government has "plenary" or complete power over who immigrates to the United States and the procedures governing this process. In 1952, the Immigration and Nationality Act (INA), 8 U.S.C. § 1101 et seq. established most of the current requirements for admission, inadmissibility, and removal from this country. Here, cases are presented on federal power over the states, inadmissibility, prerequisites for immigrant status, and removal.

For an analytical history of the forces shaping immigration and the legal responses to them, see Hiroshi Motomura, *Borders and Belonging: Toward a Fair Immigration Policy* (Oxford University Press, 2025). Julie Dahlstrom, "Commentary on *Chy Lung v. Freeman*," and Stewart Chang, "*Chy Lung v. Freeman*," *Feminist Judgments: Immigration Law Opinions Rewritten* (Kathleen Kim, et al. eds., Cambridge University Press, 2024) 15, creatively reimagine how that important early case might have recast the plenary power doctrine in an anti-discriminatory direction. A controversial inadmissibility case is recounted in Peter H. Schuck, "*Kleindeinst v. Mandel:* Plenary Power v. the Professors," *Immigration Stories* (David A. Martin & Peter H. Schuck eds., Foundation, 2005) 186. Maria-Teresa Davenport, "Deportation and Driving: Felony DUI and Reckless Driving as Crimes of Violence following Leocal v. Ashcroft," 96 *Journal of Criminal Law & Criminology* 849 (2006) critiques the Court's approach to removal in that decision.

## PLENARY POWER

### CHY LUNG V. FREEMAN

92 U.S. 275 (1875)

* * *

MR. JUSTICE MILLER delivered the opinion of the court.

* * *

The plaintiff in error was a passenger on a vessel from China, being a subject of the Emperor of China, and is held a prisoner because the owner or master of the vessel who brought her over refused to give a bond in the sum of $500 in gold, conditioned to indemnify all the counties, towns, and cities of California against liability for her support or maintenance for two years.

The statute of California, unlike those of New York and Louisiana, does not require a bond for *all* passengers landing from a foreign country, but only for classes of passengers specifically described, among which are 'lewd and debauched women;' to which class it is alleged plaintiff belongs.

The plaintiff, with some twenty other women, on the arrival of the steamer 'Japan' from China, was singled out by the Commissioner of Immigration, an officer of the State of California, as belonging to that class, and the master of the vessel required to give the bond prescribed by law before he permitted them to land. This he refused to do, and detained them on board. They sued out a writ of *habeas corpus*, which by regular proceedings resulted in their committal, by order of the Supreme Court of the State, to the custody of the sheriff of the county and city of San Francisco, to await the return of the 'Japan,' which had left the port pending the progress of the case; the order being to remand them to that vessel on her return, to be removed from the State.

All of plaintiff's companions were released from the custody of the sheriff on a writ of *habeas corpus* issued by Mr. Justice Field of this court. But plaintiff by a writ of error brings the judgment of the Supreme Court of California to this court, for the purpose, as we suppose, of testing the constitutionality of the act under which she is held a prisoner. We regret very much, that, while the Attorney-General of the United States has deemed the matter of such importance as to argue it in person, there has been no argument in behalf of the State of California, the Commissioner of Immigration, or the Sheriff of San Francisco, in support of the authority by which plaintiff is held a prisoner; nor have we been furnished even with a brief in support of the statute of that State.

It is a most extraordinary statute. It provides that the Commissioner of Immigration is 'to satisfy himself whether or not any passenger who shall arrive in the State by vessels from any foreign port or place (who is not a citizen of the United States) is lunatic, idiotic, deaf, dumb, blind, crippled, or infirm, and is not accompanied by relatives who are able and willing to support him, or is likely to become a public charge, or has been a pauper in any other country, or is from sickness or disease (existing either at the time of sailing from the port of departure or at the time of his arrival in the State) a public charge, or likely soon to become so, or is a convicted criminal, or a lewd or debauched woman;' and no such person shall be permitted to land from the vessel, unless the master or owner or consignee shall give a separate bond in each case, conditioned to save harmless every county, city, and town of the State against any expense incurred for the relief, support, or care of such person for two years thereafter.

The commissioner is authorized to charge the sum of seventy-five cents for every examination of a passenger made by him; which sum he may collect of the master, owner, or consignee, or of the vessel by attachment. . . .

If the ship-master or owner prefers, he may commute for these bonds by paying such a sum of money as the commissioner may in each case think proper to exact; and, after retaining twenty per cent of the commutation-money for his services, the commissioner is required once a month to deposit the balance with the Treasurer of the State. See c. 1, art. 7, of the Political Code of California, as modified by sect. 70 of the amendments of 1873, 1874.

If is hardly possible to conceive a statute more skillfully framed, to place in the hands of a single man the power to prevent entirely vessels engaged in a foreign trade, say with China, from carrying passengers, or to compel them to submit to systematic extortion of the grossest kind.

The commissioner has but to go aboard a vessel filled with passengers ignorant of our language and our laws, and without trial or hearing or evidence, but from the external appearances of persons with whose former habits he is unfamiliar, to point with his finger to twenty, as in this case, or a hundred if he chooses, and say to the master, 'These are idiots, these are paupers, these are convicted criminals, these are lewd women, and these others are debauched women. I have here a hundred blank forms of bonds, printed. I require you to fill me up and sign each of these for $500 in gold, and that you furnish me two hundred different men, residents of this State, and of sufficient means, as sureties on these bonds. I charge you five dollars in each case for preparing the bond and swearing your sureties; and I charge you seventy-five cents each for examining these passengers, and all others you have on board. If you don't do this, you are forbidden to land your passengers under a heavy penalty. But I have the power to commute with you for all this for any sum I may choose to take in cash. I am open to an offer; for you must remember that twenty per cent of all I can get out of you goes into my own pocket, and the remainder into the treasury of California.' If, as we have endeavored to show in the opinion in the preceding cases, we are at liberty to look to the effect of a statute for the test of its constitutionality, the argument need go no further.

But we have thus far only considered the effect of the statute on the owner of the vessel.

All passengers [other than representatives of foreign governments arriving in their official capacity] are subject to the order of the Commissioner of Immigration.

Individual foreigners, however distinguished at home for their social, their literary, or their political character, are helpless in the presence of this potent commissioner. Such a person may offer to furnish any amount of surety on his own bond, or deposit any sum of money; but the law of California takes no note of him. If is the master, owner, or consignee of the vessel alone whose bond can be accepted; and so a silly, an obstinate, or a wicked commissioner may bring disgrace upon the whole country, the enmity of a powerful nation, or the loss of an equally powerful friend.

While the occurrence of the hypothetical case just stated may be highly improbable, we venture the assertion, that, if citizens of our own government were treated by any foreign nation as subjects of the Emperor of China have been actually treated under this law, no administration could withstand the call for a demand on such government for redress.

* * *

If [the U.S.] government has forbidden the States to hold negotiations with any foreign nations, or to declare war, and has taken the whole subject of these relations upon herself, has the Constitution, which provides for this, done so foolish a thing as to leave it in the power of the States to pass laws whose enforcement renders the general government liable to just reclamations which it must answer, while it does not prohibit to the States the acts for which it is held responsible?

The Constitution of the United States is no such instrument. The passage of laws which concern the admission of citizens and subjects of foreign nations to our shores belongs to Congress, and not to the States. It has the power to regulate commerce with foreign nations: the responsibility for the character of those regulations, and for the manner of their execution, belongs solely to the national government. If it be otherwise, a single State can, at her pleasure, embroil us in disastrous quarrels with other nations.

We are not called upon by this statute to decide for or against the right of a State, in the absence of legislation by Congress, to protect herself by necessary and proper laws against paupers and convicted criminals from abroad; nor to lay down the definite limit of such right, if it exist. . . . .The statute of California goes so far beyond what is necessary, or even appropriate, for this purpose, as to be wholly without any sound definition of the right under which it is supposed to be justified. Its manifest purpose, as we have already said, is, not to obtain indemnity, but money.

The amount to be taken is left in every case to the discretion of an officer, whose cupidity is stimulated by a reward of one fifth of all he can obtain.

The money, when paid, does not go to any fund for the benefit of immigrants, but is paid into the general treasury of the State, and devoted to the use of all her indigent citizens. The blind, or the deaf, or the dumb passenger is subject to contribution, whether he be a rich man or a pauper. The patriot, seeking out shores after an unsuccessful struggle against despotism in Europe or Asia, may be kept out because there his resistance has been adjudged a crime. The woman whose error has been repaired by a happy marriage and numerous children, and whose loving husband brings her with his wealth to a new home, may be told she must pay a round sum before she can land, because it is alleged that she was debauched by her husband before marriage. Whether a young woman's manners are such as to justify the commissioner in calling her lewd may be made to depend on the sum she will pay for the privilege of landing in San Francisco.

It is idle to pursue the criticism. In any view which we can take of this statute, it is in conflict with the Constitution of the United States, and therefore void.

*Judgment reversed, and the case remanded, with directions to make an order discharging the prisoner from custody.*

---

**Questions:** What is the Supreme Court's view of federal immigration power in *Chy Lung*? Would the case have turned out differently if a federal statute, rather than an action by a state or local official, was the basis for the decision? See *Chae Chan Ping vs. United States,* 130 U.S. 581 (1889).

# INADMISSIBILITY

## KLEINDIENST V. MANDEL

408 U.S. 753 (1972)

* * *

MR. JUSTICE BLACKMUN delivered the opinion of the Court.

The appellees have framed the issue here as follows:

'Does appellants' action in refusing to allow an alien scholar to enter the country to attend academic meetings violate the First Amendment rights of American scholars and students who had invited him?'

Expressed in statutory terms, the question is whether §§ 212(a)(28)(D) and (G) (v) and § 212(d)(3)(A) of the Immigration and Nationality Act of 1952, 66 Stat. 182, 8 U.S.C. §§ 1182(a)(28)(D) and (G)(v) and § 1182(d)(3)(A), providing that certain aliens 'shall be ineligible to receive visas and shall be excluded from admission into the United States' unless the Attorney General, in his discretion, upon recommendation by the Secretary of State or a consular officer, waives inadmissibility and approves temporary admission, are unconstitutional as applied here in that they deprive American citizens of freedom of speech guaranteed by the First Amendment.

The challenged provisions of the statute are:

'Section 212(a). Except as otherwise provided in this Act, the following classes of aliens shall be ineligible to receive visas and shall be excluded from admission into the United States:

'(28) Aliens who are, or at any time have been, members of any of the following classes:

'(D) Aliens not within any of the other provisions of this paragraph who advocate the economic, international, and governmental doctrines of world communism or the establishment in the United States of a totalitarian dictatorship . . . .

'(G) Aliens who write or publish . . . (v) the economic, international, and governmental doctrines of world communism or the establishment in the United States of a totalitarian dictatorship; . . .

'(d)

'(3) [State Department or consular officers may recommend to the Attorney General that ineligibility be waived allowing the latter to temporarily admit the otherwise ineligible individual. The AG then is required to make a "detailed report" to Congress on the matter].

Ernest E. Mandel resides in Brussels, Belgium, and is a Belgian citizen. He is a professional journalist and is editor-in-chief of the Belgian Left Socialist weekly La Gauche. He is author of a two-volume work entitled Marxist Economic Theory published in 1969. He asserted in his visa applications that he is not a member of the Communist Party. He has described himself, however, as 'a revolutionary Marxist.' He does not dispute, see 325 F.Supp. 620, 624, that he advocates the economic, governmental, and international doctrines of world communism.

Mandel was admitted to the United States temporarily in 1962 and again in 1968. On the first visit he came as a working journalist. On the second he accepted invitations to speak at a number of universities and colleges. On each occasion, although apparently he was not then aware of it, his admission followed a finding of ineligibility under § 212(a)(28), and the Attorney General's exercise of discretion to admit him temporarily, on recommendation of the Secretary of State, as § 212(d)(3)(A) permits.

On September 8, 1969, Mandel applied to the American Consul in Brussels for a nonimmigrant visa to enter the United States in October for a six-day period, during which he would participate in a conference on Technology and the Third World at Stanford University. . . . The invitation stated that John Kenneth Galbraith would present the keynote address and that Mandel would be expected to participate in an ensuing panel discussion and to give a major address the following day. The University, through the office of its president, 'heartily endorse(d)' the invitation. When Mandel's intended visit became known, additional invitations for lectures and conference participations came to him from [various prestigious universities and political groups]. . . . Mandel then filed a second visa application proposing a more extensive itinerary and a stay of greater duration.* * *

The Department of State . . . recommended to the Attorney General that Mandel's ineligibility be waived with respect to his October visa application. The Immigration and Naturalization Service, however, acting on behalf of the Attorney General, see 28 U.S.C. § 510, in a letter dated February 13, 1970, to New York counsel stated that it had determined that Mandel's 1968 activities while in the United States 'went far beyond the stated purposes of his trip, on the basis of which his admission had been authorized and represented a flagrant abuse of the opportunities afforded him to express his views in this country.' The letter concluded that favorable exercise of discretion, provided for under the Act, was not warranted and that Mandel's temporary admission was not authorized. * * *

In March Mandel and six of the other appellees instituted the present action against the Attorney General and the Secretary of State. . . .All the appellees who joined Mandel in this action are United States citizens and are university professors in various fields of the social sciences. They are persons who invited Mandel to speak at universities and other forums in the United States or who expected to participate in colloquia with him so that, as the complaint alleged, 'they may hear his views and engage him in a free and open academic exchange.'

Plaintiff-appellees claim that the statutes are unconstitutional on their face and as applied in that they deprive the American plaintiffs of their First and Fifth Amendment rights. Specifically, these plaintiffs claim that the statutes prevent them from hearing and meeting with Mandel in person for discussions, in contravention of the First Amendment; that § 212(a)(28) denies them equal protection by permitting entry of 'rightists' but not 'leftists' and that the same section deprives them of procedural due process; that § 212(d)(3)(A) is an unconstitutional delegation of congressional power to the Attorney General because of its broad terms, lack of standards, and lack of prescribed procedures; and that application of the statutes to Mandel was 'arbitrary and capricious' because there was no basis in fact for concluding that he was ineligible, and no rational reason or basis in fact for denying him a waiver once he was determined ineligible. Declaratory and injunctive relief was sought.

A three-judge district court was duly convened. The case was tried on the pleadings and affidavits with exhibits. Two judges held that, although Mandel had no personal right to enter the United States, citizens of this country have a First Amendment right to have him enter and to hear him explain and seek to defend his views. The court then entered a declaratory judgment that § 212(a) (28) and § 212(d)(3)(A) were invalid and void insofar as they had been or might be invoked by the defendants to find Mandel ineligible for admission. The defendants were enjoined from implementing and enforcing those statutes so as to deny Mandel admission as a nonimmigrant visitor. 325 F.Supp. 620 (E.D.N.Y.1971). Judge Bartels dissented. Id., at 637 . . .

Until 1875 alien migration to the United States was unrestricted. The Act of March 3, 1875, 18 Stat. 477, barred convicts and prostitutes. Seven years later Congress passed the first general immigration statute. Act of Aug. 3, 1882, 22 Stat. 214. Other legislation followed. A general revision of the immigration laws was effected by the Act of Mar. 3, 1903, 32 Stat. 1213. Section 2 of that Act made ineligible for admission 'anarchists, or persons who believe in or advocate the overthrow by force or violence of the Government of the United States or of all government or of all forms of law.' By the Act of Oct. 16, 1918, 40 Stat. 1012, Congress expanded the provisions for the exclusion of subversive aliens. Title II of the Alien Registration Act of 1940, 54 Stat. 671, amended the 1918 Act to bar aliens who, at any time, had advocated or were members of or affiliated with organizations that advocated violent overthrow of the United States Government.

In the years that followed, after extensive investigation and numerous reports by congressional committees, see Communist Party v. Subversive Activities Control Board, 367 U.S. 1, 94 n. 37, (1961), Congress passed the Internal Security Act of 1950, 64 Stat. 987. This Act dispensed with the requirement of the 1940 Act of a finding in each case, with respect to members of the Communist Party, that the party did in fact advocate violent overthrow of the Government. These provisions were carried forward into the Immigration and Nationality Act of 1952.

We thus have almost continuous attention on the part of Congress since 1875 to the problems of immigration and of excludability of certain defined classes of aliens. The pattern generally has been one of increasing control with particular attention, for almost 70 years now, first to anarchists and then to those with communist affiliation or views.

It is clear that Mandel personally, as an unadmitted and nonresident alien, had no constitutional right of entry to this country as a nonimmigrant or otherwise. [Citations].

The appellees concede this. Brief for Appellees 33; Tr. of Oral Arg. 28. Indeed, the American appellees assert that 'they sue to enforce their rights, individually and as members of the American public, and assert none on the part of the invited alien.' Brief for Appellees at 14. 'Dr. Mandel is in a sense made a plaintiff because he is symbolic of the problem,' Tr. of Oral Arg. 22.

The case, therefore, comes down to the narrow issue whether the First Amendment confers upon the appellee professors, because they wish to hear, speak, and debate with Mandel in person, the ability to determine that Mandel should be permitted to enter the country or, in other words, to compel the Attorney General to allow Mandel's admission.

In a variety of contexts this Court has referred to a First Amendment right to 'receive information and ideas':

'It is now well established that the Constitution protects the right to receive information and ideas. 'This freedom (of speech and press) . . . necessarily protects the right to receive . . . .' [Citations].

* * *

Mr. Justice White, speaking for a unanimous Court upholding the FCC's 'fairness doctrine' in Red Lion Broadcasting Co. v. FCC, 395 U.S. 367, 386–390 (1969), said:

'It is the purpose of the First Amendment to preserve an uninhibited marketplace of ideas in which truth will ultimately prevail . . . . It is the right of the public to receive suitable access to social, political, esthetic, moral, and other ideas and experiences which is crucial here. That right may not constitutionally be abridged either by Congress or by the FCC.' Id., at 390.

* * *

This Court has recognized that this right is 'nowhere more vital' than in our schools and universities. [Citation].

In the present case, the District Court majority held:

'The concern of the First Amendment is not with a non-resident alien's individual and personal interest in entering and being heard, but with the rights of the citizens of the country to have the alien enter and to hear him explain and seek to defend his views; that, as Garrison (v. Louisiana, 379 U.S. 64, 85 (1964)) and Red Lion observe, is of the essence of self-government.' 325 F.Supp., at 631.

The Government disputes this conclusion on two grounds. First, it argues that exclusion of Mandel involves no restriction on First Amendment rights at all since what is restricted is 'only action—the action of the alien in coming into this country.' Brief for Appellants 29. Principal reliance is placed on Zemel v. Rusk, 381 U.S. 1, 85 9 (1965), where the Government's refusal to validate an American passport for travel to Cuba was upheld. The rights asserted there were those of the passport applicant himself. The Court held that his right to travel and his asserted ancillary right to inform himself about Cuba did not outweigh substantial 'foreign policy considerations affecting all citizens' that, with the backdrop of the Cuban missile crisis, were characterized as the 'weightiest considerations of national security.' Id., at 13, 16. The rights asserted here, in some contrast, are those of American academics who have invited Mandel to participate with them in colloquia debates, and discussion in the United States. In light of the Court's previous decisions concerning the 'right to receive information,' we cannot realistically say that the problem facing us disappears entirely or is nonexistent because the mode of regulation bears directly on physical movement. . . .

The Government also suggests that the First Amendment is inapplicable because appellees have free access to Mandel's ideas through his books and speeches, and because 'technological developments,' such as tapes or telephone hook-ups, readily supplant his physical presence. This argument overlooks what may be particular qualities inherent in sustained, face-to-face debate, discussion and questioning. While alternative means of access to Mandel's ideas might be a relevant factor were we called upon to balance First Amendment rights against governmental regulatory interests . . .—we are loath to hold on this record that existence of other alternatives extinguishes altogether any constitutional interest on the part of the appellees in this particular form of access.

Recognition that First Amendment rights are implicated, however, is not dispositive of our inquiry here. In accord with ancient principles of the international law of nation-states, the Court in The Chinese Exclusion Case, 130 U.S. 581, 609 (1889), and in Fong Yue Ting v. United States, 149 U.S. 698 (1893), held broadly, as the Government describes, it, Brief for appellants 20, that the power to exclude aliens is 'inherent in sovereignty, necessary for maintaining normal international relations and defending the country against foreign encroachments and dangers—a power to be exercised exclusively by the political branches of government . . . .' Since that time, the Court's general reaffirmations of this principle have been legion. The Court without exception has sustained Congress' 'plenary power to make rules for the admission of aliens and to exclude those who possess those characteristics which Congress has forbidden.' Boutilier v. Immigration and Naturalization Service, 387 U.S. 118, 123 (1967). '(O)ver no conceivable subject is the legislative power of Congress more complete than it is over' the admission of aliens. Oceanic Navigation Co. v. Stranahan, 214 U.S. 320, 339, (1909). In Lem Moon Sing v. United States, 158 U.S. 538, 547, (1895), the first Mr. Justice Harlan said:

'The power of congress to exclude aliens altogether from the United States, or to prescribe the terms and conditions upon which they may come to this country, and to have its declared policy in that regard enforced exclusively through executive officers, without judicial intervention, is settled by our previous adjudications.'

Mr. Justice Frankfurter ably articulated this history in Galvan v. Press, 347 U.S. 522 (1954), a deportation case, and we can do no better. After suggesting, at 530, that 'much could be said for the view' that due process places some limitations on congressional power in this area 'were we writing on a clean slate,' he continued:

'But the slate is not clean. As to the extent of the power of Congress under review, there is not merely a page of history, . . . but a whole volume. Policies pertaining to the entry of aliens and their right to remain here are peculiarly concerned with the political conduct of government. In the enforcement of these policies, the Executive Branch of the Government must respect the procedural safeguards of due process. . . . But that the formulation of these policies is entrusted exclusively to Congress has become about as firmly embedded in the legislative and judicial tissues of our body politic as any aspect of our government . . . .

* * *

In almost every instance of an alien excludable under § 212(a)(28), there are probably those who would wish to meet and speak with him. The ideas of most such aliens might not be so influential as those of Mandel, nor his American audience so numerous, nor the planned discussion forums so impressive. But the First Amendment does not protect only the articulate, the well known, and the popular. Were we to endorse the proposition that governmental power to withhold a waiver must yield whenever a bona fide claim is made that American citizens wish to meet and talk with an alien excludable under § 212(a)(28), one of two unsatisfactory results would necessarily ensue. Either every claim would prevail, in which case the plenary discretionary authority Congress granted the Executive becomes a nullity, or courts in each case would be required to weigh the strength of the audience's interest against that of the Government in refusing a waiver to the particular alien applicant, according to some as yet undetermined standard. The dangers and the undesirability of making that determination on the basis of factors such as the size of the audience or the probity of the speaker's ideas are obvious. Indeed, it is for precisely this reason that the waiver decision has, properly, been placed in the hands of the Executive.

* * *

In summary, plenary congressional power to make policies and rules for exclusion of aliens has long been firmly established. In the case of an alien excludable under § 212(a)(28), Congress has delegated conditional exercise of this power to the Executive. We hold that when the Executive exercises this power negatively on the basis of a facially legitimate and bona fide reason, the courts will neither look behind the exercise of that discretion, nor test it by balancing its justification against the First Amendment interests of those who seek personal communication with the applicant. What First Amendment or other grounds may be available for attacking exercise of discretion for which no justification whatsoever is advanced is a question we neither address or decide in this case.

Reversed.

MR. JUSTICE DOUGLAS, dissenting.

Under The Chinese Exclusion Case, 130 U.S. 581, rendered in 1889, there could be no doubt but that Congress would have the power to exclude any class of aliens from these shores. The accent at the time was on race. Mr. Justice Field, writing for the Court, said: 'If, therefore, the government of the United States, through its legislative department, considers the presence of foreigners of a different race in this country, who will not assimilate with us, to be dangerous to its peace and security, their exclusion is not to be stayed because at the time there are no actual hostilities with the nation of which the foreigners are subjects.' Id., at 606.

An ideological test, not a racial one, is used here. But neither, in my view, is permissible, as I have indicated on other occasions. Yet a narrower question is raised here. Under the present Act aliens who advocate or teach 'the economic, international, and governmental doctrines of world communism' are ineligible to receive visas '(e)xcept as otherwise provided in this Act.' The 'except' provision is contained in another part of the same section and states that an inadmissible alien 'may, after approval by the Attorney General of a recommendation by the Secretary of State or by the consular officer' be admitted 'temporarily despite his inadmissibility.'

* * *

Dr. Mandel is not the sole complainant. Joining him are the other appellees who represent the various audiences which Dr. Mandel would be meeting were a visa to issue. While Dr. Mandel, an alien who seeks admission, has no First Amendment rights while outside the Nation. The other appellees are on a different footing. The First Amendment involves not only the right to speak and publish but also the right to hear, to learn, to know. [Citations].

Can the Attorney General under the broad discretion entrusted in him decide that one who maintains that the earth is round can be excluded? [T]hat no one who believes in the Darwinian theory shall be admitted? [T]hat those who promote a Rule of Law to settle international differences rather than a Rule of Force may be barred? [T]hat a genetic biologist who lectures on the way to create life by one sex alone is beyond the pale? [T]hat an exponent of plate tectonics can be barred? [T]hat one should be excluded who taught that Jesus when he arose from the Sepulcher, went east (not up) and became a teacher at Hemis Monastery in the Himalayas?

I put the issue that bluntly because national security is not involved. Nor is the infiltration of saboteurs. The Attorney General stands astride out international terminals that bring people here to bar those whose ideas are not acceptable to him. Even assuming, arguendo, that those on the outside seeking admission have no standing to complain, those who hope to benefit from the traveler's lectures do.

Thought control is not within the competence of any branch of government. Those who live here may need exposure to the ideas of people of many faiths and many creeds to further their education. We should construe the Act generously by that First Amendment standard, saying that once the State Department has concluded that our foreign relations permit or require the admission of a foreign traveler, the Attorney General is left only problems of national security, importation of heroin, or other like matters within his competence.

* * *

In Brandenburg v. Ohio, 395 U.S. 444, . . .we held that the First Amendment does not permit a State 'to forbid or proscribe advocacy of the use of force or of law violation except where such advocacy is directed to inciting or producing imminent lawless action and is likely to incite or produce such action.' Id., at 447. That case involved propagation of the views of the Ku Klux Klan. The present case involves teaching the communist creed. But, as we held in Noto v. United States, 367 U.S. 290, 297–298:

'(T)he mere abstract teaching of Communist theory, including the teaching of the moral propriety or even moral necessity for a resort to force and violence, is not the same as preparing a group for violent action and steeling it to such action.'

As a matter of statutory construction, I conclude that Congress never undertook to entrust the Attorney General with the discretion to pick and choose among the ideological offerings which alien lecturers tender from our platforms, allowing those palatable to him and disallowing others. The discretion entrusted to him concerns matters commonly within the competence of the Department of Justice—national security, importation of drugs, and the like.

I would affirm the judgment of the three-judge District Court.

---

**Questions:** In *Kleindienst,* both the majority and the dissent recognize that some balancing is necessary between the Immigration and Nationality Act and the First Amendment. Why do they arrive at different results? Can inadmissibility be based solely on the fact of membership in an organization? See *Abourezk v. Reagan,* 785 F.2d 1043 (D.C. Cir. 1986).

## IMMIGRANT STATUS

### MATTER OF RODRIGUEZ-CRUZ IN VISA PETITION PROCEEDINGS

A-23050125

18 I & N Dec. 72 (Board of Immigration Appeals 1981)

BY: MILHOLLAN, CHAIRMAN; MANIATIS, MAGUIRE, and MORRIS, BOARD MEMBERS

This is an appeal from the March 5, 1979, decision of the District Director denying the visa petition filed by the United States citizen petitioner on behalf of the beneficiary as his son under section 203(a)(1) of the Immigration and Nationality Act, 8 U.S.C. 1153(a)(1). The appeal will be dismissed.

The United States citizen petitioner was born on February 4, 1927, in Garland, Texas. The beneficiary is a 30-year old native and citizen of Mexico. The District Director denied the visa petition based on his finding that the beneficiary was born illegitimate and had been legitimated by the marriage of his parents after he had reached the age of 18. He concluded therefore that the beneficiary could not qualify as the child of the petitioner under section 101(b)(1)(C) of the Act, 8 U.S.C. 1101(b)(1)(C), and consequently could not be conferred visa preference status as the son of the petitioner.

In order for a United States citizen to confer visa-preference status upon the beneficiary he must once have qualified as a "child" under section 1101(b). Section 1101(b) of the Act provides that:

"The term "child" means an unmarried person under twenty-one years of age who is—C) a child legitimated under the law of the child's residence or domicile, or under the law of the father's residence or domicile, whether in or outside of the United States, if such legitimation takes place before the child reaches the age of eighteen years and the child is in the legal custody of the legitimating parent or parents at the time of such legitimation."

On appeal, the petitioner argues that the beneficiary qualifies as his child since he entered into a religious marriage with the beneficiary's mother on March 13, 1949, more than a year prior to the beneficiary's birth. Contained in the record is a marriage certificate issued by the Vicaria Fija de San Miguel Arcangel in Uriangato, Guanajuato, Mexico, verifying the 1949 religious marriage of the petitioner and the beneficiary's mother. Also included in the record is a marriage certificate issued by the Guanajuato Civil Registrar which indicates that the beneficiary's parents entered into a civil marriage ceremony on November 23, 1972.

Counsel for the petitioner contends that the question of the validity of religious marriages, particularly in Mexico, is governed by the intent of the parties. He cites *Matter of K-,* 7 I & N Dec. 492 (BIA 1957), for the proposition that where the evidence of record indicates that the foreign religious marriage was entered into in good faith and recognized by the parties thereto, the validity of the marriage was presumed in the absence of evidence to the contrary, reliance being had on the presumption in favor of the validity of a marriage and that the formalities of law had been complied with.

The petitioner's reliance of *Matter of K-, supra,* is misplaced. The generally accepted rule is that the validity of a marriage is governed by the law of the place of celebration. *See Matter of P-,* 4 I & N Dec. 610 (A.G. 1952; BIA 1952); *Matter of Freeman,* 11 I & N Dec. 482) (BIA 1966). Article 130 of the Constitution of Mexico, in force at the time of the 1949 religious marriage of the beneficiary's parents, provides;

"Marriage is a civil contract. This and other acts concerning the civil status of persons are within the exclusive competence of civil officials and authorities in the manner prescribed by law. These acts shall have the force and validity attributed to them thereby."

In *Matter of A-E-,* 4 I & N Dec. 405 (BIA 1951), we held that a religious marriage ceremony in Mexico does not result in a valid marriage, notwithstanding the parties' intention that it be such. *See also Matter of*

*Magana,* 17 I & N Dec. 111 (BIA 1979). To the extent that *Matter of K-, supra,* is inconsistent with *Matter of A-E-, supra,* it is expressly overruled. Since the religious marriage in question here was not performed in accordance with civil formalities, it did not result in a valid marriage under Mexican law, despite any intent on the part of the petitioner and the beneficiary's mother that it be such.

In visa petition proceedings, the burden of proving eligibility for the benefit sought rests with the petitioner. *Matter of Brantigan,* 11 I & N Dec. 493 (BIA 1979). The law of a foreign country is a question of fact that must be proven by the petitioner if he wishes to rely on it. *Matter of Annang,* 14 I & N Dec. 502 (BIA 1973). The petitioner has not presented any evidence to establish that the 1949 religious marriage would be recognized as valid under the law of Mexico or the state of Guanajuato in effect at the time of the marriage. Since the petitioner and the beneficiary's mother did not enter into a civil marriage ceremony until 1972 when the beneficiary had already reached the age of 22, the beneficiary cannot meet the 18-year age requirement for legitimation in accordance with section 101(b)(1)(C) of the Act. Consequently, the petitioner cannot confer visa-preference status on the beneficiary as his son. The appeal, accordingly, will be dismissed.

ORDER: The appeal is dismissed.

---

**Question:** In resolving *Rodriguez-Cruz,* why did the Board of Immigration Appeals need to evaluate the origin country's law?

## REMOVAL

### LEOCAL V. ASHCROFT

540 U.S 1176 (2004)

* * *

CHIEF JUSTICE REHNQUIST delivered the opinion of the Court.

Petitioner Josue Leocal, a Haitian citizen who is a lawful permanent resident of the United States, was convicted in 2000 of driving under the influence of alcohol (DUI) and causing serious bodily injury, in violation of Florida law. See Fla. Stat. § 316.193(3)(c)(2) (2003). Classifying this conviction as a "crime of violence" under 18 U.S.C. § 16 and therefore an "aggravated felony" under the Immigration and Nationality Act (INA), an Immigration Judge and the Board of Immigration Appeals (BIA) ordered that petitioner be deported pursuant to § 237(a) of the INA. The Court of Appeals for the Eleventh Circuit agreed, dismissing petitioner's petition for review. We disagree and hold that petitioner's DUI conviction is not a crime of violence under 18 U.S.C. § 16.

Petitioner immigrated to the United States in 1980 and became a lawful permanent resident in 1987. In January 2000, he was charged with two counts of DUI causing serious bodily injury under Fla. Stat. § 316.193(3)(c)(2), after he caused an accident resulting in injury to two people. He pleaded guilty to both counts and was sentenced to two and a half years in prison.

In November 2000, while he was serving his sentence, the Immigration and Naturalization Service (INS) initiated removal proceedings against him pursuant to § 237(a) of the INA. Under that provision, "[a]ny alien who is convicted of an aggravated felony . . . is deportable" and may be removed upon an order of the Attorney General. 66 Stat. 201, 8 U.S.C. § 1227(a)(2)(A)(iii). Section 101(a)(43) of the INA defines "aggravated felony" to include, *inter alia,* "a crime of violence (as defined in section 16 of title 18, but not including a purely political offense) for which the term of imprisonment [is] at least one year."1 8 U.S.C. § 1101(a)(43)(F) (footnote omitted). Title 18 U.S.C. § 16 in turn, defines the term "crime of violence" to mean:

> "(a) an offense that has as an element the use, attempted use, or threatened use of physical force against the person or property of another, or
>
> "(b) any other offense that is a felony and that, by its nature, involves a substantial risk that physical force against the person or property of another may be used in the course of committing the offense."

Here, the INS claimed that petitioner's DUI conviction was a "crime of violence" under § 16, and therefore an "aggravated felony" under the INA.

In October 2001, an Immigration Judge found petitioner removable, relying upon the Eleventh Circuit's decision in *Le* v. *United States Attorney General,* 196 F.3d 1352 (1999) *(per curiam),* which held that a conviction under the Florida DUI statute qualified as a crime of violence. The BIA affirmed. Petitioner completed his sentence and was removed to Haiti in November 2002. In June 2003, the Court of Appeals for the Eleventh Circuit dismissed petitioner's petition for review, relying on its previous ruling in *Le, supra.* App. to Pet. for Cert. 5a–7a. We granted certiorari, 540 U.S. 1176 (2004), to resolve a conflict among the Courts of Appeals on the question whether state DUI offenses similar to the one in Florida, which either do not have a *mens rea* [guilty mind, or mental state recognizing wrongdoing] component or require only a showing of negligence in the operation of a vehicle, qualify as a crime of violence. [Citations]. We now reverse the Eleventh Circuit.

Title 18 U.S.C. § 16 was enacted as part of the Comprehensive Crime Control Act of 1984, which broadly reformed the federal criminal code in such areas as sentencing, bail, and drug enforcement, and which added a variety of new violent and nonviolent offenses. § 1001(a), 98 Stat. 2136. Congress employed the term "crime of violence" in numerous places in the Act, such as for defining the elements of particular offenses, see, *e.g.*, 18 U.S.C. § 1959 (prohibiting threats to commit crimes of violence in aid of racketeering activity), or for directing when a hearing is required before a charged individual can be released on bail, see § 3142(f) (requiring a pretrial detention hearing for those alleged to have committed a crime of violence). Congress therefore provided in § 16 a general definition of the term "crime of violence" to be used throughout the Act. See § 1001(a), 98 Stat. 2136. Section 16 has since been incorporated into a variety of statutory provisions, both criminal and noncriminal.

Here, pursuant to § 237(a) of the INA, the Court of Appeals applied § 16 to find that petitioner's DUI conviction rendered him deportable. In determining whether petitioner's conviction falls within the ambit of § 16, the statute directs our focus to the "offense" of conviction. See § 16(a) (defining a crime of violence as "*an offense* that has *as an element* the use . . . of physical force against the person or property of another" (emphasis added)); § 16(b) (defining the term as "*any other offense* that is a felony and that, *by its nature*, involves a substantial risk that physical force against the person or property of another may be used in the course of committing the offense" (emphasis added)). This language requires us to look to the elements and the nature of the offense of conviction, rather than to the particular facts relating to petitioner's crime.

Florida Stat. § 316.193(3)(c)(2) makes it a third-degree felony for a person to operate a vehicle while under the influence and, "by reason of such operation, caus[e] . . . [s]erious bodily injury to another." The Florida statute, while it requires proof of causation of injury, does not require proof of any particular mental state. See *State* v. *Hubbard*, 751 So. 2d 552, 562–564 (Fla. 1999) (holding, in the context of a DUI manslaughter conviction under § 316.193, that the statute does not contain a *mens rea* requirement). Many States have enacted similar statutes, criminalizing DUI causing serious bodily injury or death without requiring proof of any mental state, or, in some States, appearing to require only proof that the person acted negligently in operating the vehicle. The question here is whether § 16 can be interpreted to include such offenses.

Our analysis begins with the language of the statute. See *Bailey* v. *United States*, 516 U.S. 137, 144 (1995). The plain text of § 16(a) states that an offense, to qualify as a crime of violence, must have "as an element the use, attempted use, or threatened use of physical force against the person or property of another." We do not deal here with an *attempted* or *threatened* use of force. Petitioner contends that his conviction did not require the "use" of force against another person because the most common employment of the word "use" connotes the *intentional* availment of force, which is not required under the Florida DUI statute. The Government counters that the "use" of force does not incorporate any *mens rea* component, and that petitioner's DUI conviction necessarily includes the use of force. To support its position, the Government dissects the meaning of the word "use," employing dictionaries, legislation, and our own case law in contending that a use of force may be negligent or even inadvertent.

Whether or not the word "use" alone supplies a *mens rea* element, the parties' primary focus on that word is too narrow. Particularly when interpreting a statute that features as elastic a word as "use," we construe language in its context and in light of the terms surrounding it. See *Smith* v. *United States,* 508 U.S. 223, 229 (1993); *Bailey, supra,* at 143. The critical aspect of § 16(a) is that a crime of violence is one involving the "use . . . of physical force *against the person or property of another.*" (Emphasis added.) As we said in a similar context in *Bailey*, "use" requires active employment. 516 U.S., at 145. While one may, in theory, actively employ *something* in an accidental manner, it is much less natural to say that a person actively employs physical force against another person by accident. Thus, a person would "use . . . physical force against" another when pushing him; however, we would not ordinarily say a person "use[s] . . . physical force against" another by stumbling and falling into him. When interpreting a statute, we must give words their "ordinary or natural" meaning. *Smith, supra,* at 228. The key phrase in § 16(a)—the "use . . . of physical force against the person or property of another"—most naturally suggests a higher degree of intent than negligent or merely accidental conduct. See [citations]. Petitioner's DUI offense therefore is not a crime of violence under § 16(a).

Neither is petitioner's DUI conviction a crime of violence under § 16(b). Section 16(b) sweeps more broadly than § 16(a), defining a crime of violence as including "any other offense that is a felony and that, by its nature, involves a substantial risk that physical force against the person or property of another may be used in the course of committing the offense." But § 16(b) does not thereby encompass all negligent misconduct, such as the negligent operation of a vehicle. It simply covers offenses that naturally involve a person acting in disregard of the risk that physical force might be used against another in committing an offense. The reckless disregard in § 16 relates *not* to the general conduct or to the possibility that harm will result from a person's conduct, but to the risk that the use of physical force against another might be required in committing a crime. The classic example is burglary. A burglary would be covered under § 16(b) not because the offense can be committed in a generally reckless way or because someone may be injured, but because burglary, by its nature, involves a substantial risk that the burglar will use force against a victim in completing the crime.

Thus, while § 16(b) is broader than § 16(a) in the sense that physical force need not actually be applied, it contains the same formulation we found to be determinative in § 16(a): the use of physical force against the person or property of another. Accordingly, we must give the language in § 16(b) an identical construction, requiring a higher *mens rea* than the merely accidental or negligent conduct involved in a DUI offense. This is particularly true in light of § 16(b)'s requirement that the "substantial risk" be a risk of using physical force against another person "in the course of committing the offense." In no "ordinary or natural" sense can it be said that a person risks having to "use" physical force against another person in the course of operating a vehicle while intoxicated and causing injury.

In construing both parts of § 16, we cannot forget that we ultimately are determining the meaning of the term "crime of violence." The ordinary meaning of this term, combined with § 16's emphasis on the use of physical force against another person (or the risk of having to use such force in committing a crime), suggests a category of violent, active crimes that cannot be said naturally to include DUI offenses. Cf. *United States* v. *Doe,* 960 F.2d 221, 225 (CA1 1992) (Breyer, C. J.) (observing that the term "violent felony" in 18 U.S.C. § 924(e) (2000 ed. and Supp. II) "calls to mind a tradition of crimes that involve the possibility of more closely related, active violence"). Interpreting § 16 to encompass accidental or negligent conduct would blur the distinction between the "violent" crimes Congress sought to distinguish for heightened punishment and other crimes. See *United States* v. *Lucio-Lucio,* 347 F.3d 1202, 1205–1206 (CA10 2003).

Section 16 therefore cannot be read to include petitioner's conviction for DUI causing serious bodily injury under Florida law. This construction is reinforced by Congress' use of the term "crime of violence" in § 101(h) of the INA, which was enacted in 1990. See Foreign Relations Authorization Act, Fiscal Years 1990 and 1991, § 131, 104 Stat. 31 (hereinafter FRAA). Section 212(a)(2)(E) of the INA renders inadmissible any alien who has previously exercised diplomatic immunity from criminal jurisdiction in the United States after committing a "serious criminal offense." 8 U.S.C. § 1182(a)(2)(E). Section 101(h) defines the term "serious criminal offense" to mean:

> "(1) any felony;
>
> "(2) any crime of violence, as defined in section 16 of title 18; or
>
> "(3) any crime of reckless driving or of driving while intoxicated or under the influence of alcohol or of prohibited substances if such crime involves personal injury to another." 8 U.S.C. § 1101(h) (emphasis added).

Congress' separate listing of the DUI-causing-injury offense from the definition of "crime of violence" in § 16 is revealing. Interpreting § 16 to include DUI offenses, as the Government urges, would leave § 101(h)(3) practically devoid of significance. As we must give effect to every word of a statute wherever possible, see *Duncan* v. *Walker,* 533 U.S. 167, 174 (2001), the distinct provision for these offenses under § 101(h) bolsters our conclusion that § 16 does not itself encompass DUI offenses.

This case does not present us with the question whether a state or federal offense that requires proof of the *reckless* use of force against a person or property of another qualifies as a crime of violence under 18 U.S.C. § 16. DUI statutes such as Florida's do not require any mental state with respect to the use of force against another person, thus reaching individuals who were negligent or less. Drunk driving is a nationwide problem, as evidenced by the efforts of legislatures to prohibit such conduct and impose appropriate penalties. But this fact does not warrant our shoehorning it into statutory sections where it does not fit. The judgment of the United States Court of Appeals for the Eleventh Circuit is therefore reversed, and the case is remanded for further proceedings consistent with this opinion. It is so ordered.

---

**Question:** Why does the Supreme Court in *Leocal* focus on whether the Florida statute under which petitioner was convicted required proof of a particular mental state?

# CHAPTER 22

# IMMIGRATION LAW—POLITICAL ASYLUM

■ ■ ■

## CONTEXT & SOURCES

The concept of political asylum reflects the U.S. history of welcoming refugees and promoting democratic values. The INA grants permission to remain in the United States, and a path to permanent resident status, to individuals who have a "well-founded fear of persecution on account of race, religion, nationality, membership in a particular social group, or political opinion." 8 U.S.C. § 1101(a)(42)(A). Cases are included here on the definition of persecution, the meaning of political opinion, and the statutory bar against persecutors of others receiving asylum.

*Refugee Roulette: Disparities in Asylum Adjudication and Proposals for Reform* (Jaya Ramji-Nogales, et al., eds., New York University Press, 2009) is a comprehensive guide to the legal proceedings of the asylum process as well as perspectives from other countries and critiques. Yujin Chun, "Courts Shall Not Rule on Homeschool Alone: Romeike v Holder and the Intersection of Fundamental Rights and Asylum," 2 *Cornell International Law Journal Online* 60 (2014) concisely analyzes the Supreme Court's approach to the scope of persecution. In Shayna S. Cook, "Repairing the Legacy of *INS v. Elias-Zacarias*," 23 *Michigan Journal of International Law* 223 (2002), a federal judge assesses the effect of the Court's narrow definition of political opinion. For a discussion of persecutors' asylum eligibility in relation to broader issues of administrative law, see David A. Karp, "Setting the 'Persecutor Bar' for Political Asylum After *Negusie*," 61 *Florida Law Review* 933 (2009).

## PERSECUTION

### ROMEIKE V. HOLDER

718 F.3d 528 (6th Cir. 2013)

SUTTON, CIRCUIT JUDGE.

Uwe and Hannelore Romeike have five children, ages twelve, eleven, nine, seven and two, at least at the time this dispute began. Rather than send their children to the local public schools, they would prefer to teach them at home, largely for religious reasons. The powers that be refused to let them do so and prosecuted them for truancy when they disobeyed orders to return the children to school. Had the Romeikes lived in America at the time, they would have had a lot of legal authority to work with in countering the prosecution. *See Wisconsin v. Yoder,* 406 U.S. 205 (1972) (additional citations.)

But the Romeikes lived in Germany when this dispute began. When the Romeikes became fed up with Germany's ban on homeschooling and when their prosecution for failure to follow the law led to increasingly burdensome fines, they came to this country with the hope of obtaining asylum. Congress might have written the immigration laws to grant a safe haven to people living elsewhere in the world who face government strictures that the United States Constitution prohibits. But it did not. The relevant legislation applies only to those who have a "well-founded fear of persecution on account of race, religion, nationality, membership in a particular social group, or political opinion." 8 U.S.C. § 1101(a)(42)(A). There is a difference between the persecution of a discrete group and the prosecution of those who violate a generally applicable law. As the Board of Immigration Appeals permissibly found, the German authorities have not singled out the Romeikes in particular or homeschoolers in general for persecution. As a result, we must deny the Romeikes' petition for review and, with it, their applications for asylum.

German law requires all children to attend public or state-approved private schools. The Romeikes feared that the public school curriculum would "influence [their children] against Christian values." A.R. 478. When the parents chose to homeschool their children, the government imposed fines for each unexcused absence. When the fines did not bring the Romeikes in line, the police went to the Romeikes' house and escorted the children to school. That strategy worked—once. The next time, four adults and seven children from the Romeikes' homeschooling support group intervened, and the police, reluctant to use force, left the premises without the children.

The school district returned to a strategy of imposing fines rather than force. It prosecuted the Romeikes for, and a court found them guilty of, violating the compulsory-attendance law, leading to still more fines. The prosecution and the mounting fines were the last straws, and the family moved to the United States in 2008. At the time of their departure, they owed the government 7,000 euros or roughly $9,000.

The Romeikes entered the United States through a visa waiver program. Uwe applied for asylum, and his wife and five children sought relief as derivative applicants. An immigration judge approved the applications after finding that the Romeikes had a well-founded fear of persecution based on their membership in a "particular social group": homeschoolers. The Board of Immigration Appeals overturned the immigration judge's decision. It explained that "[t]he record does not show that the compulsory school attendance law is selectively applied to homeschoolers like the applicants." *Id.* at 5. It added that homeschoolers were not punished more severely than other parents whose children broke the law. It concluded by reasoning that, even if the German government had singled out people like the Romeikes, "homeschoolers" are not protected by the immigration laws because they "lack the social visibility" and "particularity required to be a cognizable social group." *Id.* at 7.

To obtain asylum, an individual must prove that he cannot return to his native country because of a "well-founded fear of persecution on account of race, religion, nationality, membership in a particular social group, or political opinion." 8 U.S.C. § 1101(a)(42)(A). In trying to meet this requirement, the Romeikes have not claimed on appeal that the German government has persecuted them in the past; they claim that the government will persecute them in the future if they return.

When it comes to showing that a foreign country's enforcement of a law will persecute individuals on the basis of religion, membership in a social group or for that matter any other protected ground, there is an easy way and a hard way. The easy way is available when the foreign government enforces a law that persecutes on its face along one of these lines. Then there is the hard way—showing persecution through the enforcement of a generally applicable law. "[W]here the law that the native country seeks to enforce in its criminal prosecution is 'generally applicable,'" that usually will be the antithesis of persecution. *Cruz-Samayoa v. Holder,* 607 F.3d 1145, 1151 (6th Cir.2010). One normally does not think of government officials persecuting their citizens when they enforce a law that applies equally to everyone, including the allegedly persecuted group and the officials themselves. That is why, generally speaking, "[p]unishment for violation of a generally applicable criminal law is not persecution." *Saleh v. U.S. Dep't of Justice,* 962 F.2d 234, 239 (2d Cir.1992). Enforcement of a neutral law usually is incompatible with persecution.

But usually is not the same as invariably. Even "[g]enerally applicable laws," we have recognized, "can be the source of a petitioner's persecution" in some cases. *Stserba v. Holder,* 646 F.3d 964, 977 (6th Cir.2011). The government, for example, might selectively enforce a neutral law, prosecuting some individuals but not others based on a protected ground or punishing some more harshly than others for the same crime based on a protected ground. *See Cruz-Samayoa,* 607 F.3d at 1151. Or the government might enact a seemingly neutral law that no one would feel compelled to break except on the basis of a protected ground, say a law banning certain clothing worn only by a discrete religious group or a law "outlaw[ing] the display of the American flag." *Beskovic v. Gonzales,* 467 F.3d 223, 226 (2d Cir.2006). In either instance, if the applicant otherwise meets the requirements for establishing persecution, the fact that the government purported to enforce a generally applicable law would not immunize it from a charge of persecution.

This, however, is the hard way to show persecution, and regrettably for the Romeikes they have not shown that Germany's enforcement of its general school-attendance law amounts to persecution against them, whether on grounds of religion or membership in a recognized social group. Because the Board issued its own decision, as opposed to summarily affirming the immigration judge, we review its decision as the final agency determination. *Khalili v. Holder,* 557 F.3d 429, 435 (6th Cir.2009). The Board's "findings of fact are conclusive unless any reasonable adjudicator would be compelled to conclude to the contrary." 8 U.S.C. § 1252(b)(4)(B). And the Board's "decision that an alien is not eligible for admission to the United States is conclusive unless manifestly contrary to law." *Id.* § 1252(b)(4)(C).

The Romeikes have not met these standards. Even assuming for the sake of argument that faith-based homeschoolers (or for that matter homeschoolers in general) are a cognizable social group, a matter we need not resolve, "[t]he record does not show that the compulsory school attendance law is selectively applied to homeschoolers like the applicants," or that "homeschoolers are more severely punished than others whose children do not comply with the compulsory school attendance law." A.R. 5. The petitioner's key witness, Michael Donnelly, testified that *all* parents who do not send their children to school face consequences ranging from fines to jail time to loss of custody. Donnelly identified parents punished for homeschooling their children for religious *and* secular reasons as well as parents punished for truant children who received no schooling at all.

The parents of Melissa Buzekros, for example, decided that it would be "better for her to learn at home." *Id.* at 272. Melissa's siblings continued to attend public school, but Melissa struggled due to "high noise levels and cancelled classes," prompting her parents to teach her at home. *Id.* at 587. In response, the government removed Melissa from her parents' custody—not to persecute her parents but to enforce the country's compulsory-attendance law. Other parents, too, have tried to homeschool their children for secular reasons, whether because they were "very unhappy" in public school, highly gifted or low performing, and they also were punished. *See id.* at 591–92 (affidavits of Tilman and Dagmar Neubronner) (explaining that they faced $9,500 in fines after trying to homeschool their kids who were "very unhappy" in public school); *id.* at 657–58 (affidavit of Jorg Grosselumern) (explaining that "people who would like to practice homeschooling" because of "educational needs of the child," such as being highly gifted or low performing, "do not dare to practice homeschooling actively because of the varied sanctions").

The parents of "school skippers," truant students who do not show up for school, face civil fines as well. If the parents fail to convince their children to go to school, the government places them in alternative learning programs or special schools for truants. This enforcement of the law has nothing to do with homeschooling, whether for faith-based or secular reasons. For better or worse, Germany punishes any and all parents who fail to comply with the school-attendance law, no matter the reasons they provide.

So far as the record shows, the only evidence of selective enforcement comes from a paragraph of an affidavit of a German lawyer, Gabrielle Eckermann. "In my experience," Eckermann says, the "parents of truant children are treated differently than parents who homeschool," as they often are "permitted to participate in home based distance learning or correspondence schools." *Id.* at 913. But the Romeikes' expert, Donnelly, acknowledged that the State runs the distance-learning programs for truant children, confirming that the State does not exempt them from a state-run education. And, as Donnelly also acknowledged, the State had ample reasons for distinguishing two groups of students: those not in school because their parents refuse to send them and those not in school in spite of their parents' best efforts to make them go. In the case of the latter, the parents do not violate the law; the children do.

All of this suggests that what seems to be true on the face of this neutrally worded law is true. "There is no indication," the Board permissibly found, that the German officials "are motivated by anything other than law enforcement. These factors reflect appropriate administration of the law, not persecution." *Id.* at 5.

* * *

The . . . finding by the immigration judge—that "animus" and "vitriol" underlay enactment of the law—[is unsupported]. For one, the judge never said that Germany enacted this law based on animus toward faith-based homeschoolers or homeschoolers in general. Nothing in the record, indeed, suggests that such groups existed in 1938. For another, the record does not include the language of the original law, the history that led to its adoption or any contemporary understanding of what motivated it, if indeed that could be identified with respect to a law supported by different legislators with different perspectives. For still another reason, the only "finding" the immigration judge made—that the law showed an "intolerant" effort to "stamp out" "parallel societies" that might arise if parents could teach their children at home—sets sail at such a high level of generality as to add little to the case. Any compulsory-attendance law could be said to have this effect. But that does not prove that this law, then or now, targets faith-based homeschoolers in general or the Romeikes in particular. If, as the Romeikes claim, the law emerged from the Nazi era, that would understandably make anyone, including the Romeikes, skeptical of the policy underlying it. But such a history would not by itself doom the law. The claimants still must show that enforcement of the law amounts to persecution under the immigration laws. They have not done so.

To a similar end, the Romeikes complain that Germany's compulsory-attendance law violates their fundamental rights and various international standards and thus constitutes persecution regardless of whether it is selectively enforced. Each argument shares an Achilles' heel: Asylum provides refuge to individuals persecuted *on account of* a protected ground. 8 U.S.C. § 1101(a)(42)(A). The United States has not opened its doors to every victim of unfair treatment, even treatment that our laws do not allow. *Stserba,* 646 F.3d at 972. That the United States Constitution protects the rights of "parents and guardians to direct the upbringing and education of children under their control," *Yoder,* 406 U.S. at 233, does not mean that a contrary law in another country establishes persecution on religious or any other protected ground. And even if, as the Romeikes claim, several human-rights treaties joined by Germany give parents the right to make decisions about their children's educations, *see, e.g.,* International Covenant on Civil and Political Rights art. 18(4), adopted Dec. 16, 1966, S. Exec. Doc. E, 95–2 (1978), 999 U.N.T.S. 171; Universal Declaration of Human Rights, G.A. Res. 217(III) A, U.N. Doc. A/RES/217(III), art. 26(3) (Dec. 10, 1948), that by itself does not require the granting of an American asylum application.

Nor does *Perkovic v. INS,* 33 F.3d 615 (6th Cir.1994), hold that a treaty violation on its own establishes persecution. Two Yugoslavian citizens of ethnic Albanian descent sought asylum after they were arrested and beaten for posting pro-Albanian propaganda and for participating in demonstrations in favor of Albanian civil rights. *Id.* at 616–17. Noting that the Board's conclusion that the Yugoslavians had not been persecuted "was directly contrary . . . to the manifest intent of Congress in enacting the asylum law," *id.* at 621, we held that the petitioners were refugees deserving of asylum. In doing so, we added in dicta that Yugoslavia's treatment of the petitioners violated international law, *id.* at 622, but that observation was neither a necessary nor a sufficient predicate to their status as refugees. Just as a petitioner cannot obtain asylum merely by proving an American constitutional violation, a petitioner cannot obtain asylum merely by proving a treaty violation.

As then-Judge Alito explained, "the concept of persecution does not encompass all treatment that our society regards as unfair, unjust, or even unlawful or unconstitutional. If persecution were defined that expansively, a significant percentage of the world's population would qualify for asylum in this country—and it seems most unlikely that Congress intended such a result." *Fatin v. INS,* 12 F.3d 1233, 1240 (3d Cir.1993); *see also Foroglou v. INS,* 170 F.3d 68, 72 (1st Cir.1999) ("The asylum statute does not inflict on foreign governments the obligation to construct their own draft laws to conform to this nation's own highly complex equal protection jurisprudence.").

The question is not whether Germany's policy violates the American Constitution, whether it violates the parameters of an international treaty or whether Germany's law is a good idea. It is whether the Romeikes have established the prerequisites of an asylum claim—a well-founded fear of persecution on account of a protected ground. *See* (citations.).

* * *

The Romeikes have not met this burden. The German law does not on its face single out any protected group, and the Romeikes have not provided sufficient evidence to show that the law's application turns on prohibited classifications or animus based on any prohibited ground.

For these reasons, we deny the Romeikes' petition.

---

**Questions:** Is the *Romeike* opinion applying a plain meaning or purposive interpretation of the political asylum statute? What concerns the court about a broader reading of "persecution?"

# POLITICAL OPINION

## IMMIGRATION AND NATURALIZATION SERVICE V. ELIAS-ZACARIAS

502 U.S. 478 (1992)

* * *

JUSTICE SCALIA delivered the opinion of the Court.

The principal question presented by this case is whether a guerrilla organization's attempt to coerce a person into performing military service *necessarily* constitutes "persecution on account of . . . political opinion" under § 101(a)(42) of the Immigration and Nationality Act, as added, 94 Stat. 102, 8 U.S.C. § 1101(a)(42).

Respondent Elias-Zacarias, a native of Guatemala, was apprehended in July 1987 for entering the United States without inspection. In deportation proceedings brought by petitioner Immigration and Naturalization Service (INS), Elias-Zacarias conceded his deportability but requested asylum and withholding of deportation.

The Immigration Judge summarized Elias-Zacarias' testimony as follows:

"[A]round the end of January in 1987 [when Elias-Zacarias was 18], two armed, uniformed guerrillas with handkerchiefs covering part of their faces came to his home. Only he and his parents were there. . . . [T]he guerrillas asked his parents and himself to join with them, but they all refused. The guerrillas asked them why and told them that they would be back, and that they should think it over about joining them.

"[Elias-Zacarias] did not want to join the guerrillas because the guerrillas are against the government and he was afraid that the government would retaliate against him and his family if he did join the guerrillas. [H]e left Guatemala at the end of March [1987] . . . because he was afraid that the guerrillas would return."

The Immigration Judge understood from this testimony that Elias-Zacarias' request for asylum and for withholding of deportation was "based on this one attempted recruitment by the guerrillas." She concluded that Elias-Zacarias had failed to demonstrate persecution or a well-founded fear of persecution on account of race, religion, nationality, membership in a particular social group, or political opinion, and was not eligible for asylum. See 8 U.S.C. §§ 1101(a)(42), 1158(a). She further concluded that he did not qualify for withholding of deportation.

The Board of Immigration Appeals (BIA) summarily dismissed Elias-Zacarias' appeal on procedural grounds. Elias-Zacarias then moved the BIA to reopen his deportation hearing so that he could submit new evidence that, following his departure from Guatemala, the guerrillas had twice returned to his family's home in continued efforts to recruit him. The BIA denied reopening on the ground that even with this new evidence Elias-Zacarias had failed to make a prima facie showing of eligibility for asylum and had failed to show that the results of his deportation hearing would be changed.

The Court of Appeals for the Ninth Circuit, treating the BIA's denial of the motion to reopen as an affirmance on the merits of the Immigration Judge's ruling, reversed. 921 F.2d 844 (1990). The court ruled that acts of conscription by a nongovernmental group constitute persecution on account of political opinion, and determined that Elias-Zacarias had a "well-founded fear" of such conscription. *Id.,* at 850–852. We granted certiorari.

Section 208(a) of the Immigration and Nationality Act, 8 U.S.C. § 1158(a), authorizes the Attorney General, in his discretion, to grant asylum to an alien who is a "refugee" as defined in the Act, *i.e.,* an alien who is unable or unwilling to return to his home country "because of persecution or a well-founded fear of persecution on account of race, religion, nationality, membership in a particular social group, or political opinion." § 101(a)(42)(A), 8 U.S.C. § 1101(a)(42)(A). See *INS v. Cardoza-Fonseca,* 480 U.S. 421, 423, 428, n. 5 (1987). The BIA's determination that

Elias-Zacarias was not eligible for asylum must be upheld if "supported by reasonable, substantial, and probative evidence on the record considered as a whole." 8 U.S.C. § 1105a(a)(4). It can be reversed only if the evidence presented by Elias-Zacarias was such that a reasonable factfinder would have to conclude that the requisite fear of persecution existed. *NLRB v. Columbian Enameling & Stamping Co.,* 306 U.S. 292, 300 (1939).

The Court of Appeals found reversal warranted. In its view, a guerrilla organization's attempt to conscript a person into its military forces necessarily constitutes "persecution on account of . . . political opinion," because "the person resisting forced recruitment is expressing a political opinion hostile to the persecutor and because the persecutors' motive in carrying out the kidnapping is political." 921 F.2d, at 850. The first half of this seems to us untrue, and the second half irrelevant.

Even a person who supports a guerrilla movement might resist recruitment for a variety of reasons—fear of combat, a desire to remain with one's family and friends, a desire to earn a better living in civilian life, to mention only a few. The record in the present case not only failed to show a political motive on Elias-Zacarias' part; it showed the opposite. He testified that he refused to join the guerrillas because he was afraid that the government would retaliate against him and his family if he did so. Nor is there any indication (assuming, *arguendo,* it would suffice) that the guerrillas erroneously *believed* that Elias-Zacarias' refusal was politically based.

As for the Court of Appeals' conclusion that the guerrillas' "motive in carrying out the kidnapping is political": It apparently meant by this that the guerrillas seek to fill their ranks in order to carry on their war against the government and pursue their political goals. See 921 F.2d, at 850 (citing *Arteaga v. INS,* 836 F.2d 1227, 1232, n. 8 (CA9 1988)); 921 F.2d, at 852. But that does not render the forced recruitment "persecution on account of . . . political opinion." In construing statutes, "we must, of course, start with the assumption that the legislative purpose is expressed by the ordinary meaning of the words used." [Citations]. The ordinary meaning of the phrase "persecution on account of . . . political opinion" in § 101(a)(42) is persecution on account of the *victim's* political opinion, not the persecutor's. If a Nazi regime persecutes Jews, it is not, within the ordinary meaning of language, engaging in persecution on account of political opinion; and if a fundamentalist Moslem regime persecutes democrats, it is not engaging in persecution on account of religion. Thus, the mere existence of a generalized "political" motive underlying the guerrillas' forced recruitment is inadequate to establish (and, indeed, goes far to refute) the proposition that Elias-Zacarias fears persecution *on account of* political opinion, as § 101(a)(42) requires.

Elias-Zacarias appears to argue that not taking sides with any political faction is itself the affirmative expression of a political opinion. That seems to us not ordinarily so, since we do not agree with the dissent that only a "narrow, grudging construction of the concept of 'political opinion,'" *post,* at 487, would distinguish it from such quite different concepts as indifference, indecisiveness and risk-averseness. But we need not decide whether the evidence compels the conclusion that Elias-Zacarias held a political opinion. Even if it does, Elias-Zacarias still has to establish that the record also compels the conclusion that he has a "well-founded fear" that the guerrillas will persecute him *because of* that political opinion, rather than because of his refusal to fight with them. He has not done so with the degree of clarity necessary to permit reversal of a BIA finding to the contrary; indeed, he has not done so at all.

Elias-Zacarias objects that he cannot be expected to provide direct proof of his persecutors' motives. We do not require that. But since the statute makes motive critical, he must provide *some* evidence of it, direct or circumstantial. And if he seeks to obtain judicial reversal of the BIA's determination, he must show that the evidence he presented was so compelling that no reasonable factfinder could fail to find the requisite fear of persecution. That he has not done.

The BIA's determination should therefore have been upheld in all respects, and we reverse the Court of Appeals' judgment to the contrary.

*It is so ordered.*

JUSTICE STEVENS, with whom JUSTICE BLACKMUN and JUSTICE O'CONNOR join, dissenting.

Respondent refused to join a guerrilla organization that engaged in forced recruitment in Guatemala. He fled the country because he was afraid the guerrillas would return and "take me and kill me." After his departure, armed guerrillas visited his family on two occasions searching for him. In testimony that the hearing officer credited, he stated that he is still afraid to return to Guatemala because "these people" can come back to "take me or kill me."

It is undisputed that respondent has a well-founded fear that he will be harmed, if not killed, if he returns to Guatemala. It is also undisputed that the cause of that harm, if it should occur, is the guerrilla organization's displeasure with his refusal to join them in their armed insurrection against the government. The question of law that the case presents is whether respondent's well-founded fear is a "fear of persecution on account of . . . political opinion" within the meaning of § 101(a)(42) of the Immigration and Naturalization Act.

If respondent were to prevail, as he did in the Court of Appeals, 921 F.2d 844 (CA9 1990), he would be classified as a "refugee" and therefore be eligible for a grant of asylum. He would not be automatically entitled to that relief, however, because "the Attorney General is *not required* to grant asylum to everyone who meets the definition of refugee." *INS v. Cardoza-Fonseca,* 480 U.S. 421, 428, n. 5 (1987) (emphasis in original). Instead, § 208 of the Act provides that the Attorney General may, "in [his] discretion," grant asylum to refugees.

Today the Court holds that respondent's fear of persecution is not "on account of . . . political opinion" for two reasons. First, he failed to prove that his refusal to join the guerrillas was politically motivated; indeed, he testified that he was at least in part motivated by a fear that government forces would retaliate against him or his family if he joined the guerrillas. See *ante,* at 482–483. Second, he failed to prove that his persecutors' motives were political. In particular, the Court holds that the persecutors' implicit threat to retaliate against respondent "because of his refusal to fight with them," *ante,* at 483, is not persecution on account of political opinion. I disagree with both parts of the Court's reasoning.

A political opinion can be expressed negatively as well as affirmatively. A refusal to support a cause—by staying home on election day, by refusing to take an oath of allegiance, or by refusing to step forward at an induction center—can express a political opinion as effectively as an affirmative statement or affirmative conduct. Even if the refusal is motivated by nothing more than a simple desire to continue living an ordinary life with one's family, it is the kind of political expression that the asylum provisions of the statute were intended to protect.

As the Court of Appeals explained in *Bolanos-Hernandez v. INS,* 767 F.2d 1277 (CA9 1985):

"Choosing to remain neutral is no less a political decision than is choosing to affiliate with a particular political faction. Just as a nation's decision to remain neutral is a political one, *see, e.g.,* Neutrality Act of 1939, 22 U.S.C. §§ 441–465 (1982), so is an individual's. When a person is aware of contending political forces and affirmatively chooses not to join any faction, that choice *is* a political one. A rule that one must identify with one of two dominant warring political factions in order to possess a political opinion, when many persons may, in fact, be opposed to the views and policies of both, would frustrate one of the basic objectives of the Refugee Act of 1980—to provide protection to all victims of persecution regardless of ideology. Moreover, construing 'political opinion' in so short-sighted and grudging a manner could result in limiting the benefits under the ameliorative provisions of our immigration laws to those who join one political extreme or another; moderates who choose to sit out a battle would not qualify." *Id.,* at 1286 (emphasis in original; footnote omitted).

* * *

In my opinion, the record in this case is more than adequate to support the conclusion that this respondent's refusal was a form of expressive conduct that constituted the statement of a "political opinion" within the meaning of § 208(a).

It follows as night follows day that the guerrillas' implied threat to "take" him or to "kill" him if he did not change his position constituted threatened persecution "on account of" that political opinion. As the Court of Appeals explained in *Bolanos-Hernandez, supra:*

"It does not matter to the persecutors what the individual's motivation is. The guerrillas in El Salvador do not inquire into the reasoning process of those who insist on remaining neutral and refuse to join their cause. They are concerned only with an act that constitutes an overt manifestation of a political opinion. Persecution because of that overt manifestation is persecution because of a political opinion." 767 F.2d, at 1287.

It is important to emphasize that the statute does not require that an applicant for asylum prove exactly why his persecutors would act against him; it only requires him to show that he has a "well-founded fear of persecution on account of . . . political opinion." As we recognized in *INS v. Cardoza Fonseca,* the applicant meets this burden if he shows that there is a " 'reasonable possibility' " that he will be persecuted on account of his political opinion. 480 U.S., at 440, (quoting *I.N.S. v. Stevic,* 467 U.S. 407, 425(1984)). Because respondent expressed a political opinion by refusing to join the guerrillas, and they responded by threatening to "take" or to "kill" him if he did not change his mind, his fear that the guerrillas will persecute him on account of his political opinion is well founded.

Accordingly, I would affirm the judgment of the Court of Appeals.

---

**Questions:** In Elias-Zacarias, how do the majority and dissent differ in their views of what counts as expression of a political opinion? How do these perspectives parallel those of the majority and dissent in the Commerce Clause portion of NFIB v. Se*belius*? Does teaching government-sponsored literacy classes opposed by guerrillas constitute expressing a political opinion? See *Cordon-Garcia v. I.N.S.,* 204 F.3d 985 (9th Cir. 2000).

# PERSECUTORS

## NEGUSIE V. HOLDER

555 U.S. 511 (2009)

* * *

JUSTICE KENNEDY delivered the opinion of the Court.

An alien who fears persecution in his homeland and seeks refugee status in this country is barred from obtaining that relief if he has persecuted others.

"The term 'refugee' does not include any person who ordered, incited, assisted, or otherwise participated in the persecution of any person on account of race, religion, nationality, membership in a particular social group, or political opinion." Immigration and Nationality Act (INA), § 101, 66 Stat. 166, as added by Refugee Act of 1980, § 201(a), 94 Stat. 102–103, 8 U. S. C. § 1101(a)(42).

This so-called "persecutor bar" applies to those seeking asylum, § 1158(b)(2)(A)(i), or withholding of removal, § 1231(b)(3)(B)(i). It does not disqualify an alien from receiving a temporary deferral of removal under the Convention Against Torture and Other Cruel, Inhuman or Degrading Treatment or Punishment (CAT), art. 3, Dec. 10, 1984, S. Treaty Doc. No. 100–20, p. 20, 1465 U. N. T. S. 85; 8 CFR § 1208.17(a) (2008).

In this case the Board of Immigration Appeals (BIA) determined that the persecutor bar applies even if the alien's assistance in persecution was coerced or otherwise the product of duress. In so ruling the BIA followed its earlier decisions that found *Fedorenko* v. *United States*, 449 U. S. 490 (1981), controlling. The Court of Appeals for the Fifth Circuit, in affirming the agency, relied on its precedent following the same reasoning. We hold that the BIA and the Court of Appeals misapplied *Fedorenko*. We reverse and remand for the agency to interpret the statute, free from the error, in the first instance.

Petitioner in this Court is Daniel Girmai Negusie, a dual national of Eritrea and Ethiopia, his father having been a national of the former and his mother of the latter. Born and educated in Ethiopia, he left there for Eritrea around the age of 18 to see his mother and find employment. The year was 1994. After a few months in Eritrea, state officials took custody of petitioner and others when they were attending a movie. He was forced to perform hard labor for a month and then was conscripted into the military for a time. War broke out between Ethiopia and Eritrea in 1998, and he was conscripted again.

When petitioner refused to fight against Ethiopia, his other homeland, the Eritrean Government incarcerated him. Prison guards punished petitioner by beating him with sticks and placing him in the hot sun. He was released after two years and forced to work as a prison guard, a duty he performed on a rotating basis for about four years. It is undisputed that the prisoners he guarded were being persecuted on account of a protected ground—*i.e.*, "race, religion, nationality, membership in a particular social group, or political opinion." 8 U. S. C. § 1101(a)(42). Petitioner testified that he carried a gun, guarded the gate to prevent escape, and kept prisoners from taking showers and obtaining fresh air. He also guarded prisoners to make sure they stayed in the sun, which he knew was a form of punishment. He saw at least one man die after being in the sun for more than two hours. Petitioner testified that he had not shot at or directly punished any prisoner and that he helped prisoners on various occasions. Petitioner escaped from the prison and hid in a container, which was loaded on board a ship heading to the United States. Once here he applied for asylum and withholding of removal.

In a careful opinion the Immigration Judge, W. Wayne Stogner, found that petitioner's testimony, for the most part, was credible. He concluded that petitioner assisted in persecution by working as an armed guard.

* * *

The BIA affirmed the denial of asylum and withholding. It noted petitioner's role as an armed guard in a facility where "prisoners were tortured and left to die out in the sun . . . on account of a protected ground." App. to Pet. for Cert. 6a. The BIA held that "[t]he fact that [petitioner] was compelled to participate as a prison guard, and may not have actively tortured or mistreated anyone, is immaterial." *Ibid.* That is because " 'an alien's motivation and intent are irrelevant to the issue of whether he "assisted" in persecution . . . [I]t is the objective effect of an alien's actions which is controlling.' " *Ibid.* (quoting *Matter of Fedorenko*, 19 I. & N. Dec. 57, 69 (BIA 1984)). The BIA also affirmed the grant of deferral of removal under CAT.

On petition for review the Court of Appeals agreed with the BIA that whether an alien is compelled to assist in persecution is immaterial for persecutor-bar purposes. . . . .

Consistent with the rule in *Chevron U. S. A. Inc.* v. *Natural Resources Defense Council, Inc.*, 467 U. S. 837, 842–843 (1984), the BIA is entitled to deference in interpreting ambiguous provisions of the INA. The question here is whether an alien who was compelled to assist in persecution can be eligible for asylum or withholding of removal. We conclude that the BIA misapplied our precedent in *Fedorenko* as mandating that an alien's motivation and intent are irrelevant to the issue whether an alien assisted in persecution. The agency must confront the same question free of this mistaken legal premise.

It is well settled that "principles of *Chevron* deference are applicable to this statutory scheme." *INS* v. *Aguirre-Aguirre*, 526 U. S. 415, 424 (1999). Congress has charged the Attorney General with administering the INA, and a "ruling by the Attorney General with respect to all questions of law shall be controlling." 8 U. S. C. § 1103(a)(1). Judicial deference in the immigration context is of special importance, for executive officials "exercise especially sensitive political functions that implicate questions of foreign relations." *INS* v. *Abudu*, 485 U. S. 94, 100 (1988).

* * *

The parties disagree over whether coercion or duress is relevant in determining if an alien assisted or otherwise participated in persecution. As there is substance to both contentions, we conclude that the statute has an ambiguity that the agency should address in the first instance.

Petitioner argues that the statute's plain language makes clear that involuntary acts do not implicate the persecutor bar because " 'persecution' " presumes moral blameworthiness. Brief for Petitioner 23–28. He invokes principles of criminal culpability, concepts of international law, and the rule of lenity. *Id.*, at 28–45. Those arguments may be persuasive in determining whether a particular agency interpretation is reasonable, but they do not demonstrate that the statute is unambiguous. Petitioner all but conceded as much at argument in this Court when he indicated that the BIA has discretion to construe the duress defense in either a narrow or a broad way. Tr. of Oral Arg. 20–24.

The Government, on the other hand, asserts that the statute does not allow petitioner's construction. "The statutory text," the Government says, "directly answers that question: there is no exception" for conduct that is coerced because Congress did not include one. Brief for Respondent 11. We disagree. The silence is not conclusive. The question is whether the statutory text mandates that coerced actions must be deemed assistance in persecution. On that point the statute, in its precise terms, is not explicit. Nor is this a case where it is clear that Congress had an intention on the precise question at issue. Cf. *Cardoza-Fonseca*, *supra*, at 448–449.

* * *

The *Fedorenko* Court held that "an individual's service as a concentration camp armed guard—whether voluntary or involuntary—made him ineligible for a visa" under § 2(a) of the IRO Constitution. 449 U. S., at 512. That Congress did not adopt a voluntariness requirement for § 2(a), the Court noted, "is plain from comparing § 2(a) with § 2(b), which excludes only those individuals who '*voluntarily* assisted the enemy forces.' " *Ibid.* The Court relied on the principle of statutory construction that "the deliberate omission of the word 'voluntary' from § 2(a) compels the conclusion that the statute made *all* those who assisted in persecution of civilians ineligible for visas." *Ibid.*

*Fedorenko* does not compel the same conclusion in the case now before us. The textual structure of the statute in *Fedorenko* ("voluntary" is in one subsection but not the other) is not part of the statutory framework considered here. Congress did not use the word "voluntary" in any subsection of the persecutor bar, so its omission cannot carry the same significance.

The difference between the statutory scheme in *Fedorenko* and the one here is confirmed when we " 'look not only to the particular statutory language, but to the design of the statute as a whole and to its object and policy.' " Both statutes were enacted to reflect principles set forth in international agreements, but the principles differ in significant respects.

As discussed, Congress enacted the DPA in 1948 as part of an international effort to address individuals who were forced to leave their homelands during and after the second World War. *Fedorenko, supra,* at 495. The DPA excludes those who "voluntarily assisted the enemy forces since the outbreak of the second world war," 62 Stat. 3052, as well as all who "assisted the enemy in persecuting civil populations of countries," *id.*, at 3051. The latter exclusion clause makes no reference to culpability. The exclusion of even those involved in nonculpable, involuntary assistance in Nazi persecution, as an expert testified in *Fedorenko*, may be " '[b]ecause the crime against humanity that is involved in the concentration camp puts it into a different category.' " 449 U. S., at 511, n. 32.

The persecutor bar in this case, by contrast, was enacted as part of the Refugee Act of 1980. Unlike the DPA, which was enacted to address not just the post war refugee problem but also the Holocaust and its horror, the Refugee Act was designed to provide a general rule for the ongoing treatment of all refugees and displaced persons. As this Court has twice recognized, " 'one of Congress' primary purposes' in passing the Refugee Act was to implement the principles agreed to in the 1967 United Nations Protocol Relating to the Status of Refugees, Jan. 31, 1967, 19 U. S. T. 6224, T. I. A. S. 6577 (1968)," as well as the "United Nations Convention Relating to the Status of Refugees, 189 U. N. T. S. 150 (July 28, 1951), reprinted in 19 U. S. T. 6259." *Aguirre-Aguirre*, 526 U. S., at 427 (quoting *Cardoza-Fonseca*, 480 U. S., at 436–437).

These authorities illustrate why *Fedorenko*, which addressed a different statute enacted for a different purpose, does not control the BIA's interpretation of this persecutor bar. Whatever weight or relevance these various authorities may have in interpreting the statute should be considered by the agency in the first instance, and by any subsequent reviewing court, after our remand.

* * *

In denying relief in this case the BIA recited a rule that has developed in its own case law in reliance on *Fedorenko:* "[A]n alien's motivation and intent are irrelevant to the issue of whether he 'assisted' in persecution . . . [I]t is the objective effect of an alien's actions which is controlling." App. to Pet. for Cert. 6a. The rule is based on three earlier decisions: *Matter of Laipenieks*, 18 I. & N. Dec. 433 (1983); *Matter of Fedorenko*, 19 I. & N. Dec. 57; and *Matter of Rodriguez-Majano*, 19 I. & N. Dec. 811 (1988).

* * *

Our reading of these decisions confirms that the BIA has not exercised its interpretive authority but, instead, has determined that *Fedorenko* controls. This mistaken assumption stems from a failure to recognize the inapplicability of the principle of statutory construction invoked in *Fedorenko*, as well as a failure to appreciate the differences in statutory purpose. The BIA is not bound to apply the *Fedorenko* rule that motive and intent are irrelevant to the persecutor bar at issue in this case. Whether the statute permits such an interpretation based on a different course of reasoning must be determined in the first instance by the agency.

Having concluded that the BIA has not yet exercised its *Chevron* discretion to interpret the statute in question, " ' "the proper course, except in rare circumstances, is to remand to the agency for additional investigation or explanation." ' "

We reverse the judgment of the Court of Appeals and remand the case for further proceedings consistent with this opinion.

It is so ordered.

---

**Question:** The Supreme Court in *Negusie* states that the BIA is entitled to deference as an administrative agency. If so, why does the Court reverse the BIA's and Court of Appeals's holdings and remand the case?

# CHAPTER 23

# CORPORATE CRIME AND PRIVILEGE

■ ■ ■

## CONTEXT & SOURCES

Issues of criminal law and procedure are not only regulated by the Fourth Amendment and state constitutional law, as we have seen in Chapters 14, 15, and 16, but come within the scope of legislation and evidence rules as well. Federal statutes cover a range of criminal behaviors by corporations and their officers, and under the Federal Rules of Evidence the attorney-client privilege is applied in the corporate context. Here we see decisions on criminal liability, dissolved corporations, perjury, and privilege.

For examples of the variety of white-collar crimes and an analysis of regulatory effectiveness, see Rena Steinzor, *Why Not Jail? Industrial Catastrophes, Corporate Malfeasance, and Government Inaction* (Cambridge University Press, 2015). Alan M. Wilner, "Continuing Corporate Liability for Federal Crime After State Dissolution of Corporation—Melrose Distillers, Inc. v. United States," 20 *Maryland Law Review* 69 (1960) concisely discusses the Supreme Court's broad approach to defining corporate crime. The theoretical and practical problems of determining perjury without convincing proof of a corporate speaker's intent are presented in Luis Lopez, "Did Samuel Bronston Commit Perjury?—A Study in Discourse Semantics," 10 *International Journal of Language and Law* 1 (2021). Paul F. Rothstein, "The Story of Upjohn Co. v. United States: One Man's Journey to Extend Lawyer-Client Confidentiality, and the Social Forces that Affected it," *Evidence Stories* 151 (Richard Lempert ed., Foundation Press, 2006) elaborates the background, legal issues, and legacy of a key corporate privilege decision.

# CORPORATE CRIME

## UNITED STATES V. DOTTERWEICH

320 U.S. 277 (1943)

* * *

MR. JUSTICE FRANKFURTER delivered the opinion of the Court.

This was a prosecution begun by two informations, consolidated for trial, charging Buffalo Pharmacal Company, Inc., and Dotterweich, its president and general manager, with violations of the Act of Congress of June 25, 1938, c. 675, 52 Stat. 1040, 21 U.S.C. §§ 301–392, 21 U.S.C.A. §§ 301–392, known as the Federal Food, Drug, and Cosmetic Act. The Company, a jobber in drugs, purchased them from their manufacturers and shipped them, repacked under its own label, in interstate commerce. (No question is raised in this case regarding the implications that may properly arise when, although the manufacturer gives the jobber a guaranty, the latter through his own label makes representations.) The informations were based on § 301 of that Act, 21 U.S.C. § 331, 21 U.S.C.A. § 331, paragraph (a) of which prohibits 'The introduction or delivery for introduction into interstate commerce of any ... drug ... that is adulterated or misbranded'. 'Any person' violating this provision is, by paragraph (a) of § 303, 21 U.S.C. § 333, 21 U.S.C.A. § 333, made 'guilty of a misdemeanor'. Three counts went to the jury—two, for shipping misbranded drugs in interstate commerce, and a third, for so shipping an adulterated drug. The jury disagreed as to the corporation and found Dotterweich guilty on all three counts. We start with the finding of the Circuit Court of Appeals that the evidence was adequate to support the verdict of adulteration and misbranding. 131 F.2d 500, 502.

* * *

The Circuit Court of Appeals, one judge dissenting, reversed the conviction on the ground that only the corporation was the 'person' subject to prosecution unless, perchance, Buffalo Pharmacal was a counterfeit corporation serving as a screen for Dotterweich. On that issue, after rehearing, it remanded the cause for a new trial. We then brought the case here, on the Government's petition for certiorari, 318 U.S. 753, because this construction raised questions of importance in the enforcement of the Federal Food, Drug, and Cosmetic Act.

The court below drew its conclusion not from the provisions defining the offenses on which this prosecution was based (§§ 301(a) and 303(a), but from the terms of § 303(c). That section affords immunity from prosecution if certain conditions are satisfied. The condition relevant to this case is a guaranty from the seller of the innocence of his product. So far as here relevant, the provision for an immunizing guaranty is as follows:

'No person shall be subject to the penalties of subsection (a) of this section (2) for having violated section 301(a) or (d), if he establishes a guaranty or undertaking signed by, and containing the name and address of, the person residing in the United States from whom he received in good faith the article, to the effect, in case of an alleged violation of section 301(a), that such article is not adulterated or misbranded, within the meaning of this Act, designating this Act.'

This Circuit Court of Appeals found it 'difficult to believe that Congress expected anyone except the principal to get such a guaranty, or to make the guilt of an agent depend upon whether his employer had gotten one.' 131 F.2d 500, 503. And so it cut down the scope of the penalizing provisions of the Act to the restrictive view, as a matter of language and policy, it took of the relieving effect of a guaranty.

The guaranty clause cannot be read in isolation. The Food and Drugs Act of 1906 was an exertion by Congress of its power to keep impure and adulterated food and drugs out of the channels of commerce. By the Act of 1938, Congress extended the range of its control over illicit and noxious articles and stiffened the penalties for disobedience. The purposes of this legislation thus touch phases of the lives and health of people which, in the circumstances of modern industrialism, are largely beyond self-protection. Regard for these purposes should infuse construction of the legislation if it is to be treated as a working instrument of government and not merely as a collection of English words. See [citations]. The prosecution to which Dotterweich was subjected is based on a now familiar type of legislation whereby penalties serve as effective means of regulation. Such legislation dispenses with the conventional requirement for criminal conduct—awareness of some wrongdoing. In the interest of the larger good it puts the burden of acting at hazard upon a person otherwise innocent but standing in responsible relation to a public danger. United States v. Balint, 258 U.S. 250. And so it is clear that shipments like those now in issue are 'punished by the statute if the article is misbranded (or adulterated), and that the article may be misbranded (or adulterated) without any conscious fraud at all. It was natural enough to throw this risk on shippers with regard to the identity of their wares.' United States v. Johnson, 221 U.S. 488, 497.

The statute (§ 303) makes 'any person' who violates § 301(a) guilty of a 'misdemeanor'. It specifically defines 'person' to include 'corporation'. § 201(e). But the only way in which a corporation can act is through the individuals who act on its behalf. New York Central & H.R.R.R Co. v. United States, 212 U.S. 481. And the historic conception of a 'misdemeanor' makes all those responsible for it equally guilty, United States v. Mills, 7

Pet. 138, 141, a doctrine given general application in § 332 of the Penal Code, 18 U.S.C. § 550, 18 U.S.C.A. § 550. If, then, Dotterweich is not subject to the Act, it must be solely on the ground that individuals are immune when the 'person' who violates § 301(a) is a corporation, although from the point of view of action the individuals are the corporation. As a matter of legal development, it has taken time to establish criminal liability also for a corporation and not merely for its agents. See New York Central & H.R.R. Co. v. United States, supra. The history of federal food and drug legislation is a good illustration of the elaborate phrasing that was in earlier days deemed necessary to fasten criminal liability on corporations. Section 12 of the Food and Drugs Act of 1906, 21 U.S.C.A. § 4, provided that, 'the act, omission, or failure of any officer, agent, or other person acting for or employed by any corporation, company, society, or association, within the scope of his employment or office, shall in every case be also deemed to be the act, omission, or failure of such corporation, company, society, or association as well as that of the person.' By 1938, legal understanding and practice had rendered such statement of the obvious superfluous. Deletion of words—in the interest of brevity and good draftsmanship1 superfluous for holding a corporation criminally liable can hardly be found ground for relieving from such liability the individual agents of the corporation. To hold that the Act of 1938 freed all individuals, except when proprietors, from the culpability under which the earlier legislation had placed them is to defeat the very object of the new Act. Nothing is clearer than that the later legislation was designed to enlarge and stiffen the penal net and not to narrow and loosen it. This purpose was unequivocally avowed by the two committees which reported the bills to the Congress. The House Committee reported that the Act 'seeks to set up effective provisions against abuses of consumer welfare growing out of inadequacies in the Food and Drugs Act of June 30, 1906'. (H. Rep. No. 2139, 75th Cong., 3d Sess., p. 1.) And the Senate Committee explicitly pointed out that the new legislation 'must not weaken the existing laws', but on the contrary 'it must strengthen and extend that law's protection of the consumer.' (S. Rep. No. 152, 75th Cong., 1st Sess., p. 1.) If the 1938 Act were construed as it was below, the penalties of the law could be imposed only in the rare case where the corporation is merely an individual's alter ego. Corporations carrying on an illicit trade would be subject only to what the House Committee described as a 'license fee for the conduct of an illegitimate business.' A corporate officer, who even with 'intent to defraud or mislead' (§ 303(b), introduced adulterated or misbranded drugs into interstate commerce could not be held culpable for conduct which was indubitably outlawed by the 1906 Act. See, e.g., United States v. Mayfield, D.C., 177 F. 765. This argument proves too much. It is not credible that Congress should by implication have exonerated what is probably a preponderant number of persons involved in acts of disobedience—for the number of non-corporate proprietors is relatively small. Congress, of course, could reverse the process and hold only the corporation and allow its agents to escape. In very exceptional circumstances it may have required this result. See Sherman v. United States, 282 U.S. 25. But the history of the present Act, its purposes, its terms, and extended practical construction lead away from such a result once 'we free our minds from the notion that criminal statutes must be construed by some artificial and conventional rule'. United States v. Union Supply Co., 215 U.S. 50, 55.

The Act is concerned not with the proprietory relation to a misbranded or an adulterated drug but with its distribution. In the case of a corporation such distribution must be accomplished, and may be furthered, by persons standing in various relations to the incorporeal proprietor. If a guaranty immunizes shipments of course it immunizes all involved in the shipment. But simply because if there had been a guaranty it would have been received by the proprietor, whether corporate or individual, as a safeguard for the enterprise, the want of a guaranty does not cut down the scope of responsibility of all who are concerned with transactions forbidden by § 301. To be sure, that casts the risk that there is no guaranty upon all who according to settled doctrines of criminal law are responsible for the commission of a misdemeanor. To read the guaranty section, as did the court below, so as to restrict liability for penalties to the only person who normally would receive a guaranty—the proprietor disregards the admonition that 'the meaning of a sentence is to be felt rather than to be proved'. United States v. Johnson, 221 U.S. 488, 496. It also reads an exception to an important provision safeguarding the public welfare with a liberality which more appropriately belongs to enforcement of the central purpose of the Act.

The Circuit Court of Appeals was evidently tempted to make such a devitalizing use of the guaranty provision through fear that an enforcement of § 301(a) as written might operate too harshly by sweeping within its condemnation any person however remotely entangled in the proscribed shipment. But that is not the way to read legislation. Literalism and evisceration are equally to be avoided. To speak with technical accuracy, under § 301 a corporation may commit an offense and all persons who aid and abet its commission are equally guilty. Whether an accused shares responsibility in the business process resulting in unlawful distribution depends on the evidence produced at the trial and its submission—assuming the evidence warrants it—to the jury under appropriate guidance. The offense is committed, unless the enterprise which they are serving enjoys the immunity of a guaranty, by all who do have such a responsible share in the furtherance of the transaction which the statute outlaws, namely, to put into the stream of interstate commerce adulterated or misbranded drugs. Hardship there doubtless may be under a statute which thus penalizes the transaction though consciousness of wrongdoing be totally wanting. Balancing relative hardships, Congress has preferred to place it upon those who have at least the opportunity of informing themselves of the existence of conditions imposed for the protection of consumers before sharing in illicit commerce, rather than to throw the hazard on the innocent public who are wholly helpless.

It would be too treacherous to define or even to indicate by way of illustration the class of employees which stands in such a responsible relation. To attempt a formula embracing the variety of conduct whereby persons may responsibly contribute in furthering a transaction forbidden by an Act of Congress, to wit, to send illicit goods across state lines, would be mischievous futility. In such matters the good sense of prosecutors, the wise guidance of trial judges, and the ultimate judgment of juries must be trusted. Our system of criminal justice necessarily depends on 'conscience and circumspection in prosecuting officers,' Nash v. United States, 229 U.S. 373, 378, even when the consequences are far more drastic than they are under the provision of law before us. See United States v. Balint, supra (involving a maximum sentence of five years). For present purpose it suffices to say that in what the defense characterized as 'a very fair charge' the District Court properly left the question of the responsibility of Dotterweich for the shipment to the jury, and there was sufficient evidence to support its verdict.

Judgment reversed.

MR. JUSTICE MURPHY, dissenting.

Our prime concern in this case is whether the criminal sanctions of the Federal Food, Drug, and Cosmetic Act of 1938 plainly and unmistakably apply to the respondent in his capacity as a corporate officer. He is charged with violating § 301(a) of the Act, which prohibits the introduction or delivery for introduction into interstate commerce of any adulterated or misbranded drug. There is no evidence in this case of any personal guilt on the part of the respondent. There is no proof or claim that he ever knew of the introduction into commerce of the adulterated drugs in question, much less that he actively participated in their introduction. Guilt is imputed to the respondent solely on the basis of his authority and responsibility as president and general manager of the corporation.

It is a fundamental principle of Anglo-Saxon jurisprudence that guilt is personal and that it ought not lightly to be imputed to a citizen who, like the respondent, has no evil intention or consciousness of wrongdoing. It may be proper to charge him with responsibility to the corporation and the stockholders for negligence and mismanagement. But in the absence of clear statutory authorization it is inconsistent with established canons of criminal law to rest liability on an act in which the accused did not participate and of which he had no personal knowledge. Before we place the stigma of a criminal conviction upon any such citizen the legislative mandate must be clear and unambiguous. Accordingly that which Chief

Justice Marshall has called 'the tenderness of the law for the rights of individuals' entitles each person, regardless of economic or social status, to an unequivocal warning from the legislature as to whether he is within the class of persons subject to vicarious liability. Congress cannot be deemed to have intended to punish anyone who is not 'plainly and unmistakably' within the confines of the statute. [Citations].

Moreover, the fact that individual liability of corporate officers may be consistent with the policy and purpose of a public health and welfare measure does not authorize this Court to impose such liability where Congress has not clearly intended or actually done so. Congress alone has the power to define a crime and to specify the offenders. United States v. Wiltberger, 5 Wheat. 76, 95. It is not our function to supply any deficiencies in these respects, no matter how grave the consequences. Statutory policy and purpose are not constitutional substitutes for the requirement that the legislature specify with reasonable certainty those individuals it desires to place under the interdict of the Act. [Citations].

Looking at the language actually used in this statute, we find a complete absence of any reference to corporate officers. There is merely a provision in § 303(a) to the effect that 'any person' inadvertently violating § 301(a) shall be guilty of a misdemeanor. Section 201(e) further defines 'person' as including an 'individual, partnership, corporation, and association.' The fact that a corporate officer is both a 'person' and an 'individual' is not indicative of an intent to place vicarious liability on the officer. Such words must be read in light of their statutory environment. Only if Congress has otherwise specified an intent to place corporate officers within the ambit of the Act can they be said to be embraced within the meaning of the words 'person' or 'individual' as here used.

Nor does the clear imposition of liability on corporations reveal the necessary intent to place criminal sanctions on their officers. A corporation is not the necessary and inevitable equivalent of its officers for all purposes. In many respects it is desirable to distinguish the latter from the corporate entity and to impose liability only on the corporation. In this respect it is significant that this Court has never held the imposition of liability on a corporation sufficient, without more, to extend liability to its officers who have no consciousness of wrongdoing. * * *

The dangers inherent in any attempt to create liability without express Congressional intention or authorization are illustrated by this case. Without any legislative guides, we are confronted with the problem of determining precisely which officers, employees and agents of a corporation are to be subject to this Act by our fiat. To erect standards of responsibility is a difficult legislative task and the opinion of this Court admits that it is 'too treacherous' and a 'mischievous futility' for us to engage in such pursuits. But the only alternative is a blind resort to 'the good sense of prosecutors, the wise guidance of trial judges, and the ultimate judgment of juries.' Yet that situation is precisely what our constitutional system sought to avoid. Reliance on the legislature to define crimes and criminals distinguishes our form of jurisprudence from certain less desirable ones. The legislative power to restrain the liberty and to imperil the good reputation of citizens must not rest upon the variable attitudes and opinions of those charged with the duties of interpreting and enforcing the mandates of the law. I therefore cannot approve the decision of the Court in this case.

---

**Questions:** In *Dotterweich,* the majority focuses both on the text and likely purpose of the statute, while the dissent refers only to the text, saying that the legislature must "specify with reasonable certainty" those targeted by the law. Is it likely that the legislature meant to exclude corporate officers from liability? Is the dissent imposing a new requirement going beyond the plain meaning rule?

## MELROSE DISTILLERS, INC. V. UNITED STATES

359 U.S. 271 (1959)

* * *

MR. JUSTICE DOUGLAS delivered the opinion of the Court.

Petitioners are corporations—two organized under Maryland law and one under Delaware law—and wholly owned subsidiaries of Schenley Industries, Inc. They were indicted with others for restraining trade, conspiring to monopolize and attempting to monopolize commerce in violation of §§ 1 and 2 of the Sherman Act, 26 Stat. 209, 15 U.S.C. §§ 1 2. Shortly after the indictment was returned, petitioners were dissolved under their respective state statutes and became separate divisions of a new corporation under the same ultimate ownership. They then moved to dismiss the indictment on the ground that their dissolution abated the proceeding. The District Court denied the motions, holding that under the applicable Maryland and Delaware statutes the existence of the dissolved corporations continued so far as prosecution of this criminal proceeding was concerned. United States v. Maryland Shate Licensed Beverage Ass'n, D.C., 138 F.Supp. 685. Petitioners then pleaded nolo contendere and the District Court levied fines against them. The Court of Appeals affirmed, 258 F.2d 726. The case is here on a petition for a writ of certiorari which we granted because of a conflict among the Circuits. 358 U.S. 878.

We start from the premise that in the federal domain prosecutions abate both on the death of an individual defendant (List v. State of Pennsylvania, 131 U.S. 396; Schreiber v. Sharpless, 110 U.S. 76) and on the dissolution of a corporate defendant (Defense Supplies Corp. v. Lawrence Warehouse Co., 336 U.S. 631, 634), unless the action is saved by statute. We need not decide whether federal law alone would be sufficient to save a federal cause of action against a corporation dissolved under state law. We have here a situation where the interplay of federal and state law makes it clear that petitioners did not escape criminal responsibility under the Sherman Act by the kind of dissolution decreed under Maryland and Delaware law.

The Sherman Law in § 8 defines 'person' to include corporations 'existing' under the laws of any State. The question whether a corporation 'exists' for any purpose is thus determined by reference to state law. We conclude that under both Maryland and Delaware law the lives of these corporations were not cut short, as is sometimes done on dissolution, cf. Chicago Title & Trust Co. v. Forty-One Thirty-Six Wilcox Bldg.Corp., 302 U.S. 120, but were sufficiently continued so that this proceeding did not abate.

In Maryland, during the period relevant here, though the dissolution of the corporation was effective when the articles of dissolution had been accepted, the corporation continued 'in existence for the purpose of paying, satisfying ad discharging any existing debts and obligations . . . .' (Flack's Md.Ann.Code 1951, Art. 23, § 72(b). It was also provided in § 78(a) that 'such dissolution' shall not 'abate any pending suit or proceeding by or against the corporation . . .' We have found no Maryland decisions interpreting these sections; but we are satisfied that the term 'proceeding,' no matter how the state court may construe it, implies enough vitality to make the corporation an 'existing' enterprise for the purposes of § 8 of the Sherman Act.

The Delaware statute seems equally clear, though again there is no authoritative interpretation of it. It provides that any 'proceeding' begun by or against a corporation before or within three years after dissolution shall continue 'until any judgments, orders, or decrees therein shall be fully executed.' Del.Code Ann.1953, Tit. 8, § 278; Addy v. Short, 89 A.2d 136, 139. The term 'proceeding' is elsewhere used in the Delaware Code as including criminal prosecutions; and that seems to us to be consistent with its normal construction. We conclude that irrespective of how the Delaware statute may be construed by the Delaware courts, it sufficiently continued the existence of this corporation for the purpose of § 8 of the Sherman Act.

Policy reasons look to the same result. Petitioners were wholly owned subsidiaries of Schenley Industries, Inc. After dissolution they simply became divisions of a new corporation under the same ultimate ownership. In this situation there is no more reason for allowing them to escape criminal penalties than damages in civil suits. As the Court of Appeals noted, a corporation cannot be sent to jail. The discharge of its liabilities whether criminal or civil can be effected only by the payment of money.

Affirmed.

---

**Question:** After *Melrose Distillers,* could a bank escape criminal liability for failing to file the required currency transaction reports by arguing that, by the time the reports were due, it had merged with another bank? See *United States v. Alamo Bank of Texas,* 880 F.2d 828 (5th Cir. 1989).

## BRONSTON V. UNITED STATES

409 U.S. 352 (1973)

* * *

MR. CHIEF JUSTICE BURGER delivered the opinion of the Court.

We granted the writ in this case to consider a narrow but important question in the application of the federal perjury statute, 18 U.S.C. § 1621[1], whether a witness may be convicted of perjury for an answer, under oath, that is literally true but not responsive to the question asked and arguably misleading by negative implication.

Petitioner is the sole owner of Samuel Bronston Productions, Inc., a company that between 1958 and 1964, produced motion pictures in various European locations. For these enterprises, Bronston Productions, opened bank accounts in a number of foreign countries; in 1962, for example, it had 37 accounts in five countries. As president of Bronston Productions, petitioner supervised transactions involving the foreign bank accounts.

In June 1964, Bronston Productions, petitioned for an arrangement with creditors under Chapter XI of the Bankruptcy Act, 11 U.S.C. § 701 et seq. On June 10, 1966, a referee in bankruptcy held a § 21(a) hearing to determine, for the benefit of creditors, the extent and location of the company's assets. Petitioner's perjury conviction was founded on the answers given by him as a witness at that bankruptcy hearing, and in

---

1 118 U.S.C. § 1621 provides:

'Whoever, having taken an oath before a competent tribunal, officer, or person, in any case in which a law of the United States authorizes an oath to be administered, that he will testify, declare, depose, or certify truly, or that any written testimony, declaration, deposition, or certificate by him subscribed, is true, willfully and contrary to such oath states or subscribes any material matter which he does not believe to be true, is guilty of perjury, and shall, except as otherwise expressly provided by law, be fined not more than $2,000 or imprisoned not more than five years, or both. This section is applicable whether the statement or subscription is made within or without the United States.'

particular on the following colloquy with a lawyer for a creditor of Bronston Productions:

> 'Q. Do you have any bank accounts in Swiss banks, Mr. Bronston?
>
> 'A. No, sir.
>
> 'Q. Have you ever?
>
> 'A. The company had an account there for about six months, in Zurich.
>
> 'Q. Have you any nominees who have bank accounts in Swiss banks?
>
> 'A. No, sir.
>
> 'Q. Have you ever?
>
> 'A. No, sir.'

It is undisputed that for a period of nearly five years, between October 1959 and June 1964, petitioner had a personal bank account at the International Credit Bank in Geneva, Switzerland, into which he made deposits and upon which he drew checks totaling more than $180,000. It is likewise undisputed that petitioner's answers were literally truthful. (a) Petitioner did not at the time of questioning have a Swiss bank account. (b) Bronston Productions, Inc., did have the account in Zurich described by petitioner. (c) Neither at the time of questioning nor before did petitioner have nominees who had Swiss accounts. The Government's prosecution for perjury went forward on the theory that in order to mislead his questioner, petitioner answered the second question with literal truthfulness but unresponsively addressed his answer to the company's assets and not to his own—thereby implying that he had no personal Swiss bank account at the relevant time.

At petitioner's trial, the District Court instructed the jury that the 'basic issue' was whether petitioner 'spoke his true belief.' Perjury, the court stated, 'necessarily involves the state of mind of the accused' and 'essentially consists of willfully testifying to the truth of a fact which the defendant does not believe to be true'; petitioner's testimony could not be found 'willfully' false unless at the time his testimony was given petitioner 'fully understood the questions put to him but nevertheless gave false answers knowing the same to be false.' The court further instructed the jury that if petitioner did not understand the question put to him and for that reason gave an unresponsive answer, he could not be convicted of perjury. Petitioner could, however, be convicted if he gave an answer 'not literally false but when considered in the context in which it was given, nevertheless constitute(d) a false statement.'

The jury began its deliberations at 11:30 a.m. Several times it requested exhibits or additional instructions from the court, and at one point, at the request of the jury, the District Court repeated its instructions in full. At 6:10 p.m., the jury returned its verdict, finding petitioner guilty on the count of perjury before us today and not guilty on another charge not here relevant.

In the Court of Appeals, petitioner contended, as he had in post-trial motions before the District Court, that the key question was imprecise and suggestive of various interpretations. In addition, petitioner contended that he could not be convicted of perjury on the basis of testimony that was concededly truthful, however unresponsive. A divided Court of Appeals held that the question was readily susceptible of a responsive reply and that it adequately tested the defendant's belief in the veracity of his answer. The Court of Appeals further held that, '(f)or the purposes of 18 U.S.C. § 1621, an answer containing half of the truth which also constitutes a lie by negative implication, when the answer is intentionally given in place of the responsive answer called for by a proper question, is perjury.' 453 F.2d 555, 559. In this Court, petitioner renews his attack on the specificity of the question asked him and the legal sufficiency of his answer to support a conviction for perjury. The problem of the ambiguity of the question is not free from doubt, but we need not reach that issue. Even assuming, as we do, that the question asked petitioner specifically focused on petitioner's personal bank accounts, we conclude that the federal perjury statute cannot be construed to sustain a conviction based on petitioner's answer.

The statute, 18 U.S.C. § 1621, substantially identical in its relevant language to its predecessors for nearly a century, is 'a federal statute enacted in an effort to keep the course of justice free from the pollution of perjury.' United States v. Williams, 341 U.S. 58, 68 (1951). We have held that the general federal perjury provision is applicable to federal bankruptcy proceedings. Hammer v. United States, 271 U.S. 620, 46 (1926). The need for truthful testimony in a § 21(a) bankruptcy proceeding is great, since the proceeding is 'a searching inquiry into the condition of the estate of the bankrupt, to assist in discovering and collecting the assets, and to develop facts and circumstances which bear upon the question of discharge.' Travis v. United States, 123 F.2d 268, 271 (CA10 1941). Here, as elsewhere, the perpetration of perjury 'well may affect the dearest concerns of the parties before a tribunal. . . .' United States v. Norris, 300 U.S. 564, (1937).

There is, at the outset, a serious literal problem in applying § 1621 to petitioner's answer. The words of the statute confine the offense to the witness who 'willfully . . . states . . . any material matter which he does not believe to be true.' Beyond question, petitioner's answer to the crucial question was not responsive if we assume, as we do, that the first question was directed at personal bank accounts. There is, indeed, an implication in the answer to the second question that there was never a personal bank account; in casual conversation this interpretation might reasonably be drawn. But we are not dealing with casual conversation and the statute does not make it a criminal act for a witness to willfully state any material matter that implies any material matter that he does not believe to be true.

The Government urges that the perjury statute be construed broadly to reach petitioner's answer and thereby fulfill its historic purpose of reinforcing our adversary factfinding process. We might go beyond the precise words of the statute if we thought they did not adequately express the intention of Congress, but we perceive no reason why Congress would intend the drastic sanction of a perjury prosecution to cure a testimonial mishap that could readily have been reached with a single additional question by counsel alert—as every examiner ought to be—to the incongruity of petitioner's unresponsive answer. Under the pressures and tensions of interrogation, it is not uncommon for the most earnest witnesses to give answers that are not entirely responsive. Sometimes the witness does not understand the question, or may in an excess of caution or apprehension read too much or too little into it. It should come as no surprise that a participant in a bankruptcy proceeding may have something to conceal and consciously tries to do so, or that a debtor may be embarrassed at his plight and yield information reluctantly. It is the responsibility of the lawyer to probe; testimonial interrogation, and cross-examination in particular, is a probing, prying, pressing form of inquiry. If a witness evades, it is the lawyer's responsibility to recognize the evasion and to bring the witness back to the mark, to flush out the whole truth with the tools of adversary examination.

It is no answer to say that here the jury found that petitioner intended to mislead his examiner. A jury should not be permitted to engage in conjecture whether an unresponsive answer, true and complete on its face, was intended to mislead or divert the examiner; the state of mind of the witness is relevant only to the extent that it bears on whether 'he does not believe (his answer) to be true.' To hold otherwise would be to inject a new and confusing element into the adversary testimonial system we know. Witnesses would be unsure of the extent of their responsibility for the misunderstandings and inadequacies of examiners, and might well fear having that responsibility tested by a jury under the vague rubric of 'intent to mislead' or 'perjury by implication.' The seminal modern treatment of the history of the offense concludes that one consideration of policy overshadowed all others during the years when perjury first emerged as a common-law offense: 'that the measures taken against the offense must not be so severe as to discourage witnesses from appearing or testifying.' Study of Perjury, reprinted in Report of New York Law Revision Commission, Legis.Doc.No.60, p. 249 (1935). A leading 19th century commentator, quoted by Dean Wigmore, noted that the English law 'throws every fence round a person accused of perjury,' for

'the obligation of protecting witnesses from oppression, or annoyance, by charges, or threats of charges, of having borne false testimony, is far paramount to that of giving even perjury its deserts. To repress that crime, prevention is better than cure: and the law of England relies, for this purpose, on the means provided for detecting and exposing the crime at the moment of commission,—such as publicity, cross-examination, the aid of a jury, etc.; and on the infliction of a severe, though not excessive punishment, wherever the commission of the crime has been clearly proved.' W. Best, Principles of the Law of Evidence § 606 (C. Chamberlayne ed. 1883).

See J. Wigmore, Evidence 275–276 (3d ed. 1940). Addressing the same problem, Montesquieu took as his starting point the French tradition of capital punishment for perjury and the relatively mild English punishment of the pillory. He thought the disparity between the punishments could be explained because the French did not permit the accused to present his own witnesses, while in England 'they admit of witnesses on both sides, and the affair is discussed in some measure between them; consequently false witness is there less dangerous, the accused having a remedy against the false witnesses, which he has not in France.' Montesquieu, The Spirit of the Laws, quoted in Study of Perjury, supra, p. 253.

Thus, we must read § 1621 in light of our own and the traditional Anglo-American judgment that a prosecution for perjury is not the sole, or even the primary, safeguard against errant testimony. While 'the lower federal courts have not dealt with the question often,' and while their expressions do not deal with unresponsive testimony and are not precisely in point, 'it may be said that they preponderate against the respondent's contention.' United States v. Norris, 300 U.S., at 576. The cases support petitioner's position that the perjury statute is not to be loosely construed, nor the statute invoked simply because a wily witness succeeds in derailing the questioner—so long as the witness speaks the literal truth. The burden is on the questioner to pin the witness down to the specific object to the questioner's inquiry. [Citations].

The Government does not contend that any misleading or incomplete response must be sent to the jury to determine whether a witness committed perjury because he intended to sidetrack his questioner. As the Government recognizes, the effect of so unlimited an interpretation of § 1621 would be broadly unsettling. It is said, rather, that petitioner's testimony falls within a more limited category of intentionally misleading responses with an especially strong tendency to mislead the questioner. In the federal cases cited above, the Government tells us the defendants gave simple negative answers 'that were both entirely responsive and entirely truthful . . . . In neither case did the defendant—as did petitioner here—make affirmative statements of one fact that in context constituted denials by negative implication of a related fact.' Thus the Government isolates two factors which are said to require application of the perjury statute in the circumstances of this case; the unresponsiveness of petitioner's answer and the affirmative cast of that answer, with its accompanying negative implication.

This analysis succeeds in confining the Government's position, but it does not persuade us that Congress intended to extend the coverage of § 1621 to answers unresponsive on their face but untrue only by 'negative implication.' Though perhaps a plausible argument can be made that unresponsive answers are especially likely to mislead, any such argument must, we think, be predicated upon the questioner's being aware of the unresponsiveness of the relevant answer. Yet, if the questioner is aware of the unresponsiveness of the answer, with equal force it can be argued that the very unresponsiveness of the answer should alert counsel to press on for the information he desires. It does not matter that the unresponsive answer is stated in the affirmative, thereby implying the negative of the question actually posed; for again, by hypothesis, the examiner's awareness of unresponsiveness should lead him to press another question or reframe his initial question with greater precision. Precise questioning is imperative as a predicate for the offense of perjury.

It may well be that petitioner's answers were not guileless but were shrewdly calculated to evade. Nevertheless, we are constrained to agree with Judge Lumbard, who dissented from the judgment of the Court of Appeals, that any special problems arising from the literally true but unresponsive answer are to be remedied through the 'questioner's acuity' and not by a federal perjury prosecution.

Reversed.

---

**Question:** When President Clinton testified before a grand jury concerning his relationship with Monica Lewinsky, he said that his lawyer's statement that "there is no sex of any kind" was, in Clinton's words "completely true" depending on "what the meaning of the word 'is' is." In light of the *Bronston* decision, was this perjury?

# CORPORATE PRIVILEGE

## UPJOHN CO. V. UNITED STATES

449 U.S. 383 (1981)

* * *

JUSTICE REHNQUIST delivered the opinion of the Court.

We granted certiorari in this case to address important questions concerning the scope of the attorney-client privilege in the corporate context and the applicability of the work-product doctrine in proceedings to enforce tax summonses. 445 U.S. 925. With respect to the privilege question the parties and various *amici* have described our task as one of choosing between two "tests" which have gained adherents in the courts of appeals. We are acutely aware, however, that we sit to decide concrete cases and not abstract propositions of law. We decline to lay down a broad rule or series of rules to govern all conceivable future questions in this area, even were we able to do so. We can and do, however, conclude that the attorney-client privilege protects the communications involved in this case from compelled disclosure and that the work-product doctrine does apply in tax summons enforcement proceedings.

Petitioner Upjohn Co. manufactures and sells pharmaceuticals here and abroad. In January 1976 independent accountants conducting an audit of one of Upjohn's foreign subsidiaries discovered that the subsidiary made payments to or for the benefit of foreign government officials in order to secure government business. The accountants, so informed petitioner, Mr. Gerard Thomas, Upjohn's Vice President, Secretary, and General Counsel. Thomas is a member of the Michigan and New York Bars, and has been Upjohn's General Counsel for 20 years. He consulted with outside counsel and R. T. Parfet, Jr., Upjohn's Chairman of the Board. It was decided that the company would conduct an internal investigation of what were termed "questionable payments." As part of this investigation the attorneys prepared a letter containing a questionnaire which was sent to "All Foreign General and Area Managers" over the Chairman's signature. The letter began by noting recent disclosures that several American companies made "possibly illegal" payments to foreign government officials and emphasized that the management needed full information concerning any such payments made by Upjohn. The letter indicated that the Chairman had asked Thomas, identified as "the company's General Counsel," "to conduct an investigation for the purpose of determining the nature and magnitude of any payments made by the Upjohn Company or any of its subsidiaries to any employee or official of a foreign government." The questionnaire sought detailed information concerning such payments. Managers were instructed to treat the investigation as "highly confidential" and not to discuss it with anyone other than Upjohn employees who might be helpful in providing the requested information. Responses were to be sent directly to Thomas. Thomas and outside counsel also interviewed the recipients of the questionnaire and some 33 other Upjohn officers or employees as part of the investigation.

On March 26, 1976, the company voluntarily submitted a preliminary report to the Securities and Exchange Commission on Form 8–K disclosing certain questionable payments. A copy of the report was simultaneously submitted to the Internal Revenue Service, which immediately began an investigation to determine the tax consequences of the payments. Special agents conducting the investigation were given lists by Upjohn of all those interviewed and all who had responded to the questionnaire. On November 23, 1976, the Service issued a summons pursuant to 26 U.S.C. § 7602 demanding production of:

"All files relative to the investigation conducted under the supervision of Gerard Thomas to identify payments to employees of foreign governments and any political contributions made by the Upjohn Company or any of its affiliates since January 1, 1971 and to determine whether any funds of the Upjohn Company had been improperly accounted for on the corporate books during the same period.

"The records should include but not be limited to written questionnaires sent to managers of the Upjohn Company's foreign affiliates, and memorandums or notes of the interviews conducted in the United States and abroad with officers and employees of the Upjohn Company and its subsidiaries." App. 17a–18a.

The company declined to produce the documents specified in the second paragraph on the grounds that they were protected from disclosure by the attorney-client privilege and constituted the work product of attorneys prepared in anticipation of litigation. On August 31, 1977, the United States filed a petition seeking enforcement of the summons under 26 U.S.C. §§ 7402(b) and 7604(a) in the United States District Court for the Western District of Michigan. That court adopted the recommendation of a Magistrate who concluded that the summons should be enforced. Petitioners appealed to the Court of Appeals for the Sixth Circuit which rejected the Magistrate's finding of a waiver of the attorney-client privilege, 600 F.2d 1223, 1227, n. 12, but agreed that the privilege did not apply "[t]o the extent that the communications were made by officers and agents not responsible for directing Upjohn's actions in response to legal advice . . . for the simple reason that the communications were not the 'client's.' " *Id.*, at 1225. The court reasoned that accepting petitioners' claim for a broader application of the privilege would encourage upper-echelon management to ignore unpleasant facts and create too broad a "zone of silence." Noting that Upjohn's counsel had interviewed officials such as the

Chairman and President, the Court of Appeals remanded to the District Court so that a determination of who was within the "control group" could be made. In a concluding footnote the court stated that the work-product doctrine "is not applicable to administrative summonses issued under 26 U.S.C. § 7602." *Id.*, at 1228, n. 13.

Federal Rule of Evidence 501 provides that "the privilege of a witness . . . shall be governed by the principles of the common law as they may be interpreted by the courts of the United States in light of reason and experience." The attorney-client privilege is the oldest of the privileges for confidential communications known to the common law. 8 J. Wigmore, Evidence § 2290 (McNaughton rev. 1961). Its purpose is to encourage full and frank communication between attorneys and their clients and thereby promote broader public interests in the observance of law and administration of justice. The privilege recognizes that sound legal advice or advocacy serves public ends and that such advice or advocacy depends upon the lawyer's being fully informed by the client. As we stated last Term in *Trammel v. United States*, 445 U.S. 40, (1980): "The lawyer-client privilege rests on the need for the advocate and counselor to know all that relates to the client's reasons for seeking representation if the professional mission is to be carried out." And in *Fisher v. United States*, 425 U.S. 391, 403 (1976), we recognized the purpose of the privilege to be "to encourage clients to make full disclosure to their attorneys." This rationale for the privilege has long been recognized by the Court, see *Hunt v. Blackburn*, 128 U.S. 464, 470 (1888) (privilege "is founded upon the necessity, in the interest and administration of justice, of the aid of persons having knowledge of the law and skilled in its practice, which assistance can only be safely and readily availed of when free from the consequences or the apprehension of disclosure"). Admittedly complications in the application of the privilege arise when the client is a corporation, which in theory is an artificial creature of the law, and not an individual; but this Court has assumed that the privilege applies when the client is a corporation. *United States v. Louisville & Nashville R. Co.*, 236 U.S. 318, 336 (1915), and the Government does not contest the general proposition.

The Court of Appeals, however, considered the application of the privilege in the corporate context to present a "different problem," since the client was an inanimate entity and "only the senior management, guiding and integrating the several operations, . . . can be said to possess an identity analogous to the corporation as a whole." 600 F.2d at 1226. The first case to articulate the so-called "control group test" adopted by the court below, *Philadelphia v. Westinghouse Electric Corp.*, 210 F.Supp. 483, 485 (ED Pa.), petition for mandamus and prohibition denied *sub nom. General Electric Co. v. Kirkpatrick*, 312 F.2d 742 (CA3 1962), cert. denied, 372 U.S. 943 (1963), reflected a similar conceptual approach:

"Keeping in mind that the question is, Is it the corporation which is seeking the lawyer's advice when the asserted privileged communication is made?, the most satisfactory solution, I think, is that if the employee making the communication, of whatever rank he may be, is in a position to control or even to take a substantial part in a decision about any action which the corporation may take upon the advice of the attorney, . . . then, in effect, *he is (or personifies) the corporation* when he makes his disclosure to the lawyer and the privilege would apply." (Emphasis supplied.)

Such a view, we think, overlooks the fact that the privilege exists to protect not only the giving of professional advice to those who can act on it but also the giving of information to the lawyer to enable him to give sound and informed advice. See *Trammel*, *supra*, at 51; *Fisher*, *supra*, at 403. The first step in the resolution of any legal problem is ascertaining the factual background and sifting through the facts with an eye to the legally relevant. See ABA Code of Professional Responsibility, Ethical Consideration 4–1:

"A lawyer should be fully informed of all the facts of the matter he is handling in order for his client to obtain the full advantage of our legal system. It is for the lawyer in the exercise of his independent professional judgment to separate the relevant and important from the irrelevant and unimportant. The observance of the ethical obligation of a lawyer to hold inviolate the confidences and secrets of his client not only facilitates the full development of facts essential to proper representation of the client but also encourages laymen to seek early legal assistance."

* * *

In the case of the individual client the provider of information and the person who acts on the lawyer's advice are one and the same. In the corporate context, however, it will frequently be employees beyond the control group as defined by the court below—"officers and agents . . . responsible for directing [the company's] actions in response to legal advice"—who will possess the information needed by the corporation's lawyers. Middle-level—and indeed lower-level—employees can, by actions within the scope of their employment, embroil the corporation in serious legal difficulties, and it is only natural that these employees would have the relevant information needed by corporate counsel if he is adequately to advise the client with respect to such actual or potential difficulties. This fact was noted in *Diversified Industries, Inc. v. Meredith*, 572 F.2d 596 (CA8 1978) (en banc):

"In a corporation, it may be necessary to glean information relevant to a legal problem from middle management or non-management personnel as well as from top executives. The attorney dealing with a complex legal problem 'is thus faced with a "Hobson's choice". If he interviews employees not having "the very highest authority", their communications to him will not be privileged. If, on the other hand, he interviews *only* those employees with the "very highest authority", he may find it extremely difficult, if not impossible, to determine what happened.' " *Id.*, at 608–609 (quoting Weinschel Corporate Employee Interviews and the Attorney-Client Privilege, 12 B.C.Ind. & Com. L.Rev. 873, 876 (1971)).

The control group test adopted by the court below thus frustrates the very purpose of the privilege by discouraging the communication of relevant information by employees of the client to attorneys seeking to render legal advice to the client corporation. The attorney's advice will also frequently be more significant to noncontrol group members than to those who officially sanction the advice, and the control group test makes it more difficult to convey full and frank legal advice to the employees who will put into effect the client corporation's policy. See, *e. g., Duplan Corp. v. Deering Milliken, Inc.*, 397 F.Supp. 1146, 1164 (DSC 1974) ("After the lawyer forms his or her opinion, it is of no immediate benefit to the Chairman of the Board or the President. It must be given to the corporate personnel who will apply it").

The narrow scope given the attorney-client privilege by the court below not only makes it difficult for corporate attorneys to formulate sound advice when their client is faced with a specific legal problem but also threatens to limit the valuable efforts of corporate counsel to ensure their client's compliance with the law. In light of the vast and complicated array of regulatory legislation confronting the modern corporation, corporations, unlike most individuals, "constantly go to lawyers to find out how to obey the law," Burnham, The Attorney-Client Privilege in the Corporate Arena, 24 Bus.Law. 901, 913 (1969), particularly since compliance with the law in this area is hardly an instinctive matter, see, *e. g., United States v. United States Gypsum Co.*, 438 U.S. 422, 440–441 (1978) ("the behavior proscribed by the [Sherman] Act is often difficult to distinguish from the gray zone of socially acceptable and economically justifiable business conduct"). The test adopted by the court below is difficult to apply in practice, though no abstractly formulated and unvarying "test" will necessarily enable courts to decide questions such as this with mathematical precision. But if the purpose of the attorney-client privilege is to be served, the attorney and client must be able to predict with some degree of certainty whether particular discussions will be protected. An uncertain privilege, or one which purports to be certain but results in widely varying applications by the courts, is little better than no privilege at all. The very terms of the test adopted by the court below suggest the unpredictability of its application. The test restricts the availability of the privilege to those officers who play a "substantial role" in deciding and directing a corporation's legal response. Disparate decisions in cases applying this test illustrate its unpredictability. Compare, *e. g., Hogan v. Zletz*, 43 F.R.D. 308, 315–316 (ND Okl.1967), aff'd in part *sub nom. Natta v. Hogan*, 392 F.2d 686 (CA10

1968) (control group includes managers and assistant managers of patent division and research and development department), with *Congoleum Industries, Inc. v. GAF Corp.*, 49 F.R.D. 82, 83–85 (ED Pa.1969), aff'd, 478 F.2d 1398 (CA3 1973) (control group includes only division and corporate vice presidents, and not two directors of research and vice president for production and research).

The communications at issue were made by Upjohn employees to counsel for Upjohn acting as such, at the direction of corporate superiors in order to secure legal advice from counsel. As the Magistrate found, "Mr. Thomas consulted with the Chairman of the Board and outside counsel and thereafter conducted a factual investigation to determine the nature and extent of the questionable payments *and to be in a position to give legal advice to the company with respect to the payments.*" (Emphasis supplied.) 78–1 USTC ¶ 9277, pp. 83,598, 83,599. Information, not available from upper-echelon management, was needed to supply a basis for legal advice concerning compliance with securities and tax laws, foreign laws, currency regulations, duties to shareholders, and potential litigation in each of these areas. The communications concerned matters within the scope of the employees' corporate duties, and the employees themselves were sufficiently aware that they were being questioned in order that the corporation could obtain legal advice. The questionnaire identified Thomas as "the company's General Counsel" and referred in its opening sentence to the possible illegality of payments such as the ones on which information was sought. App. 40a. A statement of policy accompanying the questionnaire clearly indicated the legal implications of the investigation. The policy statement was issued "in order that there be no uncertainty in the future as to the policy with respect to the practices which are the subject of this investigation." It began "Upjohn will comply with all laws and regulations," and stated that commissions or payments "will not be used as a subterfuge for bribes or illegal payments" and that all payments must be "proper and legal." Any future agreements with foreign distributors or agents were to be approved "by a company attorney" and any questions concerning the policy were to be referred "to the company's General Counsel." *Id.*, at 165a–166a. This statement was issued to Upjohn employees worldwide, so that even those interviewees not receiving a questionnaire were aware of the legal implications of the interviews. Pursuant to explicit instructions from the Chairman of the Board, the communications were considered "highly confidential" when made, *id.*, at 39a, 43a, and have been kept confidential by the company. Consistent with the underlying purposes of the attorney-client privilege, these communications must be protected against compelled disclosure.

The Court of Appeals declined to extend the attorney-client privilege beyond the limits of the control group test for fear that doing so would entail severe burdens on discovery and create a broad "zone of silence" over corporate affairs. Application of the attorney-client privilege to communications such as those involved here, however, puts the adversary in no worse position than if the communications had never taken place. The privilege only protects disclosure of communications; it does not protect disclosure of the underlying facts by those who communicated with the attorney:

"[T]he protection of the privilege extends only to *communications* and not to facts. A fact is one thing and a communication concerning that fact is an entirely different thing. The client cannot be compelled to answer the question, 'What did you say or write to the attorney?' but may not refuse to disclose any relevant fact within his knowledge merely because he incorporated a statement of such fact into his communication to his attorney." *Philadelphia v. Westinghouse Electric Corp.*, 205 F.Supp. 830, 831 (q2.7).

See also *Diversified Industries*, 572 F.2d., at 611; *State ex rel. Dudek v. Circuit Court*, 150 N.W.2d 387, 399 (Wis. 1967) ("the courts have noted that a party cannot conceal a fact merely by revealing it to his lawyer"). Here the Government was free to question the employees who communicated with Thomas and outside counsel. Upjohn has provided the IRS with a list of such employees, and the IRS has already interviewed some 25 of them. While it would probably be more convenient for the Government to secure the results of petitioner's internal investigation by simply subpoenaing the questionnaires and notes taken by petitioner's attorneys, such considerations of convenience do not overcome the policies served by the attorney-client privilege. As Justice Jackson noted in his concurring opinion in *Hickman v. Taylor*, 329 U.S., at 516: "Discovery was hardly intended to enable a learned profession to perform its functions . . . on wits borrowed from the adversary."

Needless to say, we decide only the case before us, and do not undertake to draft a set of rules which should govern challenges to investigatory subpoenas. Any such approach would violate the spirit of Federal Rule of Evidence 501. See S.Rep. No. 93–1277, p. 13 (1974) ("the recognition of a privilege based on a confidential relationship . . . should be determined on a case-by-case basis"); *Trammel*, 445 U.S., at 47; *United States v. Gillock*, 445 U.S. 360, 367 (1980). While such a "case-by-case" basis may to some slight extent undermine desirable certainty in the boundaries of the attorney-client privilege, it obeys the spirit of the Rules. At the same time we conclude that the narrow "control group test" sanctioned by the Court of Appeals, in this case cannot, consistent with "the principles of the common law as . . . interpreted . . . in the light of reason and experience," Fed. Rule Evid. 501, govern the development of the law in this area. * * *

[The Court then held that the work product doctrine, which accords special protection from disclosure to an attorney's mental processes on behalf of a client, applied to I.R.S. summonses].

Accordingly, the judgment of the Court of Appeals is reversed, and the case remanded for further proceedings.

*It is so ordered.*

---

**Question:** In Upjohn, the Supreme Court contrasts the "control group" test for the scope of attorney-client privilege with its own broader focus on whether the communications at issue were made as part of a corporate purpose to seek legal advice. Which is more practical in terms of how business is actually conducted?

# CHAPTER 24

# EMPLOYMENT LAW—TITLE VII DISCRIMINATION

■ ■ ■

## CONTEXT & SOURCES

Employment law is a growing area where businesses, public sector entities, and nonprofits often have priorities that conflict with those of the people working in these contexts. As such its statutory analysis parallels in some points what we have seen in other topics. This chapter explores the judicial interpretation of Title VII of the Civil Rights Act of 1964, 42 U.S.C. § 2000e, et seq., which prohibits discrimination based on race, color, religion, sex, and national origin. Cases are presented on disparate treatment, hostile work environment, disparate impact, and the employer's bona fide occupational qualification defense.

George Rutherglen, *Major Issues in the Federal Law of Employment Discrimination* (5th ed., Federal Judicial Center, 2012) comprehensively surveys Title VII's prohibitions, defenses, procedures, and remedies, as well as related legislation covering age and disability. A critique of the *McDonnell Douglas* approach to adjudicating disparate treatment claims is provided by Taylor Gamm, "The Straw That Breaks the Camel's Back: A Final Argument for the Demise of the *McDonnell Douglas* Framework," 86 *University of Cincinnati Law Review* 287 (2018). For a helpful dissection of a key decision, see Augustus B. Cochran, III, *Sexual Harassment and the Law: The Mechelle Vinson Case* (University Press of Kansas, 2004). David J. Garrow, "Toward a Definitive History of Griggs v. Duke Power Company," 67 *Vanderbilt Law Review* 197 (2014) reviews a recent book on the decision and discusses its background and legacy.

# DISPARATE TREATMENT

## MCDONNELL DOUGLAS V. GREEN

411 U.S. 792 (1973)

* * *

MR. JUSTICE POWELL delivered the opinion of the Court.

The case before us raises significant questions as to the proper order and nature of proof in actions under Title VII of the Civil Rights Act of 1964, 78 Stat. 253, 42 U.S.C. § 2000e et seq.

Petitioner, McDonnell Douglas Corp., is an aerospace and aircraft manufacturer headquartered in St. Louis, Missouri, where it employs over 30,000 people. Respondent, a black citizen of St. Louis, worked for petitioner as a mechanic and laboratory technician from 1956 until August 28, 1964 when he was laid off in the course of a general reduction in petitioner's work force.

Respondent, a long-time activist in the civil rights movement, protested vigorously that his discharge and the general hiring practices of petitioner were racially motivated. As part of this protest, respondent and other members of the Congress on Racial Equality illegally stalled their cars on the main roads leading to petitioner's plant for the purpose of blocking access to it at the time of the morning shift change. The District Judge described the plan for, and respondent's participation in, the 'stall-in' as follows:

'(F)ive teams, each consisting of four cars would 'tie up' five main access roads into McDonnell at the time of the morning rush hour. The drivers of the cars were instructed to line up next to each other completely blocking the intersections or roads. The drivers were also instructed to stop their cars, turn off the engines, pull the emergency brake, raise all windows, lock the doors, and remain in their cars until the police arrived. The plan was to have the cars remain in position for one hour.

'Acting under the 'stall in' plan, plaintiff (respondent in the present action) drove his car onto Brown Road, a McDonnell access road, at approximately 7:00 a.m., at the start of the morning rush hour. Plaintiff was aware of the traffic problems that would result. He stopped his car with the intent to block traffic. The police arrived shortly and requested plaintiff to move his car. He refused to move his car voluntarily. Plaintiff's car was towed away by the police, and he was arrested for obstructing traffic. Plaintiff pleaded guilty to the charge of obstructing traffic and was fined.' 318 F.Supp. 846.

On July 2, 1965, a 'lock-in' took place wherein a chain and padlock were placed on the front door of a building to prevent the occupants, certain of petitioner's employees, from leaving. Though respondent apparently knew beforehand of the 'lock-in,' the full extent of his involvement remains uncertain.

Some three weeks following the 'lock-in,' on July 25, 1965, petitioner publicly advertised for qualified mechanics, respondent's trade, and respondent promptly applied for re-employment. Petitioner turned down respondent, basing its rejection on respondent's participation in the 'stall-in' and 'lock-in.' Shortly thereafter, respondent filed a formal complaint with the Equal Employment Opportunity Commission, claiming that petitioner had refused to rehire him because of his race and persistent involvement in the civil rights movement, in violation of §§ 703(a)(1) and 704(a) of the Civil Rights Act of 1964, 42 U.S.C. §§ 2000e–2(a)(1) and 2000e–3(a). The former section generally prohibits racial discrimination in any employment decision while the latter forbids discrimination against applicants or employees for attempting to protest or correct allegedly discriminatory conditions of employment.

* * *

The District Court also found that petitioner's refusal to rehire respondent was based solely on his participation in the illegal demonstrations and not on his legitimate civil rights activities. The court concluded that nothing in Title VII or § 704 protected 'such activity as employed by the plaintiff in the 'stall in' and 'lock in' demonstrations.' 318 F.Supp., at 850.

On appeal, the Eighth Circuit affirmed that unlawful protests were not protected activities under § 704(a), but reversed the dismissal of respondent's § 703(a)(1) claim relating to racially discriminatory hiring practices . . . .

* * *

The critical issue before us concerns the order and allocation of proof in a private, non-class action challenging employment discrimination. The language of Title VII makes plain the purpose of Congress to assure equality of employment opportunities and to eliminate those discriminatory practices and devices which have fostered racially stratified job environments to the disadvantage of minority citizens. [Citations].

* * *

What is required by Congress is the removal of artificial, arbitrary, and unnecessary barriers to employment when the barriers operate invidiously to discriminate on the basis of racial or other impermissible classification.

There are societal as well as personal interests on both sides of this equation. The broad, overriding interest, shared by employer, employee, and consumer, is efficient and trustworthy workmanship assured through fair and racially neutral employment and personnel decisions. In the implementation of such decisions, it is abundantly clear that Title VII tolerates no racial discrimination, subtle or otherwise.

In this case respondent, the complainant below, charges that he was denied employment 'because of his involvement in civil rights activities' and 'because of his race and color.' Petitioner denied discrimination of any kind, asserting that its failure to re-employ respondent was based upon and justified by his participation in the unlawful conduct against it. Thus, the issue at the trial on remand is framed by those opposing factual contentions.

* * *

The complainant in a Title VII trial must carry the initial burden under the statute of establishing a prima facie case of racial discrimination. This may be done by showing (i) that he belongs to a racial minority; (ii) that he applied and was qualified for a job for which the employer was seeking applicants; (iii) that, despite his qualifications, he was rejected; and (iv) that, after his rejection, the position remained open and the employer continued to seek applicants from persons of complainant's qualifications. In the instant case, we agree with the Court of Appeals that respondent proved a prima facie case. 463 F.2d 337, 353. Petitioner sought mechanics, respondent's trade, and continued to do so after respondent's rejection. Petitioner, moreover, does not dispute respondent's qualifications and acknowledges that his past work performance in petitioner's employ was 'satisfactory.'

The burden then must shift to the employer to articulate some legitimate, nondiscriminatory reason for the employee's rejection. We need not attempt in the instant case to detail every matter which fairly could be recognized as a reasonable basis for a refusal to hire. Here petitioner has assigned respondent's participation in unlawful conduct against it as the cause for his rejection. We think that this suffices to discharge petitioner's burden of proof at this stage and to meet respondent's prima facie case of discrimination.

The Court of Appeals intimated, however, that petitioner's stated reason for refusing to rehire respondent was a 'subjective' rather than objective criterion which 'carr[ies] little weight in rebutting charges of discrimination,' 463 F.2d, at 343. This was among the statements which caused the dissenting judge to read the opinion as taking 'the position that such unlawful acts as Green committed against McDonnell would not legally entitle McDonnell to refuse to hire him, even though no racial motivation was involved . . . .' Id., at 355. Regardless of whether this was the intended import of the opinion, we think the court below seriously underestimated the rebuttal weight to which petitioner's reasons were entitled. Respondent admittedly had taken part in a carefully planned 'stall-in,' designed to tie up access to and egress from petitioner's plant at a peak traffic hour. Nothing in Title VII compels an employer to absolve and rehire one who has engaged in such deliberate, unlawful activity against it.

* * *

Petitioner's reason for rejection thus suffices to meet the prima facie case, but the inquiry must not end here. While Title VII does not, without more, compel rehiring of respondent, neither does it permit petitioner to use respondent's conduct as a pretext for the sort of discrimination prohibited by § 703(a)(1). On remand, respondent must, as the Court of Appeals recognized, be afforded a fair opportunity to show that petitioner's stated reason for respondent's rejection was in fact pretext. Especially relevant to such a showing would be evidence that white employees involved in acts against petitioner of comparable seriousness to the 'stall-in' were nevertheless retained or rehired. Petitioner may justifiably refuse to rehire one who was engaged in unlawful, disruptive acts against it, but only if this criterion is applied alike to members of all races.

Other evidence that may be relevant to any showing of pretext includes facts as to the petitioner's treatment of respondent during his prior term of employment; petitioner's reaction, if any, to respondent's legitimate civil rights activities; and petitioner's general policy and practice with respect to minority employment. On the latter point, statistics as to petitioner's employment policy and practice may be helpful to a determination of whether petitioner's refusal to rehire respondent in this case conformed to a general pattern of discrimination against blacks. [Citations].

* * *

[Respondent] had engaged in a seriously disruptive act against the very one from whom he now seeks employment. And petitioner does not seek his exclusion on the basis of a testing device which overstates what is necessary for competent performance, or through some sweeping disqualification of all those with any past record of unlawful behavior, however remote, insubstantial, or unrelated to applicant's personal qualifications as an employee. Petitioner assertedly rejected respondent for unlawful conduct against it and, in the absence of proof of pretext or discriminatory application of such a reason, this cannot be thought the kind of 'artificial, arbitrary, and unnecessary barriers to employment' which the Court found to be the intention of Congress to remove.

In sum, respondent should have been allowed to pursue his claim under § 703(a) (1). If the evidence on retrial is substantially in accord with that before us in this case, we think that respondent carried his burden of establishing a prima facie case of racial discrimination and that petitioner successfully rebutted that case. But this does not end the matter. On retrial, respondent must be afforded a fair opportunity to demonstrate that petitioner's assigned reason for refusing to re-employ was a pretext or discriminatory in its application. If the District Judge so finds, he must order a prompt and appropriate remedy. In the absence of such a finding, petitioner's refusal to rehire must stand.

The cause is hereby remanded to the District Court for reconsideration in accordance with this opinion.

---

**Question:** A female senior manager at an accounting firm is turned down for partnership because she lacks "interpersonal skills," while males similarly described are promoted. Partners also criticize her for "using foul language" and failing to walk, talk, and dress "more femininely." Do these facts constitute a pretext for unlawful discrimination under *McDonnell Douglas*? See *Price Waterhouse v. Hopkins,* 490 U.S. 228 (1989).

---

**Note:** The Supreme Court held in *Bostock v. Clayton County,* 590 U.S. 644 (2020) that an employer who fires an individual based on sexual preference or for being transgender violates Title VII.

## HOSTILE WORK ENVIRONMENT

### MERITOR SAVINGS BANK V. VINSON

477 U.S. 57 (1986)

* * *

JUSTICE REHNQUIST delivered the opinion of the Court.

This case presents important questions concerning claims of workplace "sexual harassment" brought under Title VII of the Civil Rights Act of 1964, 78 Stat. 253, as amended, 42 U.S.C. § 2000e *et seq.*

In 1974, respondent Mechelle Vinson met Sidney Taylor, a vice president of what is now petitioner Meritor Savings Bank (bank) and manager of one of its branch offices. When respondent asked whether she might obtain employment at the bank, Taylor gave her an application, which she completed and returned the next day; later that same day Taylor called her to say that she had been hired. With Taylor as her supervisor, respondent started as a teller-trainee, and thereafter was promoted to teller, head teller, and assistant branch manager. She worked at the same branch for four years, and it is undisputed that her advancement there was based on merit alone. In September 1978, respondent notified Taylor that she was taking sick leave for an indefinite period. On November 1, 1978, the bank discharged her for excessive use of that leave.

Respondent brought this action against Taylor and the bank, claiming that during her four years at the bank she had "constantly been subjected to sexual harassment" by Taylor in violation of Title VII. She sought injunctive relief, compensatory and punitive damages against Taylor and the bank, and attorney's fees.

At the 11-day bench trial, the parties presented conflicting testimony about Taylor's behavior during respondent's employment. Respondent testified that during her probationary period as a teller-trainee, Taylor treated her in a fatherly way and made no sexual advances. Shortly thereafter, however, he invited her out to dinner and, during the course of the meal, suggested that they go to a motel to have sexual relations. At first she refused, but out of what she described as fear of losing her job she eventually agreed. According to respondent, Taylor thereafter made repeated demands upon her for sexual favors, usually at the branch, both during and after business hours; she estimated that over the next several years she had intercourse with him some 40 or 50 times. In addition, respondent testified that Taylor fondled her in front of other employees, followed her into the women's restroom when she went there alone, exposed himself to her, and even forcibly raped her on several occasions. These activities ceased after 1977, respondent stated, when she started going with a steady boyfriend.

* * *

Taylor denied respondent's allegations of sexual activity, testifying that he never fondled her, never made suggestive remarks to her, never engaged in sexual intercourse with her, and never asked her to do so. He contended instead that respondent made her accusations in response to a business-related dispute. The bank also denied respondent's allegations and asserted that any sexual harassment by Taylor was unknown to the bank and engaged in without its consent or approval.

The District Court denied relief, but did not resolve the conflicting testimony about the existence of a sexual relationship between respondent and Taylor. It found instead that

"[i]f [respondent] and Taylor did engage in an intimate or sexual relationship during the time of [respondent's] employment with [the bank], that relationship was a voluntary one having nothing to do with her continued employment at [the bank] or her advancement or promotions at that institution." 23 FEP Cases, 37, 42 (DC 1980).

The court ultimately found that respondent "was not the victim of sexual harassment and was not the victim of sexual discrimination" while employed at the bank. *Ibid*, at 43.

Although it concluded that respondent had not proved a violation of Title VII, the District Court nevertheless went on to address the bank's liability. After noting the bank's express policy against discrimination, and finding that neither respondent nor any other employee had ever lodged a complaint about sexual harassment by Taylor, the court ultimately concluded that "the bank was without notice and cannot be held liable for the alleged actions of Taylor." *Ibid*, at 42.

* * *

The Court of Appeals for the District of Columbia Circuit reversed. 753 F.2d 141 (1985). . . . [T]he court stated that a violation of Title VII may be predicated on either of two types of sexual harassment: harassment that involves the conditioning of concrete employment benefits on sexual favors, and harassment that, while not affecting economic benefits, creates a hostile or offensive working environment. The court drew additional support for this position from the Equal Employment Opportunity Commission's Guidelines on Discrimination Because of Sex, 29 CFR § 1604.11(a) (1985), which set out these two types of sexual harassment claims. Believing that "Vinson's grievance was clearly of the [hostile environment] type," 753 F.2d, at 145, and that the District Court had not considered whether a violation of this type had occurred, the court concluded that a remand was necessary.

The court further concluded that the District Court's finding that any sexual relationship between respondent and Taylor "was a voluntary one" did not obviate the need for a remand. "[U]ncertain as to precisely what the [district] court meant" by this finding, the Court of Appeals held that if the evidence otherwise showed that "Taylor made Vinson's toleration of sexual harassment a condition of her employment," her voluntariness "had no materiality whatsoever." 753 F.2d, at 146. The court then surmised that the District Court's finding of voluntariness might have been based on "the voluminous testimony regarding respondent's dress and personal fantasies," testimony that the Court of Appeals believed "had no place in this litigation." 753 F.2d, at 146, n. 36.

As to the bank's liability, the Court of Appeals held that an employer is absolutely liable for sexual harassment practiced by supervisory personnel, whether or not the employer knew or should have known about the misconduct.

* * *

In accordance with the foregoing, the Court of Appeals reversed the judgment of the District Court and remanded the case for further proceedings. . . . We granted certiorari, and now affirm but for different reasons.

Title VII of the Civil Rights Act of 1964 makes it "an unlawful employment practice for an employer . . . to discriminate against any individual with respect to his compensation, terms, conditions, or privileges of employment, because of such individual's race, color, religion, sex, or national origin." 42 U.S.C. § 2000e–2(a)(1). The prohibition against discrimination based on sex was added to Title VII at the last minute on the floor of the House of Representatives. 110 Cong.Rec. 2577–2584 (1964). . . . . and we are left with little legislative history to guide us in interpreting the Act's prohibition against discrimination based on "sex."

Respondent argues, and the Court of Appeals held, that unwelcome sexual advances that create an offensive or hostile working environment violate Title VII. Without question, when a supervisor sexually harasses a subordinate because of the subordinate's sex, that supervisor "discriminate[s]" on the basis of sex. Petitioner apparently does not challenge this proposition. It contends instead that in prohibiting discrimination with respect to "compensation, terms, conditions, or privileges" of employment, Congress was concerned with what petitioner describes as "tangible loss" of "an economic character," not "purely psychological aspects of the workplace environment." Brief for Petitioner 30–31, 34. In support of this claim petitioner observes that in both the legislative history of Title VII and this Court's Title VII decisions, the focus has been on tangible, economic barriers erected by discrimination.

We reject petitioner's view. First, the language of Title VII is not limited to "economic" or "tangible" discrimination. The phrase "terms, conditions, or privileges of employment" evinces a congressional intent " 'to strike at the entire spectrum of disparate treatment of men and women' " in employment. [Citations]. Petitioner has pointed to nothing in the Act to suggest that Congress contemplated the limitation urged here.

Second, in 1980 the EEOC issued Guidelines specifying that "sexual harassment," as there defined, is a form of sex discrimination prohibited by Title VII. As an "administrative interpretation of the Act by the enforcing agency," [Citations]. The EEOC Guidelines fully support the view that harassment leading to noneconomic injury can violate Title VII.

In defining "sexual harassment," the Guidelines first describe the kinds of workplace conduct that may be actionable under Title VII. These include "[u]nwelcome sexual advances, requests for sexual favors, and other verbal or physical conduct of a sexual nature." 29 CFR § 1604.11(a) (1985). Relevant to the charges at issue in this case, the Guidelines provide that such sexual misconduct constitutes prohibited "sexual harassment," whether or not it is directly linked to the grant or denial of an economic *quid pro quo,* where "such conduct has the purpose or effect of unreasonably interfering with an individual's work performance or creating an intimidating, hostile, or offensive working environment." § 1604.11(a)(3).

In concluding that so-called "hostile environment" (*i.e.*, non *quid pro quo*) harassment violates Title VII, the EEOC drew upon a substantial body of judicial decisions and EEOC precedent holding that Title VII affords employees the right to work in an environment free from discriminatory intimidation, ridicule, and insult. See generally 45 Fed.Reg. 74676 (1980). * * *

Courts applied this principle to harassment based on race, *e.g.,*[citations], religion, *e.g.,*[citations], and national origin, *e.g.,* [citations] Nothing in Title VII suggests that a hostile environment based on discriminatory *sexual* harassment should not be likewise prohibited. The Guidelines thus appropriately drew from, and were fully consistent with, the existing case law.

Since the Guidelines were issued, courts have uniformly held, and we agree, that a plaintiff may establish a violation of Title VII by proving that discrimination based on sex has created a hostile or abusive work environment. As the Court of Appeals for the Eleventh Circuit wrote in *Henson v. Dundee,* 682 F.2d 897, 902 (1982): "Sexual harassment which creates a hostile or offensive environment for members of one sex is every bit the arbitrary barrier to sexual equality at the workplace that racial harassment is to racial equality. Surely, a requirement that a man or woman run a gauntlet of sexual abuse in return for the privilege of being allowed to work and make a living can be as demeaning and disconcerting as the harshest of racial epithets."

* * *

Of course, . . . not all workplace conduct that may be described as "harassment" affects a "term, condition, or privilege" of employment within the meaning of Title VII. See *Rogers v. EEOC, supra,* at 238 ("mere utterance of an ethnic or racial epithet which engenders offensive feelings in an employee" would not affect the conditions of employment to sufficiently significant degree to violate Title VII). For sexual harassment to be actionable, it must be sufficiently severe or pervasive "to alter the conditions of [the victim's] employment and create an abusive working environment." *Ibid.* Respondent's allegations in this case—which include not only pervasive harassment but also criminal conduct of the most serious nature—are plainly sufficient to state a claim for "hostile environment" sexual harassment.

The question remains, however, whether the District Court's ultimate finding that respondent "was not the victim of sexual harassment," 23 FEP Cases, at 43, effectively disposed of respondent's claim. The Court of

Appeals recognized, we think correctly, that this ultimate finding was likely based on one or both of two erroneous views of the law. First, the District Court apparently believed that a claim for sexual harassment will not lie absent an *economic* effect on the complainant's employment. See *ibid.* ("It is without question that sexual harassment of female employees in which they are asked or required to submit to sexual demands as a *condition to obtain employment or to maintain employment or to obtain promotions* falls within protection of Title VII") (emphasis added). Since it appears that the District Court made its findings without ever considering the "hostile environment" theory of sexual harassment, the Court of Appeals' decision to remand was correct.

Second, the District Court's conclusion that no actionable harassment occurred might have rested on its earlier "finding" that "[i]f [respondent] and Taylor did engage in an intimate or sexual relationship . . ., that relationship was a voluntary one." 23 FEP Cases, at 42. But the fact that sex-related conduct was "voluntary," in the sense that the complainant was not forced to participate against her will, is not a defense to a sexual harassment suit brought under Title VII. The gravamen of any sexual harassment claim is that the alleged sexual advances were "unwelcome." 29 CFR § 1604.11(a) (1985). While the question whether particular conduct was indeed unwelcome presents difficult problems of proof and turns largely on credibility determinations committed to the trier of fact, the District Court in this case erroneously focused on the "voluntariness" of respondent's participation in the claimed sexual episodes. The correct inquiry is whether respondent by her conduct indicated that the alleged sexual advances were unwelcome, not whether her actual participation in sexual intercourse was voluntary.

Petitioner contends that even if this case must be remanded to the District Court, the Court of Appeals erred in one of the terms of its remand. Specifically, the Court of Appeals stated that testimony about respondent's "dress and personal fantasies," 753 F.2d, at 146, n. 36, which the District Court apparently admitted into evidence, "had no place in this litigation." *Ibid.* The apparent ground for this conclusion was that respondent's voluntariness *vel non* in submitting to Taylor's advances was immaterial to her sexual harassment claim. . . .To the contrary, such evidence is obviously relevant. . . . .While the District Court must carefully weigh the applicable considerations in deciding whether to admit evidence of this kind, there is no *per se* rule against its admissibility.

* * *

We . . . decline the parties' invitation to issue a definitive rule on employer liability, but . . .Congress wanted courts to look to agency principles for guidance in this area. While such common-law principles may not be transferable in all their particulars to Title VII, Congress' decision to define "employer" to include any "agent" of an employer, 42 U.S.C. § 2000e(b), surely evinces an intent to place some limits on the acts of employees for which employers under Title VII are to be held responsible. For this reason, we hold that the Court of Appeals erred in concluding that employers are always automatically liable for sexual harassment by their supervisors. See generally Restatement (Second) of Agency §§ 219–237 (1958). For the same reason, absence of notice to an employer does not necessarily insulate that employer from liability. *Ibid.*

* * *

In sum, we hold that a claim of "hostile environment" sex discrimination is actionable under Title VII, that the District Court's findings were insufficient to dispose of respondent's hostile environment claim, and that the District Court did not err in admitting testimony about respondent's sexually provocative speech and dress. As to employer liability, we conclude that the Court of Appeals was wrong to entirely disregard agency principles and impose absolute liability on employers for the acts of their supervisors, regardless of the circumstances of a particular case.

Accordingly, the judgment of the Court of Appeals reversing the judgment of the District Court is affirmed, and the case is remanded for further proceedings consistent with this opinion.

---

**Question:** A work environment may not seriously affect an employee's psychological well-being but still detract from performance and discourage employees from remaining on the job (e.g., disparaging comments like "You're a woman, what do you know?"). Is this illegal harassment after *Meritor Savings*? See *Harris v. Forklift Systems,* 510 U.S. 17 (1993).

## DISPARATE IMPACT

### GRIGGS V. DUKE POWER CO.

401 U.S. 424 (1971)

* * *

MR. CHIEF JUSTICE BURGER delivered the opinion of the Court.

We granted the writ in this case to resolve the question whether an employer is prohibited by the Civil Rights Act of 1964, Title VII, from requiring a high school education or passing of a standardized general intelligence test as a condition of employment in or transfer to jobs when (a) neither standard is shown to be significantly related to successful job performance, (b) both requirements operate to disqualify Negroes at a substantially higher rate than white applicants, and (c) the jobs in question formerly had been filled only by white employees as part of a longstanding practice of giving preference to whites.[1]

Congress provided, in Title VII of the Civil Rights Act of 1964, for class actions for enforcement of provisions of the Act and this proceeding was brought by a group of incumbent Negro employees against Duke Power Company. All the petitioners are employed at the Company's Dan River Steam Station, a power generating facility located at Draper, North Carolina. At the time this action was instituted, the Company had 95 employees at the Dan River Station, 14 of whom were Negroes; 13 of these are petitioners here.

The District Court found that prior to July 2, 1965, the effective date of the Civil Rights Act of 1964, the Company openly discriminated on the basis of race in the hiring and assigning of employees at its Dan River plant. The plant was organized into five operating departments: (1) Labor, (2) Coal Handling, (3) Operations, (4) Maintenance, and (5) Laboratory and Test. Negroes were employed only in the Labor Department where the highest paying jobs paid less than the lowest paying jobs in the other four 'operating' departments in which only whites were employed. Promotions were normally made within each department on the basis of job seniority. Transferees into a department usually began in the lowest position.

In 1955 the Company instituted a policy of requiring a high school education for initial assignment to any department except Labor, and for transfer from the Coal Handling to any 'inside' department (Operations, Maintenance, or Laboratory). When the Company abandoned its policy of restricting Negroes to the Labor Department in 1965, completion of high school also was made a prerequisite to transfer from Labor to any other department. From the time the high school requirement was instituted to the time of trial, however, white employees hired before the time of the high school education requirement continued to perform satisfactorily and achieve promotions in the 'operating' departments. Findings on this score are not challenged.

The Company added a further requirement for new employees on July 2, 1965, the date on which Title VII became effective. To qualify for

---

1 The Act provides:

'Sec. 703. (a) It shall be an unlawful employment practice for an employer—

'(2) to limit, segregate, or classify his employees in any way which would deprive or tend to deprive any individual of employment opportunities or otherwise adversely affect his status as an employee, because of such individual's race, color, religion, sex, or national origin.

'(h) Notwithstanding any other provision of this title, it shall not be an unlawful employment practice for an employer * * * to give and to act upon the results of any professionally developed ability test provided that such test, its administration or action upon the results is not designed, intended or used to discriminate because of race, color, religion, sex or national origin. . . .' 78 Stat. 255, 42 U.S.C. § 2000e–2.

placement in any but the Labor Department it become necessary to register satisfactory scores on two professionally prepared aptitude tests, as well as to have a high school education. Completion of high school alone continued to render employees eligible for transfer to the four desirable departments from which Negroes had been excluded if the incumbent had been employed prior to the time of the new requirement. In September 1965 the Company began to permit incumbent employees who lacked a high school education to qualify for transfer from Labor or Coal Handling to an 'inside' job by passing two tests—the Wonderlic Personnel Test, which purports to measure general intelligence, and the Bennett Mechanical Comprehension Test. Neither was directed or intended to measure the ability to learn to perform a particular job or category of jobs. The requisite scores used for both initial hiring and transfer approximated the national median for high school graduates.

The District Court had found that while the Company previously followed a policy of overt racial discrimination in a period prior to the Act, such conduct had ceased. The District Court also concluded that Title VII was intended to be prospective only and, consequently, the impact of prior inequities was beyond the reach of corrective action authorized by the Act.

* * *

The Court of Appeals reversed the District Court in part, rejecting the holding that residual discrimination arising from prior employment practices was insulated from remedial action. The Court of Appeals noted, however, that the District Court was correct in its conclusion that there was no showing of a racial purpose or invidious intent in the adoption of the high school diploma requirement or general intelligence test and that these standards had been applied fairly to whites and Negroes alike. It held that, in the absence of a discriminatory purpose, use of such requirements was permitted by the Act. In so doing, the Court of Appeals rejected the claim that because these two requirements operated to render ineligible a markedly disproportionate number of Negroes, they were unlawful under Title VII unless shown to be job related. We granted the writ on these claims.

The objective of Congress in the enactment of Title VII is plain from the language of the statute. It was to achieve equality of employment opportunities and remove barriers that have operated in the past to favor an identifiable group of white employees over other employees. Under the Act, practices, procedures, or tests neutral on their face, and even neutral in terms of intent, cannot be maintained if they operate to 'freeze' the status quo of prior discriminatory employment practices.

The Court of Appeals' opinion, and the partial dissent, agreed that, on the record in the present case, 'whites register far better on the Company's alternative requirements' than Negroes. 420 F.2d 1225, 1239 n. 6. This consequence would appear to be directly traceable to race. Basic intelligence must have the means of articulation to manifest itself fairly in a testing process. Because they are Negroes, petitioners have long received inferior education in segregated schools and this Court expressly recognized these differences in Gaston County v. United States, 395 U.S. 285 (1969). There, because of the inferior education received by Negroes in North Carolina, this Court barred the institution of a literacy test for voter registration on the ground that the test would abridge the right to vote indirectly on account of race. Congress did not intend by Title VII, however, to guarantee a job to every person regardless of qualifications. In short, the Act does not command that any person be hired simply because he was formerly the subject of discrimination, or because he is a member of a minority group. Discriminatory preference for any group, minority or majority, is precisely and only what Congress has proscribed. What is required by Congress is the removal of artificial, arbitrary, and unnecessary barriers to employment when the barriers operate invidiously to discriminate on the basis of racial or other impermissible classification.

Congress has now provided that tests or criteria for employment or promotion may not provide equality of opportunity merely in the sense of the fabled offer of milk to the stork and the fox. On the contrary, Congress has now required that the posture and condition of the job-seeker be taken into account. It has—to resort again to the fable—provided that the vessel in which the milk is proffered be one all seekers can use. The Act proscribes not only overt discrimination but also practices that are fair in form, but discriminatory in operation. The touchstone is business necessity. If an employment practice which operates to exclude Negroes cannot be shown to be related to job performance, the practice is prohibited.

On the record before us, neither the high school completion requirement nor the general intelligence test is shown to bear a demonstrable relationship to successful performance of the jobs for which it was used. Both were adopted, as the Court of Appeals noted, without meaningful study of their relationship to job-performance ability. Rather, a vice president of the Company testified, the requirements were instituted on the Company's judgment that they generally would improve the overall quality of the work force.

The evidence, however, shows that employees who have not completed high school or taken the tests have continued to perform satisfactorily and make progress in departments for which the high school and test criteria are now used. The promotion record of present employees who would not be able to meet the new criteria thus suggests the possibility that the requirements may not be needed even for the limited purpose of preserving the avowed policy of advancement within the Company. In the context of this case, it is unnecessary to reach the question whether testing requirements that take into account capability for the next succeeding position or related future promotion might be utilized upon a showing that such long range requirements fulfill a genuine business need. In the present case the Company has made no such showing.

The Court of Appeals held that the Company had adopted the diploma and test requirements without any 'intention to discriminate against Negro employees.' 420 F.2d, at 1232. We do not suggest that either the District Court or the Court of Appeals erred in examining the employer's intent; but good intent or absence of discriminatory intent does not redeem employment procedures or testing mechanisms that operate as 'built-in headwinds' for minority groups and are unrelated to measuring job capability.

The Company's lack of discriminatory intent is suggested by special efforts to help the undereducated employees through Company financing of two-thirds the cost of tuition for high school training. But Congress directed the thrust of the Act to the consequences of employment practices, not simply the motivation. More than that, Congress has placed on the employer the burden of showing that any given requirement must have a manifest relationship to the employment in question.

The facts of this case demonstrate the inadequacy of broad and general testing devices as well as the infirmity of using diplomas or degrees as fixed measures of capability. History is filled with examples of men and women who rendered highly effective performance without the conventional badges of accomplishment in terms of certificates, diplomas, or degrees. Diplomas and tests are useful servants, but Congress has mandated the commonsense proposition that they are not to become masters of reality.

The Company contends that its general intelligence tests are specifically permitted by § 703(h) of the Act. That section authorizes the use of 'any professionally developed ability test' that is not 'designed, intended or used to discriminate because of race . . . .' (Emphasis added.)

The Equal Employment Opportunity Commission, having enforcement responsibility, has issued guidelines interpreting § 703(h) to permit only the use of job-related tests. The administrative interpretation of the Act by the enforcing agency is entitled to great deference. See, e.g., [citations]. Since the Act and its legislative history support the Commission's construction, this affords good reason to treat the guidelines as expressing the will of Congress.

* * *

From the sum of the legislative history relevant in this case, the conclusion is inescapable that the EEOC's construction of § 703(h) to require that employment tests be job related comports with congressional intent.

Nothing in the Act precludes the use of testing or measuring procedures; obviously they are useful. What Congress has forbidden is giving these devices and mechanisms controlling force unless they are demonstrably a reasonable measure of job performance. Congress has not commanded that the less qualified be preferred over the better qualified simply because of minority origins. Far from disparaging job qualifications as such, Congress has made such qualifications the controlling factor, so that race, religion, nationality, and sex become irrelevant. What Congress has commanded is that any tests used must measure the person for the job and not the person in the abstract.

The judgment of the Court of Appeals is, as to that portion of the judgment appealed from, reversed.

---

**Question:** Did the employer in *Griggs* intentionally discriminate by imposing its testing requirement?

## BONA FIDE OCCUPATIONAL QUALIFICATION

### DOTHARD V. RAWLINSON

433 U.S. 321 (1977)

* * *

MR. JUSTICE STEWART delivered the opinion of the Court.

Appellee Dianne Rawlinson sought employment with the Alabama Board of Corrections as a prison guard, called in Alabama a 'correctional counselor.' After her application was rejected, she brought this class suit under Title VII of the Civil Rights Act of 1964, 78 Stat. 253, as amended, 42 U.S.C. § 2000e et seq. (1970 ed. and Supp. V), and under 42 U.S.C. § 1983, alleging that she had been denied employment because of her sex in violation of federal law. A three-judge Federal District Court for the Middle District of Alabama decided in her favor. Mieth v. Dothard, 418 F.Supp. 1169. We noted probable jurisdiction of this appeal from the District Court's judgment.

At the time she applied for a position as correctional counselor trainee, Rawlinson was a 22-year-old college graduate whose major course of study had been correctional psychology. She was refused employment because she failed to meet the minimum 120-pound weight requirement established by an Alabama statute. The statute also establishes a height minimum of 5 feet 2 inches.

After her application was rejected because of her weight, Rawlinson filed a charge with the Equal Employment Opportunity Commission, and ultimately received a right-to-sue letter. She then filed a complaint in the District Court on behalf of herself and other similarly situated women, challenging the statutory height and weight minima as violative of Title VII and the Equal Protection Clause of the Fourteenth Amendment. A three-judge court was convened. While the suit was pending, the Alabama Board of Corrections adopted Administrative Regulation 204, establishing gender criteria for assigning correctional counselors to maximum-security institutions for 'contact positions,' that is, positions requiring continual close physical proximity to inmates of the institution. Rawlinson amended her class-action complaint by adding a challenge to regulation 204 as also violative of Title VII and the Fourteenth Amendment.

Like most correctional facilities in the United States, Alabama's prisons are segregated on the basis of sex. Currently the Alabama Board of Corrections operates four major all-male penitentiaries Holman Prison, Kilby Corrections Facility, G. K. Fountain Correction Center, and Draper Correctional Center. The Board also operates the Julia Tutwiler Prison for Women, the Frank Lee Youth Center, the Number Four Honor Camp, the State Cattle Ranch, and nine Work Release Centers, one of which is for women. The Julia Tutwiler Prison for Women and the four male penitentiaries are maximum-security institutions. Their inmate living quarters are for the most part large dormitories, with communal showers and toilets that are open to the dormitories and hallways. The Draper and Fountain penitentiaries carry on extensive farming operations, making necessary a large number of strip searches for contraband when prisoners re-enter the prison buildings.

A correctional counselor's primary duty within these institutions is to maintain security and control of the inmates by continually supervising and observing their activities. To be eligible for consideration as a correctional counselor, an applicant must possess a valid Alabama driver's license, have a high school education or its equivalent, be free from physical defects, be between the ages of 20 1/2 years and 45 years at the time of appointment, and fall between the minimum height and weight requirements of 5 feet 2 inches, and 120 pounds, and the maximum of 6 feet 10 inches, and 300 pounds. Appointment is by merit, with a grade assigned each applicant based on experience and education. No written examination is given.

At the time this litigation was in the District Court, the Board of Corrections employed a total of 435 people in various correctional counselor positions, 56 of whom were women. Of those 56 women, 21 were employed at the Julia Tutwiler Prison for Women, 13 were employed in noncontact positions at the four male maximum-security institutions, and the remaining 22 were employed at the other institutions operated by the Alabama Board of Corrections. Because most of Alabama's prisoners are held at the four maximum-security male penitentiaries, 336 of the 435 correctional counselor jobs were in those institutions, a majority of them concededly in the 'contact' classification. Thus, even though meeting the statutory height and weight requirements, women applicants could under Regulation 204 compete equally with men for only about 25% of the correctional counselor jobs available in the Alabama prison system.

In enacting Title VII, Congress required 'the removal of artificial, arbitrary, and unnecessary barriers to employment when the barriers operate invidiously to discriminate on the basis of racial or other impermissible classification.' Griggs v. Duke Power Co., 401 U.S. 424, 431. The District Court found that the minimum statutory height and weight requirements that applicants for employment as correctional counselors must meet constitute the sort of arbitrary barrier to equal employment opportunity that Title VII forbids. The appellants assert that the District Court erred both in finding that the height and weight standards discriminate against women, and in its refusal to find that, even if they do, these standards are justified as 'job related.'

The gist of the claim that the statutory height and weight requirements discriminate against women does not involve an assertion of purposeful discriminatory motive. It is asserted, rather, that these facially neutral qualification standards work in fact disproportionately to exclude women from eligibility for employment by the Alabama Board of Corrections. We dealt in Griggs v. Duke Power Co., supra and Albemarle Paper Co. v. Moody, 422 U.S. 405, with similar allegations that facially neutral employment standards disproportionately excluded Negroes from employment, and those cases guide our approach here.

Those cases make clear that to establish a prima facie case of discrimination, a plaintiff need only show that the facially neutral standards in question select applicants for hire in a significantly discriminatory pattern. Once it is thus shown that the employment standards are discriminatory in effect, the employer must meet 'the burden of showing that any given requirement (has) . . . a manifest relationship to the employment in question.' Griggs v. Duke Power Co., supra, at 432. If the employer proves that the challenged requirements are job related, the plaintiff may then show that other selection devices without a similar discriminatory effect would also 'serve the employer's legitimate interest in 'efficient and trustworthy workmanship.'' Albemarle Paper Co. v. Moody, supra, at 425, quoting McDonnell Douglas Corp. v. Green, 411 U.S. 792, 801.

Although women 14 years of age or older compose 52.75% of the Alabama population and 36.89% of its total labor force, they hold only 12.9% of its correctional counselor positions. In considering the effect of the minimum height and weight standards on this disparity in rate of hiring between the sexes, the District Court found that the 5$2$-requirement would operate to exclude 33.29% of the women in the United States between the ages of 18–79, while excluding only 1.28% of men between the same ages. The 120-pound weight restriction would exclude 22.29% of the women and 2.35% of the men in this age group. When the height and weight restrictions are combined, Alabama's statutory standards would exclude 41.13% of the female population while excluding less than 1% of the male population. Accordingly, the District Court found that Rawlinson had made out a prima facie case of unlawful sex discrimination.

The appellants argue that a showing of disproportionate impact on women based on generalized national statistics should not suffice to establish a prima facie case. They point in particular to Rawlinson's failure to adduce comparative statistics concerning actual applicants for correctional counselor positions in Alabama. There is no requirement, however, that a statistical showing of disproportionate impact must always be based on analysis of the characteristics of actual applicants. See Griggs v. Duke Power Co., supra, 401 U.S., at 430. The application process might itself not adequately reflect the actual potential applicant pool, since otherwise qualified people might be discouraged from applying because of a self-recognized inability to meet the very standards challenged as being discriminatory. See International Brotherhood of Teamsters v. United States, 431 U.S. 324, 365–367. A potential applicant could easily determine her height and weight and conclude that to make an application would be futile. Moreover, reliance on general population demographic data was not misplaced where there was no reason to suppose that physical height and weight characteristics of Alabama men and women differ markedly from those of the national population.

For these reasons, we cannot say that the District Court was wrong in holding that the statutory height and weight standards had a discriminatory impact on women applicants. The plaintiffs in a case such as this are not required to exhaust every possible source of evidence, if the evidence actually presented on its face conspicuously demonstrates a job requirement's grossly discriminatory impact. If the employer discerns fallacies or deficiencies in the data offered by the plaintiff, he is free to adduce countervailing evidence of his own. In this case no such effort was made.

We turn, therefore, to the appellants' argument that they have rebutted the prima facie case of discrimination by showing that the height and weight requirements are job related. These requirements, they say, have a relationship to strength, a sufficient but unspecified amount of which is essential to effective job performance as a correctional counselor. In the District Court, however, the appellants produced no evidence correlating the height and weight requirements with the requisite amount of strength thought essential to good job performance. Indeed, they failed to offer evidence of any kind in specific justification of the statutory standards.

If the job-related quality that the appellants identify is bona fide, their purpose could be achieved by adopting and validating a test for applicants that measures strength directly. Such a test, fairly administered, would fully satisfy the standards of Title VII because it would be one that 'measure(s) the person for the job and not the person in the abstract.' Griggs v. Duke Power Co., 401 U.S., at 436. But nothing in the present record even approaches such a measurement.

For the reasons we have discussed, the District Court was not in error in holding that Title VII of the Civil Rights Act of 1964, as amended, prohibits application of the statutory height and weight requirements to Rawlinson and the class she represents.

Unlike the statutory height and weight requirements, Regulation 204 explicitly discriminates against women on the basis of their sex. In defense of this overt discrimination, the appellants rely on § 703(e) of Title VII, 42 U.S.C. § 2000e–2(e), which permits sex-based discrimination 'in those certain instances where . . . sex . . . is a bona fide occupational qualification reasonably necessary to the normal operation of that particular business or enterprise.'

The District Court rejected the bona-fide occupational-qualification (bfoq) defense, relying on the virtually uniform view of the federal courts that § 703(e) provides only the narrowest of exceptions to the general rule requiring equality of employment opportunities. This view has been variously formulated. In Diaz v. Pan American World Airways, 442 F.2d 385, 388, the Court of Appeals for the Fifth Circuit held that 'discrimination based on sex is valid only when the essence of the business operation would be undermined by not hiring members of one sex exclusively.' (Emphasis in original.) In an earlier case, Weeks v. Southern Bell Telephone and Telegraph Co., 5 Cir., 408 F.2d 228, 235, the same court said that an employer could rely on the bfoq exception only by proving 'that he had reasonable cause to believe, that is, a factual basis for believing, that all or substantially all women would be unable to perform safely and efficiently the duties of the job involved.' See [citation]. But whatever the verbal formulation, the federal courts have agreed that it is impermissible under Title VII to refuse to hire an individual woman or man on the basis of stereotyped characterizations of the sexes, and the District Court in the present case held in effect that Regulation 204 is based on just such stereotypical assumptions.

We are persuaded by the restrictive language of § 703(e), the relevant legislative history, and the consistent interpretation of the Equal Employment Opportunity Commission that the bfoq exception was in fact meant to be an extremely narrow exception to the general prohibition of discrimination on the basis of sex. In the particular factual circumstances of this case, however, we conclude that the District Court erred in rejecting the State's contention that Regulation 204 falls within the narrow ambit of the bfoq exception.

The environment in Alabama's penitentiaries is a peculiarly inhospitable one for human beings of whatever sex. Indeed, a Federal District Court has held that the conditions of confinement in the prisons of the State, characterized by 'rampant violence' and a 'jungle atmosphere,' are constitutionally intolerable. Pugh v. Locke, 406 F.Supp. 318, 325 (MD Ala.). The record in the present case shows that because of inadequate staff and facilities, no attempt is made in the four maximum-security male penitentiaries to classify or segregate inmates according to their offense or level of dangerousness a procedure that, according to expert testimony, is essential to effective penological administration. Consequently, the estimated 20% of the male prisoners who are sex offenders are scattered throughout the penitentiaries' dormitory facilities.

* * *

The essence of a correctional counselor's job is to maintain prison security. A woman's relative ability to maintain order in a male, maximum-security, unclassified penitentiary of the type Alabama now runs could be directly reduced by her womanhood. There is a basis in fact for expecting that sex offenders who have criminally assaulted women in the past would be moved to do so again if access to women were established within the prison. There would also be a real risk that other inmates, deprived of a normal heterosexual environment, would assault women guards because they were women. In a prison system where violence is the order of the day, where inmate access to guards is facilitated by dormitory living arrangements, where every institution is understaffed, and where a substantial portion of the inmate population is composed of sex offenders mixed at random with other prisoners, there are few visible deterrents to inmate assaults on women custodians.

Appellee Rawlinson's own expert testified that dormitory housing for aggressive inmates poses a greater security problem than single-cell lockups, and further testified that it would be unwise to use women as guards in a prison where even 10% of the inmates had been convicted of sex crimes and were not segregated from the other prisoners. The likelihood that inmates would assault a woman because she was a woman would pose a real threat not only to the victim of the assault but also to the basic control of the penitentiary and protection of its inmates and the other security personnel. The employee's very womanhood would thus directly undermine her capacity to provide the security that is the essence of a correctional counselor's responsibility.

There was substantial testimony from experts on both sides of this litigation that the use of women as guards in 'contact' positions under the existing conditions in Alabama maximum-security male penitentiaries would pose a substantial security problem, directly linked to the sex of the prison guard. On the basis of that evidence, we conclude that the District Court was in error in ruling that being male is not a bona fide occupational qualification for the job of correctional counselor in a 'contact' position in an Alabama male maximum-security penitentiary.

The judgment is accordingly affirmed in part and reversed in part, and the case is remanded to the District Court for further proceedings consistent with this opinion.

MR. JUSTICE MARSHALL, with whom MR. JUSTICE BRENNAN joins, concurring in part and dissenting in part.

I agree entirely with the Court's analysis of Alabama's height and weight requirements for prison guards, and with its finding that these restrictions discriminate on the basis of sex in violation of Title VII. . . . . I must, however, respectfully disagree with the Court's application of the bfoq exception in this case.

* * *

The Court points to no evidence in the record to support the asserted 'likelihood that inmates would assault a woman because she was a woman. . . . . the incidence of sexually motivated attacks on guards will be minute compared to the 'likelihood that inmates will assault' a guard because he or she is a guard.

The proper response to inevitable attacks on both female and male guards is not to limit the employment opportunities of law abiding women who wish to contribute to their community, but to take swift and sure punitive action against the inmate offenders. Presumably, one of the goals of the Alabama prison system is the eradication of inmates' antisocial behavior patterns so that prisoners will be able to live one day in free society. Sex offenders can begin this process by learning to relate to women guards in a socially acceptable manner. To deprive women of job opportunities because of the threatened behavior of convicted criminals is to turn our social priorities upside down.

* * *

---

**Questions:** The *Dothard* majority and concurrence/dissent differ over whether female guards in contact positions could safely handle inmates. Could the dissent have gone further and argued that female guards may be able to command more respect from prisoners than do male guards? An airline refuses to employ male flight attendants, arguing that they would be inconsistent with its "love in the sky" marketing campaign outfitting stewardesses with hot pants and go-go boots. BFOQ? See *Wilson v. Southwest Airlines,* 517 F.Supp. 292 (N.D. Tex. 1981).

# CHAPTER 25

# EMPLOYMENT LAW—OCCUPATIONAL SAFETY AND WORKERS' COMPENSATION

■ ■ ■

## CONTEXT & SOURCES

The federal Occupational Safety and Health Act of 1970 (OSHA), 29 U.S.C. § 651 et seq. regulates workplace safety and health, while state workers' compensation statutes set recompense for employee injury. OSHA's elaborate inspection and citation process encourages employers to maintain acceptable conditions. The state compensation system was designed to replace the uncertain liability and inadequate remedies provided by the common law tort system. The following cases cover OSHA search procedures, the employer's duty to abate hazards, and workers' compensation eligibility.

Jonathan D. Karmel, *Dying to Work: Death and Injury in the American Workplace* (Cornell, 2017) surveys the wide range of risks to employees and critiques the limitations of OSHA and workers' compensation in addressing them. For a practical guide to how the Marshall's decision affected questions of warrant validity, see Mark A. Rothstein, "OSHA Inspections after Marshall v. Barlow's, Inc.," 1979 *Duke Law Journal* 63 (1979). The debate over undocumented immigrants' entitlement coverage, including worker's compensation, is analyzed in Peter L. Reich, "Environmental Metaphor in the Alien Benefits Debate," 42 *UCLA Law Review* 1577 (1995).

## OSHA INSPECTIONS

### MARSHALL V. BARLOW'S

436 U.S. 307 (1978)

* * *

MR. JUSTICE WHITE delivered the opinion of the Court.

Section 8(a) of the Occupational Safety and Health Act of 1970 (OSHA or Act) empowers agents of the Secretary of Labor (Secretary) to search the work area of any employment facility within the Act's jurisdiction. The purpose of the search is to inspect for safety hazards and violations of

OSHA regulations. No search warrant or other process is expressly required under the Act.

On the morning of September 11, 1975, an OSHA inspector entered the customer service area of Barlow's, Inc., an electrical and plumbing installation business located in Pocatello, Idaho. The president and general manager, Ferrol G. "Bill" Barlow, was on hand; and the OSHA inspector, after showing his credentials, informed Mr. Barlow that he wished to conduct a search of the working areas of the business. Mr. Barlow inquired whether any complaint had been received about his company. The inspector answered no, but that Barlow's Inc., had simply turned up in the agency's selection process. The inspector again asked to enter the nonpublic area of the business; Mr. Barlow's response was to inquire whether the inspector had a search warrant. The inspector had none. Thereupon, Mr. Barlow refused the inspector admission to the employee area of his business. He said he was relying on his rights as guaranteed by the Fourth Amendment of the United States Constitution.

Three months later, the Secretary petitioned the United States District Court for the District of Idaho to issue an order compelling Mr. Barlow to admit the inspector. The requested order was issued on December 30, 1975, and was presented to Mr. Barlow on January 5, 1976. Mr. Barlow again refused admission, and he sought his own injunctive relief against the warrantless searches assertedly permitted by OSHA. A three-judge court was convened. On December 30, 1976, it ruled in Mr. Barlow's favor. 424 F.Supp. 437. Concluding that *Camara v. Municipal Court,* 387 U.S. 523, 528–529 (1967), and *See v. City of Seattle,* 387 U.S. 541, 543 (1967), controlled this case, the court held that the Fourth Amendment required a warrant for the type of search involved here and that the statutory authorization for warrantless inspections was unconstitutional. An injunction against searches or inspections pursuant to § 8(a) was entered. The Secretary appealed, challenging the judgment, and we noted probable jurisdiction.

The Secretary urges that warrantless inspections to enforce OSHA are reasonable within the meaning of the Fourth Amendment. Among other things, he relies on § 8(a) of the Act, 29 U.S.C. § 657(a), which authorizes inspection of business premises without a warrant and which the Secretary urges represents a congressional construction of the Fourth Amendment that the courts should not reject. Regrettably, we are unable to agree.

The Warrant Clause of the Fourth Amendment protects commercial buildings as well as private homes. To hold otherwise would belie the origin of that Amendment, and the American colonial experience. An important forerunner of the first 10 Amendments to the United States Constitution, the Virginia Bill of Rights, specifically opposed "general warrants, whereby an officer or messenger may be commanded to search suspected places without evidence of a fact committed." The general warrant was a recurring point of contention in the Colonies immediately preceding the Revolution. The particular offensiveness it engendered was acutely felt by the merchants and businessmen whose premises and products were inspected for compliance with the several parliamentary revenue measures that most irritated the colonists. "[T]he Fourth Amendment's commands grew in large measure out of the colonists' experience with the writs of assistance . . . [that] granted sweeping power to customs officials and other agents of the King to search at large for smuggled goods." [Citations]. Against this background, it is untenable that the ban on warrantless searches was not intended to shield places of business as well as of residence.

This Court has already held that warrantless searches are generally unreasonable, and that this rule applies to commercial premises as well as homes. In *Camara v. Municipal Court, supra,* 387 U.S., at 528–529, we held:

"[E]xcept in certain carefully defined classes of cases, a search of private property without proper consent is 'unreasonable' unless it has been authorized by a valid search warrant."

On the same day, we also ruled:

"As we explained in *Camara,* a search of private houses is presumptively unreasonable if conducted without a warrant. The businessman, like the occupant of a residence, has a constitutional right to go about his business free from unreasonable official entries upon his private commercial property. The businessman, too, has that right placed in jeopardy if the decision to enter and inspect for violation of regulatory laws can be made and enforced by the inspector in he field without official authority evidenced by a warrant." *See v. City of Seattle, supra,* 387 U.S., at 543.

These same cases also held that the Fourth Amendment prohibition against unreasonable searches protects against warrantless intrusions during civil as well as criminal investigations. *Ibid.* The reason is found in the "basic purpose of this Amendment . . . [which] is to safeguard the privacy and security of individuals against arbitrary invasions by governmental officials." *Camara, supra,* 387 U.S., at 528. If the government intrudes on a person's property, the privacy interest suffers whether the government's motivation is to investigate violations of criminal laws or breaches of other statutory or regulatory standards. It therefore appears that unless some recognized exception to the warrant requirement applies, *See v. City of Seattle,* would require a warrant to conduct the inspection sought in this case.

The Secretary urges that an exception from the search warrant requirement has been recognized for "pervasively regulated business[es]," *United States v. Biswell,* 406 U.S. 311, 316 (1972), and for "closely regulated" industries "long subject to close supervision and inspection."

*Colonnade Catering Corp. v. United States,* 397 U.S. 72, 74 (1970). These cases are indeed exceptions, but they represent responses to relatively unique circumstances. Certain industries have such a history of government oversight that no reasonable expectation of privacy, see *Katz v. United States,* 389 U.S. 347, 351–352 (1967), could exist for a proprietor over the stock of such an enterprise. Liquor (*Colonnade*) and firearms (*Biswell*) are industries of this type; when an entrepreneur embarks upon such a business, he has voluntarily chosen to subject himself to a full arsenal of governmental regulation.

Industries such as these fall within the "certain carefully defined classes of cases," referenced in *Camara,* 387 U.S., at 528. The element that distinguishes these enterprises from ordinary businesses is a long tradition of close government supervision, of which any person who chooses to enter such a business must already be aware. "A central difference between those cases [*Colonnade* and *Biswell*] and this one is that businessmen engaged in such federally licensed and regulated enterprises accept the burdens as well as the benefits of their trade, whereas the petitioner here was not engaged in any regulated or licensed business. The businessman in a regulated industry in effect consents to the restrictions placed upon him." *Almeida-Sanchez v. United States,* 413 U.S. 266, 271 (1973).

The clear import of our cases is that the closely regulated industry of the type involved in *Colonnade* and *Biswell* is the exception. The Secretary would make it the rule. Invoking the Walsh-Healey Act of 1936, 41 U.S.C. § 35 *et seq.,* the Secretary attempts to support a conclusion that all businesses involved in interstate commerce have long been subjected to close supervision of employee safety and health conditions. But the degree of federal involvement in employee working circumstances has never been of the order of specificity and pervasiveness that OSHA mandates. It is quite unconvincing to argue that the imposition of minimum wages and maximum hours on employers who contracted with the Government under the Walsh-Healey Act prepared the entirety of American interstate commerce for regulation of working conditions to the minutest detail. Nor can any but the most fictional sense of voluntary consent to later searches be found in the single fact that one conducts a business affecting interstate commerce; under current practice and law, few businesses can be conducted without having some effect on interstate commerce.

* * *

The Secretary nevertheless stoutly argues that the enforcement scheme of the Act requires warrantless searches, and that the restrictions on search discretion contained in the Act and its regulations already protect as much privacy as a warrant would. The Secretary thereby asserts the actual reasonableness of OSHA searches, whatever the general rule against warrantless searches might be. Because "reasonableness is still the ultimate standard," *Camara v. Municipal* Court, 387 U.S., at 539, the Secretary suggests that the Court decide whether a warrant is needed by arriving at a sensible balance between the administrative necessities of OSHA inspections and the incremental protection of privacy of business owners a warrant would afford. He suggests that only a decision exempting OSHA inspections from the Warrant Clause would give "full recognition to the competing public and private interests here at stake." *Ibid.*

The Secretary submits that warrantless inspections are essential to the proper enforcement of OSHA because they afford the opportunity to inspect without prior notice and hence to preserve the advantages of surprise. While the dangerous conditions outlawed by the Act include structural defects that cannot be quickly hidden or remedied, the Act also regulates a myriad of safety details that may be amenable to speedy alteration or disguise. The risk is that during the interval between an inspector's initial request to search a plant and his procuring a warrant following the owner's refusal of permission, violations of this latter type could be corrected and thus escape the inspector's notice. To the suggestion that warrants may be issued *ex parte* and executed without delay and without prior notice, thereby preserving the element of surprise, the Secretary expresses concern for the administrative strain that would be experienced by the inspection system, and by the courts, should *ex parte* warrants issued in advance become standard practice.

We are unconvinced, however, that requiring warrants to inspect will impose serious burdens on the inspection system or the courts, will prevent inspections necessary to enforce the statute, or will make them less effective. In the first place, the great majority of businessmen can be expected in normal course to consent to inspection without warrant; the Secretary has not brought to this Court's attention any widespread pattern of refusal. In those cases where an owner does insist on a warrant, the Secretary argues that inspection efficiency will be impeded by the advance notice and delay. The Act's penalty provisions for giving advance notice of a search, 29 U.S.C. § 666(f), and the Secretary's own regulations, 29 CFR § 1903.6 (1977), indicate that surprise searches are indeed contemplated. However, the Secretary has also promulgated a regulation providing that upon refusal to permit an inspector to enter the property or to complete his inspection, the inspector shall attempt to ascertain the reasons for the refusal and report to his superior, who shall "promptly take appropriate action, including compulsory process, if necessary." 29 CFR § 1903.4 (1977). The regulation represents a choice to proceed by process where entry is refused; and on the basis of evidence available from present practice, the Act's effectiveness has not been crippled by providing those owners who wish to refuse an initial requested entry with a time lapse while the inspector obtains the necessary process. Indeed, the kind of process sought in this case and apparently anticipated by the regulation provides notice to the business operator. If this safeguard endangers the efficient administration of OSHA, the Secretary should never have adopted it, particularly when the Act does not require it. Nor is it immediately apparent why the advantages of surprise would be lost if, after being refused entry, procedures were available for the Secretary to seek an *ex parte* warrant and to reappear at the premises without further notice to the establishment being inspected.

Whether the Secretary proceeds to secure a warrant or other process, with or without prior notice, his entitlement to inspect will not depend on his demonstrating probable cause to believe that conditions in violation of OSHA exist on the premises. Probable cause in the criminal law sense is not required. For purposes of an administrative search such as this, probable cause justifying the issuance of a warrant may be based not only on specific evidence of an existing violation but also on a showing that "reasonable legislative or administrative standards for conducting an . . . inspection are satisfied with respect to a particular [establishment]." *Camara v. Municipal Court,* 387 U.S., at 538. A warrant showing that a specific business has been chosen for an OSHA search on the basis of a general administrative plan for the enforcement of the Act derived from neutral sources such as, for example, dispersion of employees in various types of industries across a given area, and the desired frequency of searches in any of the lesser divisions of the area, would protect an employer's Fourth Amendment rights. We doubt that the consumption of enforcement energies in the obtaining of such warrants will exceed manageable proportions.

Finally, the Secretary urges that requiring a warrant for OSHA inspectors will mean that, as a practical matter, warrantless-search provisions in other regulatory statutes are also constitutionally infirm. The reasonableness of a warrantless search, however, will depend upon the specific enforcement needs and privacy guarantees of each statute. Some of the statutes cited apply only to a single industry, where regulations might already be so pervasive that a *Colonnade-Biswell* exception to the warrant requirement could apply. Some statutes already envision resort to federal-court enforcement when entry is refused, employing specific language in some cases and general language in others. In short, we base today's opinion on the facts and law concerned with OSHA and do not retreat from a holding appropriate to that statute because of its real or imagined effect on other, different administrative schemes.

Nor do we agree that the incremental protections afforded the employer's privacy by a warrant are so marginal that they fail to justify the administrative burdens that may be entailed. The authority to make warrantless searches devolves almost unbridled discretion upon executive and administrative officers, particularly those in the field, as to when to search and whom to search. A warrant, by contrast, would provide assurances from a neutral officer that the inspection is reasonable under the Constitution, is authorized by statute, and is pursuant to an administrative plan containing specific neutral criteria. Also, a warrant would then and there advise the owner of the scope and objects of the search, beyond which limits the inspector is not expected to proceed. These are important functions for a warrant to perform, functions which underlie the Court's prior decisions that the Warrant Clause applies to inspections for compliance with regulatory statutes. [Citations]. We conclude that the concerns expressed by the Secretary do not suffice to justify warrantless inspections under OSHA or vitiate the general constitutional requirement that for a search to be reasonable a warrant must be obtained.

We hold that Barlow's was entitled to a declaratory judgment that the Act is unconstitutional insofar as it purports to authorize inspections without warrant or its equivalent and to an injunction enjoining the Act's enforcement to that extent. The judgment of the District Court is therefore affirmed.

MR. JUSTICE STEVENS, with whom MR. JUSTICE BLACKMUN and MR. JUSTICE REHNQUIST join, dissenting.

* * *

The case before us involves an attempt to conduct a warrantless search of the working area of an electrical and plumbing contractor. The statute authorizes such an inspection during reasonable hours. The inspection is limited to those areas over which Congress has exercised its proper legislative authority. The area is also one to which employees have regular access without any suggestion that the work performed or the equipment used has any special claim to confidentiality. Congress has determined that industrial safety is an urgent federal interest requiring regulation and supervision, and further, that warrantless inspections are necessary to accomplish the safety goals of the legislation. While one may question the wisdom of pervasive governmental oversight of industrial life, I decline to question Congress' judgment that the inspection power is a necessary enforcement device in achieving the goals of a valid exercise of regulatory power.

I respectfully dissent.

---

**Questions:** In *Marshall v. Barlow's,* why did the majority not defer to the administrative agency's view of proper enforcement procedure? Comparing the majority and the dissent, which followed the plain meaning rule in interpreting the statute? Which followed the purpose rule?

# OSHA EMPLOYER'S DUTIES

## SEAWORLD OF FLORIDA, LLC V. PEREZ

748 F.3d 1202 (D.C. Cir. 2014)

* * *

ROGERS, CIRCUIT JUDGE:

SeaWorld of Florida, LLC, operates a theme park in Orlando, Florida, that is designed to entertain and educate paying customers by displaying and studying marine animals. Following the death of one of SeaWorld's trainers while working in close contact with a killer whale during a performance, the Occupational Safety and Health Review Commission found that SeaWorld had violated the general duty clause, § 5(a)(1) of the Occupational Safety and Health Act of 1970, 29 U.S.C. § 654(a)(1), by exposing the trainers to recognized hazards when working in close contact with killer whales during performances, and that the abatement procedures recommended by the Secretary of Labor were feasible. SeaWorld challenges the order with respect to one citation. Concluding its challenges are unpersuasive, we deny the petition for review.

On February 24, 2010, SeaWorld trainer Dawn Brancheau was interacting with Tilikum, a killer whale, during a performance before a live audience in a pool at Shamu Stadium in Orlando. Ms. Brancheau was reclined on her back on a platform a few inches below the water surface. Tilikum was supposed to mimic her behavior by rolling over. Instead, the killer whale grabbed her and pulled her off the platform into the pool, refusing to release her. She suffered traumatic injuries and drowned as a result of Tilikum's actions.

The Secretary of Labor issued three citations to SeaWorld after an investigation by an Occupational Safety and Health Administration ("OSHA") compliance officer. Only the second citation is at issue. It alleged two instances of a "willful" violation of the general duty clause for exposing animal trainers to the recognized hazards of drowning or injury when working with killer whales during performances. The first instance related to animal trainers working with Tilikum being exposed to "struck-by and drowning hazards" by being "allowed unprotected contact with Tilikum" while conducting " 'drywork' performances on pool ledges, slideouts and platforms." Citation 2, Instance (a). In SeaWorld's terms, when trainers are out of the pool or on submerged ledges called "slideouts" in water no deeper than their knees, their interactions with killer whales are called "drywork." Any interaction in deeper water is "waterwork." According to the Secretary, "[a]mong other methods, one feasible and acceptable means of abatement would be to not allow animal trainers to have any contact with Tilikum unless they are protected by a physical barrier." The second instance concerned animal trainers working with killer whales other than Tilikum who were exposed to struck-by and drowning hazards when they were "allowed to engage in 'waterwork' and 'drywork' performances with the killer whales without adequate protection." The Secretary listed as possible abatement methods "prohibit[ing] animal trainers from working with killer whales, including 'waterwork' or 'dry work,' unless the trainers are protected through the use of physical barriers or through the use of decking systems, oxygen supply systems or other engineering or administrative controls that provide the same or greater level of protection for the trainers." The Secretary proposed a penalty of $70,000. * * *

The general duty clause, § 5(a)(1) of the Occupational Safety and Health Act, provides: "Each employer [ ] shall furnish to each of his employees employment and a place of employment which are free from recognized hazards that are causing or are likely to cause death or serious physical harm to his employees." 29 U.S.C. § 654(a)(1).

* * *

"To establish a violation of the General Duty Clause, the Secretary must establish that: (1) an activity or condition in the employer's workplace presented a hazard to an employee, (2) either the employer or the industry recognized the condition or activity as a hazard, (3) the hazard was likely to or actually caused death or serious physical harm, and (4) a feasible means to eliminate or materially reduce the hazard existed." Fabi Constr. Co. v. Sec'y of Labor, 508 F.3d 1077, 1081 (D.C.Cir.2007) (citation omitted). Tempering the range of potential remedies that might be imposed upon finding a violation of the clause, the court explained: "In other words, 'the Secretary must prove that a reasonably prudent employer familiar with the circumstances of the industry would have protected against the hazard in the manner specified by the Secretary's citation.' " [Citation].

SeaWorld contests only the second and fourth elements regarding recognized hazard and feasibility. In challenging the general duty citation, SeaWorld does not perforce contend that the Secretary of Labor or the Occupational Safety and Health Review Commission lack legal authority to require employers to provide a reasonably safe working environment for employees. Rather, SeaWorld takes issue with the interpretation by these officials of what constitutes a recognized hazard that would subject an employer to citation under the Occupational Safety and Health Act. First, SeaWorld contends that the finding that it exposed its employees to a "recognized hazard" is unsupported by substantial evidence. Second, it contends that "when some risk is inherent in a business activity, that risk cannot constitute a 'recognized hazard.' " Pet'r Br. at 33. Third, it contends that the ALJ's decision was based on unreliable expert testimony about the extent of killer whale predictability after SeaWorld's training and precautions. As regards the feasibility of physical barriers and minimum distances SeaWorld contends that the Secretary failed to prove feasible abatement methods (or that SeaWorld had already implemented these measures), and that the ALJ failed to consider evidence these abatement measures present additional hazards and erred because eliminating close contact changes the nature of a trainer's job . . . .

The court must uphold the Commission's decision unless it is "arbitrary, capricious, an abuse of discretion, or otherwise not in accordance with law." [Citations]. The factual findings of the Commission, "if supported by substantial evidence on the record considered as a whole, shall be conclusive." 29 U.S.C. § 660(a); see, e.g., [citation]. Under this standard, the court must "uphold Commission findings so long as there is 'such relevant evidence as a reasonable mind might accept as adequate to support a conclusion.' [Citation]. Likewise, the court "must accept the ALJ's credibility determinations unless they are patently unsupportable." Id. (ellipsis in original) (citation omitted). The court will "defer to the Secretary's interpretation of the Act and regulations, upholding such interpretations so long as they are consistent with the statutory language and otherwise reasonable." [Citations].

Whether a work condition poses a recognized hazard is a question of fact. Substantial evidence supports the finding that "drywork" and "waterwork" with killer whales were recognized hazards. Tilikum is a 32-year-old male killer whale with known aggressive tendencies who in 1991 killed a whale trainer at a marine park in Vancouver, British Columbia. SeaWorld had established special protocols for Tilikum, which prohibited "waterwork" and, among other things, required non-killer whale personnel and guests to stay five feet behind pool walls or three feet from Tilikum's head, indicating that SeaWorld recognized the possibility of harm to people standing outside of the pool on land. Although "drywork" with Tilikum continued, SeaWorld limited it to a team of experienced trainers who used extra caution. The caution with which SeaWorld treated Tilikum even when trainers were poolside or on "slideouts" in the pool indicates that it recognized the hazard the killer whale posed, not that it considered its protocols rendered Tilikum safe.

As to other killer whales, SeaWorld suggests that close contact with these whales was not a recognized hazard because all whales behave differently and its incident reports help SeaWorld improve training. But SeaWorld's incident reports demonstrate that it recognized the danger its killer whales posed to trainers notwithstanding its protocols. At the time of Ms. Brancheau's death, seven killer whales were at the Orlando park. Even though SeaWorld had not recorded incident reports on all of its killer whales, a substantial portion of SeaWorld's killer whale population had at least one reported incident. The ALJ also relied on the many comments by SeaWorld management personnel, including corporate curators of animal training, who described the need for caution around killer whales generally, not only around certain killer whales. Killer whales bit trainers' body parts on several occasions (although not generally puncturing skin) and in 2006 a killer whale pulled a trainer underwater by the foot and submerged him repeatedly for approximately 10 minutes. Although this incident occurred during "waterwork," substantial evidence supports the finding with regard to "drywork" as well. On numerous occasions, trainers fell or were pulled into the water, as later happened with Tilikum and Ms. Brancheau, or killer whales lunged out of the water toward trainers. These incidents constitute substantial evidence to support the ALJ's finding that "drywork" was also a recognized hazard.

* * *

SeaWorld's suggestion that because trainers "formally accepted and controlled their own exposure to . . . risks," the hazard of close contact with killer whales cannot be recognized, see Pet'r Br. at 40, contravenes Congress's decision to place the duty to ensure a safe and healthy workplace on the employer, not the employee. This court has long held "this duty is not qualified by such common law doctrines as assumption of risk, contributory negligence, or comparative negligence." Nat'l Realty & Constr. Co., 489 F.2d at 1266 n.36. SeaWorld's reliance on Oil, Chemical & Atomic Workers International Union v. American Cyanamid Co., 741 F.2d 444 (D.C.Cir.1984), is misplaced; the alleged hazard in that case was the employer's policy prohibiting women of childbearing age from working in high lead-exposure positions unless they had been surgically sterilized, and the court held that "the general duty clause does not apply to a policy as contrasted with a physical condition of the workplace." The court explained that the optional sterilization policy "does not affect employees while they are engaged in work or work-related activities." The potential harm to SeaWorld's trainers exists in their workplace and involves conditions over which SeaWorld has control.

The Secretary and the Commission could also reasonably determine that the remedy does not go to the essence of SeaWorld's productions. SeaWorld has had no "waterwork" performances since Ms. Brancheau's death in 2010, and it temporarily suspended "waterwork" after other incidents, such as the killing of a trainer by a killer whale in 2009 at a non-SeaWorld park in Spain. With distance and physical barriers between Tilikum and trainers during drywork, Tilikum can still perform almost the same behaviors performed when no barriers were present. The nature of SeaWorld's workplace and the unusual nature of the hazard to its employees performing in close physical contact with killer whales do not remove SeaWorld from its obligation under the General Duty Clause to protect its employees from recognized hazards.

* * *

Substantial evidence supports the ALJ's findings that it was feasible for SeaWorld to abate the hazard to its employees by using barriers or minimum distance between trainers and killer whales, most notably because SeaWorld has implemented many of these measures on its own. When an employer has existing safety procedures, the burden is on the Secretary to show that those procedures are inadequate. See [citations] The record evidence showed that SeaWorld's training and protocols did not prevent continued incidents, including the submerging and biting of one trainer in 2006, the killing of a trainer by a SeaWorld-trained and—owned killer whale in 2009 at an amusement park in Spain, and Ms. Brancheau's death in 2010. SeaWorld employees repeatedly acknowledged the unpredictability of its killer whales. This record evidence supports the ALJ's finding that existing protocols were inadequate to eliminate or materially reduce the hazard to SeaWorld's trainer employees performing with killer whales.

Abatement is "feasible" when it is "economically and technologically capable of being done." [Citations]. After Ms. Brancheau's death, SeaWorld required that all trainers work with Tilikum from a minimum distance or behind a barrier, and "waterwork" ceased with all of its killer whales. . . . . As the ALJ noted, SeaWorld had not argued the Secretary's proposed abatement was not economically or technologically feasible and had already implemented abatement for at least one of its killer whales and needed only to apply the same or similar protective contact measures it used with Tilikum to other killer whales. Consequently, the Secretary was not required to specify the precise manner in which abatement should be implemented.

* * *

Accordingly, we deny the petition for review.

KAVANAUGH, CIRCUIT JUDGE, dissenting:

Many sports events and entertainment shows can be extremely dangerous for the participants. Football. Ice hockey. Downhill skiing. Air shows. The circus. Horse racing. Tiger taming. Standing in the batter's box against a 95 mile per hour fastball. Bull riding at the rodeo. Skydiving into the stadium before a football game. Daredevil motorcycle jumps. Stock car racing. Cheerleading vaults. Boxing. The balance beam. The ironman triathlon. Animal trainer shows. Movie stunts. The list goes on.

* * *

The broad question implicated by this case is this: When should we as a society paternalistically decide that the participants in these sports and entertainment activities must be protected from themselves—that the risk of significant physical injury is simply too great even for eager and willing participants? And most importantly for this case, who decides that the risk to participants is too high?

* * *

. . . . the Department of Labor, acting with a fair degree of prudence and wisdom, has not traditionally tried to stretch its general authority under the Act to regulate participants taking part in the normal activities of sports events or entertainment shows.

In this case, however, the Department departed from tradition and stormed headlong into a new regulatory arena. The Department issued a citation to SeaWorld that effectively bans SeaWorld from continuing a longstanding and popular (albeit by definition somewhat dangerous) show in which SeaWorld trainers play with and interact with whales. The Department's SeaWorld decision was upheld administratively by the independent Occupational Safety and Health Review Commission, and the majority opinion today affirms.

Whether SeaWorld's show is unreasonably dangerous to participants and should be banned or changed is not the question before us. The question before us is whether the Department of Labor has authority under current law to make that decision—in addition to the authority already possessed by Congress, state legislatures, state regulators, and courts applying state tort law.

* * *

In my view, the Department of Labor either has authority to regulate sports and entertainment so as to prevent injuries to participants, or it does not. The fact that the Department expressly disclaims its authority over the NFL and NASCAR, and that the Department goes to such lengths to draw head-scratching distinctions between sports events on the one hand and entertainment shows on the other, shows that something is up. What's up is that the Department is treating similar cases dissimilarly, the paradigmatic arbitrary and capricious agency action.

The Congress that enacted the Act in 1970 was certainly aware of the hazards in many popular sports such as football, baseball, ice hockey, and boxing. It was also well aware of the hazards in entertainment shows such as the circus. Yet as SeaWorld correctly points out, Congress did not in any way indicate or even hint that the Clause's vague terms encompassed an implicit grant of authority to the Department of Labor to regulate and remake some undefined swath of America's sports and entertainment behemoth.

In the real world, it is simply not plausible to assert that Congress, when passing the Occupational Safety and Health Act, silently intended to authorize the Department of Labor to eliminate familiar sports and entertainment practices, such as punt returns in the NFL, speeding in NASCAR, or the whale show at SeaWorld. See [citation].

* * *

To the extent sports or entertainment activities raise concern about the risk of injury to the participants, several extant legal bodies possess significant authority to clamp down on unreasonable dangers: Congress, state legislatures, state regulators, courts applying state tort law. I take no position here on whether SeaWorld—or for that matter the NFL or NASCAR—should be subject to more stringent government regulation or liability, or otherwise should voluntarily make its activities safer. That policy question is not before us. My legal disagreement with the majority opinion boils down to one basic question: Who decides? Under current law, it is not the Department of Labor. I respectfully dissent.

---

**Question:** The majority in *SeaWorld of Florida* walks us through an OSHA investigation, prosecution, and judicial review. What aspect of the majority's statutory reading troubles the dissent?

## WORKERS' COMPENSATION

### MENDOZA V. MONMOUTH RECYCLING CORP.

288 N.J. Super. 240 (App.Div. 1996)

The opinion of the court was delivered by PRESSLER, P.J.A.D.

The question raised by this appeal is whether an illegal alien who is injured on the job is entitled to workers' compensation benefits even if he is not authorized by law to work. The judge of workers' compensation dismissed the claim petition on the ground that workers' compensation benefits are not available to an illegal alien. We disagree and consequently reverse and remand.

Insofar as we can determine from this rather sparse record, petitioner Luis Castro Mendoza entered the United States from Mexico some time in 1988. The facts surrounding his entry were never really established. Petitioner testified through an interpreter, and his illegal status was apparently regarded by the judge as proved by petitioner's own testimony. Although he conceded on cross-examination that he had entered the United States as an illegal alien, he also asserted that he had a one-year work permit when he arrived and that he had intended to return to Mexico when his permit expired. He did not do so, he claimed, because of the injury he sustained in August 1989 which is the subject of this claim petition. The inconsistencies and ambiguities in petitioner's testimony were not resolved. Nor was the date of his entry into the United States proved. Thus, had he entered in or after August 1988 with a work permit good for a year, it may well be that at the time of his injury in 1989 he was not working illegally. Since we are persuaded, however, that the legality of petitioner's status makes no difference to his workers' compensation rights, we assume for purposes of this disposition that he was an illegal alien on the date of the injury. We see no useful purpose to be served by a remand at this juncture for a status determination to be made particularly since the proofs may be elusive.

In any event, in August 1989 petitioner was working, at a compensation of $6 per hour, on an assembly line at the Monmouth Recycling Center. As we understand the record, his employer was actually Quality Labor Services, who, we surmise, supplied workers to this and other sites. Petitioner caught his right hand in a conveyor belt, sustaining a serious injury to the hand requiring four surgeries and then amputation of his little finger. Respondent initially admitted that petitioner was in its employ and that the injury was work-related. Accordingly, it provided medical and temporary disability benefits.

Prior to any determination having been made of the extent of petitioner's ensuing permanent disability, a dispute developed between the parties respecting temporary disability. Several years after the injury, petitioner consulted a psychiatrist who diagnosed petitioner's problems as post-traumatic stress disorder and severe depression attributable to the accident. Petitioner moved for medical benefits in order to continue treatment with the psychiatrist and for an extension of temporary benefits during the period of treatment, estimated by the psychiatrist as a likely period of eight to twelve weeks. It was during the course of that hearing that petitioner's alien status first came up—apparently, he had discussed it with the psychiatrist. Despite the employer's obligations under the Immigration Reform and Control Act, 8 U.S.C.A. § 1324a(a)–(h) (West 1995), to ascertain the work-authorization status of all employees, respondent had assertedly not been earlier aware that petitioner was an illegal alien, if, indeed, he was at the time of the hire. In any event, respondent then moved for dismissal of the claim petition on the illegal-alien ground, and the motion was granted.

The compensation judge's rationale in dismissing the petition relied first on that provision of the unemployment compensation law, N.J.S.A. 43:21–4(i)(1), barring the grant of benefits to an illegal, undocumented alien who is neither authorized to work nor awaiting pending work-authorization. *See Brambila v. Board of Review*, 124 N.J. 425, (1991). The judge then pointed to a forty-year-old opinion of this court, *Felice v. Felice*, 34 N.J. Super. 388, (App.Div. 1955), which struggled with the issue of whether an injured employee of a partnership who was married to one of the partners was barred by reason of the marital relationship from seeking unemployment compensation from the partnership. Rejecting earlier authority to the contrary, Justice (then Judge) Francis relied in *Felice* on the growing recognition of a partnership's status as a separate jural entity, thus placing it beyond the bar of interspousal litigation. As illustrative of that partnership status, Justice Francis noted that for purposes of taxation under the Unemployment Compensation Act, a partnership is treated as a separate entity. In this context, namely the susceptibility of a partnership to an employee's claim for statutory benefits, Justice Francis observed that "the social purposes which inspired the workmen's compensation and unemployment compensation legislation are identical." *Id.* at 392. Taking that observation completely out of context and seizing upon it as an analogical vehicle, the compensation judge concluded that since an illegal alien cannot qualify for unemployment compensation benefits, then he also cannot qualify for workers' compensation benefits.

We regard the analytical flaw in this syllogistic reasoning as evident. Obviously the Workers' Compensation Act and the Unemployment Compensation Act are both remedial social statutes designed to alleviate the financial burdens suffered by employees whose working lives have been interrupted. But their mechanisms, funding, and underlying premises are very different. The fact that unemployment compensation is not available to an illegal alien does not, by itself, answer the question of whether or not workers' compensation is. We are, moreover, satisfied that the rationale for withholding unemployment compensation from an illegal alien does not implicate the workers' compensation system. We are also persuaded that the purpose, policy and mechanism of the workers' compensation scheme are entirely consistent with the availability of benefits to illegal aliens illegally employed who are injured on the job.

We consider first the Unemployment Compensation Act. As made clear by Brambila, *supra,* that Act, unlike this state's workers' compensation legislation, expressly addresses the qualification of aliens. Thus N.J.S.A. 43:21–4(i)(1) prohibits benefits to be paid "on the basis of services performed by an alien unless such alien is an individual who was lawfully admitted for permanent residence at the time the services were performed and was lawfully present for the purpose of performing the services or otherwise was permanently residing in the United States under color of law at the time the services were performed." Aside from the express mandate of that provision, the claimant's availability for work has always been a prerequisite for eligibility for unemployment compensation. N.J.S.A. 43:21–4(c)(1). See, e.g., *Krauss v. A. M. Karagheusian,* 13 N.J. 447, 457–458 (1953); *Vasquez v. Bd. of Review, Labor and Ind.*, 127 N.J. Super. 431 (App.Div.), certif. denied, 65 N.J. 559 (1974). That condition is at the heart of the structure of the unemployment compensation scheme—that is, that when the employee's separation from the labor market is both involuntary and temporary, society bears the burden, by the unemployment tax system, of alleviating the employee's hardship until a new job is found. Since an illegal alien is prohibited by law from accepting a new job, that person must be deemed unavailable for work, thus not temporarily unemployed and therefore not qualified for unemployment compensation.

Workers' compensation, however, rests upon quite different predicates. The conceptual basis of the workers' compensation system is the substitution of the statutory remedy for a common-law right of action, the statutory remedy becoming an integral component of the contract of employment. *See Dudley v. Victor Lynn Lines, Inc.,* 32 N.J. 479, 488–489 (1960). Moreover, unlike the unemployment compensation system, the focus of workers' compensation is not the primarily prospective one of seeing a worker through a temporary period of unemployment. Its crux, rather, is the compensation of a worker who is already injured on the job both for the time lost from work because of the injury and for the disabling effect of the injury on future earning capacity. *See Medwick v. Bd. of Review, Div. Empl. Sec.*, 69 N.J. Super. 338, 340–341 (App.Div. 1961). In this state the workers' compensation system, unlike the unemployment compensation system, is not governmentally funded. Rather, it is primarily paid for by employers through their insurance premiums or self-insurance funds and the costs passed on to consumers. *See Romanny v. Stanley Baldino Const. Co.,* 142 N.J. 576, 580–581 (1995). Thus, as explained by Judge Conford in his dissenting opinion in *Marcus v. Eastern Agricultural Ass'n, Inc.*, 58 N.J. Super. 584, 596 (App.Div. 1959), *rev'd on dissent,* 32 N.J. 460 (1960), the purpose of workers' compensation is not only to provide a prompt monetary remedy for workers injured in the course of their employment, but also to do so by a system in which the cost of industrial accidents is borne by the consumer as part of the cost of the product or service. *See also* [citations]. The private-sector responsibility for payment of workers' compensation also serves the significant public purpose of encouraging employers to take steps to advance and promote workplace safety. *Eger v. E.I. Du Pont DeNemours Co.*, 110 N.J. 133, 140 (1988); *Stephenson v. R.A. Jones Co., Inc.*, 510 A.2d 1161 (1986) (Stein, J., dissenting).

As explained by Brambila, *supra,* 124 N.J. at 431–432, 591 A.2d 605, the unemployment compensation system is funded both by taxes on employers and federal and state grants.

We think it plain that none of these predicates is in the least degree compromised by the eligibility of an injured illegal alien for workers' compensation. Surely, the effect on the worker of his injury has nothing to do with his citizenship or immigration status. If his capacity to work has been diminished, that disability will continue whether his future employment is in this country or elsewhere. Moreover, his need for medical treatment and his right thereto as an incident of his employment do not derive from or depend upon his immigration status. They are, rather, a function of work he has actually performed during the course of which he sustained an injury.

We also regard the *desideratum* of workplace safety enhanced by according workers' compensation benefits to an illegal alien since an employer's immunity from payment of compensation to that class of employees might well provide a disincentive to assuring workplace safety. Moreover, such an immunity from accountability might well have the further undesirable effect of encouraging employers to hire illegal aliens in contravention of the provisions and policies of the Immigration Reform and Control Act. *See Montoya v. Gateway Insurance Company,* 168 N.J. Super. 100, 104 (App.Div. 1979).

There are, however, even more fundamental reasons, in the absence of an express statutory bar, for according illegal aliens the benefit of the workers' compensation laws. To begin with, as we explained in *Montoya, id.* at 103–104, "a well established body of law holds that illegal aliens have rights of access to the courts and are eligible to sue therein to enforce contracts and redress civil wrongs such as negligently inflicted personal injuries." We fully subscribe to that proposition. As we have pointed out, workers' compensation rests upon both contract and tort principles—the contract right in effect substitutes for the tort right an employee would otherwise have. It would not only be illogical but it would also serve no discernible public purpose to accord illegal aliens the right to bring affirmative claims in tort for personal injury but to deny them the right to pursue the substitutionary remedy for personal injuries sustained in the workplace, particularly since, in the end, the right to workers' compensation is as much an incident of the employment as the right to receive salary, and has been earned once the labor has been performed. In short, we are in full accord with the holding in *Montoya* which recognized that in respect of illegal aliens, the *sui generis* nature of unemployment compensation and the considerations uniquely relevant to its administration are not transferrable to or in any way applicable to the alien's right to prosecute personal injury claims. And workers' compensation is, in the end, a personal-injury remedy.

For the reasons we have herein expressed, we also disagree with the compensation judge's perception that workers' compensation must be denied to an illegal alien because his contract of employment is illegal pursuant to federal law. First, as we have noted, a rule of law denying workers' compensation to an illegal alien is more likely to encourage than to deter employers in employing illegal aliens. Such a rule would therefore disserve the public policy expressed by federal law. Beyond that, as we held in *Montoya, id.* at 106, in the context of an illegal alien's right to income protection benefits under personal injury protection coverage, a distinction must be drawn between "work which, in and of itself, violates law and work which, although lawful, is engaged in by a person under a disability to do it." We concluded there that as a matter of fundamental fairness, the disability under which an illegal alien nevertheless works does not justify withholding from him the privately funded benefits to which his labor would otherwise entitle him. We see no essential difference in this respect between income continuation benefits under a PIP policy and workers' compensation benefits under an employer-funded insurance program.

Finally, we note that other states that have considered this issue in the absence of an "availability for work" requirement in their workers' compensation statutes have uniformly afforded illegal aliens a compensation right. *See Gene's Harvesting v. Rodriguez,* 421 So.2d 701 (Fla.Dist.Ct.App. 1982); *Commercial Standard Fire Marine Co. v. Galindo,* 484 S.W.2d 635 (Tex.Civ.App. 1972); *Testa v. Sorrento Restaurant, Inc.,* 10 A.D.2d 133, (N.Y.App.Div. 1960); *see also* Bateman, Annotation, *Validity, Construction, and Application of Workers' Compensation Provisions Relating to Nonresident Alien Dependents,* 28 A.L.R. 5th 547 (1995). We also note that this view is generally supported by legal scholars as well. *See* Reich, *Environmental Metaphor in the Alien Benefits Debate,* 42 UCLA L.Rev. 1577, 1593 (1995); Reich, *Public Benefits for Undocumented Aliens: State Law Into the Breach Once More,* 21 N.M. L.Rev. 219, 239–241 (1991). *See also* Bosniak, *Exclusion and Membership: The Dual Identity of the Undocumented Worker Under United States Law,* 1988 Wis. L.Rev. 955, 978, 1033–1035 (1988); *but see* Miele, Note, *Illegal Aliens and Workers' Compensation: The Aftermath of Sure-Tan and IRCA,* 7 Hofstra Lab.L.J. 393, 405–408, 412–413 (1990) (arguing that eligibility of illegal aliens for workers' compensation benefits conflicts with IRCA's policy of discouraging the employment of undocumented aliens).

The order dismissing the claim petition is reversed and we remand for further proceedings on the merits.

---

**Question:** How does the *Mendoza* court view the differing purposes of unemployment compensation and workers' compensation in order to explain its award of the latter to undocumented workers?

# CHAPTER 26

# COMMON LAW REGULATION—THE PUBLIC TRUST DOCTRINE

■ ■ ■

## CONTEXT & SOURCES

In addition to public law's expression through constitutions and statutes, regulation can also function through common law created directly by the courts. One doctrine established by courts is that of the public trust—the idea that certain lands and waters should be reserved for general rather than private use. The public trust concept originated in Roman law's protection of tidelands, and in the United States was developed through U.S. Supreme Court and state judicial interpretation. Decisions are included here on public tidelands ownership for commercial purposes, the doctrine's expansion to ecological and recreational uses, and its limitations on existing property rights.

For the origins of the public trust in the context of waterfront access disputes, with particular emphasis on the *Illinois Central* case, see Joseph D. Kearney and Thomas W. Merrill, *Lakefront: Public Trust and Private Rights in Chicago* (Cornell University Press, 2021). The *Audubon* decision and its impacts are thoroughly explored in Erin Ryan, "The Public Trust Doctrine, Private Water Allocation, and Mono Lake: The Historic Saga of *National Audubon Society v. Superior Court*," 45 *Environmental Law* 561 (2015). Mary Christina Wood, *Nature's Trust: Environmental Law for a New Ecological Age* (Cambridge University Press, 2014) argues that the public trust is a more effective tool for protecting the environment than is traditional administrative regulation.

### ILLINOIS CENTRAL RAILROAD CO. V. ILLINOIS

146 U.S. 387 (1892)

* * *

[In 1869 the Illinois legislature granted underwater land within Lake Michigan to the Illinois Central Railroad, but in 1873 repealed the granting statute. Meanwhile the railroad had built harbor improvements, and continued to do so after the repeal. In 1883 the state sued the railroad on the ground that these improvements were located on state land, while

Illinois Central claimed that the 1869 grant was still valid. A federal circuit court upheld the state's title and the railroad appealed].

JUSTICE FIELD delivered the opinion of the court.

* * *

The object of the suit is to obtain a judicial determination of the title of certain lands on the east or lakefront of the City of Chicago, situated between the Chicago River and Sixteenth Street, which have been reclaimed from the waters of the lake and are occupied by the tracks, depots, warehouses, piers, and other structures used by the railroad company in its business, and also of the title claimed by the company to the submerged lands, constituting the bed of the lake, lying east of its tracks, within the corporate limits of the city . . . . The determination of the title of the company will involve a consideration of its right to construct, for its own business, as well as for public convenience, wharves, piers, and docks in the harbor.

* * *

The question . . . to be considered is whether the legislature was competent to . . . deprive the State of its ownership of the submerged lands in the harbor of Chicago, and of the consequent control of its waters; or, in other words, whether the railroad corporation can hold its lands and control the waters by the grant, against any future exercise of power by the State.

That the State holds the title to the lands under the navigable waters of Lake Michigan, within its limits, in the same manner that the State hold title to soils under tide water, by the common law, we have already shown, and that title necessarily carries with it control over the waters above them whenever the lands are subjected to use. But it is a title held in trust for the people of the State that they may enjoy the navigation of the waters, carry on commerce over them, and have liberty of fishing therein freed from the obstruction or interference of private parties. The interest of the people in the navigation of the waters and in commerce over them may be improved in many instances by the erection of wharves, docks and piers therein, for which purpose the State may grant parcels of the submerged lands; and, so long as their disposition is made for such purpose, no valid objections can be made to the grants.

* * *

The trust devolving upon the State for the public, and which can only be discharged by the management and control of property in which the public has an interest, cannot be relinquished by a transfer of the property. The control of the State for the purposes of the trust can never be lost, except as to such parcels as are used in promoting the interests of the public therein, or can be disposed of without any substantial impairment of the public interest in the lands and waters remaining.

* * *

A grant of all the lands under the navigable waters of a State has never been adjudged to be within the legislative power; and any attempted grant of the kind would be held, if not absolutely void on its face, as subject to revocation. The State can no more abdicate its trust over property in which the whole people are interested, like navigable waters and soils under them, so as to leave them entirely under the use and control of private parties, except in the instance of parcels mentioned for the improvement of the navigation and use of the waters, or when parcels can be disposed of without impairment of the public interest in what remains, than it can abdicate its police powers in the administration of government and the preservation of the peace. In the administration of government the use of such powers may for a limited period be delegated to a municipality or other body, but there always remains with the State the right to revoke those powers and exercise them in a more direct manner, and one more conformable to its wishes. So with trusts connected with public property, or property of a special character, like lands under navigable waters, they cannot be placed entirely beyond the direction and control of the State.

The harbor of Chicago is of immense value to the people of the State of Illinois in the facilities it affords to its vast and constantly increasing commerce; and the idea that its legislature can deprive the State of control over its bed and waters and place the same in the hands of a private corporation created for a different purpose, one limited to transportation of passengers and freight between distant points and the city, is a proposition that cannot be defended.

* * *

It is hardly conceivable that the legislature can divest the State of the control and management of this harbor and vest it absolutely in a private corporation.

* * *

The position advanced by the railroad company in support of its claim to the ownership of the submerged lands and the right to the erection of wharves, piers and docks at its pleasure, or for its business in the harbor of Chicago, would place every harbor in the country at the mercy of a majority of the legislature of the State in which the harbor is situated.

. . . . [T]he decisions are numerous which declare that such property is held by the state, by virtue of its sovereignty, in trust for the public. The ownership of the navigable waters of the harbor and of the lands under them is a subject of public concern to the whole people of the state. The trust with which they are held therefore is governmental, and cannot be alienated, except in those instances mentioned of parcels used in the improvement of the interest thus held, or when parcels can be disposed of without detriment to the public interest in the lands and waters remaining.

* * *

[After confirming the right of the state to the submerged lands, the court ordered the lower court to investigate whether certain of the railroad's improvements were located entirely on its own land bordering the lake, or encroached upon state jurisdiction].

*Except as modified in the particulars mentioned, the decree in each of the three cases on appeal must be affirmed, with costs against the railroad company, and it is so ordered.*

---

**Question:** In the *Illinois Central* case, why didn't the U.S. Supreme Court address the question of whether the railroad had a takings claim for compensation against the state?

## MARKS V. WHITNEY

491 P.2d 374 (Cal. 1971)

* * *

MCCOMB, J.

This is a quiet title action to settle a boundary line dispute caused by overlapping and defective surveys and to enjoin defendants (herein "Whitney") from asserting any claim or right in or to the property of plaintiff Marks. The unique feature here is that a part of Marks' property is tidelands acquired under an 1874 patent issued pursuant to the Act of March 28, 1868 (Stats. 1867–68, ch. 415, p. 507); a small portion of these tidelands adjoins almost the entire shoreline of Whitney's upland property. Marks asserted complete ownership of the tidelands and the right to fill and develop them. Whitney opposed on the ground that this would cut off his rights as a littoral owner and as a member of the public in these tidelands and the navigable waters covering them. He requested a declaration in the decree that Marks' title was burdened with a public trust easement . . .

The trial court settled the common boundary line to the satisfaction of the parties. However, it held that Whitney had no "standing" to raise the public trust issue and it refused to make a finding as to whether the tidelands are so burdened.

* * *

[The disputed property is located on the westerly side of Tomales Bay, in Marin County, California].

Questions: First. Are these tidelands subject to the public trust; if so, should the judgment so declare?

Yes. Regardless of the issue of Whitney's standing to raise this issue the court may take judicial notice of public trust burdens in quieting title to tidelands. This matter is of great public importance, particularly in view of population pressures, demands for recreational property, and the increasing development of seashore and waterfront property. A present declaration that the title of Marks in these tidelands is burdened with a public easement may avoid needless future litigation.

Tidelands are properly those lands lying between the lines of mean high and low tide [citation] covered and uncovered successively by the ebb and flow thereof [citation]. The trial court found that the portion of Marks' lands here under consideration constitutes a part of the tidelands of Tomales Bay, that at all times it has been, and now is, subject to the daily ebb and flow of the tides in Tomales Bay, that the ordinary high tides in the bay overflow and submerge this portion of his lands, and that Tomales Bay is a navigable body of water and an arm of the Pacific Ocean.

This land was patented as tidelands to Marks' predecessor in title. The patent of May 15, 1874, recites that it was issued by the Governor of California "by virtue of authority in me vested" pursuant to "Statutes enacted from time to time" for the "Sale and Conveyance of the Tide Lands belonging to the State by virtue of her sovereignty."

* * *

The tidelands embraced in these statutes extend from the Oregon line to Mexico and include the shores of bays and navigable streams as far up as tide water goes and until it meets the lands made swampy by the overflow and seepage of fresh water streams. [Citations]. No issue is here presented of swamp or overflowed lands. These are true tidelands within the meaning of these statutes, the patent of May 15, 1874, and the public trust doctrine. They are, therefore, subject to a reserved easement in the state for trust purposes.

Public trust easements are traditionally defined in terms of navigation, commerce and fisheries. They have been held to include the right to fish, hunt, bathe, swim, to use for boating and general recreation purposes the navigable waters of the state, and to use the bottom of the navigable waters for anchoring, standing, or other purposes. (See [citations]). The public has the same rights in and to tidelands.

The public uses to which tidelands are subject are sufficiently flexible to encompass changing public needs. In administering the trust the state is not burdened with an outmoded classification favoring one mode of utilization over another. [Citation]. There is a growing public recognition that one of the most important public uses of the tidelands—a use encompassed within the tidelands trust—is the preservation of those lands in their natural state, so that they may serve as ecological units for scientific study, as open space, and as environments which provide food and habitat for birds and marine life, and which favorably affect the scenery and climate of the area. It is not necessary to here define precisely all the public uses which encumber tidelands.

* * *

The power of the state to control, regulate and utilize its navigable waterways and the lands lying beneath them, when acting within the terms of the trust, is absolute [citation], except as limited by the paramount supervisory power of the federal government over navigable waters [citation]. We are not here presented with any action by the state or the federal government modifying, terminating, altering or relinquishing the jus publicum in these tidelands or in the navigable water covering them. Neither sovereignty is a party to this action. This court takes judicial notice, however, that there has been no official act of either sovereignty to modify or extinguish the public trust servitude upon Marks' tidelands. The State Attorney General, as amicus curiae, has advised this court that no such action or determination has been made by the state.

* * *

It is within the province of the trier of fact to determine whether any particular use made or asserted by Whitney in or over these tidelands would constitute an infringement either upon the jus privatum [private rights] of Marks or upon the jus publicum of the people. It is also within the province of the trier of fact to determine whether any particular use to which Marks wishes to devote his tidelands constitutes an unlawful infringement upon the jus publicum [public rights] therein. It is a political question, within the wisdom and power of the Legislature, acting within the scope of its duties as trustee, to determine whether public trust uses should be modified or extinguished (see [citation]), and to take the necessary steps to free them from such burden. In the absence of state or federal action the court may not bar members of the public from lawfully asserting or exercising public trust rights on these privately owned tidelands.

There is absolutely no merit in Marks' contention that as the owner of the jus privatum under this patent he may fill and develop his property, whether for navigational purposes or not; nor in his contention that his past and present plan for development of these tidelands as a marina have caused the extinguishment of the public easement. Reclamation with or without prior authorization from the state does not ipso facto terminate the public trust nor render the issue moot. [Citations].

* * *

Second: Does Whitney have "standing" to request the court to recognize and declare the public trust easement on Marks' tidelands?

Yes. The relief sought by Marks resulted in taking away from Whitney rights to which he is entitled as a member of the general public. It is immaterial that Marks asserted he was not seeking to enjoin the public. The decree as rendered does enjoin a member of the public.

Members of the public have been permitted to bring an action to enforce a public right to use a beach access route [citation]; to bring an action to quiet title to private and public easements in a public beach [citation]; and to bring an action to restrain improper filling of a bay and secure a general declaration of the rights of the people to the waterways and wildlife areas of the bay [citation]. Members of the public have been allowed to defend a quiet title action by asserting the right to use a public right of way through private property [citation]. They have been allowed to assert the public trust easement for hunting, fishing and navigation in privately owned tidelands as a defense in an action to enjoin such use [citation], and to navigate on shallow navigable waters in small boats [citation].

Whitney had standing to raise this issue. The court could have raised this issue on its own. "It is now well settled that the court may finally determine as between the parties in a quiet title action all of the conflicting claims regarding any estate or interest in the property." [Citation]. Where the interest concerned is one that, as here, constitutes a public burden upon land to which title is quieted, and affects the defendant as a member of the public, that servitude should be explicitly declared.

* * *

Judgment is reversed and remanded for proceedings not inconsistent with this opinion.

---

**Question:** What is the California Supreme Court's source in *Marks* for expanding the public trust doctrine from its traditional navigation and commerce purposes to recreation and ecology?

## NATIONAL AUDUBON SOCIETY V. SUPERIOR COURT (THE MONO LAKE CASE)

658 P.2d 709 (Cal. 1983)

* * *

BROUSSARD, J.

Mono Lake, the second largest lake in California, sits at the base of the Sierra Nevada escarpment near the eastern entrance to Yosemite National Park. The lake is saline; it contains no fish but supports a large population of brine shrimp which feed vast numbers of nesting and migratory birds. Islands in the lake protect a large breeding colony of California gulls, and the lake itself serves as a haven on the migration route for thousands of Northern Phalarope, Wilson's Phalarope, and Eared Grebe. Towers and spires of tufa on the north and south shores are matters of geological interest and a tourist attraction.

Although Mono Lake receives some water from rain and snow on the lake surface, historically most of its supply came from snowmelt in the Sierra Nevada. Five freshwater streams—Mill, Lee Vining, Walker, Parker and Rush Creeks—arise near the crest of the range and carry the annual runoff to the west shore of the lake. In 1940, however, the Division of Water Resources, the predecessor to the present California Water Resources Board granted the Department of Water and Power of the City of Los Angeles (hereafter DWP) a permit to appropriate virtually the entire flow of four of the five streams flowing into the lake. DWP promptly constructed facilities to divert about half the flow of these streams into DWP's Owens Valley aqueduct. In 1970 DWP completed a second diversion tunnel, and since that time has taken virtually the entire flow of these streams.

As a result of these diversions, the level of the lake has dropped; the surface area has diminished by one-third; one of the two principal islands in the lake has become a peninsula, exposing the gull rookery there to coyotes and other predators and causing the gulls to abandon the former island. The ultimate effect of continued diversions is a matter of intense dispute, but there seems little doubt that both the scenic beauty and the ecological values of Mono Lake are imperiled.

Plaintiffs filed suit in superior court to enjoin the DWP diversions on the theory that the shores, bed and waters of Mono Lake are protected by a public trust. Plaintiffs' suit was transferred to the federal district court, which requested that the state courts determine the relationship between the public trust doctrine and the water rights system.

This case brings together for the first time two systems of legal thought: the appropriative water rights system which since the days of the gold rush has dominated California water law, and the public trust doctrine which, after evolving as a shield for the protection of tidelands, now extends its protective scope to navigable lakes. Ever since we first recognized that the public trust protects environmental and recreational values (Marks v. Whitney (1971), 491 P.2d 374, the two systems of legal thought have been on a collision course. [Citation]. They meet in a unique and dramatic setting which highlights the clash of values. Mono Lake is a scenic and ecological treasure of national significance, imperiled by continued diversions of water; yet, the need of Los Angeles for water is apparent, its reliance on rights granted by the board evident, the cost of curtailing diversions substantial.

Attempting to integrate the teachings and values of both the public trust and the appropriative water rights system, we have arrived at certain conclusions which we briefly summarize here. In our opinion, the core of the public trust doctrine is the state's authority as sovereign to exercise a continuous supervision and control over the navigable waters of the state and the lands underlying those waters. This authority applies to the waters tributary to Mono Lake and bars DWP or any other party from claiming a vested right to divert waters once it becomes clear that such diversions harm the interests protected by the public trust. The corollary rule which evolved in tideland and lakeshore cases barring conveyance of rights free of the trust except to serve trust purposes cannot, however, apply without modification to flowing waters. The prosperity and habitability of much of this state requires the diversion of great quantities of water from its streams for purposes unconnected to any navigation, commerce, fishing, recreation, or ecological use relating to the source stream. The state must have the power to grant nonvested usufructuary rights to appropriate water even if diversions harm public trust uses. Approval of such diversion without considering public trust values, however, may result in needless destruction of those values. Accordingly, we believe that before state courts and agencies approve water diversions they should consider the effect of such diversions upon interests protected by the public trust, and attempt, so far as feasible, to avoid or minimize any harm to those interests.

The water rights enjoyed by DWP were granted, the diversion was commenced, and has continued to the present without any consideration of the impact upon the public trust. An objective study and reconsideration of the water rights in the Mono Basin is long overdue. The water law of California—which we conceive to be an integration including both the public trust doctrine and the board-administered appropriative rights system—permits such a reconsideration; the values underlying that integration require it.

* * *

. . . Mono Lake has no outlets. The lake loses water only by evaporation and seepage. Natural salts do not evaporate with water, but are left behind. Prior to commencement of the DWP diversions, this naturally rising salinity was balanced by a constant and substantial supply of fresh water from the tributaries. Now, however, DWP diverts most of the fresh water inflow. The resultant imbalance between inflow and outflow not only diminishes the lake's size, but also drastically increases its salinity.

Plaintiffs predict that the lake's steadily increasing salinity, if unchecked, will wreck havoc throughout the local food chain. They contend that the lake's algae, and the brine shrimp and brine flies that feed on it, cannot survive the projected salinity increase. To support this assertion, plaintiffs point to a 50 percent reduction in the shrimp hatch for the spring of 1980 and a startling 95 percent reduction for the spring of 1981. These reductions affirm experimental evidence indicating that brine shrimp populations diminish as the salinity of the water surrounding them increases. (See Task Force Report at pp. 20–21.) DWP admits these substantial reductions, but blames them on factors other than salinity.

DWP's diversions also present several threats to the millions of local and migratory birds using the lake. First, since many species of birds feed on the lake's brine shrimp, any reduction in shrimp population allegedly caused by rising salinity endangers a major avian food source. The Task Force Report considered it "unlikely that any of Mono Lake's major bird species . . . will persist at the lake if populations of invertebrates disappear." (Task Force Report at p. 20.) Second, the increasing salinity makes it more difficult for the birds to maintain osmotic equilibrium with their environment.

The California gull is especially endangered, both by the increase in salinity and by loss of nesting sites. Ninety-five percent of this state's gull population and 25 percent of the total species population nests at the lake. (Task Force Report at p. 21.) Most of the gulls nest on islands in the lake. As the lake recedes, land between the shore and some of the islands has been exposed, offering such predators as the coyote easy access to the gull nests and chicks. In 1979, coyotes reached Negrit Island, once the most popular nesting site, and the number of gull nests at the lake declined sharply. In 1981, 95 percent of the hatched chicks did not survive to maturity. Plaintiffs blame this decline and alarming mortality rate on the predator access created by the land bridges; DWP suggests numerous other causes, such as increased ambient temperatures and human activities, and claims that the joining of some islands with the mainland is offset by the emergence of new islands due to the lake's recession.

* * *

"By the law of nature these things are common to mankind—the air, running water, the sea and consequently the shores of the sea." (Institutes of Justinian 2.1.1.) From this origin in Roman law, the English common law evolved the concept of the public trust, under which the sovereign owns "all of its navigable waterways and the lands lying beneath them 'as trustee of a public trust for the benefit of the people.'" [Citation]. The State of California acquired title as trustee to such lands and waterways upon its admission to the union [citation]; from the earliest days [(see citation)] its judicial decisions have recognized and enforced the trust obligation.

Three aspects of the public trust doctrine require consideration in this opinion: the purpose of the trust; the scope of the trust, particularly as it applies to the nonnavigable tributaries of a navigable lake; and the powers and duties of the state as trustee of the public trust. We discuss these questions in the order listed.

(a) The purpose of the public trust.

The objective of the public trust has evolved in tandem with the changing public perception of the values and uses of waterways. As we observed in Marks v. Whitney, "public trust easements [were] traditionally defined in terms of navigation, commerce and fisheries. They have been held to include the right to fish, hunt, bathe, swim, to use for boating and general recreation purposes the navigable waters of the state, and to use the bottom of the navigable waters for anchoring, standing, or other purposes." We went on, however, to hold that the traditional triad of uses—navigation, commerce and fishing—did not limit the public interest in the trust res. * * *

Mono Lake is a navigable waterway. [Citation]. It supports a small local industry which harvests brine shrimp for sale as fish food, which endeavor probably qualifies the lake as a "fishery" under the traditional public trust cases. The principal values plaintiffs seek to protect, however, are recreational and ecological—the scenic views of the lake and its shore, the purity of the air, and the use of the lake for nesting and feeding by birds. Under Marks v. Whitney, it is clear that protection of these values is among the purposes of the public trust.

(b) The scope of the public trust.

* * *

It is . . . well settled in the United States generally and in California that the public trust is not limited by the reach of the tides, but encompasses all navigable lakes and streams. (See Illinois Central Railroad Co. v. Illinois (1892), 146 U.S. 387 (Lake Michigan); State of California v. Superior Court (1981), 625 P.2d 239 (Clear Lake); State of California v. Superior Court (1981), 625 P.2d 256 (Lake Tahoe); [further citations].

Mono Lake is, as we have said, a navigable waterway. The beds, shores and waters of the lake are without question protected by the public trust. The streams diverted by DWP, however, are not themselves navigable. Accordingly, we must address in this case a question not discussed in any recent public trust case—whether the public trust limits conduct affecting nonnavigable tributaries to navigable waterways.

* * *

[T]he principles recognized by [prior] decisions apply fully to a case in which diversions from a nonnavigable tributary impair the public trust in a downstream river or lake. "If the public trust doctrine applies to constrain fills which destroy navigation and other public trust uses in navigable waters, it should equally apply to constrain the extraction of water that destroys navigation and other public interests. Both actions result in the same damage to the public interest." [Citations].

We conclude that the public trust doctrine, as recognized and developed in California decisions, protects navigable waters from harm caused by diversion of nonnavigable tributaries.

(c) Duties and powers of the state as trustee.

In the following review of the authority and obligations of the state as administrator of the public trust, the dominant theme is the state's sovereign power and duty to exercise continued supervision over the trust. One consequence, of importance to this and many other cases, is that parties acquiring rights in trust property generally hold those rights subject to the trust, and can assert no vested right to use those rights in a manner harmful to the trust.

As we noted recently in City of Berkeley v. Superior Court, the decision of the United States Supreme Court in Illinois Central Railroad Company v. Illinois "remains the primary authority even today, almost nine decades after it was decided." The Illinois Legislature in 1886 had granted the railroad in fee simple 1,000 acres of submerged lands, virtually the entire Chicago waterfront. Four years later it sought to revoke that grant. The Supreme Court upheld the revocatory legislation. Its opinion explained that lands under navigable waters conveyed to private parties for wharves, docks, and other structures in furtherance of trust purposes could be granted free of the trust because the conveyance is consistent with the purpose of the trust. But the legislature, it held, did not have the power to convey the entire city waterfront free of trust, thus barring all future legislatures from protecting the public interest.

* * *

[The court then reviewed California decisions endorsing Illinois Central, concluding that private property interests in trust lands, such as oil leases, are held subject to the public trust, and that establishment of the trust does not constitute a compensable taking.]

In summary, the foregoing cases amply demonstrate the continuing power of the state as administrator of the public trust, a power which extends to the revocation of previously granted rights or to the enforcement of the trust against lands long thought free of the trust (see City of Berkeley). Except for those rare instances in which a grantee may acquire a right to use former trust property free of trust restrictions, the grantee holds subject to the trust, and while he may assert a vested right to the servient estate (the right of use subject to the trust) and to any improvements he erects, he can claim no vested right to bar recognition of the trust or state action to carry out its purposes.

* * *

Thus, the public trust is more than an affirmation of state power to use public property for public purposes. It is an affirmation of the duty of the state to protect the people's common heritage of streams, lakes, marshlands and tidelands, surrendering that right of protection only in rare cases when the abandonment of that right is consistent with the purposes of the trust.

* * *

[The court then discussed the development of California's water rights system, administered by the State Water Board, which recognizes both prior appropriation (first beneficial user of water has priority) and riparian rights (first property title holder bordering a watercourse has priority). A 1928 constitutional amendment modified this system, preventing rights holders from "waste" or "unreasonable" water diversions. Subsequent statutes and cases enhanced the Board's power to implement reasonable water use and public trust values.]

As we have seen, the public trust doctrine and the appropriative water rights system administered by the Water Board developed independently of each other. Each developed comprehensive rules and principles which, if applied to the full extent of their scope, would occupy the field of allocation of stream waters to the exclusion of any competing system of legal thought. Plaintiffs, for example, argue that the public trust is antecedent to and thus limits all appropriative water rights, an argument which implies that most appropriative water rights in California were acquired and are presently being used unlawfully. Defendant DWP, on the other hand, argues that the public trust doctrine as to stream waters has been "subsumed" into the appropriative water rights system and, absorbed by that body of law, quietly disappeared; according to DWP, the recipient of a board license enjoys a vested right in perpetuity to take water without concern for the consequences to the trust.

We are unable to accept either position. In our opinion, both the public trust doctrine and the water rights system embody important precepts which make the law more responsive to the diverse needs and interests involved in the planning and allocation of water resources. To embrace one system of thought and reject the other would lead to an unbalanced structure, one which would either decry as a breach of trust appropriations essential to the economic development of this state, or deny any duty to protect or even consider the values promoted by the public trust. Therefore, seeking an accommodation which will make use of the pertinent principles of both the public trust doctrine and the appropriative water rights system, and drawing upon the history of the public trust and the water rights system, the body of judicial precedent, and the views of expert commentators, we reach the following conclusions:

a. The state as sovereign retains continuing supervisory control over its navigable waters and the lands beneath those waters. This principle, fundamental to the concept of the public trust, applies to rights in flowing waters as well as to rights in tidelands and lakeshores; it prevents any party from acquiring a vested right to appropriate water in a manner harmful to the interests protected by the public trust.

b. As a matter of current and historical necessity, the Legislature, acting directly or through an authorized agency such as the Water Board, has the power to grant usufructuary licenses that will permit an appropriator to take water from flowing streams and use that water in a distant part of the state, even though this taking does not promote, and may unavoidably harm, the trust uses at the source stream. The population and economy of this state depend upon the appropriation of vast quantities of water for uses unrelated to in-stream trust values. California's Constitution, its statutes, decisions, and commentators all emphasize the need to make efficient use of California's limited water resources: all recognize, at least implicitly, that efficient use requires diverting water from in-stream uses. Now that the economy and population centers of this state have developed in reliance upon appropriated water, it would be disingenuous to hold that such appropriations are and have always been improper to the extent that they harm public trust uses, and can be justified only upon theories of reliance or estoppel.

c. The state has an affirmative duty to take the public trust into account in the planning and allocation of water resources, and to protect public trust uses whenever feasible. Just as the history of this state shows that appropriation may be necessary for efficient use of water despite unavoidable harm to public trust values, it demonstrates that an appropriative water rights system administered without consideration of the public trust may cause unnecessary and unjustified harm to trust interests. (See [citations]). As a matter of practical necessity the state may have to approve appropriations despite foreseeable harm to public trust uses. In so doing, however, the state must bear in mind its duty as trustee to consider the effect of the taking on the public trust (see [citation]), so far as consistent with the public interest, the uses protected by the trust.

Once the state has approved an appropriation, the public trust imposes a duty of continuing supervision over the taking and use of the appropriated water. In exercising its sovereign power to allocate water resources in the public interest, the state is not confined by past allocation decisions which may be incorrect in light of current knowledge or inconsistent with current needs.

The state accordingly has the power to reconsider allocation decisions even though those decisions were made after due consideration of their effect on the public trust. The case for reconsidering a particular decision, however, is even stronger when that decision failed to weigh and consider public trust uses. In the case before us, the salient fact is that no responsible body has ever determined the impact of diverting the entire flow of the Mono Lake tributaries into the Los Angeles Aqueduct. This is not a case in which the Legislature, the Water Board, or any judicial body has determined that the needs of Los Angeles outweigh the needs of the Mono Basin, that the benefit gained is worth the price. Neither has any responsible body determined whether some lesser taking would better balance the diverse interests. Instead, DWP acquired rights to the entire flow in 1940 from a water board which believed it lacked both the power and the duty to protect the Mono Lake environment, and continues to exercise those rights in apparent disregard for the resulting damage to the scenery, ecology, and human uses of Mono Lake.

It is clear that some responsible body ought to reconsider the allocation of the waters of the Mono Basin. No vested rights bar such reconsideration. We recognize the substantial concerns voiced by Los Angeles—the city's need for water, its reliance upon the 1940 board decision, the cost both in terms of money and environmental impact of obtaining water elsewhere. Such concerns must enter into any allocation decision. We hold only that they do not preclude a reconsideration and reallocation which also takes into account the impact of water diversion on the Mono Lake environment.

* * *

Conclusion.

* * *

The federal court inquired first of the interrelationship between the public trust doctrine and the California water rights system, asking whether the "public trust doctrine in this context [is] subsumed in the California water rights system, or . . . function[s] independently of that system?" Our answer is "neither." The public trust doctrine and the appropriative water rights system are parts of an integrated system of water law. The public trust doctrine serves the function in that integrated system of preserving the continuing sovereign power of the state to protect public trust uses, a power which precludes anyone from acquiring a vested right to harm the public trust, and imposes a continuing duty on the state to take such uses into account in allocating water resources.

Restating its question, the federal court asked: "[C]an the plaintiffs challenge the Department's permits and licenses by arguing that those permits and licenses are limited by the public trust doctrine, or must the plaintiffs . . . [argue] that the water diversions and uses authorized thereunder are not 'reasonable or beneficial' as required under the California water rights system?" We reply that plaintiffs can rely on the public trust doctrine in seeking reconsideration of the allocation of the waters of the Mono Basin.

* * *

This opinion is but one step in the eventual resolution of the Mono Lake controversy. We do not dictate any particular allocation of water. Our objective is to resolve a legal conundrum in which two competing systems of thought—the public trust doctrine and the appropriative water rights system—existed independently of each other, espousing principles which seemingly suggested opposite results. We hope by integrating these two doctrines to clear away the legal barriers which have so far prevented either the Water Board or the courts from taking a new and objective look at the water resources of the Mono Basin. The human and environmental uses of Mono Lake—uses protected by the public trust doctrine—deserve to be taken into account. Such uses should not be destroyed because the state mistakenly thought itself powerless to protect them.

Let a peremptory writ of mandate issue commanding the Superior Court of Alpine County to vacate its judgment in this action and to enter a new judgment consistent with the views stated in this opinion. Bird, C. J., Mosk, J., Kaus J., and Reynoso, J., concurred.

---

**Question:** Is there an argument that the public trust doctrine should apply not only to surface water, as in *National Audubon,* but to groundwater as well? See *In Re Water Use Permit Applications for the Waiahole Ditch,* 9 P.3d 409 (Haw. 2000).

**Note:** Not all state judiciaries have given the public trust as expansive a reading as have those of California and Hawaii. Contrary to *National Audubon,* the Nevada Supreme Court held in *Mineral County v. Lyon County (Mineral County II)* 473 P.3d 418 (Nev. 2020) that while the public trust is part of the state's water law, it could not be applied to require reallocation of existing water rights, even to protect threatened trust resources.

# INDEX

References are to Pages